Matters of Mind

A.B. McKILLOP

Matters of Mind:
The University in Ontario,
1791–1951

A Publication of the
Ontario Historical Studies Series
for the Government of Ontario
Published by University of Toronto Press
Toronto Buffalo London

ISBN 0-8020-0424-5 (cloth)
ISBN 0-8020-7216-x (paper)

Printed on acid-free paper

Canadian Cataloguing in Publication Data

McKillop, A.B., 1946–
  Matters of Mind : the university in Ontario 1791–1951

  (Ontario historical studies series)
  Includes index.
  ISBN 0-8020-0424-5 (bound) ISBN 0-8020-7216-x (pbk.)

  1. Universities and colleges – Ontario – History.
  2. Education, Higher – Ontario – History. I. Title. II. Series.

LA417.M35 1994   378.713'09   C94-930086-1

This book has been published with the assistance of funds provided by the Government
of Ontario through the Ministry of Culture, Tourism and Recreation.

To Pauline and Hamish

Contents

Figures and Tables

FIGURES

TABLES

The Ontario Historical Studies Series

For many years the principal theme in English-Canadian historical writing has been the emergence and the consolidation of the Canadian nation. This theme has been developed in uneasy awareness of the persistence and importance of regional interests and identities, but because of the central role of Ontario in the growth of Canada, Ontario has not been seen as a region. Almost unconsciously, historians have equated the history of the province with that of the nation and have often depicted the interests of other regions as obstacles to the unity and welfare of Canada.

The creation of the province of Ontario in 1867 was the visible embodiment of a formidable reality, the existence at the core of the new nation of a powerful if disjointed society whose traditions and characteristics differed in many respects from those of the other British North American colonies. The intervening century has not witnessed the assimilation of Ontario to the other regions in Canada; on the contrary it has become a more clearly articulated entity. Within the formal geographical and institutional framework defined so assiduously by Ontario's political leaders, an increasingly intricate web of economic and social interests has been woven and shaped by the dynamic interplay between Toronto and its hinterland. The character of this regional community has been formed in the tension between a rapid adaptation to the processes of modernization and industrialization in modern western society and a reluctance to modify or discard traditional attitudes and values. Not surprisingly, the Ontario outlook has been, and in some measure still is, a compound of aggressiveness, conservatism, and the conviction that its values should be the model for the rest of Canada.

From the outset the objective of the series' Board of Trustees was to describe and analyse the historical development of Ontario as a distinct region within Canada. The series includes biographies of several premiers, and thematic studies on the growth of the provincial economy, educational institutions, labour, welfare, the Franco-Ontarians, the Native Peoples, and the arts.

Matters of Mind is a thorough account of the adaptation of the concept of the university, inherited from the political, intellectual, and religious traditions of the North Atlantic world, to the changing climate of opinion and needs of provincial society. This process was shaped by a distinctive institutional framework in which the University of Toronto, sustained by the state, had a dominant role among the Ontario universities, the gradual acceptance of the legitimacy of unfettered research, the growth of professional and utilitarian studies, and the universities' inadequate financial resources.

Brian McKillop has written a scholarly and perceptive study of the establishment and growth of the university in Ontario from its modest beginning to the eve of the massive expansion of higher education in the 1950s and 1960s. He has attempted 'to de-mystify the ivory tower in order to demonstrate that it is one social institution among others, yet a very special one ... The university has always been a body with overwhelming potential for individual and social transformation, and it remains so.' This work will be indispensable for all those involved in the ongoing debate over the universities' contemporary function, the proper limits of university autonomy, and the best means of enabling the universities to fulfil their potential.

The editors and the Board of Trustees are grateful to Brian McKillop for undertaking this task.

GOLDWIN FRENCH
PETER OLIVER
JEANNE BECK
J.M.S. CARELESS

Toronto
August 1993

*The corporation known as the Ontario Historical Studies Series ceased to exist 31 August 1993. This volume was completed and approved for publication before 31 August 1993.

Preface

The idea of introducing higher education to the British North American province of Upper Canada occurred to its first Lieutenant-Governor, John Graves Simcoe, almost as soon as the colony was born in 1791. Shortly after his arrival, Simcoe spoke of the desirability of creating a university that would 'inculcate just principles, habits and manners into the rising generation.' This book is about how the university came into being in Simcoe's province, not as one institution but as several, and about the course of university education over the century and a half that followed. It is concerned with politicians and clerics, founders and the institutions they founded; with ideas and ideologies, disciplines and programs; with what was taught and, at times, what was not – and with why this was so. It is especially about students and their professors, although for a half century after Simcoe first uttered his wish neither had yet appeared on the scene. Its central theme is the human dialectic of memory and hope, affirmation and criticism, tradition and endeavour, for the university is above all an institution in which past and future meet in uncertain and uneasy combination.

At the end of the eighteenth century, Upper Canada largely consisted of a line of discontinuous settlement along the upper St Lawrence River, the north shores of lakes Ontario and Erie, and the Niagara escarpment. The population of the new province numbered approximately 35,000 people. Roughly ten per cent of its people lived in towns, the largest of which was Kingston with fewer than a thousand inhabitants. By the middle of the twentieth century, the province – now called Ontario – was the largest and wealthiest in the Dominion of Canada, with a population of four and a half million people. Over a million of these lived in the provincial capital, Toronto, and its surrounding municipalities. Twenty thousand Ontario citizens in 1951 were enrolled as full-time students in one of the five universities in the province. Forty years later, the number of universities in Ontario had more than trebled and almost a quarter of a million people attended them as full-time students.

Matters of Mind is an account of the formative years of higher education in Ontario. It is about an institution, the university, but it is not an institutional history of universities. Each university in the province of Ontario has its own interesting story to tell, and the experiences of some of them have been the subject of treatment by other historians. Several of these studies – those of Queen's and McMaster universities, for example – are very good indeed, and they merit close reading by anyone who wishes to understand the circumstances over which the universities, for the most part, have prevailed. Readers who wish to learn the detailed history of a given Ontario university, especially as viewed from the perspective of its president, principal, or board of governors, should turn to such institutional histories. My intention has been to establish and pursue several themes (some common to all institutions, some unique), to explore a number of unexamined avenues, to focus upon intellectual and social life, and to relate the university experience as a whole to the life of the province.

The universities of Ontario founded in the nineteenth century arose in different circumstances and were marked by the strenuous competition of Christian denominations. Yet beneath a surface often characterized by acrimony and difference lay a variety of deeply held shared beliefs and social convictions. All university founders, regardless of religious affiliation, saw the fundamental purpose of their institution to be the continued preservation of a social order that because of its British and loyalist origins was more conservative than that of the American colonies. The belief that British North America was an evolutionary extension of the British and European inheritance was so deeply a part of the colonial sense of social and imperial self that from the outset of academic life in the post-revolutionary British colonies there was little desire – or perceived need – for Anglo-Canadian academicians to discover or to articulate any sense that the life of the mind in colonial circumstance could or should be significantly differentiated from that of the 'old country.' The sense of a continuity of inheritance – political, intellectual, religious – was strong in the nineteenth century and was to continue beyond it.

Yet overlaying this ethic of concern for tradition, given force and direction by the conservative reaction to revolutionary excess and the power of the evangelical revival, was an acceptance within British North American society and its fledgling universities of the liberal tenets of a capitalist market economy that took substantial shape in Canada precisely in the years when the universities of Ontario were founded. To the spirit of Edmund Burke was added those of Adam Smith and Richard

Cobden, embodiments of the theory and practice of *laissez-faire* liberal-ism, and in this way colleges and universities founded to train clergy, educate a professional and citizen elite, and ensure stability also took up the ethic of material growth central to commercial and industrial capital-ism. One consequence of this was that from the middle of the nineteenth century onward, when the democratic age had dawned in Canada and the first undergraduates began to graduate from Ontario universities, the competing ethics of concern for tradition and of pursuit of material progress – of a certain past and an uncertain future – found champions in British North America in a degree of balance perhaps not found in quite the same combination elsewhere. If the dominant ethic of British univer-sities at the time was that of tradition and of their American counterparts that of social development, in the central-Canadian province of Ontario for the century after Queen Victoria's coronation both existed in uneasy equipoise.

University programs and disciplines were created against the back-drop of political, economic, and social transformation. Yet within the academy, equally momentous changes rooted in the life of the emotions and of the mind also took place. The first Ontario university professors and students assumed their roles in colleges shaped by evangelical Christianity, and they did so on the eve of the Darwinian revolution. They and their successors faced challenges to traditional religious values and academic curricula posed by evolutionary theories, biblical criti-cism, and new assumptions about the nature of social change. Operating in a North American environment that on the whole preferred the practi-cal and admired the scientific, they sought to demonstrate their social utility by creating programs both practical and scientific. Yet in common with colleagues elsewhere, at the same time they gave shape and sub-stance to distinctive variants of the modern humanities and social sci-ences. Each university in the province, with its own peculiar mission and ambience, rose to such challenges and adjusted to them in its own way. I have tried to be sensitive to this institutional distinctiveness while recog-nizing that universities share many academic values and traditions.

The University of Toronto holds a special place in this universe of separate existence but collective understanding. As the 'provincial uni-versity,' blessed from the outset by the munificence of the provincial state, it quickly became the benchmark by which other institutions mea-sured themselves and their relationship to provincial administrations. Like the Canadian Pacific Railway in the eyes of Western Canadian farmers, to those outside the pale the University of Toronto became a symbol of privilege easily attained and jealously guarded. University-government relations in Ontario began as a rearticulation in colonial circumstances of the ancient problem of the one and the many – here related to the problem of the University of Toronto and its 'regional' competitors. In this respect, as in many others, academic politics simply mirrored other aspects of provincial life. Since the University of Toronto enjoyed guaranteed provincial funding that other institutions could depend on only after the second decade of the twentieth century, the provincial university attained a level of physical infrastructure and academic pre-eminence that could not be matched by other universities in Ontario. Given this initial advantage, by the end of the Great War of 1914–18 the University of Toronto had reached an extraordinary degree of dominance in the academic and scholarly life of the province. For the half-century that followed, the Toronto professoriate made many of the most important contributions to scholarship in the province. The latter chapters of the book reflect this predominance.

Ironically, of the Ontario universities whose origins date from the nineteenth century, only the University of Toronto has not been the subject of a recent institutional biography. No general history of the provincial university has appeared since 1927. Because of this remarkable lacuna in scholarship, I have attempted to provide at least an initial outline, however skeletal and provisional, of certain elements of the largely untold intellectual and social history of the University of Toronto in this century. Yet in doing so, I have made every effort not to undervalue the contributions of other institutions. Similarly, since a comprehensive survey of key developments in all major disciplines in the professions, sciences, humanities, and social sciences has not proven possible in the space allotted to this volume, I have chosen to focus on certain key professions and disciplines that illuminate important themes and are of major significance in academic development. Inevitably there are gaps in my treatment – of the intellectual history of academic science, of the disciplines that are glanced over or ignored, of organized sports, or of agencies such as sororities and fraternities, for example. I can only hope that their existence will inspire others to fill them.

I have attempted here to convey the sense that the universities of Ontario have very much been conditioned by the provincial, continental, and transatlantic environments. In an earlier and rather more lengthy manifestation, the text of the book contained more of this contextual and comparative material, as well as additional evidence and discursive passages intended to establish atmosphere and scene. Editorial requirements resulted in the deletion of much of it; what remains will often be found in the notes. I hope that although *Matters of Mind* is in a strict sense a study in provincial or regional history it will nevertheless be seen to address themes – economic, political, intellectual, and social – that transcend provincial boundaries. In the absence of a volume in the Ontario Historical Studies Series devoted specifically to the intellectual history of Ontario, I have deliberately cast a broad thematic net. I hope that the past I have sought to recover will be regarded as part of this larger framework of ideas and influence. There is a sense in which the history of an individual university recapitulates that of the institution as a whole. In this way, the university in Ontario is also part of the history of Oxford, or Edinburgh, or Johns Hopkins, just as they, in turn, share part of a common inheritance. For this reason, I would like to think that the story told in these pages will be accepted as a meaningful part of the history of those Ontario universities founded only after the book concludes.

My approach has required an attempt to prod beneath the manifest content of academic rhetoric and action to discern individual, institutional, and social motivations responsible for conditioning them. Decisions as to what students should study, or what disciplinary 'empires' to encourage or to resist, often result from motives somewhat removed from the purely academic abstraction called Truth, even if the search for truth remains the ideal. *Matters of Mind* is an attempt to anchor the life of the mind in material circumstance in order to demonstrate that while the university is one social institution among others, it is a very special one. This book has been written by someone who believes strongly in the central place of the university in society and who can personally testify to its ability to affect lives in profound ways. The university has always been a body with overwhelming potential for individual and social transformation, and it remains so.

Acknowledgments

This book could not have been completed without a great deal of assistance and support. My primary obligation lies with the editors and the Board of Trustees of the Ontario Historical Studies Series for offering an untested young historian in the late 1970s the opportunity to undertake a difficult but challenging task. Goldwin French, Jeanne Beck, and Peter Oliver have been model editorial advisers, and they, like the members of the OHSS Board, have been paragons of patience. All have offered consistent and strong support for a project that has shifted in magnitude and taken many years to complete. A middle-aged historian now offers his deep gratitude to them.

Several people have served over the years as research assistants. I wish to thank Michael Goeres, Jonas Thor, Judy Curry, Jocelyn Buller, Peter James, and Nancy Bell for their aid. I owe a special debt of gratitude to Lin Buckland, who in 1980 uprooted herself from her family in Ottawa to do a great deal of vital research elsewhere.

I am happy to acknowledge sources of funding. Once again, the Ontario Historical Studies Series has been very supportive. Its editors and board provided a level of research assistance sufficient for a scholar initially located in Manitoba to do research in Ontario over sustained periods. I was also helped in 1980–1 by a leave fellowship from the Social Sciences and Humanities Research Council of Canada that allowed me to spend a sabbatical year based in Kingston and Toronto. Other grants making research assistance possible were provided by the University of Manitoba and Carleton University, using funds provided by SSHRCC.

Institutions can be homes, and during my research trips I have found some good ones. Massey College offered me a Visiting Senior Fellowship while I was in Toronto in 1981, so I had the good fortune to be near both the Robarts Library and the University of Toronto Press lunch table (now alas auctioned off) in the basement of the university's Faculty Club during the last term of Robertson Davies's tenure as Master of Massey. Between 1983 and 1985, the board of directors of the Jackman History of Canadian Methodism project kindly allowed me to continue my work on the Ontario Historical Studies Series project on a part-time basis.

More recently, in the academic year 1990–1 I had the good fortune to have been appointed a Fellow of St Mary's College, University of Durham, by the University's Society of Fellows. This made it possible for me to escape the ongoing drive to do 'just a little more research' on my book, and to finish most of it well away from any enticing relevant archive – always a source of seduction when the alternative is to write. The department of history in the University of Durham provided me with a comfortable garret near the cathedral, as well as with invaluable access to mailing facilities and photocopy machines that are too easily taken for granted. I am also grateful to that department for the opportunity to speak to its faculty research seminar on the subject of higher education in Ontario in the twentieth century. Similarly, I wish to thank St Mary's College, University of Durham, for the invitation to give its 1991 Fellowship Lecture on the subject of the student generation of 1914. Professor Anthony Fletcher, head of the history department, and Miss Joan Kenworthy, principal of St Mary's College, were most gracious and helpful hosts; Miss Kenworthy kindly did not complain when my son Hamish pulled up some of the college tulips while fooling around with Black Bess, the porter's dog. I would be remiss if I did not also mention the uniquely English hospitality provided by the Buffalo Head, my 'local.' Some serious editing got done there.

I wish also to thank the Carleton University committee that selected me as recipient of the Marston LaFrance Research Fellowship for 1992–3. This unique award, which allows scholars in the final stages of preparing a book for publication to be released from teaching and administrative responsibilities, made possible a year free of distractions so that an unwieldy manuscript could be turned into a book.

At times I have taxed the patience of colleagues by sending them parts or all of my manuscript to read. Paul Axelrod, Michael Bliss, Joanna Dean, Lydia Dixon, Robert D. Gidney, Charles M. Johnston, J.K. Johnson, W.P.J. Millar, Heather Murray, H. Blair Neatby, George Rawlyk, John G. Reid, Katherine Ridout, Keith Walden, and William Westfall read one or several chapters. Two anonymous readers from the University of Toronto Press and the Ontario Historical Studies Series pointed out areas of omission and weakness. Carl Berger, John Kendle, and Judith Kendle read the entire manuscript, at a time when it was some 40,000 words longer than the one submitted to the publisher. Their comments and criticisms were especially encouraging, substantive, and helpful. As in the past, I am particularly indebted to Judith Kendle, whose single-spaced typewritten responses to chapters seemed at times half as long as what I asked her to read; my work has been improved immeasurably because of her wit, wisdom, and exactitude. Collectively these critics have saved me from many errors of fact and judgment. Whatever problems of evidence, interpretation, logic, or style remain in the book, because of their efforts it is nevertheless much better than what they were asked to evaluate. I could not have kept my work in perspective over the past dozen years if these friends and colleagues had not been willing to devote their own energies to helping me. I cannot thank them enough.

The time a writer spends in the study is not a sacrifice, but a privilege. The sacrifice is made by others, usually family members, and I have done more than my share in exacting one. So I thank Pauline Johnston McKillop and Hamish Alexander McKillop. As one with long experience in the production end of academic publishing, Pauline knows enough about the idiosyncrasies of authors to have remained patient when she found her partner all too often bent over a word processor at odd hours while the curtains remained unhung. As for Hamish, now almost eight, I hope that our talks in the study about how books are written and made, what a university is, or how a mere iceberg could sink the mighty *Titanic*, have given him a sense that acquiring new words and then sharing them with others in the form of a story, even one about long ago, is something very special and enriching, akin to making music. If he has learned this elementary lesson in the life of the mind, my neglect of him will have been worth every moment of time otherwise spent.

A.B. McKillop

Part One:
Institutional Foundations

1

Education and Authority

The occasion was probably Bishop John Strachan's finest hour. The main chamber, the gallery, even the adjacent corridors of the Upper Canadian Legislature in Toronto, abandoned since the union of the Canadas three years earlier, were again crowded with distinguished visitors. For almost all of them it was a singular occasion. Despite their social eminence in Upper Canada, few had ever attended a university function. They were about to do so now, for their presence had been requested at the first convocation of the University of King's College, Toronto.

A contributor to the *Patriot*, a newspaper that supported the Lord Bishop of Toronto, was part of the throng that packed the gallery on that Friday, five days before Christmas, 1844. The scene on the chamber floor below impressed him. 'The first object, which met the eye of the spectator,' he recorded, '... was the Dais, on which were seated the authorities of the University, attired in full academic costume. In the centre, on an elevated platform, was the Lord Bishop of Toronto, President of the University ...'[1] Strachan's place was on the spot where the chancellor of King's College would normally be; but the chancellor of the college was the governor-general of the United Canadas, Sir Charles Metcalfe, and he had another ceremony to attend. The second Parliament of a newly united Canada had opened in Montreal three weeks earlier, on 28 November.

Bishop Strachan had therefore assumed the chancellor's duties as well as his seat. Seated to the left was the vice-president, the Reverend Dr John McCaul. Slightly in front of both were the proctors, the Reverend Dr James Beaven and Professor Henry Croft. So the academic hierarchy continued, with professors in stalls located in front of the dais, graduates on benches immediately behind them, tiers for the students on either side. Altogether, it was most impressive, thought the *Patriot*'s reporter. The 'coup d'oeil,' he concluded, 'was most attractive and imposing – on the Dais, the sombre yet ornamental furniture, the blaze of the scarlet and pink and blue worn by some authorities, according to their degrees, beautifully contrasted with the grave black which was the predominant colour.'

The convocation itself was not unlike hundreds that had preceded it in the ancient universities of Europe and were to follow it within the boundaries of this British North American province. Degrees were bestowed, academic prizes given, and speeches by university authorities delivered. Still, it was the first such ceremony in the province; many if not all of the guests probably left the old legislative building that December afternoon impressed with the proceedings and secure in the belief that the intellectual and cultural life of Canada West had reached a new plateau. The ceremonies that day may have stirred up pride, but they represented aspiration rather than accomplishment, for King's was a college more by force of will than by actual circumstance. The cornerstone of its one building had been laid only two years earlier, and it had begun to admit students only in 1843. The young men who had presented themselves at convocation were a mere nine in number, and they were matriculants, not graduating university students. Six degrees, it is true, had been awarded, but five of them were granted *ad eundem*, because the candidates had previously attended the universities of Aberdeen, Edinburgh, and Dublin. The sixth was a bachelor's degree in arts, awarded to F.W. Barron, principal of Upper Canada College.[2] The recipient of the first of thousands of such degrees in the province that became Ontario graduated without having attended a class at his Alma Mater.

In spite of the pomp of this first granting of academic degrees in Canada West, it was not at all certain that the University of King's College would survive. The fact was that King's was struggling for existence at a time when a new economic and political order was coming into existence. The 1840s would prove to be one of the most important decades of the nineteenth century for British North America, although it could only have been dimly seen as such at the time. Much more than an institution of higher learning was at stake in the struggle over King's College; also in question was the legitimacy of the complex, interconnected web of power and authority that had gradually come into existence after the passage of the Constitutional (or Canada) Act of 1791 and that had reached its apogee with the overwhelming victory of Lieutenant-Governor Francis Bond Head and his Tory supporters in the Upper Canadian election of 1836. Rebellion was one result, triggered in part by sheer frustration at the rigid and self-righteous exclusiveness of those in power as they attempted to maintain authority in the face of changing social and economic circumstances. It came within a year. The arrival of the Earl of

Durham to assess the nature and cause of the breakdown of existing constitutional structures was another. He submitted his famous report in
1838. The political union of the Canadas in 1841 was yet a third.

Durham's *Report* heralded a new epoch in the political and economic
history of British North America, one that was to witness a remarkable
shift in the basis of political, economic, and social authority, and it
would do so within the short span of a single decade. On 20 December
1844 the most influential members of the old colonial elite, members of
the 'Family Compact' all, had attended an academic convocation
designed to assure them that education conferred legitimate authority,
that the interests of King's College were also their interests and would
help perpetuate that authority. Like the mastodons that had once roamed
North America at will, they must have believed themselves to be imper-
vious to the changing environment, to be blessed by providence. Yet the
next day in Montreal a young Kingston lawyer, John Alexander Macdonald, made one of his first speeches in the Legislature of the United
Canadas. Its purpose was to support a 'radical' grocer's petition to have
two sitting members of the Legislature removed.[3] The man who would
later become Canada's first prime minister had assumed his place in politics, and with him a new species of politician not far removed from the
status of upstart grocers had come into political prominence. These men
of commerce, the heirs of Smith, Durham, and Cobden, dreamt of a
political process in harmony with the imperatives of the market-place.
One result would be the evaporation of Bishop Strachan's dreams for
King's College.

Simcoe and Strachan

Upper Canada's first lieutenant-governor, John Graves Simcoe, had
been fond of reminding its inhabitants that while they lived in a new
land they were not a new people. They lived in a colony but they were
part of an Empire. In numerous ways during his term in the 1790s Simcoe attempted to extend into his newly established province the principles and practices – as he understood them – of the eighteenth-century
England he had left. Filtered through his experience defending British
interests during the American Revolution more than a decade earlier,
and through his repulsion at the spectre of a French Revolution not then
ended, that understanding came to sharp focus in his resolve to establish
the western province as a pivotal British citadel in an alien American
continent. It was his utmost duty, he believed, to 'inculcate British Customs, Manners & Principles in the most trivial, as well as serious matters' in order 'to assimilate the colony with the parent state.'[4]

Simcoe knew first hand that armies and fortifications were not in themselves sufficient to guard against the potential intrusion of the republican institutions and democratic excesses he so abhorred. The source of all authority – whether political, religious, or social – was to reside, in Simcoe's schema, in the island centre of the Empire. Only in this way would Upper Canada become what he hoped it would: the very 'image and transcript' of the England in his mind. Education was central to this purpose, and Simcoe voiced these thoughts from the moment he reached Canadian soil, whether to the English naturalist Sir Joseph Banks or to colonial leaders such as Bishop Mountain of Quebec and others.[5] 'Liberal education,' he wrote to Mountain, 'seems to me ... to be indispensably necessary; and the completion of it in the establishment of a University ... in my apprehension would be most useful to inculcate just principles, habits and manners, into the rising generation; to coalesce the different customs of the various descriptions of settlers, emigrants from the old Provinces of Europe into one form.'[6]

To Simcoe higher education and social authority were inextricably linked. They were also central in the mind of John Strachan from the time he arrived in Upper Canada in 1799, three years after Simcoe's departure for England. These were men who shared many assumptions. Strachan was every bit as Scottish as Simcoe was English, yet each nevertheless held dearly to the preservation at all costs of the 'balanced' eighteenth-century English constitution – in which, they assumed, the monarchical, aristocratic, and democratic elements in society upheld and stabilized the social order by keeping each other in check. They were therefore vehement in their denunciations of the republican and democratic experiment that was the United States. They were firm in their commitment to the belief that the Constitutional Act made the Church of England the established church of Upper Canada. They were also unwilling to concede, as others had done, that this rigid extension of British institutions into a colonial environment could cause a disjunction of mental expectation and social experience. The secretary of state, Henry Dundas, expressed this when, reacting to the lieutenant-governor's educational plans, he pointed out what to him and others was obvious: 'the Country must make the University, and not the University the Country.'[7]

Such misgivings stopped neither Simcoe nor Strachan. The former left British North America in 1796 still committed to the notion of a university for the perpetuation and enhancement of the 'superior classes,' but he had been checked by the scepticism of both colonists and colonial authorities. 'In particular,' he wrote to Mountain in the year of his departure, 'I have no Idea that a University will be established though I am daily confirmed in its necessity.'[8] John Strachan directed much of his energy towards the control by the 'established' – Anglican – church of the clergy reserves, and the use of Crown lands for educational purposes. In this area, as in most others, his activities marked a direct continuation of Simcoe's aspirations. He was indefatigable in the attempt, for the transition from Simcoe to Strachan was one from enthusiasm to ambition. Strachan, in fact, was one of the few leaders of Upper Canadian society who took an active interest in educational matters, for on only four occasions from 1800 to 1827 were they raised in speeches from the throne, and only two of these (in 1816 and 1827) concerned university affairs. The arrival of Sir Peregrine Maitland as lieutenant-governor in 1818 encouraged Strachan, for Maitland was warm to the idea of a university in Upper Canada. Prompted by Strachan, now archdeacon of York and president of the board for the general superintendence of education, Maitland in 1825 solicited and received clarification from the Colonial Office that the Upper Canadian Legislature could indeed substitute some of the more valuable Crown reserve lands for existing university tracts, allocated by the Crown in 1797.[9] So impressed was Maitland with Strachan's energy and ideas that he named the archdeacon as special envoy to confer with Colonial Office authorities in England.

Strachan returned to Upper Canada in 1827 with a Royal Charter for the University of King's College in his hands. He had not always agreed with Colonial Office officials such as Lord Bathurst, and ironically enough it was Strachan who was the man of 'advanced views' during the discussions, arguing for a less strong Anglican presence than they had.[10] But by Upper Canadian standards, Strachan's charter for King's College was still strongly Anglican – too strongly for some. No religious tests were to be required of any student, but the president and the professorial members of the governing council were required to be members of the Church of England and to subscribe to the Thirty-Nine Articles. (Non-Anglican professors could therefore teach at King's, but could not participate in college administration.) What was to be administered at this point before King's had either buildings or students? To begin with, there were the 225,944 acres of Crown land set aside for its use. Even before King's existed in any meaningful sense it was therefore already an economic enterprise of no mean importance, and with that importance came political strife. Strachan's difficulties with King's College had scarcely begun. Twenty years later they would still be with him.

Between 1832 and 1851 no fewer than fourteen university bills failed to pass in the legislatures of either Upper Canada or United Canada, and not because their sponsors lacked political acuity.[11] They were drawn up and supported in debate by some of the most successful politicians of the day, including Robert Baldwin, W.H. Draper, and John A. Macdonald. They failed for other reasons, rooted in the tensions and discontentment caused by two diverging conceptions of which social and economic groups should govern. With them also came competing notions about the role of government. Should it primarily be dedicated to ensuring social stability or fostering economic change?

By the 1830s Bishop Strachan had come to epitomize the old order then still in political power in Upper Canada. He had long been insistent, for example, on the necessity of social inequality. For him, it was rooted in the natural order. Different classes of men have different capacities, he proclaimed in numerous sermons of the 1820s and 1830s.[12] As one of Upper Canada's first educators – certainly its foremost – Strachan was able to give his assumptions concrete expression. The early graduates of his Grammar School in Cornwall gradually took their places, as they were intended to do, in positions of power.[13] By the end of the 1830s, although by no means a completely united political group and under considerable pressure by moderate reformers and radicals alike, they nevertheless maintained their hegemony in the upper reaches of power, especially in the Upper Canadian Legislative Council. There the support for projects such as King's College remained unsullied by compromise on the matter of its Anglican nature. Yet people resented Strachan's charter for King's College from the outset, and their objections increased with the passing years.

Citizens from various districts presented more than forty petitions (containing almost five thousand signatures) to the Upper Canadian Assembly within a few months of Strachan's return from England with the King's College Charter in hand. When demands for revision to it were made, however, the initiative came from the Legislative Council, not from Reformers in the Assembly. Following the major victory of the Tories in 1836, led by the recently arrived Francis Bond Head, the Tory faction held a sizeable majority in the Assembly. It was now possible to introduce a limited bill of amendment. When it was passed early in 1837 it had significantly reduced the formal Anglican presence in the administration of the college. For Reform members of the Assembly, such changes were entirely too meagre. King's College still had full control over the Crown lands intended to support the cause of education in the province. Their suspicions that the changes would not affect the actual practice of religious exclusivism were not allayed when the announcement was made of the new officials of King's College. All were members of the Church of England.[14]

The abortive rebellion of 1837-8, as might be expected, strained affairs still further. On the one hand, the rebellion itself confirmed in Strachan's mind the need for proper institutional mechanisms by which to stabilize a shaky social order; on the other, Lord Durham's subsequent *Report* on the causes and implications of the insurrection severely criticized the oligarchical nature of the Family Compact, thereby strengthening the conviction of Reformers that the apparent stranglehold of the Compact needed to be broken. In addition, one further development added to Strachan's unease. In 1836 the Methodists had succeeded in founding the Upper Canada Academy, intended 'for the general education of youth, in the various branches of literature and science on Christian principles.'[15] By 1838 Strachan well knew that it was only a matter of time before the Methodist leader, Egerton Ryerson, a man every bit as energetic and ambitious as himself, made his case for a university that would meet the needs of his own denomination.

Politics, Sectarianism, and the New Economic Order

Durham's *Report* of 1838 has become well known for its indictment of the hegemony of the old colonial oligarchies, its promotion of the idea of 'responsible government,' and its argument for the legislative union of Upper and Lower Canada. Yet it was also an eloquent, sustained, and powerful apologia for an economic and social order that by the time of the Canadian rebellions was already beginning to assume definite shape. Published at the very outset of Victoria's reign, it embodied two notions central to the Victorian mind: an optimistic materialism and a firm belief in the progressive beneficence of the unfettered expansion of the market economy. It was, in the words of one historian, a socio-economic vision that 'was firmly rooted in the secular world ...'[16]

The report began and ended with attention called to the great potential for material prosperity in British North America made possible by its unexploited natural resources.[17] Durham's task, as he elsewhere stated it, was to remove the obstacles preventing Canadians from sharing 'in the progressive prosperity of a flourishing State.' Accordingly, the best way of securing continued loyalty was to 'rectify existing evils, and to produce in their place a well-being which no other dominion could give.' Greater population and more capital, Durham said, were the means of bringing this about. Immigration schemes would encourage the former; relaxation of mercantilist restrictions on commerce would help accumulate the latter.

But the crisis of the Canadas was also a crisis of leadership and of authority – a matter, put simply, of who should rule. Durham's criticism of the Upper Canadian governing class was based only in part on his dislike of oligarchy; of more importance was his belief that the Family Compact impeded the degree of economic growth that was possible. 'The statute book of the Upper Province abounds,' he admitted, 'with useful and well-constructed measures of reform, and presents an honourable contrast to that of the Lower Province.' Durham had, then, no fundamental quarrel with the legislative record of the pre-rebellion rulers of Upper Canada. His objection was instead with the fact that their monopoly on power and authority had closed the doors of opportunity to a new class of potential leaders who represented the enthusiastic and aggressive spirits of commerce, industry, and general economic self-interest. 'As long as personal ambition is inherent in human nature, and as long as the morality of every free and civilized community encourages its aspirations,' Durham wrote near the end of his *Report*, 'it is one great business of a wise Government to provide for its legitimate development.' To this end he quoted one of his philosophical mentors, the great eighteenth century moral philosopher and economic theorist, Adam Smith: 'we must provide some scope for what he [Smith] calls "the importance" of the leading men of the Colony, beyond what he forcibly terms the present "petty prizes of the paltry rattle of colonial faction."' It was Durham's fervent hope that by means of legislative union and responsible government new leaders would assume their rightful and necessary place in the corridors of colonial power. The hegemony of the unrestricted self-regulating market economy, not of democracy, was the central element in his solution to the Canadian crisis.

Durham's materialistic and secular vision was a portent of events to come. Within a decade King's College was to be closed, its place taken by a state-sponsored, secular provincial institution, the University of Toronto. Durham had seen the clergy reserves question, and by implication the King's College controversy, as one of the major issues precipitating the Upper Canadian rebellion, but he foresaw no solution to the problem short of leaving the disposal of all such lands completely in the hands of the colonial legislature. The combination of a representative government and a less dominant position of Anglican adherents in Upper Canada (because of non-Anglican British emigration), he thought, would soon make the Church of England recognize the incongruity of 'the supremacy thus given to it.' The 1842 census of Upper Canada showed a total of 107,791 Anglicans, compared with a combined total of 261,632 Methodists, Presbyterians, Roman Catholics, and Baptists, in Canada West[18] (see Fig. 1.1). Yet the conduct of Church of England politicians after the Act of Union came into effect in 1841 was scarcely one of acquiescence or philosophical resignation. Unless they decided to withdraw from politics altogether, they were now confronted

FIGURE 1.1

Religious adherence in Canada West, 1842–62

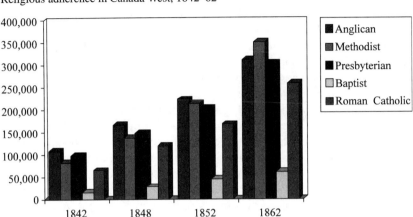

SOURCE: *Census of Canada* (Ottawa 1871)

with a serious problem in addition to that of the continued opposition of the Reform element: they were deeply divided among themselves.

A first source of division was the very issue of the Union. Many of the old guard – John Beverley Robinson, John Strachan, Henry Sherwood, and others (those strong in defence of King's College) – had bitterly opposed it. Theirs was a politics whose emphasis was on class differentiation, on deference, rather than on the imperatives of the market-place.[19] In their view the levelling implications of a united group of Upper and Lower Canadian reformers in a single legislative assembly outweighed the potential economic advantages of a restored Laurentian trade axis. But other heirs of the 'Constitutional Party' of 1836 held different priorities. During the 1840s the advocates of commercial expansion became increasingly vocal within both its leadership and its rank and file. Francis Hincks and John A. Macdonald, both of whom later became premiers of pre-Confederation Canada and whose politics largely were railroads, were two such men who entered the Legislature during the decade.

The man who dominated the new coalition of Conservatives, as they were coming to call themselves, was, however, William Henry Draper. In a very real sense he was a man caught between the shifting allegiances within his political group. Draper was by inclination a supporter of the old Constitution of 1791, a believer in both the established church and the emergent secular state. But as a director of the Bank of Upper Canada he was equally committed to the ongoing expansion of Canadian commerce.[20] As a result he became the spokesman of other men of business who supported the Act of Union. Draper's great political ambition was to foster the development of a political system that preserved conservative social values yet provided incentives to economic advancement. It was not easy, however, to wed social pedigree and economic ambition. Draper found this out when he sought to find a middle ground on the King's College question, now an unresolved issue in Canadian politics for more than a decade.

To the modern student of Canadian history, the political activity of the Union period appears Byzantine in its complexity. Political parties, in the strict sense, did not exist, the principle of ministerial responsibility was a novel theory that had not, in the early 1840s, been conceded, and the issues that dominated the political process were often ones that perplex the secular, twentieth-century mind. To discover that religious concerns shaped Canadian politics in major ways in the 1840s and 1850s is puzzling enough to such students that many avoid the subject altogether. Yet the fact remains that no politician in Canada in the middle years of the nineteenth century could survive in office without addressing religious issues, and without allying, formally or informally, with the major political lobbies of the day: the organized churches. William Draper was not the only Canadian politician who had to negotiate the dangerous shoals of the university question in the Union period. Nor was he the first. Making his difficulties worse, by the early 1840s more than one university existed in Canada West.

The Methodists had not been inactive in promoting their own plans for a college during the years of the King's College controversy. In 1841 they had secured an extension of the charter of Upper Canada Academy, founded at Cobourg in 1836, and the new Victoria College was receiving students within a year of Egerton Ryerson's appointment as its principal.[21] The story of the origins of the new Methodist college provides a capsule case study of the rather complex interaction of personalities, religion, and politics that faced William Draper – and for that matter all other politicians – in the united Canadas. One religious figure dominated the scene: Egerton Ryerson, the voluntarist counterpart to John Strachan.

Along with missions and temperance, education dominated the pages of the *Christian Guardian* in its years after 1829, when Ryerson, the young Anglican-turned-Methodist, became its twenty-six-year-old founding editor. This decision to put the need for non-sectarian general education in the province before his brethren helped generate sufficient debate on the subject that it became a matter of serious concern at the Methodist Conference of 1830. As if to prod delegates further, Ryerson had printed in June a letter from 'A Methodist Youth' that demanded to know why nothing was being done to provide education for Methodists in Upper Canada, and, as if to shame his elders, the young man had pledged ten pounds sterling towards such a project. This ploy, as well as other items on education by the *Guardian*'s editor, worked. That autumn, a five-man committee of the conference was appointed to consider establishing an institution of higher education. It was decided that the institution would be governed by a board of nine trustees and five visitors, to be chosen by the conference. Most important of all, the institution was to be based on broad, liberal principles. The committee's declaration stated that 'no system of Divinity shall be taught therein; but all students shall be free to embrace and pursue any religious creed, and attend any place of religious worship which their parents or guardians may direct.'[22] Altogether, this was a truly extraordinary declaration, given the fierce sectarian loyalties of the day. Later, after the appointment of a committee of nine, the choice of site was made by secret ballot. The lucky location was the Lake Ontario town of Cobourg, chosen from six possibilities including Brockville and York.

By the autumn of 1831, 3,954 pounds sterling had been subscribed, providing sufficient encouragement for the conference to instruct the building committee to proceed with the construction of a brick edifice not to exceed 5,000 pounds in cost. The cornerstone of the academy was duly laid by Dr John Gilchrist, chairman of the building committee, on 7 June 1832, amidst jubilant celebrations. Construction continued through 1832 and early 1833 at a pace that exceeded that of financing the venture.

A bill of incorporation failed to pass in the province's Legislature in 1835, and the next year, with the academy about to open and already deeply in debt, the president of the conference commissioned Ryerson to visit England to petition its government for a royal charter and to seek donations. C.B. Sissons's biography of Ryerson documents at length the initial rebuff he received from Lord Glenelg, the colonial secretary, and his persistent courtship of the under-secretary, Sir George Grey.[23] The visitations and negotiations at Westminster and the canvassing of London and prominent towns took nineteen long months, but when at last Ryerson returned he held the first royal charter ever granted to a non-Anglican institution. He also brought with him a colonial office promise of 4,100 pounds sterling and individual subscriptions amounting to more than 1,200 pounds. Ten of these were promised by the Duchess of Kent, whose daughter Victoria would soon assume the throne of England and provide the successor of UCA with its name.

Ryerson's role in the foundation and early history of UCA was as a general publicist of the cause of education and as a troubleshooter: whatever his other interests and duties, he was always available when needed. Once the academy was opened, under the principalship of Matthew Richey, he played no direct role in its affairs. But he was not to be apart from it for long. Richey was an Irish-born Wesleyan in Canadian Methodist territory, and he soon ran afoul of John and William Ryerson, among others, who feared that the new academy would become unduly Wesleyan in tone. As a result, he received little moral support, was accused of financial mismanagement, and had difficulty retaining staff. By 1838 the coeducational academy was near a state of 'hopeless insolvency,' and within a year Richey had all but resigned, leaving Jesse Hurlburt, a graduate of Wesleyan University in Connecticut, as acting principal.

For the brief span of a year or two, all was relatively tranquil. Instructors gave classes in chemistry, physics, and astronomy, classics and mathematics, Greek, Hebrew, and rhetoric. Then Acting Principal Hurlburt discovered and began to pursue the future Mrs Hurlburt, in the form of Miss Maria Boulter, the preceptress. The unaccountable but regular absences of both principal and preceptress from daily functions of the college led to laxity of discipline. One student boasted fifty years later that Miss Boulter's own preoccupations had made possible 'certain infringements of discipline' on the part of himself and one of the girl students. By 1841 the principal had demonstrated to his staff that he was capable of giving only varying versions of the same public speech, students were open in their disrespect for him, and the call came from members of the academy for Egerton Ryerson to take charge.[24]

Ryerson was officially offered the principalship by the Board of Conference in early September, 1841, although only after the bitter opposition of British Wesleyan delegates such as Matthew Richey. It was a fortunate, if divisive, decision, for the Church of Scotland in Canada had just obtained legislative approval for the construction of what would become Queen's University at Kingston, and was at the time pressing for a royal charter. Thus stimulated, and perhaps threatened, the conference applied for and secured by unanimous consent of the Legislature an act incorporating 'Victoria College' at Cobourg, with the power to grant degrees in several faculties. On 27 August 1841 the statute received royal assent. With it, but not part of it, came a much-needed bonus in the form of an annual grant of five hundred pounds.

Ryerson proved to be a valuable but peripatetic principal of Victoria College. He remained stationed in Toronto, and travelled to Cobourg only when necessary, as when he presided over the opening exercises of the new college in October 1841. He directed his commencement

address to the 'Gentlemen and young friends' of the college, an indication of the decision (fully supported by Ryerson) that the coeducational
experiment had failed and would not continue. Not until the 1870s
would women return to Victoria. Instead, Ryerson put forward a conception of the college that was consistent with that of other Victorian liberal
arts colleges, dedicated to producing useful Christians, citizens of sound
character. 'Education,' he warned, 'is not a license for idleness, but a
means of active, honorable and useful enterprise.' The object of all education, he asserted, is self-discipline. Time was precious, and should not
therefore be squandered: 'He that rises at five instead of seven-thirty
every morning gains fourteen of the best hours every week for study and
devotion.'[25]

For the first year Ryerson remained principal *in absentia*, conducting
college affairs primarily by correspondence. He was formally inducted
to the position in June 1842, at an unpretentious ceremony marked by
his 'Inaugural Address on the Nature and Advantages of an English and
Liberal Education,' a speech that took an hour and a half to deliver and
that outlined and justified the future curriculum of the college. It was,
altogether, a broad and balanced liberal arts program that at once recognized the growing importance of the sciences yet nowhere disparaged
the classics. Victoria was to be a college founded on Christian principles, one in which 'intellectual and moral powers' would be employed
according to the principles of reason and truth. It would educate prospective candidates for the Methodist ministry but would make no formal attempt to ensure the doctrinal orthodoxy of its staff.

Ryerson's lengthy address, a careful pre-Darwinian virtuoso performance balancing the dictates of traditional evangelical piety and the
emergence of the Victorian critical intellect, can in retrospect be seen as
one of the cardinal documents not only in the history of nineteenth-century higher education in Canada but also of English-Canadian intellectual history. For this reason alone, despite the brevity of his tenure at
Victoria College as principal, Ryerson must rank as one of its true
'founders.' He contrived the structure of Victoria and then gradually
withdrew, like the providential watchmaker of William Paley's eighteenth-century natural theology. He gave the new college shape and purpose, but let others establish its place in nature.

Another university opened its doors in 1842, one also provoked into
existence by the intransigence of spokesmen for King's College. Championed by the Brockville merchant William Morris, and supported by
the recently formed United Presbyterian Synod (of Upper Canada),
Queen's College at Kingston received its first charter in 1840 from the
Upper Canadian legislature. But when its trustees decided to petition for

a royal charter, English legal officers declared that the original legislation was objectionable since the granting of a charter was the direct prerogative of the crown.[26] Accordingly, the original charter was revoked by proclamation and a royal one granted on 16 October 1841.

From the outset, however, Queen's was beset with difficulties. In the first place, it was unsuccessful in obtaining sufficient revenues. It received no legislative endowment of land or money in spite of its supporters' claims that because of its denominational affiliation with the Established Church of Scotland it should split the Crown lands claimed by King's College for its own use. It received meagre support from Scotland, and its first endowment campaign was a very modest success, if that. This was not its only problem. In 1843 the Scottish church was rent by schism based on the question of lay patronage. The controversy soon carried over into the three-year-old Canadian Synod. In Canada the issue became linked by 1844 to the propriety of receiving patronage from any body, including the provincial government. Led by the Reverend Robert Burns in Toronto, the Free Church movement soon divided Queen's College as well as almost all Presbyterian congregations. Six of Queen's seven theology students announced that they intended to join the dissenting body and urged that a Free Church theological college be established. Five of them subsequently left for Toronto and attended classes with nine others in a room in the Reverend Henry Esson's house. That same year the new synod of the Free Church named the institution Knox College. It was to have an even more precarious early existence than did Queen's. Moving from house to house, constantly impoverished, it did not receive a charter until 1858. Instruction in it was to be confined to theology.[27]

Very soon after the Act of Union was declared, advocates of different stances on university reform began to make their positions known to religious adherents and to politicians. By 1842, for example, Principal Liddell of Queen's, supported by William Morris, had tested the possibility of amalgamating Queen's with King's College in order to solve the fledgling Presbyterian university's financial problems. Such an arrangement, Liddell thought, would allow both 'established' churches – Anglican and Presbyterian – a roughly equal footing, teaching divinity, within a single 'provincial' university. To this end, Liddell quietly sounded out the King's College council, and his proposals for amalgamation reached the governor general and his executive council. Fearing that government support would not be forthcoming unless there was participation by the growing body of Methodists, Liddell also communicated with Egerton Ryerson about the possibility of the Wesleyan Methodists entering the scheme.[28]

The religious community and its newspapers divided on the issue of university reform, as it did on almost every other matter. The King's College council (its voice being the *Patriot*) rejected the notion of union, as did most Anglicans. Ryerson rejected Liddell's suggestion that direct representation be made to the Wesleyan Methodist Conference in order to cement a reform alliance, preferring that the two churches act independently. The Free Church newspaper, the *Banner*, supported reform, if only to 'rescue the University from the grasping hand of Prelate STRACHAN.' Throughout the middle months of 1843, university reform sentiment increased, as did pressures on legislators.

Francis Hincks considered Robert Baldwin's University Bill, introduced in the Assembly on 12 October 1843, as the most important piece of legislation in the first Parliament of the united Canadas. Under its provisions, King's College would have become a non-sectarian arts college in a 'University of Toronto.' Queen's, Victoria, and Regiopolis – the last a Roman Catholic institution in Kingston founded by Bishop Alexander Macdonell in 1837 – would have retained status as essentially divinity schools, without degree-granting powers and would be relocated in Toronto. They would be granted five hundred pounds per year for four years. The new university would be administered by a board representing various 'provincial' interests. No religious tests would be required for staff or students in arts. In the public and legislative debate that followed, the university question vied with the principle of responsible government as the major issue of the day. Indeed, in 1843 the two political phenomena intersected in an important way, for William Draper defended the sanctity of the King's College charter against Baldwin's intrusions by arguing before the Assembly that the erection of universities by the Legislature effectively usurped the Crown's prerogative, as did its interference with the powers of a corporation granted by the Crown. Three days after Draper's lengthy defence of King's and the Crown, Governor General Charles Metcalfe accepted the resignation of Robert Baldwin and all but one member of his executive council.

Baldwin's first attempt at solving the university question had failed. Throughout the 1840s the Tory old guard, especially from Toronto, continued to be adamant in its opposition to any modification to the King's College charter. Others, such as Ogle Gowan of Brockville, William Morris of Perth, and John A. Macdonald of Kingston, were eager to reach some sort of *modus vivendi* on the issue, if only to allow the Assembly to turn to more pressing matters. Macdonald detested the continuing influence of the Compact in political affairs. The 'Toronto Clique,' as he sometimes called them, was an impediment to his own aching ambition and to that of others like him. As he wrote to Gowan: 'I attribute the doubt and hesitation on the part of the Government altogether to the influence of the Family Compact, who cannot abide the promotion or employment of any one beyond their pale ...'[29]

Draper tried to wend his way between these fierce antipathies by proposing, on several occasions in 1845, a moderate compromise relating to King's College. His first proposal, submitted to the legislature in March, sought to locate Queen's and Victoria in Toronto, in some vague relationship with a proposed 'University of Upper Canada,' in which King's College would be the teaching and examining body in arts and science. Proposed payment to the theological colleges was greater than that provided in Baldwin's bill, and unlike it, administration of the new university would be vested in members of the academic community. All students would have been required to belong to the college of their faith. In sum, as historian John S. Moir, has concluded, 'the Bill attempted a happy compromise between national and sectarian interests by combining at one time and in one place the advantages of the residential college and centralized university, teaching secular education in a religious setting with state endowments for religious purposes.'[30] It fully satisfied no one, although the Presbyterian Church and the Wesleyan Methodists gave their support. Opposition came, on the other hand, from Free Church Presbyterians, Baptists, Congregationalists, the Episcopal Methodists, the Primitive Methodists, and, of course, the Anglican community. By the end of the year, Draper's educational policy was in ruins, and his attempt in 1846 to reintroduce university legislation found little support.[31] The prospect of war with the United States generated by the Oregon Boundary dispute, and the fear of economic collapse as a result of English Prime Minister Robert Peel's repeal of the Corn Laws, understandably deflected public and political attention.

Both Baldwin and Draper, reform and conservative politicians, had failed to find an answer to the university question. Yet others were willing to try. John A. Macdonald was not especially devoted to the cause of university reform, but he did recognize just how emotional and powerful the issue was and feared that the electors, irate over the inability of a Conservative ministry to solve the problem, would register their objections at the polls. 'Many questions of more real importance may arise,' Macdonald wrote, 'but none which operates so strongly on the principles or rather prejudices of the public, and if the Conservatives hope to retain power they must settle it before the General Elections.'[32]

Macdonald's proposals took the form of two bills that he introduced in July 1847. The first revoked the amendments made to the King's College Charter in 1837, and gave full control of the college to the Church of England. The second provided for the creation of a board composed of one government appointee and one representative from each of the denominational colleges, whose major responsibility would be to invest and administer funds derived from the university endowment. Queen's, Victoria, and Regiopolis were to receive fifteen hundred pounds yearly, and King's three thousand on the basis of its vested rights. 'These proposals,' concludes John Moir, 'recognized the inherent relation of religion and education, and established the principle of collegiate establishments under the kind of denominational control for which the High Churchmen and Roman Catholics had consistently contended. At the same time it provided an assured income to colleges for whom finances were the prime consideration. Macdonald envisaged nothing more, nor less, than a galaxy of independent denominational colleges scattered across the province, each receiving a modest income from the state.'[33]

The non-Anglican denominations who were to be part of the scheme announced publicly their general approval of the scheme. Strachan, the president of King's College, accepted the proposed division of the endowment. Even so, it failed, in part because of the pluralism of the religious community in Canada West. Excluded denominations – the Free Church, the Episcopal Methodists, and the New Connexion Methodists, for example – protested loudly in religious newspapers. The *Globe* of Free-churcher George Brown called for a 'flood' of petitions to the legislature, and got it. 'Insist that all denominations shall have an equal claim to manage and enjoy the benefits of this great institution,' wrote Brown, 'and that not one copper of the funds shall be alienated from its original purpose.' Speaking for the secularists in the Assembly, Robert Baldwin provided a different denunciation, claiming that the matter had been 'settled' only 'by sweeping the University from off the face of the earth, and giving the Country, in its stead, a few paltry Institutions, in none of which could there be any possible pretention to those attributes which it was the highest behest to a University to possess.'[34] Faced with growing public and legislative opposition, his university bill rejected by all Roman Catholic members of his own party, Macdonald decided not to proceed to second reading with it. He, too, had failed to solve the most divisive and explosive issue of the day. In 1847, at the dawn of the era of responsible government, the university question, not ministerial authority, was the major issue on the hustings.

The accepted premises and practices of Canadian political life had changed a great deal since the beginning of the decade. In 1840 the presence of the Family Compact was a critical factor. Then, the idea of responsible government was simply a theory proposed by William Warren Baldwin and his son Robert, although it had been made a practical possibility by Durham's *Report*. Eight years later it was the sine qua non of political success. The arrival of Lord Elgin in January of 1848 and the election of a new Reform majority led by Robert Baldwin combined to give it constitutional legitimacy.

The triumph of responsible government marked the rise to dominance of the new agents of commercial enterprise, their vision of the future almost wholly a materialistic one. In the turbulent politics of their day, these men of moderate and pragmatic persuasion were drawn into factional alliance and for the most part they remained loyal to their political groups, for their era placed a high premium on loyalty. In truth, none was an unalloyed embodiment, in human form, of any eighteenth-century political 'type.' Most were like the young Oliver Mowat, who described himself in 1843 as being 'neither Radical nor Tory nor Whig.'[35] They were nineteenth-century heirs of both Edmund Burke and Adam Smith, although most had probably read the writings of neither. Philosophically, they were conservative in their general belief in a natural order of social hierarchies and liberal in their acceptance of the market-place as the equally natural fulcrum for social development in the economic realm. They were Canadian lawyers and businessmen in politics.

As such, they were character actors in a political morality play the dynamics of which were rooted in the legitimation of the moral basis of the emerging economic order. Under the practice of responsible government the dispensation of patronage, special privilege, and power was no longer to be under the control of individuals as such: they were, instead, to be distributed by an agency, the secular bourgeois state, acting as the mediator of a system of commercial exchange. The authority of persons had in an important sense been banished. In its place was substituted the authority embodied in the institutional mechanisms of Adam Smith's 'unseen hand.'[36]

Robert Baldwin's successful University bill of 1849 marked the extension of the secular state into the realm of higher education. The measure brooked no compromise on the matter of secularization. It completely removed any form of denominational presence, except a provision for the possible affiliation of church colleges with the state. The chancellor of the new provincial university was not to be a cleric; there was not to be any faculty or professorship of divinity; no Crown appointees to the senate could hold religious office or be ordained. No degrees in divinity could be conferred, and no form of religious test was to be required of any student or faculty member. As the preamble to the lengthy Bill declared: 'it is ... necessary that such Institution ... should be entirely free, in its government and discipline, from all Denominational bias, so that the just rights and privileges of all may be fully maintained, without offence to the Religious Opinions of any ...'[37] As far as the source of its social authority was concerned, the new University of Toronto was very much the 'Godless Institution' its King's College opponents said it was.

That authority was now vested in the secular state. The Crown, acting through colonial politicians, was to hold substantial powers of control over the affairs of the university, including control over the old King's College land endowment. The 'Governor, or Person administering the Government of this Province,' was to be a visitor with powers of commission. The government would appoint a number of 'Crown seats' to the senate equal in number 'in all time to come' to the number of 'college seats.' It could disallow any senate statute within two years of its passing. It would have the right to appoint a member of the university's five-man endowment board; the other four would be appointed by the senate. Finally, after consultation with the senate, it would have final authority in the appointment of all professors.[38] Baldwin's University Bill was read in the House of Assembly for the second time on 17 April 1849, and it was passed with a substantial majority. It received royal assent on 30 May. Canada West now had a centralized, state-controlled, completely secular provincial university with three faculties: law, medicine, and arts.

The Demise of King's College

'In destroying King's College by enactment, you have placed yourself in open defiance of God and his revealed word and turned an Institution in which the Saviour was worshipped into a nursery of infidelity and delivered, so far as you are able, the lands of Christ's flock into the hands of his enemy, the Prince of this world.' That was Bishop Strachan's reply to Baldwin after the University legislation was passed.[39] The Crown reserves – 'the lands of Christ's flock' – were, under Baldwin's successful measure, to be used for the purely secular, satanic purposes of the state and its agents, the 'Prince[s] of this world.' In educational affairs the division of church and state was gaining substantial ground. The Church of England was now considered a denomination not to be elevated above any other. Accordingly, Strachan fell back on a second line of defence. He would preserve 'true religion' in higher education by creating a new denominational college. Within two years his efforts had met with success. The charter of Trinity College, once again secured by a special trip to England, was accepted by the Legislature in August 1851. It was King's College by another name.

Four years earlier, the Methodist newspaper, the *Christian Guardian*, had declared its support for the university bills proposed by John A. Macdonald. Since the bills would have preserved King's College while sharing its endowment with other denominations, the *Guardian* had praised them for their 'comparative equality and liberality.' 'We believe,' said its editor, 'no reader of the Guardian would wish to have the secular education of his son severed from instruction in the principles and morals of the Christian Religion.' The separation of religion and university education, he concluded, was 'a monstrous conception' held in the province only by 'certain wise-acres ...'[40] In 1849 the 'wise-acres' had triumphed, and the *Guardian* declared that their plan was 'the most objectionable one ever submitted to the country,' since it was characterized by 'Infidelity.' Moreover, said one Methodist leader, its object was simply 'to swell up the power and patronage of the Colonial government' by obtaining the old King's College endowment.[41] However precarious their formative years, four church colleges with charters and power to grant degrees nevertheless existed when Baldwin's University bill was passed: King's, Queen's, Victoria, and Regiopolis. Together, they represented a sizeable proportion of the population of Canada West, from different regions in the province, a population clearly convinced that instruction at university should not be divorced from the guiding principles of the Christian religion. It can scarcely be said that the colleges acted as one voice in their objections to Baldwin's university bill, for each had its peculiar needs and strategies for survival. At the same time, their reaction to it reflected some fundamental shared concerns that were to become a leitmotif of much future discussion of university affairs in Ontario.

The basic objection of the colleges was, naturally, to the assumption – now embodied in provincial statute – that the training of minds could and should be divorced from the nurture of spirit. For once, all leaders of the major denominations in the province were in agreement with the words of John Strachan when in a petition he warned: 'An institution which drives away all those who from their living faith, warmth of disposition and sincerity of purpose are best qualified to train the young to all that is pure, lovely and sublime in religion, and noble in science, must become the abhorrence of all Christian parents, who can look upon it in no other light than as an infidel college, dead to all sense of religious truth and unworthy of the blessing of Heaven.'[42] Such an unequivocal dismissal of religion as the basis of social cohesion and character formation was, for Strachan and his clerical colleagues, a painful affront to their beliefs; but more politically dangerous for them was the centralist nature and implications of the Baldwin measure.

The title of the new university bill contained the words, 'to provide for the more satisfactory Government, of the said University.' The substitution of state control for that of the church was one means of establishing such 'satisfactory' government, for it made efficiency and economy in university affairs easier to monitor. Centralization of provincial university education in Toronto was another. As they viewed the matter, the church colleges now had only two choices: either to continue their separate existences or to seek affiliation with the new University of Toronto. It was not a happy choice. The former promised continuing penury (for they now could expect no support from the government); the latter offered dependence and absorption. Affiliation required the surrender of the power to confer any degree except in divinity. The dubious quid pro quo was that the college would receive only a single vote in a senate of over twenty members who would control the endowment and the expenditure of income from it. In a certain sense the Tories of Toronto had achieved a measure of victory even though King's College ceased to exist, for all its former professors now held seats in the senate of the new University of Toronto. With the Scylla of self-righteous Anglicans on one side of the senate and the Charybdis of government-appointed secularists on the other, how likely was it, thought the denominational college authorities, that their own institutional interests and needs would be met, or even survive? Only Knox College, still without charter and quite content to instruct only in divinity, took immediate advantage of affiliating with the new 'Provincial University.'

Robert Baldwin left office in 1851, but on the university question he left his successor, businessman and entrepreneur Francis Hincks, his own monsters and whirlpools to contend with. Representing the former was the liberal journalist and politician, George Brown, editor of the Toronto *Globe* and a vociferous voluntarist in religious affairs. Brown and his supporters lobbied strongly for the complete secularization of the clergy reserves; he therefore opposed any form of state aid to church colleges and supported the secular University of Toronto. Representing the latter were the leaders and supporters of the denominational colleges, equally vocal in their swirling denunciations of the 1849 legislation. Faced with such opposition, Baldwin had retreated somewhat from his wholly secular stance. In 1850, confronted with accusations of infidelity from all religious camps, he had successfully proposed an amendment to his 1849 Act requiring the University of Toronto to make adequate provision for the religious instruction of students. In addition, the amendment allowed affiliated colleges to make their students meet college academic requirements before advancing to a degree. But this compromise scarcely met the colleges' objections to Baldwin's act. It merely antagonized Brown.

During the 1852–3 legislative session Francis Hincks put forward his own compromise measure, one that at once gave the university examining and degree-granting powers and stripped it of its teaching functions. The latter were to be given to a newly created non-denominational University College that would share surplus revenues with any denominational colleges choosing to affiliate under the new scheme. It was a proposal not without merit but its single inducement to the church colleges was illusory for, as the historian of Victoria University wrote of the financial clause, 'no surplus for distribution was ever permitted to exist.'[43] The complex of buildings that eventually arose to house University College cost the extraordinary sum of 95,000 pounds sterling. University College was visible evidence, forever engraved in stone, that independent church colleges would never see any of the old King's College endowment. In the end, Hincks's compromise satisfied few other than the new residents of University College. After seeing a draft of the bill, Brown asserted that 'it would be a national calamity to split up and destroy Toronto University for a set of little paltry colleges.'[44] Egerton Ryerson concluded, however, that the reorganized University of Toronto was an institution 'defended by nobody, cared for by nobody but its salaried officers and paid students.'[45]

Baldwin's University Act of 1849 was now repealed, but in important ways its spirit remained intact. The University of Toronto was more than ever a centralized and secular institution with the full measure of state support, but also vulnerable to the whims of that state, whether leading to neglect or to control. The government-appointed members of the senate had a veto over statutes passed by both senate and the University College council and made all professional and administrative appointments.[46] In addition, the 1853 University Act removed the teaching of law and medicine from university hands and left them to what a later age would call the 'private sector.' If the intention of the political leaders of the province was to establish the authority of the state in the area of higher education, that aspiration had largely been met by 1853. Control over the provincial university was now firmly established, the sensitive issue of church and state seemingly resolved. Politicians could therefore turn without risk to more pressing and profitable schemes. The provincial university could fend for itself.

Symptomatic of the uncertain future relations between the University of Toronto and its new secular patron were the unsatisfactory circumstances of its location in the days before University College was completed. With priorities separate from those related to higher education, the Hincks government first took possession of the old King's College building in anticipation of the possible location of new parliament buildings on the site. The university, whose secular future had recently been so brightly painted in political rhetoric, was then summarily shunted to an abandoned medical building, recently gutted by the local board of works. The old college building was fitted up as a mental hospital, and was officially named 'The University Lunatic Asylum.'[47]

2

The One and the Many

The wish for a university of the first rank to serve the needs of the English-speaking population of Canada West was as old as the province itself. John Graves Simcoe had spoken of his desire for 'a college of higher class' as early as 1792. More than a half-century passed, however, before such an institution existed. Matters could scarcely have been otherwise, since English-Canadian politics and society in the first half of the nineteenth century were dominated, as we have seen, by fierce sectarian squabbles over the respective jurisdictions of church and state. The 'university question,' which sapped the energies and time of professors and politicians throughout the second half of the nineteenth century, was in spirit a continuation of the older debate over the disposition of Crown lands to protestant denominations for religious and educational purposes:

The old battles were by no means over when King's College was replaced by a state-sponsored university in Toronto. In fact, for the thirty-five years after 1853 a degree of opprobrium at least equal to that heaped earlier upon King's was visited on the new child of the state. Since under the 1853 act the new University of Toronto was technically an examining body, criticisms were consistently levelled at the most tangible evidence of its practical existence, its teaching arm. University College came to symbolize and to absorb all manner of real and perceived grievance: creeping secularism, centralization, a rejection of the college ideal, the unholy alliance between educator and politician, a displacement of religion by science, anti-Canadian prejudice, the squandering of public funds, the dismissal of regional needs and interests, and the arrogance of Torontonians.

Even as students and professors throughout the province gave form and substance to the liberal arts curriculum and spoke loftily about educational values and moral rectitude, administrators in each college were preoccupied with rather more mundane matters. Convocation addresses climbed to rhetorical heights only twice a year; daily, on the other hand, college principals or presidents who gave them faced the task of financing institutions the size of factories but with no easily discernible product with which to meet expenses, much less earn profits. It was not easy, within the climate of optimistic materialism in the mid-Victorian years, to convince the public to support the luxury of a higher education. Who, moreover, should be the fundamental patrons of higher education? Parents? Churches? Private philanthropists? The state? A dominant theme in the institutional history of higher education in Ontario in the last half of the nineteenth century, as before and after, was the search for financial stability.

A University of Toronto: For and Against

The fifty-fourth section of the 1853 act creating the University of Toronto provided the constitutional mortar with which the new University College was built. That section had provided for 'any surplus' of the University of Toronto's income from endowment to be invested annually by the bursar in public provincial securities. The year by year accumulation of the surplus was thus meant to constitute a 'Permanent Fund' that *'from time to time'* could be *'appropriated by Parliament for Academical Education in Upper Canada.'*[1] Such vague wording was guaranteed to perpetuate the scramble for funds. By the mid-1850s, however, certain roles had been reversed. John Strachan had grudgingly come to accept denominational competition as a fact of Anglican life; after the failure of King's College he had conceded that Anglicans had to struggle for state support with other denominations.[2] His earlier view, that the clear intention of the Constitutional Act was that funds so allocated should go to the Church of England in Canada because it alone was the true established church in the country, was now paralleled by University of Toronto authorities who used a secular vocabulary. Funding for the University of Toronto came from the state; the university was specifically designed as the 'provincial university': therefore, went the argument, accrued surpluses should remain within its precincts. Had the University Act not directly mentioned that the institution was to be responsible for 'Academical Education in Upper Canada'?

On the eve of the construction of University College, which began in 1856, the full-time faculty at the provincial university consisted of fifteen members. Of these, five had previously served King's College. By 1855 ten more professors were on the staff of University College, including E.J. Chapman, William Hincks, John Cherriman, James Forneri, and Daniel Wilson.[3] These fifteen men had at their disposal an income from endowments and investments of $59,352, of which $31,800 was marked for salaries. Added to this was an annual average of $4,000 in student fees, until 1866 paid directly to professors rather than to the university bursar.[4] By comparison, the faculty of Queen's College in the 1850s ranged in numbers from a total of one in 1852 to five in 1858. Gross income there in 1853 was $8,000.[5] Victoria College was equally penurious. Its gross income for the year from mid-1849 to mid-1850 was $6,412. By the mid-1850s it was running a typical yearly deficit of $3,000, not including whatever improvements were made to grounds or building. President S.S. Nelles noted in 1858 that the accumulated deficit had reached $32,000.[6] The government's annual grant of $3,000, an amount also given to Queen's and Regiopolis, scarcely began to meet expenses, much less pay off previous debts.[7]

To many observers the foundation of University College appeared to rest on a quagmire of hypocrisy and prodigality. James Beaven, who had held the chair of divinity at King's College, so detested the idea of a non-denominational college that he wrote to his chancellor publicly expressing his strong 'disapproval of the very principles upon which the University is founded ... ' It was, he added, 'an institution which I abominate,' for it was godless.[8] Beaven's principles, however, proved to be rather more malleable than his rhetoric. When the divinity chair at King's College was abolished, Beaven had been offered monetary compensation in the clear hope that he would return to England. 'He took the money,' one faculty member later recalled, 'but insisted on staying as the incumbent of the new Chair.'[9] By 1853, in spite of having been the reason for a university senate committee of inquiry because of his charges, Beaven was making $1,800 per year, much more than professors at Victoria College or Queen's University. In 1857, when total provincial grants to Victoria and Queen's were $3,000 each, the president of the provincial university enjoyed a salary of $4,000.[10] It is therefore understandable that when the chief administrators of the University of Toronto – President John McCaul, Vice-Chancellor John Langton, and Professor Daniel Wilson – laid the cornerstone of University College in 1856 they did not dare hold a public ceremony. Langton confided to his brother at the time that 'every stone that goes up in the building, every book that is bought is so much more anchorage and so much less plunder to fight for.' The cornerstone, wrote an historian of Victoria College, was 'laid stealthily.'[11]

The largesse bestowed upon the new provincial university in the 1850s and 1860s rested, in the end, less on individual greed or on graspings for power and privilege than on temptations to university officials arising out of administrative confusion caused by the University Act. Technically a great deal of power resided in the governor general in council. Not even current expenses out of income, much less capital improvements, could be paid by the university without the passing of a legislative statute and the governments of the day seldom acted quickly, given the impasse of Union politics. Having by 1854 finally secularized the clergy reserves and created a state university, Upper Canadian politicians, in their benign neglect, acted as if they wished both thorny issues would simply go away. As a result, officials of the University of Toronto simply began to spend money at will, whenever deemed necessary, in the expectation that formal assent would ultimately be forthcoming. Since Vice-Chancellor Langton, largely responsible for initiating such disbursements by the university, was also auditor of public accounts for the province, invariably it was. Langton the vice-chancellor clearly enjoyed this freedom of financial initiative; whether as auditor he lay awake at nights sorting out his responsibilities to the public and to the university is not known. He did admit, however, that the situation left much to be desired. 'The whole thing,' he confessed, 'is a mass of confusion ... '[12]

Others thought so too. The order-in-council concerning the financing of University College had provided maximum sums of $300,000 for the structure itself and $80,000 for its museum and library. By the time the building was finished in 1859 actual costs had reached $350,000 and $50,000, respectively. Needless to say, for the remainder of the decade the university found itself unable to generate any significant surplus from its revenues for distribution to other colleges. In 1855, for example, income from all sources was $49,452; expenses totalled $56,656, and this was before construction of University College had even begun.[13]

By 1856 the Legislature had received a number of petitions objecting to the 'unnecessary expenditure of the endowment of King's College,'[14] but the main campaign to stop this apparent abuse of public funds began in 1858 and 1859 when Egerton Ryerson began to orchestrate a four-front campaign for legislative action on the matter. He did so through Victoria College, the secular press, public meetings, and the Conference of the Methodist Church. President S.S. Nelles and others at Victoria did battle with George Brown in the letters columns of his newspaper the *Globe*, for Brown was a strong supporter of the provincial university. The 1858 General Conference of the Methodists in Canada passed a strongly worded resolution describing existing university policy as 'grossly illiberal, partial, unjust and unpatriotic.' And on 30 November 1859 the Methodists released a litany of complaints on university policy and governance. Called *Liberal Education in Upper Canada, Explained and Defended*, it was a densely worded and thoroughly documented attack on the provincial university. It called for 'an investigation to be instituted into the manner in which the University Act has been administered, and the funds of the University and Upper Canada College have been expended, the immense advantage and benefits to the country of several competing colleges over the deadening and wasteful monopoly of one College.' It also insisted that 'an act ... be passed by which all the Colleges now established, or which may be established in Upper Canada, may be placed upon equal footing in regard to public aid, either as so many co-ordinate University Colleges, or (which we think the best system), as so many Colleges of one University.'[15]

So severe was the Methodist indictment, and so detailed its argument, that the Canadian Assembly had little choice at the opening of its 1860 session but to strike a select committee to investigate the truth of the matter. Dozens of petitions were submitted by interested Methodist groups; others supporting the Victoria College position came from Queen's College; still more (such as one from Knox College) were written in favour of maintaining the status quo. Daniel Wilson and John Langton testified at length in response to the numerous Methodist accusations. Egerton Ryerson replied in even greater detail.[16]

Statements by the principals – particularly Wilson and Ryerson – combined detailed criticism and defence of spending, organizational structures, and curriculum with fierce vituperation and outright character assassination.[17] Beneath the invective of both sides lay an implicit criticism of government policies since 1849 on the matter of university education in the province. Much of the self-interested rhetoric concerning the necessity, direction, and abuse of funding, which so dominated the select committee's proceedings, would clearly have been obviated if the government had been able to formulate an unambiguous position with respect to state aid to denominational institutions. By 1860 the institutional and church stances on this question had been the subject of intense public debate for a decade and more, yet a solution to the problem remained as contentious and as elusive as ever. In the end the university question became one among many elements of the continuing stalemate that so characterized the politics of the Union period.

With consensus impossible, two draft reports were prepared, each replicating the basic positions rather than striving for compromise. One, presented by committee chairman Malcolm Cameron, with the aid of the president and secretary of the Conference of the Wesleyan Methodist Church of Canada, recommended that $28,000 per year be allotted to run University College with the remainder of endowment income to be distributed to the denominational colleges.[18] The other, written by John

Langton and committee member William Cayley, defended the University of Toronto's disposition of funds but did not specifically deny the possibility of denominational funding, especially if students of the colleges were subject to no religious tests.[19] The two reports effectively negated each other, returning the matter to a state no more advanced than when the pamphlet war had begun. The committee made no collective report, and it set forth no recommendations. The university question appeared as vexing as the Irish question and, it seemed, was no more capable of solution.

In spite of such political paralysis, Ryerson kept up the pressure by writing to John A. Macdonald with an implicit offer to deliver Methodist votes to Macdonald's Conservatives in return for favourable legislation or, failing that, a formal commission of inquiry. Macdonald replied that he scarcely thought it 'politic' to introduce legislation during the current session and (anticipating what would become a time-worn staple of Canadian political procrastination) asked the Governor General, Lord Monck, to appoint a royal commission. By so doing, Macdonald possibly hoped that the academic and denominational combatants would become exhausted and consumed by their own unceasing rhetoric. The commission was duly appointed in 1861 and it reported in May of 1863.[20]

The rancorous experience of the select committee of 1860 was still in the memory of parliamentarians, so the commissioners in 1862 chose not to hear witnesses but to circulate instead a questionnaire asking respondents for their views concerning the advantages and disadvantages of membership of the province's colleges on a single university board, the adequacy of the current system of affiliation with the University of Toronto, and alternative systems of association. With replies from the church colleges and responses to questions posed to officials of University College and the university senate in hand, the royal commission reported. On virtually all counts it recommended in favour of the denominations. The cost of University College was judged excessive in relation to need, as were ongoing expenditures. Its bursar was quoted as saying, rather brazenly, that there were 'no limits to the demands which the University, and of University College, might make.' Strict economies should henceforth be practiced, including a reduction of professorial staff. But the commission went even further: it suggested a reorganization of the whole university. Its name would be changed to the University of Upper Canada and that of University College to King's College. The denominational colleges would be allowed to affiliate, using a common curriculum, and they would have major representation on a reconstituted senate. The new King's College would receive

$28,000 per year to operate, the others $10,000 apiece as well as a further $20,000 each to upgrade their libraries. Finally, control over the university endowment would be placed in the jurisdiction of the Crown Lands Department of Canada West.[21]

Supporters of the University of Toronto, including a sizeable number of its alumni, were outraged. An 'Indignation Meeting' was held at St Lawrence Hall. Motions of protest (as well as 'three groans' for the commissioners) were voiced. The *Globe* and the *Leader* strongly defended Toronto's beleaguered university.[22] Nelles and others replied, but in general the various participants had by now sung their different tunes too often. Public as well as political interest in the crisis was waning. John A. Macdonald's ministry had fallen on its proposed Militia Bill in 1862, and by the time the commission reported that of another Macdonald, John Sandfield, had taken its place. Like his predecessor, J.S. Macdonald initially found inaction on the university issue to be the wisest policy, at least for his own political future. In such a state did the university question rest for a decade. But by then Canadian politicians had found larger matters to preoccupy them and the whole constitutional structure of British North America had been fundamentally altered.

The New Province and the Old University Question

'The most important date between 1861 and 1890 in the history of higher education in Upper Canada ... ,' wrote historian of education Robin S. Harris in 1976, 'was 1 July 1867.'[23] With passage of the British North America Act the Dominion of Canada formally came into being. Section 93 of the BNA Act gave unambiguous jurisdiction to the provinces over all aspects of education, public and higher. Henceforth, the university question would be debated not at the distance of Quebec City or Ottawa, the old seats of government, but within easy walking distance of the provincial university in Toronto, the capital city of the new province of Ontario.

John Sandfield Macdonald, who formed Ontario's first provincial government by forging a Liberal-Conservative coalition, now found it expedient to act quickly on the subject of state aid to higher education. Public opinion in the late 1860s clearly did not favour state support for denominational institutions. His government acted accordingly, introducing in February 1868 a resolution that declared 'the payment of any sums of money out of the Treasury to Collegiate Institutions' to be 'inexpedient.'[24] The special act which soon followed discontinued all further aid to the church colleges, but did raise their final grants (for the fiscal year 1868–9) by fifty per cent.[25] The measure provoked heated debate in the new provincial Legislature before it was passed, in part because news of the government's intentions had been leaked earlier to the *Globe*. In response to Brown's strong support for it, on the grounds of economy and voluntarism,[26] denominational lobbyists had already been at work on members of the provincial parliament by the time the act was introduced early in 1868. The old arguments and proposals therefore resurfaced. Another select committee was proposed to investigate the affairs of the provincial university and its profligate college. The virtues and vices of centralization of higher education in Toronto became a leitmotif in the refrain of debate, although the tune was already a very familiar one.[27]

Petitions for both sides circulated in the province throughout the summer of 1868. Brown's *Globe* kept the issue in the news by his continued denigration of those who 'talk much about the higher education of one or two sects,'[28] but a motion was nevertheless introduced during the autumn session of the legislature urging that 'some comprehensive scheme be devised and adopted for giving effect to the objects, and for extending the operation of the Act 16 Vict., cap. 89, in the establishment of a Provincial University, and the affiliation of colleges to be supported in connection therewith.' Thus was the university question brought back to the status it occupied in 1853, with all the ensuing arguments once again trotted out. The proceedings were duly transcribed for posterity, and they were sufficient to produce yet another lengthy pamphlet in the continuing war of words, probably to be read only by the participants and by a very few grumbling historians a century later.[29]

The dissidents' motion failed to pass. At last the proponents of the provincial university could relax from their long vigil. As the child of the province, the University of Toronto did not now have to fear the dissipation of scarce government funds at the hands of the church colleges. Professors at University College looked forward to closer relations with a government that had shown support for its cause. Yet over the next forty years the University of Toronto's contact with politicians would at times be the source of its greatest problems. Having willingly bound itself to the secular state for its main source of support by arguing strenuously against the denominational colleges for fifteen years, the University of Toronto proceeded to reap its ambiguous and at times problematic rewards.

The reaction of the main denominational colleges to the provincial government's decision to support only institutions not tied to any church was a mixture of resignation and resolve. 'I fail to see any course upon which the Colleges can now unite,' wrote Principal William Snodgrass of Queen's to President Nelles of Victoria, 'and must therefore proceed in future on the ground that it is the duty of each to set itself in order after its own fashion and with its best endeavours to fulfil its own mission.'[30] For a time this also was the attitude of Victoria. Both institutions, led by these two men, immediately started private fund-raising campaigns. By February 1869 $40,000 had been pledged to Victoria, and within four years the objective of $100,000 had been reached. At the same time, however, the effects of the public fear that Victoria might collapse for lack of state funds took effect. It awarded only seven Bachelor of Arts degrees in 1869 and only three in 1870. By 1871, with the campaign for funds meeting with success, the number had risen to fourteen.[31]

Queen's was in even more precarious financial shape. The withdrawal of the annual government subsidy had been preceded in 1867 by the failure of the Commercial Bank, which handled much of the college's modest endowment. Two-thirds of that endowment was lost, but such was the penurious state of the college that this amounted to only $1,280 a year. William Snodgrass, appointed principal in 1864, launched his financial drive by appealing first to those in Kingston, especially to the congregation of St Andrew's Church and to his own professors. Both groups gave generously, ultimately raising $15,000. With this base of support, Snodgrass and Professor John MacKerras canvassed the outlying areas. By early 1872 the campaign had raised about $114,000. This success, especially when considering its sources, convinced university authorities of the soundness of their initial assumptions about its support within the Ontario community. Both in student numbers and in finances it came from eastern Ontario and Quebec, to the extent that almost thirty per cent of campaign contributions had been donated from Protestant Montreal.[32] This would not be forgotten when proponents of affiliation with the University of Toronto later urged Queen's to move to Toronto.

Knox College, the Free Church Presbyterian rival of Queen's, had been located in Toronto from its inception. Incorporated in 1858, it attained a degree of stability with the union of the Presbyterian Church in Canada and the United Presbyterian Synod in 1861, for this meant the merger of two rival theological schools within the existing structure of Knox College. The 1858 articles of incorporation also provided it with a board of management and a senate. An 1880 amendment gave the college the power to confer degrees in theology. Although its professors believed that a liberal arts training was necessary for the preparation of divinity students, the college itself had no university-level arts department. It depended, instead, on its students' attendance at University College. 'For many years,' wrote the University of Toronto's first historian, 'the Presbyterian students in the University outnumbered those of any other religious denomination; and there were times at which it almost seemed as if Knox College kept University College alive.'[33] It is not surprising that such comfortable symbiosis found much consistent support from staff at both Knox and the provincial university. In 1855 the two agreed to affiliate, and by 1890 Knox was a fully federated theological college in the University of Toronto.

Not all Ontario colleges in existence in 1867 were Protestant ones. Roman Catholic institutions had come into existence, but they too encountered serious difficulties. Regiopolis in Kingston had been founded by the Roman Catholic Bishop Alexander Macdonell thirty years earlier, but as of 1880 it had yet to grant a degree. The elimination of financial aid by the province ensured that it would remain what it had always effectively been: essentially a Roman Catholic secondary school. Assumption College in Windsor had been established by the Jesuit order in 1857, but it closed in 1859 and was reopened only in 1870 by the Basilians. Somewhat more successful was the College of Ottawa, founded as the College of Bytown in 1848 by the Oblate order, and granted incorporation by the legislature in May of the next year. In 1861 it was renamed to coincide with the transformation of Bytown to Ottawa. Dedicated to bilingual instruction in the practical and liberal arts (teaching commercial as well as classical subjects), it was granted a university charter in 1866. But ten years later, led by Father Joseph-Henri Tabaret, fewer than a dozen students were enrolled. It had awarded only five Bachelor of Arts degrees in the years 1867–76, and by 1890 the total had reached only sixty-five. Yet as a seminary and as a bilingual institution that taught at the secondary as well as post-secondary level, it was beginning to find a constituency amidst the French and Irish Catholics of the Ottawa Valley. In 1887, the year of Tabaret's death, 400 students were in residence, and in 1889 it was recognized as a 'full-fledged Catholic University' when Pope Leo XIII issued it with a pontifical charter. The year 1889 also marked the founding of its faculties of theology and philosophy. In Toronto, St Michael's College had been established in 1852 by the Basilian order. Championed by the Bishop of Toronto, the Most Reverend Armand de Charbonnel, its object was to impart a general Roman Catholic education rather than to train theology students. In 1881 it was affiliated by statute to the University of Toronto, in the hope that its relationship would be similar to that enjoyed by those Roman Catholic colleges that by then were affiliated with Western University in south-western Ontario.[34]

Throughout the 1870s and 1880s Trinity College, like its denominational sisters, sought to be true to its college ideal while searching for private funding. The thrust of the former, that of joining academic study with personal discipline, had been given from Trinity's very opening in 1852 when Bishop Strachan had stated that 'Our desire ... is to build upon this holy foundation; to form ourselves, in so far as possible, into a large household and keep as near as may be practicable to the order and harmony of a well-regulated family. There will be daily and hourly intercourse between the youth and their instructors – reverence for superior age and attainments, and a prompt obedience to all their reasonable commands.' Cheerful conformity to 'the rules of order and regularity prescribed,' he concluded, 'will seldom fail to produce good habits.' But Trinity's provosts and professors found themselves also taking time from their disciplinary vigils in order to find benefactors. In several cases they were able to obtain substantial grants from affluent supporters. Twice in the mid-1870s individual families either gave or bequeathed amounts in the $4,000 range. By 1882 a supplemental endowment fund campaign had yielded $85,000 from Canadian and English sources, including $12,000 from the Society for Promoting Christian Knowledge.[35]

The problems of Trinity College after 1868 were not, however, solely those of finance. Theological divisions within the Anglican communion made for division of both mental and monetary resources. The first of these had dated from the early 1860s when Huron College was founded in the western town of London, following the 1857 division of the large Diocese of Toronto. Within a half dozen years the bishop of the new Diocese of Huron, Benjamin Cronyn, had founded his own 'Broad Church' counterpart to Strachan's Trinity, and by 1865, still taking strong exception to the seemingly 'Romish' teachings of Provost Whitaker of Trinity and maintaining that the survival of Huron College was essential if Church of England doctrines untainted by the heresies of the Oxford Movement were to be taught, the Huron College council asked for and received provincial aid. Huron's first principal, the Reverend Isaac Hellmuth, had good reason for believing such help to be forthcoming, since two influential Toronto politicians had been instrumental in drawing up the constitution of the college. One, Adam Crooks, was his brother-in-law; the other, Edward Blake, was the son-in-law of Bishop Cronyn.[36]

The decade-long conflict between Strachan and Cronyn, and with them Trinity and Huron, ended only with their deaths in 1867 and 1871, respectively. Hellmuth became the new bishop of the Diocese of Huron. But Bishop Hellmuth was not the only person in London with ambitious plans for the future of Huron College. Early in 1877 thirty-nine Huron graduates met at Christ Church, in the town, to form an organized lobby for the transformation of the church college into a university. Urged on by Principal Michael Boomer, Hellmuth's successor at Huron College, the group declared its 'ardent desire to establish a University and University College to facilitate the obtaining of the highest scholastic training and instruction in Evangelical truth for the future clergy of this Diocese & Dominion, & to meet the educational wants of the fast developing West by supplying it with an undenominational School of Arts, Law & Medicine ...'[37] With these twin buttresses, the needs of the diocese and the professional aspirations of south-western Ontario, the resolution of 'the Association of Professors and Alumni of Huron College' (as the group now called itself) met with the approval of both the diocesan hierarchy and the local newspaper press. A sign that the alumni and clerical campaigns were meeting with success lay in the *Globe*'s predictable warning that the project marked the emergence of yet 'another sectarian rival to the Provincial University.'[38]

Perhaps as a result of this dismissal of London's regional needs by the loudest apologist for the province's urban behemoth, a bill of incorporation of 'The Western University of London, Ontario' was presented to the provincial Legislature in January 1878. The debate that followed raised anew the spectre of the university question. It also provided ample evidence that the Liberal government of Oliver Mowat did not yet have a firm position on any aspect of university affairs except the existing one of not financing denominational institutions. More alarming still from the perspective of the University of Toronto, the government seemed to have no clear commitment to extending the interests of the provincial university. The province could not, of course, protect or enhance the University of Toronto's provincial or even national mandate by legislating the older denominational colleges out of existence. But Toronto's supporters thought it could certainly declare its support for the idea of a secular university system by refusing to incorporate yet another church-connected institution. In this sense the struggle over the incorporation of Western University transcended the issue nominally at hand.

The debate on the Western University bill was significant mostly for its implications concerning the University of Toronto. As always the university question threatened to split party ranks, and Oliver Mowat, who had become premier upon the resignation of Edward Blake from the provincial Legislature in 1872, accordingly sought to minimize possible political damage by allowing a free vote. At the committee stage the defenders of the University of Toronto argued that the creation of another denominational college would undermine the very idea of a state-supported system of higher education and the value of degrees would be cheapened. But in the House the proposed regional college found its champions, especially W.R. Meredith, member for London, leader of the opposition, and member of the University of Toronto senate. Defenders of the Western University prevailed. Denominational institutions, they argued, were an accepted fact of educational life. A population of 700,000 people in south-western Ontario would potentially be served by the new university; besides, the exclusivist arguments of the University of Toronto were little different from those of any other monopoly. In a free society committed to the laws of supply and demand, all such monopolies should be avoided. Mowat himself agreed that the new university would be 'of considerable value to the Western part of the province.' With this atypical indication of the premier's own inclinations an amendment that would have blocked the bill was soundly defeated: Conservatives voted twenty to three against it; Mowat's Liberals split badly, voting in favour by a twenty to eighteen margin. A full sixty per cent of the members of the provincial Legislature had voted against the interests of the state university. The bill itself therefore passed easily.[39]

By spring 1878 'The Western University of London' existed, but it did so as an aspiration in search of a patron. This largely continued to be the case for the next thirty years. The university began promisingly enough, for by 1880 the energetic Hellmuth was able to secure $39,933 in overseas contributions and he had obtained pledges in an equal amount from Canadian benefactors. Like all private fund-raising campaigns, however, these brought no necessary promises of long-term financial security. If Western University wished to secure its future it needed to identify and to consolidate its constituency. It could seek guarantees of support from the London business community, from the church by means of cementing its ties with Huron College, from the state through some kind of relationship with the University of Toronto, or from private benefactors such as the Society for the Promotion of Christian Knowledge (from which it had already received the promise of a grant). At each level it failed, for in return for support each source made demands that alienated other potential benefactors or found opposition within the university itself.

The relationship with the Anglican church, through Huron College, was the most obvious basis for establishing an institutional infrastructure and a base for ongoing financial support. By May 1881 the resources of the college were placed under the jurisdiction of the university senate, and Huron College became the university's faculty of divinity. Arts instruction commenced the following autumn. But the surrounding community was more concerned with producing doctors of medicine than Bachelors of Arts. As a result, although arts courses were able to continue only because Huron College professors taught extra classes under conditions of duress, money was located to found a medical school. It was operational by the autumn of 1882. By then, however, Hellmuth, chancellor of the university, clearly had realized that his institution's academic stock had been watered. From the outset he had urged the possibility of an affiliation with the University of Toronto, but its senate, in no mood to accommodate, had insisted that this must include all faculties, including medicine. The medical lobby in the Western University senate would have nothing of this apparent attempt to control, diminish, or even possibly eliminate local control over medical education in London, and it made certain by its senatorial votes that the affiliation scheme failed. Difficulties also arose concerning philanthropic aid, for the Society for the Promotion of Christian Knowledge now insisted that the university would receive no further support from it unless the University Act was altered to require all members of senate to be adherents of the Church of England. (Senate regulations already required this, but the act itself did not.) Desperate to be assured of at least some financial aid, university authorities placed the measure before the provincial legislature. It passed in 1882, and with it the university's name was changed to 'Western University and College of London, Ontario.' In this way, for the promise of a mere $4,000 from the SPCK the university diminished its potential for obtaining non-Anglican support.

The skein of Hellmuth's hopes quickly unravelled. Church support was more rhetorical than real; Huron College increasingly regarded university affiliation as a financial liability and a drain on scarce human resources; the fifteen arts students of 1882 shrank to seven in 1883. His wife desperately ill as well, Hellmuth announced his intention to resign and promptly left for England. He never came back. Leaderless and embittered, the staff of the university and its divinity school argued among themselves. In 1885, with virtually no money or students, the senate proposed to sell the Huron College building, essentially its only asset. Recognizing the fact that existence without Huron College support was impossible, it suspended all classes in arts. An attempt in 1885 to found a faculty of law also floundered, and by 1887 it, too, had ceased to be. The faculty of arts at Western remained in limbo for the next decade; hence, between 1885 and 1895 the university consisted only of its faculties of divinity and medicine. Even after arts was revived, with great difficulty, in 1895, it was scarcely a major force. At the turn of the twentieth century, only thirteen students had graduated in arts from the twenty-two-year-old university; two decades later the total had yet to reach two hundred.[40]

In the matter of higher education the Anglican community of Ontario was not divided in two ways between the supporters of Trinity and

Huron colleges, but in three. The High Church leanings of Strachan's college had alarmed Benjamin Cronyn to the extent that in 1860 he had publicly charged the Provost of Trinity, the Reverend George Whitaker, with preaching Roman Catholic 'heresies.' As late as 1878 Whitaker was still replying to such charges.[41] By then, in fact, some Anglican supporters were on their way to providing an institution for theological education, along both Protestant and Evangelical lines, to be located in Toronto. Wycliffe College was the result.

The immediate success of Wycliffe, compared with the struggles of Huron, can largely be attributed to its Toronto location. With a sizeable urban population on which to draw, Evangelicals were sufficient in numbers to form an effective and visible lobby against High Church exponents. In 1873 the 'Church Association of the Diocese of Toronto' was established, its object 'to maintain the principles and doctrines of our Church as established at the Reformation and to preserve the simplicity of her Protestant worship and the purity of her Scriptural teaching.' Moreover, as was to be expected in a centre of political and economic power, many of its 235 members were both influential and affluent. The first two presidents of the Church Association, for example, were the Honourable Chief Justice William Draper, former prime minister of the United Canadas, and Sir Casimir Gzowski, the wealthy engineer and promoter. Other members, such as Daniel Wilson and James Patton, were prominently connected with the University of Toronto. By 1879 the new college was incorporated. Five years later it moved into a newly constructed, architecturally unpretentious red brick building adjacent to the University of Toronto. Led by its first principal, James Sheraton, Wycliffe College suffered neither from financial difficulties nor from rancorous relations with the University of Toronto. In this respect its early history was rather distinctive. In 1885 the new college and the university reached an agreement to affiliate; by 1890, as with Knox College, the two were organically linked in federation.[42]

Unity, Plurality, and Dollars

By 1883 the university question had bedevilled Ontario politics for longer than most politicians and educators cared to remember. Some, dating the origins of the conundrum from the 1853 University of Toronto Act, could declare that it had been a public issue for thirty years. The more philosophically inclined might have argued that the struggle over the Crown and clergy reserves that ensued from the Constitutional Act of 1791 was marked by variations on the problem of the one and the many articulated by presocratic philosophers two millennia earlier.[43] In the years after Confederation the politicians and educators of Ontario in fact had before them a modern political model for reconciling unity and plurality: the Canadian federation embodied in the British North America Act of 1867. Was it possible to forge a similar form of federation, involving the provincial university and denominational colleges?

The university question was complicated further because it involved two constitutional entities which by the 1870s were coming to represent conflicting ideals. The college was rooted in the construction of character by means of an education in the liberal arts; the university, as it came to be redefined in nineteenth-century North America, was the coordinating agency for a wide variety of academic units only some of which were traditional in nature. Each found strong exponents in the last third of the nineteenth century. Within the University of Toronto itself this increasing divergence made for divisions and animosity within the professoriate, in part because until the late 1880s the identity of the university was necessarily wrapped up with that of University College. The result was a conflict within the Toronto academic community that (as will be seen) took the form of a struggle between two generations of men. It was also inflamed by the enlarged constituency of the university's senate after a major change in the University of Toronto Act in 1873. In this way, just as at one level the conflict between 'college' and 'university' ideals was a struggle between outlying denominational institutions and the University of Toronto, at another it could also be found within the provincial university itself – between those who wished University College to maintain the broad social and educational functions of the traditional college and those who wanted to widen the institutional division of labour in order to serve society in more practical ways. That meant meeting the needs of scientific enterprise in an industrializing society. Before science could meet social needs, however, it first had to be assured of adequate financial and institutional support.

Signs of a potential conflict between college and university ideals could be seen in Ontario as early as when presentations had been made to the 1860 select committee of the Legislative Assembly by Egerton Ryerson and Daniel Wilson. Ryerson, for his part, had presented a traditional college perspective when he declared his opposition to specialized studies made possible at the provincial university by curricular 'options.' The central purpose of the college was to provide discipline, both intellectual and social, and this could only be accomplished by presenting the student with a broad range of mandatory studies. 'The great objects of collegiate studies,' he had argued, 'are to develop the faculties of Language and Reason, and to form that intellectual discipline, without which there is no intellectual progress throughout life. An undisciplined mind increases in power as it grows in years until the decay of nature.' By insisting that students take a broad and prescribed range of courses in the arts and sciences in order to acquire a disciplined intelligence, the colleges, in Ryerson's view, would be instrumental in subordinating natural desire to a common code of culture, of ordered and self-regulated conduct. An educated community of the like-minded would be the desired result.[44]

Wilson would not have disagreed in the abstract with Ryerson's statement of purpose, for few would argue with education as a means of developing reason or of fostering intellectual or social stability. But he had defended the 'options permitted in the University' by expanding the *raison d'être* of the University significantly beyond that of collegiate functions: 'There have not been wanting men of the highest position in the intellectual world,' he countered, 'who have argued that [the classical subjects] were not merely not the only, but not even the best studies for forming the mind; whilst the practical utility of many new subjects has been forcing them into the established studies of the Universities. There has been also a growing conviction that from the narrow limits of the studies of our Public Schools and Universities, they were not fitting men for the actual business of life ... Old prejudices are not easily overcome, especially in the Universities.'[45] In this way, Wilson was an important transitional figure, adhering to elements of both college and university ideals.

Wilson was a scholar who chose his words carefully, so his phrases should not be passed over lightly. They are laden with implications that would become increasingly important in the next decades. First is the assertion that a traditional attachment to the classical curriculum constituted 'old prejudices' rather than a major function of professorial concern; second, in a shift of emphasis in favour of the dynamic and the new, is the notion that higher education should rightfully be connected with 'the actual business of life.' Much more, then, was at stake in the 1860 debate over college 'options' than the simple matter of whether or not students should be allowed to choose their own subjects. Ryerson represented the view that education provided a mental discipline fundamentally rooted in social memory. Wilson, as an historian by no means antagonistic to such ends, insisted nevertheless that the higher education of the day must also point towards the future. In addition, by forging a rough equation between education and the 'business of life,' he was only in part being metaphorical. By analogy he was implicitly setting forward the proposition that, like capitalist enterprise in general, universities were engaged in a system of production. In effect, they manufactured two commodities – knowledge and students – and as with other manufacturers in a market economy, such producers should meet the laws of supply and demand. The options so opposed by Ryerson allowed a student not only to pursue his own academic interests, but also to prepare for a career by obtaining expertise in a field that society would prize. Indeed, 'expertise' was slowly coming to be seen as the surest means that universities could devise for preparing students for the 'business' of life.

The protracted struggles of the 1860s and 1870s between the colleges and the provincial university were not, therefore, merely the result of denominational jealousies or clashes of ego. Central to the concern for state funding was the recognition by all that the teaching of science, not to mention innovative research, was an expensive enterprise. Latin, after all, could be taught at not much more expense than a professorial salary; chemistry required apparatus even at the level of simple demonstration. Finding a solution to this financial problem was critical for the church colleges, for if they failed to gather support for scientific education they might find themselves eventually teaching only theological subjects, as Goldwin Smith and others wished, or at best offering a truncated program in the liberal arts.[46] An obvious possible solution throughout the 1870s had been formal affiliation of the colleges with the provincial university. But this invariably floundered, particularly at Queen's, because of opposition to the centralization of educational resources in Toronto. It was one thing for Trinity College, located there, to make such an overture (as it did in 1875), but quite another for the colleges located at Kingston and Cobourg to do so. One university in Toronto, said the editor of the *Queen's Journal*, would doubtless 'be sufficient for that ambitious city.' But, he added, 'We certainly fail to see how the cause of higher education in Ontario would be advanced by a general migration of all the universities outside of Toronto to that city. Such a concentration, instead of extending the facilities for obtaining a superior education, would limit them. There are many graduates in Ontario today who would never have seen the inside of a University had it been necessary for them to go to Toronto to do so.'[47] There was more than a measure of truth to this: between 1861 and 1890 the University of Toronto awarded 1,290 Bachelors of Arts degrees; a total of 959 students graduated from Victoria College and Queen's University in the same period.[48]

Nevertheless, initiatives pointing towards university federation began in earnest in 1883, when George Ross became the province's minister of education. The University of Toronto became increasingly distant and exclusivist after the debate on the Western University charter, and its senate consistently denigrated suggestions for affiliation on the grounds that the University of Toronto alone carried a 'provincial' mandate in higher education. Such attitudes, narrowing the notion of a provincial university, had dubious consequences not the least of which was the isolation of the university from informed public opinion. The perceived arrogance of the 'U of T,' public indifference to higher education, and financial parsimony in university affairs by the provincial government thus entrenched themselves, for they were themes almost as old as the educational institutions themselves.[49]

In 1883, members of the University of Toronto academic community were made painfully aware of this lack of public support when a letter, given the title 'Revenues of Toronto University,' appeared in the student newspaper *Varsity*. 'Strong apathy,' said the correspondent, 'was felt by the mass of the people for any expenditure of provincial revenue upon the Provincial University or any other institution of higher education.' He went on: 'I wish to point out that the great proportion of the community are strongly imbued with the idea that the State is doing quite sufficient for the people in the way of national education when she provides free public schools, and that were the Government or any other government to introduce a bill granting a proportion of the provincial surplus to the endowment of Toronto University, or granting even an annual subsidy, the bill would not only meet the strongest opposition in the House but would be bitterly attacked throughout the Province by the electorate, not to speak of the hostility it would encounter from the supporters of the sectarian institutions.'[50] This blunt statement of political realities was, as one historian concludes, 'a classic statement of the case against aid.'[51] It also silenced those who earlier had written to *Varsity* to warn of the desperate need for state aid to the provincial university. This was partly so because university and college officials may have suspected that the author of the letter, signed only with the initial 'R,' was George Ross himself.[52]

The University of Toronto senate had forced the issue of funding to public attention when it had issued a report on the 'requirements of the university.' William Mulock, recently elected vice-chancellor of the university, kept the issue alive by declaring the need of an increase in the state endowment in a convocation address given in June 1883, much to the surprise of his Toronto colleagues. By autumn the denominational colleges had become alarmed at this new offensive taken by the provincial university on the matter of funding.[53]

The language of warfare was often present in private communications between the principal groups in this renewed crusade. James Loudon believed that by the autumn of 1883 his university was under 'a combined attack' by Queen's, Victoria, and Trinity. Daniel Wilson, who had become president of University College in 1880, confided to his diary early in 1884 his fear that 'the politicians would sell us to win the Methodist vote.' S.S. Nelles of Victoria wrote to his friend John George Hodgins about the same time that 'it is not wise to let the enemy have the last word and especially when one of them says we have beat a hasty retreat ... you know we are trying first of all to prevent the enemy from getting further aid ... the enemy is ready to negotiate and agree. Then we should try & meet them half-way, for none of us will get any money without such agreement. Apart from the money question we have no need of doing anything but go on our own way – as the fishes did under St Anthony's Sermon.'[54] It was Nelles's view that a provincially appointed commission, directed to investigate mechanisms of university consolidation, was a practical way of solving the problem. 'I think our best hopes now lie in that direction [consolidation],' wrote Nelles to Hodgins. 'Our present debt is over $40,000, and new buildings or greatly improved ones are a necessity. We can say stubbornly that we will just stay here and struggle along on the old lines, but one thing is beyond our own control, viz. *the retention and increase of students* with a huge monopoly working against us, and great improvements in the other denominational colleges.'[55] Victoria College needed state aid, but state aid required some scheme of consolidation, and consolidation was unlikely without a commission appointed to explore the possibility.

No such commission was appointed, for George Ross defused the situation by inviting leaders of the major institutions (Western University, Regiopolis, and Ottawa were excluded) to confer with him collectively but without attendant publicity. Nelles represented Victoria; G.M. Grant came in from Kingston; Wilson, Mulock, and James Loudon spoke for the University of Toronto. Wycliffe, St Michael's, Knox, and the Toronto Baptist College were also represented. The first meeting took place on 24 July 1884. The question of federation was discussed in general terms, after which each party retreated to its academic sanctuary to plan future strategy and to await Ross's call for subsequent meetings. By January 1885 Ross had produced a draft proposal for circulation and discussion. Central to it was a clear-cut division of labour between college and university. Professors and the courses they taught would henceforth be categorized as belonging to one or the other. In addition to theology, federated denominational colleges would teach only certain delineated arts subjects; instruction in all social, natural, and physical sciences would be the responsibility of the university proper. The University of Toronto would become a teaching body as well as an examining authority, and it would award all degrees except those in divinity. Students at the federating denominational colleges would be allowed to take courses not available at their host institutions free of charge. The quid pro quo for this, however, was that the state endowment would be applied solely and unambiguously to the maintenance of the University of Toronto, its faculty, and its college. Such were the outlines of the structure of federation to which the academic leaders had to respond.

The Debate over Federation

Samuel Nelles was the first principal figure to declare his stand on the university question, *circa* 1885. At the Victoria University convocation on 13 May, he spoke to his colleagues and students with considerable frankness. This man, who had been one of the first matriculants of Victoria College in 1842, and who was to leave little record of published scholarship, made the most important public statement of his career on that day, an eloquent and personal exploration of the place of the denominational college in the dawning age of the secular university. There were, he said, 'three or four currents of sentiment,' each ill-informed, abroad in the province at the time. First there were 'those who disparage the advantages of higher learning'; secondly, there were 'those who imagine that a University can be adequately sustained upon twenty five or thirty thousand dollars a year'; third, those who wished 'to give higher education an unduly practical turn'; finally, 'those who, either as a matter of preference or of expediency, would restrict the work of our national University to what are called secular studies, leaving all religious teaching and discipline to the pulpit and the Sunday-school.'[56] Each view, he argued, was represented in some degree by those who pronounced upon the university question in Toronto. His task as president was to seek a solution that would meet the needs of higher education in Ontario and those of the Methodist Church in Canada while avoiding the pitfalls, academic and financial, inherent in such public pronouncements on the situation.

Nelles's situation was not an enviable one. He had privately concluded that the woeful financial problems of Victoria could be solved only by some form of university consolidation, yet he was equally committed to a continuing religious influence in higher education. In his own way he was a stern realist. 'Every sect cannot have a genuine University,' he admitted, 'and the Legislature cannot recognize the claims of one sect over another. And thus between the necessities of the State University, and the rival necessities of a number of denominational universities, we have at last reached what may be called a kind of dead-lock in our educational progress.' Those who argued for minimal funding because of this impasse simply made the problem worse for all, for 'if we keep our Universities poor, we shall have poor Universities in more senses than one.'

Victoria's president was well aware of the reasons for the existing funding crisis in the province. University work, he noted, was expanding because of 'the progress of the Physical sciences.' Yet he insisted that while such expansion had to take place, and find adequate financial support, the traditional subjects should not be sacrificed. His words, doubtless read later by members of the Legislature, were important reminders of the essential need for a balanced university curriculum:

I have no need to set up any defense of classical studies as against modern science and literature. There is no proper opposition between the two forms of discipline, and no occasion for exalting the one at the expense of the other; but when popular sentiment runs strongly in one direction ... it is perhaps as well for us to insist a little more on that which is in danger of being unduly displaced. We may, indeed, value too highly the study of ancient literature, but we may also over-estimate ... the value of physical science. True culture is not one-sided, but many-sided ... And when men tell us that it is better to study nature than literature, as the works of God are nobler than the works of man, we can but ... say ... that man is also one of the works of God, and the highest one known to us, and that the study of man requires the study of his language and literature, and, among others, the language and literature of Greece.

This concern for preserving the old forms of knowledge and the values they embodied while furthering the new, this necessary equipoise of nature and human nature, was a theme that Nelles wove throughout his address. But beneath it was a recognition of the harsh political and economic realities faced by Victoria. Nelles was no reactionary, and certainly no fool. 'The physical and so-called practical sciences have come to the front with multiplied claims and attractions that cannot be resisted, and should not be resisted.' It was these forms of knowledge, Nelles knew, that would receive the public's blessing where funding for higher education was concerned. The age, he recognized, was one of specialization and this should not be resisted in academic work so long as the whole range of scholarship benefitted.

To further such an end some form of accommodation between competing institutions had to be made. The old quarrels had resulted only in 'a game of reciprocal obstruction and enfeeblement.' 'Sectarian divisions,' 'undue regard for local interests,' and 'sentimental attachment to an old order of things' should, in Nelles's view, be cast aside in favour of a university federation scheme such as the one then being considered. This was no easy concession for him to make, since it meant the abandonment of the Cobourg location of the college he had spent his adult life trying to preserve and enhance. The senate of Victoria University had already accepted the scheme in principle in January 1885, and Nelles looked forward to the new order of higher education, one which marked a 'liberal and Christian reconstruction of our Provincial University.' Theology would at last be taught in the reorganized University of Toronto. Varsity would be godless no more.

However much Nelles was willing to accede to the need for furthering scientific teaching and scholarly specialization, he could not give his support to a purely secular higher education. 'I plead for a national University,' he concluded, 'but such a University for a Christian people should somehow employ ... the highest and most effective of all spiritual forces known among men – the power of the Christian faith ... It is a profound and eminently Christian saying of Dean Stanley's, that all high order of thought seeks to unite the secular learning and the sacred, while all thought of a low order seeks to separate them.' University federation, he thought, might possibly achieve that end, a conclusion shared by his colleague and successor, Nathanael Burwash.

Daniel Wilson, president of University College, did not address himself to the federation proposals until the autumn of 1885. Although rested after a long summer abroad, Wilson nevertheless gave a speech that was an exasperated *cri de coeur*. What he said in the frank privacy of his diary he also told his colleagues. He was not a happy man, and he wasted little time on the rhetoric of uplift. Reviewing briefly the constitutional history of the University of Toronto since 1853, he lamented the decision of that date to separate 'university' from 'teaching' functions. The confusion that had resulted over the responsibilities of a 'university' senate and a 'college' professoriate had, he said, 'been a puzzle to outsiders ever since. Even Attorney-Generals [*sic*] and Ministers of Education have not always mastered the distinction ...' The failure of provincial university and denominational colleges to unite had been only one casualty of such ill-considered provincial legislation. By separating examining from teaching functions within the university, the 1853 act had also encouraged 'a process of examination based on mere textbooks, and not on actual teaching and college work.' Even so, he argued, standards had generally improved in spite of inadequate state funding.[57]

Now, however, the movement for university reform had seemingly taken 'a more healthful direction,' the direction of a federated system that would possibly 'utilize the national endowments ... more effectually.' To secure such proper use of state funds Wilson had entered the negotiations over federation and had been, in his own view, 'ready to make only too large concessions ...' But he was not pleased with the result. 'It certainly does not recommend itself,' he said, 'to my unqualified approval.' Wilson, like Nelles, was boxed in. Nelles needed state aid for simple institutional survival; Wilson required it if any further expansion of scientific teaching and research were to take place. The proposed affiliation scheme exacted some infuriating administrative costs. The bifurcation of function between 'examination' and 'teaching' had been bad enough, but now another source of division was to be created. The 1883 proposal was 'to break up the small staff [of University College] into two bodies, as a college faculty and a university professoriate – classified on no logical system, but confessedly arranged on a basis suggested by the still more inadequate equipment of certain confederating colleges ...' Moreover, the suggestion that federating colleges would be given major representation on the university senate appeared to Wilson as 'a proposal to trammel the free action of the University,' one that would 'organize within its Senate a sectional minority, necessarily denominational in character, with a power of veto upon the action of a large majority.'

As with Nelles, Wilson recognized that confederation was the political and organizational form of an issue that was of much greater cultural and intellectual significance: the relation of the sacred and the secular in society. But on that issue they were diametrically opposed. 'Nothing in all the experience of a lifetime,' said Wilson, 'has tended to shake my faith in the superiority of national, as compared with any denominational system ...' Denominationalism meant for him duplication of function, and therefore inefficiency; 'national' education meant centralization of resources and therefore academic improvement. Whereas in his 1885 address Nelles had suggested that the secular nature of education at the University of Toronto was something for which it should be apologetic, Wilson openly declared that this was nothing less than an education fully 'in harmony with the spirit of the age.' While nothing taught at University College, he said, should be seen as offending any Christian, it remained a grave responsibility of the University College Council to maintain 'its secular character unimpaired.'

The long peroration of Wilson's speech, like that of Nelles, directly addressed the relations of the sacred and the secular in university affairs. Invariably it also hinged on the respective spheres of science and religion. Although himself a devout Broad Church Anglican, Wilson was nevertheless unwilling to argue the cause of religion in the higher learning: 'if the history of intellectual progress after the revival of learning proves ... that the progress of scientific truth has been hindered by theological restraint, and some of the grandest revelations of science have not only been received with suspicion, but have been denounced as in conflict with religion; how much more needful is it that the spirit of speculative enquiry should have free play in an age when the bounds of knowledge have so vastly extended?'

Like Victoria, Queen's in the late 1880s was a financially strapped denominational institution trying to compete with the expanding provincial university. But unlike President Nelles and his colleagues, who from the virtual outset of Victoria's existence had considered federation as a possible means of survival, Principal George Monro Grant and those at Queen's did not. Even before he arrived in Kingston from Halifax in 1877 to become principal, resentment of the provincial university was strong at Queen's, as it had been for decades. Under Grant's energetic moral leadership the college ideal remained strong at Queen's, for Grant was in the process of assembling a strong, productive, and united faculty in the arts and sciences. But the resentment did not abate, as many items in the *Queen's Journal* illustrated whenever the question of university consolidation was raised.[58] Since becoming principal of Queen's, G.M. Grant had not asked for government aid on behalf of Queen's, although he had no philosophical objection to the idea. But after Toronto's vice-chancellor, William Mulock, unilaterally insisted in 1883 that the provincial university badly needed an increase in its state endowment, Grant was galvanized into energetic opposition. Throughout 1884 he actively campaigned against any increase in such aid to Toronto without compensation for the other universities in the province.[59]

In an inaugural address given in November 1885, he outlined his university's final position on the matter. He refused to concede any legitimacy to the distinction, usually made by Toronto supporters, between 'provincial' and 'denominational' universities. The two were not in his view mutually exclusive. There was no reason why, like Oxford or Cambridge, a university could not hold a denominational connection yet serve a national clientele or purpose. Nor did he see any virtue in centralizing higher education in Toronto or anywhere else in Ontario. There was 'no need that all the "scientific" education of a country should be at one centre ... The distributive principle is best.' As to 'the so-called "confederation" scheme,' it was a sham. It had 'not a single clause to secure the continued existence of the colleges we now have, much less a single word indicating a desire to improve them. It proposes to bring the existing colleges together, but the proposal is a ghost ... It is simply a bare invitation to the colleges to throw aside their charters, associations, dignity, local strength; to uproot themselves at their own expense, and move to Toronto ...'[60] In Grant's view, the government's proposal of January 1885 was a deceptive exercise in political legerdemain, and he said so: 'It outlined a plan that few University men could regard with enthusiasm, and even those most in favour of it acknowledge it to be a compromise based upon no intelligible principle. It was neither consolidation or confederation, nor did it grapple with the problem of how to get a system adequate to the necessities of the whole Province. It seemed to us simply a scheme to enable Victoria and Toronto to unite.' For this reason, Grant's role at the university-government meetings in 1884 and early 1885 was the self-declared one of observer, not negotiator. His view was simple: 'Queen's will remain an autonomous University.' Where the money would come from to expand the college curriculum or to construct new facilities for the emergent sciences he could not say. But one thing he did know. 'Certainly,' he concluded, 'our trust is not in politicians.'

Senator McMaster's Dream

The final Ontario university to be founded in the nineteenth century came into existence precisely when this reorientation of the relationships between competing universities and urban centres was taking place. The founding of McMaster University marked the completion of a body of institutions of higher learning that would not be significantly enlarged for half a century. Like most other universities in the province, McMaster was founded as a denominational college.

The Baptists of Ontario were predominantly concentrated in the south-west, particularly in the areas around Brantford and Hamilton, and by 1857 they had founded an educational institution at Woodstock: the Canadian Literary Institute. The Anabaptist heritage was rooted in a firm belief in absolute division between the affairs of church and those of state. As a result, the first director of the Literary Institute, the Reverend R.A. Fyfe, strongly supported the creation of a non-denominational University College in Toronto. The institute would provide a sound grammar school education for boys and girls, along with training in theology for those who wished to enter the Baptist ministry. Graduates who wished to proceed to university might then enroll at University College, since it was free from sectarian influences.[61]

That, at least, was Fyfe's ideal. But from the time the Literary Institute opened its doors in Woodstock its history reflected tensions within the Baptist community. Lacking any endowment, it was dependent upon subscriptions and tuition fees, and they were not forthcoming from those within the community who believed that literary studies should not be combined with theological ones. A second major problem lay in its site. Located near the heart of the population of rural Ontario's Baptists, the Canadian Literary Institute placed the urban brethren at a disadvantage.

Those in burgeoning Toronto, in particular, early expressed their dissatisfaction at the lack of Baptist educational facilities in the provincial metropolis. Fyfe was a strong defender of the institute's Woodstock location, but his death in 1878 resulted immediately in the emergence of vocal proponents of a relocation to Toronto.

By the late 1870s, the most important of these champions was William McMaster, an Irish-born merchant-turned-financier who had made his fortune as a provisioner of wholesale drygoods from his store on Front Street in Toronto, and who, by 1867, had gone on to become the first president of the Bank of Commerce. As historian Charles M. Johnston has suggested, McMaster was 'as good a personification as any entrepreneur at mid-century of the phenomenon known as metropolitanism.' For this reason, McMaster's economic position and urban location are as important for understanding subsequent developments in Baptist higher education as is the fact that he was a Baptist. A business partner and political supporter of George Brown, McMaster was, like Brown, an unabashed promoter of Toronto and its metropolitan potential. If economic and political power should, in his view, rightfully emanate from the largest of Ontario's cities, why should the main educational institution of his religious denomination not also recognize the virtues of relocating in that dynamic urban centre?

McMaster and his wife, Susan Moulton, widow of a wealthy Michigan lumber baron, found a willing ally for their designs to relocate the theological department of the Canadian Literary Institute in Toronto in John Harvard Castle, the American minister of the Jarvis Street Church founded in 1876 at McMaster's behest. Speaking in 1879 before an assembly of Baptists in Guelph, Castle put forward the case for removal, but he attempted in doing so to assuage the fears of many that cities, especially those as large as Toronto, were unwholesome places in which to study for the ministry. 'We are not ambitious to have the institution in Toronto for our own sakes ... ,' he said. 'But I have a very strong conviction that, looking into the future, and considering the influence of city and town upon the men who are trained respectively in each, while I am perfectly willing to grant that the country churches for the future will need excellent men, a great need which I fear will be unmet will be for men to take hold of and control the great centres.' Castle argued that training in a large urban centre such as Toronto would equip Baptist ministers to face the complexities of life in a fast-changing world, but would not make them worldly. His vague allusion to the fact that a certain benefactor might soon provide a large sum of money to finance the new institute no doubt helped some find his argument convincing. As one Baptist wrote, years later: 'The wealth of William McMaster discovered principles that we had never heard of before.'

The result of this felicitous combination of moralism and money was the relocation of the theological arm of the Canadian Literary Institute to Toronto. Advocates of the importance of Toronto had won a significant battle. More veiled was the fact that within the Baptist community, a theological world in which the second coming of Christ was central and constant, a shift in religious orientation was taking place. The relocation of the Canadian Literary Institute from a basically rural setting to an urban one also reflected a long-standing division between fundamentalist and modernist strands in the Baptist tradition, usually denominated 'pre-millennialist' and 'post-millennialist.' The former, in Ontario located largely in the Brantford district, tended to be Biblical literalists who believed that Christ might come again at any moment to issue in the millennium, and that the material world would reflect the depravity of man until that event occurred. Such a view did not encourage social activism, nor trust in values associated with city life. The latter were more optimistic, in the sense that they believed the secular world could be improved even before the second advent of Christ. The establishment of the Toronto Baptist College in Toronto, a city where some manner of social engagement was a necessity for survival, thus reflected a triumph of post-millennial enthusiasm. As twentieth-century events would demonstrate, however, it did not necessarily mean that dissenting voices would remain silent.

More material factors also helped facilitate the removal of the theological department of the Canadian Literary Institute to Toronto. Prominent businessmen, manufacturers, and politicians took their place on the new board of trustees, including Alexander Mackenzie, the former Prime Minister of Canada. McMaster donated an initial $100,000 to get the new institution under way, and promised a smaller annual contribution of $14,500. The result was the construction by 1881 of McMaster Hall on Bloor Street, a substantial building in the Romanesque Revival style. Initially, however, it housed only a small department for theological instruction comprising a faculty of three and a student population of twenty. The literary department continued to exist in Woodstock, but, as historian Charles M. Johnston states, it 'was already, in effect, being turned into a kind of preparatory school for the centralizing institute in Toronto.'

The Bloor Street location of the Toronto Baptist College, just west of University Avenue, meant that it was only a few hundred yards away from the centre of secular education in the city, University College. Throughout the 1880s, the relation of one to the other was the major issue faced by Baptist college authorities. By 1884, with negotiations over the possible federation of other denominational colleges with the University of Toronto under way, Castle and his colleagues were forced to consider their options. Castle championed what he called 'moral affiliation' with the provincial university, one in which students of his college would take university courses in arts and science at University College while their professors would receive cross-appointments. His view, expressed during the Queen's Park negotiations between Minister of Education George Ross and representatives of the different universities, was that the Toronto Baptist College should be allowed to expand its arts curriculum in order to supplement the offerings that would be available to his students by their attendance at University College. In this he was strongly supported by Professor Malcolm MacVicar, a forceful and intellectually progressive appointment to the TBC faculty. The increase in secular courses in arts at the college, MacVicar claimed, would create a level of courses occupying a curricular space between that of Woodstock College and the theological college. Such courses, he urged, would 'be unreservedly consecrated to the training of the young men and women who are to be leaders and standard bearers in the state and the churches ... they should have special power in directing every form of investigation towards the development in their students of an exalted Christian manhood.'

The University of Toronto, on the defensive throughout the 1880s, ultimately found the form of affiliation unacceptable, and nothing came of the TBC scheme. But the initiatives of the Baptist college suggested that a more profound reorientation was taking place: the willingness of the denomination's urban educational leaders to integrate a measure of secular with sacred learning. As Theodore Harding Rand, the newly appointed principal of Woodstock College, was to write to the college board in 1886, the college would continue to be as much 'a Christian school of learning ... as its future resources may permit.' But Rand, and others of his point of view, would also have agreed with a Baptist observer of the 1840s that the educational institutions of the denomination 'ought to be practical.' So did the group's greatest benefactor.

With the Federation Act of 1887 settled, as far as the University of Toronto and its affiliated colleges were concerned, the relationship of the Toronto Baptist College to the provincial university became clearer. The earlier notion of 'moral affiliation' had already been rejected by University of Toronto officials, and partnership in the federation scheme of 1887 would have limited the range of academic subjects that could have been offered at the Baptist college. The obvious alternative, therefore, was to create a Baptist university independent of any institutional affiliation. The proponents of a location in Woodstock once again saw their star rise. The Woodstock board of trustees had already met late in 1886 to arrange the constitutional procedures to allow this to take place. A 'university bill' was drawn up, one that would have united Woodstock College and the Toronto Baptist College under a common board and senate. It was agreed that the university would be named after Senator McMaster.

The spring and summer of 1887 were seasons of intense lobbying by members of the Baptist community, both at Queen's Park and within their own membership.[62] Some resented the apparent bullying of William McMaster; others complained that higher education should remain the responsibility of the state, not of any religious body. Edward Blake, chancellor of the University of Toronto, complained of the dangers inherent in the multiplication of universities in the province. Champions of the proposed university extolled the virtues of alternatives in higher education in ways distinctly reminiscent of the arguments of Samuel Nelles and George Monro Grant when arguing earlier on behalf of the claims of Victoria and Queen's. The arguments were all too familiar to any members of the academic community whose memories went back ten years or more. One factor, however, was different: the apparent availability of a large sum of private money. Rumours circulated that William McMaster was willing to provide around $600,000 as McMaster's initial endowment – an amount that would have equalled that of Queen's and Victoria combined.

Money talked. Ross quickly issued a charter to formalize the existence of the new university, with the stipulation that it would not be allowed to give degrees in arts until its endowment was $700,000. Shortly thereafter, McMaster drew up a new will bequeathing almost his entire estate to the project. On 22 April 1887 the McMaster University bill received final legislative approval. Five months later to the day, almost as if to prove that by force of will he could attain any desire, William McMaster died. He left $900,000 to the university that now perpetuated his memory and his name. In 1888 the Ontario Baptists voted against any form of affiliation with the University of Toronto and the decision was made to move the arts department of Woodstock College to Toronto. The problem of affiliation was scarcely resolved, and it would become a major issue for the new university early in the twentieth century. But a decision had been made, for the time being at least. The city of Toronto, and its promoters, had gained yet another institution.

3

Professions and Politics

With the creation of McMaster University in 1887, the last of the institutions offering the authority of a university degree in the arts and sciences had been founded until Carleton College came into existence in the 1940s. Yet the rise of colleges and universities was not the whole story of higher education in Ontario for, other than the study of theology, education in the traditional professions existed apart from the university. Physicians and lawyers were educated for decades before the first universities were founded in Ontario. Ironically, however, throughout the nineteenth century medical and legal education in the province was marked by an institutional fragility even greater than that of the universities. Both professions, like the universities, were dependent on the power of the legislative element of the state to gain formal legitimacy, but they sought to maintain control over the educational standards and practices of their members. But what form should this education take? To what extent did an education in law or medicine require the elements of a general liberal education? Throughout the nineteenth century the relationship of the legal and medical professions to university education was ambiguous and at times conflicting.

That professions and politics were so intimately linked in the nineteenth century points to a crucial social and ideological function of higher education: it not only perpetuates old forms of knowledge and helps generate new ones, but it also confers status, power, and prestige on groups that claim a privileged economic and social place within society. Universities award a form of credential that formalizes this, called the academic degree, and the traditional professions confer the right to membership and practice. To examine the claims of those organizations – such as the legal and medical fraternities – that claim the right to bestow such credit is, then, also to locate those that seek social as well as intellectual authority. As bodies for the granting of academic credit, universities were potentially in competition with them, but it was by no means certain that professional education needed to take place within their jurisdiction.[1]

The Politics of Medical Education

The first major attempts to facilitate stability in the practice of medicine and law took place in the 1790s, virtually at the outset of provincial life. The Physicians' and Surgeons' Act of the Upper Canadian Legislature, passed in 1795, attempted to protect the population of the province from 'unskilled persons practising physic and surgery therein' by prohibiting any future colonist from vending, selling, or distributing medicines by retail, or from practicing 'physic, surgery or midwifery, within the Province, for profit'[2] without examination and licencing by a medical board created for the purpose. The act did not extend to those already resident in the province or to graduates of 'any university in His Majesty's dominions.' Until the 1820s those who wished to practice medicine in Upper Canada were, in effect, screened by imperial authority. Examiners were to be surgeons of royal hospitals, the army, or the navy. The creation in 1818 of the Upper Canada Medical Board helped institutionalize this essentially Loyalist relationship.

During the same period accreditation and training in law was relatively more autonomous; yet its practitioners, too, derived their professional status by virtue of legislative enactment. The Law Society of Upper Canada was founded in 1797, by an act 'for the better Regulating the PRACTICE of the Law.'[3] Henceforth, the Law Society, whose charter members were selected as much for their social standing as for their formal legal training, was to have complete control over the education and accreditation of barristers and solicitors in the province. Just as the colony's doctors were usually trained by accompanying surgeons of the British military, so students of law in the early nineteenth century apprenticed themselves to barristers and solicitors already admitted to the bar.

In both cases, however, the adequacy of such training largely depended upon the experience and skill of the practitioner with whom the novice physician or lawyer was associated. The Physicians' and Surgeons' Act had scarcely addressed the subject of medical education. At the same time, however, the medical board of Upper Canada set standards for medical education, including midwifery, surgery, and Latin. As a result, 'a full apprenticeship never became a substitute for medical school in Canada to the same extent that it did in pre-revolutionary America.'[4] In spite of an 1822 act of the Upper Canadian Legislature that enhanced the powers of the Law Society by constituting it a 'body corporate and politic in deed and in law' (thereby giving it quasi-legislative authority in legal matters and the power to hold land and construct a building), educational standards under its jurisdiction were at times subject to acute criticism.[5] The act of 1822 softened the traditional British distinction between barristers (an elite group of lawyers allowed to argue in court) and solicitors (lawyers who maintained direct public contact by drafting wills, deeds, and other documents) by removing from the Law Society the power to create solicitors. Some worried, as a result, about the extent to which solicitors were prepared to practice their craft. As part of an ongoing campaign to reassert Law Society control over their education, the editor of the *Canadian Law Journal* reported in 1855: 'Existing laws afford no guarantee of fitness. A young man whose only qualification for entering the study of law is the ability to read and write, may be articled to an Attorney: – spend five years copying and serving papers, or idly kicking his heels against the office desk, or in doing the dirty work of a disreputable practitioner. At the end of this time, armed with a certificate of service, he claims to be sworn in as an Attorney of Her Majesty's courts.'[6] (Two years later, the Law Society regained control over the education and licensing of solicitors.) Upper Canada had its own 'inn of court' in the form of Osgoode Hall (completed in 1832), but problems of term-keeping for students outside Toronto kept attendance at lectures on a voluntary basis. The essential problem with the legal profession at mid-century was the absence of any means of guaranteeing that acceptable standards of fitness to practice would be met for all students. This was also the case in medical education, but sometimes with more dire consequences.

In 1855 Job Broom, a carpenter in his late fifties otherwise unknown to history, complained to his family of a bowel ailment. He was treated by a young medical practitioner. Powders of various colours were administered orally, but Broom's condition rapidly worsened. His stomach was pumped, and cloths soaked in boiling water were applied to his body. After frequently yelling 'Don't scald me to death,' the patient lost consciousness. Attempts to revive him, including 'slapping him in the face, striking him and pinching his legs, and stepping on his toes with heavy boots' for several hours, failed. Like his Biblical namesake, Job Broom doubtless went to his grave puzzled by the capricious nature of an obviously furious God. His faithful son was convinced that the cure had indeed been worse than the complaint and sought action by the magistrate of police. A coroner's inquest subsequently revealed that the initial 'doctor' in question had been a medical student with only a few months' training and that he had mistakenly administered a massive overdose of morphine. This alone may have been sufficient to kill the patient.[7]

The historical importance of the case lies less in the death itself than in what it reveals about the internal politics of institutional medical education. The coroner's jury ultimately convicted the medical student, James Dickson, of manslaughter and he was carted off to jail with bail denied. But by the conclusion of the trial the fate of the accused, not to mention the victim, scarcely mattered. More important issues were at stake for the other principals involved, including the daily press. The very names and backgrounds of the coroner and the doctor responsible for Dickson's training made this inevitable, for the coroner was Dr John King, recipient of one of the degrees given *ad eundem* in 1844 at the first convocation of John Strachan's King's College. The physician accused by him of 'allowing the indiscriminate use of ... medicines' by 'inexperienced students' was none other than John Rolph, one of the political 'radicals' responsible for leading the Upper Canadian rebellion of 1837. In the age of responsible government the old social and political animosities of the Family Compact years still resonated, nowhere more so than within the politics of the medical profession in Toronto. Indeed, that profession was viewed by some as the scalpel-wielding heirs of the old Tory oligarchy.[8]

Throughout his turbulent career, by no means concluded by the 1850s, Rolph played an instrumental role in the education of medical students. Even before receiving his Canadian licence in 1829 he actively practised medicine, and between 1824 and 1826 he and Dr Charles Duncombe (also to become a prominent rebel in 1837), under the patronage of Colonel Thomas Talbot, ran a dispensary at St Thomas. Part of its function was to instruct candidates in medicine and surgery. As Rolph wrote to Talbot when initiating his scheme: 'No school of that description has yet been formed in any part of the Province nor is the hospital at York ever likely under its sleepy patrons to become a source of public usefulness.'[9] By the 1820s medical licensing was somewhat systematized, but actual education continued to be conducted through an informal apprenticeship system. Shortly after the founding of King's College in 1827, John Strachan proposed to Lieutenant-Governor Sir Peregrine Maitland that a medical faculty be founded in association with it. But this plan evaporated when Rolph moved to York in 1832 and opened his own private medical school. An immediate success, his school continued until its founder fled into exile because of his involvement in the Upper Canadian rebellion.[10]

By the time of his involvement in the 1855 trial of James Dickson, Dr John Rolph, granted amnesty but neither forgotten nor forgiven by the

Tories of York, was a major force – and certainly the major figure – in medical education in Upper Canada. In 1837 Strachan had revived his plans for a medical faculty at King's College, but the rebellion turned the government's attention in other directions. A similar attempt at the end of the 1840s resulted in the disallowance of the medical college charter by imperial authorities. Undeterred, King's College officials managed to initiate instruction in medicine in 1843, but this was the year when amnesty was granted to the Upper Canadian rebels. One result was the return of John Rolph and the refounding of his medical school in Toronto. Once again, it was a success, and its students were recognized by the Medical Board of Upper Canada. In 1851 it was re-named the Toronto School of Medicine, housed in a new brick building. By then, however, Rolph faced local competition. Following passage of the Baldwin Act, the Upper Canada School of Medicine was founded in 1850 at the initiative of Dr James Bovell and Dr E.M. Hodder, both devout Anglicans. In 1851 it became the medical faculty of the University of Trinity College, Bishop Strachan's new bastion of Anglican rectitude in higher education. Rolph's institution now began to suffer from this new source of competition. Some of his students complained that they failed because of their political sympathies rather than their lack of medical knowledge; others protested that they had great difficulty in obtaining adequate access to the Toronto General Hospital, largely controlled by the Anglican and predominantly British-born medical establishment of the city.[11] Faced with this competition and obstruction, Rolph, once again in provincial politics, lobbied for the abolition of the faculties of medicine and law at the provincial university. The Hincks university bill of 1853 abolished its medical faculty. Critics suggested that Hincks's action in support of Rolph's medical schemes was based on the latter's support for Hincks's own ambitions for the Grand Trunk Railway.

By 1855 medical and educational authorities were in a state of verbal and institutional war. The University of Toronto was now restricted to being an examining and degree-granting body: instruction was the province of its colleges. Rolph's Toronto School of Medicine had become affiliated with the Methodist-run Victoria College, and was its Toronto-based medical faculty. The Upper Canada School of Medicine had become the medical faculty of the Anglican Trinity College. The Upper Canadian Rebellion may have ended, but the animosities between Reformers and Tories continued.

Then, in March, a scathing indictment by 'A Medical Student' appeared as a letter in a local newspaper, the *Daily Colonist*. At great length it accused physicians at the Toronto General Hospital of giving preference to Trinity's medical students and of treating those of Rolph's school like 'so much dirt in the wards and corridors of the building.' The editor of the Methodist *Christian Guardian* supported the accusation.[12] Cries of malpractice were hurled across the hospital's board table by supporters of each institution. Two colleagues of Rolph, doctors W.T. Aikins and H.H. Wright, were shortly thereafter dismissed from the wards of the hospital. Three months later an ailing Job Broom summoned medical help. The result was political as well as medical scandal, for the student who first attended him, James Dickson, was discovered to have been the author of the letter that had so greatly embarrassed the Tory officers of the Toronto General Hospital, and the senior colleague who administered the stomach pump to the patient had been Rolph's medical partner, Dr Aikins.

The public revelations of conditions at the Toronto General Hospital, coupled with the Broom inquest, tested the public's confidence in the medical profession. During and after the trial of Dickson the Conservative press vilified Rolph, Aikins, and Dickson with letters and editorials carrying titles such as 'Butchery and Quackery,' 'The Degeneracy of the Times,' 'Pseudo-Medical Manslaughter,' and 'Horrid Case of Cruelty.'[13] Yet Dickson, the student in question, was merely the unwitting vehicle for the public airing of personal, professional, and political rivalries. Accused of being responsible for the scalding of Job Broom because Dickson was ultimately under his tutelage, Rolph mischievously cited the coroner himself, Dr John King, as an authority on the medical application of boiling water, an area of expertise vehemently denied by King in his address to the jury.[14] His medical school and his professional reputation at stake, Rolph, perhaps aided by Aikins, resolved to redress the balance. He would get even.

It was therefore more than coincidental that a second coroner's inquest gained the attention of the daily press of Toronto in the hot days of August 1855. It investigated the untimely death of John Blackie who, found 'raving' on the streets, was bled and subsequently given morphia. He did not recover from the treatment. Another scandal ensued, and with even greater journalistic diatribes, for this time the physician at blame was a member of the medical establishment. The attending physician had been Dr Cornelius Philbrick, professor of surgery at Trinity College and a prominent member of the board of the Toronto General Hospital. It was Philbrick who had performed the autopsy on Job Broom. The public image of the medical practitioner now reached its nadir, for it was clear to all that political animosity took precedence to patients' health. 'Before that jealous discord and factious rivalry had destroyed its faith,' wrote one exasperated newspaper editor, 'the public held belief, that the

practice of medicine was one of those liberal and gentlemanly professions ... Recent revelations ... have cleansed the film from the public eye,
and clear to its astonished gaze is the unseemly strife of political faction
brought to the bed side of a dying patient ...'[15]

The medical controversies that followed the deaths of Job Broom and
John Blackie took place at a time when the privately sponsored proprietary school had gained a new measure of security as the site of medical
education. The Hincks University Act of 1853 had effectively privatized
the medical profession in Toronto by denying the provincial university
any role in the instruction of medical students, but relations within the
medical community remained tense because old political divisions
remained intact. Rolph's political views were not shared by most of his
colleagues, and they resented his assertive ways. In 1856 six of the
seven members of his incorporated board resigned on the opening day of
term, protesting against his arbitrary initiatives. While the Victoria College board supported its embattled dean the six doctors won the legal
right to continue working independently using the name of the Toronto
School of Medicine. From then until his death in 1870, therefore, Dr
John Rolph largely *was* the medical faculty of Victoria College. Five
years later, classes in the faculty were suspended and students were recommended by university officials to attend lectures in the privately controlled Toronto School of Medicine.[16]

At Trinity College matters were scarcely better. An 1855 attempt to
convince provincial politicians to reconstitute the teaching functions of
the University of Toronto and to allow members of the Trinity medical
faculty to apply for appointment to its staff failed. Initiated by members
of the medical faculty, this action was taken without consulting the Trinity College council. A crisis occurred when a medical faculty advertisement appeared, unknown to university officials, indicating in 1856 that
no religious tests would be asked of students attending lectures in the
autumn. Rebuked immediately by the college council, still smarting at
the secularization of the university, the entire medical staff resigned.
The medical faculty of Trinity College, six years old, disappeared and
did not reappear until the 1870s.[17]

The early history of medical education in Kingston was also one of
strained relations. Although interest in establishing a medical school had
existed even before Queen's College received its charter, no success was
achieved until 1853. In that year, Dr James Bovell unexpectedly
informed his students at the Upper Canada School of Medicine that in
order to graduate they would be required to subscribe to the Thirty-Nine
Articles of the Anglican faith. He advised them that those who chose not
to do so should transfer to another school. The result was that Bovell

wrote to the senate of Queen's on behalf of several students, suggesting that the college open a medical faculty that would require no religious tests. Urged on by several members of the Queen's board of trustees, in 1854 university officials reluctantly decided to do so. Some Queen's officials, including the first principal (John Machar) and vice-principal (James George), opposed the initiative strenuously and voted against it, fearing that the new faculty might acquire title to university property or otherwise deplete the institution's meagre financial resources. Lines of authority and jurisdiction between the medical faculty and the board of trustees of the university, and within the newly created medical board itself, were unclear. The two groups argued over the ownership and use of a series of provincial grants issued to the medical school in the amount of two hundred fifty pounds sterling. Dr John Stewart, the strong-willed leader of the medical faculty, consistently resisted revealing the expenses of the faculty to university officials, and after he lost his case for control of the provincial grant by the medical faculty even his medical colleagues began to lose patience with him, for he was abrasive and imperious. He further strained relations within the medical faculty and between it and the university community when serious personal conflicts developed between Stewart and Dr George Lawson, appointed jointly to both medical and arts faculties in 1858. In 1862, the medical staff at Queen's offered collectively to resign if Lawson decided to do so, after Stewart had used his newspaper, the *Argus*, to attack Lawson. The result was that Lawson remained on staff, but Stewart was summarily dismissed.[18]

Deteriorating relations within the medical school were mirrored by those between town, represented by the Kingston physicians and surgeons on the medical board, and gown, embodied in the trustees of the university. Hospital authorities came to resent the increasing use of hospital facilities for teaching by university staff. The two groups quarrelled over the power of appointment, with details made public by the *Argus*. Some people within the university community regarded medical men as 'secular, irreligious radicals' in these first years after the publication of Charles Darwin's treatise *On the Origin of Species* (1859), and they believed the raucous medical students to be a poor influence on Queen's undergraduates. Members of the medical staff objected to the possibility that a statement of faith might be required of Queen's professors. By 1866, after a series of negotiations between the medical faculty and the university's board of trustees failed to resolve the impasse, the medical faculty decided to secede. The Kingston medical community secured its independence from college authorities when it gained incorporation as the Royal College of Physicians and Surgeons, Kingston. The university soon capitulated to this demonstration of the power that could be wielded by the new monopolists of medical knowledge. It suspended its faculty of medicine, relieved to be rid of this potential drain on its meagre resources. Power and control in this critical area of human concern rested now with the doctors. The Royal College at Kingston allowed no trustees or governors to be placed above them, and for its part Queen's simply conferred the degrees earned under the tutelage of the college staff. The university continued to have little other authority in medical education until the 1890s.[19]

The history of the Ontario medical profession during this initial stage in the institutionalization of medical education indicates if nothing else that physicians and surgeons acted like mere mortals. Like others, they were capable of incompetence and chicanery, of petty intrigue and jealousy; and no less than politicians, clerics, or entrepreneurs, also of coveting power, control, and prestige. Through the nineteenth century the regulation of medical standards was of major concern throughout Canada, not only in Ontario.[20] Provincial statutes in 1865 and 1869 sought to mediate between the demands of a group of men conscious of their increasingly specialized knowledge and of the crucial nature of their skills, and those of several institutions – the universities – whose key instrument of social power was knowledge in general. In an age of growing influence of the universities in other walks of life, their failure to control such an important matter as medical education was a challenge to their sense of place within society. The creation of a General Council of Medical Education and Registration for Upper Canada in 1865 allowed members of the provincial medical profession and of the degree-granting institutions to be represented, although not in equal numbers.[21] This body quickly began to shape the boundaries of the medical community by outlining the privileges – especially the right to practice, to prescribe, and to charge fees – afforded to those accepted into the fraternity. It also controlled appointments and access to medical services in hospitals or in the militia. Moreover, it was empowered to levy fines on those not so licenced, especially those who practiced 'sectarian' forms of medicine, such as homeopaths and eclectics.[22]

The act of 1865 guaranteed professional autonomy, but it was only one stage in securing discipline and control. The initiative was expanded and consolidated by the creation of the College of Physicians and Surgeons of Ontario in 1869, again by provincial statute. A professional college now existed with an expanded governing body based mainly along lines already set. Its powers, too, were increased. New members were required to pass licencing examinations administered by the college; the college set the matriculation standards governing access to medical schools and regulated the curricula of medical studies.[23]

Legal Ideology and Training

The legal profession in Ontario had held secure and unqualified control over the education of its members since 1797. After the passage of the 1822 act enhancing and consolidating the powers of the Law Society of Upper Canada, the society was solely responsible for determining entrance standards and the content of legal studies, as well as the internal regulation of the profession. The status of barrister was the only important one in practice, and the Law Society held complete licensing power. While no law school formally existed in the early years, several attempts were made in the 1830s and 1840s to devise a system of entrance standards to obviate the problems posed by the wide variation in social and educational backgrounds displayed by candidates for admission. In 1832, for example, a 'Select Committee on Improvements in the Mode of Conducting Examinations' (consisting of George Ridout, John Rolph, and Robert Baldwin) successfully argued for a three-tiered system of entrance standards, based on the student's degree of pre-legal preparation.[24]

During this period of relative ease of access into the profession[25] in the 1830s and 1840s, the emergent liberal arts colleges and the legal profession served different missions. Consistent with British convention, members of the Law Society strongly believed that legal education was best gained by a practical, three- to five-year apprenticeship in a law firm, not by a university-based liberal education. Yet a problem existed when a university student or graduate expressed an interest in becoming a lawyer. How much credit, if any, should be given to university courses as part of the education of a lawyer? The Law Society studiously resisted 'arts courses' as a means of credit in legal education, and began to reduce entrance requirements for university graduates only when provincial statutes of 1837 and 1847 forced it to do so. After the first arts and science students of the province's colleges began to graduate, it created a university class of entering students (1846). When entrance examinations were waived in 1871 for university graduates, the measure met with great opposition from benchers, particularly in the rural areas of the province. Nevertheless, legal education was not unaffected by the founding and growth of universities in the province, if only because from the outset some members of the university community wanted legal education to be an important part of their curriculum. (King's College, for example, had appointed William Hume Blake as its first professor of common and civil law in 1843.) By the 1850s 'it was becoming obvious that law students in Upper Canada required some sort of formal training to supplement their articling experience ...' As a result, in 1855 the convocation of benchers who governed the Law Society overhauled its program of required studies. Even without any formal programs of legal education, the new universities had begun to influence the study of law. One noticeable change was the increasing use of prescribed textbooks within an 'academic' classification of student levels based on entrance qualifications.[26]

In addition to these attempts to formalize and to raise the standards of the course of studies, the 1855 reforms also initiated a series of lectures to be given at Osgoode Hall. These lectures, compulsory for all students articling within ten miles of Toronto, usually took up only two hours per week and were held only when the superior courts were sitting. Gradually, however, the practice became more episodic. Seven years later, perhaps provoked into action by the decision of Queen's University to create its own law school, the Law Society re-established one. (The Queen's venture died after a few years, because the Law Society insisted that students reside for four terms in Toronto.) Yet much of the actual education of law students continued to take place outside the confines of Osgoode Hall. As late as 1882 its student library consisted of a mere twenty-five volumes. The articled clerk, not the college student, is the best description of the lawyer-in-training throughout the nineteenth century and beyond it. The law office, not the academic classroom, remained the main site of legal education.[27]

The law student, articled to a law firm and engaged in a course of self-directed reading, was expected to concentrate on mastering the technicalities of existing common and criminal law rather than inquiring into ethical questions raised by legislation or judicial decisions. Little law was formally taught in any of the Canadian universities in the thirty years prior to 1890.[28] Yet attention must be drawn to the lawyer's sense of his place in Ontario society and to the ideological implications of his self-conceived role as a professional and as a citizen. Only by doing so can we understand the reasons for the tensions that existed between the provincial legal community, acting as educators in law, and the professoriate, which increasingly took higher education as its own preserve.

Physicians cared for the health of the human body and sought to cure its ailments. Lawyers, it was hoped, would do so for the body politic. When Archdeacon John Strachan wrote to Lieutenant-Governor Sir Peregrine Maitland in 1826 about the desirability of a university for Upper Canada, he was thinking less of a province whose future leaders were to be enriched by studying the liberal arts than one governed by lawyers.

'Lawyers must, from the very nature of our political institutions ... become the most powerful profession ... They are emphatically our men of business, and will gradually engross all the colonial offices of profit and honour. It is, therefore, of the utmost importance that they should be collected together at the university, become acquainted with each other and familiar, acquire similar views and modes of thinking, and be taught from precept and example to love and venerate our parent state.'[29] Strachan spoke here in the context of his desire for a unitary system of legal instruction in the province. Clearly he was concerned not only for the training of enough lawyers for a society whose institutions and statutes were only then being drawn up, but also for lawyers with a particular cast of mind. What became of the Family Compact after the advent of responsible government? Instead of going into oblivion, it increasingly assumed the guise of the Benchers of the Law Society of Upper Canada.

More than 200 lawyers left the American colonies during and after the American revolution. Many of them emigrated to Canada. At least four of the ten lawyers at the inaugural meeting of the Law Society of Upper Canada in 1797 were Loyalists.[30] As the civil court system of Upper Canada developed in the years prior to the outbreak of the War of 1812, appointments to the bench understandably were given to those whose Loyalist credentials were impeccable. At least a third of the fifteen judges appointed to the courts of Canada between 1840 and 1860, for example, 'were members of loyalist families, had fought in the War of 1812, and had been educated by John Strachan.'[31] In most cases those appointed to positions of judicial authority in Upper Canada were reasonably well-qualified by training to do so; but declared loyalty to the preservation of a social fabric based upon pre-revolutionary and anti-republican values was a major factor in defining those qualifications.

The tenure of John Beverley Robinson as chief justice of the Court of King's (later Queen's) Bench for the thirty-three years from 1829 to 1862 serves as a symbol of the clear lines of association between the legal profession and the conservative oligarchy of pre-rebellion days. Doctors in the province could be found, such as John Rolph and Charles Duncombe, who took part in outright rebellion in the 1830s, but lawyers seldom ventured beyond advocating slow constitutional change to the status quo – if they went that far.[32] In the case of one of the most prominent of the lawyers associated with respectable constitutional reform, William Warren Baldwin, such liberal attitudes did not extend to his sense of place as bencher or as examiner of law students. 'Although called a reformer,' one former law student recalled, Baldwin 'was a haughtily prejudiced, Protestant Irish gentleman, and wonderfully set in all his ways and notions of propriety towards young men and law students ...'[33] Thus were the overt, seemingly rigid, political lines of cleavage between 'Tory' and 'Reformer' blurred by membership in the same social class.

Lawyers of the day were trained to acquire legal knowledge and practice, essentially to affirm rather than to inquire. As will be seen, in this respect law students were little different from students of natural theology, history, or philosophy. With lawyers, however, there existed a clear connection between the knowledge and values they assimilated in the process of education and the nature of their future livelihood. The anti-republican, essentially illiberal ideological climate of the first half of the nineteenth century in Upper Canada facilitated the melding of lawyers and their Law Society into an occupational and social elite that shared the values that John Strachan had so fervently hoped for. The dedication of their profession was to the preservation of social stability and order, and to the creation of the juridical apparatus by which a fundamentally un-American society, loyal to the Crown and to its venerated institutions, would be created and expanded.[34] In this self-appointed task, the common law as interpreted by Sir William Blackstone was often their touchstone.

The first person to hold a chair in common law at an English university, Blackstone provided in his *Commentaries on the Laws of England* (published in several volumes between 1765 and 1769) a systematic and comprehensive treatment of constitutional and legal development. This masterwork taught generations of English and North American students that law was the virtual embodiment of reason, and that what was not reason could not be law. In short, the study of law in the hands of Blackstone became an eighteenth-century science.[35]

The *Commentaries* were also a codification and apologia for the ideological assumptions of the official culture of Hanoverian, and later Georgian, England. The British Constitution, that complex accretion of legal precedents anchored in the common law, was presented as a model of earthly perfection. An apologist for the Whig ascendancy, Blackstone upheld the principles of political and civil liberty but insisted that liberty must be subjected firmly to the rule of government and of law. He asserted that civil government was the best protector of natural rights, so he rejected the notion of popular sovereignty. He accepted a moderate version of Montesquieu's theory of a healthy constitution balanced by a separation of powers, although he also strongly advocated parliamentary supremacy. This essentially conservative vision became a powerful force for shaping virtually all English-speaking practitioners of law for generations, but perhaps nowhere more so than in nineteenth-century Ontario. The 'image and transcript' desired by John Graves Simcoe and the liberty sought by the Upper Canadian Loyalists were soundly based upon Blackstonian precepts and principles, for the master jurist had reflected the political ethos of his time and the Loyalists had helped export it to the colonies.[36]

Because the *Commentaries* said little about contracts, the corporation, or property and loss allocations, British North American lawyers did not often cite them in specific cases.[37] Nevertheless, Blackstone provided a broad code of shared assumptions for a nascent profession in North America; moreover, he supplied a virtual taxonomy of English law, a structural outline which law students could use to make their way through law school examinations. There was an irony in this, for while Blackstone was a strong critic of the apprenticeship form of legal study and firmly believed that it should be conducted within a university setting, much of his educational legacy rested in the fact his *Commentaries* served as excellent textbooks for part-time study by the legal apprentice. They learned the cases: he supplied the fundamental operating assumptions and the overarching conceptual apparatus. Law was law: invariable truth not inviting scepticism or inquiry, and based on reason rather than sentiment. That suited the needs of legal education, for law schools in North America were scarcely havens for the speculative mind. 'In every law school,' wrote legal historian Lawrence M. Friedman, 'the method used to teach law was dogmatic, and uncritical, except from the standpoint of the law's own inner suppositions; and in most law schools, teaching was dogmatic from any standpoint whatsoever. This kind of training could not convey to the student much sense of connection between law and life, or even of common-law evolution. Beneath sometimes brilliant lectures there was a fundamental hollowness.'[38]

During the years of the Jacksonian 'opening' of American institutions and society in the second quarter of the nineteenth century, the authority of Blackstone slowly diminished, his place taken by American-born commentators on essentially Blackstonian themes. With the rapid democratization of American life also came a loosening of the restrictiveness of its legal community: formal requirements for apprenticeship in the United States were abolished or reduced; law schools fell into disrepute; bar associations lost control over the direction of the profession (although lawyers continued as individuals to play major roles in directing public affairs).[39] Upper Canadian jurists increasingly referred to judgments rendered by American legal authorities, yet no challenge to the self-regulatory capacity or the prestige of the legal profession took place. The Law Society of Upper Canada easily maintained its monopoly in these years. By the 1850s the legal elite in this very British and scarcely democratic province had entered a period of institutional consolidation and complacency that would last for several generations.

Law, Medicine, and the Universities

The relationship between the universities of Ontario and the legal and medical professions was an uneasy one for the remainder of the century. Attendance at the Law Society school established in 1862 increased throughout the 1860s until 1868, when the society abruptly announced that classes were to be suspended and the school closed. Frequent and compulsory examinations were substituted for it. The *Canada Law Journal* gave financial reasons for the Law Society's decision, but other factors provide a more likely explanation. First, the collapse of the Queen's University law school meant that by the late 1860s the Law Society faced no competition in legal instruction from an Ontario university. Having probably drawn students of the Queen's school from Kingston to Toronto by inaugurating its own school, and by refusing to accept courses given by Queen's, the Law Society had contributed to the demise of the Queen's program. Second, it is likely that by 1868 there existed within the community of benchers in the province a resentment of the centralization of legal education in Toronto. In the late 1860s benchers from smaller centres of urban life like London argued for the creation of county law libraries and the end of term-keeping at Osgoode Hall. From the perspective of lawyers engaged in private practice in such communities, the presence of students in Toronto attending compulsory lectures meant a diminished supply of the cheap labour provided by articling. Finally, most benchers probably viewed classroom instruction as less than useful, producing little more, as the *Canada Law Journal* put it, than 'disorder and "skylarking".'[40]

In 1872, largely at the initiative of John Hillyard Cameron and Chief Justice Thomas Moss, the Law Society launched another attempt at formal legal education, The Law School of Ontario, located at Osgoode Hall. Attendance at lectures continued to be voluntary, but by enrolling in the school students could significantly decrease the duration of their apprenticeship. This time the law school lasted six years. It was closed by the society in 1878, possibly because of pressure applied by non-Toronto benchers whose constituencies bitterly resented the understaffed law offices of the countryside.[41] Fortunately, the law students themselves, perhaps desiring a degree of intellectual stimulation beyond what their school provided for them, had founded the Osgoode Hall Literary and Legal Society in 1876. In the years after 1878 that society, which held debates (for example, on Henry George's Single Tax theory) and organized social occasions, provided an important forum for student self-education. It also became a forum in which student discontent could be focused.

Discontent there was by the late 1870s, given voice not only by students but also by unhappy members of the legal profession. In November 1877 an article called 'The Law of Succession to Land in Ontario' appeared in the *Canadian Monthly and National Review*. In it, George S. Holmested launched a devastating attack not only on his nominal subject but also upon law itself, and by inference upon legal education. 'The common law of England,' he began, 'has been declared by some of its enthusiastic votaries to be "the perfection of reason," and most students of English law imbibe this exalted notion with regard to one of the principal objects of their study at the very commencement of their labours, and accept it with all the docility which becomes profound ignorance sitting at the feet of profound wisdom.'[42] Within a month a contributor to the 'Round the Table' section of the *Canadian Monthly and National Review* had enlarged the scope of the attack. Taking as his starting-point an address on 'Professional Ethics' given by Edward Blake to a gathering of lawyers and law students, the anonymous author noted that 'there was a great deal in the lecture about the nobility of the Law, and the elevating influence of its study, which, although fully "borne out by the authorities," sticks in my perverse throat, as it has always done.' He was not, he insisted, 'looking at the Law as a matter of business. It is a very fine business ... It is upon the plea that its study is noble, elevating, or intrinsically beneficial to a man, as a rational (over and above a bread-winning and dollar-accumulating) being, that unhesitatingly I join issue.'[43]

Like Holmested, the anonymous critic declared that the common law was full of the 'dead bones of details that should be buried with things put away as nationally childish,' and that it had become 'a patchwork puzzle, tangled, twisted, and wrapped up in barbarous jargon.' The chaotic state of the law was reflected in legal education itself, for law 'is studied empirically and unintelligently; walled up for professional profit ...' How could the student be truly educated when the major problems of the day were ignored in order to acquire 'a mass of undigested and lifeless facts, facts almost valueless in any broader connection than their mere professional use'? Legal studies were a sustained exercise in 'subjection to authority,' dominated by the 'tendencies to exalt the letter and word over the spirit and every thing, to join hands with precedent and tradition against even moderate progress, and to accept in all matters the dicta of authority without verification ...'[44]

There was much food for thought in this sustained, if at times intemperate, indictment of the virtual sanctification of the common law, and the issue was joined in the next edition of the *Canadian Monthly* by defenders of the integrity of law and legal education. Accepting the fact that there was 'much truth' in what had been said, one writer insisted that law nevertheless was a 'noble profession,' for it was rooted in the principles of liberty and order. Far from being a narrow vocation, it encompassed broad considerations that made it 'an essential branch of a liberal education. Burke thought so, and his mind was certainly not cramped, nor his usefulness impaired by his careful study of Blackstone.'[45]

Early in 1880, their law school now suspended, the students themselves entered the controversy. Thomas Gorham read a paper to the Legal and Literary Society indicting legal education as found at Osgoode Hall, and it was subsequently published in the *Canadian Monthly* with prefatory remarks by Nicholas Flood Davin, the feisty politician, lawyer, and journalist from the North West Territories. 'Here in Canada ...,' wrote Davin, 'it would be well to ponder the causes which have made the attorney the favourite villain and trickster of the novel and stage.' Gorham reiterated accusations levelled earlier and set them concretely into the context of the students' experience at Osgoode Hall. 'Some of us ... have shuddered at the cold and stiff embrace of the Common Law,' he wrote. 'How many of us have floundered wearily in the "Slough of Despond," as ... we have struggled through, and at last conquered ... the "barbarous jargon" of the law ... Is it any wonder that the student finishes his servitude with [a] narrowed and distracted mind, a dulled ambition and a meaner aim?' In short, Gorham concluded, the study of the law in Ontario was 'at a stand-still.' The operations of the law school had been suspended and no instruction was provided, yet the degree of Barrister-at-Law was still awarded. The benchers had pleaded financial embarrassment, but Gorham showed that its 1878 financial report indicated a permanent reserve of at least $60,000. Fees for the year from all sources totalled over $20,000. 'Let the students ... demand, in tones not to be misunderstood, a method of instruction founded on correct principles and with the design of instructing them in the art as well as the science of the law.'[46]

The attacks by Davin and Gorham created a sensation throughout the legal community in the province, and the controversy was kept alive by subsequent elaboration by both critics. Davin accused the Law Society of 'yielding to a cry short-sighted, selfish and ignoble,' from those benchers from the backwoods of the province who were envious of the educational opportunities available only in Toronto. Faced with such opposition from its rural constituency, the benchers had 'bowed the head before the boorish clamour ... The way the country benchers fulfilled their manifold trust ... was to put their knife in the Law School.'[47] Davin argued that it was now the duty of such men as Adam Crooks and Edward Blake – prominent as benchers and influential in politics – to initiate substantial change in legal education, and to have the courage not to succumb to the demands of self-seeking and mean-spirited rural lawyers. Legal education, he concluded, must somehow be made to embody the spirit of the liberal culture afforded by the university experience.

In his contribution to the controversy, Gorham supplied further facts and figures to document his accusation that law students were not a drain on the coffers of the Law Society. In fact, he asserted, while student fees constituted a significant sum, very little was expended by the society on the students. 'There is,' Gorham wrote, 'every year a large expenditure for books, but the students are furnished with a poor lending library.' In fact, he went on, the term 'library' was scarcely warranted. 'It is a motley collection of a few volumes of some of the works on the course, the most of them old editions, and of so ancient a character that one might easily be forgiven for asking if their age would not make them rare curiosities.'[48] Gorham concluded that law courses should be taught in a way that placed law into a broad social and intellectual context. All law students, whether 'three year men' who had obtained a bachelor's degree at a university or 'five year men' who had none, should be exposed to such a true legal education. 'How much better then would it be for both of these classes of students, were there lectures which they were compelled to attend – in order that the one should gain an insight into its historical and philosophical aspects, and that the other might be initiated in the mysteries of legal phraseology, both meanwhile having added to their desire for legal knowledge that zest which is so necessary.'[49]

Faced with such sustained and telling criticism, the Law Society of Upper Canada once again launched an experiment in legal education. A 'special committee' of the society recommended that lecture programs be set up by local bars and students in various towns throughout the province. Attendance was not compulsory, and Toronto students petitioned the Law Society to re-establish the lecture program as it had existed prior to 1878. For the third time in twenty years a law school was set up, this time on a three-year trial basis. The Osgoode Hall lectures recommenced in the fall of 1882; they continued to the end of the decade, but on an increasingly sporadic basis. At late as 1889 the *Canadian Law Times* could note that 'in the many years during which lectures have been delivered at Osgoode Hall no one Bencher or other member of the profession, except the paid lecturers, has ever delivered a single lecture, or appeared at a lecture delivered, or in any way manifested the slightest interest in the welfare of the School.'[50]

With such indifference exhibited by the profession, the law school drifted through the decade until 1888, when a special committee of the Law Society met to consider a proposal from the University of Toronto to collaborate in the operation of a law faculty. On 14 December 1888 it decided that it would not do so. The law school would instead be reorganized and expanded; attendance at lectures was for the first time to be compulsory. Lectures would be given only in Toronto. A permanent law school – the Osgoode Hall Law School – had at last been established. It was to have a principal, part-time lecturers and examiners, substantive lectures, weekly moot courts, and annual examinations. The Law Society of Upper Canada maintained statutory control over educational and licensing standards, thereby ensuring that professional autonomy would not be compromised by association with a university (a situation that was to continue until 1957), but the classroom now became a permanent element of Ontario legal education.[51]

The 1887 proposal from the University of Toronto to cooperate with the Law Society in the creation of a jointly operated faculty of law at the provincial university came about as a direct result of the Federation Act of that year. It had reconstituted the university as a teaching body, thereby opening up the possibility for the creation of professional faculties. Soon after the passing of the act, the Toronto School of Medicine became the medical faculty of the University of Toronto, in the obvious hope that state aid would be made available for medical education. This posed a direct challenge to the Trinity Medical College, incorporated since 1877 by provincial statute and by the 1880s the locus of medical education in Toronto.[52] Its dean, Walter B. Geikie, objected strenuously to whoever would listen. Provincial policy regarding medical education, he argued, had since 1853 been to do so by means of privately funded institutions. Not without great difficulty and sacrifice, Trinity had been successful in operating along such lines. But if the provincial government was now to change the rules and, he inferred, in effect provide state-supported medical education by allowing a medical school to exist within the jurisdiction of the provincial university, surely Trinity could expect an equal measure of provincial largesse.[53]

The fears of favouritism by Geikie and others soon seemed borne out. In 1888 the University of Toronto began the construction of a biological building (added to in 1890). Nominally for the use of arts and science students, it was open to medical students and contained dissecting rooms. Moreover, the vice-chancellor of the university, William Mulock, had instructed the architect to remove from the blueprints all indications of how the different rooms were going to be used. Geikie saw in such actions clear evidence of duplicity, and he launched a vigorous campaign of protest that was to last for years.[54] For this reason and others, Trinity remained unfederated with the University of Toronto for the rest of the century. By 1900, however, Geikie encountered opposition to his isolationist position within the staff of Trinity. In that year, its provost, the Reverend T.C.S. Macklem, following initiatives taken by his predecessor, presented him with a scheme to 'merge the Medical College with the University of Toronto Medical Faculty.' Geikie resisted, but the proposal went forward. By 1903 the charter of the medical college had been surrendered to the Trinity Corporation. Dean Geikie resigned during the negotiations, refusing to be a party to what he called 'the Niagara Falls of Amalgamation.' Full association took place in October 1903.[55] The age of proprietary medical schools in Toronto had finally ended, after a half-century of existence.

Other institutions for medical education existed in the latter years of the nineteenth century. In Kingston, relations between the Royal College of Physicians and Surgeons and the university remained uneasy for the first few years after the creation of the Royal. Fears by the university that the standards of the medical college might not be sufficiently high ended when the Royal College of Surgeons of Edinburgh approved its course of studies and recognized its graduates. Yet arts students and professors resented the continued occupation of college buildings by members of a body over which the university had no control, especially when in 1870 the Royal College refused to pay rent for the classrooms it used. Controversy over degree-granting powers continued until 1892, when Principal G.M. Grant, who believed from the time of his arrival in 1877 that the university should support medical education if it was to be worthy of the name, managed to complete an arrangement for the Royal College to surrender its degree-granting power. Its teaching members would become the medical faculty of Queen's while continuing to have full academic autonomy under the jurisdiction of their own dean, except in the matter of appointments where the university council and the principal would have representation. Nevertheless, matters of financial responsibility and jurisdiction remained problematic into the twentieth century. Only with the Queen's University Act of 1912, severing the university's formal ties from the church, was the situation resolved. Queen's could now use its endowment for any appropriate purpose. Professors of medicine thereafter went onto the university's payroll, and its faculty could claim financial support from general revenues.[56]

In London, the medical school of Western University was also associated with, but virtually autonomous from, the university. Medical instruction began in 1882, upon the conclusion of an agreement between the university, mainly in an old five-room cottage that stood on the college grounds. With the discontinuation of the arts faculty in 1885 the medical faculty virtually sustained the presence of higher education in the London area, except for instruction given in divinity at Huron College. In 1888, however, upon the completion of a new building near the London General Hospital, the medical faculty removed itself from the university grounds. Western University remained one largely in name only.[57] Medical education, in London as elsewhere, stood substantially apart from the non-medical aspects of university life.

Between 1860 and 1890 the situations of legal and medical education in Ontario were similar, for the relationships of the professional schools to the university were more nominal than real. In the case of law, the relationship could scarcely even be said to be nominal.[58] But one major difference existed between law schools and medical schools. Bed-side instruction had always been an essential element of the training of medical students, but until the latter decades of the nineteenth century those beds had usually been located in the home, or in the traditional private hospital, a place of confinement and treatment of indigent patients. Between 1880 and the Great War, however, the middle class turned increasingly to the hospital as its preferred site for treatment, for the image of the hospital was now less of a charitable institution for the poor than of one in which the latest medical technologies and methods were practiced. For the first time, the hospital was coming to be associated with health more than with disease. The wealth of the middle class provided the general hospital with an economy based on patient fees, and private physicians – often before prohibited from treating patients there – began to seek access to the new-look hospital wards. Medical men argued that the hospital ward should be the heart of the medical student's learning experience. The human body and the observation of it was his textbook. As medical technology and treatment improved with better surgical techniques, the antiseptic method, and the use of anaesthesia, the authority and prestige of the medical man grew, and the source of much of it lay in the confidence the middle class now bestowed upon the general hospitals.[59]

Beneath the surface of this reorientation, however, was the fact that the very nature of the 'medical man' – and therefore of medicine – was fundamentally changing, not because the proprietary schools had ultimately proven inadequate as educational institutions but as a result of other factors. R.D. Gidney and W.P.J. Millar have demonstrated that the criticisms of the Toronto proprietary schools that surfaced with considerable vehemence in the late 1880s did so, ironically, at a moment of significant success. By the mid-1880s they offered a wide range of clinical instruction and a constantly expanding number of courses. The Toronto School of Medicine alone provided a teaching staff of nineteen (sixteen were physicians); student enrolment at it and Trinity exceeded 500 students in 1886-7. 'The success of the proprietorial schools,' Gidney and Millar note, 'was widely recognized, moreover, at home and abroad. Their certificates, or the university degrees they prepared students for, were accepted by British authorities as equivalent qualifications.' The proprietary schools met their fate not because they had failed but because they were seen to represent a different kind of medicine, and medicine man, from those the newly federated University of Toronto, intent on the cultivation of research, wanted to attract and encourage.[60]

As will be seen, these were the years not only of university federation but also of the rise of the ideal of research as a fundamental rationale of academic life. Knowledge must be discovered in the archives and in the laboratory, not merely disseminated in the act of teaching. Gidney and Millar fully document the fact that medicine was no less transformed than were other subjects because of this 'paradigm shift.' To apostles of the research ideal, such as University of Toronto biologist R. Ramsay Wright, the 'enlightened empiricism' represented by clinical observation of the patient was no longer adequate: the methodological rigour of the laboratory was now deemed essential. Seen in this way, the conflict between Geikie at Trinity and the champions of a University of Toronto faculty of medicine reflected Geikie's role as self-imposed champion of the older, humanistic notion of the medical 'arts,' not the desperation of an anachronistic old curmudgeon intent on holding onto his personal academic fiefdom. For physicians such as Geikie, the biological and other sciences were complementary to medical practice, not central to it. But the age of the laboratory had now come to academic Ontario, and the events of 1887 in academic politics demonstrated that the provincial state was willing to finance the construction of scientific facilities and the purchase of equipment for the provincial university. Gidney and Millar conclude: 'As older notions of what constituted a liberal education began to disintegrate, as science in particular could claim that status as much as any other study, a scientific education gained respectability and put its possessor on a par with those who knew the ancient tongues. At the same time, the explanatory (and more rarely the curative) power of the biological sciences heightened the prestige of technical knowledge *per se* ... [This knowledge] won its place in the medical curriculum not least because it conferred a new degree of cultural authority, not merely upon the researcher but on the medical profession as a whole.' From the surgery of the gentleman practitioner, the locus of medicine's authority had shifted first to the hospital wards and later into hospital and university laboratories. As the twentieth century unfolded, physicians in North America still believed their profession to be a beleaguered one; yet as medical science became more complex, and as the benefits of laboratory and clinical research became apparent, the physicians who gained the most prestige in government and university circles increasingly carried with them advanced academic credentials and university appointments.[61]

From the days of the old Family Compact Ontario's lawyers had been the self-appointed arbiters of the legal requisites for orderly social change. At the end of the nineteenth century, the Law Society of Upper Canada was as securely in control of the profession as it had ever been. Moreover, law remained a man's profession, for only one woman – Clara Brett Martin – was admitted to the Ontario bar in the century that followed the formation of the Law Society. Martin attained this distinction, as will be seen, only after a protracted struggle with the benchers of the province. Yet, as individuals, lawyers no longer felt in control of either their own or the province's destiny. The power of the profession had for decades been challenged by the rise of commercial capital. By the early twentieth century, lawyers admitted openly that the real leaders of the province and of the nation were the businessmen, financiers, and tycoons whose rise to power and social authority the legal profession had earlier sought to undermine.[62] Increasingly the lawyer found his role to be a secondary one, that of adviser to businessmen. Specialization within the profession further diminished the breadth of his status as social leader. He felt less in control of his own vocational destiny: instead, he was an agent hired by powerful people to control their own financial empires. The formalism of the law now appeared to be a restrictive strait-jacket. Collectivist legislation seemed to have dethroned the common law as the moral core of jurisprudence. Government regulations had seemingly taken the place of private contract as the basis of socio-political change. 'The old family lawyer, the repository of the secrets of the family for years,' Mr Justice Riddell told the Ontario Bar Association in 1907, 'the guide, philosopher and friend of old and young, has become, largely, a thing of the past. His place has been taken by the businessman, the acute pulse feeler of the money market.'[63] Just as in an earlier generation the power of the conservative oligarchy had been eroded by the advocates of mid-Victorian commerce and expansion, so now the leaders of the legal fraternity – the professional heirs of that oligarchy – felt similarly displaced, and by the grandsons of those Upper Canadian capitalists. By the beginning of the twentieth century the Ontario legal profession was in a state of uneasy equipoise, sitting 'Janus-like with the Tory values of Upper Canada behind it and the emerging values of an urban, industrialized culture ahead.'[64]

Part Two:
Victorian Studies and Students

4

Character and Conduct

Reconstructing the world in which the first generation of Ontario students and professors in the liberal arts lived and worked is a difficult task for the historical imagination. It involves a voyage into a social, moral, and mental environment whose patterns of assumption and belief are elusive to us, for they carry a linguistic code that has become problematic to the late twentieth-century sensibility. 'The past,' as novelist L.P. Hartley wrote, 'is a foreign country. They do things differently there.'[1] Yet however difficult, it is critically important to recover and take measure of the ideas and imperatives that lay behind the largely lost world of the mid-Victorian liberal arts curriculum, for they helped give form and substance to what might be called an Ontario ethos well beyond the nineteenth century.

In Canada West in the middle decades of the nineteenth century there existed something of a disjunction of consciousness and circumstance. This was largely due to the facts of colonial life. On the one hand, Ontarians lived in a province they knew was vastly different from the England that was their cultural model. England had already undergone major industrial and urban transformation, yet Ontario was still overwhelmingly rural and had scarcely begun to witness its own industrial revolution.[2] On the other hand, a sense of membership in the expanding commercial and industrial empire gave a good number of Ontarians by the 1850s a significant degree of optimistic expectation that this good fortune would some day also be theirs. The British had experienced their railroad mania in the 1840s; the Canadian engineer and promoter T.C. Keefer called eagerly for Canadians to follow suit early in the next decade. The advent of the railway age in British North America, he urged, would bring about industrial, urban, commercial, and even moral transformation.[3]

The mid-Victorian frame of mind assumed that material progress would continue indefinitely, and that it meant inevitable improvement. Politicians and promoters in Canada West such as Francis Hincks, Allan MacNab, and Thomas Keefer exuded such belief, and acted upon it. In this respect they were representative of their age. They and others could take pride with the British in the Great Exhibition of 1851, with its Crystal Palace built of glass and steel and crammed with all manner of turbine and mechanical gadgetry, a tangible reminder of the supremacy of British industry, institutions, values, and beliefs. The inhabitants of Canada shared vicariously in this pride of achievement because the emotional, intellectual, and moral attitudes that informed Victorian Canadians may have been distant from the British in space but they were one with it in time. The force of cultural memory, that is, allowed the mind's eye to share, however vicariously, in imperial achievement. The social observer Susanna Moodie, for example, was perpetually troubled by the rudeness of her colonial surroundings, yet she was as much an agent of British beliefs and values as if she lived in an English village. She did live in one, in spirit if not in fact. Thomas Keefer's solution to the problem of Canada's future development was to champion the 'iron civilizer' – the steam locomotive; for Susanna Moodie and others concerned with the cultural development of the colony, education was 'the true wealth of the world.'[4]

For her, a true moral education extended to inhabitants of both country and town by means of schools and magazines (such as her own *Victoria Magazine*) would eventually bring about material progress and even ease class tension. 'The want of education and moral training,' she wrote, 'is the only *real* barrier that exists between the different classes of men. Nature, reason, and christianity, recognize no other.' (By implication, the ideological extremes of aristocracy and democracy, to which Moodie also took exception, were less insurmountable.) As a result, she urged her Canadian compatriots, particularly the farmers who had less opportunity than townsmen to acquire knowledge and taste by reading, to put their sons 'in a situation to acquire solid and useful information, from masters who will not merely teach them to repeat lessons like parrots, by rote; but who will teach them to think – to know the meaning of what they learn – and to be enabled by the right use of those reflective faculties, to communicate the knowledge thus acquired to others.' In this way, out of a colony of disparate immigrants would arise 'a people ... held together by the strong bonds of moral and intellectual fellowship.'

The sequence of the adjectives 'moral' and 'intellectual' should be noted, for it implies a choice of priorities not confined to Mrs Moodie. Social unity was seen to be achieved not simply by 'rational' decisions but even more by bonds of emotion and volition given direction by 'the precious code of moral laws' handed down through the generations by the Christian tradition, 'for all true knowledge is from on high ...' A first major source of conflict between nineteenth- and twentieth-century notions of the aims of education – at whatever level – lay, therefore, in the perceived nature and origins of knowledge itself. And in this search for definition, as educational institutions were developed in Canada West, traditional forms of religious belief involving the willing suspension of critical judgment – forms of religious piety and of social deference – occupied a greater place than did the fine-tuning of the intellect for the purpose of discovering new forms of objective truth. The mental life of nineteenth-century Ontario was shaped by the ethos of the evangelical revival, even as its material life continually improved. Nowhere were these characteristics more pronounced than in the struggling colleges of the province.

The New Colleges

The colleges that existed in Canada West by the 1850s – University College, Trinity, Knox, Victoria, and Queen's – were modest institutions indeed, whether judged by buildings, students, or staff. Relatives of the undergraduates of the University of Toronto in the 1850s, for example, might even have had difficulty finding the place until University College was completed in 1859. Yet once they found it visitors would have been impressed, for they would have been struck by the imposing size, solidity, and beauty of the University College complex, a strange yet markedly successful combination of Norman, Byzantine, and Italian architectural styles.[5] A powerful evocation of Old World architecture it was, set in heavily wooded, bucolic splendour near the northern boundary of Toronto above College Street. To its south could be seen the old Magnetic Observatory, built in the 1840s. Beyond it, even in the 1870s, lay open acres of farmland and forest dotted only sporadically by house or church.[6] As a graduate of 1880, reflecting on the university in the 1860s, put it: 'A wonderful stone college had been built out in the bush, at great expense ... That the college would ever be filled, even comfortably, with students, was unbelievable.'[7]

A mile and a half to the south-west of University College stood Bishop Strachan's pride, Trinity College. Located on the western edge of the city, just north of Queen Street in St Patrick's ward, it too stood in isolation from the urban environment, surrounded by 'unimproved' land and uncultivated fields. But there it was, imposing in its own austere way – a lengthy two-storey gothic structure resplendent with a variety of cupolas and complemented by an impressive provost's lodge and terrace.[8] Far less striking was Knox College, which consisted of a single small building located two blocks to the east of Queen's Park Crescent in St John's ward.

The colleges outside Toronto were modest by any standard. Victoria, located at Cobourg, was housed in a single building in the 1850s and Queen's, at Kingston, was even less imposing. One professor who arrived from the University of Glasgow in 1872 was impressed with the 'bold and impressive lines' and the 'graceful Corinthian pillars' of the university's main building – until he discovered that he had been looking at the Kingston Court House. The nearby college itself, he found to his dismay, conducted its entire business in a building 'as yet of only two storeys, with its little pepper-box on top intended as a belfry, and its general air of disdaining the meritricious advantage of architectural ornament and concentrating itself severely on what Aristotle defines as the object of a house – "to afford shelter from the weather."' With his memory securely fixed on the 'massive and imposing' buildings of the University of Glasgow, the young Scottish philosopher John Watson had to adjust his expectations to the Canadian reality. 'It was hardly surprising,' he later admitted, 'that as I looked at the plain and ugly structure in which I was to begin my labours I felt a curious sinking of the heart.'[9]

It was clearly not the physical plant of the university that kept Watson, soon to become Canada's most outstanding scholar, at Queen's for the next fifty years. 'I am afraid I whispered sadly to myself: "One-horse college, evidently!"' he noted. Nor was he encouraged by great numbers of eager students, for the size of the student population was at least as modest as its surroundings. In his first year at Queen's (1872–3) Watson had classes of four, five, and fourteen; this was a discouraging number until he discovered that it marked an increase of nine over the previous year.[10] The year before, only thirty-three students enrolled in the entire faculty of arts and science (see Fig. 4.1), and convocation at year's end recorded that only four students from the faculty took degrees. Indeed, for the whole period from 1861 to 1875 the faculty of arts and science at Queen's granted, on average, only eight degrees per year.[11]

At the other colleges in the province, student enrolment and numbers of graduates in arts and science were equally meagre in the 1860s and early 1870s. Enrolment at the University of Toronto in 1861–2 was 260; a decade later it had only increased by three. Trinity's numbers increased from thirty-nine to sixty-nine, whereas Queen's, beset by financial crisis and professorial intrigue, declined from thirty-nine to thirty-three. The average annual number of graduates in arts and science for the years 1860-75 stood at fourteen for the University of Toronto, seven for Victoria, and fewer than six for Trinity.[12] Such students as

FIGURE 4.1

Ontario enrolment in arts and science by institution, 1861–81

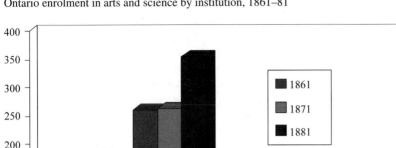

SOURCE: Robin S. Harris, *A History of Higher Education in Canada, 1663–1960* (Toronto 1976), 625–8. Note: unless otherwise indicated, enrolment statistics refer to the academic year. Thus 1861 refers to the fall and winter sessions, 1861–2.

there were came primarily, as Mrs Moodie had hoped, from rural rather than urban areas. This should scarcely be surprising since only 14.6 per cent of the population of Canada West lived in urban settings (towns and cities exceeding 25,000 in population) in 1850 and the percentage did not reach twenty (in fact 20.2) for two decades.[13] The student secretary of the class of 1880 at the University of Toronto, using letters and records in his possession, found that 'of fifty-three who graduated in that year, eight were from Toronto and forty-five came from other parts of Ontario. Of these forty-five, forty had been brought up on farms.'[14]

Those who reached university in the mid-nineteenth century, whether from town or country, shared the common attribute of literacy; but literacy in itself was no guarantor of the upward class and occupational mobility that a university education seemed to promise. Of greater significance for the potential to achieve a significant degree of upward mobility – even to aspire to a university education – were the factors of race, sex, and ethnicity. The conclusion is a hackneyed one: to go to college it helped to be white, male, and an English or Scottish Protestant.[15] The colleges of mid-century were institutions intended to educate the social and intellectual elite of Canadian society, whose education and enhancement, said presidents and principals, would bring broad public benefit. University authorities were by no means defensive about the elitism of higher education, for few members of the provincial population were democrats in the modern sense of that word.[16] The existence of such views did not mean that the colleges actively encouraged exclusionist policies. For good or for ill, it simply did not occur to most educators or politicians in British North America that universities and colleges could or should do other than prepare a relative few – the rising generation – for entrance into society.[17] Even by 1869 no one in a position of educational authority in Ontario viewed the fact that only thirteen graduates of Toronto common schools could be found in the grammar schools (meant to prepare them for university entrance) as a sign of institutional or social weakness.[18]

That colleges existed for a fortunate few was a fact of social existence scarcely of note, because the belief that society was structured by social stations into which one was born, and would probably remain, operated as often as not at the level of unexamined assumption and was therefore a powerful force for the preservation of the status quo.[19] What *did* require constant reiteration was the social purpose of those elite institutions, whether through solemn statements of the general objects of a university education or through rhetorical justification of what should be taught. Members of college boards of governors played a critically important role in this respect, for while their task was not specifically to make such pronouncements or to dictate the content of curricula, they could effectively shape both by the kinds of professors they recruited. During the middle years of the nineteenth century, careful attention was paid in Canada West to the academic pedigrees, social backgrounds, and personal connections of professors at Ontario universities in order to assure that no heretical views issued from the lectern. Family ties and letters of recommendation by scholarly acquaintances, not the open market-place of academic competition for posts, dominated academic hiring at the time.[20]

From the outset, all colleges in the province shared the common aims of transmitting knowledge and fostering social stability. But each except the provincial university also existed for the more immediate purpose of meeting the needs of its own religious denomination. The former meant that boards of governors would seek members of faculty whose character and training were known to be 'safe'; the latter prescribed the range of institutions to which they would go for faculty. The results are scarcely surprising. In what might be called the first generation of the Ontario professoriate, from the 1840s to the early 1870s, the governors of Trinity College consistently recruited staff solely from Oxford and Cambridge – bastions of Anglican orthodoxy and social privilege that could be counted on to provide clerics trained in the classical curriculum of the liberal arts. Its first three mathematics professors, for example, were drawn from the same Cambridge college.

Victoria was more eclectic, initially appointing well-respected local clerics as well as graduates of American colleges. Queen's also drew upon ministers with Canadian pastoral experience, then began to hire graduates from Scottish universities. Victoria and Queen's proved quite willing, however, to appoint their own graduates, and this became a source of both denominational and institutional pride. As will be seen, the college ideal was tied to the notion that undergraduates were in as much need of good pastoral counselling and parental advice as they were of contact with scholars with advanced academic degrees. While sharing this pastoral approach, University College chose to recruit along lines similar to those of Strachan's bastion of Anglican orthodoxy, Trinity College. In the formative years of professorial recruitment it drew almost exclusively from the well-established British universities.[21]

Student and Professorial Conduct

The students who entered the colleges of Ontario from the 1850s to the 1870s took instruction in buildings that were fairly new but for the most part were also spartan in construction and facilities. Their professors were almost invariably British in background and training except, on occasion, when recent graduates of the college (as at Trinity) were given sub-professorial appointments while college authorities contacted British universities to fill vacancies. There were exceptions, as with the Reverend George Ferguson, an 1851 graduate of Queen's who held the chair of English Language and Literature and History from 1869 to 1907 – but his wealthy father had endowed the chair. More often than not these teachers were also ordained clergymen, and at Trinity, on Bishop Strachan's insistence, they were also required (until 1859) to be celibate. This may account for the relatively short tenure of most early Trinity appointees.

Differences of denominational affiliation naturally led to differences in academic and social ambience. Life under Provost Whitaker of Trinity, a man greatly affected by the Oxford Movement in England, meant adherence to a High Church doctrine and practice that some within the Anglican communion thought to be Roman rather than Anglo-Catholic. At Victoria the atmosphere was quite different yet no less intense. The Methodist rejection of Calvinist notions of predestination meant that the burden of religious faithfulness fell directly onto the shoulders – more properly the hearts and consciences – of the individual. At Trinity, students received religious Truth catechismically from their provost; at Victoria they had to discover it within themselves as they awaited the 'new birth.' They were expected to search for the call of God from within, not from received doctrine, and the result was a great deal of undergraduate anxiety. In the 1840s and 1850s, relief from spiritual unease took collective forms, with several entire student bodies, previously unconverted, professing a 'saving faith in Christ.'[22]

The greater intellectual orientation of the Calvinist tradition made religious revivalism on a large scale less pronounced at Queen's, but there, too, the religious conscience was dominant, as it was meant to be. The decision of virtually all of its theological students to abandon their college for another during the Great Schism of 1844 clearly took extraordinary conviction and courage. Their professors tried to persuade them to stay, but 'conscience, and a sense of duty to Christ,' wrote one, 'impelled us onwards, though respecting our professors, and unwilling to give them pain. Hence, we took our stand according to our conviction.'[23] The professor of philosophy at King's College, James Beaven, had greeted the decision to create a secular University of Toronto with the accusation that the province now sponsored a 'godless university,' and this, for him, was a contradiction in terms. But there was in fact nothing godless about the newly created University College. It taught no denominational creed, but its atmosphere and orientation, like that of Ontario society itself, was still overwhelmingly Christian.

Such differences were ones of nuance, for much more united the general atmosphere of the several Ontario colleges than divided it. College life at each was specifically intended to nurture an environment in which the student would assimilate knowledge within the framework of Christian assumptions, for in the Christian *Logos* was seen to lie the source of all academic truth. Yet such a voyage of discovery could not be left to the undisciplined mental caprices of mere boys. The university student was regarded less as a young adult than as an older child; the university itself acted as a parental body. As soon as University College students registered for residence in the 1850s, for example, authorities gave them a circular to send to their parents assuring them that their sons' spiritual life would be supported by daily morning and evening prayers, regular reading of the Scriptures, and Sunday services. 'The council will afford every facility for the carrying out of your intentions, and with this view, will exercise such control over your son during his residence, as may be best calculated to effect your wishes.'[24]

All aspects of the students' lives, at whatever college, were governed by strict forms of domestic and intellectual regimentation. 'We had come from a small town where we had been thought persons of some consequence to the Church and to society,' remembered one divinity student who arrived at Trinity in 1852, 'and were very much our own masters. It was no small trial to us to be brought under strict domestic – almost monastic – discipline; to be put into a new and imperfectly warmed building in the dead of winter, and to be subjected to precise rules as to chapel and meals, and going-out and coming-in, and generally to more or less restriction of our liberty.' This student had earlier attended the Anglican Diocesan Theological Institute in Cobourg, where the educational model was an older one based on the notion of apprenticeship. Expose a student to a knowledgeable gentleman, it was thought, and that student will begin to act like one and be responsible to the larger community of which he was a part. At Trinity, students were also meant to emulate their professorial mentors, yet the emphasis there was different, for the educational culture stressed separation from society's corrupting forces.[25] Student autonomy was more circumscribed. Mandatory attendance at chapel and compulsory wearing of cap and gown at lectures and in public served as constant reminders that students were assumed to be wayward by inclination and to be in the world but not of it.

Daily life was equally regimented elsewhere. At Queen's daily morning and evening prayers were required of all students, and those in theology had, as a group, to attend Sunday evening services at St Andrew's Church. Victoria's undergraduates were also required to attend morning and evening prayer services, and these included one held at six o'clock Sunday morning in preparation for services later in the day. Meal hours were strictly observed: at University College in the 1860s, students ate at 8 a.m., 2 p.m., and 7 p.m. – or they did not eat at all. Their schedules kept them busy from early morning until after eight o'clock at night, and did not include time for private study, the completion of class assignments, or general reflection. In this way, it was difficult for them to find any substantial block of free time in order to succumb to the wiles of city life. Somers, the steward of the University College residence in the 1860s, closed its gate door at 9 p.m., and the porter recorded the names of all students entering thereafter. Students habitually (four times in a month) returning to residence after 10 p.m. were fined ten cents for each transgression – a significant sum given that forty cents would buy a hundred pounds of coal to fuel the grate fire that was the only source of heat in a dormitory room.[26]

Professors served as proctors, supervising attendance at prayer meetings, making spot checks on residence behaviour, and fining students who missed classes. Victoria College had an officer with the ominous title of 'Moral and Domestic Governor' in the 1850s. College 'wardens' were just that. The Trinity College minutes of 26 January 1854 included instructions to place bars on the basement and ground-floor windows of the College, and the practice at University College was to fix pieces of broken glass to the top of the stone walls surrounding the residence in case their steel spikes were insufficient deterrents. Their object was to keep truants in, not intruders out. At least one undergraduate, Mitchell by name, was found in the early hours of one morning 'hanging by the seat of his trousers.'[27]

In spite of such all-embracing forms of regulation and control – perhaps because of them – life in the early colleges was by no means always tranquil. Youths fresh from the farm, unaccustomed to the industrial work discipline implicit in the hourly regulation of their days and used to being required to work as men and by the rhythm of rural life from the outset of their teens, clearly had a difficult time making the adjustment. For the most part order was observed, but each college experienced its share of student unrest. Victoria's 'Moral Governor' was hanged in effigy at least once, perhaps because of the two foolscap pages of printed rules he had drawn up prescribing, with appropriate penalties, 'every movement of the student from five o'clock in the morning, when a monitor turned him out of bed, till ten at night when lights were ordered out and to bed he must go.'[28]

Nor were student frustrations vented only on college authorities. At times factional squabbles turned student against student. A prayer meeting Nathanael Burwash attended as a student at Victoria was disrupted by the 'heavy rhythmic march of many well-shod feet ascending the stairs ...' While the second hymn was still in progress, 'in they came in marching order, as if under command of a drill-sergeant ... surrounded those singing, and proceeded to pelt the candles on the black-boards first with marbles and later with pine kindling.'[29] Particularly before organized student self-government, university authorities often found themselves forced to confront disciplinary problems. Usually the disturbance took the form of 'irreverent' behaviour in chapel or 'rude and disorderly conduct' towards professors or at dinner. Such were the moral strictures of the mid-Victorian years that laughter and conversation at an unpropitious moment could result in equally serious charges.

Professorial conduct was at times not conducive to exemplary student behaviour. The Reverends James Beaven and William Hincks taught natural theology and natural history respectively at University College in the 1860s. Neither demanded more – nor less – than rote learning from his students, and each as a result was the butt of practical jokes.

Entering his classroom one day, Beaven – a firm believer in the pre-Darwinian fixity of species – found his lectern already occupied by the skeleton of an ape in academic dress. (He is said to have responded that at last his students had found an instructor suitable to the level of their abilities.) Hincks, whose brother, Francis, was premier of Canada West at the time of his appointment, was once forced to cancel a lecture after his students bored a hole through the classroom wall and filled the room with selenide of hydrogen.[30] Less amusing and of more serious import was the circulation to all first year students at Trinity of Provost Whitaker's lectures on the church catechism, which did not vary from year to year. Distributed by enterprising but anonymous senior undergraduates from notes taken by three of them, they consisted of a lengthy list of questions and answers that pupils were required to memorize.[31]

A serious affair that rocked Queen's in the 1860s probably occasioned a certain number of biting comments in student quarters. For several years in the late 1850s philosophy professor (and former Vice-Principal) James George and classics professor George Weir had feuded over a variety of institutional matters. In 1861 their private quarrels erupted into public scandal when Weir, publicly and in print, accused George of having seduced his (Weir's) sister and fathered her child. A lady's reputation was in ruins. As a result, students were encouraged by Weir and his wife to choose sides (it is not difficult to guess which one), but George (who later resigned to take a rural pastoral charge) was ultimately exonerated by college authorities. Weir was admonished for his willingness to let 'personal feeling ... prevail over concern for College discipline.'[32]

In spite of such signs of unrest within college walls, the fact is that such episodes, viewed in isolation, provide an incomplete view of college atmosphere in the quarter century after 1850. Some students did disrupt prayer meetings with flying marbles, but there were also students at prayer, and earnestly so. Student pranks and college scandals make for lively anecdote and interesting reading; moments of intense piety, of internal stress and turmoil, or of silent (and at times unsettling) discovery of new forms of truth, are more difficult to discover and to convey. Yet it is this inner life, in which reason and emotion met and mixed, that is at the heart of mid-Victorian undergraduate experience. The counterpoint to pranksterism at Victoria in the difficult year 1853–4, for example, was the beginnings of a religious revival that affected the college for literally the remainder of the century.[33]

As a result of a number of special evangelistic services held at the Christmas break by the Reverend G.R. Sanderson, remembered Nathanael Burwash, the tone of college life abruptly changed. 'Deep seriousness began to prevail and before long scores of students began to decide for a better life. The ordinary work of the students was almost completely suspended. Instead of the usual lectures, the professors were holding meetings for deeply distressed inquirers. At almost any hour of the day the voice of prayer might be heard from some student's room, where two or three earnest souls, often boys of fourteen, had met for prayer. At the end of six weeks not half a dozen students had resisted the influence of this great college revival.'[34]

The mid-Victorian undergraduate was pulled in conflicting directions. At home, in newspapers, even at college he was told that the century was one of material advance, of improving conditions, of a rising middle class with seemingly unlimited opportunity – and that he was an agent and heir of the age. To assume one's rightful place in such a society required persistence and diligence. Hard work would be met with success in life, and success, said the secular press, meant material reward. Students lived their lives, at one level, in this way. Yet these same earnest young Christians also knew that their religious faith did not equate spiritual with material success. The meek, not the powerful, were, after all, supposed to inherit the earth. What, they asked, was the basis of the civilization in which they lived? This was central to the Victorian conundrum, the attempt to strike a balance between material and moral progress. 'What Is Civilization?' was the title of a public lecture given by philosopher James George at Kingston's City Hall late in 1859. 'No mistake,' he said, 'can be greater than that wealth in its rude materiality, or in its more refined commercial forms, can of itself either produce or preserve civilization.' What *was* civilization, if not consisting in material development and acquisition? For George it was derived from 'the conscience and intellect of a people thoroughly cultivated, and the intellect in all cases acting under the direction of an enlightened conscience. This is the basis of all true civilization.'[35]

Evangelical Influences

The 'enlightened conscience' that undergirded civilized life, as James George defined it, required not knowledge but introspection. This appeal to conscience was a powerful impulse within Ontario college life in the nineteenth century, for it was a central element in a movement within European and North American Protestantism that had arisen almost a century earlier and that was by no means exhausted: the Evangelical Revival.[36] Evangelicalism transcended the concerns of systematic theology by appealing unabashedly to the emotions in the conduct of a reasonable life. This appeal to enthusiasm, said one nineteenth-century observer, was not 'merely an act or a performance; but ... a disposition, a habit, a temper: it is not a name but a nature: it is a turning of the whole mind to God.'[37] Its nature was caught perfectly by the English novelist George Eliot: 'Evangelicalism had brought into palpable existence and operation ... that idea of duty, that recognition of something to be lived for beyond the mere satisfaction of self, which is to the moral life what the addition of a great central ganglion is to animal life. No man can begin to mould himself on a faith or an idea without rising to a higher order of experience: a principle of subordination, of self-mastery has been introduced into his nature; he is no longer a mere bundle of impressions, desires, and impulses.'[38]

Without doubt, Victoria College was the Ontario institution of higher education most directly and forcibly affected by the religious revivals of the mid-Victorian years. One of its graduates and its future head, fearing a tendency to 'dissipation of mind,' asked his diary in 1861: 'The great questions with me are whence does it arise & is it sinful? It seems to me at least to arise from an overworked or overexcited mind & I think is nearly as much physical as mental. It certainly should be guarded against & never allowed to influence your acts, thoughts & feelings ... The best remedy for it seems to be not to struggle against it & work on ... but to give up work altogether & allow the mind a perfect rest. Spiritually in feeling I have made little progress today except that in studying the Word of God I found faith strengthened.'[39]

The mental anguish, the acceptance of (and battle against) sinfulness, the fear of failure, the resolute and earnest search for spiritual purity – each was characteristic of the evangelical temperament. But it was more, even, than that. It was in its broadest sense a 'call to seriousness' in all aspects of life, and as such it gave shape and direction to one of the most fundamental characteristics of the Victorian mind. Trinity may have escaped its de-emphasis of theological doctrine and Queen's may have succeeded in maintaining intellectualism in religious affairs because of the university's Calvinist legacy. But virtually no liberal arts college in the British-American transatlantic world during second half of the nineteenth century was unaffected by the evangelical appeal to high moral purpose.[40] Its aim, said one advocate, was 'to apply moral truths to practical purposes; to point out their bearings on modern opinions and modern manners; and to deduce from them rules of conduct by which the inhabitants of this country, each in his particular station, may be aided in acquiring the knowledge and encouraged in the performance of their several duties.'[41] In short, evangelicalism had the capacity to affect one's view of almost every aspect of life: character, conduct, vocation, the role of women, the place of the family, philanthropy, and mission work. It moulded the character of higher education.

Evangelicalism was not a program: it was a temper, a disposition. It was therefore capable of blending with other assumptions central to the mid-Victorian mind. Its appeal to the individual conscience broadened in the nineteenth century into a general moral seriousness that gave religious sanction to secular self-improvement.[42] Although based on an awareness of one's sinfulness it was nevertheless essentially a hopeful creed, and it helped reinforce the secular faith in material progress and economic initiative. Much of mid-Victorian entrepreneurialism gained its moral impetus because it was the cult of self-improvement operating in the marketplace. Sentiment, in addition to rationality, became a means of measuring individual worth and social conduct. Together, these seemingly disparate notions had substantially coalesced in the Anglo-American world of the mid-nineteenth century into 'the sensibility of aspiration.'[43]

In the second half of the nineteenth century the focus of evangelicalism began to shift from that of a specific religious disposition centred in the Christian revelation to a more general (and ultimately more secular) moralism concerned with ethical conduct, with 'culture.'[44] Gradually the evangelical need for personal conversion waned, but it left an important attitudinal residue: the 'high seriousness' embodied in the word 'earnestness,' itself a reflection of the larger phenomenon of an emergent middle class that was attempting to define its mission.[45] The broad system of values supported and bolstered by the evangelical temperament suited the needs of that class, for it preached the virtues of work, sobriety, thrift, duty, and the sanctity of family life and sought to adhere to them. These were the strands of mid-Victorian character formation, the major function of colleges of the day. Together, they helped formulate the social objectives that lay behind definitions and defenses of a liberal education, and they helped shape the dynamic structure, and ideological *raison d'être* of college curricula.[46]

Even at the turn of the twentieth century these larger objectives, stated in terms of educational priorities, remained substantially intact, although the evangelical imperative was increasingly expressed (as we will see) in new ways and in a more secular social milieu. The purpose of its educational program, declared Trinity College authorities in 1902, was to mould character and to furnish 'everything that is necessary to the liberal education of a gentleman.'[47] Similar statements abound for all Ontario colleges virtually from their founding. John McCaul's inaugural address at King's College in 1843 had taken the form of a fatherly lecture on the way a broad liberal education would lead to the formation of life-long good habits. Less important than the intellectual content of subjects to be studied was that the self-improvement they afforded would provide a sense of moral direction for life.[48] Almost a decade later, Provost Whitaker presided over the opening of Trinity College by beginning with the claim that 'a society has its youth, and the character then stamped upon it – the tone then given it – it will long retain. With us then, its first teachers and scholars, it rests to give to Trinity College its prescriptive character; to determine what shall be, in greater and smaller particulars, to recognize standards of morals and manners; to give a tone to the society which, if high, it may happily be difficult hereafter to lower, but which, if low, it must be doubly difficult to raise.'[49] Twenty-one years later the principal of Queen's University addressed the autumn convocation with the theme that a university education was valuable not only for what was taught and learned but also for the 'education' acquired by the experience of residential college life – 'those conditions, which are the best for yourselves, while they are necessary for the maintenance of discipline and order. I mean such conditions as these: diligent application to work, a scrupulous conformity to the laws and statutes defining your duties, a proper respect to the authorities, a frank, courteous and gentlemanly bearing towards one another ...'[50] At the convocation that marked the end of the same academic year, Principal Snodgrass returned to his theme and was even more specific. 'Let it be seen,' he said, 'that from your title to rank with men of liberal education you derive a motive power which is of a special utility, by the manner in which it constrains you to improve your life long condition of discipline and probation ... The full value of your progress in study depends largely on its relation of subservience to the practical purposes of life.' The 'full measure of an educated man,' he concluded, did not consist so much in acquired learning or intellectual discipline as 'in the formation of habits of intention, self-denial, and submission to rule.'[51]

Words such as 'discipline,' 'obedience,' and 'duty' have become shibboleths in the lexicon of twentieth century descriptions of the Victorian ethos. They were not words hollow of meaning then, but the moral benchmarks of a way of life. The kind of institutional control exacted in all colleges helped to maintain residential tranquility – and the nominal object of it – was to promote conditions conducive to moral and social discipline. In fact, however, this was ideologically only an intermediate objective. The ultimate result (however unconsciously derived) was the production and perpetuation of a society given economic direction by a middle class whose livelihood increasingly depended, directly or indirectly, on industry and commerce. We cannot understand the nature of the college curriculum as it developed, or even the full meaning of convocation rhetoric, unless we recognize and understand this implicit agenda, the tacit alliance between the rhetoric of moral worth and the dynamics of economic advance. As historian E.L. Burn said of the mid-Victorian generation: 'The age ... was devoted to the practice of "getting on"; it built that art into its system of thought and morality ...'[52]

The emotional resonances of social and moral control were in this way given tone and direction by conceptions that turned upon the relation of both university and individual to past and future. That this was so is reflected in the fact that one of the most common rhetorical preoccupations of mid-Victorian Ontario professors and students was the attempt, directly and by inference, to define the nature and meaning of civilization in a world of sometimes bewildering change. 'All things are now moving with new and amazing velocity,' proclaimed James George in a Queen's commencement address in 1853, 'while a feverish and most unhealthy state of the passions pervades every fibre of society.'[53] With life in general in such a state of flux it was all the more important not to lose one's sense of continuity with, and obligation to, the past. The leading idea of civilization, maintained one Queen's student, was that of progress – 'a progress which is continuous, and which the aim ever is the higher development of the human race, and the most extensive development of the moral and social element of society.'[54] This sense of social and moral continuity was essential to maintain, especially in an age when 'much of the spirit as well as the form of old social and civil institutions is either entirely gone or is rapidly disappearing from all civilized nations.' Antiquated forms should be allowed to die, but change for its own sake would merely destroy men's capacity to see that the '*willing obedience* which sprung from respect to authority was ... indeed that which for ages held society together.'[55] In this way, and with a certain degree of self-consciousness, professors actively promoted the subservience necessary for social stability during the flux of early industrial transformation.

The preservation and extension of civilization was impossible without the ability to discern what was worthy of keeping or discarding. Custom and the moral sentiments, like culture and self-culture, were seen as inseparable, because civilization required 'both external and internal improvement.'[56] Accordingly, one should choose a college primarily on the basis of the 'moral influence' it provided.[57] A student's duty was to grasp the opportunity of studying at the feet of professors with 'scholarly attainments, broad culture and strong personality.' For 'to come daily within the radius of their influence is the privilege of the few ... the opportunity of a lifetime,' a chance to have 'plastic minds' shaped and moulded.[58] In this way, by imitation of men of knowledge and rectitude, the objectives of the college curriculum would be met. Knowledge gained by such moral nurture would enlarge a student's views, encourage him to think for himself, 'cultivate his taste, and confirm his moral principles,' thereby making him suited to any profession he should later choose.[59]

Such virtues implied vices, and none was seen to be more threatening to the progress of civilization than a lack of earnestness or a failure to work hard. The value of earnestness was that it deflected the student's attention from 'trivial speculation' and required him, instead, to accept active faith as a form of true knowledge. 'It is the believing man,' James George said, 'who can be truly the earnest man ... Faith makes all the difference. For the soul that hath embraced the truths which this question involved, cannot but be awakened to deep earnestness.'[60] Work was seen as the vehicle of useful improvement; idleness was a form of vice. 'Seats of learning have never been more thoroughly perverted than when made the haunts of idleness. The minds of young men, dissipated by this, are thoroughly prepared for almost every other form of dissipation. The idle student is a pest in his class, a sore affliction ... and is almost certain to become a burden and a blot on society.'[61] Little wonder that students who viewed their professors as moral exemplars wrote poems called 'Nothing to Do,' with stanzas that went: 'Nothing to do – the sluggard's lament; / Are you a man and yet cannot find / Some work for you by duty sent – / Something to strive for with heart and mind?' The same 1874 issue of the student newspaper at Queen's contained a front-page article by G.H. Lewes called 'All Men of Great Genius are Hard Workers.' And in case the point had not yet been made, two pages later appeared another piece, by a student, called 'Leisure Hours.' These, it was warned, should be occupied only 'in the most profitable manner' by means of systematic study.[62]

Sixteen years later the *Queen's Journal* was no less dedicated to the value of earnest hard work. The editor exhorted fellow-students to 'grasp this opportunity while you may, and if repentance can be spoken of in a narrower sense than that in which it is implied, we would say repent; empty your mind of all carelessness and indifference, shake off indolence and neglect, so that the word may not be in vain, for the influence upon you will be in exact proportion to your capacity for receiving.'[63]

The values of evangelicalism were internalized in such ways, but students learned much more than the values of earnestness and hard work. The code of conduct provided to them by their church and university leaders was an important element in the development of the frame of mind of an emergent middle-class, and the emphasis placed on the complementarity of evangelical and middle-class values served implicitly to discount those of other groups. In their own way, the ideologists of the evangelical revival articulated their theory of social change by linking it to imperatives of moral improvement. In doing so, they sought to provide their own group with broad avenues of political, economic, and moral endeavour. Such was the college ideal in Ontario, concerned with character and conduct as much as with academic advancement, throughout the nineteenth century and beyond. But what did professors intend students to learn in their studies?

5

Mid-Victorian Arts and Sciences

One of the central functions of the nineteenth-century Ontario college, it is clear, was to help establish and preserve a dutiful, morally sound social order. The values and discipline instilled in students by means of fatherly professorial speeches, sermons in chapel, and minute regulation of everyday undergraduate life served that end well. In this insistence on the value of work-discipline the college authorities differed little from evangelical Georgian and Victorian factory owners.[1] Yet their manifest purpose was not simply to preserve order, nor to create the degree of literacy necessary to fulfil the utilitarian requisites of an enlightened electorate, but to introduce students to the 'higher' forms of learning. The reason for the existence of colleges and universities was to provide a given generation access to the inherited wisdom of the ages and to the major branches of knowledge.

What went on when the Victorian student of an Ontario college left his dormitory room or boarding house and entered the lecture hall? What did he learn, and why? Were there varieties of knowledge and belief that remained forbidden, as in Eden? If there were, why? No mere recitation of subjects taught or books read by the nineteenth-century professor and student provides adequate answers to such questions, for in order to understand what scholars chose to study we must first determine just what the mid-Victorian educator considered the process and mechanics of thinking to entail.

In his desire to inculcate the correct social and intellectual attitudes, the mid-nineteenth-century college professor placed great stress on the necessity of developing the affective – the emotional – sensibility of the student. In this way the evangelical temperament was nurtured even as knowledge was obtained. As will be seen, this was perfectly consistent with the theological and philosophical orthodoxies that prevailed before the 1860s. The purpose of thought was to acquire 'certain knowledge,' for what was its purpose if a sense of certainty did not result? Given the denominational *raison d'être* of most Ontario colleges, such knowledge was thought to come from God. Truth, in short, was seen not to be ascertainable by cognition alone. Reason was not to be divorced from sentiment, for the latter helped cultivate the pious disposition that was to give direction to rationality. Besides, a purely rationalistic form of thinking was seen to lead to criticism. The purpose of acquiring new knowledge was instead rooted in forms of appreciation. For example, when Egerton Ryerson spoke of the reasons why students should study the English language and literature he concluded that doing so would 'inspire them with veneration and attachment for Institutions and Laws which have protected and fostered, if not given birth, to Philosophers and Historians, Orators and Poets, who will hereafter be ... appreciated and honoured – and I hope imitated and emulated ...'[2]

In spite of important differences in denominational affiliation, Ryerson and others of his generation set forward quite similar views of the objectives of higher education because they shared a common understanding of the relationship between secular knowledge and religious piety.[3] Moreover, they insisted that the acquisition of the former should not be divorced from the emotional imperatives of the latter. It is important, therefore, to be wary of using such phrases as the 'intellectual life' of the student, as if merely by doing so we will have determined the locus of his mental world. In the nineteenth century the purpose of higher education was not primarily to hone the intellect, for in the educational context Christian piety channelled purely intellectual life into certain acceptable directions and prevented it from exploring others. But it was given its initial impulse by the continuing power of the Christian revelation upon the conscience and the imagination. At mid-century in the denominational colleges, academicians continued to see the ultimate function of human reason as to seek to know the mind and will of God – reason as *Logos*. Furthermore, they continued to do so in full awareness that as fallen creatures they could expect only fleeting glimpses of His truth. In short, their piety was a mental and emotional disposition that was vital to the process of thought. It was 'a portal,' in historian Perry Miller's words, 'through which ran the highway of intellectual development.'[4]

It has never been easy to reconcile the need for an understanding of reality by the acquisition of knowledge with the imperatives of Christian belief. The Ontario college student in the mid-Victorian period did not have an easy emotional or intellectual life, largely for this reason. No student who went to an Ontario college from the 1840s through the 1870s would have been exempt from some degree of academic contemplation – perhaps forced on him by his professors – of the role of reason. He would have been told in class that he must of course think and act rationally. Yet he was also reminded on many occasions that reason driven by purely 'intellectual' motives could be dangerous. In an 1855 address on 'the relation between piety and intellectual labor,' Professor James George of Queen's University stressed this point. 'For, assuredly,' he maintained, 'he who sees all things in God, or in the light that comes from Him, sees clearly the truth in things generally as well as the necessary relations among moral truths. This is, indeed, the highest form that reasoning can take, as it cannot fail under such light to arrive at certainty.'[5] This idea, that intellectual truth could be established only by determining the 'necessary relations' between Christian 'moral truths,' was characteristic of the thought of the Ontario professoriate in the mid-Victorian era.[6] The arts and science subjects taught in Ontario's colleges and universities in the middle decades of the nineteenth century were based on such presumptions, but they came into being just as the Darwinian revolution was about to take place. By the 1870s and 1880s the grounds of such belief had begun to shift.

Cultural Memory and the Liberal Arts

The undergraduate curriculum in existence in Canada West in 1859 had not fundamentally changed since university courses were first offered in the 1840s. In spite of differences of emphasis because of denominational affiliation and ecclesiastical tradition – and they were not unimportant – programs of study nevertheless bore a general similarity of structure and intention. As a result, there existed in the two decades before 1860 within each institution a liberal arts curriculum that admitted no optional subjects. All university leaders sought to create a 'balanced' curriculum based on the classical model, and they aimed to provide their students with the indelible mark of culture.[7]

When Victoria College opened its doors at Cobourg in 1841, students at the collegiate level were greeted with an arts and science program divided into five sections: 1) the ancient sciences (or classics); 2) mathematics and physical sciences; 3) moral science (or philosophy); 4) rhetoric and belles lettres; 5) theology. That structure remained intact in 1861, for Ryerson and his colleagues held firm to the view that the aim of a liberal education was not to train scholarly specialists in any one branch of learning but 'to achieve a BALANCE of character as a result of educating all the mental faculties.'[8] The program at Queen's in 1860 differed little from Victoria's. First-year students took courses in Latin and Greek, mathematics, and natural history. A similar sequence followed in second year, but with the addition of natural philosophy (or physics, as it would soon be called). Third year saw the introduction of yet another course: philosophy, consisting of rhetoric, logic, metaphysics, and moral science.[9] When Strachan's King's College had opened in 1843, its curriculum was solidly classical in nature due in part to the influence of the Reverend John McCaul, whose graduation from Trinity College Dublin (Oxford's Irish outpost) had ensured that its program would be as traditional as that of Oxford itself. The general emphasis on a broad introduction to the various branches of knowledge was testimony to the acceptance by Canadian educators of the British notion that the essence of a liberal education lay in the formation of character, the education of 'the whole man.'[10]

There can be little doubt that the culture of education in nineteenth-century Ontario was also influenced significantly by the general ethos of the Scottish intellectual and moral diaspora, for Scottish thought in the eighteenth century had produced an 'Enlightenment' as important in its philosophical understanding of humankind and society as its better known French equivalent. 'In almost every sphere of intellectual life – from literature to geology, mathematics to medicine, philosophy to economics – Scottish thinkers gained the respect of learned men everywhere.'[11] By the beginning of the Victorian era, for example, assumptions drawn from the dominant psychological theories of Scottish philosophers were gradually added to the traditional educational notion of cultivating the sensibility for moral or religious ends: the aim of giving 'discipline' to different 'faculties' of the mind. Each academic 'discipline' was valued because it was seen to stimulate a particular 'faculty,' such as those responsible for reason, the imagination, or morality.[12]

In Canada this reliance on mental faculties was pronounced because of the strong influence of Scotland on higher education in the English-speaking provinces. Educators there did not reject the English ideal of a liberal education, one that was meant to produce 'gentlemen'; on the contrary, they gave it epistemological validity by placing emphasis on the Scottish 'common sense' philosophical tradition whose foremost Scottish exponents were Thomas Reid and Dugald Stewart. Their faculty psychology asserted that moral truths could be intuited by people simply by appealing to 'common sense,' the data of their own consciousness. Most professors of philosophy in the United States and in English Canada prior to the 1870s taught their own variations of Reid or Stewart, to which they often added a good measure of the English Archdeacon William Paley's natural theology.[13] Just as the former subject taught that 'the grand object of education' was to develop and 'perfect, as far as possible,' the 'physical, mental, and moral faculties' because they represented 'the richest display of wisdom and goodness' made available by God,[14] so the latter demonstrated that proof of His existence could be found throughout the world of nature in the various examples of providential design in the fossil record.

Both Scottish common sense and Paleyite natural theology acted effectively as methodological conduits through which Christian piety could flow. What better way of cultivating the whole man than by enriching all the faculties? How better to maintain a reverential attitude in that increasingly dangerous terrain, the natural sciences, than by insisting that the very object of scientific inquiry was to affirm one's devotion to a Christian God? As Egerton Ryerson noted: 'The God of grace is also the God of nature; how delightful to trace his footsteps in the works and laws of the material universe, as well as in the pages of Revelation!'[15]

Notions that a specific region of the brain might be responsible for moral action or that nature herself might provide evidence of God's existence were intellectually exciting to contemplate, for they took the search for moral patterns in the direction of human physiology and the natural order. Yet the general importance of Scottish common sense and Paleyite natural theology was that they encouraged and gave academic credence to intellectual silence in the form of a devotional frame of mind. The student was expected to approach his subjects with a willingness to accept, a desire to appreciate; a wish to assimilate knowledge, not to reshape or redirect it. A glance at how specific subjects such as the classics, rhetoric and belles lettres, and history were viewed shows the devotional mind at work in and out of the classroom. It also reveals that within the curricula of the pre-Darwinian Ontario colleges lay important differences whose importance should not be underestimated.

It is easy to ascertain what classical texts of Greek and Roman writers the Victorian student was expected to read: the ancient names and titles leap from the otherwise arid pages of university calendars like so many fossil forms in a museum catalogue. The matriculation examination of students seeking admission to King's College in 1847 reflected the influence of classics-oriented Oxford. King's required students to have read parts or all of Homer's *Iliad*, Xenophon's *Anabasis*, Lucian's *Vita*, *Charon*, and *Timon*, Virgil's *Aeneid*, Ovid's *Fasti*, and more than this if they wished to compete for scholarships. In short, as Daniel Wilson proudly claimed some thirteen years later, they would 'have gone in fact through nearly all the chief classics of ancient times.'[16] The 1848 senior Latin class at Queen's was tested in Horace, Cicero, and Juvenal, and the Greek class in Euripedes, Sophocles, and Xenophon. Daily exercises there, by no means exceptional requirements, consisted of 'translating English into Latin and Greek,' varied occasionally 'by putting Latin into Greek and Greek into Latin.' 'It was not "morceaux choisis,"' concluded historian Hilda Neatby regarding nineteenth-century Queen's, 'but large blocks of these formidable authors that the young men read.'[17] Preliminary examinations at Victoria in the 1860s included 'the *Commentaries of Gaius*, Books I–IV, and Book IV of the *Annals of Tacitus*, with Aristotle's *Politics* I and II, together with Plato's *Republic* I and II as an option.'[18]

But what broad purpose did such study serve in an age proud of material progress and studiously practical in so many other ways? Teenage boys clearly learned to be dextrous in two ancient languages. But was that all they learned?

In the first decades of higher education in Canada West, the eighteenth-century centrality of the classics to the idea of a 'liberal education' held firm. Basically a literary education during the Georgian epoch, study of the classics naturally involved training in languages; but this was in order to gain command over a range of learning that included 'poetry, drama, biography, history, political theory, geography, ethnography, philosophy, logic, ethics, rhetoric, [and] architecture,' as well as much of the science of the day.[19] To have studied the ancients was scarcely considered at the time a restrictive enterprise, for to do so was to put oneself in touch with an inherited body of assumptions, knowledge, and values. Learning the classics made possible an empathetic entry into the great minds of the past. At the fringes of the British Empire, as elsewhere, it was in a manner to recreate and to perpetuate the seminal ideas and assumptions of Western civilization as it was then understood, and to try, in an increasingly fragmented age, 'to keep alive the notion of a community of values from which educational ideals would organically derive ...'[20] It provided a frontier society with an instant cultural and intellectual inheritance.

This stance remained a fundamental justification of the classics in Anglo-Canadian discussions of the purposes of a liberal education. But by the mid-nineteenth century, more utilitarian motives and arguments were coming to be added to it. The eighteenth-century ideal of the disinterested gentleman-scholar, broadened by acquaintance with antiquity, was not quite adequate in the years after the London Great Exhibition of 1851 and its practical wonders. To the argument that classics represented values central to a 'civilized' existence was increasingly added the more straightforward one that such study also provided a desired form of mental training.[21] Such training, argued one writer in the *Quebec Mercury*, would produce in Canada 'that healthy robustness of mind, that equally diffused intellectual vigour' characteristic of the English and Scottish frames of mind.[22] Yet there were important differences of assumption and emphasis between the English and Scottish approaches to the classical curriculum, derived from the question of whether, as in England, the university should cultivate an elite or, as in Scotland, seek to educate the general population. Such fundamental differences of ideological assumption were directly reflected in the course of studies that lay at the heart of a liberal education of whatever mould: the matter of training in languages and letters. Rhetoric and belles lettres was central to the nineteenth-century curriculum. When Egerton Ryerson established the Victoria curriculum he took responsibility for the teaching of rhetoric upon himself, as, later, did S.S. Nelles. Ryerson's inaugural speech at Victoria College had stressed the practical necessity of effective communication – in the English language.

Here was a significant point of departure between Ryerson's Victoria and approaches to language instruction elsewhere in the province, at least in the early years: Ryerson's institution was to be committed to instruction in the vernacular. Within the traditional curriculum, the role of the rhetorician was to ensure the transmission of classical learning and formal logic.[23] Ryerson's insistence on the use of the vernacular – plain English not ancient languages – was rooted in his desire to ensure the transmission of traditional knowledge and values in a common sense way. His means were modern for his day, yet his motivation was traditional. Knowledge, in his view, remained linked to revelation, shaped by the accomplishments of classical antiquity and transmitted by the rhetorician's skill in the art of persuasion. In this new commitment to the vernacular, however, lay a certain danger; for with it came a shift of assumption that effectively began to link language and learning to the present rather than to the past.

The acrimonious dispute between Ryerson and Daniel Wilson at the legislative hearings of 1860 in which Wilson introduced the system of limited student options in the senior years (for example, an undergraduate who intended to become a doctor would be allowed in his senior year to drop Latin and Greek in order to concentrate on the natural sciences) betrayed Ryerson's fear that the capacity of the curriculum to transmit traditional knowledge and Christian values would be undercut by the caprice and whim of students and the willingness of the Toronto professoriate to let them do so.[24] Ryerson had been an innovator in the higher education of British North America, but the form his innovation took lay in his commitment to use English as the primary language of instruction. Moreover, his approach to language and literature was that the study of literature provided models for good writing.

Philosophically, Wilson, not Ryerson, was the innovator when it came to changing the nature and purpose of English. He was, after all, the first professor in British North America specifically appointed to teach English language, literature, and history. His innovations of 1860, marking the beginnings of the honours program at the University of Toronto, also marked a shift away from the role of rhetoric as the art of persuasion within classics towards a new function within the study of English. Primarily an historian, Wilson stressed the history of England as a form of English literary expression; the study of the English language in Wilson's hands largely became the demonstration of the importance of its literature in the history of culture rather than as a model for good writing. In this way, the orientation of the University of Toronto's liberal arts curriculum gradually began to gravitate away from classics towards literature and history, from the languages of classical antiquity to the vernacular. In 1877 Wilson presided over a major change in the honour streams that reflected his priorities. In addition to honour classics, there would henceforth also exist mathematics, natural science, philosophy, and modern languages and history. The last area of concentration is important, for rhetoric was now associated less with classics than with history. A deep relationship between British literature and British history was beginning to emerge. It was not to be consolidated until century's end, particularly under the inspiration of W.J. Alexander in English and George Wrong in history; but when it was, it would dominate the University of Toronto arts curriculum for more than half a century. A similar shift in orientation took place at Victoria, Queen's, Trinity, and at most other colleges and universities in English-speaking Canada.[25]

Beginning in the late 1860s and continuing throughout the 1870s, exponents of the classical curriculum came to be decidedly on the defensive. Confronted with students and graduates who criticized the 'undue proportions' of such study in an expanding curriculum and a scientific age, who desired to have the power of individual choice in their studies, and who often welcomed the fact that '"practical studies" [were] so much more in demand,'[26] classics professors gradually placed greater stress on the virtues of being 'trained' in their 'discipline.' When the Reverend Professor John Mackerras was installed at Queen's University in 1867 as professor of classical literature he noted on the one hand that study of the classics was a 'redemptive process' because, by studying pagan texts, one could discern how ideas and influences 'corrupt and debase the human mind as it wanders farther and farther from the light of the knowledge of the true God.' On the other hand, he also claimed that this insight was made possible only by the 'mental training' afforded by the study of comparative philology. Linguistic training, for Mackerras, was a pathway to enriched mental culture and spiritual life.[27]

Men such as Mackerras were greatly aided by the academic respectability given to these justifications by the faculty psychology of the day, with its emphasis on the existence of separate mental 'faculties' that were presumed to be the seats of such attributes as 'reason' or 'will.' Wedded to educational concerns, faculty psychology in the nineteenth century became a theoretical basis for the Victorian preoccupation with practical self-improvement. The great 'utility' of the classics, if it required such a function at all, lay in the fact that it cultivated the various mental faculties. The first of these, said a professor of classics at Queen's, was that of language, for 'whatever awakens and develops the faculty of language, awakens and develops the faculty of thought.' But this was merely the beginning, it was said, for in a way that no other branch of university education could do the classics also cultivated other faculties, such as the memory, the reason, the taste, and the imagination. This more general nurture of the broad range of intelligence and sensibility would therefore allow 'the faithful student – I mean the student who works from a love of his subject and of the culture it imparts' – to unite his mind with those of the past. 'He lives with the great masters of learning, and makes their thoughts his own.'[28]

Languages and history were approached in much the same manner. By the early 1860s courses in modern languages were becoming accepted elements of the curriculum. At the University of Toronto, for example, James Forneri lectured on the languages of France, Germany, Italy, and Spain, and he also dwelt significantly on the literature of those countries. The study of such languages met the test of practicality, for they could actively be used; and the study of their literatures served, like those of the ancients, to help forge a community of values and a mental training. History, regarded at the time as a form of literature, served a similar purpose.

Here – in the early study of literature and history – we can see firm points of contact between academic discourse and the general sensibility of those members of the middle-class Ontario public who spoke out on literary matters. This more secular direction being taken by what was originally a Christian piety dominated the literary consciousness of mid-Victorian Ontario. When the Methodist cleric and journalist Edward Hartley Dewart published his path-breaking anthology *Selections from Canadian Poets* in 1864 he hoped that the collection would contribute to 'the formation of national character.' But his understanding of the nature of this social form of character was based on the commonly understood and assimilated constructs of faculty psychology. Those who derided literature, he said, dismissing it as 'a tissue of misleading fancies, appealing chiefly to superstitious credulity, a silly and trifling thing, the product of the imagination when loosed from the direction and control of reason,' failed to understand how the mind works. Mind, Dewart insisted, was a harmonious unity of many mental processes. Reason was not its be-all and end-all. 'Poetry is not the product of any one faculty of the mind: it is the offspring of the whole mind, in the full exercise of all its faculties, and in its highest moods of sympathy, with the truths of the worlds of mind and matter ... It ministers to a want of our intellectual nature.' Poetry, in other words, was the fullest expression of this harmonious balance of well-nurtured faculties, and it served essentially devotional ends in both the sacred and secular worlds: 'Poetry is the medium by which the emotions of beauty, joy, admiration, reverence, harmony, or tenderness kindled in the poet-soul, in communion with Nature and God, is [sic] conveyed to the souls of others.'[29]

In 1889, when W.J. Alexander delivered his inaugural lecture as professor of English in University College on 'The Study of Literature,' he insisted that English provided 'abundant scope for the highest exercise of our faculties, and leads to the profoundest investigation of human nature.' It was 'an instrument of culture, and culture comes not from the results of investigation, but from the process.' The student of literature had his mind trained to be open and flexible by maintaining an 'intellectual sympathy' with those he studied. In this way, he came into contact with an author's style and, through style, his character. Boundaries of time and space were thereby transcended. 'Fortunate it is,' Alexander proclaimed, 'that through literature we are able to feel the kindling spiritual presence of the mighty dead. It is true that but few can thus transmit themselves through the ages; but these few are among the greatest spirits of our race.'[30]

For Alexander, history performed a kindred function, although he regarded it as 'a more or less imperfect medium' compared with literature. Teachers of history, however, including those university graduates working in the province's public schools, believed that their students could benefit in similar ways. 'The great end and aim of all education is not so much *what is studied* but *how it is studied*,' said one such teacher; hence 'the formation of correct habits of thought is infinitely more valuable to the pupil than the mere knowledge imparted.' The study of history should not, therefore, be based on memorization (as it often seemed to be in the schools), but to be seen instead as 'a means of mental training and discipline' that would shed light on the great problems of the day.[31] Another teacher elaborated on these themes, noting that as well as illustrating 'great truths – moral truths of fundamental importance, upon which all creeds can unite,' history also developed the faculties of reason, morality, and memory, teaching the student 'to direct his tastes ...'[32]

In the classrooms of Victorian Ontario, whether those of the public schools or of the universities, students were of course encouraged to develop their talents. But until the latter years of the nineteenth century, the notion of 'talent' was meant to encompass the full mental spectrum – to include emotional 'feelings' and aesthetic sensibilities as well as skills derived from cognition and rational 'thought.' The academic subjects of the liberals arts curriculum, learned in the atmosphere of earnest evangelical Christianity, were approached in ways that attempted to prevent the dominance of intellect in educational life. The sciences were among those liberal arts. A major shift in the academic approach to the sciences began to take place, however, in the years between 1850 and 1880. The result was that reverential science faced evolutionary theories and intellect and emotion stood in uneasy equipoise.

Science and Emotion

Study of the sciences was an important part of the traditional curriculum of a liberal education. Of the seven professors John Strachan had hoped to appoint as the faculty of King's College, three were to have taught scientific subjects: mathematics (both practical and theoretical); natural history (including botany); and natural philosophy (including chemistry).[33] Of these subjects, the most comprehensive at the time was natural philosophy. It was what its title implied: an attempt to understand the unifying principles and laws that governed the natural world. The core of natural philosophy would later become known as physics, but for the first generation of scientific teachers in Canada West no such disciplinary specialization existed. For example, Henry Holmes Croft, who taught chemistry as a 'natural philosopher' in Toronto from the days of King's College until his retirement from University College in 1879, had studied chemistry, mineralogy, geology, botany, zoology, physics, physiology, entomology, and metaphysics as a graduate student in Berlin. During the course of his lengthy career he lectured on most of these subjects at one time or another. 'I can remember,' S.S. Nelles of Victoria College reminisced of the 1850s and 1860s, 'when a Canadian University could venture to issue its calendar with an announcement of a single professor for all the natural sciences, and with a laboratory something similar to an ordinary blacksmith's shop, where the professor was his own assistant and compelled to blow not only his own bellows, but his own trumpet as well.'[34]

When the undergraduate in the mid-Victorian years walked from his class in Latin, Greek, or literature to the science laboratory, he encountered a range of procedures and assumptions scarcely, if at all, at odds with those of his arts subjects. The room he entered may have been called a laboratory, but little experimentation would have been done in it. He was lectured to. One observer recalled that when William Mulock attended the University of Toronto in 1860

the subjects of Natural History and Zoology were taught in the lecture room upon a blackboard. Students knew nothing about the structure of living things except through occasional glances at dead specimens ... Names of animals, living, dead, and pre-historic, great or small, and infinitesmal, were memorized ... In the subject of Natural Philosophy, the modern Physics, a few pieces of ancient mechanical apparatus did for a laboratory. The theory of light and all its fundamental principles were daily taught by old professors who had never seen a lens ... Astronomy was propounded with the aid of drawing on a blackened globe, some spheres of brass that represented the sun and moon and stars, and endless formulas that filled the board ... Botany and Zoology were studied with the aid of books, filled with long and tedious lists. One large binocular microscope ... was the only sign of modern progress.[35]

This reminiscence is not an inaccurate description of the state of scientific pedagogy during the first generation of the Ontario professoriate.[36] But it is highly anachronistic. The passage presumes the existence of a research function within the university that existed at few institutions in Europe and America at the time and suggests scholarly sloth and intellectual dishonesty in its dismissive allusion to doddery old teachers of optics who 'had never seen a lens.' In its high-handed and smug dismissal of a science that placed little emphasis on theoretical or practical 'research,' the account conveys nothing of the reasons why science was taught in such a manner. Like the liberal arts, mid-Victorian science – both academic and popular – also served the purpose of God and saw truth rooted, as a result, essentially in the past. Its general aim was to verify an old truth – that of the Christian revelation – not to discover new ones.[37] In this respect, undergraduate courses in the sciences were at times as devotional as those in the humanistic disciplines. This can be glimpsed by looking a little more closely at the professors of science to whom William Mulock had been subjected.

When Mulock was an undergraduate at the University of Toronto, his professor of natural history, teaching botany and zoology, was William Hincks; his professor of natural philosophy was John Bradford Cherriman; his chemistry professor was Henry Holmes Croft. None was much concerned with experimental research, but neither were they intellectual lightweights. Before his appointment to Toronto, Hincks had held similar posts at Manchester College (York) and at Queen's College (Cork). Cherriman had placed sixth in the mathematics examinations in which the future Lord Kelvin came first. Croft had studied at the University of Berlin and had arrived at Toronto in 1853 with a strong recommendation from no less a scientist than Michael Faraday.

Did these minds calcify by simple exposure to a colonial environment? Scarcely. Cherriman, whose main love was mathematics, published in the subject, significantly helped to raise standards in the classroom, and applied his talents to the nascent science of meteorology.[38] He continued to do so in a different way when he left the university to become Superintendent of Insurance in Ottawa in 1875. Croft, like Cherriman, gave his academic skills a practical bent by serving as the chief toxological expert for Ontario criminal cases involving poisonings, wrote a textbook on analytical chemistry, and contributed frequently to the main Ontario scientific journal of the day, the *Canadian Journal*.[39] William Hincks also wrote frequently for it; in fact, he outpublished both Cherriman and Croft.[40]

Yet it was above all Hincks who was the object of scorn for teaching from a blackboard and for making his students memorize 'long and tedious lists.' In the figure of William Hincks we observe a seeming contradiction. In the classroom he offered his students, by all accounts, virtually no intellectual challenge. Yet this was the same man who, in the quiet of his study, wrote thoughtful and lengthy articles on such diverse subjects as 'Questions in Relation to the Theory of the Structure in Plants,' 'On the True ... Claims to Attention of the Science of Political Economy,' 'Thoughts on Belief and Evidence,' and 'An Inquiry into the Natural Laws which Regulate the Interchange of Commodities.'[41] What accounts for this apparent gap between the eclectic, inquiring scholar and the boring professor?[42]

In his lecture on 'Belief and Evidence' presented to the Canadian Institute, Hincks himself provided a clue. His subject was the crucial one of the relationship between cause and effect – what at the time was called the notion of 'power.' 'If there are uniform laws of Nature,' he began, 'that is, if the Author of nature governs the universe according to a plan founded on Wisdom and Benevolence, not leaving the course of events to accident or increasing change, then this existence of Law implies and renders necessary that antecedents really the same should have the same consequents. The ultimate cause is supreme and infinitely powerful intelligence, acting on a perfect plan with a view to a result.'[43] Hincks's entire range of concerns was rooted in his desire to determine the ways in which the laws of nature operated, whether in the animal and plant kingdoms or in the social and economic relationships of humans.

'Economic science,' he insisted in another essay, 'is common to mankind in all circumstances, and gives us rules of general application ... the more we study it the more thoroughly we believe that, as producers and exchangers of produce, there is only one plan which suits us all ...'[44] A Presbyterian minister who was also a convinced empiricist and advocate of the principles of associationist psychology, Hincks insisted that this 'plan' could only be discerned by collecting 'all the facts bearing on every doubtful question,' then comparing and 'harmonizing' them.[45] Since all truth was of a whole, Hincks drew similar conclusions when he taught natural history.

The pedagogical implication of such views determined the actions of Hincks and others in the classroom. Zoology and botany were not, in his view, speculative sciences. Truth was determined by observation, not experiment, and it ultimately came from God. Common sense suggested that it was best understood 'by those who know, and as being established to the satisfaction of competent judges ...'[46] But in practice this meant that in the classroom Hincks lectured, students listened, and long taxonomic lists of flora and fauna were memorized. Hincks was not alone in this decidedly authoritarian approach to undergraduate instruction. When E.J. Chapman lectured in Toronto on mineralogy and geology between 1853 and 1895 he reminded students that he was in the laboratory to give them 'an opportunity of seeing an expert at work, not to teach them to become experts.'[47]

Otherwise comfortable academic careers are occasionally disturbed by the appearance of a work in one's field that shakes its foundations. In the middle of William Hincks's tenure as professor of natural history at the University of Toronto such a book was published: Charles Darwin's *On The Origin of Species*. Appearing late in 1859, Darwin's treatise ushered in a revolution in scientific understanding. Providing abundant evidence drawn from many years of observation and research on plant and animal life, the English naturalist posited the existence of a law of 'natural selection' that, he claimed, must determine the characteristics of all species and make possible new ones. In every generation, went the theory, a degree of random variation of physical characteristics would occur. Within a species, those whose characteristics – for example, colour, size, or change of skeletal structure – were most conducive to the existing environment would be most likely to survive. Life, said Darwin in the subtitle of his magnum opus, was a matter of 'survival of the fittest' in the battle of an increasing population for a limited food supply. The social consequences of Darwinism would be much discussed in the 1870s and 1880s. What most concerned many scientists at first, however, were the implications of his views for traditional Biblical cosmogony.

Darwin's theory of the origin of species made scientific sense at the time only if the span of natural history was extended by millions of years beyond that posited by orthodox Christian observers. James Ussher, the seventeenth century archbishop of Armagh, for example, had created a chronology of world history that located the act of creation in 4004 BC. From the 1830s, after the publication and widespread influence of Charles Lyell's *Principles of Geology*, such a notion came to be challenged in a major way. Lyell had set forth the reasons for a vast extension of geological time, but it was Darwin, heavily influenced by Lyell, who put the case in terms that seemed directly to challenge the story of creation told in *Genesis*. Whereas Christian orthodoxy held that all species were forever fixed at the moment of God's creation of them (it was allowed, however, that God would at times allow them to disappear), Darwin's theory asserted that species were not fixed but in fact were capable of significant degrees of variation. The origin of new species was, he argued, rooted in the natural rather than in the divine order.

This direct challenge to the authority of Biblical revelation was also in direct opposition to the science taught in Ontario universities, as elsewhere, at the time. Just as philosophy was taught in a way that allowed a direct appeal to the Christian conscience, so science was wedded to a form of theology derived from eighteenth century clerics such as William Paley. Called 'natural theology' and given classic English expression in Paley's 1802 treatise called *Natural Theology; Or, Evidences of the Existence and Attributes of the Deity Collected from the Appearances of Nature*, this union of natural history and Christian theology set forward the argument that God must exist because everywhere in nature the evidence of design could be seen. Nature showed many signs of contrived order, both in structure and function. These contrivances must have been designed, and design required a designer. Why not call this designer God?

When Ontario students entered their science classrooms prior to the 1870s they would have heard nothing to contradict the Paleyite argument that science and religion were perfectly complementary. Two of the standard textbooks used by students of science and philosophy throughout the nineteenth century in English Canada were Joseph Butler's rebuttal of English deism, *The Analogy of Religion, Natural and Revealed, to the Constitution and Course of Nature* (1736) and William Paley's *Natural Theology* (1802). Butler provided the mode of argumentation in the form of analogical reasoning; Paley provided the evidence for design drawn from nature.

Further evidence of the importance assigned to natural theology in the Victorian period is provided by the first college textbook written by a professor in English Canada, *Elements of Natural Theology*. Published in 1850, its author was the Reverend James Beaven, who from the early 1840s to the 1870s taught an admixture of Scottish common sense and natural theology, first at King's College and later at University College in Toronto. For Beaven, natural theology served as the 'eye of faith.' In 1860 the second textbook by a member of the Toronto academic community appeared, *Outlines of Natural Theology, for the Use of the Canadian Student*. Its author was Dr James Bovell, lecturer in pathology and physiology in the Trinity University medical faculty. More than any other cluster of ideas, the assumptions and vocabulary of natural theology provided a means by which the pious disposition could find a place and a voice in the pre-Darwinian university 'laboratory.'[48]

The post hoc account of the 'backward' scientific pedagogy in Toronto in the 1860s, noted earlier, is laden with unintentional irony. The 'one large binocular microscope,' which was seen as 'the only sign of modern progress,' was thought to be brought to Canada by James Bovell, who first introduced microscopy to Canadian students. Yet while a dedicated naturalist, Bovell was also perhaps the most deeply devout member of the Toronto professoriate of his day. His *Outlines* was a sustained attempt to buttress pre-Darwinian theology, yet he managed to inspire the career of the greatest scientific mind Canada produced in the nineteenth century: Sir William Osler. It was Bovell who introduced the young Osler, then a student at Trinity College, to the world within the microscope, thereby helping in a major way to commit Osler's life to science. Such was the degree of Bovell's influence that often, to Osler's 'last days ... in moments of absentmindedness or when trying a pen, it was the name of James Bovell that came first to paper, not his own.'[49]

Bovell's mind was characteristic of those informed by a mid-Victorian liberal education, for it combined a finely tuned intellect with a highly wrought emotional sensibility rooted in the redemptive message of Christ. So it was with Osler, whose intellectual vigour forged his career in medical science, but whose own devotional frame of mind made Thomas Browne's *Religio Medici* his favourite book. As Osler's biographer suggests, a passage from it serves as the epitaph to Osler's life and career: 'Thus there are two books from whence I collect my divinity: besides that written one of God, another of his servant nature, that universal and public manuscript, that lies expansed unto the eyes of all; those that never saw him in the one, have discovered him in the other.'[50] The passage from Browne also serves as a fundamental text illustrating the precepts of pre-Darwinian academic science in Osler's Ontario.

Darwin's explanation of the origin of species challenged orthodoxy in science as well as in religion. For this reason, most professors teaching science in Canada West in the 1860s rejected it, at least at first. Some, such as Croft and Nicholson, remained silent (at least in print) on the controversy. But those who took exception to the British naturalist's views, or to those of followers such as T.H. Huxley, were quite willing to place their objections in the public record. William Hincks, for example, used the forum of a review of Huxley's popularization of Darwin's views to air his own rejection of Darwinism, and in doing so he set forward the most common reason given by Canadian scientists for doing so. 'There would be numbers,' he said, 'to whom it will appear very questionable whether he would not better have fulfilled his official duty by offering instruction respecting the established principles and interesting facts of natural science, rather than speculative views on the most recondite question his science afforded.'[51] The science of Darwin and Huxley was not acceptable because it elevated hypothesis and speculation over empirical observation and generalizations based on that observation.

Pre-Darwinian science in North America was severely Baconian in its anti-speculative empiricism.[52] One of the reasons why so little emphasis was placed upon theoretical research in Ontario universities until the 1870s (and even then it was meagre) was the prevalence of this approach. Darwin, in such a view, had not 'proven' the existence of natural selection; he had merely asserted it as an hypothesis and then suggested that the facts – such as the fossil record – led to the conclusion that some such principle must exist in order to explain them. This was methodologically unsound to scientists such as Hincks, who believed that 'it is not the business of the philosophical inquirer to form some theory respecting the origin of the various species of organised beings, unless he has first observed in them such signs of fluctuation and of being modified by causes, of which he can estimate the operation, as to turn his thoughts in that direction.' Beyond that broad – and fundamental – objection, Hincks the taxonomist could also not accept the Darwinian view that species were not 'fixed in the nature of things and only liable to modification by external causes within certain limits.'[53] Hincks insisted on maintaining the traditional distinction between 'species' and 'varieties.' Darwin and Huxley did not.

In 1860 Daniel Wilson was professor of history and English literature at University College in Toronto, but he was also the Canadian man of science probably best known abroad. In 1851 he had published *The Archaeology and Prehistoric Annals of Scotland*, an early and impressive work whose title contained the first recorded use of the word 'prehistoric.' This branch of science, including its anthropological implications, retained his interest and he found himself president of the Canadian Institute, the main forum of the Toronto scientific community, in the critical two years after the publication of Darwin's *Origins*. His own response to the book understandably dominated his presidential addresses of 1860 and 1861.[54]

Like Hincks and like geologist J.W. Dawson, Principal of McGill University, Wilson took exception to Darwin's violation of the rules of Baconian induction by his use of hypothesis. But as much as from any purely scientific objection, he disliked the way Darwin excluded aesthetic appreciation from observation of the wonders of the natural world. An accomplished engraver and watercolourist who had studied under Turner in England, Wilson was drawn to science because it held 'secret truths,' thereby preserving a sense of wonder, awe, and reverence. Science, that is, preserved and nourished the religious sensibility. It was yet another pathway for piety to take. As late as 1889, in a convocation address to the University of Toronto, Wilson, by then its president, drew attention to Darwin's admission that he had lost his aesthetic sensibilities to such an extent that he found himself unable to read Shakespeare without being bored. 'This confession,' said Wilson, 'of one, who as a student of nature has carried his assaults on many preconceived ideas into the realm of mind, cannot but impress every thoughtful specialist, when he reflects that in those very rejected pages of the great dramatist lay embodied the Caliban of Shakespeare's marvellous creation, in which Darwin would have found his own most daring imaginings anticipated in the perfect realization of his hypothetical missing link: the reasoning anthropoid merging into humanity.'[55]

This was no light matter for Wilson, and he was not speaking lightly when he claimed that Shakespeare's Caliban was 'the missing link' between man and brute. Two years after Darwin published *The Descent of Man* (1871), which asserted that mankind, too, was subject to the evolutionary process by means of natural selection (including sexual selection), thereby stirring up great public debate, Wilson gave his response. He published a highly idiosyncratic mixture of literary criticism and social anthropology to which he gave the title *Caliban: the Missing Link* (1873).

The balance Wilson sought between intellect and emotion was characteristic of his general approach to education and to life. He saw in Darwin's career 'a warning to the specialist against limitation to even the amplest single line of research.'[56] For his own part, he preferred to look for truth in its broadest sense. He saw the scholar as a kind of modern-day monk, 'earnest in chase of Truth,' satisfying his religious needs in ways not perhaps afforded by the church to which he belonged. This view found expression in Wilson's poetry:

The mighty dead revive, – poet and sage,
Historian, sophist; and philosopher.
Science unfolds her sacred mysteries;
And Art her powers; and Nature's self-coy maid –
Won by the worship that he offers her,
Her mask withdraws, and to his dazzled eyes
Unveils the primal beauties that it hid.[57]

For Wilson, science, like literature, was a form of historical investigation. Poets, sages, and historians allowed him to participate in the almost religious communion that was the heritage of Western civilization as he understood it; but it was science, susceptible to appropriately reverential advances, whose veiled wonders were most prized.

Post-Darwinian Accommodation

It would be misleading to portray the Ontario academic reaction to Darwinian evolution as one of simple retreat. Some, such as James Bovell, did return to clerical life (although he did not do so for more than a decade after the publication of Darwin's *Origins*). Others, such as William Hincks, suffered a loss of belief in the Christian faith as a result of their earnest inquiries. (Hincks ultimately became a Unitarian.) More characteristic, perhaps, was the gradual accommodation made by E.J. Chapman. In the 1860s, while admitting some misgivings about Darwin's methods and his failure to explain major gaps in the fossil record, Chapman came to accept the implications of the English naturalist's work for the origins of man. He did so reluctantly, for 'the gulf required to be bridged over is ... great: a dumb and stationary brute-intellect on the one side – speech, reason, and progress, on the other.' Yet as a scientist he had to admit, whatever the personal pains involved, that Darwin's views nevertheless had 'some strong claims to consideration.'[58] By the 1880s, even Daniel Wilson was speaking of 'the marvellous combinations of evidence and the clear inductive reasoning of the great naturalist in his chapters on the origin of species.'[59]

The accommodation of Ontario undergraduates to divergent claims made by arts and science 'disciplines' is difficult to establish. Student newspapers appeared only in the 1870s and few student diaries or classroom notes have survived. By then the debate over Darwin and science in general had widened significantly into the realm of social theory and ethics, for the narrow question of whether the principle of natural selection was valid had been transcended by larger issues. At Queen's University, for example, the student newspaper, founded in 1873, contained from the outset editorial articles with such titles as 'Finality and Opinion,' 'Belief and Knowledge,' and 'Faith and Opinion.'[60] At issue in such pieces was the matter of what constituted a proper balance between affirmation and inquiry. Is 'truth' derived from received wisdom, students asked, or is it discovered – in effect, created by each new generation? In the 1870s this crucial question was of major concern. 'The idea of yesterday,' wrote one student, 'was perhaps the best and fittest for that day, and it did its work, but may not suit the morrow. So the thought, the creed, the law which was best for one generation may not be suitable for the next. It is indeed true that truth, absolute truth never dies, never varies; but our apprehension of it may grow, and consequently vary; and the form and expression it takes in the law and creed of one age, of the fittest and best for that age, may become defeat for the next, and will practically die and be cast aside.'[61]

The idea that truth could be truths, and that they could die as well as be born, was an undergraduate conclusion revolutionary in import, and it reflected the changing views of the professoriate. But what was the relationship between belief and such truths? How could truths be established and verified? By intuition? By empirical observation? By both? For one student in 1874 the answer lay in the latter, for 'in the case of all intuitive beliefs ... the evidence is so completely bound up in the belief that it becomes indistinguishable ...'[62] What then of faith, if intuition could not be trusted to find a single form of truth? The answer, said another student, was that truth is not a form of belief, not 'an intellectual act'; it is, instead, 'a constant principle of a spiritual life.' 'The quality of faith,' he concluded, '... will depend on the nature of the conscious communion of the spirit with God as a spiritual personality, while belief must vary with the intellectual apprehension of certain philosophical interpretations of the written record; the means of which interpretation are continually changing.'[63] In such ways was a continued place for the religious sensibility preserved in an academic life increasingly dominated by science. Natural philosophy could still be seen to 'disclose' to the concerned 'in endless variety the proofs of perfection of the Great Author of creation ...'[64] But the modern age, it seemed, provided more than one pathway toward truth.

By the 1870s, then, we can witness the beginnings of a precarious consensus that a balance could and should exist between affirmation and inquiry within the arts and the sciences. In this respect the mental worlds of professors and students reflected the general concerns of some major figures among the province's literati.[65] If the classical subjects such as Latin and Greek appeared increasingly remote from the demands of everyday life, even while remaining central to the idea of a liberal education, the sciences became ever more central to a successful national future. Even the great Canadian exponents of a broad and unspecialized education as a necessary means of entrance into professional life recognized this.

Daniel Wilson had reservations about Darwin, but he had few about the practical results of science. In the same presidential addresses to the Canadian Institute in which he had voiced his criticism of Darwin's *Origins* he paid great attention to the technological accomplishments of British science. Perhaps predisposed to think along these lines because his brother George had been the first professor of technology in the British Empire,[66] he was nevertheless genuinely excited by the increasing pace of technological change in Canada by the 1860s. The engineering miracle of the Victoria Bridge, made of tubular steel and spanning the vast St Lawrence River, he said, 'well nigh annihilates for us the impediments of time and space and is already revolutionizing our whole relations of commercial and social life.' The Geological Survey of Canada allowed men a unique glimpse into past ages, whereas its new magnetic observatory helped them to fulfil their desire 'to look into the unseen truths of a great future.'[67] The successful laying in 1860 of a telegraphic cable on the floor of the Atlantic from England to North America was perhaps Wilson's greatest source of pride because of its wide range of consequences. It rekindled the 'great pulse' of the British Empire. The magnitude of its achievement reduced its participants to 'solemn awe'; it allowed naturalists associated with the project to study the nature of life beneath the ocean's depths, thereby revealing 'glimpses to us of the infinite variety of characters in which God is still writing the revelations of his creative power to shame the pretty cavils of the sceptic...'[68]

Science and technology were on the public mind in Ontario in the 1870s and 1880s, and professors – especially from the University of Toronto – were in demand to explain the consequences of the current explosion of knowledge. Henry Alleyne Nicholson gave public lectures on physical geography in relation to geology, as did Daniel Wilson on modern European history, George Paxton Young on mental and moral philosophy, and physicist James Loudon on light. 'The age teems with problems and discoveries in all departments,' remarked the editor of the *Canadian Monthly and National Review*, 'moral and physical – of the most transcendent interest and importance. To be able in any measure to follow the course of thought, and to understand its results when presented as they now are on every hand, in itself lends a new enjoyment and dignity to life. That a little knowledge is a dangerous thing is true only when you attempt to teach or criticize; for the purpose of appreciation a little knowledge may go a long way and be very useful.'[69] The future, as well as the past, was becoming an object of reverence. Increasingly, the press gave attention to science, causing the editor of another Toronto-based monthly periodical to respond to demands for a 'popularized' science by instituting a regular science column from the outset of publication. It had become 'one of the most important functions in journalism,' said the editor, 'to assist in that diffusion. Indeed,' he concluded, 'the aspect of journalism with regard to science has completely changed within the last twenty years, and now no magazine is complete without its science column.'[70]

As the Ontario student working towards a bachelor's degree in the faculty of arts and science trudged his way in the 1870s or 1880s from his Latin class to his science demonstration, he could not have been entirely unaware of the academic consequences of this transformation of public opinion and belief, for in the university setting it was reflected in the shifting authority of the disciplines. In a sense, he was at the cutting edge of this fundamental shift in public awareness. The student elite – those who wrote for the campus newspapers – were prompted to set their views on the matter into print. 'Progress,' said one, was 'the leading idea involved in civilisation,' a progress both moral and social in nature. 'If we examine history, if we inquire into the causes of civilisation, we will not fail to recognize a social activity and internal development to be the principal cause in the march of progress.' Outward improvement, he concluded, must be accompanied by development of the 'inner man.'[71]

The evidence that science and engineering led directly towards many material improvements was everywhere manifest by the 1870s. Less obvious were the signs that the progress of the 'inner man' would proceed apace. By then, students and public alike had not only Charles Darwin but also the English social evolutionist, Herbert Spencer, to contend with, assuming that they thought much about such subjects. 'Social Darwinists' such as Spencer sought to ground social ethics in the natural order rather than in theological abstractions, and in so doing they shifted the source of moral action from God to society.[72] Those influenced by such thinkers seldom saw themselves living in a world where blind chance had taken the place of God's design, but rather in one in which the nature of 'design' itself had shifted. Increasingly, God's intentions were sought less in nature than in conduct. 'Perfection must be the crown of all His works,' Goldwin Smith wrote in 1884, 'but instead of producing it at once by fiat He may have chosen to produce it by way of progress and effort, as moral excellence is produced in man. The mode of our moral development may be the true key to creation ...'[73] A fundamental shift in the understanding of social causation was beginning to take place. The authority of God was coming to be joined with that of another abstraction called Society, and the emulation of Christ with the aspiration to culture.

Signs could be seen by the 1870s that this was so, for the vocabulary of students began to change in just such a way. References to Christ slowly began to diminish in student publications, except where missionary activities were concerned. 'A high estimation of learning,' said one student journalist, 'impels to self-culture.'[74] To give the student 'that refinement and culture which at once distinguished the man of education from the illiterate ... is the object of a College Course,' said another.[75] To an extent such words simply marked the continuation of the older idea that a liberal education should nurture the whole person, but it was now expressed in the jargon of a new day. Yet such jargon, then as later, carried with it a set of assumptions that were by no means hollow. By the 1870s the unstated rationale for the notion of personal enrichment had significantly shifted. The object of a liberal education was gradually becoming less to make the self at one with Christ in an act of pious contrition than it was to establish a rightful place in society by means of social analysis or moral elevation, in however inchoate a form these aspirations may have been expressed.

This fundamental shift was symptomatic of a more general transformation in the understanding of the place of ideas and values in Western thought. Considered as 'transcendent units' derived, in the Christian formulation, from God, ideas, in the words of Hannah Arendt, had traditionally been used 'to recognize and measure human thoughts and actions.' The removal of them from the realm of the transcendent in the eighteenth and nineteenth centuries 'dissolved all such standards into relationships' between the members of society, establishing them instead as functional 'values.' With this shift of ideational conception, the notion of the Good became, in itself, a value that could be exchanged with other values, a kind of commercial transaction. 'The birth of the social sciences,' Arendt concluded, may thus 'be located at the moment when all things, "ideas" as well as material objects, were equated with values, so that everything derived its existence from and was related to society.'[76] In the history of higher education in Ontario, this moment was near at hand.

6

The Arrival of Women

The Ontario college and university was a man's domain for most of the nineteenth century. The story of women's arrival into it illuminates the constricted boundaries of male understanding as much as it does the strength of women's aspirations. When women first sought access to higher education at the university level their presence was resented in a variety of ways, and means were found to make their 'proper sphere' in university life abundantly clear, as it already was in the home and the workplace. Idealized in the nineteenth century as a redemptive, angelic figure, the Victorian woman who desired a rigorous academic education equal to that afforded to men had to face deeply engrained cultural assumptions, held by many men and women alike, that portrayed woman's biological and vocational destiny as essentially a domestic one. Nevertheless, courageous, pioneering women, persistent in the quest for educational equality, ultimately made a place for themselves. In so doing, they facilitated the broadening of academic and extra-curricular activities alike.

The Woman Question

Nineteenth-century higher education in Ontario was very much a male preserve, but so were most other aspects of social existence outside the home. For much of the century the range of acceptable public activity of women was very circumscribed, for their social role was deemed to be that of preserving the moral and spiritual unity of the family – a haven from the crassness, the corrupting influences, and the materialism that was seen to characterize the world of men in society. This was especially the case for middle-class, urban women, for whom a 'refined' and relatively leisured home existence was a possibility. (For the female factory worker or farm wife, the role of 'domestic angel' was more rhetorical than real, and certainly more difficult to achieve.) Nevertheless, pressures upon all women to assimilate values primarily associated with urban and middle class life were persistent throughout the nineteenth century. One clergyman, addressing himself to the subject of 'The Proper Sphere and Influence of Woman in Christian Society' in the 1850s, was happy to proclaim that 'woman is the equal of man, alike in the matter of intellect, emotion, and activity ...' but he nevertheless added quickly that 'It would never do ... from these premises, to draw the conclusion that woman behoves and is bound to exert her powers in the same direction and for the same ends as man. This were to usurp the place of man – this were to forget her position as the complement of man, and assume a place she is incompetent to fill, or rather was not designed to fill.'

What, then, was woman's proper sphere? The matter could be simply put: 'The sphere of woman is home and whatever is co-relative with home in the social economy.'[1] Such views were pervasive among men and women alike well into the second half of the nineteenth century, although the degree of 'separation' between the 'spheres' – whether of women and men or private and public – was as much a matter of perception as of reality.[2] Women were not necessarily happy with such a lot in life, yet lacking a wide range of vocational alternatives because of the relatively undifferentiated nature of the pre-industrial labour force, very often they made a virtue out of necessity. But what *was* 'co-relative with home in the social economy' of an industrial social order? It was precisely the relationship between domestic virtues and the needs of this 'social economy' that provided women with the desire for careers in such professions as medicine and education and for the university education that would give them a measure of educational equality with men.

Beginning in the 1870s matters slowly began to change. The English philosopher and critic, John Stuart Mill, had described and attacked 'the subjection of women' in his 1869 essay of that title, capping a decade of dispute over the 'woman question' in England. In the United States, shortly thereafter, a number of women began to link the politics of gender to those of class and race, in the form of radical political activity, as industrial capitalism moved economic production increasingly outside the household and into the factory.[3] Such tendencies did not go unnoticed in Ontario. Goldwin Smith, who had resigned from Cornell University in part because of its decision to admit women, was by 1872 comfortably married and with the leisure to pontificate from his downtown Toronto mansion, The Grange. From this sanctuary, Smith rebutted feminist arguments by denying that men were in any way responsible for the subjugation of women. Men, too, largely remained enslaved.[4]

Smith wrote with apparent relief that 'Of all the questions raised by the movement perhaps the least difficult is that which ... is alone presented to us in Canada at present – the question of Education.' He was happy to suggest that women should be allowed to take up 'any studies which have hitherto been generally confined to men,' and decried any attempts to discourage women from doing so, especially on the grounds that the female intellect was inferior to that of the male. Such a presumption, he said, was 'impertinent and absurd.' Nevertheless, he stated, the probability of academic success for women would be determined by 'the facts of physiology and by our previous experience of the relative powers of the male and female brain.' The coeducation of the sexes, he concluded, 'is a question of public expediency to be decided by reason and experience.'[5] Some female readers of Smith's' *Canadian Monthly* article may well have replied that male reasoning and past experience were precisely the problems they faced.

Women of the 1870s discontented with their lot did, however, find supportive allies. An anonymous author wrote an article for the *Canadian Monthly* in 1879 strenuously rejecting the whole range of arguments that restricted 'woman's sphere' to the family circle. 'The Woman Question,' it began, was 'one of the most interesting and important problems of modern civilization.'[6] If women, like civilized men, were to meet their 'imperative obligation to strive for the noblest goals of knowledge, wisdom, goodness, [and] power,' nothing less than complete 'freedom of self-determination' was necessary. Woman was owed the right 'to shape her own course and character, responsible only to her own conscience.' The record of past ages did, indeed, illustrate the history of women's subjugation to the will of men. The plethora of discussion of 'woman's sphere' involved an 'infinite deal of nonsense,' in which 'every fledgling in philosophy or religion felt himself fully competent to mark out with entire precision both the general course, and the specific actions appropriate to every woman.' Arguments for the biological basis of women's intellectual inferiority, it was stated, were rhetorically specious and scientifically bankrupt. The self-determination of woman required nothing less, in the eyes of the anonymous author, than the 'right to enter any employment or profession for which she has the taste and qualification,' as well as the right of suffrage. 'She can never shape her own career, never be the arbiter of her own destiny, so long as she has no voice in framing the laws under which she lives ...'[7]

Medical and other authorities in Canada proclaimed in the 1870s that the physiology of women made serious study difficult, particularly during menstruation. They also reprinted articles written by American colleagues urging physical education for girls in order to counteract the burden of mental taxation in the classroom.[8] Yet equality of education had begun to receive serious support in the upper echelons of Ontario higher education. 'Is it more unwomanly,' said Principal Grant of Queen's to the Montreal Ladies' Educational Association, 'to walk to college than to ride to hounds? More indelicate to sit in the same room with young men listening to lectures on philosophy or science, for two or three hours in the day time, than to dance fast dances with them all night? More unmaidenly to practise the healing art than to cultivate the art of husband-hunting? Is it less unworthy of the sex to know something than to know nothing, to do something than to do nothing, to cultivate faculties than to dwarf them?'[9] Grant did not suffer fools gladly, and a lot of fools, he suggested, had made pronouncements on the 'woman question.' His own view was that the education of women must be based upon the complete 'equality of the sexes,' yet he did not believe that the woman who chose to engage in traditional female pursuits was the equal of her professional and college-educated counterpart. If women, as Herbert Spencer had suggested, did suffer from an earlier arrest in physical evolution, thereby making them weaker than men, education was even more important for them. 'Ladies' colleges clearly provided an education for women, but an education, Grant claimed, that was inferior to that afforded by universities. 'I know of no reason,' he said, 'that can be urged against women studying in our recognised colleges that has not been urged from time immemorial against every step in advance taken by the race, against every reform that has ever been made in the realm of thinking or of action ... The mass of social prejudice to be overcome is enormous ...'[10]

Grant was not alone at Queen's in articulating these views. John Watson and his predecessor, John Clark Murray, were outspoken on the subject of the rights of women to university education. Watson continued to encourage the higher education of women at university. Murray, who had moved to McGill University in 1872, preached an even more strident philosophy of women's educational and social rights in Montreal for the remainder of his life, and encountered the enmity of McGill's intractable anti-Darwinian geologist and principal, William Dawson, who tolerated the idea of higher education for women but firmly opposed coeducation. Very likely it was at Murray's request that Principal Grant found himself speaking to the Montreal Ladies' Educational Association on the subject of 'Education and Co-Education' in 1879. Whether the advanced views of Watson and Murray derived in part from the fact that the former's only offspring was a strong-willed daughter, Harriet, and that the latter was married to a noted social reformer, Margaret Polson, is not yet known. It seems likely, however, that such family circumstances helped to form the social views of such liberal-minded men.[11]

The initial presence of women on Ontario university campuses was not due, however, to increasing acceptance by men of their right to be there. It was due, instead, to changing attendance patterns in provincial public education, new vocational opportunities, and the initiatives and persistence of courageous women. The need for self-fulfilment was central to such women, for whom 'higher education' and 'higher culture' were interchangeable terms. Like their British counterparts, 'they were not particularly social revolutionaries in a wider sense, they simply wanted to share fully in the benefits of their class.'[12] As Ryerson's system of non-sectarian public education took shape from the 1840s through the 1860s, the number of females attending public schools dramatically increased. Whereas earlier, girls would be educated at home or in private academies,[13] by the 1870s their number in the public school system rivalled that of boys. The supply of educated women, coupled with the discovery by school administrators that women could be employed as teachers at lower wages than men, contributed in the third quarter of the nineteenth century to the gradual 'feminization' of the teaching profession and the sexual division of labour that went with it.[14] By the late 1870s significant numbers of young women had earned educational credentials sufficient for them to become teachers, but by then few new positions were available and the profession had little prestige attached to it. Increasingly, they looked towards the universities for further advancement. Several such women pressed the issue.

By then, too, their academic performances were beginning to shatter the myth of the innate intellectual inferiority of women. Increasing numbers of women wrote the matriculation examinations sponsored by the provincial high schools, and they began to win honours and scholarships, particularly in modern languages.[15] Ladies' academies, particularly the Wesleyan Ladies' College in Hamilton, developed curricula that testified to the wishes of women to acquire a genuinely higher liberal education. Founded in 1861 on the initiative of the Reverend Dr S.D. Rice and others to provide women with an education paralleling that provided to men by Victoria College, the Wesleyan Ladies' College quickly developed a four-year course leading to the degrees of Mistress of Liberal Arts and Mistress of English Literature. Instruction was given in subjects such as geography, astronomy, mapping, ancient and modern history, natural philosophy, arithmetic, French language, drawing, and music. Yet its great strength was innovative work in the study of English language and literature. It was in advance of other institutions in the province, not only in taking this modern language seriously as an object

of academic study but also in the way it combined the 'masculine' pedagogical emphasis on linguistic rigour and discipline with an experiential
'feminine' approach that required intimate familiarity with literary texts.
In this respect, it first anticipated, and later pioneered in, the Arnoldian
criticism that (as will be seen) would come to dominate English departments in Ontario universities in later years.[16]

At Queen's as early as 1869 John Clark Murray had offered a special
class for women in English and it attracted twenty-two students. This
was soon expanded, with the approval of the senate and board of governors, to include rhetoric and logic and natural history; by 1876, with
Murray now teaching at McGill, the Queen's University senate
approved attendance of women at regular classes in chemistry and
logic.[17] At the University of Toronto matters were more difficult, for
women were not allowed to attend lectures in University College. An
influential core of professors – Murray, Watson, and later Principal
Grant – enthusiastically endorsed coeducation at Queen's, but at University College such bold initiatives were greeted with a scepticism derived
from more traditional views of the role of women in society. In 1869
Daniel Wilson of University College worried publicly about the consequences of 'thrusting woman out of her true sphere' into professional
activities and of 'transforming her into the odious modern ideal of "a
strong-minded woman."' Wilson did not declare himself to be against
the higher education of women, but rather against forms of education
that might interfere with her divinely ordained domestic destiny. 'It is an
insult to our common sense,' he told an audience of women at the Toronto Mechanics Institute, 'to tolerate the idea that the highest mental
culture need interfere in any degree with those domestic duties which so
gracefully adorn true womanhood.'[18] Several times, when support for
such views was needed, Wilson invited Principal J.W. Dawson of
McGill University to Toronto to speak on the education of women.[19]

In spite of the authority and prestige of men such as Wilson and Dawson, they were on the defensive by the late 1870s for by then much of
the controversy over women's intellectual capacities had abated.[20] In
1879 the principal and masters of the Hamilton Collegiate Institute
applied to the senate of the University of Toronto to allow Alice Cum-
ming, winner of the modern language scholarship, to attend lectures in
University College. The university's committee on applications and
memorials responded with a report that was a masterly display of academic obfuscation, recommending that no action be taken. By 1883
eleven women had applied for admission to lectures. One of the applicants was Henrietta Charles of the St Catharines Collegiate Institute.
Winner of a double first in modern languages and general proficiency in

the first-year arts examinations, Charles sought permission to attend classes in University College. Her letter was published in the Toronto *Mail* in December 1881: 'I beg to claim the right to attend lectures in University College for the remainder of the session of 1881–82. This right has hitherto been denied to women. Permit me to ask if that is quite just? The examinations of the University are open to us, but at no other institution can we obtain tuition that will enable us to compete in those examinations beyond the First Year; consequently we have either to employ private tutors or trust to our unaided exertions. Whatever rules and regulations may be imposed I am perfectly willing to submit to. Hoping you will give the matter your favourable consideration.'[21]

No action was taken on Miss Charles's request, and she was not able to obtain her Bachelor of Arts degree until 1888. But elsewhere women were more successful in gaining admittance. Annie Fowler became the first female student at Queen's University in autumn 1880, and she was soon joined by a few others. One of them, Eliza Fitzgerald, rejected for admission to University College by Daniel Wilson, graduated with the Gold Medal for classics in 1884.[22] Similarly, Nellie Greenwood became the first female student at Victoria College when she arrived in Cobourg for classes in 1880. Received with kindness and courtesy, she nevertheless felt like 'a stranger in a strange land,' even when joined by a few other female students. 'I know now,' she recalled, 'that I *was never in a position* to fully savour the spirit of Victoria. I belonged to no undergraduate societies, I knew nothing of college sports. It never occurred to me to present myself at a class meeting. I never even looked through a window at a Bob party but nevertheless Victoria is my college.'[23]

By 1883 Daniel Wilson was beginning to face the new reality in higher education. In one lengthy letter to an applicant, he affirmed his support for the notion that women should enjoy 'the privileges of higher education no less thoroughly than do men,' but then went on to find 'many grave objections' to coeducation, which in his view was 'by no means calculated to promote the best interests of women aiming at the highest culture.' The creation of a separate Provincial College for Women, situated on the university grounds, was Wilson's solution. But that, of course, depended upon financial support from the provincial Legislature.[24]

Pressure, in fact, had begun to mount in political circles for a resolution of the question of higher education for women. Several distinguished alumni of the University of Toronto favouring coeducation, particularly John Morison Gibson and Richard Harcourt, were members of the provincial Legislature. On 5 March 1884, Gibson and Harcourt moved and seconded a motion in the Legislature urging that provision be made for facilities for women 'as early as practicable in connection with University College.'[25] The motion passed after long debate and with a divided chamber. Throughout the summer and early fall, President Wilson and Minister of Education Ross engaged in lengthy, and at times tense, written negotiations concerning the form that the education of women at University College should take.[26] Ross appears to have assumed that women would be educated with men, perhaps for reasons of economy, but would have facilities such as 'retiring rooms.' For his part, Wilson insisted upon the construction of completely separate facilities, but warned of the high costs of doing so. 'No doubt if Parliament insists on our trying a plan which so many experienced educationists condemn,' he wrote with bitterness in March 1884, 'they will not refuse ample means to give the experiment the best chance of success.'[27] By June he had provided Ross with a lengthy list of expenses involved in the construction of the necessary facilities. 'I may assume that even those advocates of Coeducation who most jealously urge the free intercourse of students of both sexes in all other respects, will not recommend a common use of the ropes and ladders, leaping bars, clubs, fencing-foils, and other athletic appliances.'[28]

Ross wanted the problem resolved and Wilson wanted the money with which to resolve it. Arrangements 'to accommodate ladies,' Ross insisted at the end of August, 'can be made in a very few days.'[29] Yet by September little had been done to provide facilities for women in University College, for the Legislature had not yet voted the necessary supplies. The very least the minister could do, urged Wilson, would be to appoint a 'lady superintendent' at a suggested salary of 'not less than $600.'

On 2 October, with classes at the university about to commence, an Order in Council was approved by the lieutenant-governor authorizing 'such arrangements as may be necessary.' Two weeks later Daniel Wilson spoke on the admission of women at the university's annual convocation. 'I can only say for my colleagues, as for myself, that so long as co-education is the authorised system in University College it will be our earnest endeavour to make it accomplish for our fair undergraduates every advantage that the plan is capable of.'[30] Such words scarcely concealed Wilson's bitterness at the way Ross had managed to receive public credit while trying to avoid financing the necessary facilities. A year later the rancour was still there. Someone, he wrote to Ross in December 1885, had taken 'measurements for placing a mirror 5 feet high in the Lady Students' toilet room. This, I think is wholly unnecessary ... All that is needed is an ordinary sized mirror for brushing the hair and adjusting a neck tie, etc.'[31]

The lady superintendent whose presence Wilson thought essential was soon appointed. Letitia Catharine Salter assumed the position in 1884, at an annual salary of $500. She continued to serve the university in this capacity until 1916, when she retired at the age of sixty-seven. For most of those years she was paid directly by the government of Ontario; not until the academic year 1905–6 did she receive a salary from the university payroll.[32] More than a decade after she was appointed, William Mulock communicated with George Ross on her behalf: 'Miss Salter, the lady superintendent at the University, has called upon me in reference to her position. She has been in the service of the University for some eleven years and whilst time has touched her lightly still there is the unpoetic fact remaining that she is eleven years older and with a salary of $500.00 a year is not much richer I fear than when she entered the service. I pay my coachman $520.00 a year for looking after a few horses. Cannot you do a little better? Janitors, elevator men, engineers in public buildings all are better paid than is Miss Salter. Surely you can make it $800.00. A lady in her position must dress in harmony with her position and is no doubt put to numerous other incidental expenses for there is a system of taxation going on in connection with every office in life.'[33] Four years later Miss Salter's salary was still the same.[34]

Professional Education and Maternal Feminism

Women in faculties of arts and science enjoyed a relatively low public profile. This was not the case with those who sought to gain entrance into professional faculties such as medicine. The notion that women might gain a university degree after studying modern languages and literature scarcely challenged the continuing belief that woman's ultimate purpose was a nurturing one within the home environment to which she was expected to return. This was somewhat less the case with the study of medicine, which clearly prepared students for a life-long commitment to a specialized career.

By 1878 Queen's University had made it known that it was willing to consider the prospect of female applicants to the medical school with which it was associated. One young woman decided that she would apply to it. Elizabeth Smith, daughter of a prominent family of vegetable farmers from Winona, Ontario, had rejected the advice of her best friend that if she laid aside 'those silly thoughts' of a medical education she would be 'a better woman.'[35] She also rejected the advice of doctors Jennie Kidd Trout and Emily Howard Stowe (graduates of American medical schools) to enroll at Ann Arbor, Michigan, after being encouraged by A.P. Knight of the Kingston medical school to apply to his own institution. The provisions in Kingston for women, however, were for a summer program quite distinct from that offered to men in the regular academic term.[36]

In April 1880, Smith and three other female students enrolled for the course and survived it without great difficulty. Dissuaded from attempting to enroll in the autumn medical classes, they waited until the following April before returning to Kingston, at which point they were advised that coeducational classes would be available to them the following autumn. After spending the summer in their respective homes they returned for the fall classes. Some of them they took together with men; in others they were segregated from their male counterparts by being placed in adjacent rooms. In this full year of coeducational instruction, once again all went well.[37]

Matters changed for the worse in the 1882–3 session, which had a larger contingent of male freshmen who delighted in aggravating the female members of the class (now numbering seven). Encouraged by such support, a young lecturer in physiology began to make insulting, demeaning, and sexually provocative comments concerning women in his anatomy classes. 'No one knows or can know what a furnace we are passing through these days at College,' Smith confided to her diary in November. 'We suffer torment, we shrink inwardly, we are hurt cruelly. Not by anything in the whole range of Medicine, the awe-inspiring wonders of the human being are of deepest interest – it is not that, it is the environment. It is that encouraged current through the class of whispers, innuendo, of derisive treading, the turning of what was never meant as unseemly into horrible meaning and the thousand and one ways that can be devised by evil minds to bring responsive smiles from their own kind. Day by day it seems harder to bear for we have borne so much.'[38]

After much exasperation the women students took their case for academic harassment to the university registrar. But once the complaint was made public the offending lecturer and his coterie of male supporters responded by claiming that because of the presence of women in class lectures had to be 'garbled' for the sake of propriety. An informal caucus of male medical students insisted that women henceforth be excluded from coeducational classes. The faculty rebuked the men, in turn, by reminding them that it should be 'distinctly understood that the government of the College belongs exclusively to the Professors, not to the students.' Determined not to be intimidated, however, the students remained adamant and indicated that if women were to continue to be admitted to classes with men, they would go as a body to Trinity College. With them would also go the fees on which their professors depended for their salaries.[39] The dean of the Trinity medical school, a man who opposed coeducational medical schools,[40] declared his willingness to take the potential student strikers. Ultimately a compromise was reached whereby the faculty promised to give the women separate classes until their graduation and not to take in any more women students in future.[41]

A pathetic measure of unintentional revenge was, however, exacted upon the offensive professor of physiology by the women whose presence he so resented. Forced now to lecture to them privately, he was more than a little uncomfortable. 'It was no doubt hard for the objecting Professor to have to give us lectures without his supporting class of men,' Elizabeth Smith reminisced much later. 'The first occasion was an event. He strangled, he raced, fell headlong over phrases, splashed, struggled, and away again, and was just sixteen minutes delivering this burst of science. We made futile attempts to put down notes, but our main energies were occupied in trying to maintain a dignified decorum under such ludicrous circumstances. He endured his trial as little as possible for his lectures seldom exceeded twenty minutes and occurred sometimes only twice a week. His lectures of previous years and our textbooks were our sources of information.'[42]

Elizabeth Smith and two of her three courageous companions did graduate in 1884 (the fourth was forced, due to personal circumstances, to interrupt her medical school training and graduated in 1886), but not before they had come to call themselves 'Shadrack, Mesheck and Abednego.' Under the stress of academic sexual politics they had come to find collective strength. The *Queen's Journal* continued to debate the merits of women in medical school, and friends of medical education for women found private funding for the creation of a Women's Medical College in Kingston. It was a jerry-built institution, with rooms in City Hall used for lectures. Five women members were on the new college board, which obtained privileges with Queen's University on terms equal to those enjoyed by the Royal College of Physicians and Surgeons in Kingston. But even this academic community inspired by G.M. Grant was not yet ready for a full measure of medical education for women. Principal Grant mentioned at the 1884 convocation of medical graduates that coeducation had not worked out.

Separate and possibly inadequate medical education for women continued through the rest of the decade. When Queen's created its own medical faculty in 1892 it was decided that the Women's College was redundant and that it would be closed. Future students should apply to similar schools in Toronto or Montreal. 'Narrow prejudice,' both within the upper crust of Kingston society and within its medical community, had for the moment won out. Medical education in Kingston would remain a male preserve into the twentieth century.[43] Matters were not much different elsewhere.

As in Kingston, the admission of women into Toronto medical schools had been declared a failure. One result was the opening of the Ontario Medical College for Women in October 1883. Its facilities were meagre until a new building was opened for students in 1890 (the old college building became a dissecting room), and it possessed no degree-granting powers. Its strengths lay elsewhere, for it catered to the specific interests and needs of women, such as gynaecology, obstetrics, and childhood diseases. It established a midwifery service in 1891, and provided pre- and post-natal care, attendance at home births, and other forms of community service. In short, it provided health care by women for women. Nevertheless, by the mid-1890s the College for Women was in financial difficulty. Enrolment declined steadily from 1895 to 1905 because of the growth of coeducational medical programs in North America. It closed in 1906. Its unique combination of medicine and feminism had been built upon the assumption that separate facilities for the training of female and male physicians would provide equity in the quality of that education. This had proven not to be so, as the dean of the Ontario Medical College for Women reported in 1905. After the 1905–6 academic year women were allowed full access to regular University of Toronto medical courses, but with this 'gain' had also come loss. Female medical students now faced admission quotas and discrimination, and received in return little emotional and professional support and a great deal of sexist ridicule from male colleagues. Gone was the supportive environment of the all-female medical college as well as the unique social services it had provided.[44]

By the time Elizabeth Smith graduated from Queen's she was engaged to be married to a man who lived at the same boarding house. She married Queen's philosophy graduate and political economist Adam Shortt in 1886, upon his return to Queen's after study in Scotland. From then until its closing in 1893 she lectured in medical jurisprudence and sanitary science in the Kingston Women's Medical College; thereafter she devoted herself to her role as mother of a growing family that she wished to raise 'in innocence & purity.'[45] She practiced medicine only briefly, just after graduation, but she took a serious interest in the medical education of women and was active in various aspects of community life. In this respect, she was an advocate of that branch of nineteenth-century feminism that has been called 'maternal feminism,' characterized by the conviction that 'woman's special role as mother gives her the duty and the right to participate in the public sphere,' not because she was a wife but because of 'the special nurturing qualities which are common to all women, married or not.'[46]

Smith was well aware of the ways in which male physicians, bent upon maintaining power and prestige, put pressures upon women to find careers that were seen to utilize woman's assumed nurturing instinct. She noted in 1916 that much effort was expended within the medical community to persuade women to abandon aspirations to become doctors and to become nurses instead. 'They all knew that doctors in practice have few obnoxious things to do, and nurses have many, also that the income of practitioners exceeds that of nurses, and that nurses' fees do not in any sense affect theirs.'[47] But the pressure for women to find occupational roles complementary to their perceived nurturing qualities – midwifery and teaching, for example, as well as nursing – did not come only from men. One female correspondent to the *Queen's Journal,* in the year after Elizabeth Smith graduated, wrote:

Woman occupies at the present time a considerable share of public attention. The subject as to whether females should attend college has been widely discussed ... But education also renders fitter companions for fathers, mothers, sisters, and brothers. There is a vast field for women in which to work without infringing upon the active duties of men. Home is their proper sphere, and domestic affection their highest attribute. If women wish to be useful they may be so in many ways departed from lawyers' or doctors' offices. If they have literary taste, for instance, they may write that for which having read mankind shall be the better ... Let woman cast aside her weakness of purpose and that slavish clinging to fashion which too often characterizes her, and all she does let her aim at the highest, even though she fail, there will be no need of her vying with man.[48]

At almost every point in their education in Ontario universities, women were reminded of what, after graduation, constituted their natural function – that of mother, helpmate, and moral purifier. Sixty-six of the 146 women who graduated in medicine in Ontario before 1906 are known to have married; yet most, it appears, continued in their chosen careers.[49]

The very idea that women might seek a career in law appeared ludicrous to many people. After all, women could not vote or sit as members of any provincial Legislature. As the *Canadian Illustrated News* said in 1874: 'The idea of women mingling in public affairs ... and exercising professions which necessarily banish all maiden mawkishness, is so novel, so contrary to all notion of feminine sweetness, modesty, and delicacy, that we are tempted to be hilarious over it, even when most gravely advocated.' Only one Canadian woman, Clara Brett Martin, a graduate in mathematics from Trinity College, sought entry into the legal profession before 1900. Her initial request for admission was rejected by the Law Society of Upper Canada when it ruled in 1891 that the language of the statute that created the society had not meant the word 'persons' to include women. Undeterred, she initiated a petition to the Ontario legislature to recast the definition. Against the strenuous objection of William Meredith and others, but with Premier Mowat's backing, the resolution passed (in diluted form after committee hearings) in April 1892. Women were to be allowed to be admitted as solicitors, but not as barristers; moreover, discretion concerning the admittance of women into legal studies was to lie with the Law Society. The society quickly voted to deny Martin admission, and it was only after the premier attended Law Society meetings (as attorney-general of the province he was also a bencher) and personally moved that the Law Society 'proceed to frame Rules for the admission of women as solicitors' that the recalcitrant body passed the motion, and by the slimmest of margins. Ostracized during her articling period, ridiculed by lawyers and court reporters, and made the butt of sexist jokes by students and law professors, she turned her back on instruction at Osgoode Hall, preferring instead to continue her legal studies at Trinity College (Bachelor of Civil Law 1897) and the University of Toronto (LLB 1899).[50]

With the help of the recently formed National Council of Women and of Premier Mowat, Martin now sought the rank of barrister. Against strong opposition, Mowat successfully argued for legislation permitting this in April 1895. Once again, the Law Society denied her admission. Martin placed pressure on her opponents in the society by lobbying their major clients for support, and Premier Mowat allowed his name to stand behind a motion forcing the society to frame the necessary rules. These forms of pressure worked: many benchers simply stayed away from the crucial meeting. Of the twelve who attended, eight voted in favour of Martin. Clara Brett Martin was admitted to the bar as barrister and solicitor on 2 February 1897, the first woman in the British Empire to achieve this goal.[51]

The shape of a professional future for women who enrolled in the arts and sciences was an uncertain one. They were usually channelled into specific vocational directions directly related to the perceived nature of true womanhood. Teaching children, as earlier noted, was one such 'natural calling.' In 1865 Egerton Ryerson had stated: 'It is the general opinion of educationalists that female teachers are best adapted to teach small children, having, as a general rule, most heart, most tender feelings, most assiduity, and, in the order of Providence, the qualities best suited for the care, instruction and government of infancy and childhood.'[52] Many women had taught in private girls' academies since before mid-century, but the 1871 Ontario School Act provided them with the opportunity of teaching at a higher level by allowing them access, for the first time, to secondary education in the newly created high schools and collegiate institutes. That educationalists, particularly school boards, quickly discovered that they could hire two female teachers for every male made the presence of motherly attributes in the classroom even more attractive. Educational administrators in fact often privately resented the 'feminizing' influence of the increasing numbers of female teachers, but they could scarcely argue with the economic advantages of employing them. The result was a great influx of women into the teaching profession, especially in the lower grades. This was particularly the case in Toronto, where by the late 1880s the ratio of women to men was nine to one, up from four to one in the late 1850s.[53] By the turn of the century, the feminization of the teaching profession seemed complete. Men kept power within its ranks by maintaining administrative control: headmasters, superintendents, and school inspectors were invariably men. These were the men who hired increasing numbers of female teachers yet who also feared that the 'coming Canadians' of popular novelist Ralph Connor's robust and manly nation, whether immigrant or native-born, urban or rural, were being mollycoddled rather than moulded.[54]

Local school boards scarcely needed to hire university graduates when third-class certificates from model schools were deemed sufficient. Only one-quarter of Ontario's potential teachers in the late nineteenth century thought it necessary to enroll in one of the province's normal schools, much less obtain a university education.[55] From 1885 on, however, with the decision of the Ontario Department of Education to create an occupational category called 'specialist teacher,' the ground rules were effectively changed. Since 1871 two kinds of public secondary schools had existed in Ontario: high schools and collegiate institutes. Larger provincial grants were provided to the latter than to the former, and after 1885 school promoters sought to meet the collegiate-institute standard by obtaining at least four teachers with the specialist certificate. Gradually the academic qualifications for such a 'specialist' status became equated with the honours, as distinct from the pass, BA. By 1898 this equation was formalized, when an honours degree became a formal requirement for specialist standing. Increasingly, Ontario universities stressed the honours degree, and many of the students were women.[56] By the beginning of the decade, fourteen per cent of the teachers in Ontario's high schools, initially the preserves of men, were women, and the proportion steadily rose. The number of women teachers was much higher in the lower grades, where university degrees were not initially necessary and where maternal skills, it was thought, were both desirable and sufficient. At the university level, one of the few areas where women made substantial inroads was in music instruction, which afforded a natural extension of nineteenth-century women's studies into a university setting. Hundreds of women taught at the Toronto Conservatory of Music and the Toronto College of Music from the late 1880s to the early 1920s.[57]

By the 1890s another form of professional streaming, related both to the teaching profession and to the Victorian conception of woman's essentially domestic destiny, took its place within some Ontario universities. Led by Hamilton's energetic matron, Adelaide Hoodless, first within the circles of the YWCA movement and later within the executive circles of the National Council of Women (which she had helped to found), the campaign for 'domestic science' in the province's public schools took shape. The views of Hoodless epitomize nearly perfectly the maternal feminist ideology of the turn of the century. Concerned with the systematic and scientific education of women for home-making, preoccupied with standards of diet and hygiene, and dedicated to the creation of healthy and happy Canadian homes, Hoodless was committed to the notion that woman's natural place remained in the home. She was by no means alone in holding such views: Lillian Massey in Toronto shared them.[58] To the extent that such maternal feminists sought to enlarge the boundaries of woman's sphere, they did so in order to counter those forces within urban and industrial society that were seen to be eroding the stability of the traditional family.[59] Close examination of the campaign for home economics in Ontario schools, one historian concluded, 'reveals that its advocates and supporters saw it, not as a vehicle for freeing the new twentieth-century woman from traditional domestic responsibilities, but rather as a means of fitting her for her "God-given place in life" as custodian of hearth and home.'[60] In addition, by giving domestic chores a scientific aura, it was hoped by the champions of the movement that a 'career' within four domestic walls would gain a renewed respectability. 'Domestic science, by establishing high standards and offering certificates of competence which would justify high wages,' wrote another historian, 'would surely increase the respect of young women for this occupation and persuade them to return from the industrial labour force to the domestic sphere where they belonged.'[61] Once there, the scientifically trained modern 'homemaker' could on the one hand offer the best of nutritional advice and the soundest of home economy while on the other continue to serve her traditional function as an 'angel in the house'[62] – a veritable font of moral purity that would counteract the crassness of the world of business, industry, and finance. 'Character,' said Hoodless in 1905, 'is formed in the home, and largely under the influence of the mother, and unless women are educated so as to realize and faithfully perform the duties and responsibilities of home-makers, we cannot expect a high type of citizen ... There is no branch of education so conducive to ethical instruction as that of Domestic Science, dealing as it does directly with the home and the operations carried on there.'[63]

The campaign to have 'domestic science' taught within the public school system of Ontario required qualified teachers. For this and other reasons, Hoodless and her supporters were advocates of the further education of rural and urban women – but an education, through Women's Institutes and the universities, that would not only include the study of music or languages but also extend to the more practicable areas of 'the scientific knowledge of sanitation, food values, care of the sick, artistic furnishing, the management of children, etc.'[64] By the mid-1890s, Hoodless and lobbyists from the National Council of Women and the YWCA had convinced Minister of Education George Ross of the merits of their scheme. The institutional infrastructure for the training of domestic science teachers took shape rapidly, for by the end of the century, with the right to higher education won, the education of women in this cluster of subjects had literally become a 'motherhood issue.' Private philanthropists were delighted to help, after suitable prodding from Mrs Hoodless. In 1900 the Ontario Normal School of Domestic Science and Art opened in Hamilton's YWCA building, aided by a $2,000 contribution from Lord Strathcona. Soon after, Mrs Hoodless convinced the president of the Ontario Agricultural College in Guelph to support a formal institute of domestic science. The result, after financial assistance from tobacco baron Sir William Macdonald, and from the provincial government, was the opening in 1903 of the Macdonald Institute, which offered instruction in domestic science, manual training, and nature study. The Victor School of Household Science and Arts, established at Toronto in 1900, was renamed the Lillian Massey Normal Training School of Household Science in 1901, because of her strong interest and support of the subject. Well before the death of this daughter of the wealthy Massey family in 1915, a significant portion of her fortune was used to provide the funding for a substantial building on the Victoria College grounds, for use of the University of Toronto's faculty of household science.[65] Maternal feminists, aided by their largely male financial and political benefactors, had by the first decades of the twentieth century contributed much to the ideal of higher education for women. But in doing so they had reinforced traditional notions of 'woman's sphere' even while they extended the range of her activities – into higher education, moral, social and political reform, and into politics itself. In this way, they had provided the institutional mechanisms by which the Victorian cult of female domesticity could essentially be perpetuated, in a more subtle form, for an age of science, industry, and 'the new woman.'[66]

Power in Numbers

Had the University of Toronto's 'lady superintendent,' Letitia Salter, been paid on the basis of female enrolment her salary would have been more than $5,000 by the mid-1890s. In 1884, when she made $500, ten matriculated women students attended classes in arts at the University of Toronto. By 1888 the number had climbed to thirty-four, by 1890 it was sixty-nine, and by 1892 it had reached 107 (see Fig. 6.1). The numbers continued to climb at Toronto and other universities. A decade later the number had more than doubled, to 254, and by 1911 it had more than doubled again. Moreover, the percentage of women enrolled compared with the entire population in arts and science steadily increased: it was 18.1 per cent in 1891, 31.4 per cent in 1901 and 34.4 per cent in 1911 (see Fig. 6.2).

Increases of a similar magnitude occurred elsewhere. In 1891 at Queen's, forty-four women were enrolled in arts and science courses, 17.6 per cent of the total population of 250. In the first year of the new century the percentage had reached 25.8, women totalling 117 of an enrolment of 460. By the academic year 1911–12 the number had almost tripled, with 316 women attending classes in arts and science, compared with 881 men. Their numbers by then stood at 36.9 per cent of the total undergraduate population in the faculty. Percentage figures are less meaningful for the smaller universities. The total student population of McMaster in the arts and sciences never totalled more than 177 before 1911, but the numerical increase in women students is nevertheless significant: from four in 1891 to seventeen a decade later, rising to fifty by 1911 (see Fig. 6.3). At Western University in London, only one woman appears to have been enrolled in arts and science by 1901 (total enrolment was forty-two); a decade later a dozen women were in attendance, together with sixty-seven men.[67]

Relatively little is known about the social background or intentions of late nineteenth-century women enrolled in Ontario universities, except for the case of Queen's. The 190 women who entered Queen's between 1895 and 1900 (when the total student population was 1,006) were enrolled exclusively in the faculty of arts. Queen's students in general tended to come from reasonably well-off (yet not necessarily wealthy)

FIGURE 6.1

Female enrolment in arts, University of Toronto, 1884–92

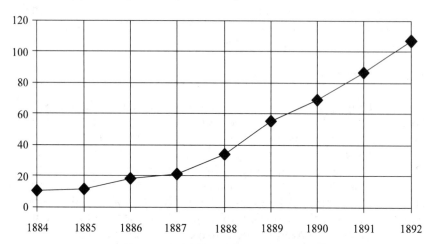

SOURCE: Department of Education Correspondence, Archives of Ontario, box 2, 'Women Students in Arts, 1884–5 to 1892–3,' report from Registrar James Brebner, University College (matriculated students only)

FIGURE 6.2

Female and total enrolment in arts and science, University of Toronto, 1891–1911

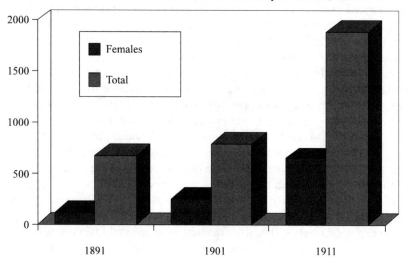

SOURCE: Robin S. Harris, *A History of Higher Education in Canada, 1663–1960* (Toronto 1976), 625–8

FIGURE 6.3
Female and total enrolment in arts and science, Queen's and McMaster, 1891–1911

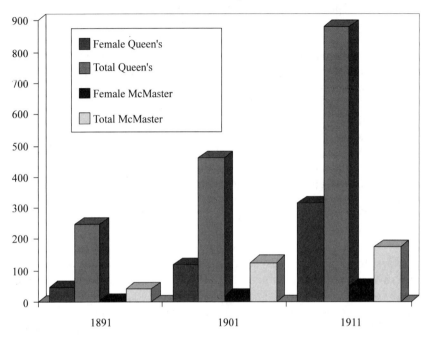

SOURCE: Harris, *Higher Education in Canada*, 625–8

families, yet the fathers of female students tended to have occupations of higher status, such as doctors or lawyers, than did those of campus men. Thirty-seven per cent of the male students came from farming back-grounds, in contrast to only twenty-one per cent of female students. Like the student population as a whole, the greatest percentage of female stu-dents – forty per cent of women, forty-two per cent of men – came from Eastern Ontario, but while only sixteen per cent of men came from Kingston, a full thirty-five per cent of women did so. In short, when family affluence and financially easy access to the university permitted it, women, it appears, were sent to Queen's; but when the expense of sending a child some distance for higher education or other forms of financial sacrifice may have been involved, families chose to send their male children to college.[68] Expense aside, that a sizeable proportion of Queen's women came from Kingston itself, and often lived at home, probably reflected the unwillingness of parents and university authori-ties to encourage women to live alone.

Men were far more certain of their vocational ambitions than women.

Two-thirds of the men stated their anticipated future occupation; seventy-one per cent of the women failed to do so.[69] Among the female students who expressed their career intentions, those from families with higher occupational status were significantly more uncertain about their future careers than those from less affluent backgrounds. If the student came from Kingston rather than elsewhere in Ontario the likelihood was even greater that she would have no clear vocational ambition – at least that she was willing to commit to paper. 'Eighty-eight per cent of female students who had attended high school in Kingston were unsure regarding their future occupations, as opposed to 67 per cent who had attended schools elsewhere in eastern Ontario and 48 per cent from schools in other parts of the province.'[70] For those students whose lives after graduation were traced, only fifty-eight per cent married, a figure much lower than the Canadian population as a whole but slightly higher than American college women. Once more, socio-economic status as reflected in the father's occupation is significant, for the rate of marriage was lowest – only fifty per cent – among those Queen's women whose fathers were not from 'professional' backgrounds – farmers or manual workers, for example. These were highly motivated women with a clear idea of what they wanted to do after graduation, and they were willing to make considerable personal sacrifices (as were their families) in order to obtain their professional goals. In contrast, more than two-thirds of women from affluent backgrounds, those also with unclear vocational intentions, married. For them, possibly, the university years were simply a pleasant interlude before marriage,[71] thereby entrenching the male-held notion that higher education for women was more closely related to courtship than to scholarship.

It may be that, as Lynne Marks, Chad Gaffield, and Susan Laskin speculate, women who chose to obtain a university education at Queen's 'contributed to a frequent rejection of the contemporary definition of women as wives and mothers.'[72] Yet the experience of women at the university at the turn of the century reflected the different social expectations of the women themselves. The ideology of female domesticity remained strong, among women as well as among men, and for every woman who expressed the desire for full and equal participation in the university's Alma Mater Society there invariably could be found another who believed such a measure to be too radical.[73] On a variety of matters ranging from political rights to career expectations Queen's women were divided, and there is little reason to believe that at other institutions circumstances were much different. Yet Queen's women were unique in one way, for regardless of ideological differences between them they participated in an organization without precise parallel elsewhere in

Ontario: the Levana Society. In a world where genders existed and operated within separate and unequal 'spheres,' Queen's women with very different views on the role of women created a common social and political space of their own.

Movement towards the creation of an organization specifically for the women students of Queen's existed by the late 1880s, a time of continued opposition from male students over the presence of women. A 'Ladies Department,' written by women, appeared in the *Queen's Journal* by 1889, so a forum existed in which they could publicly express their interests and concerns. But they lacked a space they could call their own – no common room or reading room, only a cloak room, and a tiny one at that. As members of the Alma Mater Society (AMS, with all Queen's students as members), they found that their attentions were 'diligently sought' around election time, but seldom thereafter. They lacked any class organizations or societies of their own. There were only about thirty-five of them, but that was enough for one of 'the boys' to complain in the *Journal*: 'there's an awful lot of girls in this place.'[74]

In the 1890–1 academic year, several of the senior women approached the university senate for the use of a vacant classroom in the attic of the old arts building. The senate agreed. They were given the room, and a table as well. Then they formed the Levana Society. It was informally organized at first, with a president and a secretary-treasurer, its purpose to foster solidarity and raise spirits. As one student put it late in 1889: Queen's women wanted 'that spirit of camaraderie which we admire in the boys.'[75] Levana instantly became a means by which women could use the separate spheres ideology to their advantage, whether they were intent on marriage or a career, for the small room and the one table in it represented autonomy and mutual support in the face of ongoing harassment and ridicule by men. College architecture tended, like the general college environment, to serve the interests of men. Levana served from the first as a means of helping break down this tyranny of physical and mental structures by its insistence on independent physical space for women.[76] It was also a means of communication between women students and the senate, said a Queen's woman of 1917, but 'chiefly it was a bond of union among the girls themselves.'[77]

The one room in the old arts building was exchanged in 1902 for more spacious quarters in the new arts building, just built. Levana remained there for the next fourteen years, until once again newer and better facilities were made available. For many of those years women lacked a playing field or a gymnasium for organized athletics, but they somehow made do. In the meantime, the social organization of the community of women continued to develop. The class of 1905 inaugurated formal debates, and began the Levana rites of initiation. It was in the first flush of the new century, in fact, that several venerable Levana traditions – such as its bear mascot – were invented. As the Victorian era faded into the Edwardian interlude, Levana assumed a greater range of formal responsibilities. Its council took upon itself the task of orientation and counselling that previously had been done by senior students. Early in the century, it was asked to elect not only two editors for the *Journal* but also a representative on its 'business side,' for women now comprised a sizeable segment of its readership and the *Journal,* no less than its professional counterparts, needed new subscribers. In 1911, officially sanctioned Levana candidates began to run in Alma Mater Society elections. By 1917, the year when women first won the right to vote in Canadian federal elections, Queen's women themselves gained the right to vote in the AMS elections and to secure positions on its executive. Two members of Levana were elected to the AMS executive that year. It was, students said, a 'Levana invasion.'[78]

Even the *Queen's Journal* editor who proclaimed in 1898 that he hoped 'the day was far distant' when women would 'take a full share in the discussions and the legislative and executive function of the [Alma Mater] Society' recognized that Queen's women possessed a new power of choice in determining their lives . They could now demand, as one woman did, nothing less than 'fair play, equal rights to all and special favors to none ...' They could defer to male leadership and hope, like another, that the boys would act like gentlemen and treat women with generosity.[79] But they could also go their own way, united within their own organization rather than divided in their stances toward male-dominated student organizations. They could use Levana as a means of forging an independent existence with its own structures and imperatives, one with priorities and activities that they alone would determine and organize and that would encompass the full range of university life. This is precisely what they did. Queen's University was a coeducational institution, but it was not one where formal male and female student activities were fully integrated until well into the twentieth century.

Part Three:
Transformations

7

The Gospel of Research

The academic environment in which Ontario men and women began to mingle, however uneasily at times, was one in which the imperatives of an industrial economy were beginning to make themselves felt. At the same time as male and female students struggled to come to grips with problems associated with the 'gendering' of higher education, the institutions themselves came to be transformed by public recognition that universities could be the harbingers of social change as well as social stability, and that an adjustment of universities to the conditions and requirements of industrial life was an essential ingredient in economic competition and development. No Ontario university was untouched by the province's industrial revolution and the secular gospel of research that attended it, but none was transformed in greater measure than the University of Toronto in the years before the Great War.

'Despite the compromises which it embodies,' wrote the University of Toronto's official historian in its centennial year, 'the Federation Act of 1887 must be regarded as a wise and statesmanlike measure. It has given Ontario a provincial university worthy of the name.'[1] Yet the passage of time can distort as well as clarify historical judgment, and such claims must be treated with a degree of caution. By the 1920s Ontario did indeed have such a university, and certain elements of the University Federation Act had helped in its rise to pre-eminence. But the act of 1887 also contributed directly to a degree of personal discord and administrative confusion at the University of Toronto such that by 1906 the provincial government found it essential to appoint a Royal Commission on the University of Toronto to investigate virtually all aspects of its governance.

There can be no doubt that the act of 1887 marked a major point of departure for the University of Toronto, but it was an embarkation on a course scarcely known by the participants and with very mixed blessings. Few of those involved in university affairs in Ontario for the next half-century would have described the act as 'a wise and statesmanlike measure.' The creation of new constitutional arrangements, such as the University Federation Act or the British North America Act of 1867 were in fact political responses to changing circumstances in the economic and social orders. Just as the events of 1867 cannot be understood apart from a recognition of the needs of commercial capital for a transcontinental market, those of 1887, occurring within the Ontario university community, must be seen in the context of Ontario's industrial revolution.

The period from 1873 until the mid-1890s has traditionally been characterized by Canadian historians as one of serious depression, with the Canadian economy undergoing slow and uneven growth due to unstable international economic conditions. Yet in Ontario this was scarcely the case. Production in all major industrial sectors of the Ontario economy, but especially in that of consumer goods, increased dramatically, if unevenly, between 1870 and 1890. Between 1869 and 1900, coal consumption grew more than 2,000-fold. In 1880 no electricity-generating plants existed in the province, but by 1901 there were 196.[2] Industrial production and employment expanded rapidly in Ontario's capital city. In the decade after 1881 'the total number of productive establishments in Toronto more than tripled, the number of workers doubled, capital invested increased roughly 265 percent, the annual product, 220 percent ...'[3] In the 1890s industrial growth in Ontario slowed markedly, and so did the expansion of its population: whereas it had increased by 187,399 in the decade 1881–91, it increased only 68,626 for the period 1891–1901.[4] But the provincial economy, aided by the end of international conditions of economic depression and by the beginnings of massive European immigration to Canada as a whole, revived dramatically in the first decade of 'Canada's century.' Ontario's population increased by 344,345 (from 2,182,947 to 2,527,292) between 1901 and 1911, and capital and production of consumer durables increased by 230 per cent.[5]

Increases in industrial production required advances in science and technology that were central to the nineteenth-century sense of the forces that propelled progress. Yet within the institutional setting of the university, the very nature of scientific enterprise (as well as its relations to economic life) was still very much a matter of debate. Pre-Darwinian Victorian science had largely been linked to the cause of organized Christianity, and the Darwinian debates of the 1860s and 1870s in Canada had not fully severed that association by the decade of the 1880s. Because of this, the years of Ontario's industrial revolution were marked not only by a slow and at times agonizing reorientation of the curriculum in ways suited to an industrial economy, but also by a re-examination of the nature and purpose of scientific investigation. The resulting debate, and the changes in university life that ensued, reflected the intimate link-ages between academic affairs, the needs of the provincial government, and the economic imperatives of private industrial production. It also reflected the growth in authority and acceptance of the ideal of research, of the discovery of truths and the production of knowledge.

Metaphysics and Investigation

Daniel Wilson's convocation addresses as president of the federated provincial university were models of the Victorian inclination to forge a compromise between empirical investigation and metaphysical neces-sity, between the imperatives of nature and culture. While his views probably reflected the assumptions and priorities of most members of the Ontario academic intelligentsia, by the 1870s others viewed such statements as unprogressive obfuscation hindering the real needs of the age: those of science.

Unlike some of his generation, Daniel Wilson was not convinced that new developments in science undermined religious certainty. For this reason he consistently urged the pursuit of scientific knowledge.[6] But to what end was this endeavour to be put? Wilson revealed his own view when he described the scientific community as 'a phalanx of labourers ... sharers in the glorious advancement of knowledge by which God, who has revealed himself in his word, is making ever new revelations of him-self in his works ...'[7] Here Wilson and others like him parted company with a generation of younger advocates of what was coming to be called research. For the latter, any science that continued to subordinate the pursuit of knowledge to traditional religious metaphysics – indeed any metaphysics – was no science at all.

Signs of the imminent disengagement of science from metaphysics could be seen even before the Darwinian epoch began in commentaries on the separate missions of 'practical' and 'pure' science. In the first issue of the *Canadian Journal*, the magazine of the Toronto scientific community, in 1853, an address by the British scientist Lyon Playfair was examined. It had been on 'The National Importance of Studying Abstract Science with a View to the Healthy Progress of Industry.' After noting recent improvements in the production of such items as candles and coal gas, the anonymous author of the *Canadian Journal* report paraphrased with obvious approval the gist of Playfair's message: 'the progress of abstract science is of extreme importance to a nation depend-ing on its manufactures ... Yet in our Mammon-worship we adore the golden calf, and do not see its real creator. It is abstract and not practical science that is the life and soul of industry ...'[8] Here, as with the views of Wilson, we note an overt tension between the imperatives of 'abstract' and 'practical' science. And it is one, moreover, given expression from within the scientific community itself, not from the camp of those who regarded science as a suspect, heterodox form of inquiry resulting in materialism. Debates over the nature and future of science were at first confined to the community of scientists, but this state of affairs slowly began to change in the last two decades of the nineteenth century.

In a province witnessing the uneven beginnings of industrial transformation, it was understandable that the first serious commitments of public funds to scientific research should have been made in the direction of engineering, with direct potential for application to industrial purposes and needs. Scientific men of affairs, such as T.C. Keefer and Sandford Fleming, had been urging private investors and governments to support what a later age would call 'strategic research' – research linked directly to economic, social, or political imperatives – for years, often with indifferent success.[9] By the 1880s several of the province's most distinguished academicians were pursuing the same cause. As president of the provincial university, Daniel Wilson spoke often on public occasions, and frequently his lectures touched upon the question of science and material progress. But Wilson's sensibility was as much poetic as it was scientific,[10] and as a result he would inform his audiences that support for university research in biology, electricity, optics, acoustics, and other scientific areas would lead to practical public benefit yet balance his demands with assurances that increased scientific inquiry would not distort the fundamentally humanistic aims of a university education. 'While we view with unalloyed satisfaction the due prominence given to physical sciences,' he stated in 1884, 'there is no disposition to relegate to an inferior place the study of classics, or of comparative philology and all the invaluable training which philosophy and literature supply.'[11]

Such a statement was on the surface harmless enough, for it sought to encourage scientific investigation while assuaging the fears of humanistic scholars. Yet it was also of significant import within the University of Toronto. From the early 1870s, Toronto had become an academic community highly politicized along several lines that affected the place of pure research. The University Reform Act of 1873, passed under the direction of Adam Crooks, had required the election to senate of fifteen alumni of the university, these to be voted upon by the graduates themselves.[12] The fact that this initiative took place during what historian Frank Underhill called 'the first, fine careless rapture' of Confederation, and in the heyday of the Toronto-based 'Canada First' movement,[13] simply exacerbated a tension that already existed between the proponents of more Canadian representation on the university faculty and a number of the current professors who were British in both training and outlook. Among the old guard, for example, had been William Hincks, the anti-Darwinian professor of natural history, appointed to the faculty in the 1850s. An unsuccessful candidate for the position had been the young T.H. Huxley.[14] By the 1880s the leader of this generational faction was Daniel Wilson, convinced of the superiority of British forms of higher education and sceptical of the readiness of Canadians to enter university life at the professorial level.[15]

Increasingly at odds with such men and such views was a younger generation of University of Toronto graduates led by Edward Blake, Thomas Moss, William Mulock, and James Loudon – all of whom took their degrees between 1854 and 1863. It was they who urged the election of graduates to the university's senate. They achieved their first significant political victory in 1874 when, against the strenuous opposition of Daniel Wilson, Moss was elected to the vice-chancellorship. A full sixty-eight years later, James Loudon's nephew still savoured the sweetness of the triumph when, in a biography of Sir William Mulock, he wrote: 'From that date Progress began to stretch out her hand, and although some of the members of the Senate who had lived in medieval bliss for many years fought valiantly against the new order, yet they were gradually being overwhelmed by the new representatives of public opinion. A new star of ... education was appearing on the horizon; henceforth there was to be no back-sliding. The University might stand still but there would surely be no step back toward the Past.'[16]

The old order versus the new, past against future – this was how the battle lines formed for a series of protracted squabbles that would continue to hinder the provincial university for the next thirty years. For much of that time the internal factional squabbles often attracted public attention since by virtue of the University Act all professorial appointments were made by the minister of education, not by university officials such as the president. As a result, politicians, professors, and public often sought the ear of the minister of education in order to promote their own special causes or to prevent those of their rivals.[17] Politicians wrote to the minister when the politics of prospective appointments were 'right' or when they were 'wrong.'[18] Professors wrote when their own salaries were too low or when those of their colleagues were too high. Both wrote when they sought more – or fewer – Canadians on staff.

For the remainder of the century and beyond, but especially during the uncertain years surrounding university federation in the late 1880s when the promotion of self-interest reached frenzied heights under the guise of sacrifice, the position of the president of the University of Toronto was consistently undermined. Why talk to President Wilson if one had a problem or a promotion? A brisk walk to the provincial legislative buildings could give the petitioner the ear of the minister himself. The ministry of education was not usually the originator of active interference in university affairs, although it was often accused of being so. The blame lay as much in the weakness of the University of Toronto Act, which virtually encouraged the petty and often self-serving intrigues of the university's faculty. Their acrid letters often reached the minister's desk, and they all but forced him to interfere at times in the internal affairs of an apparently ungovernable university.

The acrimony and intrigue of the day left a legacy of 'twisted beards and tangled whiskers' that playwright James Reaney found easy to satirize during the University of Toronto's sesquicentennial year,[19] but the major historical players on that stage saw nothing amusing in the state of their affairs. Associate Professor of Latin William Dale, dismissed from the university faculty in 1895 for criticizing university authorities in a public forum, was a long-time advocate of Canadian interests within the faculty. There was no hint of humour in a letter he wrote to Minister of Education George Ross in December 1890: 'In the past higher education has been repressed, almost destroyed in the Province from the apparent impossibility of any Canadian ever reaching the higher appointments. The Canadian appointments have I believe been uniformly good, while it is doubtful if the same assertion can be made respecting the foreign appointments. It must have occurred to yourself that there must be something wrong when after a generation of foreign teachers it is said to be impossible to find Canadians to fill any chair in the University, as it has been said. Doubtless we shall have to fight in the future as we have done in the past for every point ...'[20] The tangible prerequisites for the development of research at the provincial university – the acquisition of staff, equipment, and laboratory facilities, as well as the possibility of awarding a research degree (the PHD) – were debated, promoted, and resisted within this general context of institutional confusion, generational rivalries, and personality conflict. No person played a more important role in each than did James Loudon.

Born in Toronto, educated at Upper Canada College and at the University of Toronto (where he took his BA and MA degrees in 1862 and 1864), Loudon was talented, ambitious, aggressive, and therefore the most visible example of the local boy made good in the Ontario academic world. In 1875 he became the first Canadian-born scholar to occupy a chair at Toronto with the offer of the professorship of mathematics and physics. Already an acknowledged leader of the nativist (or nationalist) faction in the university – a group of University of Toronto graduates who championed the hiring of Canadian-born instead of British or American scholars – Loudon soon established himself also as an unwavering champion of the cause of disinterested scientific research. For the next fifteen and more years, as an appropriate place was sought for science within the university, the relationship between its two major exponents – Wilson and Loudon – remained very tense. Loudon had little patience and less respect for most of his former professors, at least in private, even those with whom he had associated in his early years on staff. He was curt , for example, in his dismissal of John Cherriman, who had taught him mathematics (and whom he replaced) because Cherriman 'did not believe in the possibility of any great advances in Mathematics.'[21]

The views of Daniel Wilson were also inadequate from Loudon's perspective. Loudon scarcely encouraged the older Wilson's intellectual support when he gave his first major public lecture after assuming the chair of mathematics and physics. As reported in the Toronto *Mail* on 16 October 1875, Loudon had stated: 'It is not the proper function of a scientific teacher to reconcile scientific theory with metaphysical or religious opinion – his duty being, as it appears to me, to investigate facts, to draw legitimate inferences, and declare them to the world to be accepted or refused, upon their merits.' This was a declaration of Loudon's own commitment to a complete separation of science from metaphysics; but it was also, as members of the university community would immediately have perceived, a blunt and tactless rejection of Daniel Wilson's entire approach to science and to life.

Wilson took offence at Loudon's insistence that the scientist should not take upon himself the task of reconciling science with metaphysics, and he was annoyed with Loudon's championing of the nativist cause, but he was also irritated because by implication Loudon also accused the British universities, so valued by Wilson, of having failed to harness science to the major requirements of the age. Indeed, two years later Loudon was even more direct on this subject in his presidential address to the Canadian Institute. This 1877 address is of major importance for the history of science in Canada, for it was a manifesto declaring Loudon's complete commitment to the German research ideal as found in its universities. On this matter Loudon did not waver for the rest of his long and distinguished, if constantly stormy, career.

Perhaps inspired by the opening of Johns Hopkins University two years earlier, based on the German model and therefore committed to research as much as to instruction, Loudon declared his approval. The state, as well as scientific societies, must develop ways of rewarding those engaged in independent research. It must increase the number of instructors, thereby enabling the division of labour that would make specialized professional research possible and productive. Neither British nor American universities, he stated, had yet done so. It was, however, 'the distinguishing feature of the German universities.' In them, Loudon said, 'the teacher is not relieved from the duties of the lecture-room or the work of the laboratory, but his subject lies within narrow limits, and he is thus not only enabled to teach but to devote a lifetime to his special subject ... Before the German plan, however, can be generally pursued anywhere an enormous revenue must be available; there must be a small standing army of professors, and a highly trained body of recruits.'[22] With Loudon's 1877 address, the mantle of scientific leadership at the University of Toronto began to pass from Wilson to Loudon, a man twenty-five years Wilson's junior. The future of scientific education thereby resided in the hands of a new generation.

The redirection and expansion of the university called for by Loudon was not, however, to be easily or quickly won. To begin with, the very Britishness of the university and its surrounding community had traditionally made almost any German influence suspect. 'I cannot ... even patiently sit down under the rebukes of any one who has himself drank from German fountains, and believes all wisdom to be with his masters,' William Hincks had written in 1859.[23] A certain amount of this hostility dissipated in subsequent years, especially after a philosophical idealism with origins in Germany was made both acceptable and popular at Toronto under the influence of the much-revered Professor George Paxton Young. But a residuum of British cultural distrust of German ideas and ways remained at the university and in the community; it re-emerged in the years of the Great War.[24] Second, the college ideal of a broad, humanistic, and liberal education dedicated to the instillation of 'inherited wisdom' and human values remained strong. The consolidation of the college structure in 1887 served to buttress this commitment. 'Specialization' became a synonym for challenges to humanistic values, and schemes for specialized scientific research were often regarded as evidence of the imperial and centralizing ambitions of the 'godless' university at the expense of federated colleges and regional institutions such as Queen's or Western.

Finally, even if such forms of resistance had not existed, the fact remained that financial assistance by the state was seldom forthcoming. The funds provided by the provincial Legislature necessitated by a disastrous University College fire in 1890 constituted its first significant grant in excess of the annual revenues of the university's endowment funds. The government disbursed this capital grant of $135,151 on the clear understanding that it was not to be construed by the universities as a precedent for future grants. In fact, however, each year after 1890 the Ontario government committed public funds, both for operating and capital expenses, to the University of Toronto. 'The general pattern of government expenditures ... were [sic] slightly less in 1900 than they had been in 1891 and ... fell every year between 1890 and 1896 before beginning their slow rise again ...'[25] Moreover, the financial concerns of the ministry for the university were almost entirely in the areas of academic activity of direct practical and social utility, and therefore of political benefit. Later, the School of Practical Science in Toronto and the College of Agriculture in Guelph, both under direct government control, were well financed in comparison with the universities proper; and Principal G.M. Grant's scheme to create a Kingston School of Mining and Agriculture in the early 1890s received the government's approval and support in spite of substantial Toronto opposition. In this way, a science harnessed directly to the needs of the state was encouraged while general university requirements were, by comparison, neglected.

By 1895, with a substantially increasing student body but deteriorating and inadequate equipment and facilities, the university senate issued a 'Report of a Special Committee – on claims respecting the assets and Endowments of the University.' The committee urged members of the Toronto academic community to impress upon the provincial government the need for a share of resources – in the form of land grants – sufficient to provide adequate support for the physical and social sciences and the 'Mechanical Arts.' It was critical of the government for failing to provide adequate support in the past. 'The result,' it concluded, 'is that, from poverty of means, the available resources of the university are altogether inadequate to meet the modern Educational and Scientific demands of the age.'[26]

The senate report was duly submitted to the Legislature, and the result was an 1897 act giving to the university lands in northern Ontario sufficient to increase the value of its endowment. Annual revenues generated from them were nevertheless pitifully inadequate, ranging from a low of $895 in 1898 to $8,191.81 in 1899. For these princely sums the provincial university paid a high price, for George Ross publicly justified the government's generosity on the grounds that the university was a 'child of the state,' owing its origins to 'the parliament of Ontario' and acknowledging 'no master but that parliament.'[27] In this way, the provincial state consolidated its ability to exercise either political control and direction or financial neglect whenever necessary or expedient.

Such a political climate was scarcely conducive to the successful promotion of disinterested research, whether in the sciences or in the humanities. Nor did it facilitate securing the means by which that research could best be encouraged: the creation of a sustained program of graduate studies, including the PHD. Nevertheless, progress was made – if very slowly. As might be expected, leadership of this movement was provided principally by James Loudon. Increasingly in the 1870s and 1880s, Loudon was able to point to the lead taken in American graduate studies by Johns Hopkins University, which had pioneered the German 'research seminar' in America. Moreover, he could also consistently draw upon the success and the testimonials of Toronto graduates who had gone to study there.[28] By 1883, with the aid of Edward Blake, who had become chancellor of the University of Toronto, he was able to cajole a reluctant Senate to adopt in principle the desirability of offering the PHD degree. No concrete action was taken, however, by the committee appointed to pursue the matter. The doctorate met strong resistance at the provincial university for several generations.

A year earlier the Ontario government had instituted a fellowship system, but these awards (nine in all) were intended as much to provide teaching assistance to an overworked staff as to facilitate the students' research activities. The result, ironically, was that just enough basic graduate training was made available to encourage fellowship holders to go elsewhere (usually to the United States) for the doctoral degree.[29] But along with their mentor, Loudon, these Toronto alumni were an effective lobby for the establishment of a PHD program at Toronto. They continuously extolled the virtues of American universities in academic research, particularly the practice of awarding fellowships to finance graduate study, and directly or by implication criticized their Alma Mater for its shortsightedness. Some of them – such as W.J. Alexander in English and A.B. Macallum in physiology – returned to Toronto after taking doctorates at Johns Hopkins and aided Loudon in his continuing quest for the acceptance of the new research ideal as a fundamental element in university life.

In this way, the locus of academic authority shifted away from the study of the gentleman scholar towards the laboratory of the professional researcher. Academic structures once deemed appropriate lost legitimacy to a science-minded public and research-oriented members of the academic community, even when they continued to perform well. In 1892, for example, the University of Toronto's chancellor, Edward Blake, admitted that instruction in anatomy at Trinity's medical school had always been better than that offered by his own university; yet the admission was made at the very point when general criticism of proprietorial medical schools such as that of Trinity was reaching its height.[30]

To the gospellers of research, only large institutions with major sources of funding for research and with permanent, professional staffs were worthy of support. Universities were at the centre of this ambitious vision.

Research at Toronto

Other imperatives – intellectual and social – came to their aid by the late 1880s and 1890s. The cause of specialized research was initially resisted by students and opposed by Wilson. Financial support was meagre because of the smug indifference of George Ross. Antagonisms exacerbated by the university question lingered, and the exponents of the college and university ideals concerning the purpose of higher education – transmitter of inherited wisdom or catalyst for advancing knowledge – continued. Yet the tendencies of the age favoured the ultimate acceptance of the place of research as an essential element in university education. Philosophers made heroic efforts to maintain moral and intellectual unity, but the very fragmentation of the pre-Darwinian monistic cosmology in the decades after 1859 paved the way for individualized academic routes to objective truth. The explosion of knowledge made possible by improvements in the technology of communications required the creation of well-defined academic disciplines, for by no other means could any scholar of the late nineteenth century gain command of what he was coming to call his 'field.' In spite of the financial constraints of the 1880s and 1890s, such specialization necessarily began to take place.

Earlier, Daniel Wilson could occupy a chair that encompassed all of English history and literature; Loudon could hold one in both mathematics and physics. George Paxton Young's chair in philosophy embraced not only logic, ethics, metaphysics, and the history of philosophy, but also psychology and political economy – then part of the philosopher's domain as 'mental philosophy' and 'civil polity.' Such had been the majestic sway of nineteenth-century mental and moral philosophy. But by the 1890s these chairs had each been divided – some said pillaged. In 1887 mathematics and physics were separated. The following year, English and history were effectively split with the creation of controversial chairs in English, assumed by W.J. Alexander, and political economy and constitutional history, occupied by W.J. Ashley. By 1894 history occupied a status independent of political economy with the appointment of the Reverend George Wrong as professor of history. In the case of each of these new chairs in the humanities and social sciences the lobby of Toronto nativists played a major role. In the case of most, the successful applicant was a strong advocate of the new research ideal. Political economist W.J. Ashley, for example, was a graduate of Oxford and had already distinguished himself in social and economic research of an empirical nature. An apparent exception was George Wrong, a Toronto graduate who had no obvious credentials as an historian but had the good fortune to have married the daughter of Edward Blake, the university's chancellor.

Near the mid-point in this expansion of disciplines the venerated occupant of the chair of logic, metaphysics, and ethics, George Paxton Young, died. Another major appointment was therefore necessary, and a controversy of major proportions was the result. Ultimately, the dispute touched upon each of the factors that had divided members of the university community in the 1880s: the importance of metaphysics and the value of laboratory work; the relationship of philosophy to the emergent discipline of psychology (should the latter be taught by professors of mental philosophy or by experts in laboratory experimentation?); the question of who should have the responsibility for determining appointments to the provincial university, politicians or professors; the problem of whether Canadians should be given preference over non-Canadians when such appointments were made. Moreover, the story serves as a reminder that real advances in the institutional and intellectual conditions necessary for scientific and other forms of research are at times the result of matters that, strictly speaking, have little bearing upon either science or research.

As might be expected, the Toronto academic community split largely along nationalist lines. Sir Daniel Wilson and the heads of two Toronto-affiliated theological colleges (William Caven of Knox and James Sheraton of Wycliffe) supported the candidacy of James Mark Baldwin, a young American who had studied at Princeton under James McCosh, North America's last major exponent of Scottish realism or 'common sense.' Baldwin had also studied briefly in Germany with the renowned physiological psychologist, Wilhelm Wündt. James Loudon, Vice-Chancellor William Mulock, the editors of *Varsity*, and a number of vociferous University of Toronto graduates favoured an Ontarian, James Gibson Hume, a recent Toronto graduate who was a self-proclaimed disciple of Young and who had gone for further studies to Johns Hopkins and Harvard. There he had studied variously with G. Stanley Hall, Richard Ely, Josiah Royce, and William James, and had made an excellent impression on each.

The reasons for these allegiances are relatively clear, if ironic. Loudon, faced with candidates with roughly equal credentials, favoured the native son, as did the other supporters of the nativist cause. Wilson, typically, chose the candidate with an 'international' background and therefore (in his view) cosmopolitan outlook. But he probably also favoured Baldwin as much out of reaction to Loudon's choice as out of commitment.[31] Since by virtue of the University Act the appointment of the new professor was ultimately a political one to be made by Oliver Mowat's cabinet, the controversy rapidly became a public one with academic deputations to the Legislature, letters to Toronto dailies, and front-page newspaper articles with titles such as 'Metafeesicks' and 'M'Cosh, Be Gosh.'[32] There and elsewhere the ironies inherent in the various allegiances soon became apparent. Loudon, the champion of experimental research, had rejected the candidate with laboratory experience under a German psychologist of world rank in favour of a Toronto graduate with none; the clergymen-academics, on the other hand, had rejected an exponent of a philosophy that made much of religious experience in favour of a scholar who had spent much of his time in Germany reading the writings of materialist philosophers.

The Mowat cabinet was also split, with Mowat favouring the appointment of Baldwin but his colleagues, including George Ross, strongly on the side of Hume. Mowat was further caught between the strong support of President Wilson for Baldwin and the weight of British-Canadian, imperialist, and anti-American public sentiment. Mowat's decision was truly political: he compromised by splitting Young's all-encompassing chair. Baldwin would be appointed immediately as professor of philosophy, with the understanding that he would specialize in psychological laboratory research. Hume was ordered to spend two more years of preparation abroad, after which he would return as professor of ethics and the history of philosophy. The hegemony of metaphysics – now gone from the title of the new chairs in philosophy – seemed over at the University of Toronto. By a bizarre series of events the research ideal was finally to be given a tangible presence and government support.

The days of Daniel Wilson were nearing their end. He was losing both influence and strength. He had neither won nor lost the appointment battle: he merely felt embarrassed and embittered. Although president of the University of Toronto, he lacked the power to determine appointments to his own faculty; yet he was called upon by Premier Mowat to write anonymous pieces for the *Globe* and the *Mail* praising the wisdom of the government's decision. 'And now I hope my colleagues will be considerate enough,' he wrote in his journal, 'To [let] live forever, or at least til I have shuffled off the mortal coil of Presidency or of life ... The aspect in which I find myself viewed by this pack of self seekers as a foreign intruder is comical. I am the last of the hated Hyksos kings. If they only had me safe in my sarcophagus the reign of the true native pharaohs would begin.'[33]

By 1892 both his wish and his prophecy had been fulfilled. He died in that year, his beloved University College literally in ashes. James Loudon was appointed president of the university in his place.

In a sense, James Mark Baldwin was also a victim of the controversy. The disastrous fire that in 1890 destroyed part of University College, including its library, also consumed the future location of Baldwin's anticipated psychological laboratory. His optimistic inaugural address declared him to be a true 'apostle' of the new experimental psychology,[34] but the inferno left him with little but his own enthusiasm. By literally begging and borrowing he was able to announce the existence of a laboratory for the opening of the 1891–2 academic year. Not in fact ready until the spring of 1892, the facilities – the first that were solely committed to putting the research ideal into practice at Toronto – cost a total of $919.21 Baldwin received no aid from either government or university in meeting his request for a laboratory demonstrator, and this was essential for serious and sustained experimental work. As a result he began to consider accepting one of several offers from other universities, including one from his Alma Mater, Princeton.

Baldwin (and Ashley) did choose to leave Toronto, and both enjoyed very distinguished careers.[35] In the ensuing political struggle over the leadership and direction of the philosophy department the metaphysicians and nativists exacted their revenge. Baldwin's departure for Princeton left Hume as head of the department, free to promote his own brand of Youngian idealism at Toronto. Baldwin's eventual successor in the psychological laboratory, August Kirschmann – a solid scholar specializing in experimental psychophysics – was appointed (after a replication of the original squabble) only at the level of lecturer. He did not receive professorial rank until 1898. In spite of the fact that Kirschmann managed to give psychophysical experimentation at Toronto an international reputation within a decade, he left in 1909, discontented with his treatment within the department. Meanwhile, James Gibson Hume, with the aid of Francis Tracy, a Toronto graduate molded in the image of Hume as much as Hume was of Young, shaped the department of philosophy along broadly idealist lines that were to continue well into the twentieth century in their preoccupation with ethics, history, and 'social philosophy.'

The research ideal scarcely achieved an unambiguous triumph within the confines of the university's philosophy department. Yet the episode is important historically for a different reason. It involved the question – central to many minds at the time, politics aside – of whether empirical research deserved more in the way of tangible reward than did the wide-ranging reflections of the 'unscientific' humanist sensibility. The legacy of the nineteenth century ultimately was the continued strong presence of the humanities at the University of Toronto despite the utilitarian concerns of the provincial government. It provided, too, however inadvertently, for continuation of acrimonious debate between exponents of the arts and the sciences. The institutional structure of federated denominational colleges, cumbersome as it may have been, nevertheless probably protected and even encouraged the moralistic – if increasingly secular – character of humanistic research.

Yet social and economic imperatives gave the cause of pure research increasing momentum. Throughout the 1890s university enrolment increased significantly, partly because of the success of the provincial high school system and partly because the maturing provincial economy now required university graduates with specialized skills. In 1897 Loudon, with the aid of Toronto alumni such as A.B. Macallum and W.J. Alexander (now on staff), was finally successful in getting the university Senate to pass his 1883 motion – never rescinded but never acted on – to introduce the PHD degree 'for the purpose of encouraging research.' Departments now offering the degree were biology, chemistry, physics, geology, philosophy, Oriental languages, and political science. (It should be noted that history, Latin and Greek, mathematics, and modern languages refused to participate.[36]) A turning point had been reached. From 1897 on, the university, in its attempt to meet the increasing demands of the resource-rich and industrial 'New Ontario,' was forced to declare major deficits, and the reluctant and fatigued Liberal government of the province had no choice but to respond with grants of increasing size,[37] usually earmarked for scientific facilities, training, and research of direct applicability to industry.

The year 1897 also witnessed the celebration of Queen Victoria's Diamond Jubilee. Partly to mark the occasion, the British Association for the Advancement of Science met in Toronto. Imperial fervour was near its height in Ontario, and the call of the assembled scientists for a coordinated system of research, to be led by the universities of the British Empire in order to ensure that Great Britain maintained industrial supremacy in the face of major challenge by Germany, met with general public approval. James Loudon, still the provincial leader of the cause of pure research, was therefore able to wed the needs of science to the growth of imperial-nationalist sentiment. He could support the call for more technical education, as he did in his convocation address of 1900 to the University of Toronto,[38] but he was able to insist equally, with increasing support, that 'no diffusion of technical training will in itself be effective if we do not take care to maintain the higher and highest kind of scientific instruction.'[39]

Loudon made significant progress in popularizing the need for pure research. In 1902 he began his presidential address to the Royal Society of Canada by saying 'It is now many years since I came to the conclusion that the provision of adequate facilities for research is one of the prime necessities of university education in Canada.'[40] By then he could properly claim major credit for helping convince politicians, professors, and public that his convictions regarding research were justified. But at his own university he continued to meet with frustration and to be thwarted by internal unrest due ultimately to the near impossibility of governing under the 1887 University Act. Its inadequacies played into the hands of the Liberal administrations of Mowat and Ross, both of which were quite willing to interfere in academic affairs occasionally, perhaps to remind the scholarly community of the provincial university that the security of patronage also brought the possibility of control. To them must also be apportioned much of the blame for the low state of the university's morale by the end of the Liberal regime.

Between 1887 and 1896, apart from emergency aid to University College after its disastrous fire and the continuing $500 annual stipend for its lady superintendent, the sole grant provided to the University of Toronto was $1,038.03 for a watermain. The university itself funded the construction of its biology building ($130,000), library ($60,000), gymnasium ($36,000), and chemistry building ($80,000), at the expense of a corresponding loss to its endowment. Between 1891 and 1905 only three votes on university affairs were recorded in the provincial Legislature. From 1898 to 1906, annual statutory grants to the provincial university yielded, on average, less than $10,000 annually. Only after pressure was exerted on the government in 1901, as a result of intense dissatisfaction by University of Toronto alumni, did the government begin to increase support to the university's science departments ($25,281 in 1901) and to assume the operating deficit ($10,353 in 1902).[41]

Santa Claus came early to members of the University of Toronto academic community in 1905, and he assumed the beardless yet whiskered guise of the new premier of Ontario, James Pliny Whitney, whose Conservative party had defeated the Liberals early in the year. As leader of the opposition, Whitney had long been critical of the parsimonious and capricious nature of the Liberal government's handling of university affairs, especially in matters of finance. He took almost immediate action. Within months of taking office in 1905, he personally introduced measures that he hoped would quickly end the financial and administrative problems of the provincial university. Government grants were announced to underwrite the construction of men's residences, a new physics building, an addition to the science building, a convocation hall, and hospital facilities to be shared with the city. In addition, the new government proposed further public expenditures of $30,000 annually for university construction, and it would continue for the next thirty years.[42] In the face of the announcement, the opposition Liberals were reduced largely to silence, while the public generally greeted it with praise. Even the university's friends who were long-time Liberals were drawn to congratulate Whitney privately.[43]

Premier Whitney also dealt swiftly with the administrative chaos of the University of Toronto. On 5 October 1905, he appointed a royal commission to examine the relations of the university to its several colleges and to the school of practical science, and to come up with a scheme for sound management and governance. Its membership personally chosen by Whitney, the commission was a distinguished one, consisting of Joseph W. Flavelle (chairman), Sir William Meredith (former leader of the Conservative party of Ontario), Byron E. Walker (of the Canadian Bank of Commerce), Goldwin Smith, Canon H. J. Cody (rector of St Paul's Anglican Church, Toronto), the Reverend D.B. Macdonald (principal of St Andrew's College), and A.H.U. Colquhoun (secretary). Notably absent from it was any active member of the Ontario professoriate.

Six months later, on 4 April 1906, after soliciting advice and opinions concerning university governance from several leading universities in Canada and the United States, the commissioners submitted their report to the Whitney government, summarizing their 'principal conclusions' as follows:

1 The powers of the Crown in respect to the control and management of the University should be vested in a Board of Governors, chosen by the Lieutenant-Governor-in-Council, and subject by the method of appointment and by the regulation of their proceedings, to the perpetual authority of the state.

2 The Senate, with its legislative and executive powers and based upon the principle of representation of the federated and affiliated institutions and the faculties and graduates, should direct the academic interests of the University.

3 The School of Practical Science should be united with the University as its Faculty of Applied Science and Engineering, and the same intimate connection should, as far as practicable, apply to the relations of the Faculty of Medicine to the University.

4 University College should continue as now constituted, with a Principal, Faculty Council and Registrar of its own, its administration being under the direction of its Faculty Council, subject to the control of the Governors, and appointments to the staff being made on the recommendation of the President of the University.

5 There should be created, a Council of the Faculty of Arts composed of the faculties of all the Arts Colleges and representatives of the federated colleges, and a Council for each Faculty.

6 There should be created a Caput or advisory committee, having authority in certain matters of University discipline, which may act as advisory to the President.

7 The office of Chancellor should be retained, its occupant to be elected by the graduates and to preside over Convocation and confer degrees.

8 The office of Vice-Chancellor should no longer exist, its functions and duties being transferred, in certain respects, to the President.

9 The office of President should be clothed with additional powers, making its occupant in fact as well as name the chief executive officer of the University.[44]

The commissioners rather cleverly attached a draft act to their report, and the Whitney government made only minor changes to it when preparing legislation.[45] The resulting University of Toronto Act of 1906 was, arguably, among the most important pieces of provincial legislation in the history of higher education in Ontario – certainly in the history of the University of Toronto. It provided the basis for effective management by strengthening the power of the university president and by defining responsibilities, ended (as Whitney had long claimed he would) the constitutional basis for political control over internal university affairs, made provision for effective handling of internal disciplinary problems, and recognized the necessity of adequate financial support by the state. In short, it provided the basis for ending the tragicomic performances of the previous quarter century in a remarkably abrupt fashion. Moreover, it provided a secure means of engaging more fruitfully in the central questions of university life. 'We have arrived at a critical juncture in the progress of University education,' wrote the commissioners. 'The question presents itself, whether the main object shall be, as it has hitherto been, intellectual culture, or the knowledge which qualifies directly for gainful pursuits ... Science, properly so-called, is culture of its kind and those who pursue it may in turn imbibe the spirit of culture by association. We could not pretend, in confronting this great question, to forecast or regulate the future. We could do no more than provide a home for culture and science under the same academic roof ...'[46]

Industry and Engineering

By the early twentieth century it had become rather easier to declare rhetorically that the university of the future would be one with a healthy balance between culture and science than actually to balance the equation. The authority of science was reaching its zenith. 'The nineteenth century may be described as a hundred years of human progress under the guidance of science,' declared a scientist at Queen's University confidently in 1895. 'Scientific discoveries [are] organized by the great universities, scientific schools, and industrial corporations. Science and industry are at last wed. As a consequence, there has been rapid advance in the material well-being of the civilized world during the last fifty years. In the control of physical forces man has reached a height never before attained, and is able to accomplish feats of construction, in view of which the tales of the Arabian Nights seem true. These great powers are in the hands of Christian nations.'[47] In the context of the day, it was difficult to object to such enthusiastic encomia, even if they indicated that the connection between Christianity and science was becoming one rooted in rhetoric rather than reality.

Although often portrayed as the result of inventive genius, a variation of the myth of the self-made man, nineteenth-century science, and the national well-being that resulted from it in fact derived increasingly from an institutional alliance between the growing scientific community and the leaders of the industrial order.[48] Science and industry were indeed wed by the end of Victoria's century – especially in England, Germany, and the United States. Canadian capitalists wanted their own share in the vast benefits of this modern nuptial, as did that segment of the academic community which would profit from corporate or state aid for their scientific ventures. The result, by the turn of the century, was a virtual crusade, born of necessity, for forms of education suitable for industrial advance.

The recommendations of the 1906 Royal Commission on the University of Toronto must be viewed in this context. The commission's report was remarkable not only for the way in which it set up the mechanisms by which the administrative problems of the University of Toronto could be solved, but also for the way in which it reflected the recognition by members of the business and industrial communities that the modern university, like the school system, was vitally linked to the creation of a skilled industrial labour force. The commissioners may indeed have been visionary, but what was the nature of the vision? The Canadian Manufacturers' Association believed it to be close to its own. Shortly after the commission's report was released, S. Morley Wickett, chairman of the CMA's 'technical education committee,' reported to his constituency that 'practically all' its recommendations had been accepted by the commission and could be found in its report. These included 'the definite co-ordination of practical and theoretical branches of University work ... provision for laboratory and other work by manufacturers and their employees,' and 'the need for the University to consider how it might better aid the advancement of industrial research.' Wickett declared his satisfaction that the attitude of the university towards industry had been modified. 'Your committee is of the opinion (an opinion which is evidently shared by the Government Commission) that a University, particularly in a young country like Canada, should seek to meet the wants of the country at large, and not aim at being merely a cultural institution in the older sense. We have no leisure class. Everyone, whether he enters a University or not, must be trained to earn his own living.'[49]

From virtually the moment Macdonald's National Policy was introduced in 1879, industrialists and educators in Ontario had lobbied for technical education within the provincial school system. If Canada was truly to become an advanced industrial nation skilled workmen were necessary. Particularly after 1896 the campaign for technical education, and the funding of it, became a major concern of boards of trade, the Trades and Labour Congress of Canada, and the Canadian Manufacturers' Association. Prime Minister Laurier, in particular, was lobbied by these associations and by concerned individuals to regard the question of technical education as a matter of federal jurisdiction under the Department of Trade and Commerce. Although educational matters were clearly assigned constitutionally to the provinces, under section 93 of the British North America Act, lobbyists for federal initiative concerning technical education argued that it properly fell within the intentions of section 91, which had charged the federal government with responsibility for providing the economic requisites for nation-building. Aware of the political consequences within Quebec of a decision to allow federal intervention in educational matters, Laurier took no initiative. Not until William Lyon Mackenzie King became minister of labour in 1908 did the lobbyists for federal funding and coordination of technical education find a receptive voice in the Liberal cabinet.[50] Meanwhile, the Canadian Manufacturers' Association argued consistently and often in its journal *Industrial Canada* that systematic industrial training in the nation's schools was essential if Canada was to progress economically and to be competitive in international trade.[51]

Largely as a result of the initiative and interest of Mackenzie King, who badgered both cabinet colleagues and provincial premiers into accepting that some form of action on the matter of technical education was necessary, the Laurier government announced in January 1910 the formation of a Royal Commission on Industrial Training and Technical

Education. The first volume of its report was released in 1913, promoting the desirability of industrial training in public secondary schools, stressing the relation of such education to the health of the national economy, and recommending that, while technical education should remain within provincial jurisdiction, all levels of government should be responsible for financing it. In particular, the commission suggested that the federal government create a development fund into which would be put $3,000,000 per year for ten years.[52] But by the time the commission published its report the Liberal government had fallen. The Conservative government of Robert Borden took no action. Without a champion in the Borden cabinet, posing problems of constitutional jurisdiction affecting federal-provincial relations, and overshadowed by the advent of the Great War, the matter of technical education was largely glossed over until 1919, when problems of demobilization and reconstruction made it an issue no longer possible to ignore. The result was the Technical Education Act, aimed at 'promoting the mechanical trades and [increasing] the earning capacity, efficiency and productive power of those employed therein.'[53]

Concurrent with the growth of the lobby for technical education in secondary schools was a less coordinated but scarcely less important campaign for similar training at a more advanced level. Initiatives came from different agencies and they were directed at the needs of the major sectors of the emerging industrial economy of Ontario. By the early 1870s, for example, the provincial administration had recognized the need for some form of advanced training for engineers, and after commissioning J.G. Hodgins, deputy superintendent of education for Ontario, to visit such American institutions as Harvard, Yale, and the Massachusetts Institute of Technology to investigate the state of engineering education, it passed legislation in 1871 creating a College of Technology in Toronto. The new institution was not, however, intended to be a professional school but was intended instead to produce technicians and mechanics. It conferred no degrees, and in general was an institution that reflected the traditional association of the engineer with the mechanic, the building tradesman, and the architect.[54] This reflected the fact that, in contrast to physicians and lawyers, the nineteenth century North American engineer did not occupy, in sociological terms, a 'functionally homogeneous area of the social division of labor.'[55] Translated, this means that in the public mind the services he performed were scarcely differentiated from those of the craftsmen who built and operated the canals and railroads, or who had learned their skilled trades by apprenticeship in the machine shops, mines, and forests of the nation. Historically, it also meant that the attainment of professional status by engineers was a much more difficult task than it had proved to be for the medical and legal communities. This process was made even more difficult in the twentieth century by the necessary association of most engineers with large industrial firms, a condition of dependence that effectively made many of them salaried employees. As a prominent professor at Columbia University defined engineering: it was the 'science of making money for capital.'[56]

It is therefore understandable that when the provincial government of Ontario established its College of Technology it made a point of ensuring that the institution was not connected with the provincial university. The success of the major American scientific schools, wrote J.G. Hodgins, was 'just in proportion to their entire practical separation for teaching and other purposes from the other parts of the University.'[57]

It is fair to say that for these reasons the College of Technology set up in 1871 bore more resemblance to a mechanics' institute than it did a faculty of engineering. The initial 181 registrants, most of them mechanics, were treated to evening lecture classes in drawing, physics, and chemistry. No fees were charged. But almost immediately it was recognized that the school was not adequate to the task of providing the technological leaders of an industrial society. By 1873 Adam Crooks had introduced legislation to create a School of Practical Science – one that would provide instruction in mining, engineering, and the 'mechanical and manufacturing arts.' It was a hybrid institution, performing the function of an evening school for artisans yet having the capacity for transformation into a professional school. The legislation did not place the school under the jurisdiction of the University of Toronto, but provision was nevertheless made for the lieutenant-governor in council to allow students of University College to attend lectures at it, or, conversely, for its students to sit examinations given by the university and to receive degrees and honours awarded by it.[58] Led by James Loudon, who recognized that the affiliation of the engineering school with the university was essential to the success of scientific enterprise in both, advocates of a professional and academic school of engineering directly connected with the University of Toronto began to lobby both the university community and the politicians at Queen's Park. So, indirectly, did W.H. Ellis, principal of the School of Practical Science, who stated in his third annual report (1875) that 'It would seem ... that the time had now arrived when circumstances would justify, and indeed command, the adoption of some more extended and more permanent scheme.'[59]

By 1878 the School of Practical Science was located on the University of Toronto campus. Initially it offered a three-year diploma course to full-time students in civil, mechanical, and mining engineering. Four of its six staff members were professors at the University of Toronto, leading to inevitable conflicts as university and non-university men struggled to define jurisdictions and to gain and consolidate power in the new institution.[60] Evening classes were abandoned. Its students were not now mechanics, eager for a degree of training that their jobs alone could not provide; they were drawn, instead, from the university's faculty of science, from the city's medical schools, and from the Ontario Veterinary College. By 1884 the professionalization of the school was formalized when the degree of Civil Engineer was authorized by the University of Toronto senate. The next year witnessed the founding of the Engineering Society of the School of Practical Science. After the passing of the Federation Act of 1887, further consolidation of the connection of the School of Practical Science and the university took place. With an 1889 Order in Council, the science departments of the school were transferred from University College to the University of Toronto proper; associated with this transfer was the passing of a senate statute in the same year affiliating the school to the university. This was, in turn, confirmed by provincial Order in Council. The first principal of the newly reorganized School of Practical Science, effectively the faculty of engineering of the University of Toronto, was Professor John Galbraith.[61]

By the end of the nineteenth century the politicians of the province of Ontario had come to recognize the necessity of advanced industrial training, for they had also begun to glimpse the economic and political rewards that might follow from the sound exploitation of what people were coming to call the 'New Ontario.' 'The "lure" of the North has come to rival the "Call" of the West,' wrote a student of Queen's University. This New Ontario, an Ontario whose future faced north as much as south, was a province of vast economic potential, with incalculable wealth to be gained from the full exploitation of its minerals and forests.[62] Faced with a conservative business community that was less than venturesome and a population that prided itself on its sober agricultural origins, the Ontario government of the late nineteenth century embarked on a broad educational program intended to encourage investment in the resource sector and 'purposefully to convert an agricultural into an industrial people.'[63] The Crown Lands Department began vocational and professional educational programs in lumbering in the early 1890s, and the report of the provincial Royal Commission on the Mineral Resources of Ontario, published in 1891, made advanced training in mining techniques and management a major educational issue when it expressed 'astonishment at the incompetence and ignorance of Ontario's prospectors, miners and mine managers ...'[64]

Queen's University responded quickly to the challenges of new forms of mechanical mining technology, which were making traditional mining operations conducted by a hierarchy of skilled workers using hand tools and 'common sense' appear out of date.[65] By the 1890s Queen's faced great difficulty in financing the development in the sciences necessary for the university to become the 'national' one desired by its ambitious principal, G.M. Grant. Yet as soon as the Royal Commission on Mineral Resources had reported, he was ready with a scheme for the creation of a school of mining that would serve the needs of north-eastern Ontario and be located in Kingston. A large contingent from Kingston had made a similar case in 1886, after the provincial government had announced its intention to establish the School of Practical Science in Toronto. No immediate support for the Kingston proposal was forthcoming. As a result, Grant spent the next few years superintending the financing and construction of the university's new science building, Carruthers Hall. Special courses on assaying were given in it to Ontario miners and prospectors by 1890. With the 1891 passage of legislation providing for the creation of mining schools throughout the province, Grant renewed his appeal for support to the Mowat cabinet and especially to the premier. (Besides being a Presbyterian, Oliver Mowat was also the son of a founder of Queen's and the brother of one of its senior professors.) Financial support in the amount of $25,000 for the founding of a school of practical science, associated with Queen's, had already been provided by Kingston and its surrounding districts; Grant now asked Mowat for an annual grant of $6,000. Mowat agreed, on the condition that the school instead be called one of 'mining and agriculture' rather than 'practical science' and that the word 'applied' not be used in connection with scientific subjects taught.[66]

Thus was founded the Kingston School of Mining and Agriculture, technically distinct from Queen's University but in all but name its faculty of applied science and more. W.L. Goodwin was transferred to it from the staff of Queen's, and he served as the director of the School of Mining from its inception in 1893 to 1916, when he became dean of the university's faculty of applied science. In effect, Principal Grant had contrived a means by which the provincial government would subsidize teaching and research in other sciences, for by the transfer of staff from university to school the university had virtually relinquished its departments of chemistry, geology, and mineralogy. Throughout the 1890s and continuing into the new century advocates of the centralization of advanced training in mining and forestry in Toronto, in connection with the provincial university, expressed their outrage at Grant's raid on the public coffers. Queen's was still, after all, a denominational institution. As President Loudon later wrote to Minister of Education Richard Harcourt: 'the School has developed into a School not only of General Engineering but of all the Sciences included in the Arts Faculty of a Modern University (Mathematics, Chemistry, mineralogy, Geology, Physics, biology). It is also authorized to establish a School of Forestry. In other words it has become a Technical University, and the name "Mining School" is a misnomer. Under the guise of this misleading name the School has received annual grants which now exceed those voted to the Provincial Engineering School.' Authorities at Queen's had long heard such charges, and were adept at rebutting them.[67]

Despite the outcry, the Ross administration announced its intention to finance the construction of a substantial building to house the School of Practical Science at the University of Toronto and to grant the Kingston School of Mining an annuity of $6,000. But the latter amount, declared the Toronto *Mail,* was 'equivalent to a capital investment of $200,000 ... equivalent to the sum of $200,000 which is to be spent on a Science building for Toronto University.'[68] The Conservative opposition in the provincial legislature and elements of the Toronto daily press expressed their outrage at 'the disingenuous tactics of the Premier' on the matter. Had George Ross not stealthily diverted public funds to a denominational institution, Queen's, while claiming only to be aiding the cause of industrial expertise? 'It is time,' fulminated the Toronto *World,* 'the country realized ... that Premier Ross ... and Principal Grant are working out the details of an insidious conspiracy to convert Queen's University from a denominational to a state institution ... The conspiracy began about ten years ago. The first step in the deal was to establish a School of Mining in connection with Queen's University. This occurred in 1893. This School of Mining is today the science department of Queen's University.'[69]

Aided by such alarmist reports in the daily press, the University of Toronto continued its campaign to convince the government to confine financial aid to its own School of Practical Science.[70] In the legislative session of 1903, political agitation reached a peak over the issue, with Leader of the Opposition Whitney voicing strong criticism of the Ross government's neglect of the University of Toronto and University College and of its failure 'to put the finances of these institutions on a sound, stable and permanent footing.'[71]

A mere three years later the Royal Commission on the University of Toronto made its recommendations. Closer affiliation, it said, should exist between the university and the School of Practical Science, and adequate provincial funding should be forthcoming. The same was said for the faculty of medicine. A faculty of law should be established within the university. A school of forestry should be created, as should household science, art, and music schools. In general, the commissioners took advantage of the high public profile of the technical education issue, and also, in effect, called upon Whitney – now premier – to act in office in a manner consistent with the thrust of his earlier criticisms of the Ross administration.[72] The result was a vision of a University of Toronto of the future – a university with faculties of arts and science at its centre, but surrounded with publicly funded professional faculties of all varieties. A vision it was, but one rooted in educational ideals and political and economic realities in equal measure.

The Canadian Manufacturers' Association readily provided a forum in the pages of *Industrial Canada* for members of the academic community to make their case for the value of universities to the industrial order. W.L. Goodwin, of the Kingston School of Mining, reminded the manufacturers in 1902 that as a result of an 1896 request by the provincial government for his school to study one recently discovered mineral, with a view to investment in its production in Ontario, a company had been formed that now produced it to an annual value of $100,000 a year, at a time when the province's investment was only $6,000.[73] Articles also began to appear arguing that the world's universities had, in a sense, always been 'trade schools.' The emphasis had simply shifted from an education aimed at 'the training of leaders of men' (for example the clergy) to one directed towards 'the development and progress of productive power on which the wealth, the welfare, the greatness, the very existence, of the world depends.'[74] Such assessments led to recommendations by the CMA that the universities institute a system of 'industrial fellowships' along the lines of those recently inaugurated by the University of Kansas. Few manufacturers, said *Industrial Canada*, had the time to 'work out' technological and scientific problems. 'The Universities, on the other hand, have a corps of students trained in laboratory work, and with plenty of time on their hands.'[75]

One word in addition to 'profit' served to rally the disparate interests – industrial, academic, political – into a group more or less united, if lacking leadership. The word was 'Germany.' At almost all points in discussions of technical education within *Industrial Canada*, and in virtually every speech on the subject given by President James Loudon, the example of German scientific accomplishment was mentioned, at first in admiration but increasingly in fear. Loudon never tired of reminding his audience that Germany was 'the home of technical education,' and when in 1906 the CMA petitioned the governor-general of Canada, Lord Grey, to appoint a royal commission on technical education it quickly pointed to 'The Example of Germany.'[76] German supremacy was especially apparent in the chemical industry. In 1901 Loudon estimated that the manufacturers of Germany employed at least 4,500 chemists. Four years later W.R. Lang, professor of chemistry at the University of Toronto, reminded Canadian manufacturers that the university, not the technical school, was the only location for serious chemical research.[77]

Yet in May 1913 the Canadian Manufacturing Association was still lamenting the absence of any substantial degree of advanced chemical research beyond what was conducted in the laboratories of the federal Departments of Agriculture and Inland Revenue; it urged the formation of a Canadian bureau of chemistry.[78] By December of the next year, the first of the Great War, when the Society of Chemical Industry of Canada had its annual meeting, morale within the scientific community was understandably low. 'War has broken out between the leading European nations and we find ourselves in conflict with the country which has achieved the principal successes in the domain of chemistry.'[79] However much the war itself came as a shock to Canada's scientists, the advanced degree of German preparation for the technological requirements of modern battle was well known to them. 'The Germans are fully alive to the necessity of being well prepared to engage in the struggle for industrial supremacy,' wrote a contributor to *Industrial Canada* in 1905. To this end, he quoted Prince Otto von Bismarck: "'The war of the future is the economic war, the struggle for existence on a large scale. May my successors always bear this in mind, and take care that when the struggle comes we are prepared for it.'"[80]

No Canadian was remotely prepared for the Great War of 1914–18. Canadian scientists had virtually no national institution for advanced scientific research, and the nation's politicians had proven incapable of providing even for its national naval service. The growth of university enrolment but not budgets in the pre-war years in fact hampered scientific research as students and professors alike struggled for scarce resources and space.[81] At the same time, Ontario academicians were scarcely ready to face the ironies involved in a war against Germany, at once the font of the research ideal so prized by James Loudon and of the idealist philosophy that, as will be seen, helped so much to accommodate many Canadian Protestants to the challenges of evolutionary theory.

Smaller but no less poignant ironies became apparent as the causes of science, research, and industry were advanced in Canadian university circles in the years preceding the Great War. The 1906 Royal Commission on the University of Toronto marked in an important way the triumph of the notion that science, research, and professionalism should have a vital place in the modern university, and no member of the University of Toronto faculty had done more for furthering this cause than had James Loudon. Yet one of the unstated but well-understood intentions of the commissioners was that Loudon was to be replaced and a new president appointed. Loudon knew this, and resigned shortly after the commission reported – that is, at the very moment when the university he had studied and taught at, served, and helped direct for the better part of forty years was about to take the form he had sought for it.

Premier Whitney provided Howard Ferguson with a profile of the kind of skills he wanted the new president to possess. He wanted someone 'fairly well educated, very level-headed, a man who understands human nature thoroughly and who knows something of Collegiate management. In addition, he should be a man of great force of Will, not hasty in his decisions, but firm as a rock when he has come to a decision ... an intellectual tyrant. If you take away any offensive meaning of the word "tyrant" you will have my exact view.'[82] The choice, it turned out, was a Presbyterian clergyman from Nova Scotia. Responsibility for securing 'a home for science and culture under the same academic roof' at the University of Toronto was given to Robert Falconer, former principal of Pine Hill Divinity College, Halifax. The 'intellectual tyrant' hired by the premier as president of the University of Toronto was a professor of theology greatly influenced by philosophical idealism. As the provincial university entered an era preoccupied by the triumphs and practical consequences of science, Robert Falconer began to go about the task of convincing humanists, scientists, and businessmen that science and technology did not threaten humanistic values because they embodied the best results of human thought. The modern university, he told the members of the Canadian Manufacturers Association in 1911, 'stands for the advancement of science, knowledge, the humanities, those principles that are concerned with the constitution of man as a physical being in a physical environment, as a being with a mind, a memory, an imagination, as a member of a society in which alone he attains to what on this earth we call life.'[83] Manufacturers, engineers, architects, chemists, and miners embodied 'the mind, the controlling thought of our industrial life. Through them and on their advice, the energy and will of the capitalist set into motion the machinery of our modern world.' The destructive potential of this fusion of mind and machinery, this Faustian 'will to mastery' so central to the industrial revolution in nineteenth-century Europe,[84] would be soon be tested.

8

Understanding Social Change

The face of Ontario was fundamentally changed by its industrial revolution. Between the 1880s and 1914 Canada witnessed an integration of its economy into a national entity, an increased concentration of capital into its central regions, a decline of the economic competition that was the dogma of orthodox economic theory, a wave of immigration from central, eastern, and southern Europe that permanently altered the existing ethnic balance between Canadians, and a growth of complexity in all its social institutions that the United States had experienced decades earlier.[1]

In more subtle ways, the experience of university students – who on the surface appeared to exist in the protective cloister of the Ontario university's ivory tower – also changed. Students of the 1880s returning for class reunions in 1914 would scarcely have recognized the campuses they had left, so great had been the physical expansion of facilities. The number of faculties and the range of choices of subjects available to their sons and daughters would either have excited or appalled them. The interests, values, and expectations of the student generation of 1914 were very different from those of the 1880s, for undergraduates were not left untouched by the swirl of social and intellectual change that some thought threatened to unhinge the basis of nineteenth century civilization. They did not lead in this reorientation, at least during their student days; but they were affected by it, and the shifting direction of their activities while at university indicated that the university in Ontario scarcely confirmed the myth of the ivory tower.

In many respects, the pattern of social and intellectual development in Canada during the late nineteenth century reflected that of North America as a whole. American commentators have consistently been of the view that the period from approximately 1890 to the Great War marked a major transformation of American culture and society – a transformation exceeding in degree that of previous eras. The American of the 1890s would have shared much more with his compatriot of the 1930s, for example, than he would have with his forebears of the 1830s.[2] 'The decade of the 1890s,' one historian declared, 'was nothing less than the watershed of American history.'[3] Others have since agreed. Whether discussing the general 'reorientation of American culture,' the growth of a bureaucratic ethos that sought order in social affairs, 'the nineteenth century crisis of authority,' or the origins of an American 'culture of consumption,' recent observers have accepted this view and extended it into all aspects of American society and culture.[4]

A major reorientation of English-Canadian culture and society also occurred between the 1880s and the 1920s. 'The articulate Victorian at the turn of the century' in Canada faced 'an intellectual quandary' because nineteenth-century ideals no longer seemed adequate to cope with the bewildering and complex problems of the age.[5] This was also sensed by articulate observers at both ends of the decade of the nineties. In 1888, for example, an anonymous writer noted that 'the higher a civilization may be the greater is its complexity and the more numerous are the forces which have been and are at work upon it.'[6] This sense of increased complexity in almost all aspects of contemporary life, a sense which came to special prominence in Central Canada in the 1880s, gave rise to a feeling of social, intellectual, and moral drift by the early twentieth century. In 1904 Goldwin Smith's long-time secretary, Arnold Haultain, captured this mood when he wrote that the nineteenth century seemed to have brought Canadians 'to the edge of a precipice,' and to have left them there 'gazing wistfully into outer space.' Science had given atoms and evolution to the Victorian, but had failed to solve many of the Victorian world's fundamental problems. The twentieth century, as a result, was 'an age which sees that it must find a solution for itself, but has no data for the task, and as yet can do little more than stand shivering timorously on the brink.'[7]

The intellectual basis of the reorientation of English-Canadian social thought that would take place in the first two decades of the twentieth century was laid, for the most part, in the last quarter of the nineteenth century. At issue was nothing less than an understanding of the nature and mechanisms of social change. In the years between the 1870s and the advent of the Great War, ones that witnessed the emergence of the social sciences from Victorian mental and moral philosophy, Ontario students and their professors began to address the intellectual problems raised by life in a complex and interdependent industrial society. These were years in which the life of the mind shifted in major ways. Recognition of the complexity and interdependence of economic and social relations gave rise to questions about the nature and mechanisms of social causation for which traditional Christian teleology had, it seemed, no adequate answer.

It would be misleading, however, to speak of a decline of faith as new and secular forms of social understanding gained acceptance. Faith, in the sense of suprarational commitment, did not decline in the late Victorian and Edwardian years in English Canada. Rather, the grounds of belief and authority shifted. Middle-class Ontarians associated with the province's universities experienced less a withdrawal of faith than a transformation of it. In the realm of higher education they began to encounter a question of fundamental importance that academics, students, politicians, and the public would face throughout the twentieth century: was the central function of the modern university to facilitate social cohesion by nurturing an understanding of those elements within the civilized past that were worth preserving, or was it to facilitate the kinds of social change that would serve the new industrial order?

The Problem of Causation

In 1903, the minister of education in Ontario received a memorandum prepared by a member of his staff putting forward the case for more systematic and better instruction in chemistry in the province's high schools. In concluding, the anonymous civil servant waxed eloquent: The era, he said, was a 'busy, hustling, energetic' one, dominated by commercialism but nevertheless growing more liberal and humane and in which superstition and ignorance were giving way to enlightenment and reason. 'What is responsible for the world's advancement? Nothing more so than the application of the science of accounting, which alone makes possible commercial expansion and progress.'[8]

Such a conclusion was extreme: the accountant as social saviour. It was certainly far removed from the traditional notion that by living the earnest life of a professing Christian social improvement would result and that by means of prayer God would intercede on the Christian's behalf. On the surface there appears to be no contradiction, for there was no reason why an accountant could not also be an earnest agent of a Christian God, carrying out His Will. Yet the twin examples of a sincere petition of prayer to God, asking for his intercession in human affairs, and the hard facts of the double-entry ledger serve as symbols of polar extremes of assumption regarding the nature and mechanisms of social change.

Historians have observed that in the half-century or so before the Great War a major shift occurred in the European and North American intellectual understanding of the nature of social causation.[9] It can be argued that the fundamental philosophical questions asked by the nineteenth century hinged around this central concern. What caused societies to change? How did improvement occur? Even the Darwinian debate may be seen as taking place within this larger framework. What was the role of human volition in affecting such change? What was the role of 'social forces'? For that matter, what *were* 'social forces'? How was humankind's freedom and liberty affected in an increasingly complex economic, social, and political world? Was it increased or compromised? What was the nature of that liberty? Did people control their own destiny in such a world? These were questions linked, ultimately, with assumptions that were debated and challenged in the 1870s and 1880s in Europe and the United States, generally in the context of the social consequences of evolutionary theory. In doing so, they defined the boundaries of new disciplines.[10] In Canada such questions arose relatively later. They did, however, arise, and when they did they were to have profound consequences for the reorientation of the curricula of the nation's universities.

The first sign that the question of social causation had become a serious issue in Canada occurred not within the universities but in the pages of the *Canadian Monthly and National Review*, the leading journal of Ontario's literati, in the mid-1870s. In God-fearing Ontario it was understandable that the question arose in the context of a debate between contributors on the origin and nature of morality. The publication of Darwin's *The Descent of Man* in 1871 had raised the question of whether ethical systems, like the human species itself, 'evolved' as part of the natural order. Popularizers of the new 'evolutionary naturalism,' such as England's Herbert Spencer, began to extend Darwinian science into all aspects of human knowledge. Ethics, in Spencer's view, consisted not of revelations based on metaphysical systems such as Christianity but rather on conduct, which he defined as the adjustment of acts to ends. All human beings, like animals, seek pleasure as they use the environment to best advantage and needed no reference to external authority to do so. In short, just as the numerical entries in an accountant's ledger were the 'data' on which he made financial decisions, measured reflection on whether actions would bring pleasure or pain constituted the 'data of ethics,' making a 'science of ethics' possible. But if the ethical nature of actions could be determined by reference only to the natural order, were God and Christ not superfluous? If conduct could be measured in a similar way, what was the value of petitioning God to answer prayers? Did the idea of the miraculous bear any meaning in the age of naturalistic ethics and 'social Darwinism'? Contributors to the *Canadian Monthly* faced the implications of precisely these questions in the 1870s.

When they did so, it was initially to respond not to the writings of the influential Spencer, but to a Canadian living in England: George J. Romanes. Born in 1848 on Wolfe Island, near Kingston, son of the professor of Greek at Queen's University, Romanes was a student in Cambridge when his controversial essay *Christian Prayer and Natural Laws* (1874) was published. In it, 'Romanes contended that religious apologists should not attempt to explain the manner in which God might answer prayer for that knowledge lay beyond the ken of human beings. There was no reason to believe that God could not employ natural laws to answer prayer ... He then countered naturalistic writers ... who had argued that natural law forbad the possibility of answers to prayer. Romanes declared that philosophy, by which he meant naturalistic philosophy, must "above all things abstain from the folly of asserting what the Unknown God can or cannot do – what He does or not desire: – so shall she cease to stultify herself, and to mislead the less thoughtful of her children."'[11]

Romanes's argument against dogmatism, whether of the Christian or of the evolutionary naturalist, provoked responses from both sides in the *Canadian Monthly*. Thus began the 'prayer debate,' centred on belief or disbelief in the miraculous. Agnes Maule Machar, daughter of a former principal of Queen's University, wrote on behalf of the community of Christian believers and asserted that it was perfectly reasonable for them to ask God in prayer to disrupt the laws of nature in order to meet their earnest requests. Christ himself had asked Him to 'give us this day our daily bread.'[12] In turn, the cause of evolutionary naturalism found its Canadian champion in the person of William Dawson LeSueur, an Ottawa civil servant. LeSueur argued that the Christian could not expect to live in a dualistic mental world, one in which God could capriciously violate natural laws by performing sought-for miracles and another in which those laws, in the everyday activities of life, were seen to be inviolable.[13] The debate continued, politely but in great earnestness, by Machar, LeSueur, and others. Many thoughtful articles appeared by writers from different backgrounds. Throughout the 1870s Canadian academic philosophers, school teachers, clergymen, and others debated the prayer issue, and extended it into the whole realm of ethical theory, social evolution, evolutionary naturalism, and Christian morality.[14]

W.D. LeSueur was usually at the centre of controversy, for by the mid-1870s he had become one of the foremost North American champions of Spencer's views on the 'data of ethics.' A contributing editor of *Popular Science Monthly*, his 1880 article 'Morality and Religion' summed up the views of the emergent generation of evolutionary naturalists in Canada. He could not accept the view that Christian morality was the only true morality, eternal, unalterable, and existing outside the laws of evolution. Nor could he accept the assertion that the origin of moral action lay outside the laws of the natural world. Such a view violated both common sense and the everyday experience of life. 'In a church which I lately attended,' he wrote,

I heard thanks offered for the interposition of Providence in the case of a fireman who had fallen through the roof of a burning house ... and then a petition – almost in the same sentence – that, inasmuch as in the natural order of things a certain number of firemen would perish in the pursuit of their calling, Divine grace might be extended to them and Divine comfort to their families. Here were two absolutely contradictory ideas presented almost in a breath. If, however, the reverend gentleman who prayed in this wise were to become a life insurance agent, which of the two orders of thought would he adhere to? Would he not confine himself exclusively to the human order, and charge a premium on the lives of firemen ... without the slightest reference to the chances of Divine interposition? Would he abate the smallest fraction in his rates on the score of 'special providences'? I think not; business is business, the faith of the most sceptical philosopher in the constancy of averages is not more profound or unfaltering than that of the man who ... seems to recognize Divine interposition everywhere.[15]

LeSueur's insight – that the crisis of religious authority was directly related to the probability of risk – was, as usual, a prescient one. Twentieth-century philosophers, historians of science, and intellectual historians are only beginning to explore the emergence of classical probability and its diffusion into the public mind in the century and more after the mid-seventeenth century. Champions of 'rational belief' such as John Locke, Robert Boyle, and Pierre Gassendi, who sought to counter destructive forms of scepticism, were willing to concede to absolute sceptics the impossibility of absolute certainty in most human affairs. But they had insisted that 'the conduct of daily life furnished sufficient, if imperfect standards for moral certainty. It was rational to believe or act in religious or philosophical matters if comparable evidence would persuade a "reasonable man" to adopt a course of action in his daily affairs ... Between the poles of absolute certainty and total doubt, the reasonable man interpolated and compared degrees of certainty.'[16] The scientific meaning of probability and the relationship between probability and statistics had to be redefined in the nineteenth century, in part because the French Revolution shook the assumption of scientists, philosophers, and mathematicians that a single enlightened viewpoint could exist even among men. Nevertheless, by the second half of the nineteenth century, a remarriage of both mathematical probability theory and social science was imminent.[17]

LeSueur's invocation of the actuarial tables of the life insurance agent was, in fact, testimony to his belief that the reasonable man could still find workable, approximate truths in the conduct of daily life in the late nineteenth century, a time when the probabilistic revolution met and merged with the industrial revolution, and when the notion of risk inherent in insurance schemes had largely come to be associated, in the mind of the middle class, with family and private security instead of gambling.[18] It found many echoes by the turn of the century, including the 1903 Ontario civil servant who had placed his faith in the ledgers of the accountant, and for the same reason. For neither did any appeal to supernatural authority, to data other than that of the natural order, have any predictive value. Judgments regarding social action could be made only on the basis of empirical data. The difference between them rests in the fact that in the 1870s this matter was still very much debated; by the early twentieth century it was common sense.

The seemingly arcane and abstruse debate on prayer was a popular reflection of a shift in the understanding of social causation that led to a crisis of authority in intellectual life.[19] This crisis was one in which concerned scholars sought to assess the possibilities and limitations of social analysis in a social environment that was highly interdependent but where prediction and explanation of social phenomena were extraordinarily difficult. 'Causal attribution, and the tasks of prediction and retrodiction that depend upon it,' observed one historian, 'become in a highly interdependent universe the business of specialists, beyond the reach of lay opinion ...' Within that complex environment, the possibility of autonomous action was limited; the individual was, in an important sense, the creation of society. As a result, 'nineteenth-century ethical views and the politics based on them would have to give way to a new welfare-oriented humanitarianism and a new politics.'[20]

The evangelical inheritance of English-speaking Canada, especially pronounced in Ontario, had long made the call to individual regeneration a fundamental element in social change. To transform society, or to improve one's own lot in life, required, in the evangelical view, a transformation of the soul. The traditional insistence by Methodists on 'the new birth,' for example, was considered essential for social improvement as well as for individual salvation. But by the 1880s the original evangelical impulse within the protestant community, especially Methodism, was beginning to wane as the churches sought to adjust to an increasingly complex urban environment.[21] By then, Nathanael Burwash reflected, the possibility of students living a life of 'vital religious experience' was directly undermined by 'scientific or philosophical conclusions,' often derived from historical criticism or 'philosophical Agnosticism.' First among the causes of this decline of individual spiritual renewal was, for Burwash, 'a materialistic conception of cause and effect.'[22] Faced with this self-declared 'crisis of his spiritual life,' the student was urged by religious instructors such as Burwash and others to recognize the 'limitations and imperfections of all our knowledge' by 'careful study of the processes by which we arrive at truth and may verify it in our consciousness,' to rely as much upon intuition as upon intellect in this search, and to seek 'a final harmony of all truth, spiritual and natural,' by recognizing that 'while we may for a time fail to solve a difficulty here or a difficulty there, the failure is due to the fact that we have not yet attained to the perfect knowledge of all the facts which round out the perfect unity of truth.'[23] By the late 1880s, the period to which Burwash was referring, such overtly religious appeals were increasingly hollow.

Related to such appeals, and more successful, were ongoing attempts by university authorities and student leaders to keep the development of character a central function of a liberal education. Part of the college ideal from the beginning of higher education in the province, such appeals were perhaps of even more psychological importance in the latter part of the century, for they provided an appearance of social utility for a liberal education, and for the liberal arts colleges, at a time when the social usefulness of the sciences was self-evident. But they also served a broader ideological function. In the larger society of industrial and urban Canada, the continuing insistence by religious, educational, and other social leaders that the common man could better his lot by thrift, sobriety, hard work, and other forms of internal discipline served to remind workers of whatever class that they, not the larger society, were responsible for their fate, for they were autonomous individuals. If they bettered their lot it was because they had successfully cultivated such virtues; if they failed it was because they lacked the discipline to do so. In this way, attention was implicitly diverted from structural inequities in the social system to a failure of personal will. Moreover, said such ideologists, those whose lot was little improved even after the exertion of significant moral discipline should not be discontented, since in any event they had no right to expect a major change in their lives. In short, precisely at a time when the circumscribed nature of individual effort was becoming obvious because of the growing complexity of social and economic realities, the 'myth of the self-made man' reached its height in Canada. The ideology behind the myth involved 'conceding the reality of circumstance without denying the proposition that the individual was responsible for what befell him,' and this depended on the ability to get that individual 'to accept an altered idea of what constituted success.'[24]

Throughout the period up to the Great War, just as members of the public were encouraged to accept their lot and to believe that they alone were responsible for their fate, university students were constantly reminded by college presidents, particularly in the smaller institutions, that the formation of character and the cultivation of an acceptable code of personal conduct was an essential element in their education. Students, for their part, recorded at least a formal acceptance of this ideal. 'The true aim of all education,' declared a Queen's student in 1890, 'is to develop the man, and not simply to increase the amount of what he knows.' 'I tell you honestly,' confessed a McMaster student in 1897, 'that it is not McMaster's intellectual training I value most ... But I count most valuable your nurture of true personality, your development of a generous and noble manhood.' Another student concluded in 1910 that 'We need development – that is why we come to college, but no development can equal self-development. The best men are what they are by their own right – individuals self caused ...'[25] But by the late nineteenth century, other imperatives of university life were evident to the student, and they were not always easily compatible with the idea of the individual's moral nurture. While the call for such self-culture remained part of the rhetorical refrain of college convocations and inspirational pieces in student newspapers, it was increasingly divorced from its evangelical origins.

By the 1880s students showed themselves to be well aware that their own academic environment was beginning to reach a level of social and institutional complexity mirroring life in the outside world. To begin with, the increasing range of academic choices made possible student careers that did not necessarily have anything to do with the cultivation of moral faculties or gentlemanly qualities. Students at the University of Toronto in the 1880s and 1890s, witnesses to the great expansion of facilities for study, could only have been reminded that the university was now a complex social institution. In 1888 a biological building was constructed, and it was enlarged only two years later. By 1892 a psychological laboratory existed, and by 1894 a chemical laboratory was housed in its own building. Geological and mineralogical studies were conducted in separate facilities by 1905.[26] Students by the 1890s could state, as one Queen's student did, that their university 'has ... outgrown her models,' the Scottish liberal arts universities of the early nineteenth century, for 'the advancing civilization of the latter part of the nineteenth century has made imperative the study of other subjects bearing more directly upon it.'[27] At Queen's, too, facilities for the study of the sciences, including mining and agriculture, gained prominence in the 1890s. By 1893 its fledgling faculty of applied science existed, one that would do practical work on subjects such as architecture, navigation and sanitary plumbing as well as engineering. By the Great War, new buildings dedicated to chemistry, biology, and athletics, as well as other subjects, also stood on the Queen's campus.[28]

Expansion within faculties of arts was less visible, but was at least as important. Such expansion depended less on the existence of expensive physical facilities than it did upon the increase and organization of knowledge and the appointment of staff to profess it, and it reveals much about the reorientation of intellectual life in those years. Queen's provides an illustration. When philosophy professor John Watson arrived at the university in 1872, the entire range of the arts and sciences was distributed between six chairs: classics, history and English literature, mental and moral philosophy, mathematics and physics, and chemistry and natural science. Other subjects such as French and German or political economy were taught by occupants of existing chairs – in these cases, by the professor of history and English literature and that of mental and moral philosophy, respectively. Very little in the way of an academic division of labour existed at the time, for the range of intellectual labour was herculean. No one was a specialist. But by the turn of the century all this had changed. Academic appointments to the faculty of arts and science had tripled and specialization within traditional disciplines had virtually created new ones requiring different skills. The chair of classics at Watson's Queen's was split into chairs of Latin and Greek. The single chair of history and English literature had become four – in history, English literature, French, and German. The one chair of mental and moral philosophy was taught by experts in moral philosophy, in psychology, and in political economy. In each case, this specialization also involved assistant professors and tutors.[29] This was the period in which the vertical hierarchy of professorial rank began. With rank lay status, and by the early twentieth century professorial life was dominated by a veritable aspiration of associate professors.

A similar fragmentation of traditional disciplines had occurred in science. Where once mathematics and physics had formed a single chair, there existed by 1902 'a Professor and Assistant Professor of Mathematics, a lecturer on Applied Mathematics and two tutors, together with a Professor and Associate Professor of Physics, and a Demonstrator.'[30] At the University of Toronto an even greater division of labour took place. There, too, traditional chairs were divided and subdivided in the 1880s and 1890s because of the requirements of specialization and the sheer increase in available knowledge. By the 1890s the appointment of young scholars to full professor status, simply on the basis of an outstanding undergraduate career, was becoming rare. With the recognition of the difficulties imposed on scholarship by the explosion of knowledge came the creation of divisions within professorial ranks based on experience and expertise. By 1892 the position of associate professor had been established, followed by that of assistant professor in 1913.[31] These divisions were paralleled by the increase in honours courses, forms of student specialization. Mathematics and physics were separated in 1882, and physics soon included courses on electricity, physiological optics, and thermodynamics. By 1890 English had been separated from history. Two years earlier a department of political science had been created, previously a subject (as at Queen's) within the vast domain of the professor of mental and moral philosophy.[32]

Curriculum changes reflected, in ways that brief notices in college calendars can never reveal, the shift of causal attribution that was taking place. Whereas in the 1850s and 1860s the science student was taught in his classes that all aspects of science were ultimately linked to God's purposes, initiated in the act of creation, the student of the 1880s suffered from no such illusion. Professors such as James Loudon at Toronto and Nathan Dupuis at Queen's studiously avoided the introduction of any form of metaphysical speculation into their courses, and the specialization of science itself mitigated against any comprehensive grasp of the natural world, at least at the level of undergraduate study. The world of the humanities and the arts, still dedicated largely to the elucidation of moral values, was increasingly alien to that of the sciences. Students of a practical bent could avoid such speculative studies by the simple act of choosing different courses.

It is manifestly impossible to consider the reorientation that occurred within each discipline, much less within individual subjects. Two disciplines, however, old and new, serve to illustrate the redirection of academic scholarship, the crisis of authority, and the new forms of causal assumption. Philosophy and political science were arts subjects much in demand in the late nineteenth century.

The Comforts of Idealism

By the 1870s the days of the centrality of the Scottish common sense tradition in English-Canadian universities were numbered. The philosophy of common sense had been academically popular in Canada because it asserted the existence of individual mental faculties that ranged the spectrum from the intellectual to the moral to the physical. A true education, philosophers working from such assumptions asserted, was one in which the whole man was created by developing each of these aspects of human existence. The object was mental balance, and the equal weight it gave to moral as well as intellectual training suited the needs of those who advocated the mid-nineteenth-century college ideal. Philosophical training by common-sense philosophers had been, in effect, an elaborate rationalization of that ideal in an academic guise, a form of ideological justification of acceptable forms of social behaviour. But neuroanatomical research, largely emanating from Germany in the second half of the nineteenth century, dismissed the notion of hypothetical faculties. The traditional dualism of mind and body was challenged by scientists such as Karl Vögt, who enraged traditionalists by asserting as early as 1847 that 'the brain secretes thought just as the liver secretes bile.'[33]

With the arrival of John Watson at Queen's University in 1872 another form of philosophical inquiry took its place in Ontario universities: philosophical idealism. For the next fifty years Watson advocated a philosophical outlook that held sway over generations of students. Other philosophers, such as George Paxton Young at University College and George Blewett at Victoria College, offered their own variants on the idealist view of life, and they too came to be venerated by students, lingering, as with Watson, in the memories of graduates long after they had ceased to be active or had died. Why? Why did philosophical idealism, rather than some form of evolutionary naturalism derived from the sciences, become the major force in the intellectual life of students between the 1880s and the Great War?

The answer lies partially in the extraordinary combinations of forceful personality and powerful intellect found in such men. But this alone is not enough to account for the institutional memory of Paxton Young in the University of Toronto remaining powerful enough that when a marble bust of him was completed it bore the simple inscription 'Young.' Nor does it account for the many reverential letters John Watson received in the 1930s, almost a generation after his retirement, from students he had taught half a century earlier. The key to the influence of idealism on late nineteenth-century students lay in the peculiar comfort it offered to young and earnest minds in an age of bewildering intellectual and social complexity. Idealism was, first of all, a philosophical system that was confident in the face of the multiple forms of modern scientific investigation. It rejected the problematic dualism of common sense while affirming the moral nature of man. It provided a renewed sense of design in the natural and mental worlds, a sense of purpose, and it did not depend on Paleyite natural theology. In fact, it sought to do nothing less, in Watson's formulation at least, than to provide a way of encompassing and understanding naturalistic science by placing it within the larger framework of the essential rationality of a moral universe, thereby circumscribing and taming it. Inspired by John and Edward Caird at the University of Glasgow, Watson offered students a solution to the problems of life in a complex intellectual and social world. And students, as well as others, listened. In 1898 the editor of the *Queen's Journal* marked the fact that Watson had filled the moral philosophy chair for twenty-seven years. 'Few men,' he noted, 'have been less in the public eye than he, and yet it is not too much to say that the higher intellectual life of our Alma Mater finds its dominant note in him. The honour philosophy course is the aspiration, as it is the despair, of most of the students for the Church. Moreover it is not difficult to discern that his incisive reasoning, and his comprehensive grasp of the deepest problems of life have impressed themselves upon other and younger professors, to their advantage and ours.'[34]

Watson's students could make sense of the complexity of modern life because he stressed, above all, the interrelationship of all phenomena, and took great pains to point out the nature of that relationship.[35] He offered coherence. The philosophical outlook he had inherited from Edward Caird was one which, in spite of being called idealism and stressing the supremacy of the spiritual life, was in fact rooted solidly in an understanding of actual experience. For both men, philosophy had 'ceased to be a mere academic theory, or even a special investigation into a particular section of human life,' but had 'expanded into the nobler discipline of an interpretation of social and political life and institutions, of art and religion, as these developed into ever higher and more perfect forms in the great secular process of history. And philosophy itself ... was in no sense to be divorced from the concrete life of man. It had a law of its own, no doubt; but this was the law by which human reason gradually unfolded itself.'[36]

Watson and colleagues of a similar mind had an interpretation of social reality that seemed to meet the needs of the age. In the light of science and of empirical investigation, denominational differences were coming to be seen as matters of declining importance, and Watson claimed that idealism was aimed at protecting the essentials of Christianity, not its denominational forms. In an age of increasing differentiation in academic subjects, his leading idea was 'the internal relation of all entities.'[37] In an increasingly secular era he sought to relate the ideal life to that very secularity, without proclaiming the secular world to be a threat. In decades when emotional states were coming to be seen as less important in academic life than intellectual rigour, the moral life was, in the idealist formulation, rearticulated as being the very embodiment of reason.[38] Watson elaborated these themes in numerous influential works, most notably *An Outline of Philosophy* (1895), *Christianity and Idealism* (1897), and *The Interpretation of Religious Experience*, given as the prestigious Gifford Lectures at major universities in his native Scotland and published in two substantial volumes in 1912. It is not difficult to see why he became the most popular professor at Queen's, if at the same time the most intellectually feared. In the 1880s and 1890s students clamoured to get into his classes, and no one complained that his Junior Philosophy course was mandatory for all arts and divinity students or that passing Senior Philosophy was necessary in order to graduate with a Queen's honours degree.[39]

The philosophical idealism of the late nineteenth and early twentieth centuries was an elaborate and elegant edifice intended to provide a sense of intellectual and moral unity in an age of increasing pluralism and fragmentation. But it was also more than this: it was also a sustained and heroic attempt to prove that the individual could still be a meaningful moral agent, in control of his own destiny, at a time when impersonal and unseen social forces seemed to be propelling society in directions seemingly beyond individual control. In this task, a rearticulation of the free will versus determinism debate for an industrial age, Watson's was the most articulate and sustained voice, but not the only one. Virtually all university-based philosophers in Ontario in the late nineteenth century addressed the question – by no means an academic one – in their own ways. How can people be free in an interdependent social universe?

The answer of each emphasized self-realization, a major characteristic of late nineteenth-century thought given expression by those who believed that man was by nature a progressive being. Exponents of self-realization believed, in various ways, that 'mankind had undergone a self-transformation through forces rooted in the individual's nature; furthermore, they all tended to hold that the talents and powers of individuals were capable of continuing to transform virtually all aspects of men's social existence. Changes which had been achieved, and were still to be achieved, were regarded as constituting mankind's progress. They were progressive not merely in the sense that men were gradually learning better ways of mastering their environments and achieving their goals, but in the sense that these goals were themselves becoming higher in value. Thus, human nature was viewed as changing, with new and nobler ends coming to dominate the lives of individuals.'[40]

To several generations of Queen's students, Watson taught that one's freedom was realized by the rational search for the 'true good of the individual,' and that this was firmly rooted in the objective social order. 'For the moral consciousness,' he said, 'always involves the recognition of a higher than individual good, and, because this higher good is partially realized in social laws and institutions, the individual feels himself constrained by his reason to submit to it. It is by reflection upon this good as realized in outward laws and institutions that the individual becomes conscious of moral law.'[41] While at first the individual might think that 'custom and external law' should have no 'authority over him' since his first duty is rationally to obey 'the law of his own reason,' upon reflection he would recognize that those externalities in fact represent the social realization of that 'law of reason.' Only by a commitment to the social good, Watson concluded, could self-realization take place. Only then would people be truly free.[42]

The morality of Watson and other Ontario idealists was a social morality; the freedom that flowed from it depended on a commitment to the larger good of the community. Watson's words are worth noting, since they embodied and articulated fundamental premises of early practitioners of social science in Ontario and they inspired a generation and more of students eager to serve: 'It is still true that only by identifying himself with a social good can the individual realize himself. And the reason is that in the community the idea of humanity as an organic unity is in process of realization. That the community has not reached its final form only shows that the moral life is the gradual realization of the ideal life ... Hence the individual man can find himself, can become moral, only by contributing his share to its realization. He must learn that, to set aside his individual inclinations and make himself an organ of the community is to be moral, and the only way to be moral.'[43]

Until his death in 1889, George Paxton Young at University College in the University of Toronto taught a form of idealism inspired by similar concerns and with similar conclusions. Among his first published works was one on the problem of 'Freedom and Necessity,' and a posthumously published collection of his undergraduate lectures was given the title *The Ethics of Freedom*.[44] Like Watson's, Young's was a philosophy of self-realization. He learned 'to distinguish the appearance of things – and persons – from their true nature, to see in human desires and activity not simply the blind play of natural forces but the struggle to realize an ideal essence,' and 'discovered that man is capable of change, of improvement, and that his social, economic, and political institutions must be designed accordingly.'[45] Moreover, Young and other British idealists offered their followers, in place of a Spencerian naturalistic ethics, 'an index for measuring the quality of existing behavior against superior standards that ought to exist.'[46]

Yet idealism exacted its own price. While they did not see their philosophy as inconsistent with the Christian revelation, neither was it dependent on orthodox Christian notions of causality. Theirs was a liberal Protestantism that was relatively easily detached from traditional Christian theological assumptions.[47] Moreover, 'when stripped of its metaphysical associations and treated as a basic psychological concept, the notion of self-realization or self-development [was] unfortunately empty.'[48] In the hands of the less intellectually able, or the gullible, it had the power, as we will see, of forging a 'new Christianity' profoundly different from the old.

Idealism was but one way of trying to comprehend the complexity of the new industrial world propelled by science, and there is no doubt that as expressed by such powerful figures as Watson and Young it helped resolve problems inherent in the material world of science and the moral world of religion as students encountered them in the classroom. Young, said one of his admiring former students thirty-eight years after the master's death, 'had placed more than one sinking and wavering belief on the solid rock of scientific truth.'[49] Those students less capable of understanding the subtleties of the monistic embrace of idealist systems might have accepted the general thrust of the message – that there was no real conflict between science and religion, if both were properly understood – but they still had to face a future life in the post-graduate world. They went to church on Sunday and increasingly they purchased life insurance. Idealism, from this less-elevated perspective, provided a measure of intellectual comfort if no practical solutions to the problems of daily life.

It was capable, however, of changing lives. A glimpse of this is afforded by a rather unique source, *Miriam of Queen's*, a romantic novel about student life at turn-of-the-century Queen's. It is of little literary merit but is good grist for the intellectual historian, for its author, Lilian Vaux MacKinnon, had in fact attended Queen's between 1899 and 1903, graduating with an MA degree in political economy. The novel is primarily concerned with the social scene at the university, but it conveys an accurate glimpse of Watson's dominating presence, for as an honours student Miss Vaux was obliged to take both junior and senior philosophy from him. 'I never worked harder in my life than I did over Senior Philosophy,' Miriam confides to her friend Hugh at one point. Both Miriam and Hugh conclude that the intellectual struggle of studying the doctrines of Immanuel Kant or John Stuart Mill, 'which gripped the very nerve of you, and wrenched the fibres of your brain in that wild clutch after the intangible,' was exhilarating. Yet for others it could be unsettling. At one point, lounging around with a 'freshette,' Miriam hears a sophomore discussing Watson with a friend. 'The Professor has a great way of mixing you up. They say he means to do it. He furrows up your mind in the Junior so that the seed can be sown in the Senior.' Miriam's companion, who has also overheard the conversation, turns to her and says: 'It must be an awful class, that Junior Philosophy. Do you know there was one man took it, who was intending to be a minister, and he lost all his faith and religion, in the lectures, and had to go into Political Science and Law.'[50]

The Quest for a Science of Society

Concurrent with the rise of the intellectual status of idealism within Ontario's universities was a movement for a more down-to-earth approach to such problems. Throughout the country by the 1880s and the 1890s the newspapers provided daily graphic evidence of the increasing sources of division and conflict within the new social order: the entrance of women into the work force, increasing tension between capital and labour, competing interests of urban and rural groups, and sectional and racial conflict.[51] The newspapers themselves generally preached an ethic of consensus, but this was the desired end, not a means of obtaining it. The failure of existing institutions of all sorts to understand and accommodate themselves to such social polarities was by the last decades of the century apparent to many, especially in large cities such as Toronto. Increasing social inequality and class division (symbolized, for example, in a growing differential between salaries and wages[52]), the rise of pro-labour mayors such as W.H. Howland in Toronto, growing discontent of industrial workers over conditions in the workplace, and the state of urban social conditions in general contributed to a state of unease within the middle class, the traditional constituency of the university.[53] Pressures began to mount by the 1880s for the universities to address themselves to the origins of such problems and, if possible, to offer solutions for them. The age was that of science, the avenue of solution was that of the political arena. Universities, it was urged, should attempt to cultivate a science of politics.

Traditionally, theories of politics had been taught by professors of mental and moral philosophy as civil polity. Plato's *Republic*, understandably, was usually the starting-point in student reading. The heavily constitutional nature of the study of history also served to introduce students to political matters. Lectures were given on 'The Development of Monarchy' and 'The British Constitution,' and textbooks such as William Stubbs's *Constitutional History of England*, E.A. Freeman's *Growth of the English Constitution*, and J.G. Bourinot's *Constitution of Canada* were in use, as at Queen's, by the 1880s. But it concerned some by that decade that such works, descriptive and celebratory, did not directly address themselves to current social and political problems.[54]

In the University of Toronto, pressure to provide a more practical approach to politics came from a variety of sources. By 1884, William Houston, an 1872 graduate of the university, librarian of the Ontario Parliament, and a member of the nativist faction within the Toronto alumni, had convinced Chancellor Edward Blake and Vice-Chancellor Mulock (leaders of that faction) to propose the introduction of a course on political science to senate. Senate accepted the proposal, but the University College council refused to act on the grounds that it might introduce 'party politics' and politically sensitive issues such as free trade and protectionism into the classroom.[55] Education Minister George Ross had good grounds by 1887 for fearing that Houston was not the man to teach such a possibly controversial course, for in correspondence with the minister Houston declared that he now preferred the term sociology to political science and proposed to teach a course in a way that closely connected it with the work of Comte and Spencer, thereby, he claimed, making the subject 'a real science' dedicated to the inductive method and social laws. '"Sociology," as thus defined,' he said, 'is extremely important for practical life.'[56] Clearly, Houston, in spite of the best intention to be academically disinterested, would have linked his course to a commitment to social reform. In this respect, he represented that strain within emergent North American social scientists of the 1880s which was more concerned with moral advocacy than with scholarly objectivity.[57]

Two strategies existed for depoliticizing such an appointment. One was to associate the teaching of political science with the newly proposed faculty of law, where the ethical aspects of social and political relations were, given the preoccupations of the profession, of less than pressing academic concern; the second was to appoint a scholar who had no connection to the Ontario political scene. Both avenues were used. Vice-Chancellor Mulock suggested that political science should be made a responsibility of various professors of law.[58] President Wilson had already expressed his concerns to the minister. 'It is most desirable,' he had written in 1887, 'to secure the permanent appointment of a Professor who, giving all his time to the duties of his Chair, shall hold himself entirely aloof from Party politics.' A major concern of Wilson was the possibility that undergraduates might become politicized. To the new appointment, Wilson continued, 'I should entrust the control of the Student's Association and Club; which requires careful handling to keep out of trouble.' Wilson feared that the use of temporary lecturers in political science could damage the university's reputation if they engaged in political controversy.[59] The spectre of William Houston, lurking amidst the rows of books in the Legislative Library, was clearly on Wilson's mind, for Houston was at the time the president of the University College History and Political Science Association.[60] When Ross's department advertised in *Varsity* for the position of professor of political economy early in 1888, it led to a number of excited letters on the question of whether or not the new appointee should be a Canadian.[61]

The decision was made – and at the highest level. In the summer of 1888 Premier Mowat himself, accompanied by Chancellor Blake, went to England, interviewed, and secured the appointment of William James Ashley of Oxford.[62] Ashley, later cross-appointed in arts and law, was clearly apprised of what was and was not expected of him. He indicated to Ross, in correspondence marked 'Private,' that he wished to set up a monograph series similar to one initiated by the Johns Hopkins University, assuring him that 'Each piece of work should be primarily a scientific investigation, and tho' of course the authors would shew their own opinions I should as Editor take care to eliminate all merely partisan expressions – & try to give the Series an altogether non-party character.' This was a reassurance that went beyond addressing the understandable desire by government officials to obtain a serious scholar, dedicated to objective academic research, for among the subjects of proposed monographs were the development of the factory system and the study of poor relief in Toronto.[63] Ashley promised 'objective' scholarship on subjects that some thought required moral judgment, yet he was perfectly willing to be judgmental on other issues. The new science of ethnology was replete with racial and moral pronouncements, but Ashley told Ross that he thought it to be of more value to students of political science than a knowledge of Roman law. Ethnology, he wrote to Ross, 'would help them in dealing with the Chinese, the Indian, & the Negro problems.'[64] The University of Toronto had obtained as its first full-time professor of political science a man who was already an advocate of social reform and would become a very distinguished scholar; but it had also secured someone who, in his attempt to avoid partisan politics, wished not to rock the political boat. Ashley's new program, he assured the minister, would be set up 'in consultation with eminent lawyers.'[65] The Toronto banking community, in particular, took a special interest in the new department.[66]

Queen's University also established the teaching of political science as a subject separated from philosophy or history in these years. Set apart from the intrigues of the provincial capital, Queen's had a less political reason for doing so. John Watson, who had long taught political economy as an element of mental and moral philosophy, found that high student enrolment in his courses required more and more of his time, and his own interests were turning increasingly, by the 1880s, to the philosophy and psychology of religion. Moreover, by then he had a disciple to whom he could entrust instruction in political economy, elsewhere now a subject in its own right. The disciple was Adam Shortt, whose early career as student and as professor says much of the way in which the social sciences emerged from the elaborate edifice of nineteenth-century academic philosophy.

A boy born on a farm near Kilworth, Ontario, Adam Shortt enrolled at Queen's in the 1880s after hearing an inspirational talk in Walkerton by Principal Grant. Soon he fell under the spell of Grant, Watson, and Nathan Dupuis. Intending initially to enter the Presbyterian church as a minister, he soon abandoned such plans, perhaps because of the influence of Watson, his favourite professor. (Is it possible that he was the inspiration for the student who lost his faith in *Miriam of Queen's*?) He specialized in philosophy and science instead, writing his graduating essay on 'Recent English Psychology' – the 'most complete critical statement,' said his mentor, Watson, 'of the Psychology of Mr Herbert Spencer to be anywhere found.'[67] It must be remembered that nowhere did Watson attack science as science; he merely sought to place the scientific perspective in the context of the rational construction of social reality. For this reason, after Shortt's graduation Watson had no difficulty in recommending that Shortt be appointed, in 1885, as instructor in philosophy, and chemistry and botany, at the university. He continued in this role until 1888, when Watson secured for him an appointment to teach political science. The stars of the instructor and his subject had risen by then. In 1889 Shortt was given the John Leys lectureship in political science; in 1891 he assumed the newly created John A. Macdonald professorship in the subject. He continued to occupy it when Lilian Vaux, novelist *manqué*, graduated with the MA degree in political economy he supervised.

In the early career of Adam Shortt we witness the convergence, curious at first glance, of two of the major sets of philosophical assumptions that late nineteenth-century intellectuals utilized to gain command of the complexities of an interdependent industrial society: idealism and empiricism. The Macdonald professor of political science embodied both. It has been argued that the two epistemologies could not be resolved, that idealism and empiricism represented a conflict of 'world views.'[68] What such an interpretation ignores is the fact that the objective idealism of Watson, and, in less technical form, of G.M. Grant, involved no such incompatibility. Watson taught that the social universe was rational, that one could comprehend its essential coherence only by rational thought, not by intuitive beliefs. God, in this view, was the virtual embodiment of reason, and all forms of intuitionist epistemology were accordingly rejected. This suited the personal needs and the academic ambitions of the young Adam Shortt. While increasingly convinced that his future lay in some kind of commitment to factual as distinct from spiritual knowledge, Shortt did not regard the former as a threat to the latter. Concerned, as with Watson, always with the relationship of particular aspects of knowledge to the whole of social reality, his emphasis was simply on the former. 'I am not one of those,' he wrote, 'who believe in running a country or a great organization on theory. You have to run it on facts ... I have no faith whatever in a policy built on sentiment.'[69] With this, too, his mentor, Watson, would only have concurred.

By his own admission Shortt was no social theorist; but he had been educated well by Watson, and he had observed Principal Grant combine an evangelical spirit, a commitment to public service, and idealist principles in a highly active life. Accordingly, Shortt held views on the nature of society, and of the place of human volition within it, that were perfectly consistent with objective idealism even while his own career took him in the direction of a genuine commitment to empirical investigation, and he did so with the energy of an evangelist. Certain general laws, he believed, governed the evolution of any civilization: 'the individuality of each person must be respected ... But this is not the individuality of isolation and independence. It is just because society requires of the individual to forget himself with the social objects and purposes that it can make so much of him in the end, and give him a new and infinitely richer individuality which is the common product of the whole world.'[70] In this way Shortt began to take the premises of objective idealism to their logical conclusions. Rejecting individualism because of the idealist repudiation of any form of subject-object dualism, regarding society as a complex and interdependent series of relationships, and viewing the fullest expression of individuality as a form of self-realization attained by means of a personal identification with social objects and purposes, Shortt, like so many others of his generation, sought to establish a niche for individual social action within the bewildering complexity of social institutions.

The students who entered Queen's and the University of Toronto in the 1890s were, in this way, exposed to a very different approach to the study of society than were those of earlier generations. Increasingly, Shortt turned his attention, and that of his students, to the empirical study of the evolution of the country's economic, political, and financial institutions: tariff and transportation policy, war industries, currency, municipal government, taxation, trade, railways, industrial monopoly, and many other aspects of the 'real' life of Canadian society came under his acute attention.[71] Although highly specialized in their dedication to specific institutions, such studies attempted to place the history and status of each subject into the context of the larger social whole. Inevitably, since many of his conclusions bore implications for possible governmental policy, Shortt rapidly drew the attention of the federal government. By the early twentieth century he was often found in Ottawa on government-related business. In 1903 he was appointed chairman of the Ontario Commission to Investigate Railway Taxation; soon he was intensively involved with the federal department of labour, acting as conciliator between capital and labour in disputes that fell within the jurisdiction of the Industrial Disputes Investigation Act. In 1907 alone he presided over no fewer than eleven conciliation hearings. His impartiality under such conditions resulted in his resignation from Queen's in 1908 to become Civil Service Commissioner. The idealist commitment to public service, stressed so much by Watson and Grant, had not been lost on Shortt. When in the spirit of objectivity he initiated civil service examinations, it was to Watson that Shortt sent the philosophy questions to be marked.

At the University of Toronto a similar reorientation of student and professorial attention away from metaphysical abstractions and towards the empirical bases of contemporary problems and institutions took place in the 1890s. Yet here, too, the shift arose out of the influence of idealists. W.J. Ashley had been a student at Balliol College, Oxford, when T.H. Green was at the height of his influence, and he was an advocate of the 'New Liberalism,' inspired and given direction by Green and the idealist social ethic, that in the mid-1880s found concrete expression in Toynbee Hall and the University Settlement movement. Although he remained apart from partisan politics in Ontario, he brought with him to the University of Toronto the spirit of idealist social reform.[72] Ashley stayed at Toronto only three years, for in 1892 he accepted an appointment at Harvard University. But the pattern and assumptions of political economy at the university had been set.

In his inaugural lecture, given in 1888, Ashley had stated clearly his approach to the subject. He would stress the German historical method rather than classical economic doctrines. The best work in the subject would not be done not by using 'the abstract deductive method which has done as much service as it is capable of, but in the following new fields of investigations – historical, statistical, inductive.'[73] To be of real value, political economy must be predictive, capable of being utilized by governments and citizens alike in order to address 'the perils of an ignorant democracy.'[74] As at Queen's the conditions were being set in place for the universities of the province to provide experts ready and willing to provide advice and service to the state. 'I will not here lay stress,' Ashley concluded, 'on the advantages of such a course to the man who intends to "enter politics," to the man who looks forward to journalism, to the future civil servants of the country ...'[75] A new kind of intellectual was finding its place within the groves of academe, in part propelled into prominence by the social ethic of British idealism.

When Ashley left Toronto in 1892 he suggested the appointment of a like-minded successor, James Mavor, and Ross accepted his suggestion in spite of the submission of a signed petition by graduates of the University of Toronto insisting on a Canadian-born scholar.[76] When Shortt left Queen's in 1908, he too had an heir apparent in mind, a brilliant former student named Oscar Douglas Skelton. The two new appointees, with Shortt, dominated the teaching of political economy in Ontario before the Great War. An eccentric Scot, Mavor had as a youth been drawn to study the sciences; but soon, in the Glasgow of Watson's mentor Edward Caird, he was drawn to the study of idealist philosophy. He was also drawn towards socialism. By the time of his appointment to Toronto, however, his enthusiasm for collectivism and with social reform was on the wane. Indeed, so far did his commitments swing that he ultimately came to embrace a philosophy of anti-collectivist libertarianism. Related to his ongoing interest in the history of Russia, he corresponded with Tolstoy, studied the Doukhobors, and encouraged Wilfrid Laurier's minister of the interior, Clifford Sifton, to welcome their emigration to Canada.

As a scholar, Mavor's Canadian writings were voluminous. His textbook *Applied Economics* and his *Economic History of Russia* appeared in 1914, and his study of state ownership of the Manitoba telephone system, *Government Telephones* (1916), and of hydroelectricity in Ontario, *Niagara in Politics* (1925), secured his reputation as a vigorous enemy of collectivist state policy. 'In the course of his labours,' economic historian Ian Drummond wrote, 'he may be said to have invented social-science contract research in Canada.'[77] Mavor was more than willing to hire himself out to various governments, and he happily accepted covert financing of his attacks on government-owned utilities by privately owned American corporations.[78] His approach to the study of political economy was, therefore, a mixture of genuine academic commitment and convenient self-interest. As with Shortt, he stressed, as he put it not long before he moved to Toronto, 'the close interdependence of the parts of our highly organised society, and the dependence of the groups which constitute the commercial world upon each other and upon the public.'[79] 'Impartial study of the facts,' he believed, was the basis of knowledge.

Governments would soon have to depend on the advice of applied social scientists, not theorists or metaphysicians or moralists, to guide their steps in the making of policy.'[80] The ongoing commitment of the University of Toronto to a structured curriculum that allowed students a range of choice between programs but not within them, coupled with Mavor's thirty-one years as professor of political economy and constitutional history, made him the 'permanent monarchical Head of the nascent Department ...'[81]

It was that department, under Ashley and Mavor, that helped form the ideological assumptions and the understanding of social dynamics of the university's most illustrious student of the 1890s, William Lyon Mackenzie King. In the summer of 1895, just after graduating in honours political science under Mavor, the twenty-one-year-old recipient of a fresh Toronto BA degree confided to his diary: 'I would like to give all my time to Political Science ... I might as well record here thoughts that are constantly flooding my mind. I feel that I have a great work to do in this life ... As yet I do not know where it is to be, I believe it may be as a professor of Political Economy, an earnest student of social questions. Or it may be in public life, parliament perhaps ...'[82]

King, too, was a product of the fusion of idealism and empiricism in the 1890s. An advocate of social research, he was also an apostle of self-realization. Speaking to his home church in Berlin, Ontario, on the 'Social betterment of the slums in large cities,' he could assert that 'abundant life' meant 'the realization of our natures and endowments in their many sides, moral, intellectual, spiritual ...'[83] The intellectual capital for King's 1918 book, *Industry and Humanity*, had been generated many years before.[84]

King symbolized the emergence in his own generation of a new class of intellectuals who not only sought to understand the complexity of an interdependent industrial and urban society but were also willing to serve the state in order to help facilitate social harmony. A new, secular clerisy was coming into a position of influence, because industrial society was changing the character of social relations within it. Industry and commerce required expertise; so did the political system that served industrial and commercial needs. Academic life followed suit.[85] In effect, the new political economists of the turn of the century served the function of helping to legitimize, as much as to improve or to criticize, the existing structures and values of industrial society. Nor were they 'the less such because they were for the most part unaware that this was the role they were performing. In other words, they not only propagated but shared to the full in the illusion of universalism ... of any class which cloaks its partial interests, deliberately or not, in the garb of universal principles, sacred and eternal verities, the national interest, and so on.'[86] If it can be concluded that in an earlier epoch those who preached a Baconian natural theology helped legitimize the authority and prescriptions of Christianity by giving it a basis in natural science, it does not seem unreasonable to conclude that the new political scientists, dedicated to the systematic gathering of empirical information that was itself derived from the Baconian model,[87] served a similar function for a new social order based not on Christianity but on the secular state system.

Adam Shortt was to O.D. Skelton what John Watson had been to Shortt: an academic mentor who vitally affected the future career of his protégé. Born in 1878 at Orangeville, Ontario, the son of a high school principal, Skelton had attended Queen's in the 1890s, graduating with an MA (first class honours) in classics in 1899. Thereafter, he spent a year studying classics at the University of Chicago but, intellectually unsettled, he travelled to England in 1901. Between 1902 and 1905 he found himself in Philadelphia, engaged in editorial work for *Booklover's Magazine*, his true vocation still in doubt. While there, he struck up a correspondence with his mentor Shortt, and his attention turned to political science. In 1905 he returned to the University of Chicago for graduate studies in the subject. He was lecturing at Queen's on Shortt's invitation in 1907, just before Shortt resigned to become civil service commissioner in Ottawa. In 1908 he was appointed professor of political and economic science, having turned down academic offers in America as well as the post of deputy minister of labour, recently vacated by William Lyon Mackenzie King.[88] Soon, inspired by Skelton, Queen's was pioneering in a new kind of university education, in the form of extension courses in commerce and banking offered by the department of political science. Such courses were welcomed by the Bankers' Association of Canada.[89]

As with Shortt, Skelton ultimately became a career civil servant. After seven years as dean of arts at Queen's between 1919 and 1925, the last of them spent as adviser to Prime Minister King at the Imperial Prime Ministers' Conference (1923) and as special counsellor at the Department of External Affairs (1924–5), he accepted the post of under-secretary for external affairs. He held this important position until his death in 1941. For our purposes, the career path is important for the intellectual trajectory it reveals. Watson had stressed the positive social functions of the state and the necessity that university graduates be willing to serve it; Shortt had acted out Watson's dicta, and he was willing at times to utilize the language of idealism in order to justify social service; Skelton followed Shortt's example, but while his actions bore witness to the impulse to service generated by the idealists, his statements contained nothing of their rhetoric. As he had written to Shortt as early as 1907: 'strikes, trusts, taxes, socialism, tariffs, banking, bulk a great deal larger in the public mind than the authenticity of St John's gospel or the wherefore or the whyness of Hegel. Possibly they shouldn't, but here for once Providence and the stream of tendency is with the righteous, otherwise the political scientists.'[90]

In saying this Skelton knew that he no more offended the idealist side of his mentor Shortt than Shortt had offended Watson when choosing to study banking and transportation systems instead of ethical theory. In their own ways, both Shortt and Skelton were simply fulfilling the logic of nineteenth-century idealism, and in so doing they helped shape a liberal-democratic ethic by taking the sense of mission and stewardship they had learned and acted out at the university into the public realm.[91]

By the early twentieth century the new political scientists were among the groups in academic life most visible to the public. They had taken the basic task of nineteenth-century idealist philosophers – to elucidate and examine the interrelatedness of modern society – and were beginning to do so, but without recourse to the Christian religion or, for that matter, to any traditional form of providential design. The idea of the miraculous did not exist as an operative principle in their working lives. The new sense of the nature of social change was not monocausal, but interdependent.

Skelton caught the essence of the new approach not only to society but also to history in a paper he gave on the philosophy of history. His own approach to both, he said, was sociological: 'Sociology tends to stress the causable view of history. It seeks to determine the influences which have helped to mould history and finds that climate, the geographical nature of a country, presence or absence of domestic animals and common cereals, race and many other factors have played an important role.'[92] No single factor sufficed to explain history, whether the inspiration of Christianity, the actions of great men, or the forces of economic change. 'The economic interpretation of history has received considerable attention in recent times,' he said. 'History, however, is too many-sided to permit of a single method of explanation.'[93]

Indeed it was by 1912. By then Skelton was involved in empirical research on a number of socio-economic questions with a bearing on political issues. So, too, were his colleagues at the University of Toronto. A few years earlier the Toronto *Globe* had noted one of the characteristics of the teaching of the new political science at universities: that its assumed mantle of scientific objectivity effectively sanitized the investigation of sensitive social problems. 'The academic pursuit' of political science, pointed out the editor of the *Globe*, 'if this is carried out in the proper spirit, tends to free politics from prejudice, to make patriotism more rational, and to cause the duties of citizenship to appear more imperative on those who enjoy its privileges.'[94] If encouraged in this direction, agents of the state would learn, the new political science could become a powerful force for social conservatism and control. But these academics, of a different order from those who had come before them, were not necessarily easy to direct or control.

By 1912, the new men of social science at the University of Toronto had put forward an ambitious program heading clearly in the direction of social reform. A proposal submitted to its senate by members of the faculty of arts began: 'There is ... a growing demand for persons who are, by reason of personality, experience, and training, able to help in the difficult work of alleviating social misfortune and remedying social maladjustment.' It then proposed the creation of a school of social service that would 'investigate problems of poverty and philanthropy, crime and its prevention, and government and administration.' Each heading, noted the Toronto *Star*, embraced 'a very large number of distinct, specialized activities.'[95] On the eve of the Great War, the emergent social sciences in Ontario universities, inspired in part by the new political science, had not resolved the question of whether they should be disinterested observers of empirical phenomena or compassionate advocates of social reform. But they seemed to promise a future that could be shaped by the minds and hands of people, in an earthly kingdom ruled increasingly by statistical probability.

9

Christianity and Culture

Professors and students searched earnestly for intellectual stability and order in the years prior to the Great War, and much of that search concerned the applicability of Christian ethics to industrial and urban society. In this age of rapid change they wanted to determine the essentials of their faith, and then to act in accordance with them. This continued to absorb much of their attention, and it is reflected in the pages of student newspapers. Inspired by their professors, many of them idealists, students turned gradually away from traditional evangelical concerns and towards the 'spirit' of Christianity. The advent of the higher criticism – a quest for the historical Jesus and for a critical understanding of the biblical record – met with different responses in different institutions, but in each case the effect was ultimately to challenge evangelical religious assumptions by pointing in the direction of historical relativism and a liberal ethical religion. Paralleling this was the remarkable rise of English as a major academic discipline dedicated to the study and criticism of literature and concerned with culture. For some, as will be seen, it became a surrogate religion, fulfilling deep psychological and ideological needs met in the past by Christianity. Exactly when the 'timeless' values of religion were being brought to earth and placed within history rather than beyond it, professors of English emerged as apostles of a new discipline that promised moral transcendence in the form of the universality of literary culture.

By the early twentieth century, the liberal arts community was as preoccupied with culture as it was with Christ. This reorientation of attention was facilitated by the pronouncements, both behind the lectern and before the public, of professors in the humanities who increasingly found themselves beleaguered by the crusade of some of their colleagues for practical applications of university activity. The concern for culture, which at times resembled a secular articulation of an essentially

Christian sensibility, also turned student attention towards cultural and social rather than personal norms. At the same time the emergence of professors vocal on social and political issues convinced a number of students that they too should be concerned about such questions. In these years when Christian social reformers sought to root the Kingdom of God in earthly ground, the view of Christ held by many members of the university intelligentsia began to have less to do with heaven and more with the attributes of a secular and urban middle-class citizen.

Christian Authority and the Higher Criticism

Late Victorian and Edwardian exponents of the evangelical ethos in Ontario colleges made earnest efforts to reconcile their tradition of scriptural authority and inerrancy with changing intellectual assumptions. They asserted that the bible story and universal history were inextricably linked, but found that their theological commitment to a providential dispensation which assumed divine intervention in human affairs – the idea of the miraculous – was increasingly at odds with the claims of secular reason and with notions of social progress. They claimed that the realms of the sacred and the secular, divine history and human history, were part of a single moral order, but found that the new historians told a very different story than theirs. In order to account for historical change that seemed at odds with religious assumptions and priorities, they divided history into 'dispensations' that, however different on the surface, were united by the conflict of sin and salvation and by the decline and revival of religion. They built on the authority of a Christian past and proclaimed that history was on the evangelical side, but they also looked steadfastly to the future and attempted in so doing to absorb notions of social, intellectual, and scientific improvement into their tradition of biblical prophecy. It was a profoundly precarious undertaking, built upon the moral and intellectual contradictions of the age.[1]

'Certain people have talked so much about the *fin de siècle* that they have come to cherish the delusion that the foolish phrase means something.' So wrote one undergraduate in January 1901. 'We are told that we know nothing,' he continued, 'that we have lost intelligent idealism and true sentiment, that the whole business of human life is a delusion and a snare, and, sad to say, Christianity has been destroyed once more.'[2] The student would have nothing of such pessimism. In spite of the evidence of international imperial rivalries, scepticism in modern philosophy, and the 'rarified' air of modern theology, he said, there still existed the university itself as an anchor for non-material values in a materialistic world. Because of its existence, students could meet the new century 'thankful that we are not doomed to the *fin de siècle* nightmare, that life for us is still full of hope, that those who really live in any large sense prove the worth and the joy of life, and convinced that in all forms of knowledge and in all the movement of life there is a divine meaning which we may realize through the manifestation of our higher self in loyalty to the social relationships which are both our safety and our strength.'[3]

The assertion that in knowledge and in life 'a divine meaning' is present, and given expression in the 'higher self,' scarcely differentiated this student from hundreds of others who had gone to Ontario universities before him. What does separate him from previous students is how he believed this higher self was given meaning. The day of evangelical pietism as a dominant and directing force in Ontario college life was on the wane by the beginning of the twentieth century. Taking its place was a sense of moral identity increasingly distant from a reliance on internal nurture requiring private prayer and reflection. This new sense of Christian identity was intensely social, and it became more so. As the student of the new century had said, the new identity involved a 'loyalty to the social relationships' from which he or she derived both safety and strength. In the quarter-century from 1890 to the advent of the Great War that identity became a major force in the emergence of a discernible student culture.

The same years witnessed the emergence, within North American public life generally, of a liberalization of Protestantism generally referred to as the 'social gospel.'[4] Based on a belief in a God immanent in the secular world, striving to realize the Kingdom of God on earth by means of numerous political and social reform activities, minimizing traditional denominational distinctions, the social gospel became a major force in Canada in the first three decades of the twentieth century. In Canada the way to such a commitment was paved in the last decades of the nineteenth century by the many activities of women within the organized churches. Traditionally excluded from direct participation in the theological issues of their churches, and segregated from the councils of formal theocratic power, church women had, by the early twentieth century, long accepted and given expression at the congregational level to the practical Christianity discovered by their husbands and sons in the years of the social gospel.

Intellectually, gradual acceptance of the higher criticism helped shape the commitment to a social gospel, although it did not come without controversy and pain within theological schools, academic departments, and churches.[5] At Victoria College, for example, Professor George

Coulson Workman ran into severe opposition to his views in the early 1890s. The valedictorian of the college in 1875, Workman had studied theology at the University of Leipzig before rejoining his Alma Mater's faculty of theology as a teacher of metaphysics and theology. Shortly after the publication of his doctoral dissertation, as *The Text of Jeremiah* (Edinburgh 1889), Workman gave a lecture in Toronto on 'messianic prophecy.' It offended many Methodists, particularly the Reverend E.H. Dewart, the influential editor of the *Christian Guardian*.[6] Firmly committed to historical criticism of the Bible, Workman asserted that Old Testament prophecies reflected the authors' observations rather than their predictions of the coming of the Messiah.[7] Outraged, conservative members of the Methodist community and of the Victoria College board of regents insisted upon Workman's dismissal. In spite of Nathanael Burwash's attempts to dispel concern, the pressure on Workman was sufficient that he tendered his resignation two years later.[8] In the wake of the Workman affair other Methodists, such as Burwash, continued to search for a means of reconciling the higher criticism with Methodist doctrine, and they did so by balancing the Wesleyan tradition's belief in biblical inerrancy through 'the written Apostolic word' with its equal reliance on 'a continuous tradition of teaching, which expands and enlarges the truth to be gathered from the written word.' Such liberality of interpretation allowed some conscientious Methodists who possessed the evangelical assurance of an inner light to expand the unchallenged word of God to include the expansive realm of human interpretation and teaching of it, all in the name of orthodoxy.[9]

At one level the Workman affair may be seen as the first controversy regarding academic freedom in an Ontario college or university. At another it reflected the implication of the higher criticism's liberal view of Christ: that Christ offered an ethical form of salvation. This was a theological position that, in the words of one historian, 'was a ready-made foundation for the developing social gospel ideology.'[10] Workman formally disappeared from Victoria College in 1892, but by the mid-1890s within the Methodist community the higher criticism was coming to have an increasing number of supporters.[11] Few, if any, who encountered it embraced it as a release from theological shackles, for they sought to shore up the grounds of the beliefs they had inherited, not to discover alternate forms of faith. For this reason, the higher criticism was often approached cautiously. This was the experience of Salem Bland in 1893. But whatever the motivation of those who examined it, the higher criticism – like idealism – was capable of unsettling beliefs and taking them in directions unanticipated by those who held them. By the mid-1890s even clergymen such as S.D. Chown, who were to become major figures in the twentieth-century Methodist church, were on the defensive when it came to discussing the Bible as an inerrant work of divine inspiration. 'I know it is inspired,' said Chown in 1895, 'because it inspires me.'[12]

Within the Methodist church, and at Victoria College, however, powerful advocates of traditional evangelical religion did continue to exist and to defend their views against modernism.[13] The Reverend George Jackson found that out in 1909 when, having just accepted a post at Sherbourne Street Methodist Church and at Victoria College as professor of English Bible (a title that indicated that the holder of the position did not have to be an expert in Greek or Hebrew) in the faculty of theology, he was attacked by the Reverend Albert Carman, chairman of the board of regents, for having given a liberal interpretation of the first chapters of Genesis to a YMCA audience in Toronto. To an important extent Carman's attack on Jackson's theological heresy was in fact a means by which Carman sought to exact revenge on certain influential members of Toronto's Sherbourne Street congregation – Newton Wesley Rowell and Joseph Flavelle, for example – who in 1906 had attempted to unseat the aging general superintendent in favour of someone younger and more in sympathy with the times. Carman's objection was thus not only to a higher critic (whose theological views on Genesis scarcely differed from those of Nathanael Burwash) but also to the plutocrats who had imported him from England. The board of regents and the general conference of the Methodist church, divided and rancorous, debated Jackson's 'heresies' for two years. Carman remained adamantly opposed to Jackson's continued association with Victoria, but a powerful and sustained defence of the recently appointed professor at the 1910 Methodist General Conference by Nathanael Burwash and Newton Rowell carried the day. No proceedings were instituted against Jackson. He continued to teach at Victoria and became a highly respected member of the international Methodist community.

The year 1910 marked the last time that any group attempted to interfere with theological teaching at Victoria College. Those most adamant in resistance to the new ideas were representatives of an older generation of ordained clergy, not those who listened to the Sunday sermons. 'It was often not the layman in his pew, but the preacher in the pulpit who felt most threatened by the higher criticism.' As Rowell stated to one audience of Methodists in 1910: 'Brethren, let us go forth as men to preach that God is able and willing to save men from their sins, and let us cease this haggling about non-essentials.'[14]

At Queen's University, the higher criticism generated little if any controversy. Both G.M. Grant and John Watson, the moral leaders of the university, were strong advocates of critical inquiry and firm opponents of dogmatism. 'After pointing out that the only possible result of honest criticism is the discovery of truth,' wrote one student who reviewed Grant's 1892 Sunday afternoon address called 'The Bible and Higher Criticism,' the Principal 'urged that instead of exciting alarm it should be welcomed by believers and encouraged to spend all its energies in establishing the true interpretation of Scripture.'[15] For his part, Watson was content to echo Grant's pleas for open-mindedness. The 'true mental attitude of the biblical critic,' he said, should be one 'who comes to his study without other preconception than the legitimate one of faith in the saving power of Christianity.' In his view, the end of biblical criticism, like that of literary criticism, should be the removal of obstructions 'which prevent the mind of the reader and of the author from coming into immediate contact.'[16] Why should one worry about reconciling 'minute and apparently trivial enquiries into dates and authorship,' he wondered, 'so long as these are guided by an earnest desire to realize with vividness and clearness from what manner of man and what manner of age a given literary product proceeded?'[17]

The relative absence of religious controversy at Queen's was an inversion of the situation at McMaster University in the early years of the twentieth century. There, a major rift developed within the religious and academic communities that made the years between 1905 and 1910 ones of strife.[18] The issue was less the higher criticism, as such, than it was modernism in general university instruction. The major protagonists were the Reverend Elmore Harris (affluent son of the implement-maker John Harris, pastor of Walmer Road Church, and a member of the university senate) and the Reverend Isaac George Matthews (an 1897 McMaster graduate and editor of the *Western Baptist Monthly*). The appointment of Matthews to the faculty of McMaster in 1904 as professor of systematic theology provoked the crisis. The two men represented two strains within contemporary Baptist practice. Harris was an evangelical pre-millennialist, suspicious of denominational colleges that taught both theology and the liberal arts. For this reason, he was a strong supporter of a federation agreement between the University of Toronto and McMaster. McMaster could thereby fulfil its basic mandate – theological instruction – and education in the liberal arts could be left to the institutions funded by the state.[19] For his part, Matthews represented the liberal strain within the Baptist community, with the Rockefeller-inspired and funded University of Chicago its educational jewel.

The decision by the McMaster senate to permit Matthews more than a year of preliminary study at Chicago irked Harris and his fundamentalist supporters, who regarded the newly founded American university (pointed firmly in the direction of the modern investigative scholarship necessary for a secular, industrial society by its first president, William Rainey Harper) as a source of rationalist and materialist heresy.[20] Clearly, a degree of fundamentalist anti-intellectualism was one element in the opposition voiced by those who feared the appointment of 'pretty tall heretics'[21] such as Matthews or historian George Cross, who were either supporters or (like Cross) products of Chicago. In retrospect, it appears that there was little that was starkly heretical in the views expressed by either Matthews or Cross. But to men like Harris, for whom there was only one true and inerrant faith, the claim by Cross, an historian of comparative religion, that the 'problem for the theologian was how to conserve the true Christianity while at the same time admitting that there were elements of truth in other religions,' did constitute heresy. As Charles M. Johnston observed of the controversy: 'In a good many quarters any reference, however oblique, to the study of comparative religion was enough to spark apoplectic debate.'[22] In several rural areas of Ontario, such as the Ottawa and Elgin districts, criticism mounted over the heterodoxy of McMaster's curriculum. Faced with such opposition, Cross resigned in May 1909 and shortly thereafter took an appointment at the University of Chicago.

The full force of fundamentalist criticism, bolstered by rural support, was then directed at I.G. Matthews. Harris, as a member of the senate, formally questioned the commitment of Matthews to the articles of Baptist faith and fumed that it appeared that at McMaster 'we have no standard; anything in the world can be taught in the University.'[23] Clearly, Harris was not simply after one academic hide, for by his own admission he had larger game in sight. That Matthews had more than once indicated to his students that the early chapters of Genesis were a 'little folklore ... exactly in line with the folklore of every people under the sun'[24] was offensive to Harris, to put the matter lightly. His intention was to purge the McMaster faculty of any and all 'modernist' forms of teaching in whatever discipline. But the fundamentalist insurgency within the university senate was not successful. The investigating committee reported to the senate that charges against Matthews were not proved, and that his teachings were consistent with the intentions of the university's founder. Moreover, the committee issued a statement that was to become a continuing academic creed with respect to religious instruction at the university:

McMaster University stands for freedom, for progress, for investigation. It must welcome truth from whatever quarter, and never be guilty of binding the spirit of free enquiry. As a Christian school of learning under Baptist auspices, it stands for the fullest and freest investigation, *not only in the scientific realm but also in the realm of Biblical scholarship*. Holding fast their historic position on the personal freedom and responsibility of the individual, refusing to bind or be bound by any human creed, rejecting the authority of tradition and taking their stand on the word of God alone as the supreme and all-sufficient rule of faith and practice, the Baptists have ever been ready to accord to all students of the Sacred Scriptures the largest possible measure of freedom consistent with loyalty to the *fundamentals* of the Christian faith.[25]

More than most other strands in the Protestant inheritance, the Baptist tradition was one that resembled a double-edged sword. One element within it, stressing the inerrant fundamentals of Christianity, had sought to suppress critical inquiry at McMaster in the years of strife from 1905 to 1910. Yet another, suspicious of the inherited authority of tradition, had issued the judgment that the cause of truth would prevail at the university, and it had prevailed. There proved to be a good deal of support from within the Baptist community for the decision that was made, although discontent with modernist tendencies of academic life at McMaster did not die away completely. It would resurface within the next generation, once again straining the relations of McMaster University and its denominational constituency. But Matthews, vindicated by 1910 not only by his university's senate but also by the Baptist Convention, was, in ways that only the future would reveal, an unwitting symbol of the course his university would later adopt. Sensitive to the 'practical side of life,' committed to understanding 'the basal [*sic*] principles of human development,' and impressed by the contributions made by the natural and physical sciences, this Baptist minister and professor struck a note with a decidedly modern ring: 'it is not sufficient that [the] teacher possess exact knowledge of the past only ... he must be able also to reinterpret the message in terms of the present. A modern theological seminary ought not to be divorced from the world to-day – and what a world for a theologian to come to.'[26]

The world of the university student, even one in divinity, was not necessarily that of his professor. Debates raged in university senates and boards of governors, as well as in annual denominational conferences, over heretical teachings and heterodox lectures given by members of academic staffs, and students at the various institutions involved were aware of the problems of their professors. Clearly, the teachings of men such as George Workman, George Jackson, George Cross, and I.G. Matthews – each greatly respected by those who took their lectures – helped to alter the conceptions students held of the biblical basis of Christian authority. But student views about the nature of Christianity, and of its relationship to life, were also altered in other ways. Certainly a concern with religious convictions continued to be a major preoccupation of the students in Ontario universities in the quarter-century after 1890. The pages of the student newspapers of institutions such as Methodist Victoria and Presbyterian Queen's provide, in fact, a striking documentation of the reorientation of religious and social belief, and it was one that reflected in microcosm shifts in assumption that were occurring within the Canadian middle class as a whole.

Idealism and 'Essential Christianity'

Canadian Protestants continued to seek ways of maintaining customary means of faith in order to maintain continuity of tradition into the twentieth century. They did not necessarily think their religion to be in decline, but they often saw it challenged by new intellectual and social forces and wanted it better to serve a new and different age. Accordingly, particularly in theological colleges, they were often willing to countenance the new historical and philosophical approaches to the Christian faith. But by the 1890s it was recognized that traditional evangelical religion and certain elements of college life were increasingly difficult to reconcile. The latter now introduced doubt, the exaltation of the intellect, and the removal of home restraints to students. The main solution, said one student, was to develop 'a broader sympathy' in the form of association with other students and with humanity as a whole.[27]

This larger view was complemented by the growing conviction that denominational differences were impediments to such a social sympathy. 'No one denomination in this or other lands,' declared the valedictorian of the 1893 Queen's class in divinity, 'is holding itself aloof from this friendly compact [between denominations] ... They all feel deeply interested in humanity's common cause – religion. In a word *Theology is becoming more international and interprofessional.* Theological teachings are being stripped of their eccentricities and eternal verities alone are being brought out in bold relief.'[28] Such views were accurate reflections of the ecumenicism of Principal Grant and of John Watson's disdain for denominational distinctions, just as they also mirrored the convictions of participants at the alumni conferences held by the Queen's faculty of theology, inaugurated in 1892. As the radical social gospeller Salem Bland said of the alumni conferences in which he participated in the 1890s: 'No one thing, I think, has ever done so much as these Conferences to liberate the mind of the Protestant ministers in Canada from the narrowness, the excessive subjectivity, and the uncritical traditionalism of the evangelical Protestantism then prevailing.'[29]

The idealist's refusal to recognize dualisms in any sphere of life provided students of the time with a philosophical argument for diminishing
the importance of both denominational differences and systematic theology. As one said, when reviewing a major theme of the 1894 Queen's
theological alumni conference, 'our attitude towards all presuppositions,
theological, scientific, psychological, is no longer scholastic and dogmatic, but philosophical ... It takes a long time to understand that human
life cannot be split up into sections, between which impassable gulfs are
fixed ... Any one who understands the meaning of modern philosophy,
which is God's best gift to man for the true appreciation of Christianity,
knows that abstract theology is doomed and that it must give place to a
theology built on the moral nature of man, and which will truly be "bone
of our bone and flesh of our flesh."'[30] Or, as another Queen's student put
it in the same year, using sound idealist vocabulary, 'the God of the
nineteenth century, unlike the God of Deism, is immanent in the world,
and the world is regarded as the progressive revelation of His nature.'[31]
The lesson to be gained from this, he said, was that students of theology
must obtain 'all the culture within their reach' by means of a sound
training in arts. Theology was, in this way, not only broadened in conception but also democratized. 'Every man is a theologian now,' wrote
an alumnus of Queen's to his Alma Mater in 1897. 'He thinks out his
own doctrines and recasts the religion presented by preachers and reli-
gionists to suit himself ... The age of free thought has set in and we must
abide by its consequences ... The mechanic can discuss any political
question with his employer, the servant girl can talk of the latest news or
the last novel with her mistress. It follows that we have on all social,
political or religious questions a freedom of expression and of criticism
such as the world has never seen. And we are all the better for it.'[32]

Queen's was more affected by the philosophical idealism of the late
nineteenth century than were the other denominational colleges and universities, and its students gave forceful expression to the idealists' powerful intellectual justification of such views. For this reason, the erosion
of denominational distinctions was given fullest expression there. But
other universities were scarcely exempt from the impact of similar views
held by their own professors. George Blewett at Victoria College and
James Ten Broeke at McMaster University, both idealists, provided their
students – in their classrooms and in their several books – with a perspective that was not profoundly different from that of Watson. Their
books included Blewett's *The Study of Nature and the Vision of God*
(1907) and *The Christian View of the World* (1912), and Ten Broeke's *A
Constructive Basis for Theology* (1914) and *The Moral Life and Religion* (1922).[33] In the years from 1906 to 1912, when George Blewett

taught at Victoria College, the religious atmosphere within the student population at 'Vic' was very similar to that of Queen's, for evangelical piety had come to be seen as something of an embarrassing reminder of a stage of religion now superseded by modernity. 'The new force attracting the young mind draws it away from the sentimental religion of our fathers, the usefulness of which lies now in the past,' wrote 'A.L.B.,' in a lead editorial for *Acta Victoriana*. 'The ancient eye grows alarmed to see the religion of the age swing from the bright color of old sentimentalism to the greyness of modern materialism ...,' he continued. 'As half a century ago every man had to feel for himself, so now that we to a large extent have substituted in our religion thought for feeling, each must do his own thinking ... Unless we firmly anchor ourselves to the solid rock of intellectualism, the first wave of sentiment will carry us out into the open sea beyond. The religion of sentiment would not be so unenviable if we always rode on the crest of the wave, but the trough was ever wider than the crest.'[34] The author, A.L. Burt, was at the time on the editorial staff of *Acta*, in charge of 'Personals and Exchanges.' Like a number of other students from a Methodist background concerned with the relationship between emotional character and material circumstance, then and later, he would ultimately find his vocation not in theology but in history – and like them become a distinguished historian.

The extent to which a commitment to denominational boundaries diminished at Queen's and Victoria between 1890 and the Great War was great. One student at Queen's in 1907 noted that chance expressions of his fellow students indicated that when they spoke about religion they expressed 'religious opinions' rather than 'religious faith.' The new Christian student, he said, gathered meaning from Christianity not by faith but by seeking ways of establishing relationships between the Christian tradition and various forms of fellowship.[35] To some this clearly involved a sense of loss. 'We live in an age when culture represses and intellect frowns on impulse and even religion looks with contempt upon enthusiasm,' admitted a Victoria graduate in 1910. 'It is true our lives are regular. We think we are refined. Our sentiments are well within control. But what we have is bookish, worked over, secondhand. We are tiresomely monotonous. Life for us has a dead level. We have no individuality.'[36] Or, as another Victoria student had put the matter a few years earlier: 'Religion has its place with us. We all think so, and if we do not feel so we will not confess it.'[37]

By 1911 Christianity at Victoria was being stripped to what were regarded as its fundamental elements. 'Essential Christianity' was the subject of an address by Professor Albert H. Abbott, of the University of

Toronto philosophy department, to the YMCA of Victoria College. It was possible, said this expert on experimental psychology, to discuss the subject by means of three simple points:

1 *Christianity cannot be essentially a dogma or creed, that is, a system of doctrines ...*
2 *Christianity cannot be essentially a particular form of worship or of life if it be a universal religion ...*
3 *The essence of Christianity can only be found in the attitude (mental or spiritual attitude) of a man in his daily life ...*[38]

Christianity considered basically as a 'dogma or creed,' said Abbott, was to throw it 'into the battles of the philosophers as a contending system in whole or in part.' Defining one's Christianity by adherence to a particular form of worship provided him with 'no proof that one is not a Christian.' After all, Abbott said, 'all who recognize that the Jews in Old Testament times were Christian in all but name, must also recognize that not even a knowledge of the historic Christ is necessary for one to be a Christian in his life.'[39] Christianity stripped to its true essentials, he concluded, involved little more than a daily attempt to act like the ideal man by elevating the spirit of life. 'Essential Christianity is the Holy Spirit. As men live to-day in the Spirit of Christ they are Christians, and in so far as they fail of doing this they are not Christians. He is truly fighting for Christ, he is truly laboring for Christ, he is truly doing the work of Christ who goes about his daily task in the spirit in which Christ went about His life.'[40]

Just how it was possible to go about doing Christ's work in daily life when it was also possible, as Abbott had claimed earlier, to be a perfectly good Christian without any knowledge of the historic Christ he did not say. A clue to his beliefs on the matter was perhaps provided in his reference to the quest for the ideal man, the perfect citizen. Whereas students at McMaster University, living in a smaller, more intense Christian college environment, continued to stress the redemptive power of Christ in religious life early in the twentieth century,[41] this was less so at either Victoria or Queen's. When Jesus or his disciples were mentioned at all by students, as often as not the image that resulted bore a closer resemblance to the one extolled by American advertising executive Bruce Barton, the master exponent of twentieth-century therapeutic Christian culture. Barton's Jesus, as set forth in *A Young Man's Jesus* (1914) and later in *The Man Nobody Knows* (1925) was 'a young man glowing with physical strength and the joy of living,' with 'our bounding pulses, our hot desires,' as well as 'perfect teeth.'[42] Barton's Christ was young, urban, and professional. One might also note that the new Christ was very male, different in image from the humble, meek and feminine Christ of the nineteenth century.

Meaning was given to Barton's Christ by ascribing to him values and characteristics that were increasingly dominant in secular North American society. This was, to be sure, an abject view of the meaning of the Christian revelation, but it was not much different from the image of St Paul's ideal Christian put forward by the Reverend W.T. Herridge of Ottawa in an 1896 baccalaureate sermon at Queen's: 'To his [Paul's] thought, the Christian, so far from being an unnatural growth, or a cold and colorless nonentity, is the true type of man, pre-eminent in all manly qualities; a warrior who is not afraid to go forth to hazardous combat, trusting in his good sword, wielded by a strong right arm, to hew his way to victory; an athlete who submits himself to long and severe discipline, having his muscles trained to endurance, that he may run and wrestle in the joy of his strength, and win the laurel crown.'[43] The new middle-class Christ was not far removed from being a twentieth-century advertising man's dream.

Canadian idealists concerned with preserving 'essential Christianity,' such as John Watson or James Ten Broeke (who assumed the chair of philosophy at McMaster in 1898)[44] thought that they were reshaping Christianity for the age of commerce and industry. In fact their general message, once shorn of technicalities, inadvertently helped pave the way for a secular, self-help therapeutic ideal that served the needs of the developing consumer culture of corporate capitalism at the time.[45] Whereas in the mid-nineteenth century the spur to moral action derived from the internalized values of Christianity within the individual, by the early twentieth century, largely due to the idealist proponents of the philosophy of self-realization the idea of the good was increasingly equated with the process of self-realization itself. The new socially constructed North American self was derived less from inner moral resources than from the expectations of others. The good was coming to be equated with the natural, leading to a cult of personality development epitomized by American psychologist G. Stanley Hall, when in 1920 he declared that 'the true and living god is the development urge.'[46] The sacred and the secular, said the Canadian social gospeller Salem Bland in 1918, were but aspects of the same social reality. Self-development and social development were identical. Because of this, 'it is only as it is materialized' that Christianity 'reveals itself.' Christian fellowship, in the end, was for Bland 'to be found in the process of industry and commerce. Cooperation in commerce and industry is the real Holy Communion.'[47]

Similar views were found in Canadian universities at the same time.

Within such a conceptual framework, ethics was coming to be seen as the science of good conduct, its relationship to the 'orthodox' theology of previous generations increasingly attenuated. One undergraduate in 1910, urging student participation in college activities, expressed the rationale of therapeutic culture: 'We need development – that is why we come to college, but no development can equal self-development. The best men are what they are by their own right – individuals self caused ...'[48] The social ideal of Christianity, said the Canadian professor of philosophy who published books with the revealing titles of *Self-Realization: An Outline of Ethics* in 1913 and *Faith Justified by Progress* three years later, was simply the creation of a society in which 'the divine spirit of justice and benevolence prevails and each individual is given an opportunity for the fullest personal development.'[49] By the early decades of the twentieth century the content of such approaches to what had once been the domain of the Christian religion was not remarkably different from the moral homilies in magazines of popular edification such as the *Ladies' Home Journal* or, by the 1920s, *Reader's Digest*.

With Christ's meaning as a redeemer of sin receding, his role as ideal citizen increased. 'Jesus was a doctor, albeit one who employed unusual methods,' said the Reverend Joseph F. McFadyen, professor of New Testament literature and exegesis at Queen's University in 1917. 'Jesus was a religious teacher ... Jesus was not a lawyer, but on at least one occasion He was asked to decide a disputed inheritance ...'[50] McFadyen's Christ projected the perfect image for ambitious middle-class university students in the age of the social gospel. He possessed appropriate middle-class occupational skills, yet chose to identify with the poor and the oppressed in a life of social service, thereby giving range at once to ambition and conscience. He was well known to 'many social circles' and 'was no stranger in the homes of the rich. He knew the glamour of the big house where hospitality involves no fine calculation of resources, of the luxurious appointments, the arrangements for comfort, the surroundings where there is everything to please and nothing to offend the cultured taste.' He chose to keep less elevated company, but had well-honed middle-class social skills that could be put to use when necessary. 'Only twice do we see Him as host, but when He entertained He entertained with royal hospitality.' Moreover, while He was a realist He was also an optimist.[51] One is tempted to capitalize the 'o' in 'optimist.'

In such an environment theories about the divinity or the Atonement of Christ were rather less than central to university students or, for that matter, to the clergymen who were called upon to speak to them. 'Formerly the transcendence of God was the prevailing idea, now the immanence of God is the thought which largely holds the theological field.'[52]

The speaker, addressing the Queen's theological society in 1911, ascribed much of this change to 'ideal philosophy,' which led towards 'a more spiritual view of the universe.' The universe, he said, is a rational one, and 'human self-consciousness' stood related to it. But life in a rational universe required rational acts, and the traditional notion of Christ's Atonement was no longer acceptable. The best interpretation of that act was that Christ taught sacrifice, and Tolstoy's dictum, 'Give everything and ask for nothing in return,' was as good a rule for social conduct as any. 'This,' said the Reverend James Binnie, 'is the very heart of a working Theology. I cannot define the meaning of Christ's sacrifice. No theory of the Atonement is adequate. I try to keep the great fact before me. I see in it the joy of forgiveness, the possibility of a new start in life for the hopeless ... and the hope both sure and steadfast of advancing towards the full development of all the powers of my being. Here I recognize that the true principle of life for me and all mankind is love, and service, and sacrifice.'[53]

For some contemporaries, such a statement was evidence of the growing secularity of the age. Yet Christianity remained a vital, adaptable religion, and others doubtless viewed Binnie's views as simply one attempt to remain true to the core of the faith. To some it was a sign that the spark of evangelicalism was virtually extinguished; to others it was a sign of renewed vitality. It was, perhaps, an indication that the power of the evangelical ethos had now taken it far beyond its personal and introspective roots, beyond the capacity of the Protestant churches to control it, beyond even the framework and vocabulary of formal religion itself, to reside in new guises within the institution that had become a powerful guardian of culture: the university. Important ground had shifted, and with it the institutional location of moral authority. Evangelical religion had, in a sense, provided the means by which others might implicitly redefine and build upon it. The romantic rendering of Christ articulated by the evangelicals in their reaction to the Enlightenment was now burlesqued by the new-look Christ provided by those such as Bruce Barton and Joseph McFadyen for the age of the consumer. This Christianity was clearly more secular. But was it really less religious to those who believed?

Christian Culture

Phrases such as 'the full development of all the powers of my being' were, by the early twentieth century, associated as much with cultural fulfillment as with religious enrichment. In the 1860s Matthew Arnold had given classic definition to the notion of culture with his assertion, in *Cul-*

ture and Anarchy (1869), that it originated 'in the love of perfection ... It moves by the force, not merely or primarily of the scientific passion for pure knowledge, but also of the moral and social passion for doing good.'[54] By the early twentieth century, as much attention was being paid to the relationship between culture and religion as between Christ and Christian. Arnold had also said, in the same passage, that culture's best motto was expressed in the following words: 'To make reason and the will of God prevail!' In an age when God was seen in Ontario idealist circles as the virtual embodiment of reason, and in an atmosphere in which many students and professors believed that the object of Christianity was to become the ideal man, Christian by inspiration but propelled by a social passion for doing good, it was perfectly understandable that a degree of confusion existed as to what differentiated Christianity from culture and that to some they meant largely the same thing.

Major exponents of this shift from Christ to culture taught not only theology or religion but also classics and English. The spectacular rise of English to a position of pre-eminence within the liberal arts curriculum in the span of a generation is no less part of the story of the shifting relations between Christ and culture than is that of the higher criticism or of British speculative idealism. In fact, its place is a central one.

The advent of curricular choice in the 1860s and 1870s, and with it student initiative and choice, facilitated the undergraduate gravitation away from classics and classical languages towards instruction in the vernacular, thereby drawing the study of English language and literature in from the periphery of academic life. The growing influence of post-Darwinian science on the one hand gave professors in humanistic subjects new, methodologically rigorous, 'scientific' approaches (such as a German-inspired philology) to their subjects, thereby, they hoped, regaining an authority that had been in relative decline. But on the other hand humanists within the academy were often shaken by the seeming 'triumph' of science – and also of its practical value, its materialism, and the epistemological authority it had conscripted – and they saw in the study of English literature a means of recovering and rearticulating threatened or lost moral absolutes. The last decades of Victoria's reign witnessed, as a result, the triumph of English literature as well as that of Victorian science. In this quest for centrality, its proponents found key allies in the twin forms of idealism then dominant in British intellectual circles: Matthew Arnold's Christian humanism and neo-Hegelian speculative philosophy. By the end of the Edwardian era the study of English literature had become, for many, the embodiment of British cultural ideals. For some, it served as a virtual substitute for orthodox and absolute Christian values.[55]

Signs of a movement in this direction can be seen in the teaching and administrative career of Daniel Wilson in the 1860s and 1870s;[56] but it is in the next generation of professors dedicated to the study of English, those whose careers began in the mid-to-late 1880s that the triumph of an idealist approach to English can best be witnessed. In Ontario professors of English, such as W.J. Alexander at the University of Toronto and James Cappon at Queen's, substantially set the nature and direction of English studies in the province for a full half-century and more. Their lives and views, therefore, deserve scrutiny.

James Cappon arrived in Kingston, fresh from an education in philosophy at the University of Glasgow under Edward Caird, in 1888. His University of Toronto colleague, W.J. Alexander, took up his position in University College the following year, after five years at Dalhousie. Like Cappon, Alexander was not a specialist in English literature. He had studied English language and literature at the University of London, but his advanced degree from Johns Hopkins had been in Greek philology. Yet from the time they assumed their Canadian posts they became (with Archibald MacMechan at Dalhousie, a former student under George Paxton Young and Daniel Wilson in Toronto) the major apostles of Arnold's idealist culture in Canada. Like Arnold, throughout their lengthy careers they preached a form of social citizenship inspired by a pursuit of the ideal that ultimately imbued culture with moral significance equal to that of the Christian religion itself. They did not feel threatened by the idealist philosophers such as John Watson or George Blewett. On the contrary, they believed themselves to be allies in service of cultural ideals and the essentials of the Christian message. Arnold was to them what Hegel was to the philosophers, for both forms of idealism provided them with a metaphysic suitable for the age and for the study of its literature. As one scholar has observed: 'It [philosophical idealism] easily encompassed the Christian orthodoxy of George Herbert and Alexander Pope, the morally active Nature of Wordsworth, and neo-platonism and "the everlasting universe of things" of Shelley, the "universal HERE" and the "everlasting NOW" of Carlyle, and the "culture" of Matthew Arnold. An easy transfer of ideal values from Christianity to literature now led to the new literature course as a replacement of the Christian philosophy and ethics and rhetoric courses that had been the capstone in many of the old, unified, classical programs.'[57] The Canadian apostles of Arnoldian humanism were not converts to an idealist ethic; they merely came to transpose it from its roots in Christian theology to the new creed of culture.

The immediate reason for the creation of a new academic chair of English language and literature at the University of Toronto in 1889 came about, however, for a more mundane reason.[58] The City of Toronto had reneged the year earlier on a 999-year lease on that portion of the provincial university's grounds called 'Queen's Park.' As part of an out-of-court settlement, the city agreed to provide $6,000 annually to support two new chairs. In September 1888 President Daniel Wilson noted in his diary: 'The City claims to determine what the chairs shall be with a view of extending the benefits of a National University to the wage-earning classes who have not hitherto shared in an equal degree with the rest of the community in its educational advantages. The object was to try and secure a useful application of the money. I put in for a chair of English language and literature for one, and for another suggested applied electricity.'[59] Wilson got half his wish. The city fathers of Toronto opted for a chair in mineralogy and geology rather than in electricity; but the chair in English language and literature was established. W.J. Alexander was appointed to the position, and began teaching in Toronto in autumn 1889.

Inspired by the Canada First movement of the 1870s and by an ardent desire to give a Canadian literary expression to the romantic nationalism of the first decades of Confederation, the student generation of the 1880s wanted Canadian professors to teach them modern literature, for this was the means to the discovery of their own literary past. They wanted their views to be heard. Student writers complained bitterly of the philological and grammatical approaches to the study of language and called for the greater use of original texts instead of literary histories. Writing in 1893, Archibald Lampman, an 1882 graduate of Trinity College, reflected critically on the approach to literature characteristic of his days in Toronto:

The study of literature is carried on in many universities and higher institutions of learning in a very stilted and academic manner. The courses of instruction, including as they do grammar, philology, the study of the growth of modern languages, the history and analysis of literary masterpieces, conducted mostly in a spirit of barren ingenuity, produce scholars simply – too often pedants – rarely men of original energy or even of true literary taste. This is particularly so in universities like our own ... In the English courses one professor has usually to cover the whole ground, and in order that a man may be found properly equipped for a position from an academic point of view a sacrifice has generally to be made on the side of critical and artistic attainment.

This was indeed true: Daniel Wilson's first assistant, D.R. Keys, taught Italian as well as English after his appointment in 1883.[60]

Other University of Toronto graduates in the 1880s continued the campaign against the philological 'gradgrinders.' Thomas Haultain complained in 1881 that studying English by means that were appropriate to the classics was 'like oxidising the diamond to prove it carbon, dissecting the body to discover the soul.' Three years later Archibald MacMechan published a detailed critique of instruction in modern languages, complaining that 'all the knowledge of literature' its examinations demanded '[was] to be gained in reading *about* books, not in reading the books themselves.' (In contrast, students of the Wesleyan Ladies' College in Hamilton were at the time required to be thoroughly familiar with literary texts – including novels, which in Toronto were not yet deemed to be of sustained literary merit.[61]) MacMechan continued his appeal for a more liberal approach to the study of literature. His clarion call inspired *Varsity* to keep up the pressure for a change of approach for the remainder of the decade. They railed against examinations that required them to regurgitate names, dates, and the literary opinions of others. 'We can scarcely speak here of the "depression" of English,' said a *Varsity* editorialist in 1885, '... for a subject cannot be depressed until it has first been elevated ...'[62] The same year its editor chided Toronto professors that even they 'might perceive that there can be no hopeful education without an awakening of interest in the mind of the learner, and that this can only be done by placing him in close contact first with the living throbbing literature of his own day.'[63]

Thus, by 1888 student sentiment coincided precisely with the kind of appointment W.J. Alexander represented. He was a Canadian and he was not a philologist, but a romantic nationalist who advocated literature as a means to culture. The new appointee could scarcely have described his own approach better than the editors of *Varsity* did in the autumn of 1888: 'The business of a Professor of English and English Literature in a Canadian University must be not mainly the mechanical dissection of word and sentence and paragraph in the works of our great authors; not mainly the dull drilling of wearied students in the facts of literary history, but the cultivation in the minds of the undergraduates of that taste for literature which we so sadly lack, and of an intelligent appreciation of the best work of the best English men of letters ...'[64] Further 'instructions' from the students continued even after the announcement of Alexander's appointment. In February and March, 1889, they expressed their wish for modern writers. One of these students, Pelham Edgar, reminded the new appointee: 'Wordsworth, Coleridge, and Shelley are not considered too modern for a denial of admittance to the Fourth Year literature. These great names unjustly, though brilliantly, end the chronological list of poets. The names of immortal contemporaries are not as yet, by virtue of their bearers' respective and obliging demises, rendered sufficiently holy for consideration.'[65] When Alexander gave his first lecture at the University of Toronto, two weeks later, the young Edgar got his wish. Alexander's subject was Robert Browning, who was then still alive.

W.J. Alexander's inaugural address at Toronto bore the same title as his one in 1884 at Dalhousie: 'The Study of Literature.' In it he insisted that while study of the English language was important, and should at some point even have its own chair, the study of English literature was more central to the nurturing of liberal culture. His emphasis, therefore, was to be on the study of literature itself, rather than on its history (as in Wilson's day), and even less on the English language. Literature embodied the elements of the highest and purest form of culture, and it held the power to provide men with a harmonious balance of intellect and emotion and to inspire them to perfection by example. Each author's style embodied his character. It captured his soul. Appreciation of good style was a window to that soul: 'When style in that highest degree is present, we are not merely told how the writer felt, but his feelings are communicated to us; not how he saw, but we are enabled to see as he did; not what manner of man he was, but we are introduced into his very presence.'[66]

The power of literature was more, even, than this: it also held out the promise of a comprehensive understanding of the vast sweep of civilization itself and of the role of university faculties of arts whose core discipline would now be English. Alexander's 1889 inaugural address was, then, a statement of late nineteenth-century academic belief as important and insightful as Egerton Ryerson's declaration of the nature and meaning of a liberal education in his first inaugural address to Victoria College half a century earlier:

When we have read a book with interest we are ... led from the study of single works to the study of writers – from books to men ... To complete our understanding of the work, or our conception of the writer, we must know something of the intellectual atmosphere which surrounded him, of the current of thought, and of the spirit of his time. In doing this, we pass from the study of the individual writer to the study of the period in which he lived – to the history of literature. Arrived at this stage, we find that books and authors possessing but little in themselves to merit our attention have now, as links in the chain of literary development, a new interest and importance through their influence upon greater writers and through the insight which they afford into the current thought of the age. Thus starting from single authors, with a desire of fully understanding their works, and of forming a complete and true likeness of them as men, we find a new conception and a new aim dawning upon us – the conception of the solidarity of literature, the aim of forming a complete image of the thought of an age in all its manifold relations ...[67]

Literature, for Alexander as for Arnold, was part of the civilizing process, an ever-widening progression of moral enlightenment from book to
author to writers to ethos to epoch, a great chain of reading rather than of
being whose canonic nature linked past and future to make a fractious
present bearable. Where once the unity of Christendom had been the
vessel responsible for the voyage of moral continuity from age to age,
this duty was now seen to lie in a tradition of English literature. It would
be very difficult to locate in English-Canadian writing a better illustration than Alexander's inaugural address, of the broad cultural and social
mission of English literature as it existed near the end of the nineteenth
century and would persist well into the twentieth.[68]

Arnold had stated in *Culture and Anarchy* that religion, however
important it was, could not embrace the totality of human affairs. Culture, however, could do so.[69] For Arnold, and for his acolytes such as
Alexander, literature, and particularly poetry, was the conduit to culture
and to civilized existence. 'The future of poetry is immense,' Arnold had
written in 1880, 'because in poetry, where it is worthy of its high destinies, our race, as time goes on, will find an ever surer and surer stay.
There is not a creed which is not shaken, not an accredited dogma which
is not shown to be questionable, not a received tradition which does not
threaten to dissolve ... We should conceive of poetry worthily, and more
highly than it has been the custom to conceive of it ... More and more
mankind will discover that we have to turn to poetry to interpret our life
for us, to console us, to sustain us. Without poetry, our science will
appear incomplete; and most of what now passes with us for religion and
philosophy will be replaced by poetry.'[70] Alexander and others echoed
the master: as the purest form of literature, poetry alone could lay claim
to universal and everlasting truth.

The views of James Cappon at Queen's were variations on these
themes. Like Alexander, he was marked for life by the thought of Matthew Arnold.[71] But Cappon's education in philosophy under Edward
Caird at the University of Glasgow had provided him also with a Hegelian brush that gave his idealist portrayal of literature a philosophical
patina and an enhanced authority, especially at Watson's Queen's.[72] The
Hegelian world spirit or absolute was the Christian God transmogrified
and under another name, for it embodied all universal principles, including aesthetic and ethical ones. Cappon accepted the philosophical premises, but chose to see them best revealed in the literary record rather
than in philosophy or theology. 'The average man's knowledge of what
is going on in the world around him ... is derived from literature,' he
wrote; 'It is really literature which binds men together in a spiritual
world and gives such solidarity of moral consciousness to society as it

has attained ...'[73] Cappon's commitment to the spirit of British imperial adventure, articulated when the Empire was at its height, gave the civilizing mission of English literature additional ideological force.[74]

While Cappon doubtless shared Alexander's views about the capacity of the canon of English literature to facilitate social harmony and to elevate the human condition, he ascribed to imperialism a parallel function. 'The Empire,' he proclaimed, in a passage that combined the civilizing process of Arnoldian humanism and the unfolding of the progressivist Hegelian world spirit, 'represents an ideal of high importance for the future of civilization, the attempt to assemble in a higher unity than even that of nationality the forces which maintain and advance the white man's ideals of civilization, his sense of justice, his constitutional freedom, his respect for law and order, his humanity. It is an attempt to transcend the evils of nationality ... without impairing the vigour which the national consciousness gives to a people.'[75]

Men such as Alexander and Cappon were emblematic of their generation of humanists. Their reorientation of the study of literature away from philological analysis towards the study of culture and its history, within the context of a British Empire then at its zenith, found allies in disciplines such as classics, philosophy, and history. Classicists such as W.S. Milner and Maurice Hutton at the University of Toronto or T.R. Glover and John MacNaughton at Queen's may have objected to the increased use of English as a language of instruction in classical subjects, but they were one in their fusion of Christian and other forms of idealism and they, too, spoke in the lexicon of Arnoldian humanism. Hutton was devoted to the Hellenic ideal and, as with Alexander and Cappon in English, he took his department away from a primary concentration on linguistic instruction toward an appreciation of the philosophy and history of the classical tradition. For this reason, although English was beginning to supplant classics at the heart of the liberal arts curriculum, the years between 1880 and the Great War were the golden years of classics at Toronto – in part, testimony to the sheer power of Hutton's own force of personality. The classics program at Toronto, as a result, produced some of the best, most cultivated, and most literate minds of several generations of English-Canadians: Charles W. Gordon, B.K. Sandwell, C.B. Sissons, Charles Norris Cochrane, and Frank Underhill were among them. A classical education in the age of Hutton was fundamentally an introduction to the cultural antecedents of Western civilization, with Hutton's own emphasis on character and taste – in short, it was an introduction to Western manners and morals as well as to the rise of imperial Europe.

Hutton delighted in all matters Greek. Yet he nevertheless found a certain hollowness at the core of Greek thought that he proceeded to fill with Christian moral nostrums. 'Faith,' he said, 'accomplishes more than knowledge; hope more than experience; charity more than caution.' His blend of Greek and Christian ideals was an uneasy one, and it led him perilously near the brink of cultural and ethical relativism. Hutton came to believe that the Christian's truths were 'only true in some mythical sense; that is ... they are the highest truths a man can reach at present, and true to his heart's needs and the needs of his conscience.' However, he accepted the challenge of demonstrating the essential compatibility and continuity of Greek and Christian messages: 'These meeting points,' he said, 'these junctions, so to speak, of the divergent highroads of Religion and Intelligence, of Christianity and Literature, spirits never identical ... and indeed often vehemently ... opposed to each other – these junctions have always appealed to me ...'[76]

Like Cappon and others at century's end, Hutton saw in the British Empire the embodiment – possibly even the culmination – of the moral and cultural ideals to which he subscribed. That empire relied in the end, like all empires, on communal sentiment – in this case a sentiment based on 'community of ideals, community of traditions, community of language, community of spiritual atmosphere.' In this belief he was supported by George M. Wrong, an avid supporter of imperial federation, in the Toronto history department.[77] Hutton was probably the most ardent and articulate of Toronto imperialists, and his commitment to the British Empire as the best protector of Christian ethics and political freedom hardened in the new century into an unapologetic defence of the martial spirit as, in his words, 'an innate facet of human nature.' The many students of this eloquent and persuasive spokesman for the just war as an act of moral purpose were to reap the harvest of this black whirlwind of words.

It is wise not to underestimate the possible influence of men such as Alexander, Cappon, and Hutton on the late Victorian and Edwardian generation of teachers and students. Their careers in the lecture hall were lengthy ones. Appointed in 1889, Alexander did not retire until 1926; Cappon's career in Canada spanned from 1888 to 1919; Hutton taught from 1880 to 1929. They held positions of great eminence within their institutions for many of these years: Alexander as head of the English department at Toronto from his appointment in 1889 until 1912, and after that as the doyen of English literature in the country; Cappon as dean of arts at Queen's from 1906 to his retirement in 1919; Hutton as principal of University College from 1901 until his own retirement almost thirty years later. In spite of such administrative and other duties (such as Cappon's editorial and authorial contributions to *Queen's Quar-*

terly for nearly twenty years) their teaching loads were enormous. Often they taught almost all of the students in their departments and many of those in their faculties. Alexander regularly lectured to hundreds of students, at every level, and Cappon's load was not much lighter. 'For many years,' Cappon wrote Principal Gordon in 1909, 'all my classes (except two Honours Classes of about 70 each) were 100 or over. Having to teach such classes twice a day and keep their interest active all the time, not only ruined my individual and exercise work, but has had, I think, a good deal to do with that peculiar nerve exhaustion from which I now suffer.'[78] Whatever one concludes about the nature or legacy of their academic mission, these were academic figures of heroic stature and they were revered by several generations of students.

English was by 1920 a core subject in virtually every arts and science program in English-speaking Canada, a subject required for graduation with a Bachelor of Arts or Bachelor of Science degree. At some institutions it was mandatory in all four years of undergraduate study. The popularity of English has been attributed in part to its provision of practical skills in written English[79] but this is only part of the explanation for its spectacular rise to eminence within a generation, for the priorities and emphasis within departments of English were away from practical development of linguistic skills derived from the art of rhetoric and overwhelmingly towards the study of literature, and towards criticism as a new form of academic endeavour that linked appreciation with scholarship. Its initial market was, ironically, those who were on the margins of society – as it had been earlier in England. As the poor man's classics, intended for those who could not gain access to university because of their lack of Latin or Greek, English found support among those involved in the education of workingmen, women, and immigrants, or those who sought access to the British or, later, Canadian civil service.[80]

The *fin de siècle* triumph of English was especially marked by the redirection of English studies to literature from language; as such, it served as a comfortable surrogate for some who no longer found certainty in orthodox Christian beliefs but who still possessed the will to believe. In 1913 the author of a *Queen's Quarterly* article on 'The Philosophy of Matthew Arnold' reproduced Arnold's poem 'The Future' in his concluding pages. It went, in part:

> This tract which the river of Time
> Now flows through with us, is the plain.
> Gone is the calm of its earlier shore.
> Bordered by cities, and hoarse
> With a thousand cries in its stream.

And we on its breast, our minds
Are confused as the cries which we hear,
Changing and short as the sights which we see.
. . . .
Haply, the river of Time –
As it grows, as the towns on its marge
Fling their wavering lights
On a wider, statelier stream –
May acquire, if not the calm
Of its early mountainous shore,
Yet a solemn peace of its own.

'It is verse like this,' said the essay's author, 'that gives Arnold his
unique power of appeal to men of this generation. We are so close to the
old faith we have lost that a strange yearning for something sure, something definite, still makes us vaguely uneasy and melancholy. Arnold is
the voice of that wistful longing ... Indeed even now the faith of the
Christian churches is changing into a form which comes nearer, at least
to giving peace, and even something of joy, to men who could not rest in
the old dogmas. But there is not as yet that "Common wave of thought
and joy, Lifting mankind again" for which Arnold looked. Until it comes
the poetry of Arnold must continue to appeal, even to be a comfort and a
source of strength to many a kindred spirit.'[81] The Christian apostles of
an idealist approach to English literature, whether Arnoldian or neo-
Hegelian, still willed to believe in religious absolutes; but as often as not
their search for them led to the literary, not the biblical, record.

By the 1890s even Alfred Henry Reynar, a Victoria College rhetorician whose lengthy career spanned the balanced general approach to language studies of the 1860s (he was appointed professor of modern
languages and English literature in 1868) and the English specialists of
the twentieth century (he was dean of arts from 1891, retiring in 1910),
had been swayed by Arnold's vision, and his lectures increasingly provided Christian sermons disguised as lectures on literature. The ancient
and modern classics, he told one audience, demonstrated that the 'best
writings of the Anglo-Saxon race' provided the finest expression of the
biblical admonition, 'thou shalt love thy neighbor as thyself.' In an
address to the Ontario chapter of the Modern Languages Association in
1889 he set forth his Arnoldian views: 'Culture is a law written in the
heart and in the mind,' linked to both by the sentiments and the imagination. 'The imagination,' he said, 'is simply that faculty by which we
form true ideals, perfect images, faithful concepts of things – that faculty
in fine by which we see things as they are in their eternal archetypes, and

not merely as they may be imperfectly realized or discovered by experience.' Tennyson's *In Memoriam*, he claimed, embodied the elevation of the world of the secular to the realm of the sacred: 'The love that had once seemed human only and that had been associated with the "sweet human hand and lips and eye" is now seen to be the expression or the outgoing of the divine principle or passion rather that pervades nature and guides and rules the world. The human love, however, is not absorbed and lost in the higher divine love, but it is exalted, glorified and made immortal. This high experience of the poet is in keeping with the prayer of the promise of the Great Son of Man ... "If I go and prepare a place for you, I will come again and receive you unto myself, that where I am ye may be also."' As Henry Hubert so aptly says of this passage: 'The conflation of English literature with Christianity here was total. The ideals of one were the ideals of the other.'[82]

The end-of-century linkage between Christianity and culture was rooted in a gradual shift from piety to moralism – that is, from inner spirit to outward conduct – that had been taking place for years, but it became most apparent in the decades that preceded the Great War. The idea of the good was ceasing to be conceived as a series of transcendent truths but instead was coming to be seen as functional values rooted in the historical or literary record. The fulcrum at which this shift took place, as we have noted, was the point at which one can locate the birth of the modern social sciences. In European history this point was reached in the eighteenth and early nineteenth centuries. In Canada it came after 1870, and we can see it in the history of English studies as well as in the realm of social analysis. The fact that the shift from Christ to culture took place in Ontario precisely in the years when men such as Adam Shortt and O.D. Skelton extolled the virtues and preached the moral and social utility of the emergent discipline of political economy, or when W.J. Alexander and James Cappon talked of the civilizing mission of English in the face of an increasingly materialistic society, is by no means a matter of coincidence.[83] Students realized this. 'Professor Skelton's paper on "The Church and Social Questions" we cannot praise too highly,' wrote one of them after Skelton's address to the 1910 Queen's alumni conference. 'Amazing in its scope and sympathetic in its treatment, it impressed us as a unique combination of scholarship, experience and spirituality. While the church's duty must ever be the "renewing of a right spirit," in the individual, to-day more than ever it must be alive to social needs of the community and the nation – and Prof Skelton set this forth in a manner that made his paper indispensable to the best success of the conference.'[84]

Students at Victoria College in the mid-1890s were already talking about Christian culture in ways that indicated that both Christianity and culture involved self-development. Their English professors, no less than philosophers or theologians, were responsible for such views. Culture, for almost all members of the province's faculties of arts, had come to mean more than outward graces of manner. It was neither refinement nor genius. It was, rather, the use of human rationality to develop the whole being in such a way that knowledge gained in college was applied to all walks of life. 'Culture must come to the rescue of society,' said one student, 'with the self-abandonment of soldiers in the time of battle ... Culture is not a lamp to study by, but a beacon light ... Culture has to exercise a divine fellowship. Modern society is a network of interests. No human being stands entirely alone. There is and must be fellowship in our culture.'[85] By the early twentieth century, the notion of culture had come to be synonymous with the earlier idea of a liberal education – to denote the 'well-balanced, harmonious development of all our faculties.'[86] But by then, in the view of the man who was to succeed Principal Grant after his death in 1902, culture also involved a basic aim of religion – to aspire to perfection – and it was rooted in the literary record.

Twentieth-century religious leaders such as Daniel Miner Gordon had difficulty addressing the relationship between culture and religion because whenever they sought to define the aims of the religious life they found that modern advocates of culture across a range of disciplines had already conscripted religious attributes. Gordon, for example, found himself embracing the culturalist vocabulary of the day, arguing, for example, that a fuller religious life was necessary 'to carry the treasures of culture for our own true welfare and for the good of others.' Unable or unwilling to argue that the pursuit of culture instead of religion should be discouraged, he – and one suspects others in his position – could only plead that culture tended 'to make the most of self, simply for the sake of self and by reliance on the powers of self,' whereas religion (Christianity is nowhere mentioned by name), sought 'to make the most of self, yet not by the efforts of self, but by the surrender of self to God.' Gordon was astute in his recognition that modern students, drawn to culture and to religion, had a serious choice to make even though both aimed at the achievement of human perfection. He struck a practical balance between the two when he said 'Culture and religion both look on human nature as capable of being developed into perfection. Culture says that this depends on the labour and effort bestowed; religion says that it depends on the surrender of our being to God.'[87]

What Gordon addressed was that at the turn of the century earnest young Christians at his university were surrendering themselves as much to society as to God, for their embrace of culture testified to their belief that it embodied society's ideal face. The children of the progressive generation wished to serve God as fervently as their parents and grandparents had before them, but the ethos of social service that informed and shaped their consciousness in so many ways convinced them that their Christian duty was to find a helpful vocation in life and to surrender themselves to lives of social commitment and moral elevation. Their professors, whether teachers of philosophy or religion, the new political science, or the equally new English, preached a commitment to the larger social and ethical good, and many university graduates heeded the call. They became teachers, social workers, clergymen, civil servants, and professors of English and history. They did so because they continued to respect the views held by their professors and also because the nature of modern society – complex in its economic and social relations, abundant with information about political issues and social problems – made it difficult for the students of the new century to be immune from the concerns of life when they chose to look beyond the ivy-covered walls of their respective institutions. For some, particularly those who felt in some way threatened by the increasing dominance of secular science, the new linkage between the essentials of Christianity and the nature of culture also offered a new means of spiritual rebirth and social resurrection.

10

Marching as to War

At the beginning of the twentieth century a vibrant student culture existed within the universities. Undergraduate social organization increasingly reflected the changing world outside campus grounds. Just as the university had become more specialized and more complex, so, too, the extracurricular life of students expanded. At times their activities complemented the pronouncements and priorities of professors, but not always. By the eve of the Great War, they were, on the whole, less willing than previous generations had generally been to submit placidly to paternalistic professorial control in their social or academic lives.

Students gained a sense of identity from social groups more than from individual moral nurture or religious conversion. As the presence of women on university campuses increased, usually in the faculties of arts, male undergraduates met the challenge by turning to aggressive 'manly' activities in the form of organized sports that helped preserve a sense of the campus as the domain of men. Women, in turn, gravitated towards an interest in mission work, and they were aided in doing so by conventional social definitions of their role as well as by an ardent desire, shared by the turn-of-the-century male, to engage in some form of useful social service. Finally, by the early twentieth century a degree of military presence existed in the form of appeals for organized martial training on the university campus.

In the intellectual and social climate of late Victorian Ontario, the values and assumptions associated with each of these clusters of activity – sports, missions, and the military – at times converged. Sports were often portrayed as a form of warfare; Christian missions to 'heathen' nations took on military precision and required no less dedication; and, most tragic of all, warfare was seen as a manly game to be played with missionary zeal. The student generation of 1914 was unprepared for the reality that followed the firing of weapons after 4 August 1914. Dancing, not war, was then the major issue at most Ontario universities. In the spring of 1914 students, university authorities, and the public were debating the sexual implications of the tango. By the beginning of the next school term, with the first undergraduates beginning to fall in Flanders, the matter had become a source of silent embarrassment.

Turn-of-the-Century Student Culture

One must be wary of making generalizations about student activities and concerns at Ontario's universities in this period, for they differed in nuance and degree from institution to institution. Moreover, the evidence necessary for sustaining such judgments exists in greater measure for universities such as Toronto, Victoria, and Queen's than it does for others.

Student activities and concerns at Western University, for example, are known primarily from whatever reports were made on university affairs by the London press. A scrapbook of such clippings for the years 1903 to 1906, compiled by historian Fred Landon during his years as an undergraduate there, reveals an institution dominated by genteel social activities: meetings of the literary and musical society, the debating society, the modern language club, 'at homes,' various field sports, and the annual field day. Clearly, the highlight of the year's activities (apart from convocation) was the annual conversazione – an evening of innocent social amusements and conversation, closely chaperoned, that marked the continuation of late Victorian activities into the Edwardian age. 'The annual conversazione of the Western University, held last night,' went one account, 'must be classed as one of the most brilliant and successful social events of the season in this city. There was a numerous assemblage of guests, who were afforded an evening of cultured enjoyment, one of the features of which was an excellent programme of music.'[1] Ushered into rooms festooned with white and gold muslin suspended from the ceilings, guests were welcomed by London's finest matrons, enjoyed 'civilized conversation' as they wended through a dining room 'adorned in the daintiest manner with red, white and blue draperies,' and made their way ultimately to the Convocation Hall dominated by the platform from which the concert was given. This, too, was decorated with 'an artistic blending of the British and United States flags surmounted by the Royal coat of arms in colored relief, palms and ferns being arranged at suitable points.' The first of two concerts began at 8:00 p.m., with instrumental solos on violin and piano, a male vocalist, and a dramatic reading. Then, while the Cortese Orchestra inaugurated a promenade concert, the guests inspected 'the many objects of interest from many lands' that were on display throughout the room.[2]

One searches almost in vain for reports on student interests at Western other than those just described. One formal debate took place between students from Western and the Ontario Agricultural College on the resolution 'That the present leadership of Japan is likely to produce a retrograte [sic] movement in the civilization of the world' (won by the affirmative), and the London press noted that the local university's students highly favoured its secularization and were willing to be vocal about it.[3] But the undergraduate clippings of Fred Landon, who was to join the university's staff as a lecturer in history and would later become its librarian and dean of arts, reveal little else by way of social concern. The margins of social life at Western were largely marked by sleigh rides, memorable performances of 'The School for Scandal,' and the making of 'Edwardian fudge.'[4] This was understandable, given the tiny size of the student population, which declined from seventy-five in 1904–5 to forty-one in 1908 and was to reach only 108 by 1914.[5]

Undergraduate culture at the bilingual University of Ottawa was one that by the beginning of the new century shared forms of associational activity with institutions elsewhere. The Oblates had provided students with a sizeable gymnasium and outdoor playing fields, and by the mid-1880s various forms of athletic activity, especially football but including basketball, volleyball, and hockey, occupied an important place. Social activities such as skating parties and the annual ice carnival aimed at uniting the student body. This much Ottawa shared with other universities in the province. But there were also very important differences. The student population remained exclusively male, since Roman Catholic women seeking secondary or post-secondary education continued to attend convent schools or affiliated colleges. (The first women who 'graduated' from the university, in 1911, were in fact high school matriculants who had attended Notre-Dame and Bruyère colleges, recently affiliated with the university. The first female undergraduates did not appear in Bachelor of Arts courses at Ottawa until 1919, when the university senate approved their enrolment.) Moreover, this male student body was itself divided by ethnicity and language, for most were either English-speaking Irish or Franco-Ontarians.[6]

It is unlikely that students escaped the division and discord that characterized relations between those who provided spiritual guidance, supervised, or taught them. French- and English-speaking Roman Catholics in Ontario had long been deeply divided on the issue of bilingual schooling, nowhere more so than in Ottawa. In the late nineteenth century this rift became personalized in the bitter struggle between J.T.

Duhamel, who became Archbishop in 1886, and Michael Francis Fallon, the University of Ottawa vice-rector who was summarily removed from office in 1898. In the careful wording of the official history of the University of Ottawa: 'The linguistic balance at the College, always delicate, leaned away from French and favoured English from about 1874 to 1901, partly because of simmering rivalry between the francophone Oblates and their anglophone Irish colleagues, and partly because English-speaking students made up the majority of the student body. Although francophone students continued to take courses in French literature and religion in their own language, the sciences and the classical courses were offered in English.'[7] Two academic solitudes based on linguistic and cultural difference, it appears, had developed within the Ottawa academic community by the early twentieth century, and matters were to get much worse by its second decade when the bilingual school issue pitted Catholic against Protestant and widened the existing rift within the Catholic community itself.[8]

The student population at McMaster University increased by sixty per cent between 1905 and 1911, when just under 300 students were enrolled and its academic staff numbered twenty-one. More students meant a greater diversity in undergraduate interests and a corresponding division of labour in the organization of activities. The *McMaster University Monthly*, first published in 1891, provided an ongoing record of what students were doing and what they could do. By 1900 students could become members of its literary society, thereby listening to debates on 'The Single Tax and the Present System.' So many students wanted to debate in 1900 that a formal debating club was created. Its first subject was 'Resolved, That the Reading of Novels is not Commendable,' but no decision was reached. Students could join its glee club or its ladies' literary league, play on one of its football teams, or attend meetings of one of the most important of campus groups, the Fyfe Missionary Society.[9] Most of these organized group activities had arisen in the 1890s, in the first exciting years of the new university's existence. They continued into the new century, but university officials began to note that the student body had poor morale and lacked a sense of direction. On the few occasions when students did take initiative, it tended towards disruptive forms of behaviour. 'Perhaps we are getting a different class of freshmen now than we used to get ten or fifteen years ago!,' wrote one graduate in 1908.[10] Hazing was officially banned on the McMaster campus, and disturbing college yells and hooliganism in the chapel building occurred at times, but apathy and listlessness were more representative of student life. The British cause in the Boer War had created much campus excitement early in the century, but by 1911 even a debating club resolution that 'Free Trade between Canada and the United States would be detrimental to the best interests of the Dominion' resulted in only an unemotional, 'lackluster performance' by the participants.[11]

The acrimonious dispute generated by Elmore Harris over modernism in religious instruction certainly did nothing to raise student morale. Some thought that the confined Bloor Street location of the university prevented it from providing the athletic and other facilities that might have regenerated student interest.[12] Professors attempted to stimulate student interest in the expansion of clubs, but their rewards were meagre. The *McMaster University Monthly* fully documents this sense of drift in the half dozen years preceding the Great War. 'In our endeavors to fill up the required space in this issue,' wrote the 1913–14 editor of the 'College News' section of the *Monthly*, 'we have expended much energy and thought ... We have investigated and considered the activities of the college organizations; but through it all nothing satisfactory was presented to our mind.'[13]

The prevalence elsewhere of *fin de siècle* ideas, said one graduate, resulted in 'little perceptible change' in student life at Trinity College as it entered the new century. Nevertheless, the decade of the 1890s left something of a mark. The first issues of the *Trinity University Review*, inaugurated in 1888, had contained sober articles on church choirs and organ music. 'Later,' admitted the Trinity graduate, 'these became the subject of chapel jokes. The men stepped out of their cloisters and became more worldly. It was, after all, "the gay nineties."'[14] Compulsory chapel services, held twice daily, were a source of acrimony every year by the turn of the century, especially the one that began at 7:30 a.m. But some traditions continued to engender respect. The annual conversazione was pronounced Trinity's most famous social institution by far. Dancing became all the rage, and 'Trinity men indulged ... whenever possible. They danced after concerts, after teas, after plays, after debates, after matches. After the turn of the century, with the appointment of a new provost intent on bringing Trinity into federation with the university, the future of Trinity was uncertain; but the main student concern at the time was his banning of beer, for beer had come to be for Trinity 'what nectar was to the Gods ... dispensed in the Buttery and drunk at meals.'

In the years prior to the Great War, Trinity students gradually adjusted to the consumption of milk. Wrote one wag: 'Old Trinity's past's been *disgraceful*, / So we'll throw all malt liquor away. / Instead of the vulgar beer supper / We'll now have a *concert au lait*.' Elsewhere in the Anglican college students performed Aristophanes' *The Frogs* in the original

Greek during a period of its history marked by a 'uniquely halcyon quality' quite unsullied by concern about the implications of the Russo-Japanese War or other outside matters. Life at Trinity continued to resemble a prolonged Edwardian soirée.

A mile or so north-east of Trinity student life was not so tranquil. University College had entered the decade of the 1890s with a conversazione that produced more heat than light. An exhibition of microscopic slides was to have been provided, but shortly before the display was to open an attendant upset one of the oil-fed lamps that were to give the necessary lighting. Fuelled by the upset oil, the fire spread rapidly. With the guests of the conversazione aghast, and President Wilson in tears, the blaze engulfed the eastern wing of the building, destroying the entire library of 33,000 volumes, as well as much of the biological and ethnological collections and all of those in mineralogy and geology. By 1892 the facade of the building had been restored more or less to its original state, and the interior had been rebuilt with greater utility but at the loss of architectural detail.[15] The conflagration was devastating, but for two brief years staff, students, and supporters of University College had a common cause. It was to be perhaps the only unifying force on the campus for the next fifteen years.

Various factors conspired to prevent social cohesion within University College. Not least of them was that after federation one of its central functions was as a centre for instruction in arts and science of students from Victoria College and several professional schools, such as the Royal College of Dental Surgeons (affiliated in 1888), the Toronto Conservatory of Music (1890), and the Ontario College of Pharmacy (1892). Students in arts within the college regarded it as 'the one important, not to say essential element of the University, the motherland of that intellectual empire,' but in their collective disdain for snobbish Trinity or self-righteous Victoria, they tended to cultivate few ties with them. 'At the end of my college career,' remembered B.K. Sandwell, a graduate of 1897, 'I probably knew more about the Royal Military College at Kingston ... than about any of the sister institutions included in the University of Toronto.'[16]

Most regular students at University College in the 1890s and the early twentieth century continued to have denominational loyalties, but during the decade from 1894 to 1904 the number of students who were not Christians, or who did not declare religious affiliation, more than doubled – from four per cent in 1893–4 to nine per cent in 1903–4 . Moreover, many of the students who were attracted to University College, perhaps not only those in this undeclared group, held a different attitude towards college authority than did those enrolled in the denominational colleges. As graduates of the nascent high school system in the province entered the provincial university's main teaching college, they brought with them a more sceptical attitude than that of their predecessors. 'Coming as I did from England, where the excellence of the work of the universities had not been greatly questioned for some generations,' B.K. Sandwell reminisced, 'I was not a little surprised to find that many of my fellow students, whose childhood had been spent among the echoes of the violent controversies about education which filled the '80's, were entirely unwilling to accept the proposition that University College now represented all that was best in education in the best of all possible worlds.'[17] Although Ontario university students of the mid-1890s represented only one-half of one per cent of the provincial population, the students were drawn from a wider socio-economic base. The high school system undercut the role of well-funded private schools or grammar schools as the basic feeders of the university system, and it helped increase the number of younger students from urban areas. By the late 1890s University of Toronto officials estimated that only between one-third and one-quarter of the university's students were from farms.[18]

The 1895 student strike at the University of Toronto, centred in University College, reflected the refractory atmosphere that had arisen and was to continue to exist there for another decade. Numerous circumstances contributed to this event, but prime among them was the unwillingness of this 'new type of student' to accept 'conditions which had worked well enough with the old type but were destined to become outmoded.'[19] University officials such as President Loudon, and Daniel Wilson before him, had acted as surrogate parents for their students; the new students resented such paternalism. Daniel Wilson's refusal in 1886 to allow students to invite 'the infidel tailor,' labour leader Alfred Jury, to speak to their political science club had met with little more than minor grumbling.[20] A similar invitation to Jury in 1894 (along with one to political radical Phillips Thompson) was stopped by James Mavor when he cancelled the entire program, and it became a major source of student grievance. Added to this undergraduate discontent was President Loudon's suspension of James Tucker, editor-in-chief of *Varsity*, as a result of his refusal to apologize formally for articles in the student newspaper (written and published by the previous editor on 17 and 31 October, and 7 and 28 November 1894) highly critical of the seeming nepotism involved in the recent appointment of George Wrong, the son-in-law of Chancellor Blake, to the newly created professorship of Canadian history. Tucker subsequently made the struggle between the students and the administration known to the general public and to the government by presenting his case, signed 'James A. Tucker (class of

'95),' in a letter to the *Mail* (23 January 1895) and the squabbles within University College were kept in the public eye when William Dale, associate professor of Latin, supported the student cause and aired grievances of his own in a long letter to the *Globe* (9 February 1895). Dale was summarily dismissed by President Loudon shortly thereafter. On 15 February students held a mass meeting, articulating their grievances, requesting Dale's reinstatement, and urging a boycott of classes until this was done. Articles attacking Dale, assumed to have been written by officials from the university council, appeared the next day in the *Globe* and the *Mail*. Through the superintendent of ladies, Letitia Salter, Loudon threatened women students with dismissal if they abstained from lectures. The creation of the 1895 provincial royal commission to inquire into 'disciplinary and other matters in the University of Toronto' was an indication that the problems were not only of major proportions but had also become of public concern.[21]

Although the royal commission concluded that most of the student accusations were based more on innuendo than on hard evidence, and therefore absolved the university authorities from any fundamental wrongdoing, there was still a great deal that was clearly unsatisfactory at University College. As the students put the matter in their formal brief to the royal commission: 'The sentiment ... is a feeling that President Loudon is unworthy of belief, that no confidence can be placed in the truth of his statements, and further that in approaching him, the student feels that he is approaching one who is lying in wait to entrap him, and not one who is desirous of assisting the student in his difficulties, or smoothing over matters of irritation, to one who is more anxious arbitrarily to exercise authority than to remove causes of complaint.'[22] William Lyon Mackenzie King, one of the student leaders of the strike, certainly supported this view. For him, the student rebellion of 1895 was the larger struggle of 1837 in microcosm, with James Loudon playing Francis Bond Head while he assumed the role of his grandfather, William Lyon Mackenzie, in a struggle for liberty and responsible government. Little wonder that, a few months later, when the newly graduated King read Charles Lindsey's biography of the Upper Canadian rebel, he confided to his diary: 'I imagined I could feel his blood coursing through my veins ...'[23]

In the decade and more after the student strike of 1895, student life at University College remained one of alienation and discontent, lacking much sense of common purpose except perhaps that of survival until graduation. A remarkable exception was the raucous annual celebration of Hallowe'en by Toronto students. Beginning in 1884 this social ritual, in which at times scores of undergraduates marched the downtown streets, disrupted performances at the Grand Opera House, harassed citizens, and tangled with police, inverted the structures of accustomed social authority and perhaps served as a means of assuaging the sense of student alienation. 'Faced with change, many university students in Toronto may have used Hallowe'en as a means of addressing tensions and experimenting with new conditions. Through Hallowe'en festivities, they turned their world upside down in ritualistic fashion, and by so doing, fostered a sense of identity and community, asserted a degree of power, and tested the makeup and limits of the city and society that were coming into being.'[24]

The growth of student numbers, combined with the increasing need for scientific building space, created a crisis in residence facilities near the end of the 1890s. The existing building was inadequate in size to house the number of students who desired to live there, and the result was, by the turn of the century, a great deal of antagonism between the few who could be accommodated and the great number of resentful outsiders. But after the abolition of the student residence in 1899, nominally because 'it was found impossible to maintain the institution without financial loss' but more likely because room for scientific facilities was needed, student sentiment in its favour increased.[25] The loss of a residential locus undermined the informal activities that fostered whatever sense of community existed in the University College student body. 'It is a matter for great regret,' said one person to the 1906 provincial royal commission investigating the university, 'that the associations which had grown up around the residence should have been so ruthlessly torn up as they were.'[26] Student relationships with their professors remained distant. Consciously Canadian and resentful of the 'old country' men who largely staffed their college, interpreting their cultural attitudes as a matter of putting on airs, students became deliberately stand-offish. 'There was, I think,' wrote B.K. Sandwell, 'a greater distance, a smaller degree of intimacy, between the student body and the really big men of the professoriate, in the Arts courses, than there has ever been before or since.' Sandwell penned those words in 1953.[27]

In the years just prior to the appointment of the 1906 royal commission, student discipline continued to be a major problem at University College, for reasons that were apparent to those who remembered the student strike of 1895. As Professor Albert H. Abbott complained to the commissioners, there existed 'no representative and responsible body of students' with which university authorities could negotiate when matters of student discipline arose.[28] For their part, in their brief submission to the 1906 royal commission the students asserted their hope that 'each College or Faculty should look after its own discipline'; the commissioners took note, observing that 'the absence of proper machinery for the direction of the student body in its various relations and for the maintenance of order' was a 'source of difficulty.'[29]

An Edwardian Trinity: Missions, Sports, and Militarism

Student ambience at different colleges and universities varied. Yet the growth of organized student activities in the late nineteenth century indicates that an important common element in the turn-of-the-century life of students was their desire to gain a measure of autonomy over their own affairs and activities. In 1890 the editor of the *Queen's Journal* lamented the 'spirit of individualism' among students that threatened to 'zap out all true college spirit' by subordinating collective social life to studies; but only four years later, life at Queen's had changed dramatically, with the existence of a host of campus organizations including a banjo club of twenty members.[30] By 1910 the individualism of 1890 that cared little for student collective activity had become a pluralistic democracy of interests that threatened to get out of control. 'We hear much of the "democracy" which prevails at Queen's,' wrote the *Journal*'s editor ... However, there is a growing danger that this "democratic spirit" may run riot among a countless number of organizations and societies. That society which will have for its object the "elimination of most of the existing organizations" is the one that is urgently needed ...'[31]

At University College, with the largest student body in the province by far, a similar range of student activities existed. In response to an 1899 accusation by the Toronto *Mail* that 'there was not the proper unanimity and heartiness' that should prevail (it cited a lecture given by urban reformer Morley Wickett on city government attended by only two faculty members and not many more students), President Loudon noted the existence of more than forty literary, scientific, musical, social, and athletic societies at his institution. By 1910 the Toronto *Star* could note the 'multiplicity of events in university life.' The university, it concluded, was 'a city, a community unto itself. It has its work and its play, its humdrum and its excitement.'[32] Even at the smallest of institutions the diverse range of student interests was reflected in numerous organized activities in which students could occupy their extracurricular time, and at each university the common seasonal rhythm of twentieth-century campus life developed. 'The average ... student's life,' wrote one journalist, 'can safely be divided into three periods. In the fall the social development has the floor and city manners and every-day culture is absorbed. In the winter sports and social events are less freely indulged in and time becomes more valuable. In the spring cramming, plugging, grinding become the keenest desire of the most lackadaisical.'[33]

Within the dynamic of provincial student life, organized activities in the years prior to the Great War ranged from those embodying high seriousness to others aimed at simple amusement and social intercourse. At Queen's University and at Victoria University students demonstrated their awareness of, and concern for, the problems of national and international life. They complained about 'blind adherence to party' in national politics; they recognized that socialism, while perhaps 'chimerical,' was 'a very plausible remedy for the ills of humanity'; they worried about the jingoistic, expansionist spirit of the United States; they railed at the fact that the prohibition question, which had begun as a moral movement, had become 'more and more a football for second-rate politicians, and a subject for mockery by men who have no faith in morals'; they decried the social costs of industrial combines.[34] Invariably, a major theme of student editorialists was one that sought to define what the essential responsibility of the modern student should be: active participation in the search for amelioration of such problems or temporary disengagement from them in order to pursue their academic studies and participate in extra-curricular social events.[35]

One of the first and most important organized student activities in Ontario universities, found at virtually all of them, was that of Christian missions. With the opening up of the Canadian West in the 1870s, the extension of evangelism into the 'heathen nations' of the Orient in the 1880s, and the discovery of the New Ontario of mining towns and logging camps early in the twentieth century, the major Protestant denominations in Canada sought to extend their religious influence. Denominational colleges were a major source of recruitment. At Queen's, Victoria, and McMaster, missionary societies were early and continuing outlets for student energy and Christian conscience.[36] Since relations between women and men were distant and formal after the admission of women into higher education, missionary organizations proved to be one social arena in which mutual interests could be shared. In years when the occupational spheres of both sexes continued to be distinctly separate, the widespread interest in foreign and home missions exhibited by women and men alike resulted in a common forum and a rough measure of equality. Canadian women who entered religious or missionary work as a life-long commitment gained the opportunity of operating outside the maternal feminist nexus, for thus engaged they could secure a measure of personal and vocational independence from men while not necessarily having to abandon their beliefs in Christian gentility and Victorian womanliness.[37] In any event, the first joint society of men and

women at Victoria University was its missionary society, founded in
1891.[38] On its executive board the next year were three men and two
women.[39]

By the twentieth century a number of organized agencies existed for
the generation of interest in missions and the recruitment of missionaries. The mission departments of the separate denominations, the Young
People's Forward Movement for Missions, the YMCA and YWCA, and
the Student Volunteer Movement, as well as alumni who had become
missionaries, provided a steady stream of speakers to campus organizations on conditions, folkways, and opportunities in China, Japan, Africa,
and Canada itself.[40] The appeal for Christian missionary service worked.
By the second decade of the twentieth century, Ontario denominational
colleges had provided scores of missionaries for overseas and home service – in Korea, India, and China, as well as in poverty-stricken districts
of Canadian cities. Others devoted themselves to service as labourer-
instructors for the 'Frontier College' that Queen's arts and theology
graduate of the late nineteenth century Alfred Fitzpatrick had founded at
the turn of the century to provide basic literacy skills and lessons in citizenship for the continental European immigrants who so largely populated the lumber and mining camps of northern Canada.[41]

The missionary spirit among students reflected the genuinely altruis-
tic sensibility of those who took part, directly or indirectly; but actual
missionary activity involved a great deal of competition on the part of
the different denominations for the heathen souls which constituted a
source of moral capital for them. Yet in the late nineteenth and early
twentieth centuries, the Christian soldiers who marched into benign missionary warfare for converts were not the only ones who imbued the
spirit of competition with moral attributes. A second major form of
extracurricular student activity in Ontario universities was that of organized sports. As with missions, such sports were conducted and justified
within the framework of an informal moral code derived from the muscular Christianity of mid-Victorian England.

Late-Victorian and Edwardian university sports in Ontario were conducted with a mixture of missionary zeal and martial ardour. In a complementary inversion of the way in which the 'Christian soldiers' of the
period were 'marching as to war' in their attempts to convert other races
and to Canadianize the European immigrants within Canada, rugby and
hockey players did manly battle as muscular Christians in the name of
moral virtue.[42] In the middle decades of the nineteenth century, sporting
activities could be found on Ontario campuses; but these were usually
conducted as occasional social events: students of Trinity might challenge the Toronto Cricket Club to a match; students of Queen's might

compete for prizes offered by citizens of Kingston on their annual field day.[43] Organized competitive sports such as football could be found by the early 1870s in Ontario, but it is perhaps significant that real enthusiasm for the sport did not take place until the 1880s – precisely when women began to gain entrance to universities.[44] A football club was founded at Queen's, for example, in the 1871–2 year, and by 1874 an athletic association had been formed; but on several occasions in 1879 student journalists found it necessary to remind the student body that the team and the association still existed.[45] Yet by 1885, just after Elizabeth Smith and her two female colleagues became the first woman graduates in medicine at the university, and with a growing number of women enrolled in arts at Queen's, male interest had picked up considerably. Suddenly, manliness became a necessary attribute of student life: 'If a man be weak and puny in body,' said one student journalist, 'he will, in nine cases out of ten, be weak and puny in his studies.'[46]

Women began to enter Ontario's universities in 1880, and by the time the first of them graduated organized athletic competition had become a major part of extracurricular life. Rugby football matches between Queen's, McGill, and Toronto were regular occurrences by the end of the decade, organized under the auspices of the Ontario Rugby Football Union until the Intercollegiate Rugby Football Union was formed in 1898. Organized hockey appeared at Queen's in the 1888, and similar clubs were begun elsewhere. Formal campus athletic associations began to be organized. The Trinity College Amateur Athletic Association was founded in 1892; at Victoria, an athletic union appeared in 1894. At Queen's informal student political parties developed in the early 1890s within the Alma Mater Society. They were known as 'the Sports' and 'the Christians.'[47] By the early twentieth century university sports such as hockey and rugby football were major public entertainment events.

In the world of Thomas Arnold, to be muscular meant also to be manly, and the public school games ethic of which such traits were a part was of enduring influence within the British Empire, including Canada, well into the twentieth century.[48] Yet the nearly simultaneous growth of interest by male undergraduates in organized extramural sporting competition and the appearance of women on campus may also be linked. Scholars of American history have noted that the cult of manliness occurred at a time when genteel culture was in the process of being feminized with the sentimentalism of the liberal arts increasingly equated with feminine attributes.[49] Novelist Henry James captured the fear of male members of the American gentry when, in his 1886 novel *The Bostonians*, one of his characters complained that 'the whole generation is womanized; the masculine tone is passing out of the world; it's a feminine, a nervous hysterical, chattering, canting age, an age of hollow phrases and false delicacy and exaggerated solicitudes and coddled sensibilities, which, if we don't look out, will usher in the reign of mediocrity, of the feeblest, and flattest and the most pretentious that has ever been seen.'[50] Within such an anxious milieu, in which Victorian males were increasingly uncertain as to how best to assert themselves as men, the cult of games and the articulation of the characteristics of manliness were of therapeutic value. In such a context, manliness was less the opposite of childishness than it was of femininity.[51]

Charles W. Gordon (the popular novelist 'Ralph Connor'), a student at the University of Toronto in the 1880s, made a direct connection between organized sports, manliness, and femininity in his autobiography, *Postcript to Adventure*. In 1879, he recalled wistfully, 'a keen rivalry' had existed between the boys of Toronto, McGill, and Queen's in sporting as well as academic matters. 'I say "boys" for up till 1882 the sacred portals of universities in Canada had not been opened to female students. While I personally voted for the extension of university privileges to women I was conscious of a secret feeling of which I was somewhat ashamed, that something of the lofty splendor of university life had departed with the advent of women. It was a little like playing baseball with a soft ball ... Though we found the young ladies charming, if somewhat exclusive in their ways, there remained an indefinable regret at the passing of a certain virility from university life at the coming of "the skirts."'[52]

'There was a time,' wrote a Victoria University senior in 1904, 'when the popular conception of a college man was a near-sighted and spindle-shanked individual, wearing a brow "sicklied o'er with the pale cast of thought," and carrying in his hand some volume of the classics or of philosophy. *Tempora mutantur* and to-day the mental picture most readily called up ... is, perhaps, that of a husky fellow in a padded suit with a rugby ball under his arm.' By then, the athletic and social side of university life was threatening, in this student's view, to 'overshadow the scholastic side.'[53] But the impulse towards athletics and action threatened more than that: it also threatened the status of the clergy in the way it portrayed them as physically weak and emotionally overwrought. By the latter part of the nineteenth century what had occurred rather earlier in the United States was also happening in Ontario. The image of the clergy – and for that matter of the 'artsman' – was becoming feminized. In the age of the robber baron, the clergyman gradually lost 'his role among his society's leaders; his place was increasingly in the Sunday School, the parlor, and the library, among women and those who flattered and resembled them.'[54]

One woman student at Western University in 1908 wrote a fictional-ized girl-meets-boy scene for her student newspaper. After 'playing a lone hand nearly all evening' at the university's conversazione, a young man summons his courage and strikes up a conversation with a beautiful young lady. The author takes up the dialogue: 'He stopped for want of breath, thus giving the girl the chance to ask "You aren't another of those Meds., are you?" Deeply humiliated by her tone he had to reply, "Oh, no Miss, worse than that – I am a divinity student, but I assure you I have some redeeming points."'[55]

By the end of the century ministers in Ontario were conscious of their tarnished image and their damaged status, and some sought to rectify matters. 'The day is long gone by,' said one student in *Acta Victoriana*, 'when an unhealthy frame and physical weakness are part of the stock in trade of the ministry.' He went on to stress the physical demands made on the ministry, the 'commanding physical appearance' of ministers of yesteryear, and urged his readers to acquire, if necessary, the physical stature necessary to command respect: 'The necessary elements are ... an upright carriage – square shoulders, bright eye and clear complexion – those outward signs which tell of steady nerve and good blood.'[56]

By the early twentieth century, a student writing on 'Athletics and Religion' could approvingly quote President Theodore Roosevelt's statement that athletics at Harvard were valuable because they helped turn out 'vigorous men' instead of 'mollycoddles.' Moreover, continued the student, athletics and religion were compatible because both culti-vated virtuous habits: courage, self-confidence, control of temper, and, above all, 'the idea of fair-play,'[57] that cardinal virtue of muscular Christians. Ontario students often talked of their sporting activities along such lines. 'Let the game be played for its own sake,' said a McMaster student in 1914, 'and if a victory cannot be gained by fair means, then surely it should not be gained at all.'[58] The attitudes of American college students toward athletic competition, stressing victory rather than the cultivation of character, often came under heavy criticism. 'Football is not a bowls, but a game in which hard knocks must be given and taken,' said one smug Queen's student of the 1890s. 'Nevertheless in Canada it is as yet, we are glad to see, a manly game, and as such wholly free from the caddish tactics which disgrace American football. We hope that it will long be so, and that any changes which may be made in the Cana-dian game will be toward the British style of play, and the British spirit of honest, manly sport, rather than toward the American spirit, which in effect says: win, fairly if you can, but if not, win at any cost.'[59]

The cultivation of a spirit of fair play was fine, but by the early twen-tieth century students also recognized that the real world of careers in business and commerce was a harsh and competitive one. Advocates of manly sports also stressed that student athletics prepared young men for such a world. The old image of the university student as 'a wizened old book-worm shut up in the gloomy recesses of a dingy library, familiar only with a race of dead men' increasingly reflected a reality of university life that was perceived to be passing out of existence. 'Students are now trained for the battle of life rather than polished to meet the requirements of drawing-room society.'[60] The successful man was one who embodied the resources made possible by physical education: courage, endurance, aggressiveness, quickness of judgment, and the capacity to sacrifice one's self for the sake of victory for the team.[61] Such attributes were essential for success in the empires of businesses or nations. Their cultivation would develop a healthy and vigorous citizenry and prevent moral decay. An occasional broken bone or forced joint was surely a small price to pay, for in the process of engaging in strenuous athletic activities the student would learn 'To set the cause above renown, / To love the game beyond the prize, / To honor while you strike him down, / The foe that comes with fearless eyes.'[62] In this way, to the notion of sport as an essentially male affair, characterized by fair play in the heat of competitive battle, was added the suggestion that athletics was a peaceful substitute for the ultimate manly game: war.

Games as war, wars as game: the rhetoric of the fifteen years that preceded the Great War reflected the perceived affinities. The use of such elevated diction often carried with it, as in England,[63] an innocent, romantic, pseudo-medieval imagery – whether expressed in the context of athleticism or of military action. When students of Queen's left Kingston to play the University of Toronto in football, they 'went forth ... to enter the lists with the Blue Knights of Varsity'; when they returned from such competition, it was a 'sturdy band of warriors' that was welcomed home.[64] Sports columns at Western University carried inspirational poems, similar in their martial imagery, derived from the presumption of personal control, Christian self-abnegation, and nobility of purpose: 'I will go forth 'mong men, not mailed in scorn, / But in the armor of a pure intent.'[65] University sermons were given on 'the game of life,' extolling the virtues of playing it 'fairly and worthily,' and urging that young men put their best self forward. 'To play the game,' the Reverend Professor S.W. Dyde told an audience of Queen's students, meant following the example of the English schoolboy. 'To play the game is for him to subordinate himself to the team, to be manly, straightforward, fair to the other side.' His spirit, on the cricket field or in war, was embedded in the words of the poet who wrote:

> The river of death has brimmed his banks,
>   And England's far, and Honour a name,
> But the voice of a school-boy rallies the
>   ranks,
> 'Play up! play up! and play the game!'[66]

The Christian idealism that was so vital a part of nineteenth-century university life in Ontario could be put to many purposes, and Dyde as well as others in positions of power and responsibility played not only upon the students' spirit of youthful enthusiasm and their willingness to dedicate themselves to a righteous cause, but also upon the meaning of life itself, and of the place of the university in it. 'The Game of Life,' said one Ontario professor, 'is an ideal working in them; it is the spirit of devotion to truth and goodness, it is a mystic and invisible society of truth-seekers.'[67] The linking of the ideals of war, of games, and of the university, was put forward by Queen's History Professor J.L. Morison when arguing in 1910 for military training at the universities: 'Military training for defensive purposes is our purer duty, a privilege to be demanded as a right, and one of the manliest and most fascinating forms of recreation.'[68] Students assimilated such values. 'Our business in the field of fight,' wrote the 1913-14 sports editor of the *McMaster University Monthly*, 'Is not to question but to prove our might.' By then, the imperial spirit, dedicated to martial vigour, had already long taken its place in the Ontario school system, both in the classroom and on playing fields tranformed into military parade squares.[69]

Athleticism and militarism were supported in university circles. In 1911, upon the election of a federal Conservative government intent upon increasing Canada's military capacity, Canadian universities formally considered the formation of an officer training program to be patterned after the Officers' Training Corps, created in England in 1908. After negotiations with the Canadian government, McGill University formed a unit of the Canadian Officers' Training Corps in 1912. At Queen's, after an offer of private funding by Major R.W. Leonard for the construction of a residence for COTC recruits on the university grounds, Principal D.M. Gordon privately promoted the scheme while publicly professing his abhorrence of war. Under Leonard's proposal, the residence was to be superintended by a military officer from the Royal Military College, and military discipline would have been expected. O.D. Skelton, for one, objected privately, but strenuously, to the 'cheap bribery of bed and board offered to induce students to join,' stressing the divisive effect such a scheme would have on the student body. 'It would do much to shift the whole centre of gravity of the university.' Deeply disturbed by these developments, Skelton could find no defence for them on either 'physical or moral grounds: a university which cannot train a man in self discipline & self control otherwise than by teaching him the goose step has failed in its mission.'[70] Skelton's objections, which found support within the university, prevailed: Principal Gordon refused to diminish the university's power to control its students, and Leonard withdrew his offer to finance the proposed residence. This would not be the last time that Major Leonard's anger would tax the head of an Ontario university.

Well-known university officials such as Principal William Peterson of McGill University continued, in speech after speech, to urge the necessity of military preparedness by wedding the English-Canadian identification with British imperial spirit to the destiny of the Canadian nation. Advocates of the humanities also extolled the virtues of empire. Professor of English James Cappon of Queen's eulogized the British Empire. 'The Empire,' said Cappon early in the century, 'represents an ideal of high importance for the future of civilization, the attempt to assemble in a higher unity than even that of nationality the forces which maintain and advance the white man's ideals of civilization, his sense of justice, his constitutional freedom, his respect for law and order, his humanity.' On the eve of the Great War, classicist Maurice Hutton, principal of University College, set forward a similar idealistic imperial vision that portrayed British imperialism as the world's defender of Christian ethics and political liberty. Wars, he told his students, 'were fought by professional soldiers full of love of fighting, full of joy of adventure, full of a certain honourable spirit and chivalry about the rule of fair fighting, full of a very real and universal feeling of sportsmanship and fair play.'[71]

The Last Victorian Tango

To portray student life before the Great War as entirely given over to athletics or to militarism would be to misrepresent it. By 1914 a rich array of activities quite distinct from those of the classroom or the library was available to Ontario university students, and the evidence suggests that they took advantage of them. No single student type existed – whether in moral attributes or in dress. Campus newspapers in Ontario changed from magazine to newspaper format in these years,[72] and the new-look student newspapers saw themselves less as forums for discussing ideas or publishing serious writing than as mirrors of the fashions and fads that attracted the interests of students. Retailers began to take the university student seriously as a consumer. Display advertising increased dramatically, and students were bombarded with pitches for underwear, hats, coats, dry cleaning, cooking ranges, shoes, sporting goods, pianos, flowers, and books. By 1914 advertisers in the *Queen's Journal* were attempting to sell 'Society Brand Clothes' by means of lithographic portrayals of variations of the self-confident and vivacious 'Gibson Girl' and her well-groomed male companion, embodiments of the new woman and the affluent man.[73]

Woman's perceived social role was still relatively circumscribed, but by now it had expanded beyond the domestic sphere and into forms of service to the secular state. The female undergraduate continued to be channelled, however, into particular academic departments and faculties, mainly arts and education. At Queen's University in 1912–13, for example, of 250 women registered intramurally, 233 were in arts and the remaining seventeen were in education. A year earlier, of thirty-two students enrolled in education, twenty-three were women.[74] 'Women's Department' columns in student newspapers, as often as not, supported and justified such limited roles, with the essence of womanliness portrayed as 'a divine quality which subtly reveals itself in tone, glance, and act.'[75] It may be that at times, faced with the increasingly aggressive, manly persona projected by male undergraduates as a social image, females found comfort, security, and a degree of camaraderie in the cultivation of distinctly 'feminine' traits. In this sense, tea parties organized by associations of women students could become political acts in the battle of the sexes.

The female undergraduate of the early twentieth century was by no means placid and submissive. At times, in exasperation, she took public exception to condescending male vocabulary. As one irate 'coed' wrote: 'And about "fairness" and "beauty" – when will the masculine mind grasp the fact that girls don't live and move and have their being on pretty speeches! The average man thinks that if he says something neat on "beauty" or "grace" that no sane girl can withstand him. We would like to educate you out of that.' University women did not want to be patronized. They wanted an equal voice and equal power.[76] The year 1913, noted the editor of the 'Women's Department' of the *McMaster University Monthly*, had been one of great advances in the 'Woman's Cause,' especially with respect to the suffrage. 'But for us,' she said, '"Woman's Cause" has the wider meaning – the opportunity for the expression of women's newly-found selves. Woman is an individual, else why were two beings created instead of one? Individuality is her birthright; and so is the expression of this individuality.'[77]

This new-found freedom was more than simply an example of the battle of the sexes. It was a manifestation of an important dynamic in the relationship between them. During the nineteenth century, English-

Canadian young adults consistently enlarged the social space in which courtship took place. While chaperonage continued throughout the century, youths – especially women – increasingly assumed control over the organization of their social lives. 'By the later nineteenth century the sexes held much courtship territory in common. The parlour remained women's courting preserve, but men and women had greater access to one another in public places, spaces free of restrictions on entry and free of close oversight.'[78] In this way college activities involving a mixing of the sexes can be seen, in part, as necessary social rituals leading towards courtship, and they carry many of the same tensions between youths and chaperones inherent in the alteration of the forms of social space. As with the department store and the public exhibition, the university became an important arena for expanding the physical public space available to women, thereby also increasing their visibility and social opportunities.[79]

The new individuality on campus was expressed in many ways, but none more so in the years immediately prior to the Great War than in the resistance of students to the quasi-parental control of their social activity by university officials. By the second decade of the new century, both sexes were willing to state outright that they wanted more social contact, and this usually meant pressure on authorities for an increased number of dances. In 1911, 285 students from the Ontario Agricultural College and the Macdonald Institute petitioned the minister of agriculture to rescind the prohibition on mixed dancing in Guelph. 'This has resulted,' they complained, 'in a great deal of wholesome pleasure being lost to the students, and has made our social functions very lacking in enjoyment ...' The same year a major issue at Queen's was whether the university's senate would continue to permit two dances per month. Students at the University of Toronto worried in 1912 whether the demolition of the old gymnasium would result in an absence of facilities for the union dance, the rugby dance, the medical 'at-home,' the arts dance, and the school of applied science dance.[80]

The craze for dancing was a major issue in the university and daily press in Toronto during the last, lingering months of Victorian innocence. The fact was, however, that the sense of innocence existed less at the universities than it did in the expectations of the public. In December 1913 the Toronto *News* broke the story that a tango party, involving five men and some 'chorus girls,' had apparently been held in the North Residence Building of the University of Toronto.[81] From that point on during the academic year, both the *News* and the Toronto *Telegram* kept a watchful eye on campus life, reflecting their readers' fear of possible sexual impropriety on the part of students who were expected to be models of youthful innocence. Organized dances were closely monitored by the press, and, sure enough, students were seen to be doing the new and dangerous dance, which allowed 'a lingering close contact,' not always in a vertical position.[82] Fear of the tango represented the fear of society that previously well-defined sex roles, particularly that of the sexually antiseptic, angelic woman, were disintegrating. The tango was not a dance; it was an omen.

The Toronto daily press portrayed the tango craze in tones combining sarcasm and titillation. 'That naughty yellow-haired maiden, the Tango,' wrote a *Star* reporter, 'is having a sort of peekaboo dance round the college halls this winter, and every time she gets up quite close to the patronesses and professors they discretely close their eyes and pretend they don't see her.' President Robert Falconer of the University of Toronto denied in reply that student dances were indelicate, and assured the public that they were 'in the hands of the patronesses' who, he was certain, 'would not countenance such a dance as the Tango.' *Varsity* also came to the aid of student virtue, but in terms that scarcely reassured the public: 'The Tango, as everyone knows, includes a great number of dances, some of which are objectionable and some are not. If the Tango maid mentioned in the *Star* is to represent all the modern fancy dances, they are quite right in saying that the Tango maid has appeared around the college halls.'[83] By February 1914 even students were caught up in the near hysteria. The University of Toronto undergraduate committee, in charge of dances and being lobbied intensively by both male and female students, banned the wearing of corsages on the grounds that it had become necessary to curb the 'unreasonable custom of young ladies being decorated in a semi-barbarous manner with vivid bouquets at all the dances.' The *News*, which carried the story, added that the committee, acting under advice of university authorities, had 'found it essential to issue an injunction against the indulgence in the new dances.'[84]

By then, not even the Methodist atmosphere of Victoria College was immune to the dance craze. At officially sanctioned 'promenades,' some imaginative student organizers managed to position the orchestra on the landing of the second floor of the college building, where the promenade was held. Then, with music wafting up to the third floor, 'many couples ... danced to their heart's content while clergymen and Methodist supporters paced the lower floors in blissful ignorance.' In the end, however, Methodist discipline prevailed. The culprits got caught, and the institution, for the moment, was scandalized. The student body and the women's literary society passed resolutions banning student dancing in the college. The result was 'barricaded stairs, and a dark third floor.'[85] They were still barricaded and in darkness at the outbreak of war.

11

The Great Divide

When the Great War began in the late evening of 4 August 1914, most Canadians and their leaders were eager to honour imperial obligations and to defend the British Empire. England's war was Canada's war, and Canadians were eager to serve. Within three days the Canadian government had committed itself to raising and sustaining a contingent of 25,000 volunteer soldiers. In those first, romantic days promising a distant and brief imperial adventure, volunteers were not difficult to find. The realities of the Great War proved, however, to be vastly different. As a war of movement in continental Europe it lasted for only a few months; as one of deadlock and attrition it lasted four more years.[1]

In early October 1914 thirty transport ships carrying 31,200 Canadian soldiers sailed for England from Halifax. Very soon, as battle lines became entrenched in Western Europe, the fact that the war would not be quickly over or decisively won became evident. By July 1915 the Canadian government had revised its commitment of recruits upward, to 150,000; by October the level stood at 250,000. In January 1916 the total was raised to 500,000. Patriotic recruitment and moral suasion by voluntary agencies, families, clerics, politicians, and educators throughout the nation brought the total number of Canadians wearing Canadian or British uniforms almost to that number by 1917,[2] but by then the rate of voluntary enlistment had drastically fallen. In May 1917, following a trip to England by the prime minister, the Borden government announced the necessity of conscription. This was followed by the formation of a Union government, comprised of the Conservative party and a number of Liberals committed to the conscription cause. The federal election of December 1917 was fought on the issue, rending the social fabric deeply by dividing anglophone and francophone. Soon after, the Military Service Act came into effect, with ambiguous results. Of 404,395 men between the ages of twenty and thirty-four who were called to service in October 1917, 280,510 applied for exemption. Only 24,100 Canadian conscripts actually saw combat in France before the end of the war in November 1918.[3] Yet by then more than half-a-million Canadian men and women had worn the uniforms of the nation's Expeditionary Force, its Navy, or the British armed services. Almost 60,000 of them died; another 173,000 were wounded.

Ontario contributed heavily to the cause. By the end of the war, nearly a tenth of the nearly three million people of the province[4] had been in uniform, mostly as volunteers. Sixty-eight thousand Ontarians had been killed, wounded, or listed as missing. The proportion of the population between the ages of fifteen and thirty-four dropped from thirty-six per cent in 1911 to 32.7 per cent ten years later.[5] The number of women between the ages of twenty and twenty-four increased from 118,342 to 123,382 in that martial decade, but the number of men in this prime age for military service dropped from 127,908 to 116,080.[6] Many of the names of these missing men, and some women, can be found on the commemorative cairns, still lovingly tended, in cities, towns, and villages throughout the province. Still others are etched in stone walls or on bronze tablets within the cloistered grounds of Ontario universities, mute testimony to the last student generation in Canada for whom romance, idealism, and an evangelical sense of mission formed the wellsprings of military commitment. As a nation, Canada was not prepared for war in 1914; but many of its university students – and certainly those of Ontario – had been psychologically readied for battle tacitly, as we have seen, by the social import of their studies, by the martial rhetoric of their evangelical Protestantism, and even by their organized competitive play. The years between 1914 and 1918 put those values and the civilization upon which they were built to the ultimate test.

Professors, Press, and Public

The universities of Ontario, like those of the Dominion as a whole, were quick to offer their services to the war effort. On 29 September 1914 President Robert Falconer of the University of Toronto opened the academic year with stirring words: 'This is the greatest of moral struggles. Are there to be free democracies who only need to police themselves against the force-attacks of the barbarous? Or will force tower arrogantly above freedom and enslave intellect? The struggle had to come. It is well to have it decided one way or other finally, for our own sakes and for our children's.' In this and many other speeches, Falconer called the new generation of students to a life of idealism and sacrifice, whether in the classroom or on the battlefield. The Great War, he said, would 'purge our selfishness' and bring social redemption, for it was nothing less than 'a clash of two views of life, and one or the other must go.'[7] What went, by war's end, was idealism, largely discredited in the public mind as a social creed.

Falconer's words were echoed by virtually every other university president or principal in the province. The horrors of the war, said Principal Daniel Gordon of Queen's in mid-October 1914, were almost beyond the imagination's grasp. But 'through it all there comes a great quickening of our sense of public duty, of devotion to country, of the necessity laid upon us to do our utmost for the Empire that maintains our national life and liberty and progress ... And whatever may be the material preparation, or lack of preparation, to meet the hour of trial, the supreme requisite is the ready spirit of service and self-sacrifice that counts not the number of its foes, but gives itself freely in defence of that which it holds dearer than life.'[8] McMaster University's Baptist supporters, traditionally critical of European militarism, quickly aligned themselves with the British cause; indeed, evangelical ardour at the denominational Christian colleges was reinvigorated by the advent of war. 'All our forces,' said Dean J.H. Farmer of McMaster, 'must be mobilized for the winning of the war into which Christ's commission has sent us.'[9]

Pacifist professors were few in numbers, but they were not silent. One of these was Lewis G. Horning, professor of classics and Teutonic philology at Victoria College, who even before the war had been warning the public of the menace of militarism. As president of the Canadian Peace and Arbitration Society, Horning undertook a speaking tour in the spring and summer of 1914 lamenting the rivalry among nations and preaching the gospel of cooperation and social service. 'We in Canada and the United States have a mission in this world,' he told one group. When the war broke out Horning – like most others involved in the post-Edwardian peace movement – found himself unprepared for it. He accepted the view that it was a struggle between democracy and nationalism, and continued to attempt to reconcile it with his own social Christianity.[10] At Queen's University, O.D. Skelton, too, lamented the advent of war and chose to see in it the means of resuscitating a failed peace movement. Accordingly, in his sanguine way, he accepted the necessity of the conflict but sought throughout the war years to conceive a realistic basis for lasting peace.[11] These were the voices of a small minority, but to advocates of jingoistic imperial adventure pacifists seemed to lurk everywhere in the first months of the war. 'The air is so full of pacifism,' Maurice Hutton warned, 'that it is necessary to urge upon the country the duty of national defence.' Another critic spoke of 'the debauch of pacifism now sweeping over the country.'[12]

Rising to the national emergency, professors appealed to patriotic instinct, to imperial sentiment, to democratic values, to the lessons of history and the words of the poet, and to religious conviction as they sought to mobilize the student body to martial action. 'When we look at the immense European war,' said theologian W.G. Jordan of Queen's University, '... it is an appalling spectacle; into this great struggle the British Empire has been drawn because there was no other honourable course ... Queen's men will be in their native atmosphere in a battle against an arrogant tyranny ... They are fighting for individuality, for diversity, in other words for life and liberty against a narrow nationalism, a mechanical view of Empire, and a drill sergeant's idea of "culture."'[13] 'What is the meaning of history?' Jordan asked, in a university sermon. 'History reveals true men, and there is a something in it greater than any mere nationality or sect. The immortal truths of today have been set up through the blood and tears of men. By sacrifice they have come and sometimes by sacrifice they must be kept.'[14]

Such exhortations transformed poet into recruitment officer. The editor of the *Queen's Journal* reprinted Kipling's poem, 'Stand Up and Meet the War,' with its appeal to imperial sentiment: 'There's but one task for all – / For each one life to give, / Who stands if Freedom fall? / Who dies if England live?' For good measure, the same issue of the *Journal* reprinted equally stirring words from Tennyson: 'Nine hundred thousand slaves in arms / May seek to bring us under; / But England lives, and still will live, / For we'll crush the despot yonder.'[15] Such thoughts, as often as not quoted without editorial comment in the first months of conflict, reflected the romantic appeal of war to the lingering Edwardian imagination. They became one of the casualties of the Western Front, silenced after Canadian engagements at Ypres, Messines Ridge, Mont Sorrel, and the Somme.[16]

In the first years of the war an almost chivalric commitment to the noble cause and patriotic duty reigned, fuelled at the level of intellect by the insistence of academic idealists such as John Watson that a British yet German-derived idealism had not been put in question by Prussian militarism.[17] It was fed emotionally by the continuing presence of evangelical Christianity, which, like idealism, was nearing its apogee. All the powers of moral suasion that clergymen could muster were focused on the university students, as on the population as a whole. Everywhere the refrain was the same: true Christianity required the ultimate sacrifice. 'True vision is through the will,' insisted one Toronto minister in a convocation sermon on 'The Blessings of Purity.' 'It is determined by character ... The cry of pain goes forth from the homes of our Empire. But if the vision of God comes to purified hearts the price is not too great. For us the University will never be the same again. It will be more sacred. Our heritage has been made sacred through the life blood of our boys shed in freedom's cause.' 'Life has a new sacredness,' proclaimed Dr

Bruce Taylor, who was to become principal of Queen's before war's end, 'and though we have felt the Armaggedon but slightly, yet we are already a better people ... Not wealth and comfort but sacrifice and death for a cause, this is the call to the higher life.' The Reverend Dr Herridge concluded a university sermon at Queen's with the warning that 'the victory will not be the triumph for all of arms but the energy of a new civilization christianized by the baptism of blood.' A visiting English speaker, in a sermon entitled 'Cross-makers and Cross-bearers,' warned that 'No nation can rise to greatness but by the blood of its bravest sons and the tears of its finest women. There are multitudes who are dying in battle today to give victory to a principle of righteousness, justice and liberty, and none of them, let us thank God, die in vain.' 'Jesus,' said another speaker, 'always impressed his contemporaries as a man of power.'[18] In such ways was the Lamb of God sacrificed to the image of Mars.

Students eagerly responded to such appeals. 'Most of us thought that Democracy had secured its decisive victory during the nineteenth century,' wrote the editor of the *Queen's Journal*. 'The present war shows how false was our conclusion ... As Canadians we feel that it is our duty to place ourselves at our country's disposal at any time she may require us. As students we feel that if the training necessary could be continued with our college work we should reap a double benefit.'[19] A year later the idealism remained high. 'The greatest business of our university this year is war,' wrote the editor of Victoria's *Acta Victoriana*, 'and we are all in it ... [I]t may be said that if we did not believe that the future will be moulded on the foundations of truth and love, those great spirits which our alma mater herself has breathed into us, our men would not so readily offer themselves. Our ideals are fixed, at least for the foundations of the future structure of our civilization; and because these foundations were jeopardized by a spoiler, we have taken up arms.'[20]

As representatives of a privileged class, largely cloistered from the harsher realities of the outside world, Ontario university students were expected to aspire to noble ideals, and their enthusiastic acceptance of lofty appeals to duty from professors and presidents simply fulfilled the expectations of society. The response of that society to the advent of war was more visceral in nature and at times more vexatious in action. On the eve of the declaration of war, a civic holiday in Ontario, crowds roamed the streets of Toronto in what the *Globe* called 'a pitch of patriotic fervour.'[21]

In such an emotionally heightened atmosphere, and in a city that was still overwhelmingly British, xenophobic reactions were inevitable. At the commencement of the public school year, E.W. Hagardy, principal of Harbord Collegiate, roundly condemned Germans and 'Germanism' at a school assembly in an attempt to stir the patriotism of his youthful charges. Three of them, however, were emotionally mauled by the speech and physically roughed up by a fellow student after it. They reported the unhappy events to their father, Paul Wilhelm Mueller, associate professor of German at the University of Toronto. To the Mueller family, Hagardy's denunciations were both personal and unfair. The boys had been born in Canada and had been patriotic part-time cadets for nearly a year; the father had been in Canada for more than twenty years, was no longer a German citizen, had graduated from the University of Toronto, and considered himself in all but formal citizenship a Canadian. After unsuccessfully attempting through Hagardy to have his children transferred to another school, the frustrated and angry father expressed his disappointment to the press. By the time a meeting of the Toronto Board of Education was held to consider the charges, seven of Mueller's university colleagues had signed a petition objecting to 'such outrageous conduct'[22] by the public schoolteacher, while the staff of Hagardy's school had rallied to their principal's defence.

The board took no action on the petition, and refused to hear from the teachers. Hagardy, it transpired, had refused to make the public apology demanded by Mueller but he had allowed the professor to speak to his students in assembly, and had warned them not to bully the Mueller boys. For his part, Mueller had scarcely been either tactful or sensitive to the heightened emotions of the day.[23] The principal, not the professor, won the battle for public support.[24] 'Getting Ready for Vengeance to Come, – Britain Gathers Evidence for Trial of Ferocious German Officers,' proclaimed a front-page *Star* headline that day.

There the matter might have ended had Mueller not been supported by his seven university colleagues. The story was a good one from a journalistic point of view, and all of the Toronto dailies covered it, gradually broadening the focus from one of parental ire over a teacher's verbal abuse to one in which the provincial university's role in the war was at issue.

At various points since the 1880s, when the appearance of the heterodox co-founder of Darwinism, Alfred Russel Wallace, at the University of Toronto had raised the spectre of campus atheism, Toronto newspapers and their readers had been on the lookout for subversive movements at the provincial university. In the academic year before the war the *Globe* had covered an indignant speech given by Arthur VanKoughnet, president of the South and Centre Toronto Conservative Club, to his group. VanKoughnet had warned his audience that the University of Toronto was 'a hotbed of sedition, privy [sic] conspiracy and rebellion, false doctrine, heresy, and schism' and had declared that 'the Ontario Government should require that these disloyal utterances should cease or should withdraw the aid given by the Province to the institution.' For its part, *Varsity* defended Toronto students with the voice of dispassionate reason, saying: 'There are those who believe in the singing of "O Canada" rather than "God Save the King" and those who believe in the development of Canadian nationality as opposed to the proponents of Imperial federation. Such beliefs are defensible and cannot truly be characterized as disloyal nor as "sedition, privy conspiracy," and so on. They arise from a conception of Canadian before Imperial patriotism, and any interference from the local politician or any of those in authority will only serve to accentuate the ideas ...' Other Toronto students upheld the sentiments expressed in *Varsity* in eloquent and articulate interviews given to the *Globe*.[25]

Student sedition simply made a good story, but possible subversion by German nationals in time of war with Germany was *news*. In the autumn of 1914 the 'German professor' question made the transition from story to news. Each of the Toronto dailies pressed its own angle and staked its own editorial position on the matter. 'Germans in Canada deserve courtesy, but not coddling,' went the title of a *Telegram* editorial on 19 September. 'The scholars in Queen's park,' said the editor, 'have a unique opportunity to exult the name of their University. The British Empire has been forced into a bloody war, and the learning of the University professors is of little avail if it does not show them the justness of its cause ... In the hour of an empire's crisis, every seat of learning is on trial.'[26] Four days later he fanned the flames of controversy by asking, rhetorically, 'Shall the Toronto School Teachers Bow ... to a German Professor?' The same editorial accused the *Globe* of sitting on the fence by condemning German tyranny on the one hand while defending the rights of the German professor on the other.[27] For its part, the *Star* applauded a decision of the Toronto Board of Education that strongly criticized the petition of the University of Toronto professors, while the *Globe* suggested that in his 29 September speech to students on Germany and militarism President Falconer had not been critical enough of the German lack of concern for human values and welfare.[28]

By November the controversy had come to focus almost entirely on the University of Toronto, for the one German professor had now become three. Dr Immanuel Benzinger, professor of oriental languages, and Bonno Tapper, lecturer in German, were now also objects of suspicion, especially the former. Benzinger, a German national hired in 1913, had gone to Germany in the spring of 1914 to gather his family, only to find his son conscripted into the German army. When he returned, alone, on 14 October, he was met by a reporter from the *Globe* who proceeded to extract from him a number of comments concerning the official German position on such matters as the invasion of Belgium and the destruction of Louvain. Later, in the *Globe's* editorial offices, the Benzinger interview became journalistic evidence of the German's treachery. The story reached the desk of the newspaper's editor, J.A. Macdonald, a member of the University of Toronto's board of governors and a friend of Falconer; the two conferred and a decision was made to suppress news of the interview.

But the damage was done. Someone leaked the story and articles accusing Benzinger of disloyalty appeared in the *Telegram* and the *World*. On 16 November, Falconer, under direct pressure to resolve the problem from a premier whose backbenchers were threatening to get out of control on the question of enemy aliens,[29] finally broke his public silence by issuing to the press a statement that provided the backgrounds of Mueller, Benzinger, and Tapper, and defended their loyalty. 'After the fullest inquiry that I have been able to make,' he said, 'I am of [the] opinion that they have done nothing that should arouse any suspicion that they are injurious alien enemies.'[30] Perhaps hoping that the affair would thus be ended, Falconer left on a speaking tour of Western Canada. He was mistaken. No one was satisfied and the public was in no mood to accept such blithe assurances.[31]

Newspapers took advantage of Falconer's absence to fan the flames. The *World* shook its editorial head in amazement at the university's response to the crisis. 'It is a matter of wonder in Toronto,' stated an editorial entitled 'Varsity vs. King George,' 'that the University authorities can be so thick-headed, for they can be excused on no other ground, as to maintain alien enemies of Britain on the staff and to expect the people of Ontario to pay these alien enemies and support them while their friends and relatives are engaged in deadly strife with the sons and brothers of those who are asked thus to support and nourish them.' The *Telegram* went further, insisting that it was 'time to put personal feeling and friendship away.' The time had come, instead, for public duty to be done: 'The Ontario Government should demand proof that no German or Austrian reservist is on the payrolls of the University of Toronto. Or the Ontario Government should direct its Attorney-General to prosecute the University Governor or others in authority for violation of their Royal Proclamation against trading with the King's enemies.'[32]

By the end of November the university's board of governors was deeply divided, with a faction led by Sir Edmund Osler insisting that the German professors should either be asked to resign or be dismissed outright. With the board of governors known publicly to be in a state of deadlock, the *Telegram*, reporting that 'an overwhelming majority of the governors were in sympathy with Sir Edmund Osler,' called upon the president of the university to return immediately from Western Canada to resolve the controversy.[33]

Falconer presented his case to the board of governors on 3 December. A reiteration and amplification of his earlier defence of Mueller in the press, it stressed the difficulties of filling academic positions in time of war, denied that the three professors were risks to national security, ensured that they would make no controversial public statements, and concluded by urging that 'their services be retained.'[34] The next day, after much acrimonious dispute,[35] the board decided to grant the three professors a leave of absence with pay until 1 July of the next year. Public reaction was swift. 'I cannot see why we should be paying Germans salaries here when thousands of the young men of Britain are being killed by Germans at the front,' said a still-outraged Osler.[36] Once again, only the University of Toronto student newspaper, *Varsity*, remained dispassionate: 'Are we to have a reign of terror in Toronto? Is each person to accuse everyone else of being pro-German, when everyone else refuses to become infected with undiscriminating, flag-waving, traitor-denouncing hysteria?'[37] The voice of *Varsity*, however reasonable, was that of a distinct minority. In that jingoistic and anxious autumn the daily press more accurately reflected public sentiment concerning the war and the university's role in it. 'The University makes a mistake,' the *World* had said on 2 December, 'in holding itself aloof from public opinion. We have commented upon this attitude before. The gods occasionally come down and mix with common men. The impression is abroad that the University Dons never do.'[38]

From his perspective, Robert Falconer had probably done more than his share of mixing with 'common men.' He well knew that the presidency of James Loudon before him had failed in part because the president of the university did not have final authority over power of appointment or tenure at his own institution. During the current crisis Falconer had faced a renewed challenge to his authority as president to determine the composition of his own staff. He was aware that the issue was of sufficient gravity to warrant a threat of resignation if the board of governors did not meet his wishes, and he might have won the battle of nerves had he done so. But he was astute enough to recognize that the consequence of losing and carrying out the threat would be to precipitate a crisis of political leadership at his university during wartime. Accordingly, he stood firm and refused to capitulate to public pressure, and he won the respect of his staff and students in doing so.[39]

In the strict sense, however, he had failed in his mission since the three German professors no longer taught at the university. Tapper resigned in December, to do post-graduate work at the University of Chicago; so did Benzinger, who went to stay with friends in Princeton and soon found an academic position at Allegheny College. Ironically, Mueller, who had started the controversy, was the least disrupted. His own departure involved the distance of only a few hundred yards northwards to Bloor Street and McMaster University. Not supported by the public purse, McMaster offered relative security from pressure by press and public. A year after the war, University of Toronto supporter John Squair wrote bitterly to a McMaster official: 'In the midst of the wild madness of our time I am deeply thankful that one Institution at all events kept its head and was kind to unfortunate people who were not responsible for the harm done the world by the German Empire. I am ashamed by the part played by our Alma Mater in such affairs and am glad that McMaster was able to show the true Christian spirit.'[40]

This was not quite the whole truth. Victoria, Queen's, and Western, as well as McMaster, had employed professors of German ancestry and none had been threatened with dismissal. Only at the one university financially beholden to the province did Germanophobia influence academic staffing policy, and at it the professoriate, increasingly understaffed and overworked, was rendered mute on the issue. The uncertain and xenophobic context of the day helps explain why this was so, but the fact remains that the provincial university remained provincial in ways far transcending definitions of political jurisdiction.

The Great War also brought the issue of bilingual schools in Ontario to a state of crisis, with great consequences for the University of Ottawa. Its vice-rector, Michael Francis Fallon, had been removed to the United States in 1898 because of his objection to Archbishop Hamel's apparent desire to convert the Ottawa university to a predominantly French-speaking institution reflecting the significant increase in the French-speaking population of the province (it grew from approximately five to almost ten per cent of the provincial total between 1880 and 1910). After the election of the Conservative Whitney government in 1905, the Orange Order had launched a vigorous public campaign for the province's schools to reflect the Protestant and English-speaking character of the majority of Ontarians. It found unlikely support from Irish Catholic leaders such as Fallon (Bishop of London from 1909), who hinted at a French-Canadian conspiracy to control church and state. These leaders were determined to raise educational standards by ensuring the supremacy of English-language schooling within their jurisdictions. The linguistic, ethnic, and religious passions central to such views produced acrimonious public debate throughout the province in 1910.[41] The issue was very much alive when the Great War began, and the situation soon grew worse.

Bishop Fallon's previous association with the cause of the English language at the University of Ottawa, and his ongoing involvement with it, ensured that the University of Ottawa, with its Irish and French leadership, remained deeply divided over the language issue. This was particularly so after the Ontario government, under pressure from its ultra-Protestant wing, introduced the measure popularly known as 'Regulation 17' in 1912. This circular of instructions issued by the provincial ministry of education appeared to prohibit use of French in all Ontario schools beyond the first two years, and it was nowhere more strenuously resisted than within the Ottawa Separate School Board. The board was threatened with the withdrawal of public funding because of its intransigence, while English-speaking Roman Catholics who sent their children to public schools were threatened with refusal of the sacraments. In September 1914, as if to prove it was not to be bullied, the board closed all its schools. The issue became a matter of heated debate in the federal parliament, because on the one hand it served as evidence for Henri Bourassa's assertion that the bilingual ideal was under siege; on the other, it became ammunition for those who accused French-Canadians of a half-hearted contribution to the war effort. A resolution introduced into the House of Commons by Ernest Lapointe in 1916, urging 'the necessity of every child being given a thorough English education' but also that 'the privilege of the children of French parentage of being taught in their mother tongue not be interfered with,' was soundly defeated. Resistance from the French-speaking Roman Catholic community scarcely diminished even after a papal encyclical of 1917, *Commisso divinitus*, urged moderation; English-speaking Ontario Protestants were somewhat mollified in the same year when the Judicial Committee of the Privy Council ruled that Regulation 17 was constitutional.[42] The issue began to recede from the public eye, but it continued to widen the two linguistic solitudes in the Roman Catholic church, including those at the University of Ottawa.

Much damage had been done in the relationship between the two main groups, and the continuous festering of the language issue at the University of Ottawa affected it deeply. 'From 1866 to the 1940s,' wrote the main historian of Catholic post-secondary education in Ontario, '... the university was rather undistinguished. It was a small bilingual, liberal arts college, racked by nationalist problems and maintaining rather indifferent schools of philosophy, theology, and canon law. Officially bilingual, the overall tendency was to adopt a French rather than an Anglo-Irish flavour.' The almost total destruction of the university in 1903 by fire lowered morale further. 'The years 1905–20,' Laurence Shook concluded, 'were particularly dismal.' The heightened emotions of wartime merely exacerbated existing tensions. After the war, Irish Catholics in Ottawa began to talk about creating an institution to serve their own needs. The founding of St Patrick's College in 1929 was the result. Formally affiliated with the University of Ottawa in 1932, but existing as a virtually separate entity, it offered its own liberal arts program, and the language of instruction was English.[43]

Mobilizing the Troops

The Great War mobilized and gave unity of direction to the complex apparatus of the industrial state in Canada for the first time in the nation's history. Press and pulpit, industry and legislature eagerly declared their willingness to contribute to the war effort in whatever ways possible. The country's universities were no exception.[44] But what would the universities do? What was their duty? The Toronto *Globe* trumpeted loudly. 'Have the Presidents of Canada's great universities no national message for a great national occasion when the Nation is involved with the Empire in a life-and-death war of the World?' asked its editor. 'What about the greatest Canadian university, the Provincial University, with its seat here in Toronto and its lines going out into all the earth? Has war brought it no new occasion? no fresh fields? no widening horizons? no enlarged responsibilities for the Nation, for the Empire, for the World? What, indeed, is a university?'[45]

During the four long years that followed, those questions were amply answered by virtually every university in the country. If the Great War, as is often claimed, marked the years in which a national frame of mind emerged in Canada, so too were they years when the nation's universities began to enter the public consciousness. The university in Ontario proved itself to be an institution with unheralded resources that could be marshalled in order to win the war that was to end all wars. The most precious of those resources were human.

At Queen's University the Fifth Field Company, a corps of engineers organized in 1910 by Professor Alexander Macphail, was quickly mobilized. This was no rough body of raw recruits. Since its formation, the company, the only one in the country that had regular standing with the militia department, had been given regular rifle and infantry drill, signals training, and instruction in bridge and fortification construction. The university administration had been sufficiently accommodating to allow the hours between three and five on Thursday afternoons free of classes. For its part, the militia department provided uniforms, caps, rifles, bayonets, and technical equipment. In the academic year 1913–14 alone, twelve lieutenants and thirty-two sergeants were qualified. Within three weeks after the declaration of war, 120 members of the company were sent to Valcartier, Quebec, to prepare it as a site capable of mobilizing 30,000 men by repairing roads, planning tent sites, and installing a water supply system. Soon their numbers swelled to 170. Fifty of these students went overseas with the first Canadian contingent; by December 1914 a further eighty officers and sappers and thirty drivers and mechanics had left with the second. From the outset, university companies proved themselves to be visible assets to the nation's armed services.[46]

Other attempts to organize university military units fared not so well. In London before the war, Colonel W.E. Hodgins, commander of Number 1 Divisional Area, had attempted to convince authorities at Western University to establish two companies of the COTC, without success. Only after hostilities had commenced did Dr E.E. Braithwaite, president of the university, offer to form a contingent, and even then the proposal was refused by the acting adjutant-general, Colonel J.B. Dunbar. Thwarted by official channels, London military men engaged in a less formal tactic: Lieutenant-Colonel Thomas J. Murphy, a member of Western's board of governors, wrote directly to Sam Hughes, minister of militia. Hughes's reply was that 'I have handed the communication to my Quartermaster-General for consideration.' But the instructions that eventually went with the letter read: 'QMG please oblige in this.' The result was the authorization of two companies of the COTC at Western University.[47]

With the formation of the units, equipment was needed. One hundred rifles, originally intended for overseas units, were issued to the corps, but the university had no place to store them, or for that matter facilities for indoor drill or instruction. The corps therefore could not use its rifles. Not until 1915 did the City of London provide adequate space for the storage of arms, but by then the Lee-Enfield rifles had been allocated to others. With no arms to store, the group lost its civic space. In spite of such travails, the corps soldiered on, its housing paid for by Murphy, its arms borrowed or purchased by corps members themselves. Volunteers were not formally required to be members of the university community, but throughout the war most of the corps was drawn from it. The university's policy 'was to make the slate of officers as exclusively as possible members, teaching or student, of the University itself.' As much as was possible, the university wanted to control military activities conducted by its own staff and students.

Invariably, in London and elsewhere, such a desire resulted in tensions. By the spring of 1915, Murphy was beginning to receive what the historian of the COTC at Western diplomatically chose to call 'wafts of complaint from the abyss of the civilian mind.' Dr H.A. McCallum, dean of the medical school and chairman of the military committee, complained of the presence of non-students in the corps. The student recruits, for their part, had become, in the words of Murphy's reply, 'unreasonably impatient, forgetting that the men who are preparing to go to the front must be served before those who are training to stay at home and teach others the science of self-defence and the defence of their home and country.' Put simply, they had discovered that military training was dull and repetitive, and that it did not challenge the intellect because it sought to divorce thought from behaviour. As one historian of the Great War put it: 'Experience in business or at university tended to produce men more mature and complex than the army had had to deal with before.'[48]

At Queen's, the question of whether or not a COTC contingent should be established was debated throughout the autumn of 1914. In spite of an appeal by history professor J.L. Morison for the formation of a Queen's University battalion, and patriotic pronouncements on the virtues of loyalty to the empire by the president of the Canadian Medical Association and Sir George Foster,[49] voluntary enlistment remained alarmingly low. On 26 October, the editor of the *Queen's Journal* found it necessary to state that 'There still seems to be some doubt in the minds of our students as to the immediate necessity for military training.' While many 'realized the gravity of the situation' and therefore were 'preparing themselves to meet any crisis that may occur,' others – 'a great number' – were seen to be 'looking on the military training merely in the light of personal advantage or disadvantage' and were 'asking whether it will interfere too much with study or with recreation.' The *Journal* editorial ended with a blunt paragraph in bold typeface: 'Every student should be in training or be able to give a valid reason for not being so.'[50] A few days later, Principal Daniel Gordon sought the answer to the same question. 'How is it that the students are so slow in volunteering for military drill and musketry instruction?' Stressing the fact that such training bound the student neither to overseas service nor even home defence, his was a call to student honour and pride: 'Is it that they are unwilling to serve in defence of their country? It may be that in the prolonged enjoyment of peace our fibre has been enfeebled, and our spirit relaxed, that in our fancied security we have grown apathetic, but one of the first claims on every citizen is for the defence of his country, and this war is ours as truly as if we were citizens of London or Edinburgh?'[51]

By then, however, the university's board of trustees had already approved the formation of a COTC unit. By the spring of 1915, more than 250 earnest student soldiers, sharing fifty or sixty rifles, lacking uniforms, manuals, or bayonets, were hard at drill. Some of them demanded course credit for doing so, but they and those that followed them were generally appeased by the vague promise of the university senate that their military training would be taken into consideration when their year's work was evaluated.[52]

The military tradition at the University of Toronto went deeper into the past than it did at Queen's. From 1861 until the late 1880s K company of the Second Regiment, Queen's Own Rifles, was known as the 'University Company.' Students and professors had participated in the resistance to the Fenian raid of 1866 and the suppression of the second Riel rebellion in 1885. Even after the formal link between the company and the university was severed in the early 1890s, students and graduates of the university continued to serve in it, especially in the South African war at century's end. Although the Department of Militia had proposed the establishment of officers training corps at Canadian universities in 1911, the University of Toronto's board of governors decided to provide no funding or armory, and the university senate rejected the overture by proclaiming that the 1906 University Act and its predecessors made it appear 'that the people of Ontario had never contemplated military training as part of the work of the University.'[53] With the declaration of war in 1914 university men began training with the Queen's Own Rifles and other city regiments, and by the end of August about 250 graduates and students of the provincial university had left for Valcartier in the first contingent. Before the end of September roughly twenty junior members of staff were taking drill and instruction in anticipation of enlistment as officers. President Falconer wrote to the commanding officer of the Second Division, Toronto, on 30 September offering on behalf of university authorities to furnish a contingent of the COTC. Falconer's objectives included the raising of nine companies of 100 men each, and supervision of enrolments in the colleges and faculties by university staff, but with control of training and organization by the military. Falconer offered the basement of the medical building as locker space for arms for 600 men, but noted that no covered accommodation was available for drill purposes.[54]

By October the University of Toronto contingent of the COTC had been formed. It was organized and led by Colonel W.R. Lang, professor of chemistry,[55] Other institutions in Toronto swelled its ranks. More than 200 undergraduates of Victoria University eventually enrolled in it, forming two companies led by Captains Vincent Massey and G.M. Smith, lecturers in modern history and, respectively, the dean and a don of Burwash Hall. A McMaster unit of 100 young men, drilled by librarian Stewart Wallace, added to the groups from Victoria and Wycliffe Colleges.[56] By the early spring of 1915, as chairman of the military committee as well as president of the University of Toronto, Robert Falconer proudly reported to the officer commanding the Second Division that the university COTC had been 'organized by Faculties and Colleges in 12 companies each of 116 all ranks and 1 supernumerary company of graduates resident in the city.' Enrolments, he noted, had 'greatly exceeded this establishment' but were being trained as supernumeraries; the corps was officered entirely from members of the university staff, along with a few senior students 'with previous military experience in the junior ranks.' Altogether, weekly lectures on Field Service Regulations were regularly attended by over 900 undergraduates.[57]

The university companies raised in 1914 and 1915 seldom managed, however, to maintain a permanent identification with the universities that had provided their initial training.[58] Troop requirements of the Canadian Expeditionary Force (CEF) and imperial forces often meant dispersal into different units and limited, when necessary, the number of those given commissions. The militia department had no difficulty in obtaining sufficient numbers of officers, yet the major demand was for infantry reinforcements. As a result, the McGill and Toronto Companies in effect became sources of enlisted footsoldiers for Princess Patricia's Canadian Light Infantry (PPCLI). This meant that these former undergraduates, graduates, and academicians experienced some of the fiercest battles of the Great War in their first engagements. University reinforcements after May 1916, wrote the historian of the PPCLI, 'saved the Regiment from practical extinction ... [I]t was they who beat the Württembergers in Sanctuary Wood on June 2, 1916.'[59] Other recruits went elsewhere. A number of former University of Toronto students, for example, joined 43 Howitzer Battery or the Fourth and Fifth Divisional Signal Companies.

The *University of Toronto Roll of Service, 1914–1918*, a memorial volume published in 1921, documents one university's wartime diaspora. More than 6,000 people associated with the provincial university – undergraduates, graduates, and staff – were on active service during the Great War. One in ten (621) died in action or on service, to be memorialized in the university's roll of honour. By the conclusion of the war, those from the University of Toronto still on active service stood as shown in Tables 11.1 and 11.2.

Similar contributions, although on smaller scales, were made by the other universities in the province. At McMaster University by the fall of 1915, twenty-one undergraduates – twelve per cent of the student body – had enlisted; by war's end the number, including graduates, would reach 237. Of these, twenty-two made the ultimate sacrifice. In spite of the fact that at Queen's in 1915–16 forty-six per cent of men, on average, were declared physically unfit for military service, four in ten male undergraduates were in uniform. By war's end more than 1,500 Queen's men were on active service: 631 graduates; 599 undergraduates; 167 alumni; 84 bankers; 21 staff: a total of 1,502. Of these, a significant proportion were commissioned officers, a proportion that rose for graduates or those who had specialized scientific or medical skills. The names of 179 such men – those who lost their lives – would later be memorialized on a

TABLE 11.1
Distribution of University of Toronto armed service enlistment during Great War,
1914–18

	Officers*	Other Ranks	Total
Present and former staff	133	16	149
Graduates (exclusive of staff)	2,453	387	2,840
Undergraduates	980	901	1,881
Former students	469	127	596
Faculty of Education	4,113	1,538	5,651

*Of the officers, 726 were promoted from the ranks.
SOURCE: G. Oswald Smith, 'Canadian Educational Institutions in the Great War.'
VIII University of Toronto,' *Canadian Defence Quarterly* 5 (1927–28), 228–9.
Statistics taken from University of Toronto *Roll of Service*

TABLE 11.2
Distribution of University of Toronto armed service enlistment during the Great War,
1914–18, by area of service

	Canadian	Imperial	Allied	Total
Army	4,019	722	108	4,849
Navy	47	119	4	170
Air Force	3	558	3	564
Auxiliary	9	34	13	56
Uncertain				12

SOURCE: G. Oswald Smith, 'Canadian Educational Institutions in the Great War.'
VIII – University of Toronto,' *Canadian Defence Quarterly* 5 (1927–8), 228–9.
Statistics taken from University of Toronto *Roll of Service*.

plaque in the students' memorial union. At Western, the student body almost disappeared during the war.[60]

The war altered all aspects of campus life. The buildings and grounds of the University of Toronto resembled an armed services base. The men's residence at Devonshire Place, the university dining hall, part of Convocation Hall, and the old engineering building were used by the Royal Air Force. The Hospital Association and the Red Cross occupied parts of the library and physics buildings. Space was provided in the chemical and mining building for the Invalided Soldiers Commission, led by Professor H.E. Haultain (head of the University of Toronto's school of mining engineering). Called upon to provide staff, finances, and equipment for a base hospital with 1,000 beds, the university community rallied. Staffed by the medical faculty and its associated hospitals, funded by more than $100,000 raised by alumni and friends, and sustained especially by the University Women's Hospital Supply Association (headed by Mrs Falconer), and with volunteer groups throughout the province contributing bed linen, surgical dressings, and clothing, Number 4 General Hospital was mobilized by the spring of 1915 and served for almost two years in Salonika, and then (until July 1919) at Basingstoke in England. Altogether, the supply association alone gathered $121,000 in subscriptions, and sent over 300,000 items of hospital clothing and linen, as well as 1,808,257 units of surgical supplies.[61]

Queen's contributed in similar ways. By May 1915 Number 7 General Hospital had left Canada for overseas with enough personnel (initially totalling 129, including thirty-five nursing sisters) and supplies for 200 beds. Soon enlarged to a 400-bed capacity, the Queen's Hospital unit served in Egypt and France, ultimately housing 2,100 beds. Its medical personnel was supplied almost totally by the Queen's University medical faculty, and it was financed and supplied by the volunteer work of Queen's graduates and students. Two of the university's main buildings – Grant Hall and the arts building – became a military hospital for up to 600 patients, and its mechanical laboratories and equipment were used by the federal Department of Soldiers' Civil Re-establishment.[62]

By 8 November 1916 few members of press or public any longer harboured doubts about the degree of commitment to the war effort of the province's universities. The *Globe*'s general description on that day of the grounds and activities of the provincial university applied equally to what was happening and could be seen in London or Kingston: 'No matter ... in what direction the University was approached the touch of Khaki and the signs of national service were much in evidence. Much of Victoria's residences have been converted into a school of musketry, and men drill on both north and south campuses on either side of University College.'[63]

Institutions in Crisis

Activities on the grounds and in the buildings of the province's universities, purposeful and of obvious public utility, in fact masked the internal crises faced by all of them. To begin with, the patriotic enlistment of professors and students meant a crisis of enrolment. Total university enrolment in Ontario dropped steadily from 8,431 in 1914–15 to 5,884 in 1916–17. At the University of Toronto – which educated almost half of the students in the province – enrolment dropped from 4,428 in the first year of the war to 3,246 in 1916–17, and would not reach pre-war levels until the 1919–20 term. Enrolment also plummeted at other universities and colleges. Two thousand and nine students began the 1914–15 term at Queen's, but by 1916–17 their number had dropped to 1,225; at McMaster enrolment for these years fell from 268 to 205; and at Western it fell from 192 to 138. Victoria College attendance decreased from 685 to 331 (see Figs. 11.1–11.3).

Such dramatic drops in enrolment largely reflected the degree of enlistment of men for the war. At the University of Toronto, the number

FIGURE 11.1

University of Toronto and total Ontario university enrolment, 1914–19

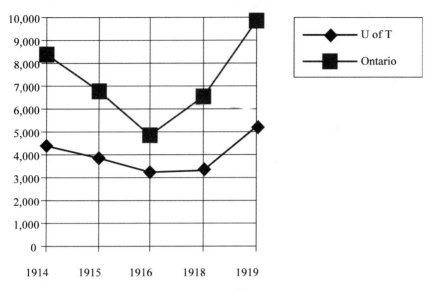

SOURCE: *Canada Year Book* (Ottawa 1914–20). Note: Because of the war, no separate volume was published for the year 1917.

FIGURE 11.2

Total enrolment at University of Toronto, Victoria, and Queen's, 1914–19

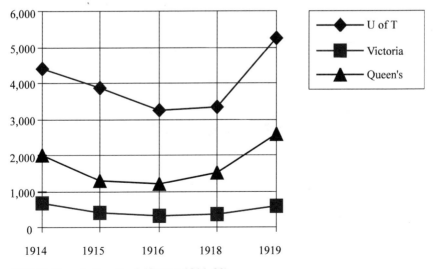

SOURCE: *Canada Year Book* (Ottawa 1914–20)

FIGURE 11.3

Total enrolment at McMaster and Western, 1914–19

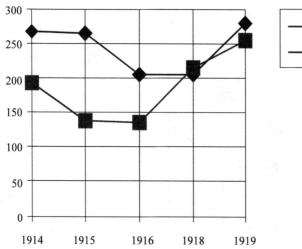

SOURCE: *Canada Year Book* (Ottawa 1914–20)

FIGURE 11.4

Male and female enrolment, University of Toronto, 1914–19

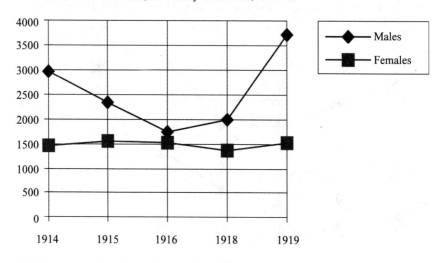

SOURCE: *Canada Year Book* (Ottawa 1914–20)

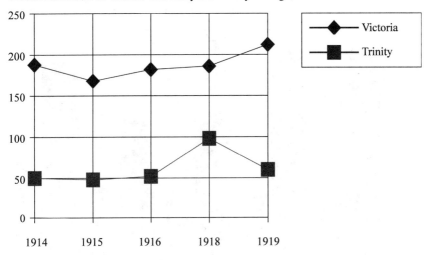

FIGURE 11.5

Female enrolment at Victoria University and Trinity College, 1914–19

SOURCE: *Canada Year Book* (Ottawa 1914–20)

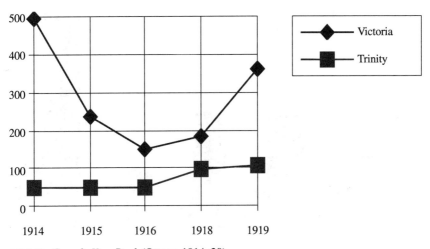

FIGURE 11.6

Male enrolment at Victoria University and Trinity College, 1914–19

SOURCE: *Canada Year Book* (Ottawa 1914–20)

FIGURE 11.7

Male and female enrolment, McMaster University, 1914–19

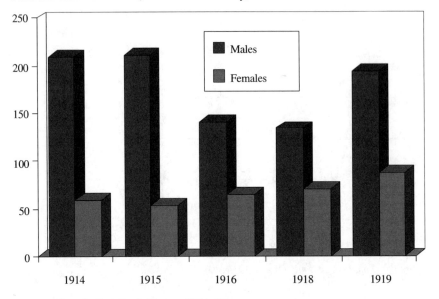

SOURCE: *Canada Year Book* (Ottawa 1914–20)

FIGURE 11.8

Male and female enrolment, Queen's University, 1914–19

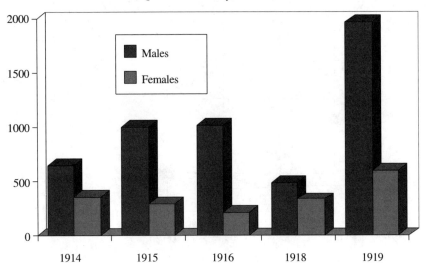

SOURCE: *Canada Year Book* (Ottawa 1914–20)

of women registered increased by only fifty from 1914–15 to 1916–17; in the same period attendance by men dropped by almost half. Similarly, at Victoria University and Trinity College female attendance remained relatively constant. Attendance by men at Victoria plummetted from 497 to 149, while at Trinity it remained virtually constant. At McMaster enrolment of men decreased from 209 in 1914–15 to 140 in 1916–17; enrolment of women increased marginally. Only at Queen's did attendance by women decrease significantly. By the 1918–19 academic year 332 of the 810 students at Queen's were women (see Figs. 11.4–11.8).

Yet such figures can mislead. By not distinguishing between full-time and part-time students, for example, they can appear to exaggerate the number of students actually attending a university on a day-to-day basis. The case of Queen's in 1914–15 makes the point. In the first year of the war there were 1,653 male students and 356 female students. Yet once the numbers are broken down by area of study the number of students in full-time attendance diminishes. Of the original total of just over 2,000, 419 were extramural (part-time) students in arts, involved in evening and extension courses. A further 497 were part-time students enrolled in what was effectively a correspondence course in accounting and related subjects for bankers.[64] Taking these figures into account allows us to see just how few students actually made up the daily life of the university in 1914–15. Full time arts students totalled 539, with women outnumbering men 290 to 249,[65] and these figures are very high compared with those of the 1916–17 academic year, when first-year intramural undergraduate registration totalled ninety-six in arts and eight in science. Enrolment in Queen's Theological College in 1916–17 had declined to fifteen.[66]

As we have already seen, the years of the Great War did not witness a sudden influx of female undergraduates to fill the void left when men enlisted. This was especially the case at Queen's, where the number of women in fact fell. If a sense of a greater presence of women on Ontario campuses arose, it did so largely because, as the war exacted its toll on enrolment of male undergraduates, the relative proportion of women increased dramatically; their numbers did not. At Victoria University in 1914–15, for example, 188 women and 497 men were enrolled. Two years later (1916–17) there were thirty-three fewer men (149) than women (182). In the 1918–19 academic year, the ratio was virtually equal, with 184 women and 185 men, but by the next year, while female enrolment continued to increase (to 211), the proportion of women to men had begun to return to its 1914–15 level with the registration of 364 men (see Fig. 11.9).

Although enrolment declined, the number of academic staff appointments at Ontario universities increased throughout the war. Total teaching staff in the province increased from 678 in 1914–15 to 751 in

FIGURE 11.9

Male and female enrolment, Victoria University, 1914–19

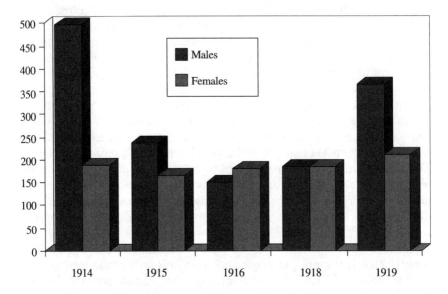

SOURCE: *Canada Year Book* (Ottawa 1914–20)

FIGURE 11.10

Teaching staffs: University of Toronto, Queen's, and Ontario total, 1914–19

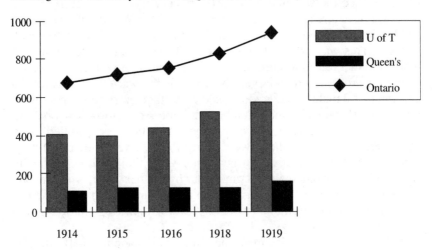

SOURCE: *Canada Year Book* (Ottawa 1914–20)

1916–17. At the University of Toronto, teaching staff increased from 401 to 440 in these years; at Queen's, from 105 to 127 (see Fig. 11.10). The vast majority of these were men, but a significant number of them were absent on military service, their places reserved until they returned. As a result, the statistics do not quite reflect the reality.

An implicit commentary on the degree to which women were acceptable as members of the academic staff lies in the numbers of female appointees. At Toronto, academic positions for women increased from fifteen at the outset of the war to forty in 1916–17, rising to sixty in 1919–20. At Queen's, however, in spite of male attrition, few women found a place behind the lectern. Not until 1916–17 were the first female staff members appointed, and then only in extreme circumstances. The absence of male staff members in the classics department had resulted in a breakdown in the health of the one remaining senior professor. Desperate, Principal Daniel M. Gordon sought an able male replacement in England, only to be told that none was available and that the only choice was between a disabled veteran, probably over forty years of age, and 'female labour.' Provided with a name by his British counsellor, Gordon appointed Miss M. Macdonnell in 1917. The first appointment of a woman to the academic staff of Queen's had taken place only one year earlier. Miss Wilhemina Gordon began teaching in the English department in 1916. She was the daughter of the university's principal. In this way, through the back door and the principal's office, female academics found a place at Queen's. Although the number of women on the teaching staff at Queen's had increased to twelve in 1918–19, within a year only four remained. The men were back (see Figs. 11.11, 11.12).[67]

The rate of increase in the number of women appointed to academic positions was not insignificant, yet their number was small. In 1914–15 only twenty-two women had university teaching positions in the province. By 1919–20 the number had reached seventy.[68] Most were associated with the faculties of arts or household science. In 1920 only six of a staff of 189 in the medical faculty at Toronto were women. Within academic ranks, women were almost always at or near the bottom of the academic ladder, and promotions were 'either very slow or non-existent.'[69] No woman held the rank of full professor at the University of Toronto at the beginning of the 1920s; only two (of forty-nine) were associate professors; all thirty-five assistant professors were men. No more than a half-dozen women could be classed as senior administrators, but forty-four (of a total staff of 290) were women who fell under the vague category of 'other' in the university's system of ranks.[70]

Even in the category of 'senior administrator' labels could deceive. One of these in 1918 was presumably Miss Salter, appointed lady super-

FIGURE 11.11

Teaching staff, University of Toronto: female and total, 1914–19

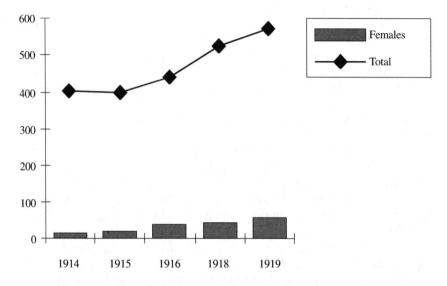

SOURCE: *Canada Year Book* (Ottawa 1914–20)

FIGURE 11.12

Female teaching staffs: University of Toronto, Queen's, and Ontario total, 1914–19

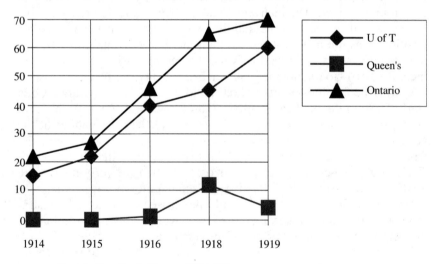

SOURCE: *Canada Year Book* (Ottawa 1914–20)

intendent by Daniel Wilson in 1885 and still on duty more than thirty years later. As historian Marni de Pencier has noted, 'The title of Superintendent, recognition in the President's reports, and long service all seemed to indicate a significant appointment.' Yet one of the women who had known Miss Salter and was aware of her duties deflated such a view. She told de Pencier that the Superintendent's function was mainly 'to provide adequate chaperonage for the women students and she did this by sitting all day behind a table in the ladies cloakroom.' Such was the unhappy professional reality masked by Robert Falconer's words of appreciation in his *President's Report* of 1920, the year after Salter's death: 'For 33 years she gave to the women of University College in unsparing labour the most faithful and kindly guidance.'[71]

Superintendent Salter's starting salary in 1885 had been $500, and evidently it was not substantially higher thirty-three years later. Just as promotions for women were slow (it took twenty-six years for Mabel Cartwright to be promoted from lecturer to associate professor in English at St Hilda's), salaries were low and lagged behind those of men in similar ranks. Clara Benson and Annie Laird, appointed as associate professors in the faculty of household science in 1906, held the same rank at the outbreak of the Great War. Their salaries at first appointment had been $1,575, when male associate professors were receiving $2,200. Benson and Laird earned that amount in 1915, but by then their male counterparts received between $2,500 and $3,000.[72] By way of contrast, President Robert Falconer had been appointed in 1907 at a salary of $10,000.

In spite of the increase in the number of the teaching staff, full-time studies at the University of Toronto were at times on the verge of collapse during the war. Departmental and faculty programs seemed to implode under the external social pressures of a civilization at war. With three exceptions – the general course in social service (which more or less maintained its numbers between its introduction in 1913–14 and 1917–18), the honours courses in modern languages, and in English and history (which remained comparatively stable) – virtually all other courses, whether in arts, science, or the professions, declined badly, often dropping by fifty per cent or more. Enrolment also declined drastically in the department of political science and economics, where graduate studies virtually disappeared.[73] Yet most courses survived, at least formally – including those in Greek and Hebrew, in which no one enrolled in the latter half of the war.[74]

Professional enrolment at the University of Toronto also declined severely during the war years. It did so precisely because the kinds of skills provided by medical and engineering faculties were so much in demand by military authorities. An indication of the magnitude of the problem can be given by comparing the numbers of first- and final-year examinations written in the war years. Medical training was at the time a five-year program[75] and applied science took four. In late spring, 1913, approximately 100 students wrote their first-year final exams in medicine; about 20 remained long enough to write their finals in 1917. General enrolment in applied science and engineering at Toronto declined from over 600 in 1913–14 to 164 in 1917–18. Other professional units faced similar fates. Enrolment in household science dropped, and the faculty was in effect closed down, its students re-enrolled in the faculty of arts – thereby inflating the numbers of those who appeared to be studying the liberal arts. The forestry program had only ten students in both 1916–17 and 1917–18.[76]

The loss of students and the collapse of programs meant that, in spite of increased public pressure for academic support of the war effort, universities in the province had a diminished capacity to provide it. This was made worse by the financial crisis they faced. The withdrawal of students meant a decline in revenue from tuition fees. At the University of Toronto, such income fell from $269,836 in 1914–15 to around $185,000 in the third and fourth years of the war. Even after revenues increased in 1918–19 to $235,000, they were well below pre-war amounts. By 1916 tuition and boarding fees at McMaster had declined by more than $1,000.00. At Queen's authorities in 1917 were forced to approach their Chancellor, James Douglas (who had succeeded Sir Sandford Fleming in 1915), for a million-dollar gift necessary to stabilize the university's precarious finances.[77]

Student fees at no Ontario university were nearly enough to operate the institution. The expansion of university enrolment and activities since the 1890s had made state aid the virtual *sine qua non* of university existence, and the Whitney years in provincial politics had been good ones for most of them. In the abstract, the Conservative premier had held to the traditional political policy of not aiding denominational universities. But he had made certain exceptions, meant to be unique cases. The University of Ottawa had received a grant of $10,000 in 1905, after a disastrous fire. Queen's had been given $50,000 to help build a new medical building in 1906, and this had been followed from 1907 to 1916 with annual grants, in amounts ranging from $5,000 to $12,000, to establish and sustain a program in pedagogy.[78]

If this meant that the traditional reluctance of provincial administrations to aid denominational institutions was waning, it was equally the case that several of them had come to the conclusion that survival of the university necessitated the ending of formal religious ties. In 1908 West-

FIGURE 11.13
Provincial operating assistance to Ontario universities, 1891–1914

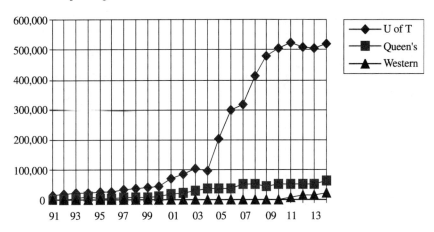

SOURCE: Derived from E.E. Stewart, 'The Role of the Provincial Government in the
Development of Universities in Ontario,' EDD thesis, University of Toronto (1970),
Tables 2 and 3

ern University, for example, had secured provincial legislation stipulat-
ing that 'the Government of the University shall be absolutely
undenominational and under public, municipal or provincial control or
any or all of them.' Within a year, the provincial government had contributed almost $25,000 to Western for the construction of a building for
the study of hygiene. Similarly, after lengthy and divisive debate within
the academic and Presbyterian communities, in 1912 Queen's sought
and obtained federal legislation that changed its name from 'Queen's
College at Kingston' to 'Queen's University at Kingston,' in part so that
it might qualify for Carnegie Foundation funding for academic pensions.
The parliamentary act specified that 'the management and discipline of
the university shall be in every respect free from all denominational
restrictions.' Parallel legislation in the same year had established
Queen's Theological College, to take the place of the university's theology faculty.[79] By 1914 operating revenue from the province to these two
newly secular universities amounted to $25,000 in the case of Western
and $65,000 for Queen's (see Fig. 11.13).

The University of Toronto had benefitted substantially from Whitney's approach to the financing of higher education. The 1906 legislation had provided for the university to be supported mainly by its fifty
per cent share of provincial succession duties, and from 1905 to 1911 the
result had been a dramatic increase in operating revenues (from

FIGURE 11.14

Provincial operating assistance to Ontario universities, 1915–20

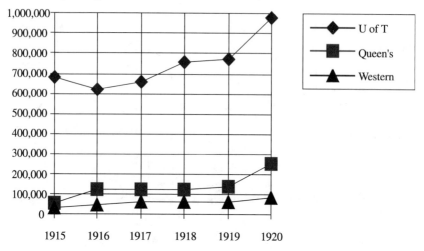

SOURCE: Derived from Stewart, 'Provincial Government'

$202,444 to $525,267). But the immediate pre-war years, marked by a nation-wide recession, witnessed a decline in such sources to $505,792 in 1913 (see Fig. 11.13). By 1912 the chairman of the board of governors spoke publicly of the 'financial crisis and the need of the Province to come once again to the aid of the institution.'[80] Matters seemed critical. But no one anticipated the events of 1914.

James P. Whitney, fresh from an election victory in June, died in September of 1914. Faced with financing the province in wartime, his successor, William H. Hearst, almost immediately passed legislation limiting the total revenues the University of Toronto could receive from succession duties to $500,000. Moreover, none of the universities could have been heartened by the statement by Provincial Treasurer I.B. Lucas in the spring of 1914 that 'as an outsider I cannot view with favor a proposal to place upon the finances of the Province the burden of maintaining two other universities. The University of Toronto might be relieved by transferring students to Queen's and Western Universities. In this way co-operation or co-ordination might be worked out.'[81] The provincial government recognized the necessity of expanding grant assistance to universities, but seemed to have no clear sense of how this could be done. During the war years – precisely when political leadership and direction were necessary for the universities to plan their own programs and activities – the provincial administration entered a period of ad hoc measures and a return to the relative drift of the Ross years.[82]

By 1916 the practice, if not the principle, of provincial operating grants to secularized institutions had been established, although in no instance did the government acknowledge responsibility for regional institutions or guarantee a continuing level of support for the University of Toronto. By 1918 operating assistance to the provincial university had reached $755,362, an increase of $234,269 over 1914. Similar support to Queen's had doubled, from $65,000 in 1914 to $122,000. Grants to Western had increased from $25,000 to $60,000 (see Fig. 11.14 and compare with Fig. 11.13 for 1891–1914 period). Each year, the government strategy for funding universities was to do so by means of the supplemental estimates, declaring on the one hand that a portion of the original estimates for university grants would not be required in the new fiscal year and then, on the other, coming forward later with sufficient supplementary funds to equal the original amounts. In each of the years from 1914 to 1918 the University of Toronto was forced to run a deficit, but these were met by supplementary government grants: $80,000 in 1916, $100,000 in 1917, and $200,000 in both 1918 and 1919.[83] No state funds were available for capital expenditures. Such procedures made planning by academic authorities all but impossible.

Nevertheless, the public had been made aware of the social utility of the universities. Working in overburdened facilities and with under-financed programs, individuals and groups did their best to contribute to the war effort. Thus, McMaster University's professor of chemistry, John Bishop Tingle, a Manchester- and Munich-educated expert at spectrum analysis and carbon compounds, trained scientists who found positions with the Imperial Munitions Board and was instrumental in placing three of his prize female students – Marion Grimshaw, Ruth Baker, and Bessie Cooke – as research chemists at the munitions board's new explosives plant at Nobel, near Parry Sound. At Queen's, S.F. Kirkpatrick of the department of metallurgy conducted research on the recovery of cobalt from Ontario ores, and chemists W.L. Goodwin and W.O. Walker investigated flares used at the front and suggested to the munitions board a way of improving them.[84] At the University of Toronto, faculty members conducted research on pectic acid, helped produce high explosive shells for the Imperial Munitions Board, tested and inspected steel, developed plugs and sockets for shrapnel, and worked on the manufacture of magnesium. Commissioned by the board of inventions of the British Admiralty, the head of physics, J.C. McLennan, investigated the possibility of producing helium in Canada. (It was produced, and in 1923 McLennan and his staff succeeded in liquefying the gas.) Other projects undertaken by McLennan and his staff included aspects of anti-submarine research such as testing glass prisms for periscopes and developing anti-mine devices.[85]

The efforts of another University of Toronto scientist, John G. Fitzgerald, associate professor of hygiene, led in the direction of saving rather than destroying lives. Appointed in July 1913 after a decade of study in Europe and the United States, Fitzgerald was dedicated to research in the areas of hygiene, preventive medicine, and public health. He had become convinced that Canada should produce its own vaccines and serums for the treatment of infectious diseases, instead of relying on the importation of foreign-made (mainly American) antitoxins. His initial proposal for the establishment of an antitoxin laboratory at the University of Toronto had met with sympathy by President Falconer but was rejected by other members of the university community on the grounds that such a commercially oriented operation would threaten the academic reputation of the university. Undaunted, and with Falconer's tacit consent, Fitzgerald established his own laboratory on Barton Street, produced a diptheria antitoxin during the winter of 1913–14, and obtained a contract from the provincial board of health for the production of it in greater quantity. (In 1915 the Ontario-made diptheria vaccine was distributed without charge throughout the province.) Faced with Fitzgerald's self-financing and possibly even profit-making *fait accompli*, the university's board of governors formally supported the institution's sponsorship of the antitoxin laboratory, with Fitzgerald as director, on 1 May 1914. At the outbreak of hostilities in Europe it was fully operational. By May 1915, aided by a $5,000 grant from the federal Department of Militia and Defence, the laboratory was supplying much of the tetanus antitoxin required by the Canadian Expeditionary Force, and was doing so at a considerable savings over imported vaccines. Inspired by the laboratory's literally life-saving work, Alfred E. Gooderham, a member of the University of Toronto board of governors, purchased a fifty-eight-acre farm in Downsview, some twelve miles north-west of the university campus, and provided $75,000 for the construction of new and enlarged facilities on it. A year later, in October 1917, the operation was formally opened and renamed the Connaught Antitoxin Laboratories, after the governor general of Canada. At the opening, Premier Sir William Hearst announced that the province would match Gooderham's gift by creating a $75,000 endowment fund in aid of medical research.[86]

Such success stories heightened public awareness of the university's practical value and diminished its image as a cloistered, almost monastic community that prided itself on its separation from the larger life of the world. 'The war is doing one thing,' the Toronto *Globe* editorialized in

January 1917: 'The standard of greatness for the universities is now seen to be ... in the quality and the range of the service rendered to the public. The university is not a thing apart ... The war has made it very plain in Canada, plain even to the Philistines, that, if Canada is to recover from the war's fearful dislocation of business and of industry, there must come into our life not less of the university's technique, of the scientist's method, and of the specialist's knowledge, [but] ... more devotion to precision in the application of science to industry ...'[87] The public little knew, however, that such successes as the Connaught Laboratories masked the reality. The fact was, as university administrators, industrialists, and governments were well aware, that frighteningly little pure or industrial research was actually being done in the country.

Recognition of the meagre and haphazard nature of Canadian scientific research had preceded the advent of war, but the war forced action and galvanized resolve. Prompted in part by a 1912 lecture on 'The crying need for Industrial Research' by the Reverend George Bryce (chairman of the Royal Commission on Industrial Training and Technical Education), the council of the Canadian Institute proposed in 1914 that a 'Bureau of Scientific and Industrial Research' be created. Spurred by J.C. McLennan, this bureau was created, with a council consisting of representatives of the universities, the boards of trade, and other interested organizations.[88]

Paralleling and fuelling this increase of interest among professional scientists was the ongoing lobby of the central Canadian industrial community. The pressing need for industrial research had become, and was to remain, a leitmotif of the Canadian Manufacturers Association's journal, *Industrial Canada*. In 1915 it had noted the concerns expressed at the National Conference of Canadian Universities that inadequate facilities for advanced research led Canadian university graduates to complete their training in 'foreign universities,' especially American ones. University plans to promote graduate education, said *Industrial Canada*'s editor, coincided with 'the long-standing demands of Canadian manufacturers for the encouragement of research work in the higher branches of technical knowledge'; accordingly, he pledged 'the strong support of the manufacturers of this country' if the proposals of the national university association were 'presented in a practical form.'[89]

The president of Canada Sugar Refining Company, A.T. Drummond, provided the first serious suggestion during the war that the federal government should cooperate with universities. By the beginning of 1915, Drummond had written the first of a several 'prodding letters' to Robert Falconer of Toronto, William Peterson of McGill, and various government officials, exploring the possibility of setting up a series of government-sponsored scholarships and subsidies for the improvement and advancement of manufactures. Concurrent with this initiative T.H. Wardleworth, president of National Drug and Chemical Company, acting on behalf of the Society of Chemical Research, suggested to the minister of trade and commerce, Sir George Foster, that the universities might contribute valuable research if they were to receive state financial assistance.[90] The result was a meeting held in Foster's office on 25 May 1915, attended by representatives of universities and industries. The former comprised mainly men from Toronto and McGill; the latter included T.H. Wardleworth, acting as a representative of the Canadian Manufacturers' Association, and Frank Arnoldi, president of the Royal Canadian Institute.[91]

Within six months Foster had learned from his commissioner of commerce the sobering fact that total expenditures on university research by all federal government departments from 1912 to 1915 had amounted to only $277,000. Pressure continued to be exerted on Foster, by both industrialists and university men, for the creation of a commission on industrial research. But the minister acted only after William Peterson announced on 1 May 1916 that he intended to place before the annual conference of Canadian university presidents (initiated in 1911 and institutionalized as the National Conference of Canadian Universities) a motion to associate the universities with the United Kingdom Research Council, founded the previous year. Challenged to act, Foster replied to Peterson that while the imperial scheme was a 'comprehensive' one, 'it seems to me that first and foremost each Dominion should organize itself and through that organization, work with the Imperial scheme.' Almost immediately he recommended to the Privy Council that a committee of the Privy Council be appointed to oversee any expenditure of monies for scientific and industrial research and recommended, as well, that an honorary advisory council, consisting of nine representatives of science and industry, be created. Of the latter group, he wrote to Toronto's J.C. McLennan: 'We want men of science, of course, but we also want men of a practical turn who have business in them.' The Order in Council approving the research plan was issued on 6 June 1916.

Soon after the national scientific community divided on the question of what sort of institution should coordinate and house the research. Prime Minister Borden wrote to Foster expressing Sir Clifford Sifton's 'apprehension that too much reliance would be placed upon the work of the Universities.' Sifton (and presumably Borden) believed that 'research work should be conducted upon a national scale and in institutions established and maintained by the Government.' In this, the Canadian Society of Civil Engineers concurred: they wrote to Borden urging him to build government testing laboratories at Ottawa. Robert Falconer privately expressed to Joseph Flavelle the opposite view. 'There is another side to this question,' he wrote, 'and that is the extent to which a properly organized movement might make use of the laboratories that already exist in the University.'

Possibly because of the likelihood of objections by the universities and the provinces, no decision was made by the Borden cabinet to establish government laboratories in Ottawa. Similarly, the appointment of the advisory research council was postponed until 29 November 1916, when George Foster recorded in his diary: 'Got my Advisory Council though most members of [Privy] Council utterly indifferent or antagonistic.' The industrial representatives on the advisory committee were T. Bienvenu, vice-president and general manager of La Banque Provinciale du Canada; R. Hobson, president of the Steel Company of Canada; and R.A. Ross, a Montreal consulting engineer. Academic representatives included Frank Adams, dean of applied science, and R.F. Ruttan, professor of chemistry, from McGill; and A.S. Mackenzie and W.C. Murray, presidents of Dalhousie University and the University of Saskatchewan, respectively. From Ontario, only the University of Toronto was represented – by J.C. McLennan, professor of physics, and A.B. Macallum, professor of biochemistry. Of great significance, however, was the further appointment of Macallum as full-time chairman to be located in Ottawa. His starting salary of $10,000 exceeded that of the minister of trade and commerce.

Macallum went about setting up the research council offices, initially three rooms in the West Block replete with lavish furniture that had once graced the Senate chambers. Surveys were sent out to 2,800 Canadian industrial companies as well as to universities, inquiring into their research facilities and activities. The results were depressing. Roughly thirty-seven firms in the country had research laboratories, usually with a staff of one. Canadian universities had granted fewer than a dozen PHD degrees in pure science. The whole country, Macallum estimated, contained probably 'not many more than 50 pure research men all told.' The annual budget of the Massachusetts Institute of Technology was greater than the total annual expenditure of all Canadian faculties of applied science. Adding to the pressures faced by Macallum, *Industrial Canada* stepped up its campaign to obtain federal leadership in industrial research.[92]

To make matters worse, universities soon began to engage in acrimonious competition for research council funding of research projects, graduate programs, and research institutes. Visions of future scientific empires grew in the imaginations of the ambitious. 'I am convinced more

than ever,' J.C. McLennan wrote to his former University of Toronto colleague Macallum, 'that such an Institution [a Bureau of Industrial
Research] should be in Toronto and that its organization should be similar
to what I so frequently indicated. It should be near the University and
should have on its staff Members of the University staff, at least in the
capacity of Consultants ...' While Macallum understandably wanted
research to be centralized in Ottawa, McLennan had in mind a Canadian
equivalent of the Mellon Institute in the United States, with branches in
Montreal and Winnipeg as well as Toronto. Moreover, administration of
the proposed institutes should ultimately rest with the government and
manufacturers.[93] On one matter McLennan and Macallum agreed:
smaller institutions within central Canada, such as Queen's, should have
no share of the pie. For its part, the Kingston university resolved not to
remain passively acquiescent over its exclusion from the councils of
national science. Meanwhile, with a total yearly budget of only $120,000,
Macallum could do little more than establish research and funding priorities, and hope that interuniversity squabbling would lessen. He was probably sustained somewhat by the consoling words of Walter Murray of the
University of Saskatchewan, written near the end of the war: '... I thoroughly approve of your efforts to do what you can to get assistance for the
research work of the Universities. The jealousy between some of the eastern Universities is quite unworthy of them. It is contemptible among
small Colleges; between large Universities it is beneath contempt.'[94]

The Great Divide

Forty years after the Great War began, Canadian scholar A.S.P. Woodhouse wrote: 'Up to 1914, though danger signs were not wanting, a
sober optimism prevailed ... Then came 1914 and, as now appears, the
Great Divide.'[95] This was largely so. Yet the disruptions caused by the
war took small forms as well as large. Sometimes the simple gravity of
war imposed burdens of self-restraint on otherwise ebullient youth. In
November 1914, news was published of the death of R.M. Richards
(school of forestry '14). Richards, it was believed, had been the first
Toronto student to die in the war. The result was the refusal by female
students of the 'Women's Lit' to participate in dances. There would be
no dancing at Trinity or University Colleges – no University College 'at
home,' no formal arts dance, no Trinity Rugby or Queen's Hall ball. By
the end of the war dances once again took place, but without official university sanction.[96]

   Other pre-war undergraduate social patterns persisted through the war
years, in either muted or exaggerated forms. Sports suffered greatly,

although military activities continued to be described in the vocabulary and with the assumptions of the English public school.[97] Rushes, scraps, and inter-faculty rivalries continued. Two hundred science and medical students engaged in battle during the medical rush of 1914. Ontario Agricultural College students scrapped with police and soldiers in 1915 at a local opera house, with many injuries. The Alma Mater Society at Queen's was forced in 1916 to abolish its old system of rushes to prevent 'the dangerous, and in some instances, extremely offensive, ancient form of initiation' from threatening students. Scraps and rites of student custom continued to be a means of alleviating frustration. 'Sir Robert Falconer and the Students' Council,' wrote one medical student, 'are apparently of one mind in desiring to convert this place of learning into a machine akin to the sausage machine into one end of which the verdant freshman is cast, to emerge several years later a man of letters or a scientist.'[98]

The year 1917 is synonymous with desperation and struggle – the German announcement of unrestricted submarine warfare in January; food riots at Petrograd in March; the American declaration of war on Germany and the Canadian victory at Vimy Ridge in April; the third Battle of Ypres, known to Canadians as Passchendaele, from August into November. By the beginning of the year, sons of Professor George Wrong and Chancellor Sir William Meredith had become part of the 'ultimate sacrifice.' A section entitled 'Killed in Action' now appeared in each issue of the *Queen's Journal*. The world seemed unhinged, individual destiny beyond individual control, leading either to a sense of helpless drift or to stoic resignation. Robert Borden's May announcement of conscription, to take effect as soon as possible, served to crystallize such attitudes. 'We are told,' wrote the editor of the *Queen's Journal*,

that the nation and the universe are a seething mass of breaking customs, changing epochs, and tottering institutions; that the university is but a reflection of life in general; that when men know not where or how their next month will be spent, or whether their whole life's course shall be altered by the act of the Military Tribunal they cannot concentrate on petty things of present time and space; that the women of the College cannot but feel the general spirit of uncertainty, indecision and helpless inactivity in the face of odds too great for mortal comprehension ... The seriousness of the age has caught us in its veil ... And therein lies the explanation of our helplessness, of our 'ambitionless' inactivity, of our questioning uncertainty, of our too readily accepted discouragement – we are feeling the war, – we are not living the war. We have adopted the feeling attitude, and in the conscious satisfaction of our intense regret, even sorrow, and sincere dismay, we have lulled the spiritually intellectual impulses, that 1914 awakened, to a serene slumber.[99]

Once the promise of conscription became a reality, however, students experienced an almost tangible sense of relief. That aspect of their uncertainty was over. They had consistently been willing to do their duty, whether responding to compulsory military registration or, if necessary, to conscription.[100] By 1918 student life was once more granted a sense of direction. 'A changed spirit in the students since the Military Service Act was put into force is reported by some of the professors,' the *Globe* reported in March. 'Before the act, the students were in a state of doubt and lost much of their habitual cheerfulness, but now that the uncertainty is ended and they definitely know what part they are to play in the great struggle, they have perked up. As one professor remarked, "they go around whistling now, and we are glad to note the change."'[101]

Few if any Ontario professors whistled in the last years of the war. A chastened Robert Falconer, whose idealist rhetoric had done so much to encourage enlistment, concluded sadly in 1916 that 'the world has come to be less moral than it was and there is a great deal less honour among the great civilized nations than we thought there was.'[102] In such a world, of what use was scholarship or higher learning in general? By February 1917 Falconer was forced to address such large questions, as members of his own board of governors were pressing for the University of Toronto to be closed for the 1917–18 academic year. Significantly, Falconer's rejection of this suggestion contained no arguments other than those based on practical utility.[103]

Just as the operations of his own university were threatened, so, too, was the scholarship that had done much to shape the intellectual outlook of Falconer and others. The magisterial edifice of German thought in theology, philosophy, and the sciences that had influenced Canadian professors for almost half a century had lost much of its moral and intellectual authority. In the first years of the war, professors such as philosopher John Watson, theologian Ernest F. Scott, Falconer himself, and others had sought to separate German scholarship from German militarism,[104] but such voices became increasingly muted. In 1916 the 25th annual Queen's theological alumni conference, formerly a major collective voice of German-derived British idealism in Canada, was held. 'The war note was not lacking,' wrote one observer. '... German Philosophy was only occasionally alluded to.' By then, even James Loudon, Ontario's scientific apostle of the German research ideal, had altered his long-held views and joined the newly formed Anti-German League of Canada – its motto, 'No More German Immigrants, Shipping, Labour, Goods [and] Influence.' By the end of the war his son Brian would become yet one more military mortality statistic.[105] 'This eclipse of Germany as an intellectual power,' Queen's theologian Ernest F. Scott concluded after the war had ended, 'is not altogether to be regretted.' Yet Scott did not speak without a measure of genuine sadness. 'It cannot be denied that this falling out of Germany as one of the great intellectual producers of the world, will mean an enormous loss. We shall miss those German books, crawling like sluggish rivers through every field of knowledge, and depositing their muddy sediment of foot-notes all along their course. They irrigated if they did not beautify, and the harvest will be poorer without them.'[106]

'The war has circumscribed us,' Scott concluded, and in some respects he was correct. At no point in the next half-century would German or Austrian scholarship influence the Ontario professoriate as it had in the years since the 1870s. Names such as Marx, Freud, Mannheim, or Weber remained foreign ones. In other respects, the war seemed in fact to have diminished the range of human possibility. 'A hurricane smote Western civilization' in August 1914, Falconer told an American academic audience, 'and ever since, the comfortable home that we had reared for ourselves out of our axioms, opinions and assumptions has been swaying so violently that broad fissures are appearing in its walls ...' He found himself asking 'Is the Idea of Progress Valid?' and he offered no firm answer. Nor did Maurice Hutton, who began a 1916 convocation address to the University of Manitoba by proclaiming that 'Our world has fallen to pieces, the academic world most of all ... Books and learning, self-culture and rationalism seem now to smack of Germany where indeed were their temples and their priests.' Two years later Hutton's Knox College colleague Robert Law told the graduating class of the same Western Canadian university that he could find 'no basis for optimism except in that interpretation of life which we call religious faith ...'[107]

The world ushered in by the Great War appeared like the world of Alice – bewildering, disproportionate, seemingly out of control. 'We are amazed at the changes, social, political, industrial, that have come about in Britain, in Russia, in France,' Principal Gordon told the graduating class of Queen's in the spring of 1917. 'Changes seem to have been crowded and condensed into three years that would scarcely be accomplished within a generation in times of peace.'[108] But Gordon was a man in his seventies whose Victorian world, like that of Maurice Hutton, seemed to have vanished. Others, younger men, had been left to wander among the shards of nineteenth-century civilization in search of the new day. Symbolic of those left with the task of reconstruction and renewal were the founders and early staff members of the *Rebel*, a University of Toronto-based magazine of iconoclastic opinion – C.B. Sissons, professor of classics and ancient history, Barker Fairley, who taught German, and S.H. Hooke, professor of Oriental languages.

No less than Gordon and Hutton, these younger academics were aware of the Great Divide marked by the Great War. 'One of the most disquieting things about life as it is to-day,' wrote one early contributor to the *Rebel*, 'is the way in which values are being hastily jettisoned, relegated to peace-times, as though life were not a unity, whether in peace or war. The only logical issue seems to me to be the acknowledgement either that our values were wrong, were not essential, and have been tried and found wanting in the *ultima ratio* of war, or that we ourselves have never really held them for values; it was only a pose, a garment which was stripped from us.' The task of these rebels, therefore, was not to jettison old values but to test them in the world of peacetime reconstruction. These young men held no brief for abject traditionalism, for in their view the Great War had not been caused by Germany but by the past itself. Nineteenth-century civilization had produced, not been betrayed by, the events of 1914–18. Academic lessons could be learned from this and university structures and programs be shaped by it. 'The life of an Arts student in the University,' wrote a *Rebel* contributor in 1918, 'seems very largely taken up with the study of the past, of the great men and their accomplishments. But the University that simply gives a student an appreciation of history even if it be an intellectual appreciation which will enrich all his life, has only begun his task. For the student should be fired with the ambition to create.'[109]

The balance between tradition and innovation, past and future, had been tipped, and the post-war university was to be a major forum in which much of the complex nexus of modern culture was to be played out. Yet hindsight allows us to see that in fact the fundamental elements of such substantial change had existed and were growing in the last several decades of the nineteenth century. From the 1880s on, the jagged edges of modernity increasingly broke the artificially calm surface of late Victorian and Edwardian academic life. Until the Great War, however, the proponents of the Ontario university's role as agent of a social and intellectual transformation firmly rooted in the industrial order had been on the defensive, for the authority of the past, rooted in the biblical record, remained the fundamental basis of moral force in higher education. At the Armistice of 11 November 1918, much of that authority was gone, and professorial apostles of the new academic order were readying themselves for the brave new post-war world.

Part Four:
Higher Education and the Interwar State

12

Reconstruction, Consolidation, Expansion

The universities of Ontario did not easily return to normal after the end of the Great War. Returned soldiers made unpredictable and potentially disruptive civilians. 'It is that terrible restlessness which possesses us like an evil spirit,' said one veteran – 'the indefinite expression of a vague discontent, the restlessness of dying men, little children and old soldiers.'[1] University authorities throughout the province were uncertain whether students who had disrupted their studies to go overseas would resume their education and, if so, in what numbers or in what frame of mind. Academic life was further disrupted from 1918 through 1920 by a serious outbreak of Spanish influenza in the province. Queen's University was completely closed for several weeks in 1918–19, with several student deaths. Classes were poorly attended. At the University of Toronto fewer than twenty-five per cent attended lectures as the disease infiltrated college residences. Over sixty cases were reported at St Michael's College, and several colleges closed their doors. As late as February 1920, all social functions of the provincial university remained cancelled.[2]

Much initial activity just after the war took on the character of a sustained memorial service. In October 1919 Victoria College survivors gathered on the college grounds for a two-day reunion that lingered for decades in the minds of some. Victoria's chancellor, the Reverend R.P. Bowles, asked his audience to remember 'the mightiest army that ever had trodden the earth, its sweep westward beyond its own borders, death and destruction, terror and anguish going before and following after ...' He asked it also to recall the student voices that once filled the campus with laughter and shouting. As students had once done on the playing field, on the battlefield they had also 'played the game with skill and prowess and with a clean and chivalrous spirit, fair and generous alike in defeat and victory.' Some had led in the college's scholastic or theological life; all had led in sacrifice and valour. The memorial service ended with the roll-call of sixty-seven names, followed by the haunting notes of the Last Post.[3] In December 1921 McMaster University unveiled a war memorial tablet to its men killed in the war, twenty-two in number.[4] The alumni association of the University of Toronto collected a substantial sum of money after the war. Some of it was used to establish scholarships and to provide loans for ex-servicemen; but primarily it was used to erect a war memorial, Soldiers' Tower, adjacent to the newly opened Hart House.[5] Similar testimonies to the need for remembrance took place throughout the province, the nation, and the empire. The rhetoric of chivalric sacrifice continued to be heard at remembrance day services, but it was now clearly associated with an era that was over. It belonged to history.

Although the years after 1919 witnessed the initial reconstruction of society, uneven prosperity, and ultimately economic depression, the course of higher education during this period was relatively smooth: continuity and modest expansion, rather than disruption, was the rule. Indeed, for one later historian the years between the wars were 'relatively quiet' ones in which, for most Ontarians, matters of higher education were of little concern. 'In Ontario,' wrote E.E. Stewart, 'there was as yet no recognition of the need for co-ordination of university effort ... nor had the Province awakened as quickly as the British were said to have done to a recognition of the importance of the universities in the general development of the state ... [A]part from a few isolated incidents that thrust universities into public prominence from time to time during the 1920s, 30s, and 40s, when it came to higher education, it was not far off the mark to say that "nobody gave a damn."'[6]

The *Canadian Annual Review* noted the existence of twenty universities in Canada in 1919. Their endowments were valued at $22,000,000 and their buildings at $28,000,000. Annual government grants to them totalled $1,400,000 and their total income reached $3,500,000, modest sums even for modest Canadians. Sixteen thousand students attended them. Of these universities, five were in Ontario. The University of Toronto had been the dependent child of the province from birth; Queen's University and Western University of London, Ontario, had divested themselves of denominational connections before the war in order to make their cases for state funding. The result had been government grants issued on a yearly basis, but such measures provided no measure of security or basis for planning. McMaster University and the University of Ottawa, more or less content with their connections to the Baptist Convention and the Roman Catholic Church, sought destinies independent of secular government.

Yet these were not uneventful years, whether measured by physical growth, curricular and disciplinary development, public attitudes towards academic life, professorial views regarding the role of the intellectual as citizen or critic, or the evolution of student culture. The social and intellectual disruption caused by the Great War altered expectations and moved universities into closer relation to the political and socio-economic life of the provincial state. The first step in this gradual, unplanned, and indeterminate linkage took place in the 1920s, when the imperatives of post-war reconstruction forced university presidents and provincial politicians alike to face the problem of financing universities with slowly increasing but expensive links to the world of scientific and technological research.

Reconstruction

When the students returned, they did so in numbers that taxed the already strained resources of the province's universities.[7] Total provincial university enrolment by the 1919–20 academic year stood at almost 10,000 (9,892), up from 8,431 at the outset of the war. University teaching staff during the same period grew from 678 to 940.[8] But the reconstruction of Ontario's institutions of higher education after the war involved more than finding the means of accommodating an influx of new and returning students. It involved, as well, coming to grips with the reality that Ontario had, in fact, no system of higher education, if by the word is meant a rational and consistent application of coherent policy, based on firm principles, intended to address a plurality of interests. The leaders of the province had continually acted in matters of administration and policy in an ad hoc manner, addressing each crisis as it arose. Even the apparently progressive direction of James P. Whitney's 1905 university policy had proven illusory. One senses that after the passage of the University Act of 1906, legislators had breathed a great, collective sigh of relief: the provincial university would at last be able to take care of itself.[9] Yet even before the war the finances of the University of Toronto were again in disarray and the question of whether secularized institutions such as Queen's or Western should receive state operating grants as a matter of principle rather than expedience was still not resolved. The death of Whitney at the outset of the war, and the dislocations of the war itself, made certain that such matters would remain unresolved for the rest of the decade.

Every university principal or president in Ontario welcomed the end of the war but lamented its immediate legacy. The 1920s threatened to be ushered in with many more students but fewer financial resources, and these fiscal uncertainties were made worse by political reorientation in the province. Only two parties had ruled Ontario since Confederation, Liberal and Conservative refractions of the British political tradition. The Great War, which exacerbated existing strains within what previously had seemed to be a permanent two-party system, had changed all that. Rural alienation from the two traditional parties, labour disaffection in the cities – these and other factors had forged a discontented and volatile post-war electorate at the level of both federal and provincial politics.

In 1919 disaffection with the political status quo in the province resulted in the election of the first third-party government in Canadian history, E.C. Drury's United Farmers of Ontario. Within three years Alberta and Manitoba were also led by Farmers' governments, and the federal election of 1921 witnessed the return of no fewer than sixty-five members of the newly formed Progressive Party of Canada as members of Parliament, a number large enough to form the official opposition in federal politics (although they chose not to do so because they objected to the very idea of 'party' politics). In Ontario, as elsewhere in the country, a new and untried political force had been unleashed by the winds of post-war discontent, fanned in part by high unemployment combined with an unprecedented increase in the cost of living.

The universities of Ontario suffered like other institutions from such inflation, and one result was the call for increases in salary. In his 1919–20 annual report, the principal of Queen's wrote that the large wage increases of the previous few years had 'brought about a revolution in the position of learned men.' At Queen's, he went on, 'an Assistant Professor receives from $2,000 to $2,400; an Associate Professor from $2,500 to $2,900; a Full Professor from $3,000 to $3,500. These sums, which would have been relatively large a few years ago, are almost absurdly small compared with the rewards of industrial life.'[10]

The dire necessity of increased industrial production during the war had helped push up industrial wages. Workers were catching up to professors, whose social status was seen to be threatened. Yet the 1921 federal census demonstrated that in fact professors did rather well within their own class. Salaries of the few university teachers aged between twenty and twenty-four were only marginally higher than those of teachers and engineers, but as the university professor aged and acquired higher rank his earnings grew appreciably greater than those of his professional peers. The average professor between twenty-five and forty-nine in Ontario could expect to earn somewhat over $3,000 per year ($3,078); his schoolteacher and engineering colleagues on average made almost a thousand dollars less ($2,119 and $2,206, respectively). The

FIGURE 12.1

Average annual professional earnings in Ontario by age profile, 1921

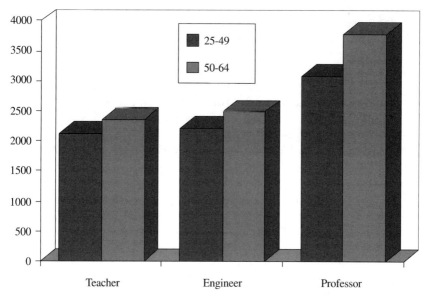

SOURCE: *Census of Canada* (Ottawa 1921), vol. 3, Table 40. Note: based on average weekly wages for these professional groups in Hamilton, London, Ottawa, and Toronto

professor sixty years old might well expect to make close to four thousand dollars (the average for the fifty to sixty-four age group was $3,778), but teachers and engineers the same age still earned on average less than twenty-five hundred dollars ($2,487 and $2,360, respectively; see Fig. 12.1).

Anxieties grew as the sense of declining status increased. George Wrong, fifty-nine years old in 1919 and the University of Toronto's senior historian, fell in the age group of salaried senior professors that was in fact very well off compared with the same age group of teachers or engineers. A man of no little social pretension, son-in-law of former Chancellor Edward Blake, neighbour of the influential Masseys, Wrong was not one to harbour his discontents even though he was among the best-paid professors at Toronto. 'I do not know whether our old civilization is to be bowled over,' he wrote to a friend at Oxford of his sad decline in circumstance. 'I could make my own bed and black my own boots quite well, but I am doubtful about cooking my own dinner! Anyone, however, who can learn to run an automobile can learn to cook a dinner.'[11] Wrong's sense of declining expectations for the professorial class was real enough at the time. Servants had become difficult to obtain or retain.

Falconer realized that pressures for an increase in salary were based on a legitimate sense of grievance, for no significant adjustment to the university's salary structure had taken place since the first year of Falconer's presidency in 1907; the last increase before that had been in the early 1890s. But the harsh reality was that such demands, however worthy, simply added to the university's financial crisis in straitened times. The university's budget estimates for 1919 declared a deficit of a quarter of a million dollars, and estimations for 1920 predicted a loss that would add up almost to a million. Toronto's president found himself in trying fiscal circumstances when the Conservative Hearst government fell and that of Drury took over. Hearst's Conservative ministry had at least met the university's basic needs (see Fig. 11.14).

The new populist administration of Drury, however, had unknown plans, a cost-cutting mandate, and a host of grudges against urban and other vested interests, not the least of them related to education. Everyone was feeling the pinch. The brother-in-law of one of the province's most prominent farmer-politicians put the annoyance privately: 'At a time when farmers' incomes are cut in two, it seems to us that some curb should be put on the amount of appropriations [to education]. A good deal ... are along the lines of Fads and go largely to the cities. Why should such large grants be made to Technical Education, to Dental Inspection and Nurses? ... It seems the interests of those who wish to see money spent has [sic] prevailed.'[12]

Falconer had experienced difficulties even with the Hearst government during its last months in office. The premier had accepted the university's 1920 estimates, which included a twenty-five per cent salary increase for all faculty and staff, but only with reluctance. He wrote privately to Falconer that it would prove 'impossible for the Province having regard to its present sources of revenue to continue making increased yearly grants to the University.'[13] After the election of a government whose platform was parsimony, Falconer and the university's board of governors must have been concerned about the financial aspects of university administration – one suspects – almost to the point of panic. Drury's first months in office were understandably occupied, however, with securing the reins of power while trying to discipline a largely inexperienced caucus and cabinet and attempting to accommodate a number of farm, labour, and other organizations whose interests had, from their perspective, previously been ignored. Drury was no enemy of higher education, but he did not want to alienate his provincial treasurer, Peter Smith. He had been elected to cut costs, and the annual grants to Toronto, Queen's, and Western already exceeded all other educational grants combined. No action on the 1920 University of Toronto estimates was taken even by the middle of the year. Twice the new premier avoided interviews with the university president.

Finally, after making arrangements for a meeting with Premier Drury through members of the board of governors, Falconer obtained a financial settlement. The budget was to be approved, but the salary increases were to be made on a merit basis only, to teachers alone (thereby excluding support staff) and to a maximum of $500. To address the large question of the financial problems and needs of the provincial university, the minister of education, R.H. Grant, announced that a royal commission would be established 'to report upon the whole question of provincial aid to the universities in order that a definite and comprehensive basis may be arrived at.'[14] Eventually, however, the government more or less accepted Falconer's suggestions concerning salaries. Permanent salary arrangements awaited the findings of the proposed royal commission.

When the membership of the royal commission was announced on 27 October 1920, the anxieties of Falconer and others were probably diminished somewhat, for Falconer himself could scarcely have chosen commissioners better suited to take university interests and needs into serious account. Its chairman was to be Canon H.J. Cody, former Conservative minister of education, and at the time a member of the board of governors of the University of Toronto. Another member of the university's board on the commission was T.A. Russell. Joining them were journalist and politician Sir John Willison, a trustee of Queen's University, and C.R. Somerville of London, a member of Western's board of governors. Eastern Ontario was represented by A.P. Deroche. J.A. Wallace, a United Farmers of Ontario member who appeared to have no particular institutional or regional interests, was a graduate of McMaster. Intentionally or not, the commission's membership clearly had the effect of undercutting criticism from the university community and the regions. Drury had provided an ideal opportunity for the three secular universities of the province – Toronto, Queen's, and Western – to make their cases for state funding on a permanent basis and on firm principles.

It was clear, too, that this was to be a commission whose purpose was to resolve problems, not to evade them. Its mandate spoke implicitly of the fact that the great expectations held for the royal commission of 1906 had resulted in a legacy of uncertainty and disappointment in matters of finance. Drury gave the commissioners very broad terms of reference:

(a) to inquire into and report upon a basis for determining the financial obligations of the province toward the University of Toronto, and the financial aid which the Province may give to Queen's University of Kingston and the Western University of London;

(b) to recommend such permanent plan of public aid to the said Universities as shall bear a just and reasonable relation to the amount of the legislative grants to primary and secondary education, and

(c) to make such suggestions on any of the above subjects as may seem, in the opinion of the Commission, to be desirable.[15]

Queen's and Western welcomed the creation of the Royal Commission on University Finances. Their post-war problems were different from those of Toronto mainly in degree. All suffered from over-enrolment and under-financing. Student numbers at Queen's had doubled in the 1919–20 academic session. New appointments increased the number of staff to 110 and the increase in the university's endowment income, made possible by a fund-raising drive in 1918–19, had quickly evaporated. In spite of increases in the annual provincial operating grants from $122,000 in 1916–17 to $177,000 in 1919–20, by that year Queen's was faced with an operating deficit of $41,000. That year, too, the province withdrew its financial support from the university's faculty of education, thereby closing it. For Queen's the prospects of the new decade looked bleak. 'The Million, which we have just raised,' reported Principal R.B. Taylor in 1920, 'and the revenue ... which we thought would relieve us from difficulty for many a year, has practically disappeared, in the increased cost of carrying on the institution. The point has been reached at which an institution which has become a truly national affair, must be carried in an increasing degree by the state.'[16] Queen's, like Toronto, viewed the creation of the provincial commission with relief, for its existence held out at least the possibility of progress in solving the problems of post-war reconstruction. The attitude of Western was similar, for its plans for the building of its new campus, postponed by the war, would largely be determined by the commission's findings.

Since receiving its charter in 1878, the Western University of London, Ontario, had led a precarious existence in the old Huron College buildings. Its future remained uncertain as it entered the 1920s. Following the rather acrimonious resignation of its president, E.E. Braithwaite, in 1919, no successor was appointed for the better part of a decade: the university was directed by a triumvirate of deans (arts and science, medicine, and public health).[17] Financially it had managed to survive separation from the Anglican Church, largely by successfully cultivating and cementing its ties to the London community. Grants from the City of London had risen gradually from $5,000 in 1908 to $20,000 in 1919.

These were not small amounts for a city the size of London to award, and from its perspective the money was well spent since it kept a faculty of medicine, founded in 1881, in the immediate area. Moreover, the investment of civic funds had paid off with the creation of an Institute of Public Health in the city, dating from initiatives taken in the early years of the Whitney government. In 1907 the provincial legislature had appropriated $50,000 for this purpose. This was followed, in concert with support from Western's medical faculty, by grants of $10,000 for equipment and $15,000 for maintenance of the agency, by then called the Institute of Public Health.[18]

The university's claim to be a centre of liberal education, however, was neither obvious nor secure. Upon secularization and reorganization in 1908, one of the professors inherited from the days of church control held the omnibus title 'Professor of Mathematics, Lecturer in Physics, Economics, Logic, [and] History of Philosophy' – a range of subject-matter that would have taxed the knowledge and pedagogical skills of the most erudite scholar. Arts instruction and resources were, to under-state the case, meagre if well-intentioned. In 1913–14 less than $9,000 was necessary to maintain work in arts. As late as 1918 the university library contained only 3,500 volumes; its annual budget was $2,000 (up from $150 previously). In the same year, the arts enrolment totalled only ninety-three. As one observer pointed out: 'In 1917 the University had no buildings of its own ... Very few London citizens knew either Huron College or the old medical school as seats of university activities and when asked by visiting strangers to be directed to Western University replied with a blank stare or – "I don't know where it is myself."'[19]

Size is, of course, relative and Western ultimately experienced the same post-war pressures as other institutions of higher learning: by 1921 arts enrolment had risen to 285. Space in the Huron College building, once adequate, was now more than cramped and by the time the provincial commission on university finances reported in 1921 classes in arts were given at locations throughout the city, including a building known as the Annex, purchased from the Women's Christian Association for $6,500 and previously used as a women's refuge and infants' home.[20]

The provincial Royal Commission on University Finances was as modest in size and conduct as its mandate was important. Its six members visited each of the three secular universities and listened to presentations from each. It also received, and took as part of its record, briefs from the Workers' Educational Association, the United Farmers of Ontario, and the Royal Canadian Institute. Altogether, it received eleven formal submissions from interested parties (five representing interests within the University of Toronto). It heard of the case for advanced research based on the successful German model, and of the desire for 'a proper [educational] policy on the part of the Government and the universities.' It was told that 'Every progressive country is spending an increasing amount on education ... Everywhere, at least in all English-speaking countries, the same factors are at work – increased numbers of students, lengthened periods of attendance, higher standards of instruction, higher costs of building and maintenance, and with these factors a growing public conviction that the meeting of these needs is the most indispensable and the most fruitful of government activities.' From Toronto it received Falconer's seventy-two-page brief, summarizing his well-known case for increased funding along lines originally intended by the commissioners of 1906 but not followed by subsequent politicians. O.D. Skelton of Queen's, similarly, called for universities to be financed by succession duties. The United Farmers of Ontario lamented the urban and 'foreign' constituency of the University of Toronto and urged 'greater frugality and extensive decentralization.' All in fact were concerned with the same problem. As the Queen's presentation put it, succinctly: 'The main question that faces the province is simply, how, given the existing conditions, can we ... produce the maximum results?'[21]

The royal commission tabled its thirty-one page report, a model of brevity, on 10 February 1921, less than four months after it had been created. Working from the assumptions that social progress was a concomitant of education and that higher education was a necessary and vital part of the educational experience – by no means insignificant challenges to provincial thinking – it pleased all three universities. It recognized the necessity of new facilities and increased financial support and proposed the means of obtaining them. It noted the inadequacy of the 1906 report's limit of $500,000 on the amount the University of Toronto could receive from succession duties, and it recommended continued and increased support for Queen's and Western. The commissioners summarized their recommendations in twelve points that constituted, as events turned out, a virtual blueprint for the renewal and expansion of higher education in Ontario for more than a quarter century:

1 That for the maintenance of the Provincial University and of University College there be restored the basis of support in the Act of 1906, viz., a yearly sum equal to 50% of the average of the succession duties for the three preceding years ...
2 That annual maintenance grants be paid to Queen's and Western Universities out of Consolidated Revenue, and that these grants be readjusted every five years by a Court of Reference to be appointed by the Lieutenant-Governor in Council.

3 That grants on Capital Account for buildings urgently needed be given to the Provincial University ($1,500,000); to Queen's ($350,000); to Western ($800,000).

4 That if increased revenues for education be required in future, the Government consider the advisability of levying a direct tax of one mill on the dollar on the municipally-assessed value of the rateable property of the province (excluding incomes), ear-marked for general educational purposes.

5 That in any University aided by State funds no new faculty be established and no new building (paid for by public funds) be erected without the consent of the Lieutenant-Governor in Council.

6 University Day be provided for in the Legislature, on which the Heads of the various Universities shall appear to report on their work.

7 That a Department of Graduate Studies and Research be organized in the Provincial University as soon as practicable.

8 That if the future increase of candidates seeking admission to the Universities should be so great as to make still further increase of staff and buildings necessary, the Department of Education and the Universities of the Province be asked to consider the transfer of the present First-Year University work to the Collegiate Institutes and High Schools.

9 That University College be given its historic academic building, and that the Administrative Offices be transferred to a new building.

10 That certain necessary additions be made to the buildings of the Ontario College of Education.

11 That certain extensions be made to the Royal Ontario Museum.

12 That the Provincial University continue to be controlled by a Board of Governors, and that such Board be truly representative of the whole Province.[22]

The commissioners' proposed policies were an adroit mixture of centralization and diffusion, control and autonomy. They appeared to advocate the centralization of graduate studies in the University of Toronto, and gave the university the possible means of encouraging advanced research. Yet by accepting the principle of state support for Queen's and Western they had also implicitly questioned the dualistic nature of the old university question – the notion that there should on principle be only one provincial university receiving public support and that other institutions should fend for themselves. Representatives of Western University, in particular, had made a strong regional case, written substantially by librarian and history professor Fred Landon, to the provincial commission, and it was one that was bound to be listened to carefully by a populist government. Unlike Queen's, Western made no claim to national importance. It was a small institution serving the counties of south-western Ontario and substantially dependent upon the local community for survival. Of Western's 534 students, 335 came from the City of London. Even at Queen's, the Western brief pointed out, twenty-two per cent of the students came from the Kingston area, while a full fifty-eight per cent were from eastern Ontario.[23] Clearly, the provincial government could not politically afford to leave such regional needs unattended. In its search for solutions the commission spoke directly of the need for 'a well-balanced system' of higher education 'for the whole Province' and it urged the government to exercise a measure of control over individual universities in order to achieve this crucial aim.[24]

The financial implications of the report caught the Drury government off political balance. With more than two million dollars in capital grants suggested for building-construction alone, not to mention the proposed allocation of a substantial portion of the province's succession duties to meet ongoing expenses, Drury was reported to be on the verge of panic at such excessive liberality. Both he and his minister of education, R.H. Grant, immediately distanced themselves from the commission, saying to the press they felt that 'owing to various reasons, they [could not] or should not at this time fully endorse that Report.' They also declared that any financial improvements for the current year should be considered solely as a temporary measure pending 'more exhaustive consideration on the part of the Government.'[25] But by the autumn of 1921, prompted by a generally positive reception of the commission's report by the provincial press and by further deputations from the universities, Drury had regained a measure of political courage. Operating grants of $415,000 and $200,000 were announced for Queen's and Western – up, respectively, from $257,000 and $84,000 in 1920. (A portion of the increased grant to each was intended for capital construction.) The University of Toronto received the substantial total of $1,606,199, but the Drury government balked at accepting the report's major financial recommendation concerning Toronto and steadfastly refused succession duties to be used for university support. As a result the provincial university was forced, as in the past, to beg the legislature each year to meet its annual deficits. Queen's and Western were in the same position as continuing supplicants, but were significantly better off than they had been. After 1921 it was to become exceptionally difficult for any government to refuse to receive a deputation from the regional universities. A strong case for support of regional institutions had been made by the institutions themselves and by the commission whose task was to determine the legitimacy of that case. Nothing less than a formal government statement of policy that only the University of Toronto should receive state support would now keep the regional university lobbies from the government's door. This was scarcely possible for any provincial political party after 1921.

The University of Toronto had received no assurance of long-term financial stability. Nevertheless, in spite of the government's refusal to endorse the commission's report, a milestone of sorts had been reached. The commissioners had at least laid the basis for an eventual end to the patronizing *noblesse oblige* that had characterized state aid for higher education in the province. 'We believe,' they had written, 'that a united public opinion will be created in support of Higher Education in the Province by two broad lines [of] policy: (a) Adequate support for the Provincial University, for which the State is primarily and solely responsible. (b) Such reasonable support to the other two Universities as will be just to them and to the districts of the Province which they specially serve, and will extend the benefits of Higher Education to a wider circle of students.'[26] The five-year period suggested for financial allocations promised at least the possibility of a measure of long-range planning for the universities.

The volatile nature of the provincial political scene was such that, in the immediate view, the commissioners appeared politically naive: there was little substantial political or public support in 1921 for greatly increased expenditures on university education. But in the broader context of the general reorientation of attitudes and expectations brought about by the war, the commissioners were most certainly correct – even prescient. The war had not been won by valour alone: its outcome had largely depended, as anyone who read the daily press recognized, by scientific and technological know-how, by industry, experts, engineers and chemists, as well as by foot-soldiers. The war that had begun with cavalry and carbines had ended with aeroplanes and tanks. Clearly, if industrial economies were to thrive and grow they could not afford to neglect the universities that were essential for the supply of experts in science, technology, and management.

Collegiate Gothic

The three Ontario universities eligible for grants acted quickly to secure tangible gains from the 1921 increase in finances, for there was no formal guarantee that such generosity would continue beyond the year. One senses an element of calculated daring by presidents and boards of governors of the day as they discussed whether to forge ahead with this project or that. One of the players in this gamble, Sherwood Fox, then dean of arts and science at Western, caught the spirit of the academic boardrooms of 1921 in his memoirs: 'The Governors spiritedly pressed the work, buoyed up by hope and faith that something would "turn up" to relieve them of the debt they were deliberately incurring. Happily, they read the omens aright.'[27] This was not the last time such academic poker would be played in Ontario.

For Western University the next few years witnessed a dramatic transformation. Since its secularization in 1908 the university had sought a site other than that of Huron College. Its property committee (established in 1910) had gradually acquired several farms north of London, north of the Thames River. By 1920 these properties totalled about 230 acres – sufficient, the board of governors confidently (but erroneously) predicted, to meet the university's needs for the next two centuries. Postwar penury and the lack of an endowment, however, had kept the university from moving to its new site. The Cody Commission changed things. It had recommended a grant of $800,000 to the university for 1921, $200,000 for each of the next two years, and $250,000 for the last two years of the five-year period. It had recognized the need to construct a new arts and science building and a new library. Buoyed by the commission's recommendations, the County of Middlesex contributed $100,000 for a war memorial, and the voters of London overwhelmingly approved a $250,000 capital grant from the city.[28] On 15 April 1922 the governor general of Canada, Lord Byng of Vimy, together with the chairman of Western's board of governors, turned the sod for the new site, although in an orientation soon rejected after the city planner of Glasgow, in London on a chance visit, suggested that the campus face east rather than west as intended.[29]

Facing in whatever direction, new structures soon began to be constructed. The arts building, convocation hall, library and administration offices, and natural science building took form. Following from a suggestion of the recently appointed dean of arts and science, Sherwood Fox, the architecture of the buildings echoed that of his Alma Mater, Princeton – a modified collegiate Gothic or 'Ivy League' look.[30] These stone buildings, made of Credit Valley stone from a quarry near Guelph, became the first of Western's new dispensation. To guard them, gargoyles were carved, including 'the devil, a boy with mumps, the Indian chief and British brigadier, Tecumseh, and everybody's favourite mythical soldier, "Old Bill," of Bruce Bairnsfather's famous war-time cartoons.'[31] Premier Drury, accompanied by his treasurer Peter Smith, laid the cornerstones of the arts and natural sciences buildings on 18 June 1923.[32] A year later, in the autumn, the buildings were fully occupied and the Memorial Tower, now also finished, was dedicated in a ceremony presided over by General Sir Arthur Currie, principal of McGill University. Together with the new medical school facility, completed in 1921, these buildings on its new and spacious grounds symbolized the university's second life. As if to embody the enlargement of body and spirit, the board of governors obtained in 1923 a new University Act, which decreed that henceforth the institution was to be called 'The University of Western Ontario.'[33]

Queen's University also embarked on a program of capital expansion once the Cody Commission had reported. Immediately after the war Queen's faced two necessary capital expenditures. Pressure existed to expand its medical facilities, in cooperation with Kingston General Hospital; and this required a new central heating plant (replacing that of 1909) near the lakeshore and of sufficient capacity to serve both university and hospital. Such was the inadequate state of clinical facilities that even such a friend of Queen's as Adam Shortt proposed to Principal Taylor that the two final years of the medical course be given not at Queen's but in Ottawa in connection with its new general hospital. Faced with a threatened revolt by some within the university and medical communities, the university managed to obtain significant donations from James Douglas and Senator Henry W. Richardson, and a grant of $150,000 from the Kingston city council. The university received more promises of private aid, and the expansion of medical facilities began. The need for further grants – for the cost of financing medical facilities was a crippling drain on scarce university revenues – was part of the Queen's University brief to the Cody Commission. As with the efforts of Western, those of Queen's were rewarded: the government ultimately promised the university and the hospital $400,000, to be allocated over five years. To this it added a grant of $125,000, to go towards the costs of the central heating plant.

In the expansion of the 1920s, university authorities did not ignore the ordinary interests of the students of Queen's. The Douglas Library, funded by provincial government grants of 1921–2, opened in 1924, with a reading room, administrative offices, and stack-space for 300,000 volumes. Once again, as with Western, the 1921 increase in government funding acted as a catalyst. James Richardson of Winnipeg donated $100,000 towards the construction of a football stadium dedicated to the memory of his brother, George Taylor Richardson, who had died in the war. Family and friends of Jock Harty, a former Queen's sportsman, gave funds for a hockey and skating arena to be named after him. In 1923 the women's alumni association obtained from the university's trustees a sum matching the $80,000 they had raised. The result was Ban

Righ Hall, a residence and dining facility for Queen's women that was opened by Lady Byng in 1925. Finally, in spite of an inconclusive campaign for a war memorial launched immediately after the war by students and staff and a decidedly less-than-successful endowment campaign run by a professional fund-raiser, the Queen's board of trustees authorized the construction of a Students' Memorial Union building. In 1928, riding the crest of expansionism that characterized the Ontario universities in the 1920s, Queen's realized its dream. It was a male dream, for women of Queen's were not allowed to join the union.[34]

Following the Cody Commission report the University of Toronto also embarked on a program of sizeable expansion, much of it recommended by the commissioners. The university's growing administrative staff was to obtain its own building, thus releasing space in University College. Additions had also been recommended for the Ontario College of Education and the Royal Ontario Museum, whose board of trustees had had representatives on the University of Toronto's board of governors since its creation in 1912, and whose various sections – archaeology, paleontology, zoology – were under the supervision of a professor from the university. The result was the construction during the decade of some dozen new buildings: a modest structure for the university's nascent publishing house (1920); Simcoe Hall (1924), constructed as a wing of Convocation Hall, to house the administration; an anatomy building (1925) for the faculty of medicine; the faculty of forestry's first building of its own (1925); a hygiene building (1926), made possible by funds from the Rockefeller Institute; and a university arena (1926) with a seating capacity of 5,000, complementing the university's Varsity Stadium, built in 1911, and by the 1920s enlarged to accommodate 17,000 football fans.[35]

Another major addition to the University of Toronto's post-war look was the presence by the mid-1920s of Trinity College. By war's end urban North American civilization had surrounded the lingering remnants of John Strachan's academic empire on Queen Street West. Once set in semi-rural surroundings, by 1919 it was in the middle of an industrial city, surrounded by cheap movie theatres, news-stands, and pawnshops. Noted one observer: 'Amid the roar of traffic, urchins played on the curbstone or waded in the gutter after rainstorms; and above them, indifferent to the filth, the tousled hair and snotty noses, moved young men with cigarettes dangling from their mouths, red-lipped girls, and old women in shawls. The denizens of this world by night overflowed into the College grounds.' The proud old building, he said, resembled 'the last survivor of an impoverished nobility.' The staff and students were well aware that the building, however noble, had fallen into serious disrepair and lacked adequate heating and ventilation. Moreover, it suffered from a 'dank and musty' inner atmosphere, worn doors, and 'cases of dead birds' that gave one wag the impression that 'this was indeed the British Museum.' Altogether, wrote this Trinity graduate of the 1920s, it 'was all curiously redolent of an age gone by.' Trinity was decidedly ambivalent about its entry into the age of the flapper and the 'vamp,' as will be seen. But central heating was another matter, and the prospect of new and more comfortable premises at the Queen's Park location of the University of Toronto was sufficient to overcome the suspicion of some that Trinity traditions and spirit might be submerged in the vast 'sea of Varsity life.'[36]

General discussions about a possible move to the University of Toronto campus had begun well before 1914, but the war delayed serious planning. After the Armistice, Trinity officials revived their plans to move, and on a bitter winter's day in December 1922 they turned the first sod for the construction of the new Trinity complex. They laid the cornerstone the following May. In 1925 it opened, on Hoskin Avenue, in collegiate Gothic style, haughtily facing the plain but sturdy Victorian red brick practicality of its Evangelical Anglican sister, Wycliffe College – right across the street and looking decidedly dowdy by comparison.

The most important of all post-war construction at the University of Toronto was Hart House. Its moment of conception, however, pre-dated the war and owed its existence not to planning in the board room but to one undergraduate's imagination. The University of Toronto had always suffered from a certain lack of soul. It had no centre, no common meeting point. University College had proven to be an imperfect means of melding the congeries of interests and groups that constituted what had become, even early in the twentieth century, a pluralistic and fragmented place of higher learning. Students socialized in several places: the university dining hall, the Undergraduate Union (a 'poky little place, designed as a collection of bed-sitting rooms off a central wooden staircase' in University College), or the overtaxed and decrepit redbrick gymnasium, in the 1890s a model of its kind. Many gathered in the five-room Young Men's Christian Association headquarters, Moss Hall.[37] This last place, with its many non-denominational activities ranging from Bible classes and physical activities to helping with registration, was perhaps as close as the provincial university had to a focal point for campus life. In the mind of one student, it was not enough.[38]

A prominent and wealthy Ontario Methodist family, the Masseys had made their fortune in the burgeoning agricultural machinery business of the late nineteenth century. Several Masseys had graduated from Victoria College, and the family had been generous to its Alma Mater. The will of Hart A. Massey had made $50,000 available for the construction of a women's residence in 1896. Land was not made available by University of Toronto trustees until 1901, but in 1902 the cornerstone of the new women's residence was finally laid, located on the Victoria College grounds. It was named Annesley Hall, after the mother of John and Charles Wesley. Massey benevolence at Victoria continued with the opening in the 1913–14 school year of Burwash Hall, four linked houses of men's residence together with a dining hall. This was a donation of Chester Daniel Massey.

Vincent Massey chose to attend University College. He was a second-year student there in 1909 when he conceived the idea of constructing a building that would serve to unite the activities of the various social organizations at the University of Toronto. Unlike most students, however, he possessed the financial power to act immediately upon his dreams, for the year before, on turning twenty-one, he had become a trustee of the family estate. After Vincent had consulted with family members and with President Falconer, a plan was announced. The Massey estate would construct and equip 'a building for the University Young Men's Association, also for the Students' Union, the two buildings to be connected by an Assembly Hall ...' The estimated cost was $300,000; the building itself was to be named after Vincent's grandfather, Hart Massey. The Toronto firm of Sproatt and Rolph was hired as architects. Vincent postponed his plans to study modern history at Oxford and for the next year offered close advice to the principals of the firm.

By the summer of 1914 the walls and roof of the structure were up, but the modest original idea was long gone. In its place stood an expansive and imposing complex of Credit Valley stone that masked its social utility in an austere early Gothic style. On a site of 70 by 120 yards Sproatt had managed to construct a building that would hold 'a dining hall to seat 350 men and three smaller dining rooms for senior members, with extensive kitchen and service areas; a swimming pool; three large and several small common rooms; a rifle range; a music room; a theatre; a library; a billiard room; a lecture hall; two gymnasiums; quarters for boxing, wrestling, and fencing; squash courts; a running track; locker rooms for 2,000 athletes; a small chapel; photographic darkrooms; a studio suitable for sketching and exhibitions; a barber shop; offices for various organizations within the House; quarters for the warden; guest-rooms on the top floor – all grouped round an elegant court.' Its completion postponed by the war, Hart House opened officially on 11 November 1919, the first anniversary of the Armistice.

First in war, and then for the next half-century, Hart House was given over to the activities of men. Its founders' prayer sought 'a common fellowship' for the university community and expressed the hope that its members would find 'true education' in the 'conversation of wise and earnest men, in music, pictures and the play, in the casual book, in sports and games and the mastery of the body ...' The women of the University of Toronto formed no part of that 'common fellowship,' for they were excluded from membership in Hart House, as they had been from the undergraduate union that had preceded it. From the first, Hart House had been imagined, then planned, as an exclusively male domain, equipped, its biographer bluntly states, 'as a men's club.'[39] In this respect it differed little from facilities elsewhere, whether Burwash Hall at Victoria or, later, the Students' Memorial Union at Queen's.

The University of Toronto obtained additional space in the decade after the war by the move of McMaster University to Hamilton in 1928. The move had been contemplated for years, but financial difficulties and divisions within the Baptist community had made the move impossible until the war was over. McMaster's close relationship with the Baptist Convention precluded acceptance of any state aid on religious grounds, and this made matters even more difficult. As a Protestant denominational college, McMaster found no place in the discussions of the Cody Commission.

When new overtures to the university and the Baptist community concerning a possible move to Hamilton arose in 1920, they came from relative outsiders. In the spring of 1920 the organization of a branch of McMaster alumni in the Hamilton and Dundas area, together with support from the Reverend W.W. McMaster of James Street Church in Hamilton, brought renewed support for the move. Like the Hamilton religious and business communities, the city's medical association also saw possibilities in such a possible move. There were good reasons for contemplating one. The population of the Hamilton had reached 120,000 by the early 1920s, an increase of more than 50,000 people since 1911, and nearly eleven thousand Baptists lived within a thirty-five mile radius. Removal there would draw substantial support from this community, it was said, and would put to rest forever the possibility of federation with the University of Toronto, the behemoth that remained in some eyes the godless university.

Throughout the early 1920s the support for relocation to Hamilton flowed and ebbed, then flowed again. During 1921, Hamilton supporters, using the offer of the city's chamber of commerce of the free gift of a site, lobbied members of the Baptist Convention (on the approval of which the move to Hamilton depended), and staved off renewed interest from Toronto residents and solicitations from those who still wished to see Woodstock College given university status. By the autumn of 1921 the convention had authorized the McMaster board of governors and senate to investigate proposals for a new location.[40] By the spring of 1922 an arrangement had been worked out. Support from the City of Hamilton would be considered a voluntary subscription rather than state aid, thereby relieving Baptists of problems of conscience over their traditional insistence on a rigid separation of church and state. University officials estimated that nothing less than $800,000 would be required for initial construction. A doubling of the university's endowment would also be necessary. Nevertheless, proponents of the move remained optimistic.[41] But then in 1922 the Hamilton economy, like that of the nation, went into recession. Negotiations, built now on hopes and dreams, continued.

Not a small factor in keeping the momentum for change alive in this period of recession was McMaster's new chancellor, H.P. Whidden, appointed in 1923. Educated at Acadia University (BA 1891) and McMaster itself (BD 1894), Whidden had done graduate work at the University of Chicago and had been president of Brandon College since 1912. He was the latest in a series of McMaster chancellors[42] increasingly 'modernist' in orientation. McMaster's chancellor at the turn of the century, O.C.S. Wallace (1895–1905), had sought to make Christianity relevant to the modern age by viewing critical scholarship from within Christian imperatives. His successor, Alexander C. McKay (1905–11), had tried to maintain this balance by stressing the scientific search for a Christian truth and by thwarting those who sought to federate McMaster with the University of Toronto. The university's war-time chancellor, A.L. McCrimmon (1911–22), who had studied at Chicago, had travelled rather further down the secularist road, accepting the necessity of critical inquiry but also stressing that the religious atmosphere of McMaster still made a Christian culture possible. The sixth chancellor, Whidden, kept McMaster firmly in this cultural trajectory.[43] A natural administrator and a consummate academic politician, he had little use for the vocabulary of Christianity. His concern was with more material realities. 'The chief business of the smaller university,' he said in his 1923 inaugural address, 'is to furnish a liberal education ... Liberal education should seek to relate the individual to his universe. I refer more specifically to the universe of things ... The whole development and structure of material things in past ages is brought within our ken [as a result of the application of scientific knowledge]; the life of plant and animal is so much better understood that human life is conserved in previously unthought of ways. In connection with all this there has gone on steadily an emancipation of the mind of man with regard to the dominance of the material.'[44]

From the outset of his chancellorship, Whidden was an outright advocate of the notion that McMaster could only achieve true progress by moving to Hamilton. He was immediately confronted with an extraordinary adversary in the figure of the Reverend T.T. Shields, minister of the large and influential Jarvis Street Baptist Church since 1910 and a staunch opponent of modernism in any form. Shields' vision for McMaster was essentially to turn it into a Christian Bible college. Throughout the 1920s, as he had earlier, Shields had looked with grave suspicion at McMaster's secular ways. He was resentful of the apparent preference for McMaster theological graduates over non-university-educated clergy; he opposed in 1922 any civic land grant to McMaster as strenuously as in 1925 he did the appointment of the theologian L.H. Marshall – far too progressive to his liking – to McMaster's chair of pastoral theology. 'We shall ask the Lord,' he exhorted in 1924, 'to arise in His might and by His own power to deliver the University out of the hands of those whose principles have blighted the denomination for so long, and to deliver it to the management of those who will be true to "the faith once for all delivered to the Saints ..."'[45] Whidden, especially, became Shields's symbol of secularist error and arrogance. Yet Shields, too, was a symbolic figure. Emblematic in Ontario of the North American fundamentalist resurgence of the 1920s, he was elected and re-elected to the McMaster board of governors by the Baptist Convention, with the support of a strong and loyal constituency. Since any change to McMaster's situation needed to be taken through the convention, it was through such fundamentalist shoals that Whidden needed to steer his educational barque.

The mid-1920s were years of hesitation, struggle, and stalemate in Whidden's battles against attacks by Shields and for the move to Hamilton. The financial depression continued into 1926. Then, later in the year, the recession began to lift and new life was breathed into the idea. Discussions reopened between city and university officials, and the Hamilton Committee presented modified terms for its proffered gift: $500,000 would be designated as a voluntary gift, and the city would also provide a free site of between fifty and seventy-five acres. Encouraged, Whidden led the call for a university financial campaign, possibly amounting to $1,500,000. The momentum for change had been regained.[46]

By 1927 the religious dissension that had desperately taxed the emotions and the resources of Ontario Baptists had begun to abate. T.T. Shields and his followers quit the Baptist Convention in 1926, disgusted at its acceptance of the Marshall appointment. In the early summer the decision was made by the university's board of governors (with strong senatorial approval) to move to Hamilton. The decision was taken to the October meetings of the Baptist Convention. On 17 October 1927, at the very meetings that formally expelled T.T. Shields's Jarvis Street Church, the Baptist Convention endorsed the university's proposal to move to Hamilton. Whidden's leadership had been vindicated and he did not now delay. Within a month he had acquired approximately seventy acres of land for the university in the Westdale district of Hamilton, and had announced a $1,500,000 fund-raising campaign to increase the endowment and provide buildings and equipment at the new location.[47]

A year later, Viscount Willingdon, governor general of Canada, laid the cornerstone of the first new McMaster building at the Hamilton site. Whidden's fund-raising campaign had been a successful one. Promises of contributions were made by wealthy patrons such as Cyrus Eaton and Gordon C. Edwards, Hamilton's five Baptist Convention churches, the city's Central Labour Union and its leading industries and corporate citizens, the Women Teachers Association, and others. The original university endowment was almost doubled, architects and landscapers were hired, and plans emerged for six new stone buildings in the fashionable collegiate Gothic style of the day. They included 'an arts and administration building, a science hall, a refectory, a men's residence of one hundred beds, and a women's residence of sixty beds.' The plans also called for a sizeable chapel, standing above and connecting the main arts and science buildings. The chapel, Chancellor Whidden recognized, would be 'a silent symbol of the place of true Religion in relation to the study and pursuit of truth as contained in the Arts and Sciences.'

This symbol held a different portent than the one Whidden originally envisaged. The onset of the Great Depression in October 1929 reduced potential revenue. Cyrus Eaton's promised donation, for example, was never given. A scaling-down of plan was the result. The university opened at its new site in the autumn of 1930, as scheduled. Now missing from the complex of residences and lecture halls was the chapel, its construction cancelled by Whidden himself with genuine regret.[48] In such ways did the place of religion slowly recede in the hierarchy of priorities of this university and others. The Great Depression had just begun, but it was already beginning to exact its toll. Yet for McMaster students in the fall of 1930 all things still seemed possible. 'McMaster Undergrads Reach Promised Land After Forty Years,' read the headline on the front page of the first edition of the new student newspaper, the *Silhouette*, at the beginning of this new dispensation.[49]

Universities and the State

The fall of the Drury government in the provincial election of June 1923, as a result of internal dissension, disappointment, and confusion, marked the end of farmers' government in Ontario but not of its legacy in higher education. A funding pattern had been set – and with it the basis for a systematic approach to higher education in the province. The election saw the return of the provincial Conservatives under G. Howard Ferguson, acting minister of education in the war-time Hearst administration, with a majority government. Now premier, Ferguson took upon himself the education portfolio. Although he spent much of his time as minister on matters related to public education, particularly expanding the province's system of vocational schools,[50] Ferguson kept a close personal watch on its universities. As leader of the opposition in the Legislature he had argued that universities should be treated generously; as premier he was more or less true to his word, but not without letting academic supplicants know that he wished matters were different and that he would have preferred a return to the pre-war relationship between the province and Queen's and Western. 'I give them notice that they should look around for some money,' he told the Toronto *Star* in 1926, when the last of the five years of grants suggested by the Cody Commission had been awarded. Two years earlier his minister of finance, W.H. Price, complained that the University of Toronto's grants – totalling $2,696,217 – meant that 'no matter what it is for, we are going too fast.'[51]

But these were the years of the 'new era' in Canada. Ontario and its economy was still growing. Its people had increased from two and a half million in 1911 to almost three million a decade later, in spite of losses from the war. By 1931 the population of the province was almost three and a half million.[52] Because of the war the number of university-aged males (twenty to twenty-four years old) had declined between the censuses of 1911 and 1921 to under 120,000, but the 1920s witnessed a significant rise in the numbers of students in the secondary school and university age groups. In 1921 there were 493,593 Ontarians between the ages of fifteen and twenty-four; by 1931 their number reached 510,069 (see Figs. 12.2, 12.3). These were not population increases as great as those of the generation before the Great War, but they provided every indication that Ontario's universities did not lack for potential clients.

With the graduation of the last of the war veterans by the mid-1920s university enrolment in Ontario declined slightly, but not as much as many observers expected. Full-time undergraduates in the province

FIGURE 12.2

Ontario population age 15–19, by gender: 1911, 1921, 1931

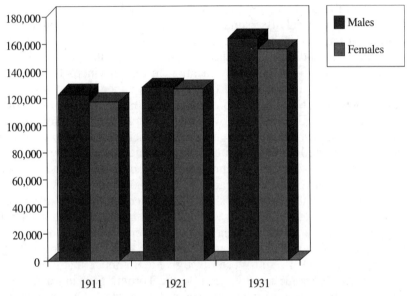

SOURCE: *Census of Canada* (Ottawa 1921), vol. 1

FIGURE 12.3

Ontario population age 20–24, by gender: 1911, 1921, 1931

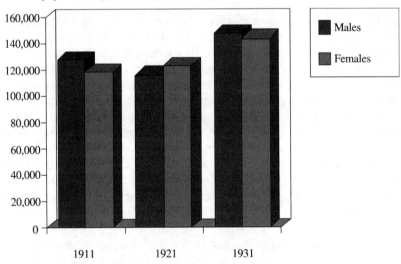

SOURCE: *Census of Canada* (Ottawa 1921), vol. 1

FIGURE 12.4

Full-time undergraduate enrolment in Ontario and Canada, 1920–50

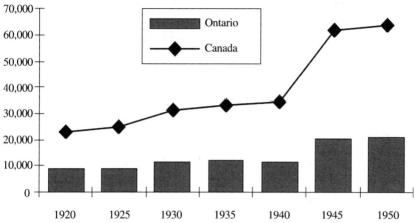

SOURCE: *Historical Statistics of Canada,* 2nd ed. (Ottawa 1983), series 340–438

numbered 9,050 in 1920 and increased to 11,414 by the end of the decade. The advent of the 'Dirty Thirties' scarcely altered this pattern of relatively stable enrolment. In the country as a whole the undergraduate population increased from 31,576 to 34,817 between 1930 and 1940; in Ontario it increased slightly between 1930 and 1935, from 11,414 to 12,066, but fell to 11,693 in 1940, with young men beginning to volunteer for overseas military service. In general, during the interwar years, the rate of increase in the Ontario undergraduate population was less than that of the nation. In 1920, Ontario undergraduates represented 39.7 per cent of the whole, but they were only 33.6 per cent in 1940 (see Fig. 12.4).

During the 1920s the Ontario economy grew unevenly – the decade was marked by surges and recessions – yet on the whole these were prosperous years.[53] The Drury government had inherited a surge of revenue, and spent accordingly. Ferguson became premier during an economic slump and was initially cautious over expenditures, but ultimately he could afford to treat the universities with generosity – and he did. The annual grants to Queen's and Western did not end, for the principle of state aid for all of the province's non-denominational universities had, in effect, silently been conceded by the fact of the established practice and was entrenched by the political reality that cutting off such established funding would alienate regional voters. The last operating grant awarded to the University of Toronto by the Drury administration was a substan-

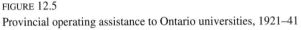

FIGURE 12.5

Provincial operating assistance to Ontario universities, 1921–41

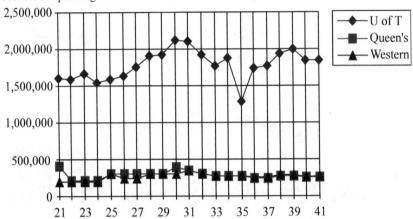

SOURCE: Derived from E.E. Stewart, 'The Role of the Provincial Government in the Development of Universities in Ontario,' EDD thesis, University of Toronto, 1970, Tables 2 and 3

tial one, $1,669,824 in 1923. As if to demonstrate that he would not be profligate, Ferguson presented the provincial university with a net decrease in funding in 1924. But thereafter, and to the end of his administration in 1930, grants to the University of Toronto grew significantly. Grants to Queen's and the University of Western Ontario did not increase as dramatically, but were enough to keep the universities operational, if not always happy. In Ferguson's last year as premier, provincial aid to the University of Toronto had climbed to $2,127,028, and Queen's and Western had reached $402,100 and $300,000, respectively, in several stepped increases (see Fig. 12.5).

Ferguson's Conservatives won the provincial election of October 1929 with an increased majority and an opposition in disarray. Buoyed by the victory, Ferguson participated actively and successfully on behalf of R.B. Bennett's Conservatives in the federal election of 1930. His reward, complementing his increased interest in international and imperial affairs, was his appointment by Bennett as high commissioner to London. He virtually bequeathed the premiership to his long-time friend and companion, George S. Henry. Provincial inheritor of the full brunt of the Depression, and declining revenues, Henry could have done nothing but curtail expenditures on higher education as on much else. During the 1930s provincial grants to the three qualifying institutions declined, but they did not end.

The principle of state aid had been won, but not without cost. By seeking state aid, the universities also courted dependence on the swings of the market-place and could just as easily suffer as benefit from shifting political priorities. Thus, the beneficent increase in funding under the United Farmers government dropped significantly during the Depression, and continued to fluctuate around the three-million-dollar mark until almost the end of the decade. Higher education was scarcely high on any political agenda during the Depression years. By 1939 the $2.4 million spent on universities represented only 2.4 per cent of the provincial budget. It had been seven per cent in 1914. Total provincial spending had increased by $130 million in this period. If the experience of the universities with state-supported funding demonstrated anything during the interwar years, it was that higher education had proved very much to be, in the words of an historian of the provincial economy, 'the stepchild of the exchequer.'[54]

13

The Culture of Utility

With the end of the Great War, Canada's past met and mingled with its future. In politics, in art and culture, and in the nation's intellectual life, people weighed the value of existing practices and traditions against challenging forms of innovation that might promise a better future.[1] In no social institution was this more evident than in the university. The *Canadian Annual Review* noted as much in its assessment of the 'Higher Educational system of Canada' in 1919: 'Primarily the system is based upon British ideas and traditions. Latterly it had, super-imposed upon these, a fabric of up-to-date, modern, technical, commercial, industrial, agricultural and business instruction; in effect it has combined something of the best in both British and American institutions.' The key word in that sentence was 'something,' for Castell Hopkins, the energetic editor of the *Canadian Annual Review*, felt obliged to qualify his approval of the nation's institutions of higher learning. While the universities were formally at the 'apex of a theoretical structure' in which public school and high school were to lead to university, 'practically,' Hopkins reflected, 'things have not quite worked out as expected.'

Such hesitation to pronounce and to judge, even by such an astute observer as Castell Hopkins, suggests that the actual functions of the universities in Canada were no longer entirely consistent with their traditional roles. 'These institutions of Canada,' Hopkins said, 'were, in 1919, keeping up many of the traditions and much of the culture of the Old World; they were trying, also, in an age of development and industry, commerce and invention, to keep up with the practical realities around them; they were being guided by public opinion to give in some measure a final touch of knowledge to a great process of development in agriculture, in the building of railways, in the sinking of mines and scientific work of Mining, in the transforming of water-power into plants of electric energy, in the organization and technique of finance and industry, in the transformation of the raw material into marketable, usable, products ... This was not exactly the mission of Oxford or Cambridge ...' It was, however, the mission of the industrial state in post-war Canada, as elsewhere.

By the 1920s, Canadian universities had deviated from both British and American models. In general, they did not quite embody the Oxbridge ideal that continued to stress the importance of an unapologetically class-based character formation aimed at shaping succeeding generations of political and cultural leaders; nor yet were they, like the American land-grant colleges, shrines to practicality and technological know-how.[2] The simple answer in the Ontario case is that by the end of the Great War its universities embodied variations of both, according to their individual imperatives and traditions. As an observer in the Toronto *Mail* put the matter in 1923: 'In education we are very properly very much influenced by the English tradition, but we are scarcely less affected by the educational progress in the United States.' The result, mirroring the Canadian conundrum itself, was an uncertainty regarding the university's fundamental purpose as it sought to mediate between cultural models in this new era, setting out to explore uncharted cultural and intellectual terrain: 'Influenced by the prestige of things British and things American, the Canadian university man is sometimes bewildered; he does not know how to align himself or what policy to support; he desires above all things to be British, and yet he feels that British university traditions are not all workable in Canada; he is impressed, on the other hand, by some aspects of the American university life and repelled by others. When Canadian universities fail to solve their problems, they fail as a general rule because they house under the same roof British and American ideals of academic administration, ideals essentially divergent. The tug and strain between the advocates of one system and the advocates of the other neutralizes the energy which should drive forward to success. Meantime, the Canadian point of view is barely recognized.'[3]

To an extent, these observations reflected the day's lack of cultural self-confidence, for in fact British observers of the 1920s cast a positive, at times even envious, eye at the Canadian academic scene. From the British perspective, the country's universities were financially and culturally accessible and academic standards were high.[4] Canada, said the *Irish Independent* in 1927, was 'amongst the most progressive of nations educationally.' Noted the *Times* of London three years later: 'The feature in Canada which most impresses visitors is the fully developed sense of nationality. Not merely is Canada producing its own manufactured goods as well as its food and raw materials, but it has also achieved already a high degree of political and educational maturity; it is, in fact, rapidly developing a culture of its own, which though materially very close to that of the United States, is in other ways a blend of British and North American tradition ...'[5] Such comparisons with Great Britain and the United States dominated public commentaries on university life in Ontario and in Canada.

As is so often the case, rhetorical accounts only approximate the empirical reality. Opinion makers, whether journalists or college presidents, tended, then as later, to approach higher education from the viewpoint of enterprise or system. In the twentieth century, particularly after the Great War, the search for system in the enterprise of higher education increasingly produced oral or written statements about the nature of the university that assumed and searched for its essential unity. Presidential pronouncements tended, as a result, to reveal an increasing diffuseness of assumption and purpose as they sought to describe and comment upon an ever more complex university environment characterized by variety and even apparent disorder.[6] This was because fundamental change and reform was initiated and gained its strength from outside the executive suites. For beneath the executive level lay the operational world and the creative confusion of the competing and ever-changing constituencies of the living university.

The bottom end of academic life, the end at which the actual work of universities occurs, is that of disciplines and departments.[7] The quiet and gradual academic reorientation of the 1920s and 1930s originated at this level, that of the academic trenches not of command headquarters. Initiatives in curriculum change took place here, new disciplines emerged, others gained or lost authority; small but real empires were won and lost. Conditions at the working level of the university, that of the disciplinary units, differed significantly from the academic reality described by presidents or journalists when trying to explain the meaning of contemporary higher education. An adequate account of the success or failure of new disciplines must, then, assess the relationship between institutions and ideas and the relative authority of each. As one historian has noted: 'While organized institutions do not necessarily create disciplines, they can produce a "resonant and echoing intellectual environment" that transmutes a fragmented subject into a tradition through continuing discussion, influential publications, and a significant number of students.'[8] Of most importance is the context in which such an environment is created and the conditions by which it comes to be accepted.

What occurred in Ontario, as elsewhere, in the interwar years, was the gradual public acceptance of the idea of social utility and of the professional ideal as determining and essential forces in society.[9] The full implications of this slow shift in attitude would not be witnessed until well after the Second World War, when demographic factors propelled Canadian universities to the very heart of socio-economic transformation, but its key elements were set in place between the fall of the Kaiser and the fall of Hitler. The universities of the nation, but especially of Ontario, were the laboratories in which that transformation first began to occur. Gradual curricular reorientation, not a vast increase in student numbers, was the dominant note of academic life in Ontario universities in the interwar years. It came about not because of visionary initiatives from the offices of university presidents, or even of deans,[10] but as a result of the anticipation of new opportunities by those who worked in existing academic departments.

A commitment to the centrality of a liberal education remained important to every Ontario university between the First and Second World Wars. The rise in importance of professional programs took place, at first, as a way of educating an expanding middle class in ways that were meant to be complementary to it. In these years the culture of utility gained a secure foothold in the institutions of higher education in the province. It was becoming an influential academic force, but it was not yet a dominant one. The humanities, as will be seen, remained the formal base of the scholarly pyramid.

Nevertheless, as in the United States, the world of business, industry, and the professions found more than enough Ontario professors interested in developing new fields of professional endeavour, or in furthering the interests of old ones, in the interwar years. The coming of age of Gramsci's 'organic intellectuals' – those involved in the production and reproduction of the industrial, social, and cultural infrastructure of the state – had begun. The political and academic culture of Ontario and Canada was not, however, entirely like that of the United States, although the many generalizations of opinion-makers made it seem so. Within the Ontario university the student of the professions operated in an environment that continued to be dominated by the language and beliefs of Arnold and Mill, even as the virtues of commercial and professional utility gained the attention of public and academic communities. In the public mind the age belonged to the businessman and the engineer, for this was the era of Henry Ford and Herbert Hoover.

Commerce and Industry

The post-war Ontario world witnessed the expansion of its urban middle class and of the range of skilled, work-related activities. By 1921 those employed in white-collar occupations linked to trade and finance, the traditional professions, and clerical, domestic and personal service were greater in number than those engaged in agriculture; by 1941 they constituted 38.4 per cent of the gainfully occupied of the province, an increase from 31.9 per cent in 1921. By the beginning of the 1940s more than thirty per cent of clerical, trade, and finance workers and fifty-six per cent of those in professional or recreational services had completed more than thirteen years of formal schooling –that is, had some education beyond the public schools. The constituency of North American universities, including those of Ontario, increased with the expansion of the occupational categories of the middle-class,[11] but it was the universities that largely made such expansion possible, for increasingly they provided the professional credentials.

As the age of the self-taught, self-made entrepreneur and of the apprentice – icons of a less complex age – drew to an end, professors and public alike began to recognize that industrial society required specialized skills that could not easily be acquired below the level of the university but that had not traditionally been taught in it. 'If I read the signs of the time aright, after the war education is going to come into its own,' the registrar and treasurer of Queen's University confided to his principal in 1917, 'but it is going to be a higher type of education than we have heretofore given, especially along the scientific and medical lines.'[12] 'Business success,' wrote an American student in the 1920s, 'no longer involves a mere doing of the right thing by intuition or experience, but is only obtained by those whose minds are trained to recognize the entire implication of the affairs with which they deal.' The banker of the new era, wrote the dean of the Harvard business school, now needed 'his trained investment counsel, his advertising manager, and his men trained in engineering and production methods. He cannot wait for the long, hourglass method of training these men by apprenticeship.'[13] The day of the expert, geared to efficiency, had arrived in North America, and parents as well as prospective undergraduates gradually came to recognize the fact.

Even those who were less apologists for the industrial order than critics of its social consequences readily admitted that the age of economic efficiency, social utility, and specialism had dawned and should not simply be dismissed by those with nobler motives. 'The maximum of efficiency has been accepted so widely as the deciding standard in modern organization,' wrote Charlotte ('Lottie') E. Whitton, MA, editor-in-chief of the *Queen's Journal* in 1917, 'that generalization is becoming more and more the attribute of the impracticable idealist. Specialization has become the key word of individual and social effort. In every hub of activity, and even in the strata of lethargic indifference, the tendency to specialize is assertively present.'[14] In this recognition of the interconnectedness of modern life, propelled by the special skills of experts increasingly centred in universities, Whitton's words reflected what was becoming the public view. 'The war is doing one thing,' wrote an editorialist in the Toronto *Globe* the same year: 'it is relating academic culture more vitaly [*sic*] with business life and industrial activity. Every day's experience is making plain the interdependence of the man in the class-room and the man in the street ... The university is not a thing apart. It stands in the midst of the crowd ... The war has made it very plain in Canada, plain even to the Philistines, that, if Canada is to recover from the war's fearful dislocation of business and of industry, there must come into our life not less of the university's technique, of the scientist's method, and of the specialist's knowledge, but more ...'[15]

As the *Globe* editorial suggests, by the end of the Great War the importance of universities as institutions that could perform public services of great practical value had finally begun to penetrate the consciousness of the general public. Moreover, the war had increased the value of the intellectual capital of some academics more than it had others, and some of them began to consider how they could profitably meet these new public expectations. Like the public at large, many members of the academic community were convinced of the vital need to address the highly complex political and social problems arising out of the war. Near the end of the war Principal R. Bruce Taylor of Queen's University received a 'Memorandum on Economic Research and Social Business Training,' urging him to increase the university's teaching and research in these areas. The memorandum (the work of O.D. Skelton) warned that the country's post-war problems were complex and urgent. 'The burden of taxation, the insistent demands for social reconstruction, the dangers of class and sectional cleavage, the problems of land settlement and of provision for returned soldiers, the task of keeping and extending the share we have won in the world's trade, our modest part in the problems of international reorganization – these and many more such issues demand all the thought and study we can give. We have found that Canada cannot longer escape the difficulties of an advanced industrial system. We have found ourselves with some surprise in days of billion dollar budgets, of IWW's and trade boards that ration or shut up great industries. The days of happy-go-lucky ease, the days when we had a continent to burn, are gone for good and all.'[16]

President Loudon of the University of Toronto had put the case for commercial education at the university level before the academic community as early as 1901. As usual, Loudon had stressed the German example and its American equivalents. 'Looking at the tendencies of the times,' he said, 'I feel like advising the young men before me not to consider it as decreed by the fates that they shall inevitably become ministers, or doctors, or lawyers, or schoolmasters, but to keep their eyes open to the possibilities of a business career, and to the possibility of equal usefulness and perhaps much greater remuneration in such a career.'[17]

Others, encouraged by such support at the top, put the case for a business program at Loudon's own university. At the urging of the Canadian Manufacturers' Association and the Toronto Board of Trade a two-year diploma course was inaugurated in 1901. In 1907 S.J. McLean, appointed as an assistant professor in the department of political economy a year earlier, addressed himself to the 'school of commerce idea' in the *University of Toronto Monthly*. 'Belief in the importance of studies which are purely disciplinary and cultural must remain,' he conceded. 'But along with this there has had to be faced the question: can there be education for vocation, in the narrower sense, as well.' His answer was resounding and unapologetic. 'Without venturing any opinion on the thorny question of the utility of culture, it may be said that we have come to recognize the culture of utility.' Those who would criticize such a venture should, he noted, recall that civilization depended on 'the stability of the industrial foundation,' and that 'self-interest is the mainspring of human activity.'[18] A demand clearly existed, and was increasing, for courses that would provide specialized skills in banking, commerce, and accountancy.

By 1909 the two-year diploma course at the University of Toronto had blossomed into a full four-year degree program coordinated by the department of political economy, leading to a Bachelor of Arts degree in commerce and finance. Indeed, it was the arrival of business courses that made possible the significant growth of the department in the last years of James Mavor's long headship. The political science side of the department's activities, which had arrived in Toronto as an adjunct to instruction in law, continued to meet with no little suspicion. In a Toronto Empire Club speech given in 1906, James Emery of the Citizens' Industrial Association of America had dismissed the discipline of political economy as something that took place 'when a man who knows nothing on any subject talks to one who knows less than he does on something which they both know nothing about.'[19] Sensitive to doubts by some of the academic legitimacy of their discipline, Mavor's department made certain that those studying commerce also received important elements of liberal education; their studies included, for example, mandatory courses in English and in two modern languages. The curriculum also reflected Mavor's own dislike of undergraduate specialization. In addition to economics and accountancy, commerce students at

Toronto studied economic history, economic geography, and commercial law.

Between 1919–20 and 1931–2 enrolment in the commerce and finance section of the department increased from 60 to 352. The proportion of the university's students enrolled in the department shot up – from 7.4 per cent in 1907–8 to 8.3 per cent in 1912–13 – and it averaged 20.5 per cent in the 1920s and early 1930s, especially after the inauguration of a Bachelor of Commerce degree in 1920.[20] Interest in business-oriented education continued to increase throughout the country. The number of commerce graduates between 1937 and 1941 totalled 1,065, more than three times the number (334) who graduated in the five years from 1922 to 1926.[21]

The advent of commerce in the University of Toronto's department of political economy, and with it increases in general enrolment that hovered around the thousand mark throughout the 1920s and 1930s,[22] made it possible to hire new staff members. By the time of his retirement in 1922, Mavor had eight academic associates in economics and political science, and the total departmental complement (which included instructors in law) stood at thirteen. Among them were men, hired during or shortly after the Great War, who were to dominate the department and their profession for the next two generations: Gilbert Jackson, R.M. MacIver, Vincent Bladen, C.R. Fay, and Harold Innis. In 1924 the department's growing multiplicity of fields was reflected in its structure and in that of its honours courses – by then the economics division was virtually coequal with political science, and was soon to predominate. (Between 1922 and 1937 the department appointed two political scientists, one sociologist, and nineteen economists.)[23] By the late 1920s law, like economics, had become a separate division that was on the verge of establishing its own degree-based autonomy.

The foundations of a business-oriented educational program at Queen's had been laid even before the war by O.D. Skelton, Shortt's successor as head of the department of economics and political science. In conjunction with the Canadian Bankers Association Queen's began in 1913 to offer extension (correspondence) courses in banking and allied subjects, presided over by Skelton himself but with organizational participation from senior members of the Canadian banking community. Skelton did not distrust specialists or specialization; indeed, under Adam Shortt's leadership the department had taken a specialist direction. So while the Queen's extension banking courses were relatively elementary in level (teaching business arithmetic, for example), they also gave lip service to, but otherwise made little pretence at providing, elements of a liberal education.[24] By the time the veterans returned from the Great War almost two thousand students were enrolled in them.[25]

Skelton was the brightest academic star in the post-Grant firmament at Queen's and, like Grant before him, he inspired fierce loyalty among his followers. In 1916 one such former Queen's honours undergraduate and disciple, Clifford Clark, returned at the request of Skelton, his mentor, from a brilliant graduate career under F.W. Taussig at Harvard to teach international trade and administer the correspondence courses in banking. Together the powerful combination of Skelton and Clark, which put together the 1918 memorandum arguing for a major expansion of economic research and business training, won its case. They had pointed, on the one hand, to the success of the extramural banking courses and, on the other, to the fact that by initiating courses in commerce and finance and creating a department of social service, the University of Toronto had taken the academic lead in Ontario.[26] Few developments were more guaranteed to galvanize Queen's administrators into action than initiatives taken by the provincial university. In spite of the uncertain socio-economic climate of reconstruction Canada, Skelton's dean, English professor James Cappon, accepted the Skelton-Clark proposal. A Bachelor of Commerce program (the first of its kind in Canada) was in place by the fall of 1919.

In his official capacity as dean, Cappon announced the new course in commerce in the university's *Principal's Report* for 1918–19, but he did so with a singular lack of enthusiasm: 'The establishment of Commercial Courses leading to the degree of B.Comm. is another instance of Vocational Education in the University. The instruction in these courses includes a few humanistic subjects but is mainly economical, commercial and actuarial.' Cappon's description was followed by a warning: 'It must be kept in mind, however, that in the Arts Faculty at least education should always have more than a merely vocational purpose ... In the midst of all our practical modern developments this original and most characteristic function of the University, that of training a large-minded citizenship, remains properly the chief function, the function which distinguishes it from a Technical or Business College.'[27] Privately, Cappon was even more bitter, for he believed the advent of such courses at Queen's symbolized its capitulation to commercial and material values – symptomatic of the direction of modern civilization itself. As he wrote to Principal Grant's son, W.L. Grant, in the autumn of 1919: 'We seem to have reached the decadent days of that great middle-class mercantile civilization that was so proud of itself ... even twenty years ago ... Quite a half of the legislation and movements we think progress ... are merely the movements of a sick man tossing on his bed.'[28] That same autumn marked the retirement of Dean Cappon after thirty-one years of service to the university, the last thirteen as dean of arts. His successor was O.D. Skelton.

Within a short time Dean Skelton had both consolidated and expanded his academic empire. By 1921 he reported that the commerce courses were 'taking effective shape,' with an enrolment of 271. The extension courses in banking, with a registration of 406 (and a field secretary who visited cities in eastern and western Ontario) were supplemented by ones in accounting, established in cooperation with the Institute of Chartered Accountants of Ontario and obligatory for all Ontario Chartered Accountancy candidates.[29] By the end of the 1920s, economics and political science was the largest department in the faculty of arts at Queen's.[30]

If anything, the arrival of the Depression increased the importance of such courses to the university. Registration in banking and chartered accountancy courses continued to increase in 1932. Clifford Clark returned in that year as professor and director of commerce and administration courses, to be joined a year later by Norman Rogers in political science and history. The departure of both for Ottawa by the mid-1930s, Clark as deputy minister of finance and Rogers as member of Parliament for Kingston and minister of labour in the new King government, diminished the Queen's department in manpower but added to the lustre of its reputation as one with important and influential links to the very centre of federal power. In spite of the Depression, the university managed to make replacement appointments in its key arts department, especially after the appointment of R.C. Wallace as principal in 1936. In the fall of that year the addition of J.A. Corry, for example, strengthened the staff in political science (he had taught law at the University of Saskatchewan).[31] The links between the commerce program and the business community continued with the creation in 1937, at W.A. Mackintosh's instigation, of an industrial relations unit and chair within the department of economics and political science. At the same time, the Skelton-Clark-Mackintosh commercial empire on the St Lawrence acquired the status of a school within the faculty of arts. Mackintosh became its first director. 'With completely up-to-date data, the [industrial relations] division will serve as a clearing house on methods and procedures in industrial life,' wrote Mackintosh for the 1937–8 *Principal's Report*.[32]

W. Sherwood Fox, dean of arts and science at the Western University of London, Ontario, announced his intention to set up a course in commerce and finance in the same 1920 chamber of commerce speech in which he suggested changing the university's name to The University of Western Ontario to reflect its service to the south-western region of the province. A commerce course similar to those in existence at Queen's and Toronto, but with specialized elements such as advanced statistics and 'the principles of efficiency engineering,' Fox promised, would also meet the region's needs. Students wanted such a course at Western, and 'there were doubtless many more,' said Fox, 'that would eagerly embrace the opportunities offered in the proposed course.' He estimated that such a program would bring a possible twenty-five per cent increase in overall enrolment.[33] With enthusiastic support from the local business community the university set up a department of commerce in the fall of 1920, with a broad program that reflected the wishes of its businessmen advisers. Courses included not only accounting and business organization and efficiency but also 'principles of advertising, buying and marketing, credits and collections, and theory and practice of banking.'[34] The hiring of the new department's first full-time faculty member set its tone and direction. E.H. Morrow possessed a Bachelor's degree from Queen's University but also a Master's degree in Business Administration from Harvard University. From the first, the Western approach to business studies differed significantly from those of Toronto and Queen's, for Morrow imported the Harvard case-study method.

The Western Ontario commerce course proved to be a great success. The Harvard method appeared to students to provide effective management skills because it focused on actual business cases rather than academic theories.[35] The Western program was a four-year honours degree, unusual at the time. Enrolment steadily increased, and with it the size of the department's teaching staff. Its name was changed to reflect its expanding status within the university, becoming in 1927 the department of business administration. By 1931, students such as graduates in engineering could also pick up a diploma in business administration after a year's intensive study.[36] 'More and more young men are entering university hall with an idea of obtaining a practical training for a business career,' remarked the London *Free Press* in a 1930 editorial applauding the University of Western Ontario's business education program. By the mid-1930s it was the largest in the university, rivalled only by medicine in size and prestige. Even at the worst of the Depression almost all its graduates, it was claimed, found employment: eighty-nine per cent in 1932, ninety-four per cent in 1933, and 100 per cent in 1935.[37]

The high demand for people trained for the worlds of commerce, finance, and industry, combined with the increasingly specialized and complex nature of the study of these areas, helped these subjects gain academic legitimacy and disciplinary status as social sciences between the wars. Professorial experts on commerce, finance, accounting, and statistics had been inspired and given courage by the industrial expan-

FIGURE 13.1

Full-time Ontario enrolment in commerce, by gender, 1920–37

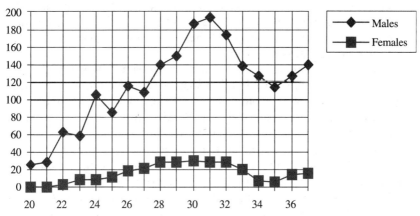

SOURCE: *Higher Education in Canada, 1936–38* (Ottawa 1939)

sion of the pre-1920 period. They had managed to help sustain the steady demand for their product after the war. The numbers of students, mostly male, increased fairly steadily throughout the 1920s. The impact of the Depression of the 1930s was severe, but enrolment began to pick up again by 1935. Thereafter, it increased at a steady rate (see Fig. 13.1).

The new-style business professors had created their own intellectual environment, complete with the vocabularies as well as the skills of the modern expert. They had also begun to produce a body of scholarship that helped legitimate their academic enterprise. In the 1920s alone, more than forty books on Canadian economics were published. This outnumbered the total scholarly production of the nineteenth century on the subject. During the 1930s the number of publications tripled again.[38] Canadian economists also cultivated those important links with the business and government communities that provided themselves with a *raison d'être* of great social utility and their students with jobs.

Even the economic collapse of the 1930s failed to shake the growing alliance between business and the academy. In the depths of the Depression the Queen's Commerce Club held weekly luncheon meetings, listened to lectures from executives of Canadian General Electric, General Motors, Goodyear Tire and Rubber Company, and 'other leading corporations of the country,' and its sponsoring department (economics and political science) promised to 'continue to develop its intimate contact with Canadian business ...'[39] Yet for others this apparent capitulation of the academy to commerce had gotten out of hand. A disillusioned and embittered principal of Queen's, Hamilton Fyfe, told his board of trustees in 1935 that even the students had come to view their education as a commercial transaction, oriented to successful employment. 'The miasma of industrial commerce has soiled the face of many academies. They have adulterated the quality of their products and have tried to disguise the defect by advertisement.'[40]

The expanding commerce idea was but one channel by which the university in Ontario, like those in other industrialized countries, was gradually transformed into what Harold Perkin has called 'the axial institution of modern society.'[41] As Perkin observes: 'Before 1900, despite many undercurrents of change, the universities are still in the world of leisured gentlemen and the gentlemanly professions; after 1920, despite many hangovers from the past, they are in the bustling, strenuous world of business and the competitive professions, where serious preparation for high status and incomes is channelled increasingly through higher education. By the 1920s the university is no longer a finishing school for young gentlemen; it is the central power house of modern industry and society.'[42] In Ontario between the wars, universities served both functions. The boys at Upper Canada College, as elitist as it had been in John Strachan's days, were courted as possible recruits by professors of commerce and told that, while years ago only doctors, ministers, and lawyers went to university and were therefore in a class apart from the rest of society, matters had substantially changed. 'The majority of fellows in the University are almost sure to go into business,' Professor Gilbert Jackson told them; 'they are not set apart, but are just the same as everyone else.'[43] This was a key element in the reorientation that took place between the wars: the gradual and at times grudging acceptance of the university not as a place apart, but as a crucial if at times peculiar institution in industrial society, especially, and increasingly, as the only one that could adequately provide the training of those expected to serve society's social needs. The result was an expansion between the wars not so much of the student population as of the number of different programs that aspired to professional status.

Practical and Other Science

While university-level programs geared towards social utility and industrial efficiency pre-dated the Great War, they significantly expanded after it. The case of engineering serves as a prime example. Toronto's School of Practical Science, founded in the early 1870s, had formally become part of the University of Toronto in 1906, and the government-sponsored Kingston School of Mines, created in the 1890s, was amalgamated with Queen's in 1916 to become its faculty of applied science. The Great War heightened the engineer's sense, originating in the nineteenth century, that his was 'the master spirit of the age.'[44] In the same year that Queen's formally gained its faculty of applied science, the *Queen's Journal*'s editorial page reprinted with obvious approval the rapturous words of W.J. Francis, a civil engineer: 'It is the engineer who harnesses the Niagaras of the world to transform the night of our cities into noon day and to turn the wheels of commerce. It is the engineer who develops the mining and furnishes the metal with which he builds machines that by their ingenuity compel us to stand in awe and admiration ... It is the engineer who furnishes the worker in the golden west with the machines whereby millions of bushels of wheat are each year made ready to enter the hopper that the engineer has constructed [who] has made Canada of to-day what she is.'[45]

Such wondrous testimony suggests that the distinction between the practical materialist and the romantic idealist can at times be a semantic one. During the Great War, such excessive rhetorical self-promotion must largely have seemed to reflect a self-evident social reality. In 1917 the general manager of a major nickel company held an audience of 250 male students at Queen's in 'most complete and rapt attention' when he spoke of the heavy social and moral responsibilities of the engineering profession. 'It rests with the electrical engineer and the capitalist,' a student journalist wrote in 1918, 'to save our country from a repetition of the present heat, light and power shortage.' An article on mechanical engineers concluded: 'In engineers in general, hope must be placed for the future, and all credit must be given for the great advancement made in Science, which has brought conveniences, luxuries and happiness to mankind.' The engineering society of Queen's was told, in a speech on 'professional ethics as applied to engineering,' that 'the keynote of the national engineering societies has been "service,"' and that 'In many respects the engineer should be, so to speak, a "public utility" ever striving to increase and spread abroad, acquired knowledge which when applied tends to make mankind the happier and life more worth living.'[46] No doubt the practical orientation of such idealistic appeals helped returned soldiers in 1918 and 1919 decide that their futures lay in engineering.

At the end of the war, deans of practical science at both Queen's and the University of Toronto reported alarming increases in enrolment. The immediate source of the increase was, of course, the influx of war veterans. Ex-soldiers comprised more than fifty per cent of those engineering students who wrote Toronto examinations in the spring of 1919 (see Table 13.1). Their average ages from first to fourth years ranged from

TABLE 13.1
Ex-soldiers and non-soldiers who wrote examinations in practical science at the
University of Toronto, spring 1919

	Total	Ex-soldiers	Non-soldiers
First year	376	173	203
Second year	164	82	82
Third year	139	79	60
Fourth year	93	60	33
TOTAL	772	394	378

SOURCE: A.M. Reid, 'The twenties,' in Robin S. Harris and Ian Montagnes, eds.,
Cold Iron and Lady Godiva; Engineering Education at Toronto, 1920–1972 (Toronto
1972), 53

FIGURE 13.2
Enrolment in School of Practical Science, University of Toronto, 1919–39

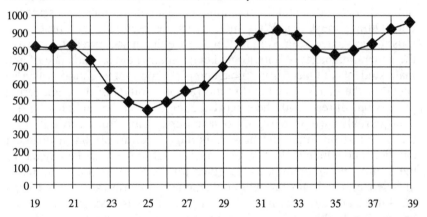

SOURCE: Marni de Pencier, 'A Study of the Enrolment of Women in the University of
Toronto,' research paper, University of Toronto (1973), PUH A83-0036/001, University
of Toronto Archives

21.6 to 25. From a pre-war figure of 627 in 1913–14, enrolment in practical science at Toronto surpassed eight hundred in 1919, 1920, and
1921 (see Fig. 13.2).

One can see the vicissitudes of both the influx of veterans and of the
business cycle in subsequent years. The Toronto engineering students
who had been in the middle of their studies at the outbreak of war and
resumed their education in the autumn of 1919 had graduated by 1921 or
1922, and the freshmen engineers of 1919 wrote their last examinations
in the spring of 1923. The boom of 1919 had turned to bust by the mid-

1920s. In 1925–6 a low of 445 students registered, partly because of a downturn in the economy but also because admission standards for the faculty had been raised in 1923. Entering students now required senior matriculation standing in English and mathematics. But with the more prosperous years of the late 1920s, enrolment again soared. Numbers in fact hit their peak at a time when, elsewhere, the Depression was at its worst. In the 1932–3 year enrolment in practical science at Toronto reached 914, a figure not to be achieved again until the Depression was virtually over and another war loomed on the horizon (in 1938–9 enrolment reached 924).

The increase in post-war enrolment reflected, however, two longer trends. First, from the beginning of the century the number of engineers in Canadian society had increased at a rate greater than other professions, the labour force, or even the Canadian population. Possibly this was because they were indeed seen as the occupational life-force of the industrial age. The second trend, of more direct significance for the education of engineers, was the corresponding decline of the apprenticeship system in the same period. Whereas 67.1 per cent of engineers in Canada learned their trade by apprenticing and 32.9 per cent by attending university in 1887–90, by 1919–22 the proportions were reversed: only 30.0 per cent apprenticed, 70.0 per cent were enrolled in a university degree program. A full eighty-seven per cent of the council members of the Canadian Society of Civil Engineers were university graduates by 1921.[47] By the 1920s, the 'virtual scientific revolution in technology' that took place between the 1880s and the end of the Great War had helped transform engineering 'from an empirical art to a scientific profession.'[48]

The shifting demands of an industrial economy resulted in a reorientation of enrolment patterns in engineering away from civil engineering, traditionally the heart and soul of the profession, towards chemical, mechanical, and electrical engineering. The highly technical nature of these areas further eroded the apprenticeship system: it was one thing to learn to make a sturdy bridge or a graded road at a work site rather than in the classroom; it was quite another to produce industrial chemicals there.[49] Throughout the interwar years at Toronto the number of civil engineering students tended to run fourth, sometimes fifth to electrical, chemical, mechanical, and, at times, mining students.[50] A similar tendency existed at Queen's, but it was less pronounced because of the university's much smaller size. By the mid-1920s more Queen's students were enrolled in electrical engineering courses than in any other branch. Forty second-, third-, and fourth-year students had decided to become electrical engineers by enrolling in such courses in 1925–6. This compared with thirty-three in civil engineering, twenty-nine in mechanical, twenty-eight in mining (the university's traditional strength), and twenty-three in chemical/metallurgical engineering. These numbers effectively reflect the full range of scientific study at Queen's: in the same year only nine students were enrolled in chemistry courses and only two in physics.[51]

The engineer, whether student or professional, saw himself as the primary agent of industrial society, and for this reason the nature and problems of engineering education often reflected the development of the profession itself as well as the self-image of the engineer. Engineers had come to see themselves as the shock troops of British civilization. Increasingly inspired by the technocratic management techniques of modern industrial corporations, they exhibited little faith in the democratic political process or in politicians, at whatever level. They tended instead to accept capitalism and the 'free market' on faith, to hold a mechanistic view of the economy, and to view the traditional professions as anachronisms that helped little in the generation of material wealth. An increasing problem for the twentieth-century engineer was, as a result, whether engineering was a profession or a business. Because so much of his work depended on the financial ventures and priorities of business entrepreneurs, professional independence was difficult to obtain; and because the social role of the engineer was so ambiguous a professional identity was difficult to articulate.[52]

Engineering education in Ontario universities between the wars mirrored the ambiguities and dilemmas of the profession itself, especially when people – whether businessmen, industrialists, university administrators, or professors of engineering – tried to tell students just what the role of the engineer in society should be as well as how he should be educated. The essential problems were outlined at the very outset of the period by men such as Dean C.H. Mitchell of Toronto and Frank D. Adams, Acting Principal of McGill University, in addresses called 'The Future of Applied Science' and 'The Problems of Engineering Education,' printed in the *Journal of the Engineering Institute of Canada*. In both instances, the demands – social and self-generated – made on the modern engineer were obvious. On the one hand, the purely theoretical and technical knowledge demanded of the engineer in the new post-war world was such that there were scarcely enough hours in the day to acquire it; on the other, the kinds of jobs engineers secured after graduation – in many cases, not even in engineering fields[53] – required an education that went well beyond engineering itself. As Dean Mitchell put it: 'if, when he is at the University, he has not been able to co-ordinate science and practice and obtain a sense of the economy of their application, he is going out into the world ill fitted to take his place alongside the men who are already there; much less to attain to be a leader amongst them. More than this, the complex industrial conditions of to-day are understandable only by long, careful study by thinking men living in close contact with industry.'[54] Or, as Frank Adams put it: 'The question is as to whether you shall endeavour to give every engineer good sound knowledge of engineering without endeavouring to specialize, or whether you shall start specialization earlier and turn out a man who knows more about, (say) civil engineering and nothing about other branches of the engineering profession,' not to mention knowledge of economics, business practices, accounting, or the modern languages in which international business was by then conducted.[55]

The rhetoric of these and other commentators on engineering education gave universal lip-service to the need for engineering graduates to be men of broad liberal culture. In fact, however, the direction of reorientation in engineering curricula went the other way, towards increased attention to engineering skills, both theoretical and practical. Outlining his program for curricular change at the University of Toronto, Mitchell illustrated the conundrum: first, because of the demands upon the engineering student's time, 'less essential subjects' should be eliminated; but, second, equally pressing was the need for that student to be introduced to 'broader humanistic subjects' – such as English, sociology, logic, philosophy, modern languages – to round out his education. Nor was this enough, for the modern engineer needed to acquire the practical skills that would allow him to apply himself to his area of employment after graduation: subjects such as finance, engineering law and jurisprudence, commercial engineering, industrial management, and engineering economics.[56] These were all laudable ideals. The problem was, as one observer put it in 1926: 'help is limited by the fact that no university savant has yet discovered how to get more than twenty-four hours into a day.'[57]

Throughout the interwar years, educators struggled with the problem.[58] Engineering deans and professors continued to worry about the proportions of time spent studying liberal arts along with engineering subjects, and to debate the balance within their engineering courses between classroom and laboratory work. All observers agreed that the demands placed on the student were too heavy, but they could suggest no solution. The observation made in 1932 by one junior engineering professor might well be taken as a reflection of the collective frustration of generations of engineering students in the twentieth century: 'Under the present system we compel the student to take down lecture notes all morning and to spend all afternoon in the laboratory or draughting room:

little wonder that at the end of the day his brain is in no condition for further study. He develops no true appreciation of his work, and consequently rapidly forgets the superficial knowledge, crammed into his brain a few weeks before the examinations, for which we give him the dignity of a degree.'[59] This, he concluded, was a lamentable state of affairs. Yet his own idealized view of the engineer, whose 'chief responsibility is to posterity,' was so broad as to be unattainable. The engineer he had in mind should be a man 'of sound health and character, of broad sympathies and vision, with an intelligent interest in all that concerns human life and welfare, earning our rightful place in society by the practice of engineering and bending our surplus energies to the development of a healthier and happier world.' But the thirty or more weekly hours of the Canadian engineering student's studies left virtually no time for courses other than in engineering – whether in English or in business – and no Canadian university made serious provision for them within the engineering curriculum.[60]

If these problems were not enough, there was the sober fact that after graduation the engineering student between the wars was guaranteed no secure future in his profession, or even in Canada. Educators, politicians, and industrialists in Ontario were greatly concerned by the late 1920s about the problem of wastage in the nation's engineering schools. Students either failed to graduate or, once they had graduated, found themselves not doing engineering, going into business for themselves, or not living in Canada. One result of the patriotic desire to keep Canadian boys in Canada was the 1927 creation in Toronto of the Technical Service Council, at the instigation of H.J. Cody, chairman of the board of governors of the University of Toronto. Propelled into action by a group of concerned engineers, particularly Professor Herbert Haultain, a mining engineer at the provincial university, Cody convinced a dozen important Ontario businessmen to spearhead the funding of an organization dedicated to maximizing the efficient production of engineers for Canadian industry, especially in Ontario.[61] Manufacturers, professors, and captains of commerce had pleaded hard and often during and after the Great War for Canadian universities to produce the engineers and scientists essential to the emergent techno-scientific society.[62] Certainly the professors heeded the call, for Canadian engineering schools produced a steady stream of graduates throughout the interwar years.[63]

The problem was that, in the view of some members of the same commercial and industrial lobby, the universities had proven to be selfish and callous: 'Our universities and colleges,' wrote a correspondent to the *Canadian Engineer* in 1923, 'appear to have an eye chiefly to increase the number of graduates they can turn out per annum, without a thought as to what is to become of the young men who have been induced to take up engineering professions, largely through a false conception as to the demand for engineers as well as a certain amount of romantic glamor which has been attached to engineering work during recent years.'[64] It was believed by many that engineering schools in Canada simply produced too many graduates for the economy to absorb – at least as engineers. Moreover, reported patriots, many Canadian engineering graduates of the 1920s ultimately found employment in the United States (twenty per cent in 1923 and twenty-six per cent in 1925).[65]

Such criticism of universities reflected the business and industrial community's unwillingness to look into its own soul. Part of the problem of student wastage in engineering rested on vestigial views, held within the private commercial and industrial sector, that the school of hard knocks, not effete academic theory, was still sufficient for entry into such branches of engineering as mining. Certainly Herbert Haultain complained of this. In addition, the business and industrial communities were better at offering moral support for industrial education than they were at financing it – whether by offering aid to universities or even sponsoring fundamental research within their own establishments. The growing branch plant pattern of Canadian industrial life during the interwar years further undercut incentive to conduct such research in Sarnia rather than Seattle. The dominant attitude was one of naïve complacence.[66] The Technical Services Council floundered because of a lack of private-sector financial enthusiasm as much as from irresolution concerning its central purpose.

A parallel effort in Ontario, the Ontario Research Foundation, was marginally more successful. Its origins, too, lay in the concern in the 1920s over the lack of scientific research in the province. From its conception in 1927 it received the enthusiastic personal support of Premier G. Howard Ferguson, who at a Toronto meeting of the Canadian Manufacturers' Association declared his intention, in the absence of initiatives elsewhere, to create an industrial research institution with an initial endowment of approximately two million dollars. Its purpose, in the words of the premier, was to solve 'scientific problems of production and processing for Canadian industries and natural resource developers.'[67] The foundation was quite successful at the outset in raising funds – it established an endowment of almost four million dollars – particularly when the popular premier used his powers of political 'moral suasion' on friends from 'the whole spectrum of industrial and commercial activity – banks, insurance companies, the great retail merchant houses, the railways, oil companies, Bell Telephone and, of course, the manu-facturers.'[68]

Ferguson may have made friends among the manufacturers with his speech announcing the formation of the Ontario Research Foundation, but he had annoyed potential supporters elsewhere. Henry Marshall Tory, president of the University of Alberta and an increasingly influen-tial member of the National Research Council, noticed that the speech was a virtual reiteration of one he had himself just given at a dominion-provincial conference. As the National Research Council's historian noted of the affair: 'It was a very effective speech on both occasions.'[69] Tory was less miffed at the Ontario premier's audacity than he was that the many political delays in Ottawa in establishing the National Research Council on an adequate foundation had made possible Fergu-son's pre-emptive strike. 'We have delayed so long at Ottawa in foster-ing a real institution while at the same time public opinion was being built up with respect to it,' he wrote to the Honourable James Malcolm, 'that now Premier Ferguson sees the political soundness of such a scheme and is therefore simply setting himself to steal the thunder and the consequent political kudos which rightly should belong to the Dominion Government.'[70]

Historical interpretation depends on the perspective of the interpreter. The historian of the Ontario Research Foundation and biographer of Pre-mier Ferguson has noted that 'To a rather unique degree, the Ferguson government was the ally, some would have said the tool, of the business community and its financial commitment to the ORF was one measure of the extent of that friendship.'[71] From the perspective of an historian of higher education, his venture carried with it decidedly less helpful con-sequences. The premier's initiative was that of a politician whose per-sonal commitment to the cooperative nature of the project was dubious. The foundation itself produced in its first quarter-century only very modest results, and its first chairman was forced to note a 'rather surpris-ing disinclination of manufacturers to evidence much interest' in the foundation's activities, to help in its organization, or to finance contin-ued research.[72] Such political initiatives served to deflect both public attention and private industrial and commercial interest in Ontario away from the possibilities of investing in the province's universities as agents of fundamental and practical scientific research.

Leaders of 'federal science' in the National Research Council, from A.B. Macallum to Henry Marshall Tory, scarcely helped the universi-ties in this respect. They had consistently stated that the universities of the country should not be involved in industrial research, but should instead train the nation's scientists and engage solely in research in the pure and practical sciences. Even then, serious advanced research was meant to be concentrated in one or two universities, clearly Toronto and McGill, as Principal Bruce Taylor found out in 1919 when Queen's was given no representation on the advisory council set up to give direction to the National Research Council.[73] Tory explained the state of affairs in the universities in 1926: 'The facts are that in Canada to a very large extent our university appointments are based on the idea of teaching only and research incidentally and most teachers are so burdened with teaching work that leisure to think and work on research problems is exceedingly difficult to get.'[74] In fact, Tory's actions did little systematically or seriously to alleviate such a state of affairs. Aid from the National Research Council was limited to the provision of a few scholarships and modest research grants to individuals, upon application and adjudication by the council. The NRC research fellowships (first awarded in 1917) and bursaries (initiated in 1919) quickly became 'virtually the preserve' of Toronto and McGill.[75] Otherwise, universities were shut out from federal support. Tory agreed, in this respect, with his arch-enemy on the council, A.B. Macallum, who had stated in September 1918 that 'The Government will not give money directly, or through the Research Council, to the Universities to assist them in developing research.'[76]

While Tory and his ambitious colleagues at the National Research Council may genuinely have sympathized with the difficulties of the university professor of science in finding time to engage in research, such a state of affairs was consistent with the council's self-interest. The problem of science, academic and industrial, had become a national one. In 1928 Principal Sir Arthur Currie of McGill University wrote to Henry Marshall Tory, just appointed chairman of the NRC, complaining that Tory's plans for the expansion of industrial research had the potential effect of diverting funds from university-based research. Tory replied: 'All state universities are still struggling with the problem of necessary funds to carry on anything but the most elementary teaching work, simply because government officers who have control to a certain extent of the amount of money voted are always watching to prevent anything being done that could have the slightest appearance of conflicting with their own ambitions.'[77]

The result was that, on the whole, little basic scientific research was conducted in the universities except at Toronto and McGill.[78] The funds available to the science research committee of Queen's University in 1929, for example, amounted to only about two thousand dollars, and important initiatives there in radiation and nuclear physics faltered because of the unwillingness of the board of trustees to allocate the $3,895 (the sum remaining after private donations) needed for the purchase of a charged particle accelerator.[79] The lack of financial resources at the university level made for timidity. At the University of Toronto, J.C. McLennan, who had struggled to undertake pure research in physics for years, was forced to tender his resignation in 1931 after his attempt to transform Toronto's school of graduate studies into a faculty failed. Nevertheless, in spite of the problems associated with finding research funding, McLennan and his colleagues at Toronto had established a solid record of research in physics, most notably in projects related to atomic spectroscopy, superconductivity, and low temperatures. Half of all NRC bursaries awarded between 1918 and 1932 went to University of Toronto students, and McLennan himself received more NRC grant money than all the McGill professors combined. The University of Toronto awarded twenty-seven doctorates in physics during these years, twenty-five of them supervised by McLennan.[80] McLennan's record testified to the fruits of academic research, yet the university's council of the school of graduate studies concluded that research should be conducted independently within the university but that no formalization of the research function was necessary: 'the relation of the School ... to research is incidental; not all graduate students engage in research ...'[81] McLennan's resignation as dean of science and as professor of physics was accepted.

In 1928, according to one estimate, scientists in Canada numbered 604, approximately 4.5 per cent of the total of more than thirteen thousand scientists listed in the biographical directory *American Men of Science*.[82] Most striking is the way that in spite of its own problems in furthering scientific research the University of Toronto had come to dominate Canadian science by the interwar years. In addition, it was evident that the brain drain to the United States was now serious. A full half of the 513 Canadian scientists (254) had been trained in Toronto, but forty-two per cent of the total no longer lived in Canada. Of Toronto graduates listed in the American directory, forty-two per cent were no longer domiciled in Canada; nor were thirty per cent of the forty-seven Queen's graduates that were listed.

These numbers, however, included those who held only Bachelor's degrees – scarcely a good indicator of the professional scientific community engaged in research. Using the gross total of Canadians listed in the American directory, the commentator isolated those who possessed the PHD degree. This left 264 professional scientists, including 120 who were graduates of the University of Toronto, thirty of Queen's, twenty-eight of McGill, twenty-one of Dalhousie, seventeen of McMaster, and nineteen of Acadia. Of their doctorates, thirty-eight had been conferred by Toronto, seven by McGill, and 219 by non-Canadian universities, mainly in the United States (especially Chicago).[83] Seventy of the 242

TABLE 13.2
Distribution of Canadian scientists with doctorate by field of specialty and place of occupational residence, 1928

Department	Canada	Foreign	Total
Agriculture	7	10	17
Anatomy	6	6	12
Astronomy	14	0	14
Bacteriology	5	5	10
Biochemistry	7	1	8
Botany	15	8	23
Chemistry	16	16	32
Engineering	2	3	5
Entomology	9	4	13
Geology	16	7	23
Mathematics	6	10	16
Medicine	9	8	17
Pathology	1	2	3
Pharmacology	2	0	2
Physics	13	10	23
Physiology	4	3	7
Psychology	4	3	7
Zoology	6	4	10
TOTAL	142	100	242

SOURCE: J.P. McMurrich, 'The Distribution of Canadian Men of Science,' National Conference of Canadian Universities *Proceedings* (1928), 63

Canadian scientists holding doctorates in their specialty had found employment outside the country. As in engineering, chemists dominated the profession, with thirty-two, equally divided between residents and non-residents. Botanists, geologists, and physicists (twenty-three of each) followed, but there the difference lay in the fact that botanists and geologists tended to stay in Canada – probably because these were fields of strength in the Geological Survey of Canada and the Survey was a major employer of scientists – whereas ten of the twenty-three physicists had gone overseas or to the United States for employment (see Table 13.2). The statistics indicate clearly just how modest the progress in advanced research had been in Canadian academic life, beyond the rhetorical acceptance of the research ideal. In continental Europe and the United States, possession of the doctoral research degree had come to confer professional status in all branches of academic life. Judged by this standard, Canadian universities, and the scientific community at large, had scarcely begun to be professionalized. In the twenty-three years up to 1917, only eleven doctoral degrees in all fields of science had been conferred by Canadian universities.[84] By 1928 Canadian uni-

FIGURE 13.3

Full-time graduate enrolment, Ontario and Canada, 1920–50

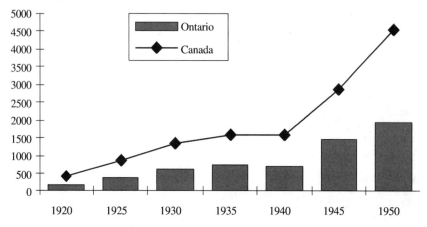

SOURCE: *Historical Statistics of Canada*, 2nd ed. (Ottawa 1983), series 340–438

versities employed fewer than fifty professors of physics, and in no year had they awarded as many as ten doctorates in the field.[85]

Such a paucity of numbers was characteristic of the parlous state of graduate studies in Ontario and in Canada. In 1920 total enrolment in all graduate programs in the country was 423, of which 190 were at Ontario universities. By 1930 Ontario enrolment had increased to 633, and by 1940 it had reached 717, when total Canadian graduate enrolment was 1,569 (see Fig. 13.3). These numbers, however, included those enrolled in Master's degrees in different fields. Of the 423 graduate degrees conferred in 1920, only twenty-four were PHDs – gained from either the University of Toronto or McGill University, the only institutions that offered the degree. By 1940 the number of doctoral graduates had tripled, to seventy-five. In that year, the University of Toronto had a hundred students enrolled at the doctoral level. By then, it had awarded a total of eighty-five doctoral degrees in physics.[86]

While the numbers were small there was some real growth. In the twenty years from 1920 to 1940 the percentage of graduate enrolment to total enrolment rose from 1.8 to 4.3. Full-time graduate enrolment also roughly tripled, and the number of doctorates doubled in both decades.[87] Research, whether in science or other areas, did take place, often of a heroic nature, undertaken by solitary scholars in inadequate laboratories after long days of teaching and not infrequently at their own expense. Modest progress was made. In the early 1930s, chemist Charles Burke had struggled at McMaster to find a place for serious science and to form a science club, and, in the absence of any but a few graduate students, confined himself to undergraduate teaching. Yet by the mid-1930s matters had changed, even at struggling McMaster. In part because of Burke's concern and leadership, science students were coming to see themselves, self-consciously at first, as distinct from – perhaps superior to – other students. In 1936 Burke admitted that because of his preoccupation with his own research and that of his advanced students his 'teaching work had probably been neglected somewhat.'[88] Perhaps behind the regret lay a smile. By the end of the decade Burke had secured approval for a course of studies at McMaster leading to the Bachelor of Science degree. Until then, Professor Burke's graduating scientists were Bachelors of Arts. This marked the kind of modest, cumulative advance in scientific teaching and research that characterized most Canadian universities, small and undercapitalized. Still, a corner had been turned in Ontario's universities by the end of the 1930s, and not only at McMaster.

The Healing Science

One event more than any other in Ontario between the wars demonstrated the value of the university as a servant of society. In doing so, it helped link the practice of medicine and the conduct of medical research to the interests of the state. This was the discovery of insulin in 1922 in the laboratories of the University of Toronto.

On the surface, the story is simple and heroic. In 1920 Frederick Banting was a young physician attempting to establish a medical practice, employed as a laboratory demonstrator in surgery and anatomy at the Western University in London, Ontario. While preparing to speak to his class on the subject of the pancreas, he had an idea. At the time it was thought that the pancreas was involved in two important forms of secretion: an external secretion of digestive enzymes and an internal one that regulated the level of blood sugar. Late one night Banting conceived that possibly, by experimental ligation of the pancreatic duct (which would cause degeneration of the pancreas), he could isolate the internal and external secretions from each other. An extract made from the internal secretion might then be used to treat diabetics, who suffered from abnormally high levels of blood sugar and often died as a result. Excited by this idea Banting talked to medical authorities first at Western University and (at their suggestion) at the University of Toronto, his Alma Mater. He was provided with laboratory space and a student assistant, Charles Best. After a year's trial-and-error experimentation on many dogs, Banting and Best at last found an extract that worked on dogs and in 1922 it was injected into human patients. Once made sufficiently pure, it worked. Diabetes could at last be successfully treated. The first of the twentieth-century's wonder drugs had been discovered, and the result was the first Nobel Prize won by Canadians, awarded in 1923.

Historical reality, however, is rather more complex than this picture allows us to see. Banting was in fact an inexperienced and at times inept researcher whose laboratory results could not always be verified or were inconclusive. His interest in the isolation of the internal pancreatic secretion was, as matters turned out, in the correct direction; but his hypothesized means for producing the extract – by ligation of the pancreatic duct – proved unnecessary, since insulin could just as easily be made from the whole, healthy pancreas. It was J.B. Collip, a biochemist associated with the medical faculty, not Banting, who created the first insulin pure enough for it to produce wondrous results, and when Collip somehow lost his formula for a pure enough insulin it was probably Best who eventually recovered it. In fact, Banting was increasingly marginalized in the research and clinical trials until Best provided him with the rediscovered formula so that insulin could be used with patients of his choice. Only then did Banting emerge permanently as the central figure in the process of discovery.[89]

The Banting myth is interesting, but it is not as central to the historian of higher education as the institutional and political settings in which the discovery of insulin took place. The fact that it took place at all is most striking. As we have seen, scientific research in Canadian universities was very weak throughout the interwar years. Banting conducted his insulin research at the University of Toronto only because Western University authorities confessed that their own facilities were inadequate for experimentation. The Toronto facilities for much of his basic research consisted of a dirty, poorly ventilated garret at the top of the medical building.[90] Yet the facilities, however rude, were adequate for the task at hand and the capacity of the University of Toronto to conduct medical research was better, in fact, than many other North American institutions. The institutional infrastructure that made possible the conditions for ultimate success did exist, however much Banting himself may have resented or denied it.

At the University of Toronto, Banting had taken his idea to J.J.R. Macleod, professor of physiology and associate dean of the faculty of medicine. An experienced medical researcher with a prolific publishing record and an international reputation as an expert in the field of carbohydrate metabolism, Macleod provided Banting with laboratory space, along with an adroit mixture of encouragement and scepticism. It was possibly the presence of Macleod that attracted the biochemist Collip to the University of Toronto on his sabbatical leave from the University of Alberta. While it was Collip who made the big breakthrough in the purification of the extract, it was Macleod, the academic administrator as well as the clinical expert, who provided the essential direction, telling Banting and Best when to slow down and repeat essential experiments and when to press ahead. And it was the cultured and distinguished Macleod, not the shy and awkward Banting, who was the best publicist and apologist for the project at learned gatherings of medical experts. As the biographer of Frederick Banting concludes: 'Insulin emerged in 1921–22 as the result of collaboration among a number of researchers, directed by J.J.R. Macleod, who expanded upon and carried to triumphant success a project initiated by Banting with the help of Best. The single most important technical achievement was that made by Collip in the purification of the extract. On their own, Banting and Best would probably not have reached Insulin. Their work would have been taken over and brought to a triumphant conclusion somewhere else.'[91] For this reason, the award of the Nobel Prize in Medicine to Macleod and to Banting in 1922 is understandable, although Banting was outraged that Macleod and not Best was named the co-recipient; and it appears appropriate that Macleod should have shared credit for the discovery with Collip just as Banting insisted on doing with Best.[92]

There was more to the resentment of Macleod and Collip by Banting, however, than mere pique at the dilution of glory. Banting represented a kind of medical man whose authority in the university setting had been progressively undermined since the 1880s: the generalist physician and surgeon who practiced medicine as a skilled art, and whose independent judgment and common-sense experimentation, arising as often as not out of the needs of his patients, had come to be challenged by the rise of the medical man as professional researcher.[93] Banting was part of the solitary and heroic age of medicine, but he was working by 1921 in a university setting coming to be controlled by men for whom medical science, not medical practice, was the heart of the profession. For men such as Macleod and Collip, the practice of medicine required intimate knowledge of a cluster of overlapping academic disciplines that demanded scientific rigour, not amateur enthusiasm. In the public mind, Frederick Banting the Nobel Prize winner combined the attractive images of both the healing physician and the modern scientific researcher, the promises of consolation and progress.[94] But his University of Toronto colleagues knew better. At best, as his University of Toronto degree indicated, Frederick Banting began his search for the treatment of diabetes with a surgeon's hands but an undergraduate's knowledge of medicine as science. For this reason, as much as any other, Banting found control over laboratories or experiments taken out of his hands by those who controlled medical science in Toronto. This was why Banting was offered no permanent position on the University of Toronto medical faculty during this crucial stage of his insulin research.[95]

Banting was not the only medical practitioner in Toronto who felt threatened. At the very time the combative and insecure surgeon was searching for the secrets of the treatment of diabetes, a medical controversy threatened to topple the university's administration, for Banting's resentment of professional researchers such as Collip and Macleod was in fact an individualized form of a larger set of similar professional antipathies. The institutional background to the discovery of insulin is in fact part of the larger story of the transformation of medicine and medical education in the province, especially at the provincial university.

From the outset of his tenure as president of the university, Robert Falconer had supported efforts to improve the education of physicians, and this was coupled with his determination to complete the transformation of Toronto into the research institution that had been envisioned by James Loudon. Since the nineteenth century the University of Edinburgh and Johns Hopkins University had pioneered in the association of university-based medical education with hospital-based clinical instruction. In Baltimore, an endowed hospital was fully integrated with the Johns Hopkins University medical faculty, and medical men there sacrificed substantial private medical practice in order to provide medical instruction in hospital wards and to conduct clinical research. In 1908, at Falconer's initiative, the University of Toronto, arguing that such reforms meant greater efficiency and anticipating Dr Abraham Flexner's forthcoming evaluation of North American medical education for the Carnegie Foundation, attempted to initiate changes in the direction of clinical instruction and medical research. The initiatives supported by Falconer met with strenuous protest from a number of doctors who feared that reform would merely make their access to hospital wards more difficult and who probably resented the notion that a class of 'superior' medical practitioners bent on 'research' was about to be given elite status in 'their' institution. Experts on their subject in their patients' eyes, they now felt threatened by those who possessed superior expertise within their own guild. Nevertheless, through the efforts of Sir Joseph Flavelle an agreement was worked out between the University and the Hospital Board of Toronto to assign full responsibility in certain ward services to the medical faculty. In this way, professors came to exercise greater administrative control and to supervise treatment and clinical research in such areas as surgery, gynaecology, ophthalmology and laryncology.[96]

In 1910 the Flexner Report was published. It was scathing in its condemnation of the poor quality of instruction and facilities in many North American medical schools, but concluded that the University of Toronto's medical faculty, like that of McGill, was one of the best ten institutions on the continent.[97] Such a good report card, issued by a man dedicated to the German-derived research ideal, allowed Falconer and university officials to press ahead with their reforms. In 1911 the Toronto General Hospital Act was amended so that while the hospital board formally made all appointments to the hospital staff they could only be made after recommendation by a joint hospital-university committee, each with four members.

In 1918 Falconer once again renewed the initiative with a tentative proposal for medical reorganization that for the first time urged the creation of a full-time professorship in medicine within the university's faculty of medicine. The suggestion was backed by the promise of a donation of $500,000 from Sir John Craig Eaton for the endowment of the position. The time appeared right for the successful implementation of the faculty's reorganization, since a number of senior men were still in the armed forces and others were due to retire.[98] The proposal became an established fact: Duncan Graham, a bacteriologist, was appointed to the chair on the condition that the university's professor of medicine also be the physician in charge at the hospital, responsible for all appointments in medicine to the hospital's staff. As a result, all aspects of the clinical teaching program and the supervision of junior resident staff effectively came under university control, and the University of Toronto gained the first full-time clinical professor in the British Empire.[99]

Two years later, in 1920, Falconer supported the reorganization of the department of surgery along similar lines, with Clarence L. Starr (since 1911 surgeon in chief at the Hospital for Sick Children) in charge. The new initiative came after G.E. Vincent of the Rockefeller Foundation wrote to the university in December 1919, with the news that the American foundation was in a position to provide five million dollars for the development of medical education in Canada. Toronto quickly submitted an application for a million dollars of this money, and by November of the next year, after the university agreed in negotiation that it would substantially increase its financial commitment to medical education, the large sum was awarded. With such tangible encouragement Clarence Starr, like Duncan Graham, quickly created the basis for a department that stressed clinical investigation over practical experience. Accordingly, new men oriented towards serious scientific research came in and older physicians were shunted aside and their honoraria discontinued.[100]

The whole direction of the medical faculty now pointed towards medical practitioners interested as much in full-time research and clinical instruction as in private practice. Indeed, Toronto's was among the first medical faculties to put into place a 'whole time system' of clinical training, by using income from its Eaton endowment to support several 'clinicians in training' for three to five years. The new approach, said Duncan Graham, 'affords the head of this department more adequate time than was possible under the former system to properly administer the department, both in the University and the hospital: to coordinate the teaching and to supervise the training of the junior whole time members of the department. It, further, provides a better opportunity for graduates to receive an adequate training and a definite attempt is being made to train such men as teachers and clinical investigators.'[101] The day of the private practitioner who engaged in teaching and research as if it were a hobby – like Frederick Banting – was coming to an end. Medical research was becoming too complex to be left solely to the physician.

Banting and Best conducted their experiments on dogs in the summer and fall of 1921, and it was just at this juncture that Robert Falconer began to receive decidedly unpleasant letters at his University College office. First came one from Dr F.W. Marlow, associate professor of gynaecology, who objected strenuously to having his association with the medical faculty, along with his honorarium, discontinued. A past-president of the Ontario Medical Association, Marlow warned Falconer of the university's lack of support in the medical fraternity. His letter concluded, ominously: 'One is forced to believe that there is something radically wrong with the institution somewhere.'[102] By early 1922, Falconer had received like-minded letters from other physicians formerly associated with the medical faculty on a part-time stipendiary basis. Then, not receiving satisfaction from the university's president, they went to their friends in the press and at Queen's Park. The president, it was said, was an autocrat who preferred 'German' methods to the traditional and established pragmatic methods of the 'British School.'

In these first years after the Great War such arguments were emotionally powerful ones, and they proved to be more so because some of the physicians dismissed from the University of Toronto's medical faculty were war veterans. Thus it was that J.F. March, dominion secretary of the Grand Army of United Veterans, levelled the charge of discrimination against returned soldiers and drew the matter to the attention of Premier Drury. March demanded a full investigation into the matter. J.R. Nicholson of the Great War Veterans Association demanded of Drury that 'no further monies be paid to the University until this matter has been investigated by a Representative Commission, and the matter satisfactorily explained or rectified.'[103] As with the controversy surrounding the appointment of philosopher Paxton Young's successor in 1889, a single event at the University of Toronto, reflecting several different kinds of self-interest, became a matter of public controversy because of its symbolic value. Who gave the university the legal, much less the moral right to appoint Graham and Starr to positions of such power and control? Was the university being run by the Eatons and the Rockefellers, in concert with the researchers? Why were the university's graduates not directly represented by their alumni association on its board of governors so that they could guard against such encroachments by outsiders?[104]

Faced with such public and professional clamour for investigation into the apparent high-handedness of the University of Toronto, in June 1922 Premier Drury appointed a select committee of the legislature to examine and report on the problem. But its mandate was not confined, as Falconer thought it would be, to procedural matters related to the medical appointments and dismissals. It was empowered, instead, 'to inquire into and report to this House in regard to any matters concerning the organization and administration of the University of Toronto including its relations ... with the Toronto General Hospital.'[105] Premier Drury himself was to chair the committee's proceedings. The entire range of affairs at the provincial university appeared to be subject to potential scrutiny. A shocked Falconer now knew how James Loudon must have felt when he learned of the appointment of the provincial Royal Commission of 1906. The select committee met, with substantial public interest in its proceedings, from October 1922 to the end of January 1923. Irate physicians complained of the university administration's high-handedness; the alumni argued for greater formal influence in its management; the Toronto District Labour Council raised the old cry that taxation required adequate representation – which, for them, meant labour representation on the university's board of governors.[106]

The legislative committee submitted a unanimous report – even the leader of the opposition, G. Howard Ferguson signed it – in May 1923, to the gratification of the university's irate alumni association and the critics of the university and its medical faculty. The faculty's reorganization, it concluded, was illegal because the changes had not been authorized by the Government through an Order in Council, as required by the Toronto General Hospital Act of 1911. The reorganizations should be reconsidered, senate approval should be secured for future changes or substantial gifts received, and a new agreement should be struck between university and hospital. The cause of medical reform had been rebuked, as indeed had the university, its president, and its board of governors, for the recommendations pointed in the direction of renewed control by the provincial legislature. But the censure proved to be as brief as it was harsh. The report was submitted on the last day of the legislative session, and the next day the House was prorogued. The fall of the Drury government in the election that followed gave medical reform at Toronto an unexpected second life, for discussion of the report ended and with it any prospect for action. The university administration and the medical faculty went on as they had before, saved unintentionally by a discontented provincial electorate most of whom – had they been polled on the matter of medical reform – would probably have backed the cause of the critics, many of them family physicians.[107]

The increasing association of medical education with university-based medical experts who relied on state or foundation support existed at small institutions as well as large ones such as Toronto or McGill. Between the publication of the Flexner Report in 1910 and the return to a semblance of pre-war normalcy in the mid-1920s, the medical schools of both Queen's and Western underwent substantial change. At both institutions, however, the relative absence of the research ideal in medicine allowed a greater degree of continued control by local physicians and surgeons over medical education in hospital settings.

The problems of Queen's were four-fold. First, located in Kingston, it was midway between the two first-class medical schools at Toronto and McGill. Flexner wondered openly whether a medical school at Queen's needed to exist at all.[108] Second, situated in a relatively small town it lacked what later medical administrators would call an adequate 'patient base.'[109] Third, facilities at Kingston General Hospital were woefully inadequate for clinical instruction – or even medical treatment.[110] Finally, veterans of the Great War, many with first-hand experience of foreign hospitals, were able to compare Kingston's facilities with others and were not prepared to put up with those they judged inferior. A $100,000 gift for hospital improvement from the university's chancellor, James Douglas, the 1918 upgrading of the school from Category C to B by the American Medical Association,[111] and the agreement reached the same year between Queen's University and Kingston General Hospital that recognized the hospital as a 'major teaching unit, autonomous but affiliated with the university' all failed to deter the critics of the medical school at Queen's.[112]

Critics found powerful support on the Queen's board of trustees. Adam Shortt, who with his wife, Dr Elizabeth Smith Shortt, had lived in the nation's capital since 1908, favoured association of the medical faculty with Ottawa Civic Hospital. Yet the efforts of Shortt and others did not succeed. By 1920 the Kingston community, including its board of trade, had united and offered its support. For its part, the university's board of trustees drew up a resolution aimed at reorganizing the medical school and keeping it in Kingston. The stated reforms included appointment of a full-time dean and full-time professors, maximization of the school's control in the Kingston General Hospital, creation of a hospital pathology department with systematic records-keeping, appointment of a hospital superintendent under the supervision of the university, and the raising of substantial sums of money from public and private sources for the rebuilding of the hospital, enlargement of staff, and creation of the pathology department.[113]

A basis had been laid at Queen's for a closer relationship between members of the medical fraternity and the university, but the alliance proved to be an uneasy one at best for a number of years, and it worked primarily to the advantage of the medical side of the equation. From the perspective of Principal Taylor, the pressure by private physicians, influential citizens, and community organizations to maintain the medical school in Kingston and in association with Queen's at almost any cost did not serve the best interests of the university as a whole. Taylor's political problem, a delicate one, was that every Kingston member of the university's board of trustees was also on the hospital's board of governors. 'The Hospital and the University through its Finance Committee has [sic] an interlocking directorate,' the principal complained, 'and the Finance Committee, being composed of local men, is not unnaturally anxious to build up the Hospital even if it be at the cost of the University.' The result was that Queen's kept its medical faculty intact, but at the cost of a continuous drain on the university's meagre financial resources. When provincial government grants were at last made to the university for improvement in hospital facilities in 1923, largely as a result of the recommendations of the royal commission of 1921, they constituted – from the government's perspective – part of the university's general grant. The harsh reality was that improved hospital facilities meant the delay of capital expenditures on other faculties.[114]

The medical fraternity in London, Ontario, exercised an even greater degree of control over medical education in the area, in spite of its formal existence as a medical school of the Western University. One of the reasons why in the nineteenth and early twentieth century Western's medical school managed to survive while virtually the rest of the university closed down was the fact that the medical faculty had existed since 1882 as a proprietary school, owned by local doctors who ran the faculty as if it were a business venture. Responsible to the university's senate only in the most formal sense, the physician owners of the Western medical school were virtually free to develop medical education as they saw fit. In 1910 Abraham Flexner observed the results: a four-year course requiring only the most nominal requirements to enter, attended by 104 students; a teaching staff of twenty, more than half of whom held no professorial status; a school with no means of maintenance other than eleven thousand dollars or so in student fees. Even in 1910 such a sum would not buy much. Flexner noted that the medical school's facilities consisted of only three rooms and appeared to contain virtually no equipment, not even a microscope. 'There are a few hundred books, locked in cases to which the janitor carries the key.' The school's clinical facilities, Flexner wrote, were 'entirely inadequate ... confined almost wholly to a small number of beds in the municipal hospital.' In short, the faculty had 'no present function' and could only be judged as one of the worst in North America.[115] Judged from the heights of Flexner's own commitment to the research ideal, this may have been true: the lack of facilities for medical research was a reality at Western. Yet had Flexner examined the institution from the perspective of its function as a training ground for physicians who intended to enter general practice, his conclusions might have been less harsh. Western's graduates had seldom if ever been accused of being inadequately educated as general practitioners. Flexner's judgement, in the end, was not without bias, and it was the bias of academic modernity.

Flexner's report doubtless rocked and embarrassed the medical community of London. Certainly, changes in the direction of higher standards quickly followed: the 1911 extension of the medical course to five years; the 1912 requirement of junior matriculation for entrance; the 1913 sale of the school and facilities to the Western University so that it could secure full faculty status, a full-time dean, and provincial grants; the creation between 1913 and 1924 of eight departments (anatomy, gynaecology and obstetrics, medicine, pathology, physiology, surgery, pharmacology, and biochemistry) with a number of full-time staff; the expansion of facilities for clinical instruction to include not only Victoria Hospital but also others in the London area; and the new medical building that opened in 1921. By the 1920s, under its more secure administrative base in the university, the medical school had recovered from the loss of external rating and recognition. In 1919 the university senate lengthened the medical course to six years (like Toronto and McGill) and initiated post-graduate studies. By the 1930s the university's medical school easily bore comparison with others of similar size on the continent.

The physical conditions at each of the province's universities had significantly improved by the mid-1920s and the rise of the full-time, salaried medical researcher based in the local teaching hospital and the university gave students significantly more access to clinical instruction.

In the four decades since the 1880s, the medical community in Ontario had secured state-sanctioned autonomy in the training and certification of those who wished to enter their guild, the right to discipline errant members, and the capacity to regulate what had become a monopoly of knowledge in a market-place of medical services. Strategies had been developed for occupational self-definition and group advancement,[116] yet medicine, like law, remained a troubled profession. It was uncertain of its mission, had difficulty in disciplining errant members, and continued to lack a sense of collegiality.

Medical students had more immediate problems. To begin with, there was so much to learn, and so little time in which to learn it. The student needed to have a basic knowledge of biology, chemistry, pharmacology, anatomy, mathematics, and much else – it was hoped at the point at which formal medical studies began. Yet educational authorities often stressed that medicine was as much art as it was science, and that the successful medical practitioner must be a man of broad liberal culture as well as sound science. Views about how this twentieth-century renaissance man could be created by the universities varied. Often focusing on the preliminary education of the medical student – education in high schools or universities before acceptance into medical school – educationalists and spokesmen from the medical community generally agreed that high schools could not provide sufficient scientific background for direct entry into medical studies; yet providing prospective medical students with sufficient scientific preparation meant that little time (as with engineers) would be left for the acquisition of humanistic learning. Who had time for philosophical or moral reflection when so many facts remained to be acquired? As Principal Fyfe of Queen's said, in a 1933 convocation address to the medical graduates: 'I expect some of you feel to-day that you are earning your title by a sort of miracle, and indeed it does seem miraculous that any human being can contain so many facts as a medical student is obliged to do. You have been swallowing them for six long years until you feel, I dare say, that you can hardly look a fact in the face.'[117]

The problem of acquiring enough facts would not have been as acute in medical education if it were not for the fact that most people recognized that medical practice continued, in truth, to be as much art as science. It was therefore difficult to dismiss the assertion that a doctor with broad humanistic knowledge and moral concern would be a better doctor for perhaps having acquired a sense of human nature and the human predicament through the ages. Accordingly, the interwar years witnessed an ongoing debate within medical circles about the proper balance in training the medical student in the arts and sciences. In the

1920s, for example, the University of Western Ontario experimented with curricular reorganization in its medical faculty as it sought to reach a balance between medical knowledge and humane learning. Reflecting general trends, including reaction against over-specialization, the university had extended the medical course from five years to six in 1919 (except for returned soldiers) in order to allow more study in the liberal arts. In 1923 medical students at Western were required to take two years of premedical studies in arts, followed by four years of medicine. Yet several years later the result was perceived to be the worst of both worlds: students had acquired sufficient skills in neither arts nor medicine. Accordingly, by 1929 the curricular pendulum at Western had swung back towards an emphasis on areas of medical specialization alone.[118] The general trend in medical education between the wars was towards the acquisition of medical facts. Courses and examinations dealt with little other than increasingly narrow medical specialties. As with the training of engineers or lawyers, little time was allocated in the education of physicians for any reflection on the social implications of what they did for a living or how they went about doing it.

The dilemma proved, of course, to be an irresolvable one, at Western and elsewhere. After discussing the problems of preliminary education in medicine, one frustrated dean talking to the National Conference of Canadian Universities drew two conclusions about the problem of balance between a liberal education and medical training. 'If I were to be pressed for a declaration of my preference,' he said, 'I should have to say a complete course in Arts or Science purposively designed with the object of reducing the number of years of professional study.' But two sentences later, when turning to how the status of medicine might be improved, he concluded that 'the hope for progress lies in scientific investigation, and that he who is not well versed in the Sciences upon which Medicine is founded and is being constructed, even though he may not consciously attempt investigation himself, must always remain handicapped in his endeavor to make practical use of what the investigations of others may bring forth.'[119] The competing claims on limited study time made by professors with ambiguous priorities must have been irksome to students of the professions as they listened to convocation addresses – if they listened at all – on the way to their degrees.

Those who graduated in medicine in Ontario between the wars were the students who proved themselves adept at memorizing a myriad of facts and remembering them until examination time. Some, no doubt, were people of broad general culture, but probably most had come to specialize rather more than they had anticipated. Even the University of Western Ontario, small in size, listed some thirty areas of academic specialization by the 1930s.[120] While medical research increasingly preoccupied their professors, not many students actually pursued a postgraduate research degree. Beginning in 1920 the University of Toronto MD degree was awarded one year after the receipt of the bachelor's degree in medicine, upon the submission of an approved thesis embodying original research. But in 1929 the MD degree was withdrawn as a form of graduate work (some twenty had been awarded by 1927) and it subsequently took the place of the Bachelor of Medicine degree, as in other jurisdictions in North America. The reality of medical licensing in the province was that as far as the leaders of the medical profession were concerned the only necessary qualification for hospital and teaching positions was a fellowship in the Royal College of Physicians and Surgeons in the United Kingdom. This license was obtained not from the universities but by passing examinations set by the college. During the 1920s those with undergraduate degrees understandably set their sights on passing these examinations, not on enrolling in a post-graduate university program in medicine. In spite of the increase in medical specialization at the level of professorial research, interest in post-graduate research degrees in medicine was generally not strong between the wars.[121]

Enrolment in medicine increased dramatically immediately after the Great War, rising at Toronto from 828 in 1918–19 to 1,284 in 1919–20; but then it steadily decreased until it was 798 in 1924–5. There it stayed – fluctuating between seven and nine hundred – throughout the interwar years. The onset of the Depression in 1929 witnessed no decrease in numbers: in fact, at Toronto enrolment increased from 746 in 1928–9 to 846 in 1931–2 (see Fig. 13.4). Very few of these students were women. At no point in the period did they exceed the eighty-eight women who enrolled in the peak year of 1920–1: the average number of female medical students at Toronto in the twenty-one years from 1918–19 to 1938–9 was seventy-one, with numbers decreasing slightly in the early years of the Depression as financial and domestic pressures on women grew. At the University of Western Ontario, where numbers were far fewer, the rate of increase was much greater: the 113 in 1921–2 became 140 students by 1928–9 and reached 229 by 1931–2, no doubt largely because of the organizational changes and improvements to facilities that took place at Western in the 1920s.[122]

Ontario medical graduates were overwhelmingly Christian as well as male. In his biography of Frederick Banting, Michael Bliss draws attention to the 'genteel anti-semitism' that existed at the University of Toronto between the wars, noting at one point Banting's observation to his secretary that, 'You know, if I'd known so many Jews had diabetes, I

FIGURE 13.4

Total and female enrolment in medicine, University of Toronto, 1921–38

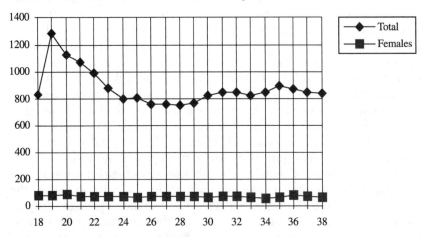

SOURCE: de Pencier, 'Enrolment of Women'

don't think I'd ever have gone into it.'[123] This was, as Bliss also notes, Banting at his worst – for on other occasions he proved to be selfless and magnanimous. But such remarks were part of a more general pattern of racial prejudice. In major Canadian universities Jews were enrolled in numbers greater than their proportion in the Canadian population.[124] Yet the figures misrepresent the reality: one is faced, for example, with J.J.R. Macleod's forthright letter to Robert Falconer in 1928, concerning his replacement ('Samson Wright is a Jew and may not be acceptable on that ground')[125] and the fact that at the University of Toronto Jewish women studying physiotherapy were not permitted to fulfill their required course in clinical training at the Toronto General Hospital.[126] By the 1930s the presence of Jews had become a subject of ongoing discussion at the highest levels of the University of Toronto's administration. The university's registrar referred in correspondence with the new President H.J. Cody to the 'Hebrew problem which has been giving you so much trouble lately,' and he began to assemble a yearly statistical breakdown of Jewish enrolment at the provincial university. Cody received a number of letters from members of the public complaining of the number of Jews at the University of Toronto – some teaching Marxism, others treating patients. Cody himself wrote in 1934 to one member of the public, General C.F. Winter, of his personal priorities in these times of financial restraint: 'Frankly I think that when a student has no means at all he should not attend the University but rather should remain out until he can earn money sufficient to pay his way. This has always been the way in which the people of our stock have acted in the past. Our chief difficulties in the present time have come from a small group of [the] Hebrew race.'[127]

Between the First and Second World Wars, Ontario's universities gradually came to recognize the extent to which public and politician alike now expected them to serve broad public needs. Institutional and curricular developments in commerce, engineering, and medicine were only the most obvious reflections of this shift in direction. These changes were important, and with hindsight the historian of the late twentieth century can properly portray their advent and note their symbolic value as signs of things to come. Yet to leave the matter without qualification would misrepresent the reality of everyday academic life in Ontario universities between the wars. One needs to provide an important reminder: that the nineteenth-century liberal arts orientation of the university, with its origins in religious affiliation, was one that persisted beyond the Great War into the era of secularized academic life. As important as it was, and despite the high public profile it enjoyed, the scholarship of utility nonetheless still constituted for many within the academy a form of intrusion. The fact is that when one looks at the areas of study most students chose between the wars, the university in Ontario remained dominated by faculties of arts. The relatively small size and limited resources of outlying universities and the college structure of the University of Toronto imposed by the university federation of the 1880s permitted a continued strength of the liberal arts ideal even as the idea of social utility continued to enlarge its sphere of influence in academic life.

14

The Piper and the Tune

Stepchildren are sometimes abused, especially when their acceptance into family life is based on self-interest rather than love. Between the wars in Ontario, the academic stepchild of the exchequer was watched closely by its public guardians. When professors or students got out of line they were usually reprimanded by stern, self-appointed masters of public morality and academic rectitude. University leaders, especially those of the provincial university, were placed in a particularly delicate position when citizens or politicians mounted crusades to discipline or to sack errant members of their academic community. The financial requirements of the modern university had made it necessary for them to seek aid from the state in order to survive and grow. Now they began to discover that the security they coveted carried with it a potentially heavy price in an age increasingly dominated by the culture of utility, and when political leadership was coming to depend on votes obtained in what in 1922 the American journalist and social critic Walter Lippmann called the 'pseudo-environment' of public opinion and perception.

Universities such as Western or Queen's were relatively protected from state encroachments on academic freedom because of their status as relatively small, independent institutions that had only recently begun to seek state support. This could not be said of the University of Toronto, for many believed that a provincial university should come, when and if necessary, under provincial scrutiny and control. Historian and civil servant E.E. Stewart has portrayed the interwar years as the 'quiet hour' in the history of higher education in Ontario. But they were quiet mainly for provincial civil servants, required to deal neither with problems attendant upon major expansion in the universities of the province nor with the consequences of recorded votes on university affairs in the provincial legislature. As we have seen, no great expansion of enrolment occurred; and no such vote took place between 1917 and 1950.[1] Most of the province's professors, it is true, went quietly about their academic tasks. Few were entirely satisfied with their socio-economic status, much less their salaries, and even fewer risked their positions in order to defend their freedom in academic matters. A few did, though, and as a result their activities ultimately meant that these were not quite the years of untroubled silence that Stewart's generalization suggests.

The temper of the times following the Bolshevik Revolution, the Winnipeg General Strike, the challenge to the two-party system (symbolized by the dramatic rise to national prominence of the Progressive Party of Canada), and the general sense of social dislocation that followed the Great War did not require wholesale professorial revolt in order for public fears to be expressed that all was not as it should be in academe. One errant and vocal professor was usually sufficient to create major public controversy. President Robert Falconer and the Reverend H.J. Cody (a member of the University of Toronto's board of governors since 1918 and its chairman from 1923 to 1932) discovered this very quickly whenever one of their professors was seen to step out of line. At times they even found themselves under attack. The so-called quiet years in Ontario higher education were in fact often controversial ones.

On Academic Freedom

In May 1919 R. Bruce Taylor, principal of Queen's University, addressed the graduating students of the University of Manitoba. It must have been a rather tense occasion. The Winnipeg General Strike was just over a week old. The city had virtually closed down when tens of thousands of workers left their jobs, and political life in the community was deeply divided between pro- and anti-strike forces. No members of the Manitoba academic community were leaders of the general strike, and only a very few would have sympathized with the workers' claims.[2] Even the local police force and fire-fighters had joined the picket lines, so this was scarcely the most hospitable moment for a visiting speaker from Ontario to speak, as Taylor did, about the necessity of safeguarding freedom of expression and the right to dissent from the prevailing assumptions of society.

Taylor chose to avoid making any direct reference to the chaos of social relations that then engulfed the local community. But in this first, strident spring of the post-war era, he nevertheless found himself responding to the storm signals of the dawning age. Academic freedom, like industrial relations, he stated, was inescapably linked to the increasing role of the state in modern society. First centred in conflict between church and state and later in that between science and religion, such freedom had come to be located, in his words, in 'matters economic and social.' Queen's University, he said, greatly valued the liberty that the beginnings of state aid had made possible. But this liberty was not to be purchased without a price: 'if the State support a University, is the State entitled to control the type of teaching within the university? Will the administration of a University be likely to depend for its academic existence upon the whims of the Legislature?'[3]

In choosing the subject of his convocation address, Taylor was probably less inspired by any specific examples of Canadian infringements on academic freedom than by several sensational cases that had risen to public prominence in the United States in the late nineteenth and early twentieth centuries.[4] By the beginning of the Great War, earlier attacks by radical academic reformers on individual capitalists or by figures of established authority on individual radicals had broadened in America to include condemnations of the whole ethos of either business or academic culture. To this, once America joined the war effort in 1917, were added accusations of disloyalty directed towards those who preached pacifism or isolationism. Nothing more clearly exemplified the nearly paranoid division of opinion by war's end than the publication of Thorstein Veblen's *The Higher Learning in America* (1918), a devastating and strident critique of the increasing domination of higher education by a crass, predatory, and crudely utilitarian business culture, whose ethos, in Veblen's iconoclastic view, was one of 'quietism, caution, compromise, collusion and chicane.'[5] It seems highly likely that Principal Taylor was aware of Veblen's damning analysis of the way in which the structure of American universities was coming to resemble the hierarchical and bureaucratic forms of business management that threatened to reduce the status of the scholar to that of a factory employee. Like Veblen, he too noticed the alienation of the contemporary professor and observed that 'behind it all there is the sense that administration tends to become political and to be infected with the carefulness of politics.'[6]

The problem of academic freedom in a business-oriented world was more easy to address than to solve. Taylor identified the crucial nexus of twentieth-century academic development. 'It is universally recognized,' he told his audience, '... that education is the business of the State.' Yet how, he wondered, could academic institutions

develop under the wing of the State and yet maintain their academic freedom? The constant danger is that the administration becomes so cautious and conservative and temporizing in its nature that it loses sympathy with freshness and originality of view. Instead of being the sponsor of fresh knowledge it takes itself so seriously as a branch of the Civil Service that it has no kindly welcome for the inconvenient and original thinker. One cannot but be sensible of the fact that in many of the Universities of the States there is a broad and apparently broadening chasm between the administrative and the educational branches ... There are signs not a few that within a democracy there may be a real intellectual tyranny and under the State supervision of education an encouragement of the thing that is only safe and tractable. In the matters of the mind officialism is the enemy, whether it be in the form of a University administration that is only politic or of a general educational system which has lost the human touch its founder intended it to have.[7]

These were courageous words to speak in Winnipeg that particular May, ones that carried elements of Veblen's critique if not his tone. They were prescient ones as well. Taylor fell back, it is true, on the notion that if professors remained responsible citizens and moral exemplars they would not only be able to exercise their freedom but also be forces for social stability. But his fear and his criticism of the potential of the universities' rich new patron – the modern state – to instil academic self-censorship and political quietude must have reduced his audience mute. Within a matter of weeks, the full apparatus of the Canadian state was forcefully and successfully used to suppress the Winnipeg strikers' brief new dawn.[8]

Principal Taylor was not alone among Ontario university leaders in fearing possible encroachments upon academic freedom by the lengthening arm of the secular state. President E.E. Braithwaite of Western University addressed the spring convocation of his own university on the subject, alarmed – as Taylor had probably been – at accounts in the *Nation* and the *New Republic* of the attacks on American academic life by state legislatures and boards of regents. He, too, fixed upon the socioeconomic rather than religious or scientific realms as the area most vulnerable to external attack. He did not fear that professors might be subject to persecution over the higher criticism or materialistic views of society – at least he did not mention them – but he did single out the possible plight of the professor of political economy, concluding that when such a scholar 'must make his conclusions conform to the ideas of the capitalists who may occupy a seat on his governing board, the usefulness of the institution is seriously impaired.' He mentioned no local instance of such self-censorship, but did warn that in Canada 'well authenticated cases could be cited where expressions of opinion on the part of the visitors to academic halls have been fiercely resented by trustees whose own position has not been too highly complimented by the speakers.'[9] President Braithwaite's fears of 1919 were prophetic, for when the first major post-war attack on an Ontario university professor occurred, two years later, it was a professor of political economy who was at the centre of the controversy. In early December, 1921, Reuben Wells Leonard, now a Colonel, wrote to President Falconer of Toronto to complain about the dangerous scholarly activities of Professor R.M. MacIver, a member of his department of political economy.[10]

Leonard was an irascible millionaire philanthropist who was on the boards of governors of both Toronto and Queen's, and he was as reactionary in his politics as he was conditional in his philanthropy. In the wry words of Robert Falconer's biographer: 'To describe Colonel Reuben Wells Leonard as a conservative would be to understate his devotion to the established order of society.'[11] Having just read Professor MacIver's 1919 book *Labor in the Changing World*,[12] Leonard was alarmed, and told Falconer so. 'I am of the opinion,' he wrote, 'that if, for any reason, it is considered necessary by the board to have such teaching in the Provincial University as is indicated in MacIver's book, then we should be honest with ourselves and true to the trust imposed upon us by the people of Ontario and establish a Chair of Political Anarchy and Social Chaos, so that the people of Ontario, who pay for the University, and the students who take the courses, will know what is being taught under its proper name, instead of under the name of "Political Economy."' To increase pressure on the university's president, Leonard sent a copy of his letter to H.J. Cody of the board of governors, the Anglican cleric who had become the chief power broker in Ontario higher education.[13]

Falconer responded to Leonard's criticism by letter – and at length. Political economists, he noted, would for some time be at the storm centre of university life in Britain and North America because the problems they examined and the theories they put forward concerned the changing conditions of society. *Labor in the Changing World,* which Falconer had read carefully, was not in his view subversive. The best place for intellectual radicalism, he told Leonard, was the university, for extreme views were invariably tempered within the academy by challenges from colleagues and students, the latter scarcely as docile or as accepting of received opinion as Leonard seemed to believe. Finally, the president concluded, his long experience with matters of declared belief within universities, dating from the days of conflict between orthodox Christians and Darwinian critics, led him to believe that 'the only safe and sound position was to allow men to state their views and maintain them in the Universities under the criticism of the world at large.' Besides, Falconer told the angry philanthropist, young men 'grow more conservative as they grow older.'[14]

Leonard was not mollified: 'To my mind,' he wrote Cody a few days later in correspondence that carried with it a copy of Falconer's letter, 'it is a great pity that the seething brain waves of these academic thinkers could not be tempered with some practical knowledge and experience of human nature through the handling of men, which these people who do all the writing seldom possess. How much attention Toronto University is bound to pay to the Marxians and other cranks and lunatics is, to my mind, very questionable.'[15]

R.M. MacIver was no crank or lunatic, much less a 'Marxian.' The son of a prosperous and pious merchant from the island of Lewis in the Outer Hebrides, and educated at the University of Edinburgh and Oriel College, Oxford, by 1921 the thirty-nine-year-old MacIver had already established a solid reputation as a serious scholar.[16] He had published three books and a dozen articles in prominent academic and popular journals.[17] *Labor in the Changing World* had been preceded by publication of his doctoral thesis, *Community – A Sociological Study*, in 1917, and at the time of Colonel Leonard's charge that MacIver was a 'Marxian' lunatic his path-breaking book *The Elements of Social Science* had just appeared.[18] MacIver's career at Toronto between 1915 and 1927, and subsequently at Columbia University in the United States, would provide ample evidence that this pioneer of Anglo-American sociology was not the kind of prophetic voice from which violent revolutions are made. Nevertheless, while not working within the Marxist tradition he recognized – and stated bluntly in *Community* – that 'class distinction based on the possession of income-yielding property' was an intractable problem which had, as yet, resisted 'democratic criticism.' 'No openminded observer,' he noted at one point in the middle of his lengthy book, could fail '... to observe on the one hand the passionate devotion to this order of the privileged classes or on the other the no less passionate revolt of the unprivileged. Such an antithesis, where it is stripped of all modifying factors, inevitably breeds revolution.'[19] These views, especially when accompanied by sympathy for the labouring classes, were bound to infuriate men such as Colonel Leonard.

MacIver's writings were not, however, the only reasons for Leonard's fears that the Toronto professor was a source of potential social unrest. His academic duties at Toronto required him to be involved in establishing and developing ways social service could be studied and conducted, and the very nature of the historical evolution of social service involved some sort of direct relationship to the well-established contemporary movement for social reform. MacIver accordingly became involved with activities of the Workers Educational Association almost from the moment of his arrival in Canada, and by 1917 he was one of several faculty members at the University of Toronto – such as C.R. Fay and Gilbert Jackson – dedicated to a social reconstruction that would enhance the dignity and power of labouring men.[20] By 1922 Leonard's letters, probably viewed by Falconer at first as merely meddling, threatened to precipitate a crisis in which the freedom of academic expression at the University of Toronto was at stake.[21]

Since Leonard's accusations had become increasingly strident and showed no signs of abating, Falconer decided that the time had come to attempt to pre-empt further interference. Accordingly, he called a meeting of the Toronto academic community at convocation hall, and delivered his first and only formal statement on the nature and meaning of academic freedom. One can only speculate whether Colonel Leonard was present. He may well have been, since this was an irregular meeting of great moment and Leonard was a member of the university's board of governors. Certainly, many of the professors and a good number of students were gathered to hear what Falconer had to say. It was Valentine's Day.

Falconer began disarmingly enough by discussing his subject in the context of the contemporary state of academic freedom in Great Britain and the United States. The issue was not a matter of great consequence in Britain because of the traditional and continuing alarm with which British academics greeted 'any attempt by a government office in London to increase its authority over their internal affairs.'[22] This could not be said, however, of American institutions of higher education, especially those newer universities of the Western states whose supporters among the public little appreciated the historic independence of the traditional university. There, political partisanship had infiltrated the government of universities. 'President after President has been discharged without warning and often most unjustly, because he happened to be on the wrong side of politics or had fallen out with a stubborn and powerful Superintendent of Education who had greater influence.' Even private foundations had been affected by the criticisms of outside influences, such as 'the reactionary views of graduates' who were inclined to cling to a romanticized view of a superior and more stable academic past (the days when they were undergraduates) that had somehow given way to an inglorious and fractious present. 'Happy is that institution,' Falconer concluded his introductory section, 'which possesses friends broad-minded enough to recognise that their personal proclivities, desires, likes and dislikes should not determine the policies or the appointments of the university which their generosity has endowed.'

In much of his address, Falconer sought to establish a larger view. Academic freedom, he asserted, 'is in fact one chapter in the history of

Toleration, and is best understood as a phase of the general course of a people's development in liberty of thought.' The struggle for academic freedom was thus inextricably linked to the struggles and writings of people such as John Milton, Jeremy Taylor, John Locke, Lord Acton, and John Stuart Mill. 'We may fairly say that in our State at least,' said Falconer, quoting John Morley, '"within a single generation, a law of tolerance – not indifference, not scepticism, not disbelief, but one of those deep silent transformations that make history endurable – has really worked its way not merely into our statutes and courts of justice, but into manners, usage, and the common habits of men's minds."' In short, those who currently grumbled about threats to the social order emanating from the university in fact undermined the very freedom that they claimed was under threat. And in no institution was the notion of freedom, and with it truth, more treasured than in the university:

It exists for imparting ascertained knowledge and truth, for educating by this means those who shall become highly equipped citizens, many of them special-ised for professional service, and to produce and maintain those whose primary duty is to investigate truth and to extend the boundaries of knowledge. By its very nature the university may become a focus of unrest and disquietude for the timid, for unless in it truth is being enthusiastically pursued and boldly faced it has lost its right to the glorious name: and men as a rule shrink from new views; they are too upsetting ... The genuine university man is too earnest in his search for truth to think that it is to be furthered by flippancy. He should have one fun-damental enthusiasm, that Truth does exist, that the human mind has arrived at what it is justified in calling truth, and that Science can devote herself unreserv-edly to the investigation not only of the material world, but of the whole life of man in the certainty that its reasonableness will be confirmed.

Falconer believed that rationality ultimately prevailed in the worlds of nature and humanity alike. Truth would emerge from the mutual exchange of freely held belief. Yet he was also well aware, like some of the most thoughtful minds of his generation, that people's actions were not solely driven by intellectuality or enlightened self-interest. Echoing the first line of *Human Nature in Politics* (1908), by English Fabian socialist and critic Graham Wallas, Falconer warned his audience – par-ticularly the members of his academic staff – that they must not forget 'that life is more than a bundle of intellectual propositions, the truth of which is demonstrable to all right thinking persons.' It is veiled in preju-dices, refracted by the many perspectives of social circumstance, pro-pelled by instincts and emotions, and portrayed by a consumer-driven daily press whose objective was not truth but to sell newspapers.[23] This was the psychological world of which Walter Lippmann had just written with telling effect in his new book *Public Opinion* (1922), inspired in part by the writings of Graham Wallas. It was a world in which the pictures of the world inside people's heads seldom conformed to the complex reality outside. It was a reality informed by the half-truths and special pleading of journalistic statement, one in which 'the essential problem was how to work out some successful relationship between misguided or apathetic "outsiders" and knowledgeable "insiders,"' one where 'men could rarely clearly see their interests or pursue them rationally.'[24]

Falconer went on to say that natural science could gain relative immunity from social controversy by its quest for the nature of the material conditions of the objective world of nature. Not so the social science of the university historian, or economist, or political scientist. Theirs was an academic pursuit of pluralistic truth invariably requiring some form of moral stance. It involved, therefore, not simply the disengaged intellect but also questions of 'temperament, mental quality, ingrained tradition' – in short 'the character of him who judges' the matters at hand. Because of this, the facts 'that appeal to one man do not appeal to another.' Theories of society put forward from the perspective of such disciplines could therefore only be semi-scientific, their public reception dependent 'chiefly upon the cast of mind of the reviewer.' And this was the case regardless of whether conservative or radical propositions were under scrutiny. Truth, in the complex and irrational world of public perception, had become multitudinous, a function of particularized social value, and the only way its many-sidedness could be discerned was to allow private truths to be pursued in the directions in which professors themselves were driven. No university true to its calling would allow itself to become the 'pontifical college' of any form of dogmatic doctrine. Truth, or truths, would out. Modern universities needed to be nothing less than 'self-governing Dominions inheriting assured truths which they test anew extending also the boundaries of knowledge.'[25]

Some in Falconer's audience would have recognized that they had just heard a polite but blunt rebuke to those who presumed to meddle in the complex question of the academic search for truth. Robert MacIver would clearly have felt comforted when Falconer declared that 'It is one of the most sacred privileges of a university that its professors shall enjoy academic freedom,' that 'a university in which professors are overawed by political, social, or sectarian influence cannot aspire to an honourable position in the Commonwealth of Learning,' or that 'we can measure the rank and stability of a university by the security given to a professor to pursue and expound his investigations without being compelled to justify himself to those who differ from him.' Besides, the possible subversion represented by the radical professor was more apparent than real. Twentieth-century students, Falconer said, taught to think and to decide for themselves, would not be seduced by academic dogmatists or by specious social theories.

Yet Falconer, educated in Germany as well as in Scotland, meant something quite precise, and circumscribed, when he spoke of the professor's freedom. In the German universities a clear distinction lay between the professor's freedom to pursue truth and his engagement in partisan politics, for the latter was not within the realm of academic freedom. The complicating factor in applying the subtle notion – that professors should somehow be intellectually of the political process but not, like normal citizens, in it – was that in the American academic context the original German notion of academic freedom had become transformed. Secure in the guarantee of freedom of expression by the First Amendment of their Constitution, American professors under pressure from outside attack because of their political or economic views came to use the notion of academic freedom as a means of protection as they engaged in partisan politics and public debate.[26] Falconer's problem was that as a university supported by the state, the University of Toronto was subject to the same outside pressures as its American counterparts, and therefore – unless he wished to deny the utility of the broad American definition in staving off attacks on professors from irate regents – there were cogent reasons why a similarly broad definition should be applicable in Canada.

His tactic was to meet this argument from expedience with the reply that it was equally expedient for a professor in a state university 'to take no active share in party-politics.'[27] His academic freedom would not be compromised; and his freedom as a citizen would be no more circumscribed than that of a judge or a senior civil servant. Professors, he reminded his audience, ceased to act solely for themselves as soon as they made public pronouncements; and it was understandable for the public to believe that such a professor's university backed his views. Moreover, the security and self-interest of the entire academic community was threatened whenever a single professor came under public attack.

Here in his speech Falconer guaranteed himself professorial attention. 'The thoughtless or ill disposed portion of the public,' the president warned, 'will find only too good grounds for an attack upon the whole university in the political utterances of the indiscreet or thoughtless professor; and a government might without giving any reason easily show its displeasure in such a way as to affect adversely the fortunes of the

institution and the financial positions of many guiltless and wiser colleagues. A professor in a State university cannot have it both ways, and
be both an effective member of the staff, in which he will enjoy full academic freedom, and at the same time be an exponent of party views or of
burning political questions. He should in the latter case take the risks of
other citizens and not rely on a security which by his injudicious action
he is endangering for others.'

Falconer had now taken his argument beyond warning, towards
implicit intimidation, for his appeal now went from expedience to naked
self-interest. Radical views on political questions, stated publicly, threatened the jobs of all – the timid and mediocre as well as the courageous
and brilliant. He concluded by outlining briefly his views on the responsibilities of governing bodies, who as trustees should recognize that 'a
university whose professors were chosen by popular vote would soon
lose its freedom, and its prestige would disappear were their liberty to be
dependent upon political issues ...' He had warned against interference
in academic affairs sufficiently in his address effectively to have
silenced Colonel Leonard, whose crusade against MacIver now came to
an end. MacIver later went on to become head of the department of
political economy at the university and, after his move to Columbia University in 1927, one of the most prolific and influential social scientists
in the United States. To the end of his life he maintained a strong interest
in academic freedom.[28]

Perhaps the greatest significance of the Leonard-MacIver dispute, and
of Falconer's discourse on academic freedom, was the lasting effect it
may have had on those who were at the time on the fringes of the controversy, not at its centre. Falconer's stark declaration that impolitic or
extreme utterance by a single errant professor threatened the very livelihood of all and invited state intervention in academic affairs was, at the
very least, an invitation to voluntary political quietude on the University
of Toronto campus.[29] It tacitly encouraged collegial peer pressure in the
direction of academic conformity to prevailing social norms. It gave
implicit sanction to sarcastic criticism in the senior common room of the
wayward, or eccentric, or publicity-seeking professor, the kind who
stooped to journalism in order to awaken a sleeping or complacent public. It gave practical legitimacy, as similar presidential warnings had
done in the United States, to 'the assumption within the academic walls
of a posture of neutrality on controversial matters,' so that in the classroom the professor increasingly 'used his professional competence and
his scientific knowledge of the facts to present controversial questions in
such a way that his own neutrality protected the students from indoctri-
nation.'[30]

In this way the ideal of objectivity became, in effect, a kind of political stance, a means of practicing a form of self-censorship while its exponents proclaimed – and honestly believed – that their studied silence made possible the conditions for pursuing a morally and politically neutral truth. Controversies concerning academic freedom between the wars centred around one or two outspoken professors who insisted on letting their views be known. But how many more kept silent because they did not wish to be seen as too radical or unpatriotic, or risk the disfavour of their colleagues or their deans, or lose their jobs? With a few notable exceptions, the University of Toronto professoriate was a quiet group that taught and did research apart from the din of public controversy and debate. Falconer's address on academic freedom provided them with reasons for doing so, for it implicitly testified to the ways the culture of the university itself could legitimize some ideas and behaviour and marginalize others. In doing so it helped set the boundaries of acceptable professorial belief and the public expression of it by faculty members at the University of Toronto between the wars.

Forms of Subversion

Robert Falconer's tactful defence of academic freedom worked in the short term. For a while, public accusations of leftward leaning in the provincial university died down. Nevertheless, certain people and institutions continued to act as public watchdogs, guarding against activities at the provincial university that might compromise the virtue of the citizens of Toronto. Within a year they began to voice their concerns not simply about the activities of professors but also about those of students. In February 1924 *Acta Victoriana*, the student newspaper of Victoria College, noted that the *Financial Post* had been particularly 'zealous of late in its tracking down of disguised Bolshevism in the university.'[31]

Beginning late in 1923 the *Financial Post*, reflecting the patriotic sentiments of its editor, Colonel J.B. Maclean, began to wage a campaign in its influential pages against subversive activities at the University of Toronto. 'The foreign campaign ... against Canadianism and Capitalism in the colleges, and particularly in Toronto University,' went one *Post* account, 'keeps up.'[32] Maclean's newspaper feared that students at the University of Toronto were subjected to a barrage of subversive speakers, sponsored by equally threatening organizations. The Student Christian Movement (viewed by the *Post* as a 'more or less immoral youth movement'), the Workers Educational Association, the League for Industrial Democracy, and other such groups had – said the *Post* – sent radical and foreign speakers to Hart House to preach revolutionary communism in wood-panelled rooms intended for silent study and reflection. For his part, Robert Falconer attempted to make light of the charges. 'Our students are really a most conservative and homogeneous lot,' he told the *Star Weekly*. 'There may be troubles with foreign students in American universities. We have none of that here.' The *Star Weekly* reporter was satisfied with Falconer's defence: 'He showed statistics of enrolment. There were scarcely 200 non-English students out of 5,000.' For his part, Colonel Maclean, when interviewed for the same article, disclaimed any attempt to discredit the University of Toronto. His objection, he said, was solely to the intrusion of 'insidious propagandists' who arrived to speak at Hart House under false colours, and whose 'sole purpose [was] to breed sedition and disrupt the British Empire.' Those who doubted his views, he said, should encourage officials of the Mounted Police, as he had done, to search Hart House – including its cellars – for evidence of subversive activities.[33]

The basis for the bombastic charges of Colonel Maclean was that room in Hart House had indeed been afforded to dissident groups and speakers in the autumn of 1923. Paul Blanchard of the New York-based League of Industrial Democracy had spoken to Toronto students in November, and had been seen to encourage 'those interested in the question of industry' to stay around after the meeting. Nineteen young men did so. Denials by University of Toronto officials that the League for Industrial Democracy had any form of official status or sanction at the university, and the statement by a 'distinguished labour leader in Toronto' that one of its main speakers, while unquestionably anti-capitalist, could probably not even 'be described as Socialistic in the commonly accepted meaning of the term,' did little to diminish the outrage of the *Post*. A *Varsity* reporter asked a representative of the league for a clear statement of its aims. It received the following declaration: 'We are an Educational Society existing to promote a social order resting on production for use and not for profit. We believe that this end can be best attained through social ownership with a larger measure of self-government in industry, as opposed to the autocracy of absentee owners.'[34] This, to the *Financial Post*, was more than sufficient evidence to justify its strident campaign. It continued throughout 1924. 'The Post not only has no desire to suppress sincere radicalism,' said one of its editorials early in 1925, 'but thinks the natural radicalism of students a very good symptom – the radicalism that produced Dr Banting, or Mackenzie King.'[35]

With the limits of radicalism so seriously circumscribed by major public opinion makers, members of the academic staff such as R.M. MacIver continued to be objects of suspicion. By the end of 1924, Toronto political economist Harold Innis was sufficiently worried by the threat to academic freedom that he attempted privately to get the *Grain Growers' Guide,* no friend of the *Financial Post,* to enter the controversy. The *Guide*'s associate editor chose to remain outside the Toronto maelstrom, declaring that he 'would rather see [MacIver] in a Canadian university, even though he has to put up with a little occasional sniping from reactionary organs, than take part in a fight which might have unfavorable results for him personally ...'[36]

There were good reasons for Innis to worry, and not only because of Maclean's attack upon MacIver. The 1906 University Act had sought to eliminate political meddling in university affairs by strengthening the position and powers of the president and establishing a board of governors that could act as a buffer between the presidency and the Ministry of Education. But the Cody Commission of 1921, while holding out the promise of potential financial security for the universities of Ontario, had not done so without qualifying the conditions of its generosity. No university that accepted state funding would be able to create an academic faculty or construct a building without the permission of cabinet. And the sense of protection to the university afforded by the creation of the board of governors in 1906 was reversed by the wording and the tone of the 1921 commission's recommendation 'That the Provincial University continue to be controlled by a Board of Governors, and that such Board be truly representative of the whole Province.' The further suggestion that there should in future be a regular 'University Day' in the Legislature, in which 'the Heads of the various Universities shall appear to report on their work,' indicates clearly that this shift of tone from one of liberation to one of control was deliberate and reflected the prevailing political mood.[37]

As one raised in the Baptist tradition, Harold Adams Innis was particularly concerned with the role of the state in society. He may well have been aware that a significant proportion of the correspondence that crossed his president's desk reflected the increasing willingness of the agents of the provincial state to diminish the distance between political concerns and academic affairs. A good deal of Robert Falconer's time and energy was spent in the 1920s addressing or deflecting correspondence that, in Premier Drury's office, was filed under 'Premier's suggestions,' on such diverse matters as the composition of the medical faculty, university extension work, convocation, appointments, promotions and retirements, powers of the board of governors and senate, alumni representation, and so forth.[38] When G. Howard Ferguson replaced Drury as premier in 1923, the formal and informal suggestions increased and became more strident. His frequent written messages to the university president reflected his public proclamation – tactless yet revealing – that 'I am the boss of the Toronto University.'[39] Moreover, the appointment of his political crony H.J. Cody to the chairmanship of the University of Toronto's board of governors in 1923 (when B.E. Walker became chancellor) gave him a loyal, powerful, and obedient voice in the university's inner councils. In this way, when political economist C.R. Fay was thought to be preaching Marxist doctrines in 1925, Ferguson could write to Cody: 'Appropos [sic] of talk the other night about the spread of communism, I am enclosing you [sic] a clipping from the *Financial Post* of Nov. 27.' The clipping contained what purported to be two or three sentences from a speech by Fay. 'If it is true that he holds these views,' Ferguson continued, 'and gives expression to them, I do not think he is the sort of man that should be on the staff. Surely our Educational Institutions should not be expressing approval, much less encouraging the activities of the communist.'[40] Similarly, when another political economist, Gilbert Jackson, had earlier assigned *The Communist Manifesto* as reading for the daughter of a person Ferguson described as 'an outstanding businessman,' the Premier wrote to Falconer: 'I think you will agree that not only should these be exterminated, but if it is true that members of the staff either encourage or condone this kind of doctrine, they should be summarily dismissed.'[41] For his part, Falconer noted that Jackson was in fact a vociferous anti-Marxist, that *The Communist Manifesto* was no longer (as Ferguson had claimed) on the list of banned publications in Canada, that Jackson's use of it was in a course that covered the full range of economic history, and that after attending the course several radicals had in fact abandoned Marxism.[42] Ferguson backed off.

There was a good deal of post-war 'bolshie hunting' in these and other such attempts to root out radicalism in academic life, but there was more than this. Behind the wiliness of a politician as astute as Ferguson lay the power of public opinion. It is clear that few members of the public held any brief for the university as an institution independent of public control, and Ferguson knew that, if anything, his political capital would increase if he were seen to be firmly at the helm of the provincial educational apparatus. It was only the university officials, not the public, that he had to mollify even as he directed them. A sign that public attitudes and Premier Ferguson were at one in viewing the university as the servant of the state can be seen in the many requests Ferguson received from members of the public for special favours relating to educational services and the willingness with which Ferguson obliged them by acting on their behalf.

Thus, a student was turned down for the University of Toronto's medical school because his marks were too low. He had a member of the provincial parliament write to Ferguson on his behalf, saying that 'Dr Kellam who is President of the Ontario Medical Board states that he should not be blocked on the subjects.' The MPP appealed to Ferguson's 'elastic attitude on these affairs' and asked if the premier 'can arrange for this chap to be admitted to the University.' The chairman and the secretary of the Ontario Ministry of Education special revising board subsequently informed Ferguson by memorandum that the board 'has not granted, and would not feel justified in granting,' standing to an applicant with such a poor record (he received only 26% in algebra and 38% in French composition, for example). Ferguson wrote to the MPP a month later, 'I had the matter up before the Special Revising Committee, who went fully into it, and I am glad to be able to advise you that he has been granted standing in Upper School Algebra and French Composition.'[43] Whether or not the rehabilitated applicant was accepted into the University of Toronto's medical school, or bothered to improve his mathematical skills, is not known.

Similarly, the managing editor of the Toronto *Globe*, Harry W. Anderson, wrote Ferguson in 1930 – as minister of education rather than as premier – to obtain admittance of the son of a *Globe* executive into the University of Toronto Schools. Ferguson's reply stated, properly, that the university's school was not under the jurisdiction of the Department of Education. But, he added, 'I know the Principal very well and those in authority.' A very long waiting list existed, he warned; but 'I will, however, use my best efforts' on behalf of the boy's mother. A week later, the distraught mother received a letter from J.G. Althouse undertaking to admit the boy into the university schools upon completion of his current studies, and promising that 'his admission to this School will be without the usual ordeal of a competitive examination.'[44]

Every Ontario premier between the wars received many such letters of request. Moral judgments aside, one can readily understand how a harried political leader could move unthinkingly from getting mediocre students accepted into medical school to seeking the suspension of a radical professor. One suspects that for the twentieth-century politician in the age of 'normalcy,' such public solicitations, whether from irate mothers or outraged newspaper moguls, were seen as but larger or smaller waves in a rising tide of unrestrained democracy.

At the end of the 1926–7 academic session, Professor George Wrong decided to retire, after thirty years of service to the University of Toronto. His replacement was one of his former students, Frank H. Underhill.[45] The appointment did little to diminish the suspicion of politicians or public that the provincial university continued to be a den of ideological iniquity.

Although an Ontarian and an alumnus of the University of Toronto (BA Honours in classics 1911), Frank Underhill was in a sense an outsider upon his return as a member of staff. Two years at Balliol College, Oxford, four years of service in the Great War, and almost a decade of teaching at the University of Saskatchewan had separated him from his years as the most distinguished Toronto honours student of his generation.[46] It was Underhill the undergraduate who was still in Wrong's mind when he sought the advice of Walter Murray, president of the University of Saskatchewan, on the question of Underhill's suitability as his successor. 'My doubt in respect to him,' confessed Wrong, 'is whether he is not too quiet and retiring to be an effective leader in such a community as this. By leadership I mean a person who would make his influence felt as a factor in the life of the University.'[47] The old professor knew very little of his former student's intellectual growth.

A decade in the Canadian West had transformed Frank Underhill. He was wounded in the Great War, but emerged from it still an Ontario nationalist with strong imperial sympathies.[48] In the early 1920s Underhill was a direct witness to the fate of prairie political and economic grievance, and he became increasingly dissatisfied with the 'Tweedledum-Tweedledee' ideologies of the nation's traditional political parties and the parochial nature of much of the country's nationalist expression. A voracious reader, while at Oxford he had worked his way through many of the late Victorian and Edwardian generation's books on the means by which the British and American liberal traditions might adapt to an increasingly collectivist society but not lose sight of their ethical aims. Among these books had been *Liberalism* (1911) by the British sociologist L.T. Hobhouse, and *The Promise of American Life* (1909), by the American Progressive social critic Herbert Croly. Sparked by annoyance and frustration over the evidence of drift and lack of mastery in Canadian politics in the early 1920s, he devoted most of the academic year 1924–5 to reading scholarly and journalistic work on the relationship between the economic and political processes, and he was especially impressed with those of Fabian or Progressive historians such as R.H. Tawney and Charles Beard. Such works gave him the intellectual capital and historical perspective necessary to transform his sense of general dissatisfaction with society into an articulate critique of its underlying socio-economic structures. His reading of Walter Lippmann's *Public Opinion*, with its rejection of human rationality as the basis for political judgment and its criticism of 'the politics of the herd,' increased his suspicion of many of the accepted socio-political nostrums of his day. A half-sabbatical leave spent in Toronto beginning in December 1925, during which he was troubled by the city's high cost of living, its increasingly materialistic ways, and the smugness of its citizens, provided Underhill with an object-lesson in the practical relevance of his academic reading. In this way, this heir to the Enlightenment tradition of sceptical rationalism was propelled by the rigour of his own intellect to become the most trenchant social critic of his age in Canada. By 1927 he was intellectually and emotionally set to become Canada's counterpart to Baltimore's great iconoclast H.L. Mencken.

Frank Underhill got himself into trouble almost as soon as he settled into his Toronto home on Walmer Road. Within a year he had antagonized the classics department by producing a written review of the classics program that criticized both its overemphasis on grammatical structure and the complacent aloofness and lack of imagination of its staff. (The review was meant to be a hymn of praise for the long career of Maurice Hutton, just retired.) And he was just as unhappy with the history department, to which he was attached. Underhill's views were decidedly anti-imperial by 1927, but History, as taught at Toronto, remained largely an extension of the British imperial adventure. The Canadian and American pasts, when taught at all, continued to be treated as colonial variants of the course of empire, and the idea of national self-determination for Canada tended to be dismissed as subversive of British imperial interests.[49] Moreover, Underhill's training as a classicist gave him a philosophical perspective that transformed the sweep of history into the history of ideas. W.P.M. Kennedy, a member of the Toronto history department, warned H.J. Cody about Underhill when he tried to prevent the Saskatchewan scholar's appointment: 'I have no idea of your plans; but I hear of Underhill. Underhill has a *distinguished* mind & is a *first class classical* scholar. He has absolutely no interest in history; & his whole enthusiasms are for philosophy ... He could *not begin to do* the Canadian Constitutional History, nor help our graduates. He is "bored" with Canadian History ... I am convinced that, as far as we are concerned, Underhill wd [sic] be no use, as he is *not an historian.*'[50] There was as much envy as insight in Kennedy's self-serving letter. But one thing was clear: Underhill was certainly no historian of the W.P.M. Kennedy mould, and his cast of mind found little intellectual sympathy in Baldwin House, whose historians narrated the nation's political evolution from empire to commonwealth safe from the hurly-burly of public political engagement.

Underhill found intellectual companionship with some of the more politically adventurous members on the University of Toronto staff, including professor of ancient history C.B. Sissons of Victoria College, professor of German Barker Fairley, economist Gilbert Jackson, educationalist Peter Sandiford, and religious scholar S.H. Hooke. All were closely associated with the left-leaning journal of opinion *Canadian Forum*, some from its founding in 1920. Underhill himself was invited to write for it. His first 'O Canada' column began to run in the March 1929 issue of the *Forum*. He was in trouble by the beginning of April. Although Underhill's column had been unsigned, it was well known that much of the magazine was written by members of the University of Toronto's staff. Underhill had already caught Premier Ferguson's eye in 1928, when someone reported to him that the recently appointed historian had given the impression in lectures 'that the British were as much if not more to blame for the war than the Germans.' Ferguson complained to Cody: 'I should feel compelled, if I thought it [such apparent disloyalty] was true, to take steps that might be thought drastic.'[51] Reacting now to Underhill's *Canadian Forum* heresies (the article associated the success of rum-running with the anti-Americanism of Canadian politicians), an angry and frustrated Premier Ferguson wrote again to Cody: 'this gentleman should be able to find opportunity for exploiting his talents on the job he is being paid for ... Some day when the estimates are brought over here I will be tempted to tick off a number of salaries of some men who seem to take more interest in interfering in matters of public policy and public controversy than they do in the work for which they are paid. I am writing you this personally as I think you should look into it.'[52] Ferguson's views were shared by many, including members of the university's board of governors.[53] Thus began a decade and more of almost constant antagonism between political and university authorities and Frank Underhill.

Central to the history of academic freedom between the wars, Underhill was a feisty and colourful weathercock whose movements can be used to gauge the winds of acceptable dissenting opinion. Yet it is as important to keep an historical eye on the activities of the owners of the barn as it is on the rooster shifting with the winds at its peak. Ferguson's threats to professorial livelihoods, as predictable as they were blustering, are less revealing than is his account of the reason for his annoyance – that his attention was 'called at such frequent intervals to the activities of members of the University staff.' It is difficult to escape the conclusion that Ferguson acted at times as the harried if unwitting agent of those in the business and journalistic communities, such as Colonel Reuben Wells Leonard and Colonel John Bayne Maclean, whose power and influence no premier could afford to ignore. Newspapers of the day were usually the privately owned fiefdoms of business tycoons, and Colonel Maclean was one of the most powerful of them.

The culture of utility heralded the age of the consumer. Well over sixty per cent of the space in post-war newspapers consisted of advertising . Dependent on the advertising revenue and the goodwill of the business community and its leaders, newspapers increasingly competed for the audience of readers, whom they now saw as consumers. Flashy layouts, subscription cuts, more photographs, more comics, more prizes and contests, more women's features, but particularly massive coverage of local news items with human interest or a unique or bizarre angle – these sold newspapers.[54]

The public controversy surrounding Frank Underhill and others in the 1920s and 1930s must be seen in this broad context. Public bites professor was good citizenship; professor bites public was news. Such stories – ones about bolshie professors were as good as those about philandering ones – had all the titillating allure of limericks about bishops and actresses: rectitude gone wrong. They therefore served a double function. Accounts of professorial wrongdoing attracted readers, and therefore sold newspapers and advertising. Editorial coverage of such stories also served to censure the renegade academic. The clever newspaper owner or editor could achieve both aims by marshalling and shaping public opinion on the letters-to-the-editor page or by saturation and sensationalized coverage of the story itself. An extraordinary illustration of these powers of the press occurred in January 1931 when a letter signed and drafted by Frank Underhill (with classicist Eric Havelock) appeared on the editorial pages of the four main Toronto dailies. What made it so remarkable was that it contained the names of sixty-seven other members of the University of Toronto's usually stoic academic staff.

The issue was central to the British heritage in which most Canadian professors were reared: freedom of speech and assembly. An international and inter-denominational association named the Fellowship of Reconciliation, whose stated purpose was 'to create international, interracial, inter-class fellowship,' had been unable to secure rental of a meeting hall. Supporters learned that this was because members of the Toronto police force had convinced the owners of such halls that to let their property to the group meant that their facilities would be used as a front for communist activities.[55] Toronto membership in the fellowship included, however, several well-known clergymen (such as Salem Bland and G. Crossley Hunter) and a few professors (among them Henri Lasserre, professor of French at Victoria College). Particularly disturbing was that the effective prohibition of the fellowship's meetings was simply the latest example of what had become an enduring campaign by certain Toronto public officials to stifle political dissent in the city.

In 1928 the Communist Party of Canada significantly increased its activities in the Toronto area. Fearful of political violence (the memory of the Winnipeg General Strike was still very much on officials' minds),[56] Toronto's chief constable, Brigadier D.C. Draper (a Great War veteran), strongly supported by the city's three-member Police Commission, began his own crusade against what he perceived to be a foreign-inspired communist menace. In January 1929 all political meetings conducted in languages other than English were prohibited; that August, police used clubs to break up a crowd in Queen's Park. During it a professor of Oriental studies at the University of Toronto, Theophile J. Meek, was manhandled by police. A charge for damages by the professor was dismissed for lack of evidence, Meek replied with the accusation that the constitutional right of free speech was being denied, and the matter became one of public controversy in the press and on the university campus. A Hart House debate in November 1929 concluded by sustaining the motion that 'Toronto is deserving of her reputation for intolerance.' The vote was 211 to 56.

To those concerned with freedom of expression, the harassment of the Fellowship of Reconciliation in 1931 was a sign that the police commission had finally taken its anti-communist campaign too far: beyond the activities of the Communist Party itself into those of respectable religious groups with broad and peaceful concerns. At the end of November 1930 Frank Underhill wrote to J.W. Dafoe, the influential editor of the *Manitoba Free Press*, that he had contacted a few 'radically minded professors' at the university and that a petition in defence of 'free public expression of opinions, however unpopular or erroneous,' was in circulation.[57] On 15 and 16 January 1931 the petition appeared as a letter to the editors of Toronto's main newspapers. It read:

The attitude which the Toronto Police Commission has assumed towards public discussions of political and social problems, makes it clear that the right of free speech and free assembly is in danger of suppression in this city. This right has for generations been considered one of the proudest heritages of the British peoples, and to restrict or nullify it in an arbitrary manner, as has been the tendency in Toronto for the last two years, is short-sighted, inexpedient, and intolerable. It is the plain duty of the citizen to protest publicly against such curtailment of his rights, and, in doing so, we wish to affirm our belief in the free public expression of opinions, however unpopular or erroneous.[58]

The text of the letter was innocuous enough, but the list of signatures below it was explosive. This was no idle protest by a few disgruntled radicals. Convinced that the Toronto Police Commission had finally gone too far, and that the principles of freedom of speech and of assembly were at stake, the Toronto professoriate broke its usual political silence. A sizeable and influential number of the academic staff at the provincial university had signed the petition: twenty-four full professors, seventeen associate professors, eight assistant professors, and fifteen lecturers; the heads of the departments of philosophy, French, history, political economy, English, and biochemistry; the supervisor of studies in commerce and finance, the dean of residences, the registrar of Emmanuel College, the director of classical studies, the secretary of the council, the principal of University College, even the university registrar. They included the best-known and the most promising of what had come to be a distinguished staff in the arts and sciences, including Irene Biss, Vincent Bladen, Alexander Brady, George Sidney Brett, E.K. Brown, George Brown, Harry Cassidy, Donald Creighton, Barker Fairley, Eric Havelock, Harold Innis, Gilbert Jackson, Chester Martin, Edgar McInnis, Norman MacKenzie, A.F.W. Plumptre, E.J. Urwick, Malcolm Wallace – and of course Frank H. Underhill.[59]

The Toronto newspapers quickly took advantage of the letter, for this was a story of the 'professor bites public' variety, and therefore of lucrative sales value. The clashes between radical demonstrators and police in the late 1920s had already established rival editorial lines on the issue of public order versus freedom of speech and assembly. Joseph Atkinson's *Star* had consistently defended the rights to free speech and assembly, even for communists, and it had been dismissed by its main rival for readers and advertisers, the *Evening Telegram*, as 'the Big Brother of the Little Reds.' The *Globe*, in spite of the quotation from Junius on its mast-head warning of the danger to liberty of arbitrary submission to the Chief Magistrate, had taken its stance in defence of law, order, and Toronto's policing policy. Both the *Telegram* and the *Globe* had been strongly critical of the unfortunate Professor Meek in 1929. Upon the publication of the letter of 'the sixty-eight,' as they became known, those editorial stances stayed intact. The *Star* agreed with the professors' views. The *Globe* initially dismissed the letter (and by implication the professors) as ridiculous, but soon led the chorus of public condemnation and suggested that 'the tender-hearted bosh about the Bolsheviki ought to be stamped out once and for all.' After a four-day delay, the *Mail and Empire* ultimately agreed with the statement by the president of the Canadian Bank of Commerce, Sir John Aird, that the professors should 'stick to their knitting.' All the newspapers kept public interest high by publishing letters from their readers, usually outraged at the professors' actions. On the University of Toronto campus, however, a *Varsity* poll found eighty-three per cent of its student respondents to be in support of the sentiments expressed in the letter of the sixty-eight. The letter of protest had become part of an ongoing and escalating newspaper subscription war. In the process, professorial defenders of British liberties had been transformed, in the eyes of the *Telegram*, into defenders of the godless cult of communism.[60]

Reaction from university officials to the controversy varied. Falconer, who had been incapacitated during the previous summer with a severe heart condition, said little except to defend 'the British habit and practice of free speech' in public and to express his fears that 'the American spirit' of public intrusion into academic affairs was beginning to be witnessed in Ontario. Cody stressed to journalists that the published views of the professors did not reflect the position of the university. Chancellor Mulock was outraged at the embarrassment to the institution over which he presided, while Sir Joseph Flavelle, long a member of the board of governors, reminded George Wrong privately that 'every teacher in the University is a trustee for the institution, that no act of his resulting from hasty and unreflective impulse shall jeopardize the progress and development of the University.' For his part, Wrong reassured Flavelle with the thought that 'in the main the Universities of the western world are strongholds of Conservative thought and a steadying force in our society.'[61]

The new premier of the province, Howard Ferguson's successor George Henry, prudently remained silent and left the university to resolve the affair. Cody, Flavelle, and Mulock conferred privately on 21 January to set strategy for the full meeting of the board of governors called for the next day. That meeting – which went unrecorded – struck a committee of eight, including Vincent Massey and Dr F.W. Merchant (deputy minister of education), as well as Cody, Flavelle, and Mulock; its purpose was to produce a formal public pronouncement by the board. When it met at the chancellor's home on 27 January the decision was made that no public censure would be made of the professors but that President Falconer would be asked to confer privately with the central figures in order to prevent further instances of embarrassment to the university. On 12 February Cody sent Premier Henry the text of the board's resolution, which noted that, while those who had signed the letter had acted as private citizens, the document had come to be associated in the public mind with the university. 'This interpretation,' it concluded, 'has been given to the communication in question by sections of the Press and by many citizens, and causes the Board to fear that the public may regard it as an expression of opinion by the University of Toronto, therefore the Board deems it its duty publicly to state that such is not the fact.'[62] In decidedly less-than-provocative wording, the university had dissociated itself from the views of its errant professors. It did not fire them, as some members of the public, and the *Globe*, wished,[63] yet neither did it made any statement in defence of academic freedom.

Press and public had not, however, satisfied their thirst for campus scandal. Thus when an otherwise innocuous *Varsity* editorial on 24 February mentioned that many members of the academic community practiced 'practical atheism,' the *Globe* fulminated that if the article was correct 'the University of Toronto needs purging with unrestrained ruthlessness, or closing up altogether,' while the *Telegram* insisted that 'until the university has been purged of the mongers of atheism, it has ceased to be a worthy recipient of state funds.' The university's student administrative council swiftly suspended the student newspaper for the remainder of the academic year and sacked its editor. Copies of the *Globe* and the *Telegram* were burned on the Hart House grounds. In the Legislature, Liberal opposition member Harry Nixon echoed the *Telegram*'s view that perhaps state funding to the provincial university – still, alas, godless – should be reconsidered. Premier Henry, fully aware of the extent to which the matter had been sensationalized by the press, reacted in calm measure: 'Unfortunately at times parents of under-graduates occasionally find some theory being advanced which is not according to the accepted tenets. This does not work to the advantage of the University, and such an incident as last week, if allowed to go unanswered, might have a very serious effect on the attendance at Varsity. I trust, however, that the newspapers who have been seeking to fan the question will not be successful and that we have heard the last of the incident.'[64] The public and the newspapers were on the whole satisfied when early in April Robert Falconer reassured them that there was 'no cause for alarm,' for his university was 'a healthy place, morally, physically, spiritually and industrially,' populated by students who were of 'the finest stock on this continent.'[65]

The president's health was certainly not helped after he returned to duty, for yet another public controversy involving the university surfaced within weeks of the accusations of 'practical atheism.' This time Frank Underhill had made the headlines of Toronto's daily newspapers on a matter that involved federal political policy on imperial and economic affairs. During the federal election campaign of 1930, R.B. Bennett of the Conservatives had promised that, if elected, his party would drastically alter the national tariff in the direction of imperial preference in order to 'blast' Canada into the markets of the world. He had won the election, and as prime minister called for a Commonwealth Conference to be held early in 1931. In a piece entitled 'Canada in the Great Depression,' written for the British journal *New Statesman and Nation* (13 June 1931), Underhill was strident in his criticism of Bennett (and his high commissioner to Britain, Howard Ferguson), calling for the cancellation of the conference on the grounds that it would only weaken imperial-commonwealth relations. First communist sympathizers, then academic atheists, now an enemy of empire: the editors of the Toronto dailies must have blinked their eyes in wonder at such continuing good fortune. The Tory *Mail and Empire* demanded that Underhill 'be called upon the carpet by someone in authority at the university' for his unseemly criticism of political policy. The putatively liberal *Globe* therefore came to the defence of the British tradition of freedom of speech. 'The *Globe* does not always agree with the views of university professors,' its editorial proclaimed, 'but can see no reason why an attempt should be made to keep academic thought within the bounds of party exigency.'[66]

Bolstered by such an unexpected source of support, Underhill felt confident enough to reply to a cautionary admonition by Falconer that political journalism threatened university autonomy. He pointed to the fact that he was scarcely the first professor to have engaged in political discussion and debate in a public forum. In England the tradition was a venerable one, and members of his own university department (such as George Wrong, Chester Martin, George Glazebrook, and W.P.M. Kennedy) had contributed political items to prominent newspapers and political journals. 'In the light of all these cases,' he told Falconer, 'I fail to see what is so particularly reprehensible in my own conduct ... If professors at Toronto must keep their mouths shut in order to preserve the autonomy of the University then that autonomy is already lost. A freedom that cannot be exercised without danger of disastrous consequences is not a real freedom at all. In the midst of all the intolerance which is rampant in the world at present a University plays a sorry part if it does not raise up its voice for freedom of speech.' Falconer, who had by then announced his intention to resign as president because of ill-health, was not impressed. 'Your letter leaves me still of the same opinion as to the inexpediency of professors in the University of Toronto taking part in political journalism, by which I mean discussing current politics in such a way as to bring party criticism upon the writer.' Perhaps Carleton Stanley, president of Dalhousie University, best summarized the circumstances Falconer had faced over the past dozen years. 'I began to realise last winter,' he wrote Falconer, 'what a difficult time the university administrator has with the yelping, yowling pack of average minds whose first instinct is to hunt down anything original or critical or independent.'[67] It is significant that his disdain was not for the troublesome professor but rather, by implication, for the practitioners of a crass, predatory, and hypocritical journalism.

Calling the Tune

The announcement that Canon H.J. Cody was to become Robert Falcon-er's successor as president of the University of Toronto was made in the autumn of 1931. Rumours had circulated within the university commu-nity since the spring that Cody might arrange for his name to be put for-ward, prompting Frank Underhill to write to his friend, Brooke Claxton: 'He has refused so many archbishoprics now that he must be reserving himself the University – damn him. If he does get the job I expect that those of us who are connected with the Forum will have to watch our step.'[68] From other Toronto colleagues Cody received letters of congrat-ulations, including one from W.P.M. Kennedy thankful that the presi-dent-designate was someone with 'the immediate knowledge and ability necessary to play out his marvellous administrative hand.' W.L. Grant, son of Principal G.M. Grant and principal of Upper Canada College, urged the appointment of an 'assistant to the president' (did he have himself in mind?) so that he might be freed 'to come more closely into contact with the individuals who really count.'[69] Cody received no mes-sage of congratulation from Frank Underhill.

Always the ironist, Underhill may well have smiled when the leader of the Liberal opposition, W.E.N. Sinclair, stated in the provincial legis-lature that Cody's appointment was 'a great mistake' because, in part, he was too overtly 'partisan in his political leanings' – having 'participated in all election campaigns since the war on the side of the Conservative party.' (Political partisanship on the part of university presidents or prin-cipals was scarcely new: Robert Falconer and William Peterson of McGill had received knighthoods during the Great War not least because of their support for the Conservative party in its guise as Union government. But what was acceptable in wartime was not necessarily so in days of peace.) Moreover, Sinclair went on, Cody had no academic post-graduate education and was too old for the job. Only a year younger than Falconer, he was about to become president at age sixty-three. Sin-clair's attack on Cody might have had more telling effect had he stuck to the issue of political partisanship; but by criticizing him on grounds of his formal education and his age he was judged to have stepped beyond the bounds of propriety. Accordingly, Cody found defenders not only in the Legislature (Premier Henry among them) and in the Tory press, such as the Toronto *Mail*, but also in magazines of relatively disinterested cultural and political observation such as *Saturday Night*.[70]

Underhill had scarcely watched his step in the months prior to Cody's appointment, for from the fall of 1931 to the summer of 1932, encour-aged by the soon-to-be Co-operative Commonwealth Federation leader,

J.S. Woodsworth, he had begun to organize an association for spiritually homeless radical intellectuals that both hoped would more or less correspond to the English Fabian Society and serve, informally, as an advisory body to the CCF.[71] In Montreal professor of law Frank Scott had secured the affiliation of economist Eugene Forsey, law student David Lewis, United Theological College member King Gordon (son of novelist Charles W. Gordon), and others. At the University of Toronto, Underhill found support from a number of those who in 1931 were among 'the sixty-eight,' including economic historian Irene Biss and classicist Eric Havelock, as well as others such as Harry Cassidy of the department of social science.[72] The first meeting of the Toronto branch of the group, calling itself the League for Social Reconstruction, took place in mid-January 1932, in the genteel ambience of Wymilwood, the women's residence of Victoria College that had once been the palatial home of entrepreneur E.R. Wood.

By the end of his first month in office, a worried Cody had written Premier Henry informing him of the activities of the League for Social Reconstruction, for which he was thanked with the suggestion that 'The Board of Governors might well raise the question as to whether any organization should use the name "University of Toronto" without your consent.' By the end of the year Underhill and Havelock had been told by the university that their membership in the executive of CCF clubs was unacceptable. Both resigned these executive positions, although Underhill did so under protest. Early in 1933 the principal of McGill University, Sir Arthur Currie, wrote to Cody: 'I note that Underhill and another professor have resigned from the Executive Committee of the CCF. Why is this? Have you been looking fiercely in their direction?'[73]

By 1933 President Cody scarcely needed to look fiercely at his staff in order to obtain the silence of most on matters of political utterance. His view that professors should not engage in partisan politics was as well known as the names of those in his powerful circle of political and social acquaintance. Most academics at the provincial university therefore stuck to their academic knitting, as Sir John Aird had suggested two years earlier. Others voluntarily resigned political positions; at least one of them chose to inform his leader that his apostasy had ended. 'I know that the trials of the President of a great university are numerous, wrote Harry Cassidy after resigning from a CCF club, 'and that I might have contributed to them on occasion. I can assure you that I appreciate very much your tolerance of faculty members such as myself expressing unorthodox ideas and of our being given genuine freedom in the University of Toronto to discover and express the truth as we see it – even if we may be wrong.'[74]

Canon Cody kept his eye on professorial political involvement, but he also spent a good deal of time early in his presidency reassuring members of his political and academic constituencies that he was the correct choice as president. He pledged the university's support for the provincial government's efforts to effect economies in expenditures, while telling the University College alumni that 'we can rest assured the government will not allow this great institution to become maimed or weakened.' Indeed, he insisted that the university's greatest need was for the expansion of non-laboratory facilities and the purchase of more books. In a radio address he reassured the community of scholars that while public service was a major part of the modern university, the University of Toronto's main role would be in 'the realm of research.' Higher education, he stressed, was an investment. By the summer of 1933 he had gained praise from the city and university press. 'The interest which the President has shown in student activities ...,' wrote *Varsity*, 'and his sympathy with the students not only as a body but as individuals, has been manifested time and again.'[75]

Earlier in the year Cody's good friend Howard Ferguson, now Canada's high commissioner in London, had written him of the 'chaotic' state of European affairs. 'So much, of course, depends on Germany, and nobody seems to be able to analyse that situation or prophecy its future. I am not so greatly alarmed about it as I was a while ago. I think the Hitler movement, with all its enthusiasm, will keep up an active agitation and disturbance for some time.'[76] The previous half-dozen years had not been easy ones, professionally or personally, for Cody, for his wife and son had died. So, perhaps inspired by Ferguson's account of Europe and wishing to see his old friend again, Cody decided to see the situation for himself. In the summer of 1933 he took a much-needed vacation in England and Italy.

While Cody was in Europe, Frank Underhill attended the second annual meeting of the Canadian Institute on Economics and Politics, later to be called the Couchiching Conference, at a YMCA camp near Orillia, Ontario. It was, at the time, perhaps the Toronto history professor's idea of heaven: a gathering of academics, politicians, and public-spirited citizens who wished to discuss Canada's economic and political problems. Doubtless he felt intellectually unleashed, shorn of the academic caution that existed in the shadow of Queen's Park. The local newspaper, the *Orillia Packet and Times,* editorialized on Underhill's observations. He had derided Canadian political leaders, criticized the two old parties and tariff and imperial trade policies, and declared that 'Canada's economic interests lay with the United States, not with the British Empire, the States being our best customer ...' 'From beginning to end,' the *Packet and Times* concluded, 'there was not one kindly or appreciative word for the mother country.'[77] While perhaps insensitive to the fact that Underhill consciously over-generalized and used highly charged turns of phrase in order to provoke his audience into a critical frame of mind (an experienced lecturer's ploy), the newspaper's characterization was probably not far off the mark. Underhill had become an unrelenting iconoclast. Nothing – no person, institution, or belief – was immune from his critical eye, and he was heedless of consequences. Upon his return to Toronto, Cody made it known that he was displeased at this latest chapter in the lengthening history of Underhill's academic indiscretions. Even the historian's retired mentor George Wrong felt obliged to write to him: 'I do not regard your opinions as "deplorable" though I should have such a word in mind, I fear, if I were discussing your mode of expressing them.' Continued personal attacks, he warned, might cost Underhill his job.[78]

In the eyes of even some of his friends, Underhill's disrespectful and tactless attacks had become socially irresponsible. He offended some people as much because of his sarcastic style as for the substance of his criticism. Yet by the autumn of 1933 he was not the only University of Toronto figure whose public utterances were impolitic and controversial. President Cody had returned from his European sojourn full of admiration for Benito Mussolini, and he proceeded to extol the dictator's virtues in public as well as in private. Mussolini 'had removed the slums that once obstructed the view of the antiquities,' he enthused to a *Varsity* reporter; and he told the Hamilton branch of the Canadian Club that the Italian 'statesman' was 'a very efficient man, who had a plan and the necessary faith in it to carry it out.' A *Globe* reporter summarized the gist of President Cody's public message: 'Security was vouchsafed the people of Italy under Mussolini's program, and state control had proved a success. Mussolini also was preparing for the future by training the youth of his country along progressive lines, Dr Cody stated.'[79] One might say that there was now a loose canon on the upper decks of the provincial university as it faced the dangerous swells of the Great Depression.

Cody's public messages in the autumn and winter of 1933–4 were two-fold: first, that spiritual renewal under inspired leadership was needed, leading to dedicated service to the community; and second, that professors should refrain from engaging in partisan political debate. A year earlier he had told an international conference on 'The Obligation of Universities to the Social Order' (held in New York's posh Waldorf-Astoria Hotel) that there was 'a general realization that something is rotten in the state of Denmark' and that 'the conditions of national and international life today are demonstrative that we do need something beyond the pursuit of abstract truth.' Neither the university nor the church could or should exert a direct influence upon political, social, or economic matters; their purpose, instead, was to provide inspiration for spiritual growth.[80] Now, having been both frightened and inspired at what he witnessed in Europe, he could be more precise. 'In this time of darkness,' he told a September commencement gathering at Convocation Hall, 'we have learned a truer sense of values.' Matters of the spirit and the mind remained supreme, but 'The youth of to-day must understand that there is the "mark of blood" on everything they do – everything is purchased at great price ... Every university has a patriotic and national service to render, and every student must carry out that service to his community and to his fellow men.'[81]

In his commencement address Cody encouraged students to take an active interest in the social, moral, and political problems of the day. But he also remained vehement in his public condemnation of political engagement by professors. Indeed, in a December speech to the Montreal branch of the Canadian Club he went even further, to include not only the university but also the church as an institution that should refrain from leaping 'into the arena of practical politics or active economic and industrial questions.'[82] The good canon now found himself under substantial public attack. Had Cody himself, while chairman of the university's board of governors, not given a political radio address during the 1929 provincial election campaign, supporting Howard Ferguson?[83] The United Church of Canada's Board of Evangelism and Social Service publicly criticized him, declaring that the church and the university had an obligation 'to speak out its mind on all matters relative to social "ends and spiritual values."'[84] Professor Norman Rogers of Queen's University dismissed the Toronto president's remarks as 'inept and inopportune and wholly inaccurate ... as a description of the true function of the Church, university and the State of this or any other country to play the role of the Pharisee in the parable of the Good Samaritan, and pass by on the other side.'[85] The Toronto *Globe* was among Cody's few public defenders. Dr Cody was surely right, wrote its editorialist, in stressing that churches and universities should confine themselves to ethical ends rather than material means.[86]

Cody was undeterred by the barrage of public criticism levelled at him. He had seen the future, and its trains ran on time. Early in January 1934 he again addressed a capacity audience in Convocation Hall. The occasion was Toronto's 'Italian Week.' He wished, he said, to convey his impressions of the Italian fascist regime, personally witnessed the past summer, and to draw some lessons. 'Canadians are inclined to emphasize too strongly the "rights" of the individual and the "duties" of the government,' he said, 'rather than to recognize that the Government, which represents all individuals, has rights and the individual has duties toward it. This is a lesson,' he concluded, 'which the "spirit of co-operation" existing in Italy today offers the rest of the world.' The national ideal should be 'co-operation for the common good,' and the example of Italy had shown that 'there is no antagonism between the individual and the state and that the state represents the interests of all ...'[87] Cody noted that he was not advocating fascism; but he was also without criticism of the Italian regime or its leader's solutions to the problems of life. Quite the contrary: he had nothing but praise to offer. Education had become a 'potent instrument for unification and inspiration.'[88] One senses just a whisper of regret in his voice when he told his audience that fascism would probably not work in North America.

Historical retrospect can cast any figure of the past as a knave or a fool. Cody's infatuation with fascism in the very year of the destruction of the German Reichstag should not particularly shock us. What should be of concern, however, is how convenient it was that he managed to remain so oblivious to the clear political implications of speeches he delivered as university president in the very days when he carried out a campaign to halt the political activities of his professoriate (not to mention the church at large). He surely must have recognized that his position at the pinnacle of academic life in Canada was secured not by any particular academic or even clerical achievement but by his astute alliance with – and publicly stated support for – the dominant imperial-conservative politicians of his day. His many utterances on party matters had, in fact, often been made in the very realms – the church and the university – that had made his own career possible, but that he expected to remain untainted by partisan politics when led by others.

In 1933 Henry J. Cody was no more a fascist than Frank Underhill was a communist. But his enthusiastic efforts to stifle radical political dissent, combined with his equally enthusiastic embrace of the spirit – if not the jackboots – of Italian fascism, points to darker resonances in his speeches at the time. Many groups across the country, secular and religious, invited this man to address them. In a time of political and economic crisis they wanted to hear inspirational and thoughtful words from the leader of one of Canada's leading institutions of higher education. 'Public men are undergoing a complete change of mind and reconstruction of character,' he told one group of young adults. 'The only panacea for the present ills of the world lies in a complete personal reconstruction ... Reverence for law and order must be widespread.' This was the message of the Canadian social gospel stood on its head: for justice now stood order; for liberation, control. In the intellectual and social context of the day, when uniformed Canadian fascists and their supporters could and did pack Toronto's Massey Hall, Cody's calls for greater 'reverence for law and order' were scarcely out of the ordinary. Given the benefit of hindsight, however, and with it the knowledge that the road to fascism led to Auschwitz, such phrases bring a chill to the bone.[89]

President Cody turned to more academic concerns for the remainder of the 1930s as he sought to define the characteristics of Toronto's future academic excellence and to give shape to it. In his first annual report to the university, he reiterated what since 1922 had effectively been its official position on academic freedom. 'While academic freedom is rightly held to be essential to true university teaching,' he wrote, 'academic responsibility accompanies it, and is equally imperative. The teacher to whom freedom is gladly given must realize and practice the responsibility which its possession imposes within and without the academic walls.'[90] For Cody and Robert Falconer alike, it was a policy of plain common sense.

If Underhill heard his president's words, he took little heed of them. Cody's own controversial outspokenness on ideological matters in the winter of 1933-4 may have left Canada's Mencken of the left thinking that Cody would not dare seriously threaten him because of his own extreme political views. Moreover, Underhill recognized that when the Conservatives under George Henry lost the provincial election to Mitchell Hepburn's Liberals in June 1934 Cody's political capital at Queen's Park diminished significantly and that he would soon have more important concerns than Underhill. Associated as closely as he was with Hepburn's political enemy, Howard Ferguson, Cody would find few natural allies in the new government.

Whatever their inspiration, Frank Underhill's rhetorical flourishes at the 1934 Couchiching Conference were even more inflammatory than those of 1933. The ever-vigilant Orillia *Packet and Times* once again reported the Toronto professor's offences. Both the British Empire and the League of Nations, Underhill had apparently said, should be consigned 'to the scrap heap.' It was further reported that he had even called those who fought in the Great War 'suckers' and 'boobs' – dupes of imperial interests.[91]

Faced with influential and outraged citizens threatening to disassociate themselves from the university because of Underhill's latest indiscretion, Cody called him onto the presidential carpet and obtained the promise of a year's moratorium on public speeches. The promised year of political silence was observed in neither letter nor spirit. 'You might be interested to know,' wrote RCMP Commissioner J.H. MacBrien to Cody on 4 April 1935, 'that the above named Professors [Underhill and Eric Havelock] took part in the conference of the Toronto and District League Against War and Fascism which was held on 23rd and 24th March, 1935. Professor Underhill when addressing the meeting requested that his speech be not quoted in the Press as he had given an undertaking to his President not to make public speeches. Our report says that he was nervous and guarded in his remarks and admitted that he was a Socialist. He spoke for about 20 minutes and seemed rather relieved when it was all over.'[92]

Such reports – public and private – could not have come at a worse time for the provincial university. The Depression had now lasted for five long years, university finances throughout the province were stretched to the breaking-point, and the new administration carried little brief for higher education. Hepburn's brand of populism had a boorish and anti-intellectual face; it made that of farmer-premier E.C. Drury look positively patrician by comparison.[93] In spite of the fact that economic and employment conditions in Ontario had improved significantly since 1933,[94] Hepburn's 1935 budget announced a major cutback in provincial grants to the University of Toronto. Operating grants to Queen's and Western were reduced by only $1,900 and $3,500, respectively, but that of Toronto was cut by $587,681. The university's total operating grant fell from $1,878,962 to $1,291,281, and for the first time in the century it received no capital grant at all (the grant had been $209,222 in 1934).[95]

The Hepburn government struck the universities hard again in 1939, when its budget cut the University of Toronto's special grant by $100,000 and those to Queen's and Western by $25,000 each.[96] Students at Western and Queen's – but particularly at Western, to which $25,000 was an enormous sum –protested loudly and at length. In a move that a London newspaper announced as 'unprecedented in all Western's history,' they paraded in demonstration through the city's streets and demanded an interview with the premier. Hepburn replied with a telegram that read: 'OTHER UNIVERSITIES RECEIVING DECREASED GRANT. REGRET UNABLE TO GRANT INTERVIEW ON MATTER.'[97] Students, parents, and civic officials wrote irate and worried letters to the premier and to their provincial political representatives. A London journalist no doubt reflected the fears of many university supporters in the province when he wrote: 'Without intervention or suggestion from the faculty who will, more than the undergraduates, feel the blow which places the local colleges' grant $90,000 below its [pre-]depression level, the student organizations have risen in a determined, concerted effort to save their school from slipping, through inadequate funds, to the status of a third-rate college.'[98]

Yet Hepburn had a lot of public support for his educational measures. An anonymous resident of London, calling himself 'small taxpayer,' complained that students with assured jobs after graduation and fathers with good salaries should not complain. A woman from Aylmer, who began her letter with the salutation 'Dear Mitch,' told him that 'The Universities are fine in some respects but there is a lot of tosh and nonsense taught there, too, and a good deal of snobbery is tolerated.' The secretary-treasurer of the University of Toronto alumni association noted the hardship imposed by budget cuts on poorer students, but concluded that 'it is undoubtedly true that many rich men's sons are attending the University ...' An insurance broker from London went further. 'The agitation locally ... to maintain the usual grant for the University of Western Ontario,' he told Hepburn, 'can be turned by you into a mighty triumph.' The budget cuts would make the universities realize how dependent they had become for government support; perhaps in future they would not take such support for granted. As for Western itself: 'You will find that in this University, the overhead is very heavy, primarily because they have a lot of dead wood in their organization.' He suggested that the premier send a financial controller to London. The 'university would function much more smoothly,' he concluded, 'when some of the dead wood is removed.'[99]

At the very time of the announcement of the 1939 budget, the University of Toronto was embroiled in yet another controversy centred on Frank Underhill's continuing outspokenness on public issues. Relations between universities and the business and political communities had deteriorated since the mid-1930s. The publication in 1935 of the League for Social Reconstruction's collectivist manifesto, *Social Planning for Canada*, may have been the catalyst that provoked the president of the Canadian Pacific Railway, Sir Edward Beatty, to tell students of the University of Western Ontario in the autumn that academic thought in Canada had become 'deeply colored by socialist ideas' and that professorial radicalism was based not only on 'a lack of adequate knowledge of the structure of the existing economic society' but also on 'an emotional desire for the correction of admitted defects in our society which outruns the slower but safer processes of logical reasoning.' Underhill's response had been to accuse the Montreal tycoon, in a *Canadian Forum* article entitled 'Beatty and the University Reds,' of being a 'traffic cop' inhibiting the free exchange of ideas.[100] The offences continued, especially in 1937: a damning indictment of Premier Hepburn by Eric Havelock for his anti-labour stance during a major strike in Oshawa; an isolationist Underhill article that offended many readers of *Maclean's*; an Underhill complaint on the radio, following the merger of the *Globe* and the *Mail,* that he was tired of 'reading at [his] breakfast table every morning whatever a couple of gold-mining millionaires may think is good for the people of Ontario.' (The reference was to owner William Wright and editor George McCullagh.)[101] Once more the Toronto dailies, led understandably by *The Globe and Mail*, were up in arms over Toronto's disloyal and disrespectful professors.

By the summer and fall of 1938 influential figures in Montreal, Toronto, and Ottawa had had enough of professors playing politics.[102] In Toronto, George McCullagh – a friend of Premier Hepburn – used his newspaper's editorial page to demand that 'certain professors, like Mr Underhill, [be] turned out *en masse* and [that] the public [be] relieved of the burden of supporting the kind of "education" they support.' Cody warned Underhill (as if the latter did not know already) that the irate newspaper magnate was 'after [his] scalp.'[103] In November 1938, when yet another of his anti-British pronouncements came to light, Underhill became the subject of sustained discussion at a meeting of the university's governing body. No disciplinary action was taken.

The University of Toronto's board of governors had changed significantly over the past thirty years. In 1908–9 it had consisted of fourteen educationalists and four businessmen, but by the end of the Second World War the proportions were exactly reversed. Among the several financiers on the board in 1939 was former premier Howard Ferguson, who now numbered among his business interests not only the presidency of the Crown Life Insurance Company but also memberships on the boards of Toronto General Trusts Corporation, the British American Insurance Company, the Western Assurance Company, and Brazilian Traction. Since the 1920s the Ontario Tory chieftain had detested Underhill's views on the Great War and the British Empire.[104] With that empire threatened by imminent war in Europe, the last year of the decade was not the time for Underhill to test the strength of support for his political views in the university or in the community at large.

In mid-April 1939, when university officials throughout Ontario were attempting to convince provincial political leaders that the cuts in grants to higher education should be eliminated, or at least be significantly eased, the Legislature itself became the scene of severe and unanimous condemnation of 'irresponsible' Toronto academics. George Grube, a League for Social Reconstruction member who taught classics at Trinity College, was accused by the minister of education, Dr L.J. Simpson, of seditious behaviour. Grube had apparently said that monies spent on

Canadian rearmament was 'a waste of public funds in the interest of British imperialism.'[105] Colonel George Drew, leader of the opposion, broadened the attack by reading into the legislative record the final paragraph of a discussion paper Underhill had been requested to write in 1935 for the Canadian Institute of International Affairs. It had appeared in the 1938 book *Canada Looks Abroad*, from which Colonel Drew read: 'We must therefore make it clear to the world, and especially to Great Britain, that the poppies blooming in Flanders Fields have no further interest for us. We must fortify ourselves against the allurements of a British war for democracy and freedom and parliamentary institutions, and against the allurements of a League war for peace and international order. And when overseas propagandists combine the two appeals to us by urging us to join in organizing "the Peace World" to which all the British nations already belong, the simplest answer is to thumb our noses at them.' More subtle ways existed for Underhill to make his anti-imperial point than to speak of the irrelevance of Flanders' poppies – by now central to the iconography of the Canadian experience in the Great War – or to thumb one's nose at advocates of the empire and the League of Nations. He had been told this often, and by some of his closest friends.

To Drew's insistence that the public had the right to be protected against those who sought to subvert the empire and its ideals, Hepburn replied by shifting the target of attack: 'I am disappointed that the University Board of Governors has not up to now disciplined Underhill in a manner befitting the crime he has committed. It smacks of rank sedition.' Accordingly, the premier assured the house that if university authorities failed 'to bring these men into line' the government would do so. The Liberal premier's real target may, in fact, have now become the members of the old Ontario establishment in the university's administrative structure, particularly President Cody and Chancellor William Mulock. Frank Underhill wrote to Howard Ferguson that Hepburn's attack on him had proven to be a convenient way 'to get at Cody by making his position so uncomfortable that he will be forced to resign.'

In the ensuing public controversy, neither Underhill nor Grube found a defender in the Toronto daily press, although *Saturday Night*, under the distinguished (and, under the circumstances, courageous) editorship of B.K. Sandwell, was one. In several articles, it attempted to establish the longer and troubled perspective of academic freedom in the province. In one, Sandwell himself warned of the danger that the provincial university might shortly come to be run by the premier.[106] *Canadian Forum* also came to the defence of free expression of opinion. Reacting to the fact that not one politician had stood up in the Legislature during the Underhill-Grube debate to defend the right of free expression, one of its authors wrote: 'Are the members of our legislatures themselves so intimidated by their own infernal party machines that they cannot recognize a fundamental issue when they see one? If our political representatives are so incapable of identifying the embryo of totalitarianism this is no time to be reducing grants to Provincial Universities; the doors of a liberal education must be thrown wide open in the hope that at least one or two who have enjoyed its benefits will find their way into a future Provincial Legislature.'[107] Doubtless, Underhill was also somewhat relieved, if not gratified, when Harold Innis and Samuel Beatty (the dean of arts), spokesmen for the university's faculty members, told Cody and the governors that, while they viewed Underhill's comments as 'ill-advised and offensive,' they strongly opposed any attempt by the administration to fire him. A student petition with 1,014 signatures also defended his right to free speech.[108] Given that the crisis took place at the end of the university year, when students were either writing examinations or had already departed, this was a sizeable portion of the student body.

Yet in the end it was perhaps the threat to Cody's own position that saved Underhill's career. While very angry, the president accepted his explanation that the remarks quoted by Drew were not meant to have been published and he presented a judicious and comprehensive report of the affair to the board of governors. Indeed, in his final report on the matter to the board on 22 June, Cody found himself defending the university's intellectual freedom against outside 'tyranny and assault.'[109] Frank Underhill was surprised that Howard Ferguson, 'of all people, was operating with his usual smoothness to prevent any trouble.' Ferguson's biographer concluded that this was doubtless 'to help Harry Cody out of a tight spot.'[110]

By June 1939 the university's crisis had passed. Colonel Fred Fraser Hunter, MPP for its own St Patrick riding, had by then withdrawn his 13 April motion that the 'rats who are trying to scuttle our ship of state' by 'hurling insults at the British Empire'[111] should be dismissed from the university, and its board of governors had once again decided to take no action on Underhill. But much damage had more than likely been done to the provincial university, not only to its public image but also to its financial position.[112]

The story of academic freedom in Ontario between the wars is ultimately less about freedom than it is about control. At the smaller universities in the province, professorial radicals in matters of religion and politics, such as Martyn Estall and Gregory Vlastos at Queen's, or economist K.W. Taylor at McMaster, or classicist R.E.K. Pemberton at the University of Western Ontario (all members of the League for Social Reconstruction), did not suffer from the wrath of their community leaders or university administrators. Estall and Vlastos, in fact, later praised their university for its supportive attitude.[113] The indignation of public and politician was instead reserved almost entirely for the institution that from its founding was viewed as the educational creation of the provincial state. By the 1930s Queen's and Western, although private and secular institutions, were themselves overwhelmingly dependent on state funding for their existence. As much as the University of Toronto, they, too, had become semi-voluntary provincial wards. But they did not have Toronto's image as *the* provincial university. The step-child of the state was also expected to be its servant.

Some, it is true, defended the right of individuals – whether professors or legislators – to utter unpalatable views in the tradition of free British subjects. An open meeting of church and professional leaders organized by the Canadian Civil Liberties Union did, as did the Labour party of Ontario, the board of evangelism and social services of the United Church of Canada, and others, at the height of the Underhill-Grube controversy.[114] Yet many more who wrote to Premier Hepburn in the spring of 1939 wanted unpatriotic dissent stifled and the professors and universities put under stricter control. 'It is the feeling of the Association that these men should not be allowed to continue in a position where they have the opportunity to influence our young people,' wrote the secretary of the Canadian Corps Association. 'I do want to offer my congratulations on the attitude you took the other day in disciplining some of the loose-talking professors in the City of Toronto,' wrote the secretary-treasurer and manager of the Canadian Brass Company. 'It was long overdue, and will, I hope, be a damper on those in this country who have little else to do but air their views.' 'Surely our resources, of money, duly contributed could be put to better use than supporting men who are poisoning the minds of the youth of our country,' bellowed the Ontario and Quebec district secretary-treasurer of Lions International of Canada. 'This type of loose and disloyal talk has ... gone on far too long,' said the secretary of the Stratford Board of Trade, in another letter of congratulations to the premier; 'and University professors seem to be the chief offenders ... The writer trusts that you will continue your efforts to silence these disloyal utterances, especially when the Universities are being substantially subsidized by the Government ... More power to you Mr Hepburn.'[115]

Some individuals who wrote to Hepburn, like a Paris (Ontario) man of self-proclaimed United Empire Loyalist stock, simply urged that 'these vipers whom this country has warmed, fed, and protected, should be stamped out ...' In such stark statements the underlying basis of the interwar controversy over dissident professors was laid bare. In power and influence lay control, and it was those who held it as the world seemed on the brink of catastrophe who were marshalled against advocates of civil liberties, church leaders, students, and professors. The suggested way of stifling unwanted dissent was through the purse strings of the state. 'The University of Toronto is a State Institution, and professors are in the class of civil servants and judges,' went part of a letter from a Toronto resident that April. 'They must be neutral on all political issues.' Premier Hepburn had carried a telegram from the Newmarket Lions Club in his suit pocket when he met the Legislature on the day that Underhill and Grube were attacked. He read it into the Legislative record: 'AS TAXPAYERS, WE SUBMIT ONTARIO'S PRIME MINISTER MIGHT WISELY FURTHER REDUCE GRANTS TO ONTARIO'S UNIVERSITIES UNTIL SUCH TIME AS THE BOARDS OF GOVERNORS OF THESE INSTITUTIONS SEE FIT TO WEED FROM THEIR STAFFS MEN WHO DELIGHT IN PARADING THEMSELVES BEFORE THE PUBLIC, AS TRAITORS TO OUR DOMINION AND EMPIRE. SURELY OUR HARD EARNED DOLLARS MIGHT BE PUT TO BETTER USE THAN SUPPLYING SALARIES FOR MEN OF THIS TYPE WHO YEAR IN AND YEAR OUT ARE POISONING THE MINDS OF ONTARIO'S FINEST YOUNG MEN AND WOMEN.'[116]

In the light of so much apparent public support for severe political and economic measures to be taken against errant professors, the arguments of those few who sought to defend freedom of expression in the university, using the rhetoric of social values rather than of public utility, must have appeared pitifully weak to those who dealt daily in hard political currency. Did Mitch Hepburn, whose bodyguard's nickname was 'Bruiser,' give any serious weight to the view of the Hamilton university student who took exception to what he called the 'well-meant but perverted patriotism' of the Newmarket Lions Club? 'Every nation is judged by its culture,' that student wrote to his premier. 'If the seat of Canadian culture, Canada's universities, is to be forcibly subjected to unnecessary suppression, it speaks very poorly for the intelligence of the Canadian Legislature, for, in censoring unduly those institutions, it is unduly censoring the epitome of Canadian intelligence. In this vein, it seems a pity that education should have to be the first victim of parliamentary economy; for, by decreasing the university grants, the legislature is swinging the axe at the root of the flower of learning.'[117] It is much more likely that Hepburn and his supporters took the view of the son and namesake of one of Canada's most wealthy and influential men. In a letter to the Ontario premier, Clifford Sifton wrote: 'There can be no doubt that the people who pay the piper have the right to call the tune, nor that where the public funds support an institution the people's political representatives may exercise control ...'[118]

That Sifton, whose family held enormous power, made such a statement should surprise no one. Economic influence was a potent lubricant in the manufacture of consent, whether in the universities or in other provincial and national institutions. The supreme irony is that although Sifton was one of the patrons of the piper, in this case he was one who came strongly to Underhill's defence in yet another and worse crisis over academic freedom. But by then, in 1941, the very civilization that had produced the tradition of free academic expression was under siege.

Part Five:
Between Past and Future

15

Students between Wars

The memory of student life in North American universities between the wars has been haunted since the 1920s by the ghost of F. Scott Fitzgerald. In his first novels, published shortly after the Great War, Fitzgerald depicted a hedonistic yet cynical society that worshipped material success and devalued wisdom and experience. Particularly in *This Side of Paradise* (1920), Fitzgerald portrayed student life in contemporary Ivy League colleges as given over to quests for social status, membership in the best clubs, and dates with the smartest debutantes – a world of fast cars and fast women, of petting parties and nightclubs, jazz and gin. As portrayed by Fitzgerald, the student generation that followed the Great War and ushered in the Jazz Age lived, like Amory Blaine, on the shimmering surface of life, driven yet enslaved by impulse and desire, coveting popularity, and resentful of all forms of authority, including that of the past.[1]

Fitzgerald's provocative use of the symbols of his generation and his portrayal of the shocking behaviour of contemporary youth alarmed, yet also teased, his readers. To traditionalists, young Americans seemed out of control, free from the restraints of custom and authority – frivolous, licentious, and disrespectful. At the same time, Fitzgerald's novels reminded people of how distant the post-war world was from the perceived stability of nineteenth-century civilization. His books told their audience 'what it was eager to know but unable to condone,' and his art helped push the culture of youth in America to the forefront of national consciousness. Newspapers, magazines, critics, politicians, and parents became absorbed by the post-war generation. Public reaction to the new culture of youth tended to polarize into those who damned them for their outrageous behaviour and others who saw in their repudiation of convention the elements of a new and more progressive social order. *This Side of Paradise*, said one observer, 'haunted the decade like a song.'[2]

Fitzgerald's portrayal of the 1920s as the Jazz Age gripped the imagination not only of the public but also of journalists and popular historians, such as Frederick Lewis Allen, whose book *Only Yesterday: An Informal History of the 1920s,* published in 1931, was a Book-of-the-Month Club selection high on the best-seller lists. Allen's 1920s were a new era, bereft of meaning and shorn of traditional values because of the disillusioning effect of the war. Youth responded to this vacuum by inaugurating, he claimed, a 'revolution of manners and morals' characterized by social experimentation and a preoccupation with every passing fad or craze. Allen's historical portrayal of the decade became the dominant one, and other historians, novelists, journalists, and movie-makers maintained the characterization for the next half-century, depicting a world of 'hip-flasks, rumbleseats, raccoon coats, crossword puzzles, marathon dances, and ticker tape through which whirled a slightly demented citizenry.'[3] One canonical text for such accounts, by Allen and others, was that drawn from the final paragraphs of Fitzgerald's *This Side of Paradise,* when the novelist spoke of 'a new generation dedicated more than the last to the fear of poverty and the worship of success; grown up to find all Gods dead, all wars fought, all faiths in man shaken ...'[4] The novels of Ernest Hemingway, particularly *The Sun Also Rises* (1926) and *A Farewell to Arms* (1929), seemed to bear witness to the truth of Fitzgerald's bitter observation.

Recent interpreters of the decade, however, have taken issue with this portrayal. They have found that social experimentation in the 1920s coexisted with a concern for recovering or preserving the traditions and values of the past. The Great War shook the confidence of many thoughtful North Americans but, while its apocalyptic nature made them believe that a point of departure had been reached in Western culture, it masked the fact that traditional ways of thinking, inherited social values, or forms of social organization in fact persisted into the new era and helped shape it. In the realm of social thought, the aftermath of the war therefore brought an anxious mingling of concerns for past and future. Tradition was at once an inheritance and a burden – and this obtained in politics, religion, education, and family life. The post-war generation was less disillusioned than it was uncertain, less cynical than nervous; an ambivalent and tense generation living at a time when old and new forms coexisted uneasily.[5]

The culture of Ontario university students in the 1920s was marked by the Great War, but undergraduate behaviour resumed much of its pre-war pattern. This was most noticeable in the continuation of rites of initiation, in the form of hazes, pranks, and stunts, throughout the war and the decades that followed, and in the persistence of established attitudes towards relations between the sexes. The range of academic programs expanded greatly between 1919 and 1939, but it was difficult for women to gain entrance into many of them, or to obtain the kind of encouragement – whether from parents, teachers, or professors – that they needed in order to enrol in programs that were the continuing preserve of men. Notions that university women were really mothers-in-waiting or that they should enrol in programs suitable to such 'inherent' attributes as nurturing or care-giving were ones that many talked about and a good number of women still believed in. Teaching and forms of social service continued to be the professional separate spheres of many university women.

At the same time, the great increase in the circulation of American mass magazines after the war meant that Canadian readers were increasingly exposed to the American fascination with college fads and fashions.[6] Journalists working for large Ontario dailies, mainly in Toronto, often got ideas for campus articles from their own reading of the American press, and they assumed that the mores and preoccupations of American and Ontario students were similar. Life in Ontario was not yet, however, if it was ever to become, simply a cold replication of the American experience. Toronto was, after all, the city described by American anarchist Emma Goldman on a visit in 1927 as 'deadly dull ... because it is church-ridden. Toronto people are smug and don't think for themselves – look at the way the university has been forced to withdraw into itself away from the life of the city. I have never seen any other university town in which the life of the university is so separate and distinct from that of the townspeople. Toronto students lose by this.' Asked by a journalist whether radicalism was more prevalent in the University of Toronto than Torontonians believed, she replied: 'Possibly, though I think it may be largely the radicalism of high living.'[7]

Academic life in Ontario universities between the wars, especially during the Great Depression, reflected a reality significantly removed from that of flappers and gin flasks. The coming of the Great Depression in 1929 did not fundamentally affect patterns of student interests, either social or academic, that had emerged after the Great War. Student attention shifted from fashion and fads towards the polarized realities of a world near chaos. But Ontario's university students still danced and dated even when they were forced by society to address matters such as the rise of fascism and communism, or the apparent collapse of capitalism. The world of the Bennett Buggy and of Hitler and Mussolini certainly made them less frivolous. We do not find them beckoning to the 1920s as a golden age, free of obligation, to which they would rather return. Their extracurricular lives mixed the youthful exuberance that was in their nature with the deep seriousness that had become their fate. The first generation of twentieth-century Ontario war babies came of university age between 1935 and 1939. Unlike their own children, they were a generation tempered by economic collapse and the imminent prospect of war, not by the transcendent luxury of peace.

North of Paradise

Denominational origins still heavily marked the ambience of Ontario's universities after the war, in tone if not in creed, mitigating their gravitation towards prevalent American college norms. The war's sombre legacy for institutions of higher education had also been far greater in Ontario than it had in the United States. Enlistment had threatened Ontario universities almost with collapse, yet enrolment in American liberal arts colleges during the war declined by only ten per cent.[8] The six hundred names inscribed on the University of Toronto's Memorial Tower were the equivalent of almost ten per cent of the total number of American college student losses (6,500).[9] The deep sense of loss that followed the war helped temper Ontario's entry into the jazz age.

It did not, however, put an end to traditional forms of student social behaviour. Rites of initiation – 'a key instrument for generating group consciousness, inculcating the values of college society, and pin-pointing the anxieties of student life' – had been a major part of Ontario campus life since the 1880s.[10] A year before the war, Toronto firemen were forced to turn their hoses on a gang of unruly Toronto students behind Trinity College, who thought the fire behind their college was amusing.[11] The onset of war only partially muted the exuberance, driving male initiation underground. Campus warfare between different years was briefly suspended by students themselves, in the face of real battles between nations. Well before the war's end, however, student scraps had reasserted themselves and had become, if anything, more frantic – and more violent.[12] By 1918, University College had once again inaugurated formal initiations, and freshmen in arts cavorted that autumn with various combinations of green paint, molasses, axle-grease, and lampblack decorating their bodies.[13]

Before the war students had been involved in a broad circle of activities, usually revolving around athletics. Increasingly during the war, though, the major campus combatants were those in the professional faculties – medical and engineering students, precisely those most in demand for service at the front. Since many of the upper-year male students had enlisted for war service, the focus of attention understandably became the hapless freshmen. The student administrative council at the University of Toronto attempted to regulate such activities, but with indifferent success. Medical students continued to do battle with those from the School of Practical Science even when, in 1917 and 1918, the war had reached its most horrific stages. Possibly such activities helped expiate the sense of guilt harboured by some who remained at home, helping to displace their fear of overseas service even as the battles expended youthful energy. With conscription imminent, one medical student chafed at the continuing attempts of university authorities to dampen his faculty's annual battle with the engineers. 'Sir Robert Falconer and the Students' Council,' he wrote in October 1917, 'are apparently of one mind in desiring to convert this place of learning into a machine akin to the sausage machine into one end of which the verdant freshman is cast, to emerge several years later a man of letters or a scientist.'[14] Unrestrained physical activity of some kind was possibly a psychological necessity for the male undergraduate in the war years. Certainly, the medical students experienced something like physical-cum-psychological release when, because of the war, they found themselves for once greatly outnumbering the engineers and took advantage of the fact by battling them. The wars between the professions that year were remarkable for the fact that arts students, now underdogs psychologically in the pecking order of undergraduate life, actually came to the aid of their traditional enemies, the engineers.[15]

Student leaders after the war sought to channel such activities into more benign forms by organizing formal activities – for regulation, it was thought, would bring control. The School of Practical Science initiation in 1919 was a private affair, held behind closed doors. Even the dean, it was said, would participate. The strategy of arts leaders was different: their initiation was held at Varsity Stadium, complete with organized activities such as tug-of-war, push ball, and 'a burlesque Rugby game.' 'It is really an outcome of the war,' one student council member told a reporter for the Toronto *Telegram*,' – this strong development of feeling against the old scraps ... The men have a new seriousness of mind, and while they must have some form of initiation, they are willing to carry it out in accordance with the views of their own discipline committee.'[16] Medical students were probably the most rowdy ones in postwar Toronto, tormenting theatre audiences, restaurant-goers, and patrons of posh hotels such as the King Edward.[17]

The unruliness of medical students was the exception. The rule at many universities was the fact that spontaneity had come to be organized – and not everyone liked it. Something, including a degree of student freedom, it seemed, had been lost. 'Time was when freshmen moved fearfully from one classroom to another, not knowing at what moment their seniors might fall swiftly upon them,' reported *Varsity*. 'Now all is changed. The element of surprise has been entirely obliterated and freshmen walk in fear no longer. Under the rules of the Students' Administrative Council all powerful is student discipline – to-day – trench raid tactics are forbidden the sophomore. They must acquaint the enemy beforehand of the time, the place and the weapon to be used. The "Hazing" element has almost entirely disappeared.' Interviewed for the article, McGill political economist Stephen Leacock was critical of such prearranged initiations. 'I don't like it,' he said. 'It is like everything else in our college life to-day, – mechanical organization instead of the promoting of the spirit. The old fashioned enthusiasm is replaced by organized hysteria.'[18]

On other university campuses in the province students and staff sought to respect the sacrifices made by men overseas by seeking to curb excessive frivolity. The Queen's Alma Mater Society (AMS), for example, voted in the spring of 1918 to abolish all rushes and initiations, and the decision was reconfirmed the next year, when the newly elected AMS president and six other members of its executive were returned soldiers. By 1922, however, the tradition had reasserted itself. In their annual reports that year, both Principal Taylor and Dean of Arts Skelton found it necessary to comment on the 'the intrusion of social activities upon study' and 'the growing frivolousness of a proportion of the rising generation.' The 1921–2 AMS Executive pronounced initiations in the various faculties to be 'unsatisfactory,' and found it necessary to discover some means of ensuring that initiations would be 'safer, saner, and more satisfactory.'[19] While harmless pranks such as those condoned by its Nip and Tuck Society were also a part of McMaster's life, initiation of freshmen there did not begin until 1926, and when it did student leaders insisted that 'no bodily harm or vulgarity' be part of it. 'The roaring twenties did not roar loudly ... for McMaster students.'[20]

Extracurricular initiations, scraps, and stunts, particularly in Toronto, continued throughout the 1920s. Students battled at length after elections, football games, and banquets, or, as in one case, when engineering students decided to harass the sleeping students of Victoria College by battering down a residence door at midnight with a tree. Possibly such activities were less extreme than the sensation-driven daily press in Toronto seemed to suggest – catching the public's attention with headlines such as '500 Rioting Students Storm Downtown Show' and 'Students Engage in Fierce Combat.'[21]

In fact, Ontario student culture echoed the larger culture of English-speaking Canadians of the day. The 'spinning vortex' of Canadian life in the 1920s 'was the opposing drives of ... the nostalgic and propulsive elements in Canadian society. Canadians, looking backward with sentiment, were being driven forward by desire.'[22] Ontario university students neither rejected tradition nor applauded it. They did not feel themselves to be lost. They were, however, disoriented, and precisely because of this they were no more willing to jettison the past than they were willing to throw themselves heedlessly into an uncertain future. 'What ... is the benefit of Tradition?' concluded a 1924 article in the *Varsity Literary Supplement*. 'There is undoubtedly a great deal that might be said for and against it, but the fact remains that even were an institution completely to abolish all forms of Tradition and traditional usage, it would never the less creep back very soon, unnoticed, perhaps, but inevitable, for we cannot abolish part of our own nature. Tradition, like war, love and other things, cannot be done away with by legislation. Though one may not be conscious of it, it is nonetheless there.'[23] In giving voice to such sentiments, students were little different from the cautious progressives – some of them their professors – who wrote for the newly formed *Canadian Forum*. Even though we often hear that civilization is doomed, said one *Forum* contributor, we can nevertheless 'say confidently that the most important things in our civilized world are not going to be lost .'[24]

Post-war university life often appeared too regimented, compared with pre-war years. Institutions seemed too large; students lacked sufficient academic motivation. 'Modern Society,' proclaimed one student editorialist shortly after the war, 'is composed of many classes, each a little wheel in the great machinery of civilization, each with its own useful function.'[25] The industrial metaphor threaded its way through campus commentaries during the decade. Toronto students debated whether or not their university had become 'a "factory" which "turns out" many graduates who [had] been changed but little by their years at college, and who [felt] no affection for their university.'[26] Victoria students were more certain of Toronto's fate, reminding themselves at the end of the decade that increasing registration and overcrowding, along with 'harassed professors teaching masses, not minds,' risked turning their college into 'just another subdivision of some great factory for the mass production of polished collegians or just another section of some efficient but mediocre department store of education.'[27] Even university leaders complained about the regimentation of university life. Speaking at the autumn convocation of the University of Western Ontario in 1929, Principal Taylor of Queen's attacked 'the modern tendency towards standardization,' which, in his view, threatened student individuality. Moreover, he said, universities were becoming flooded with students who lacked any 'intellectual curiosity.' His declaration that education was 'aristocratic,' not 'democratic,' brought sustained applause from the London audience.[28]

Students and presidents alike recognized the fact that there was a production-line aspect to the post-war university. Students themselves admitted that many of them would lay 'no claim to the love of learning,' much less 'to the profession of genius'; their defence was that this marked the increasing complexity of modern life. 'There have been many changes in the world in the past forty years,' said a *Varsity* editorialist in 1923. 'The world is becoming a more complex place to live in, necessitating that man's equipment becomes correspondingly more complex; and so comes a flood of students to universities the world over; not led on by the pure love of learning, but driven to college by the pressure of the times and the widening field of man's activity. This is not a sign of degeneration, it is a sign of progress.'[29] Going to university, concluded the dean of arts at Queen's in 1930, had become a commonplace extension of the general educational experience; many students were simply sent there by parents, and brought with them the belief that study was a task rather than a pleasure or even a duty. 'Keenness and curiosity are the main elements in any education,' concluded the dean, 'and, if these are not present, there is no likelihood of any intellectual distinction.'[30]

As the decade progressed, student leaders found the task of leadership increasingly difficult. By 1927 freshman numbers were judged to be too great at Victoria College for 'The Bob,' a traditional variety night in which individual students were spoofed, to be successful. 'There is no indifference like the indifference of multitudes,' lamented *Acta Victoriana.*'[31] By the end of the decade student activity and morale at Queen's was at a low ebb. Participation in elections was poor, and the AMS executive had a difficult time reviving the College Frolic.[32] Even the students of McMaster, newly resident in their promised land in Hamilton in the autumn of 1930, found themselves less than happy. 'Student government in McMaster cannot be called a myth,' wrote an editorialist in the first edition of the new student newspaper, the *Silhouette*; ' – it is a significant ruin of worn-out traditions and the cumbersome machinations of a decadent democracy. After having succeeded in attaining a certain prestige, it has gradually dissipated ...'[33] The lament points towards two characteristics of undergraduate life in the post-war world: first, its multifaceted nature, which seemed to diffuse student energies; and second, the uneasy coexistence of old and new forms of social expression and organization.

University life was constantly expanding. There seemed to be a formal or informal club for every activity. At McMaster in the 1920s, for example, clubs existed for the enjoyment of choral singing, modern literature, natural history, chemistry, photography, and debating. Teams of organized sports added another layer to the formal organization of student interests. Fragmenting the student body further, such clubs ran on parallel lines, separated at one point by the barrier of sex, and at another by groups that aimed at taking advantage of inter-faculty or inter-collegiate competition – such as the Women's Inter-collegiate Debating Union. The problem of student government was therefore less one of complacence than of fragmented energies. There was only so much time in the day. By the end of the 1920s, undergraduate government at McMaster reflected this; its legislative efficiency, not its enthusiasm, had diminished – because its many new student organizations had helped create 'a pyramiding of executive bodies, and overlapping representation on the council, and a top-heavy, much amended constitution.'[34]

At Trinity College, where the long shadow of Bishop Strachan was fading, life was an uneasy mixture of old and new. Post-war student activities continued to revolve around long-established organizations or annual events, such as the literary institute, the glee club, and the 'Conversat,' but such pre-war inheritances proved less than satisfying in the post-war world. Formal readings of literature and essays at the 'Lit,' previously important, were abandoned because they were considered too boring. Activity in the 'Lit' turned instead to political debates along studiously parliamentary lines, and student politicians roamed college corridors at election time making grandiose promises and distributing free cigarettes to undecided freshmen. For Trinity students, the new age demanded a greater degree of expression than the glee club – now seen as lingering on from an age that was past and judged to be out of tune with the times – could allow.

Even the annual 'Conversat' no longer seemed quite as special as it once was; its ambience now, in its own way, reflected the cultural ambivalence of the 1920s in Ontario. At one moment it seemed to be a lingering remnant of late-Victorian or Edwardian innocence, college corridors decorated with blue and gold banners and *rouge et noir* bunting, students strictly chaperoned, and a dance that ended promptly at one o'clock with the playing of 'The Home Waltz.' Yet in the next, the gas mantles of Convocation Hall, where the event was held, managed to get shattered, leaving the ballroom in darkness except for the glow of cigarettes – fireflies of the new era. Few Scottish ballads were any longer played by the orchestra; students danced instead to 'The Charleston,' 'Running Wild,' 'I'll See You In My Dreams,' 'The

Wabash Blues,' or 'The Sheik of A-ra-by.' As one Trinity College graduate recalled, wistfully: 'Ahh ... did ever saxaphones [*sic*] moan more sweetly?' Trinity prided itself on being the most elite of the Toronto colleges, and its activities set forward more starkly than elsewhere the symbols of the age. It was, said one of its historians, 'after all ... the last outpost of a way of life firmly rooted in the Victorian tradition,' and because of this it 'deplored the boisterous excesses of the "lost generation."' Yet while its students would have ridiculed the appearance of a coon coat in its precincts, the syncopated strumming of banjos or ukeleles was not unknown there. It was even rumoured that the bob-haired vamp could occasionally be seen haunting the halls of St Hilda's College. Its students also dabbled, rather self-consciously, with the avantgarde literature of the day – whether of Lawrence, Eliot, Verlaine, or Rimbaud – as likely as not, it was said, to avoid studying the formal curriculum as out of intrinsic interest.[35]

Nothing shaped the dynamic of student life in Ontario universities after the Great War more than the relationship between young men and women. By 1920 women had been present in the universities of the province for generations. In English Canada as a whole, their numbers had increased from eleven per cent of the student population at the turn of the century to over sixteen per cent by 1920.[36] In this way, however slowly, they continued to widen the range of social territory they occupied. Men may have continued to rule the Victorian market-place, but by the end of the nineteenth century women controlled access to the parlour and largely determined what went on in it. This was a form of domestic empowerment they would not easily surrender. Yet the world outside the home was also attractive and in a different way, for it held the potential for a different kind of freedom. Cities allowed escape from the close supervision of elders. The anonymous character of urban life provided greater ease of movement and therefore an increased capacity to meet potential partners and to court them in the privacy of public space.[37] Those who attended university were not, then, simply increasing their educational attainments: they were also continuing to expand, wittingly or not, the traditional territories of courtship, with the potential in the case of women for a greater degree of access to, and control over, male terrain. The preoccupation with dances, and the excitement and controversy that ensued from the tango craze on the eve of the Great War, reflected an emerging potential for reciprocity in gender relations where social activity was concerned, for men and women organized, attended, and enjoyed college dances in equal measure. It took two to tango. The question posed by the post-war generation was – who would lead?

The answer is an ambiguous one. The first years after the war were marked by a release of student energies, but in different directions. Some who enrolled in the autumns of 1919 and 1920 were impatient with the more juvenile forms of hazing and of initiation rites. At postwar Trinity, where 'the flavour of the times trickled into the life of the College' almost in spite of itself,[38] some male collegians began to be drawn to the conspicuous consumption characteristic of Veblen's leisure class or Leacock's idle rich. But their pocketbooks usually reflected a different reality. Estimating the costs of university life at the beginning of the year could be a sobering experience even in a decade of formal sobriety. The yearly costs of male students in arts at the University of Toronto were about $700. Expenses, of course, varied greatly from faculty to faculty, according to the level of tuition fees. Annual costs for the dental student were over $900, and for those in medicine $810. Any student who belonged to a fraternity could figure on spending an additional $200 more per year than other students. Since *Varsity* estimated that very few men earned more than $350 during their summer vacations, the average student budget in the 1920s obviously did not allow for much roaring (see Table 15.1).[39] Nevertheless, possibly influenced by media portrayal of American college students as self-indulgent seekers after pleasure, some students sought prestige by stretching their budgets to the breaking-point in order to impress their dates. Certainly the many advertisements for clothing, books, typewriters, jewelry, banks, and cigarettes in student journals and newspapers such as *Acta Victoriana* or *Queen's Journal* did little to discourage conspicuous consumption and much to create the adult consumer.[40] Men began to insist on taking women to and from dates in taxis, rather than using public transit or simply walking. University of Toronto women were divided in 1923 over the taxi issue. The matter was a trivial one, yet it reflected the division of opinion among students about the extent to which economic capacity was acceptable as a means of purchasing the attention of women – and also that some women were not willing to let a free taxi ride be the sign of a successful date. But theirs, it must be noted, was a minority view.[41]

While some women began to adopt the fashions of the 1920s as a means of attracting men, others waged a counter-campaign. A movement advocating the return to formal academic gowns grew in popularity among women at the University of Toronto in the mid-1920s. Some stated that such a reform would promote dignity and uniformity among students; others pointed to the sense of tradition or heightened status it promoted. By January 1925 the initiative had gained the formal sponsorship of the women's undergraduate association of the university.[42] It is more than likely that women's rediscovery of the academic gown was implicitly linked to the high costs entailed in social competition based

TABLE 15.1
Estimated average costs of a male student in arts, University of Toronto, 1922–3

Tuition	$40
Books	25
Board and Room (plus minor clothing and incidentals, $10/wk. for 30 wks.)	300
Laundry ($1/wk. for 30 wks.)	30
Socks	5
Collars and ties	5
Movies (2 tickets twice a month)	15
"Real" dances (two)	12
Pants pressing ($.50/wk.)	15
Attendance at various games	5
Clothing (1 suit, 1 overcoat)	70
Shoes (2 pair)	15
Shirts (half dozen)	12
Hat	6
Underclothing	10
Visits home	30
TOTAL	$595

SOURCE: Costs derived from 'What Does it Cost Student for a Year? Detailed Information Secured By "The Varsity" Shows Wide Variation,' Varsity (25 October 1922).

on possession of the latest wardrobe, although no student at the time was willing to give this reason to Varsity. Certainly, the general cost of living for a female student was at least as anxiety-inducing as for men – except that their virtual absence from enrolment in professional faculties meant that tuition fees were lower. Varsity's 1922 estimate of student expenses hinted at the pressure of fashion in its ridicule, for it included costs of several items of social attire. 'Think of it ye males – the fair sex must perforce spend at least $25 per year for hats.' Total yearly expenses for women students were thought to be about $750.[43]

Financial pressures on student pocketbooks, male or female, did not come simply from the initiatives of competitive men, eager for membership in the local fast set. Young men acted, as often as not, on the basis of social expectation: they wanted to know how women wanted them to behave. They sought to please, and they followed as much as they led. 'The girl of to-day,' the newspapers told them, had acquired 'seemingly expensive wants and habits' that had to be met.[44] In the new age, man continued to be seen as provider; but it was woman who was regarded as the essential ingredient of the culture of consumption. 'The proper study of mankind is man,' the advertising industry told the newspapers, 'but the proper study of markets is woman.'[45]

Changes in women's fashion or deportment were marked by men with more than idle curiosity. Bobbed hair, shortened skirts, and the smoking of cigarettes were important cues in the ritual of post-war North American romance. They were interpreted as signals from women not only that they had, in various ways, emancipated themselves from the social confinements of the home, but also that the rules regulating family life had been relaxed in the urban world of higher education. Whether men read such signals accurately or not is less important than the fact that they perceived university women to be always ready for a good time. 'The coeducational campus became the scene of heterosexual play – at the soda fountain, the movies, and college dances ... While dating had its own rules that kept most college women technically virgins until engagement, it allowed large doses of foreplay and enough ambiguity to keep college men trying.'[46]

A good deal of attention was given to the coed in the 1920s in the university press and in Toronto daily newspapers. Male reporters – reporters were overwhelmingly male – kept a journalistic lookout for female fads and fashions in articles that as often as not were patronizing and mocking. Both the Toronto *Star* and the Toronto *Telegram* noted in 1923 how far coeducation had changed from the days of the first entry of the bluestocking into university life. Now, declared the *Star*, they constituted a veritable fashion-conscious multitude in which individuality was inconspicuous.[47] *Varsity* also reported on the difference that had emerged between the serious and single-minded woman undergraduate of yesteryear and the coed of the new day. The very term 'woman undergraduate' was considered by 1924 to be too sombre to describe the 'more pleasure loving, more decidedly feministic sister' on the modern campus. How could such a pompous term adequately describe 'the sweet young girl, muffled up in snug fur coat whose saucy little hat nods and bobs every few minutes to the steady flow of serious young men whom she meets as she madly dashes over to lectures'? How could the girl who thinks lectures are either 'a bore' or 'fun,' and for whom 'college means ... the acquirement of a certain amount of miscellaneous knowledge and a ripping good time in all sorts of social activities' be called a woman undergraduate? Clearly, *Varsity* proclaimed, she was a coed. The term would apply, it concluded, 'as long as we follow our restless, seeking-the-easiest-way-out neighbour to the south and as the ever increasing social activities continue to draw a certain type of girl to college.' The fact that some people in Ontario persisted in using the term woman undergraduate, it was said with some pride, reflected the continuing presence of 'sufficient conservative British instincts ...'[48]

Journalists were far more interested in the coed than in the woman undergraduate, and they went to considerable lengths to discover a Fitzgeraldian fast set in Toronto. Women students discovered to be smoking, for example, were newsworthy. After reading an article in which an American professor expressed his alarm over the conduct of his country's youth – cosmetics, booze, and petting especially preoccupied him – a *Telegram* reporter decided to determine the extent of moral decay in Ontario universities. Doubtless he looked forward to a titillating assignment, but if so he was disappointed. University authorities admitted the existence of a 'gay set,' but the clear consensus was that the pace of social life had, if anything, slowed considerably since the immediate post-war years. Miss Addison of Victoria College's Annesley Hall declared: 'There isn't a speck of drinking and very little smoking and make-up, while as for scanty dressing, the gowns are for the most part cut rather high – quite different from the backless creations of the immediate post-war period.' College activities of 'a wholesome and helpful nature' at Victoria, the *Telegram* reporter was forced to conclude, were 'abundant.' The reporter had no better luck elsewhere. McMaster University, on Bloor Street, reported that there was no evidence of any 'fast set' there. The files in newspaper morgues were of little help. When *Varsity* searched in 1926 for the 'dissolute college boy' – the kind who carried a hip-flask – it found that the phenomenon was virtually unknown on campus, and that students of the mid-1920s drank far less alcohol than students had just after the war. (By then, of course, the last of the war veterans had gone.) Reporters also found that little, if any, gambling took place. What about a decline in classroom manners? In 1928 the question of behaviour by students who 'were rather more careless in their habits in a classroom than they would be in a night club' – yawning, sprawling, and stretching, for example – had been hotly discussed at the University of Michigan. Once again, no evidence of similar behaviour was found.[49] No doubt university authorities who declared so confidently that none of their students smoked, drank, gambled, or were rude erred on the side of rectitude. No generation of university students was ever quite that angelic. Yet the thrust of the evidence is clearly that, in general, university students in the province generally lived on the sober side of paradise. This was Ontario.

One reason why Ontario students were less adventuresome than their American counterparts was that university and college authorities continued to keep a close check on the residential and social lives of students. But there proved to be limits in the 1920s to student acceptance of the kind of *in loco parentis* control that university authorities had managed to exert before the war and now sought to re-establish. Officials at Queen's discovered this in 1928 when a student revolt helped bring about the downfall of a principal. That man, Bruce Taylor, was capable at times of turning a blind if concerned eye to the incursions of gown into the territory of town, whether in the form of snake dances on Princess Street, disruptive invasions of movie theatres, or the decoration of Kingston streetcars with the red and yellow Queen's colours. But he could not cope with the decade's apparent obsession with other forms of frivolity. 'It is a dancing and frivolous age,' intent on nothing more than a good time, the exasperated principal told the university's trustees at the decade's end, 'It requires apparatus, whether it be an automobile or a dancing floor, or a hired orchestra of a minimum number of pieces, or a taxicab to take a maiden across the street from Ban Righ to Grant Hall.'[50]

Faced in 1928 with a number of student infractions – such as the hospitalization of two male students after they challenged each other to drink a full bottle of rum – Taylor and the university senate reacted sternly. The incident became news in Toronto. A *Star* headline read: 'Bottles Empty, Contestants "Tight," When Queen's Lads Stage Rum Fight.'[51] Thus, when Queen's students in 1928 decided to hold their annual review – the 'Frolic' – under the private auspices of three students, at a downtown location (whose name, 'The Venetian Gardens,' sounded suspiciously like that of a nightclub) and with any interested party to be admitted, the university sought to prevent the imminent breach of acceptable conduct. Taylor was not particularly aided by the university's senate. Largely reduced to a rubber-stamping body after university reform in 1912 had divested it of real power, the senate had sought in the 1920s to re-establish its power and authority by focussing on student improprieties. When the crisis of the off-campus 'Frolic' occurred, the senate had already suspended the two errant student tipplers without a hearing, much to the annoyance of the Alma Mater Society. It now suspended the organizers of the 'Frolic' – which took place without incident – for two weeks, and outraged students decided to go on strike until the student organizers were reinstated. A senatorial gesture reducing the suspension from two weeks to one served only to weaken its already diminished authority. The students stayed home from crucial end-of-year classes. The university's insistence that it held the right to regulate student conduct on and off campus squared off against the students' objection to being 'interfered with in [their] private lives.'[52]

The matter was resolved after students were assured that no punishment would be meted out to the offenders after their week's suspension was served. They reluctantly returned to classes. From their perspective, they had won. Had the Kingston *Whig-Standard* not declared that 'the question of discipline' had 'been applied in a slip-shod manner lately'? That the rest of the Ontario daily press was solidly on the side of the university's right to provide quasi-parental discipline was, for the students, irrelevant. Principal Taylor, whose support on the university's board of trustees was already weak for other reasons, had now completely lost its confidence. Within a year, under direct pressure from its board chairman, he resigned.

In fact, Ontario students in the 1920s bore little resemblance to those portrayed by the American media. They were neither morally out of control nor in revolt against a meaningless past. They would not, however, accept authority for authority's sake, and they were at times willing to express their resentment of paternalistic moral guardianship, especially where extracurricular activities were concerned. What Marion Wood of Havergal College observed of the college girl of 1925 probably characterized the student generation of the time. On the whole, she concluded, the Ontario college girl of 1925 had more common sense and a more definite aim in life than could be said for her counterpart at the turn of the century. Yet students were by no means complacent. 'One sees in the modern girl much less readiness to accept things on trust. She wants to get to the bottom of things. She questions everything. There is a tendency to resent authority, and perhaps a failure to take advice. She prefers to experience for herself rather than to accept the experience of those who have gone before.'[53]

Pattern, Program, Gender

The notion that the woman of the new era preferred to shape her own academic life rather than let tradition dictate her future may have been true, but it also masked a harsher reality. Pressures on women after the war to return to the traditional security of home, hearth, and husband were very great. The media depiction of the Jazz Age heightened women's vocational dilemmas, for their new day appeared to offer new kinds of opportunities and experiences yet witnessed the reassertion of older attitudes towards the sexes. After the fragmentation of family life brought about by the war, how many people would not have wanted to see stable home lives re-established? When in 1923 the Toronto *Star* reported the presence of the fun-loving coed in large numbers on campus, its headline writer felt obliged to assure his readers with a subtitle that read: 'STILL, THEY MARRY!'[54]

The world between the wars was still very much a male preserve, and girls and young women were routinely socialized at home and in school, as they had been before the war, to believe that marriage and motherhood should be their ultimate ambition. Few would have denied that Canadian women had made a substantial contribution to the domestic war effort, whether in factories, offices, or farms; but many believed that, now that the war was over, women should return to their traditional role as home-makers. 'Do you feel justified in holding a job which could be filled by a man who has not only himself to support, but a wife and family as well?' read a federal government poster. 'Think it over.'[55]

Many Canadian women, especially those marginalized by having little education or by poverty, had little opportunity to choose the direction of their lives. Those enrolled in universities after the war, the privileged of Canadian society, were among the few who could. Increasing numbers of young women after the war sought to maximize their opportunities by staying in school. The proportion of those between fifteen and nineteen who did so rose from twenty-seven per cent to thirty-six per cent between 1921 and 1931, and reached thirty-seven per cent by 1941, consistently a few percentage points higher than the number of boys of the same age who remained in school.[56] As a result, more women than ever before held the requisite qualifications for university entrance.[57]

Theirs was a beleaguered minority on campus, for it faced male opinion that ranged from quiet tolerance to outright misogyny. Throughout the 1920s university women were ridiculed if they partied too often or studied too much,[58] if they sought entrance into professional faculties or confined themselves to arts,[59] if they indicated that their post-graduate ambition was to marry or to have a career.[60] In 1925 the Toronto *Star* asked twenty-five university men what they wanted in a wife. It found that they wanted women to have 'amiable, pleasant dispositions, be reasonably neat and tidy in clothing and general appearance, be endowed with good health and most important of all ... "not attempt to run things."'[61] Given such a general attitude among its male readers, *Varsity* scarcely needed to add editorial commentary or qualifications when it quoted the popular British historian and novelist H.G. Wells as claiming that 'education suffers because too much instruction is given by women.'[62] Statement of the facts – at that moment only sixty-one women were among the more than seven hundred University of Toronto staff members[63] – would scarcely have changed the attitude. For some, any women on the staff or among the students were too many. The 1929 editor of *Acta Victoriana* lamented the increasing number of women: 'Is Victoria about to become a ladies' finishing school with a few pre-theological students and a few sons of loyal graduates as the sole remaining male adornments?' The editorial was not meant to be ironic, for it continued with dire warnings about what would happen to 'Vic' if too many women continued to come.[64]

By the 1920s coeducation had been a fact of academic life in the major Ontario universities for almost half a century, yet what had been its outcome? At the University of Toronto, women were not welcome at its student centre, Hart House, at least not as members. They could not participate in its debates, study in its reading rooms, use its athletic facilities, or dine in its Great Hall. At every Ontario universiy what facilities women had paled in comparison with those afforded to men. In spite of an increase of interest by women in previously male-oriented sports, intermural or intercollegiate sports programs remained overwhelmingly dedicated to competition between men.[65] Throughout the interwar years they continued to complain about such discrimination, but with little effect.[66] Some minor achievements were made, as at McMaster, where women initiated their own hockey league and field day after the war.

Even then, however, parallel activities scarcely resulted in equal treatment. When Miss E. Gilmour was judged to be the top McMaster female athlete in 1920, the year of the first women's field day, her reward was a box of Laura Secord chocolates and a medal.[67] Only men could receive the coveted university 'letter.' The first female residence at McMaster, Wallingford Hall, which opened in 1920 as a result of William Davies's gift of $32,000, brought women a measure of autonomy but also a degree of supervision not applied to the university's men. In addition to a desire for 'a well-trained mind' its residents were relied upon to have 'a controlled and cultured personality, and, underlying it all, a high sense of Christian indebtedness to all of the world ...' McMaster's women students were expected, like all its students, to subscribe to the university's motto – 'In Him all things consist.' For a few of the university's women, those words may have epitomized the prevailing gender relations of the day.[68]

In the face of such obstacles, a strategy favoured by some university women was for extracurricular activity to be officially segregated on the basis of gender. If women could not gain equal access to activities dominated by men, perhaps a solution was to create the conditions by which women could govern their own extracurricular lives. Many University of Toronto women refused to attend student meetings at which they had no voting rights. Sparked by reports that the segregation of women and men had become very popular on a number of American campuses, including that of Cornell, in 1923 the University College council discussed the merits of formal segregation as a means of creating greater student spirit and unity. The matter became a subject of debate at Toronto in the 1922–3 term. Women claimed they were marginalized on the current University College executive and that the existence of a separate body would remove the discrimination. Men replied that campus women would not organize because they lacked the initiative or skill to do so. Women students held a referendum. The issue may have been on every tongue, as *Varsity* claimed, but it was apparently not of sufficient importance to galvanize the majority of University of Toronto women students into political action. Of the 1,812 female students enrolled in the university, only 123 voted: eighty-five favoured separation; thirty-eight were satisfied with the status quo.[69] The initiative went nowhere.

Queen's University prided itself on being in the forefront of the coeducational movement. Its new principal, Hamilton Fyfe, crowed in 1932 that 'there is much to be said for Women's Universities which exclude all men; and a good deal of it seems to have been said lately. But segregation is not in our Canadian tradition. Queen's blazed the trail of co-education and has no intention of turning back on it ... Queen's is unrepentantly co-educational.'[70] That, at least, was the legend. The reality was quite different outside the principal's office, as it had been for decades.

By the 1920s Levana operated almost like an independent faculty within the university. Formally, of course, it was simply an organization of women students; yet descriptions of the student population, whether in *Queen's Journal* or in student handbooks, invariably mentioned Levana in the same way it mentioned arts, science, or medicine. Queen's women were overwhelmingly enrolled in the faculty of arts, but everyone knew and acknowledged that their primary affiliation was to Levana. This helps explain the description of the arts society in the *Student Handbook* of 1926–7 as 'the student organization of all male students registered in Arts or Commerce.' Nevertheless, in spite of Levana's faculty-like stature, formal relations between it and the Alma Mater Society – that is, between female and male students – were those of inferior to superior. Permission had to be asked of the AMS, whether to use the gymnasium or to organize athletic events. Female representation on the main student body, as on the *Journal* editorial board, was minimal, yet still it was resented. 'Why not let the women have a "government" or a Mother Institute or a Dancing Club all of their own,' one male student complained, 'and let the men have a real government of their own to be run by men for the interest of the men only?' In a sense that was what already existed, for Levana was the women's 'government' at Queen's, and now that the AMS wall had been breached, the Students Memorial Union – from which women were still barred – became the local fortress in which male privilege would be defended. 'In the midst of the invading feminine movement,' said one exasperated student, the time had come for men to 'make [their] last stand and keep the Union as the safe and sacred retreat of men.'[71]

Throughout the 1920s at Queen's it was mainly the men who discussed the coeducation issue. They accused women of undermining educational standards by distracting men from their studies. Women were preoccupied with social rather than academic life, one student complained, content with organizing 'the multitude of class parties and tea dances which punctuate the College Year.' The presence of coeds in a classroom of men 'handicapped' professors, said another, by causing them to 'emasculate' their lectures 'to suit the women. Who has not watched the professor lead up to a debateable [*sic*] subject and then slide around? Here is an instance where the presence of the coed is undesirable.' Another spoke in a similar vein: 'While the gentry of the class are all seated in orderly array devouring the words of their hungry professor,' he noted, 'one by one the butterflies flit in late ... They fail to interpret the applause which greets them in the spirit in which it is given.'[72]

At best, women at Queen's could expect to receive a reluctant and passive acceptance of their presence, whether from students or staff. It was one matter for earlier generations of students or professors to state, at the level of principle, their acceptance of women's rights to higher education or to the vote. Theory seldom interfered with reality, especially in academic life. It was quite another matter to argue for equality of treatment or of condition between men and women when – the principles no longer at issue – the struggle took place at the level of ordinary experience. Here social practices altered to accommodate women might involve irritating and inconvenient changes to the comfort of men and to the routines of daily life heretofore dominated by male convention. Principal Taylor, who struggled throughout the decade with students he regarded as supercilious, scarcely provided leadership on the issue: 'Whether coeducation is a means to further the education of the brute, or whether it is a waste of time,' he told the student newspaper in 1927, 'whether there is a period in a man's life when he should be entirely away from women, I refuse to say. I have never been quoted on any views of coeducation.'[73]

Continuation of the ideology of separate spheres invariably meant that men were provided with better physical resources, such as gymnasia or common rooms, than were women. But the notion went beyond the extracurricular into the heart of the curriculum itself. The problem was not simply that lectures were watered down because of women in the classroom; it was that different subjects were coming to be seen as the academic domain of either men or women. 'What are the non-compulsory classes that are attended by men?' said an angry student in 1928. 'Natural science, math, economics, etc., are largely filled with them. Language and history are regarded as women's subjects and it is a brave

FIGURE 15.1

Total male and female enrolment in Canadian universities, 1920–50

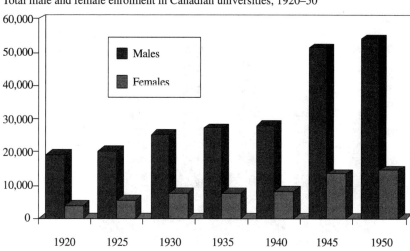

SOURCE: *Historical Statistics of Canada*, 2nd ed. (Ottawa 1983), series 340–438

or foolish male who majors in these.'[74] The pursuit of knowledge itself continued overtly to be conditioned by assumptions that linked gender and vocation.

The proportion of women attending Canadian universities increased significantly during the 1920s. In 1920, for every woman enrolled there were five men; by the end of the decade there were just over three. Total enrolment of men in the country in 1920 was 19,390; that of women, 3,824. Ten years later the numbers stood at 25,146 and 7,780, respectively. Most of the increase in the proportion of women occurred in the first half of the decade, not because there was a lower rate of increase, but because between 1925 and 1930 the number of men enrolled had jumped significantly. With the onset of the Great Depression in the 1930s, enrolment increases by both women and men virtually ended: only 653 more women and 2,807 more men were enrolled in Canadian universities at the end of the decade than at its beginning. The proportion of women to men in 1940 remained at thirty per cent (see Fig. 15.1).

Throughout the interwar years the level of enrolment in Ontario universities remained at least thirty per cent of the Canadian total. In the second half of the 1930s the socio-economic impact of the Depression took its toll on university enrolment in the West and the Maritimes, yet total Canadian enrolment remained stable, even growing slightly, from 35,108 to 36,386, between 1935 and 1940. Enrolment in Ontario, with a diversified economy that was hard hit but resisted the worst effects of

FIGURE 15.2

Total university enrolment, Canada, Ontario, University of Toronto, 1920–50

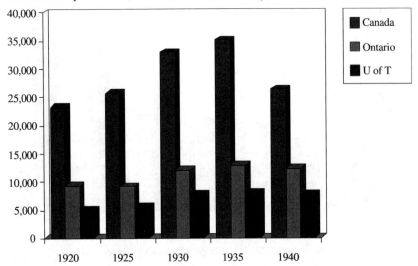

SOURCE: *Historical Statistics*, series 340–438; Marni de Pencier, 'A Study of the Enrolment of Women in the University of Toronto,' research paper, University of Toronto (1973)

the boom or bust Canadian economy,[75] remained stable: it was 12,817 in 1935 and 12,410 in 1940. In that year, 31.1 per cent of all Canadian university students attended an Ontario university. Here, one cannot help but notice the importance of the University of Toronto. Throughout the 1920s and 1930s more than half of Ontario's university students were enrolled at the University of Toronto, and by 1940 Toronto students amounted to sixty-two per cent of the total. Ontario's provincial university accommodated more than twenty per cent of the *national* university enrolment in its programs in both 1920 and 1940 (see Fig. 15.2). If any university in the country could legitimately have claimed national status in the years between the wars, it was the University of Toronto. Its sheer numbers and the increasing diversity of its program could not be matched anywhere else in Canada, except perhaps at McGill.

Because of this it is worth dwelling on the University of Toronto as we consider the relationships between gender and academic programs. To begin with, the proportion of female students as a percentage of total enrolment increased slowly but steadily throughout the 1920s. Whereas male enrolment in fact decreased from 1921 through 1924 (reflected in total enrolment figures) as returned soldiers graduated, that of women

FIGURE 15.3
University of Toronto enrolment, total and female, 1919–39

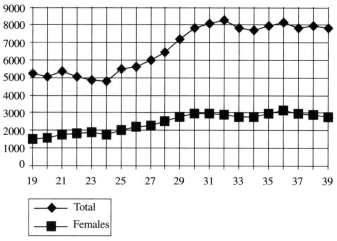

SOURCE: de Pencier, 'Enrolment of Women'

increased. In the second half of the decade, enrolment of both sexes began to increase, that of men at a greater rate than women. The Depression caused enrolment to level off, and then to fluctuate. Female students were thirty-two per cent of the total Toronto enrolment in 1920, increasing to thirty-seven per cent in 1925 and thirty-eight per cent in 1930. After falling again to thirty-seven per cent in 1935, their numbers recovered so that at the end of the 1930s the female-to-male ratio was where it had been at its beginning (see Fig. 15.3).[76]

To those men at the University of Toronto who resented the presence of women, or who for whatever reasons felt threatened by them, it doubtless seemed as if the number of women on the campus was more than thirty-five or forty per cent. And there were good reasons for such a perception. The daily cycle of male-female contact occurred in the college and the classroom. If membership in the major colleges is therefore taken into account, a rather more dramatic picture emerges. Forty-six per cent of the members of University College in 1920 were women. In the 1930s the rate of attrition for male students was greater, particularly until 1937, when enrolment of both men and women began once again to increase. By decade's end, fifty-one per cent of the student population in the college were women (see Fig. 15.4). A similar but slightly more exaggerated pattern existed between 1919 and 1939 at Victoria College.

FIGURE 15.4

Membership in University College, total and female, 1919–39

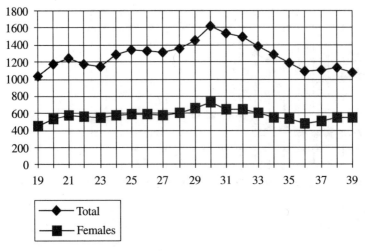

SOURCE: de Pencier, 'Enrolment of Women'

FIGURE 15.5

Membership in Victoria College, total and female, 1919–39

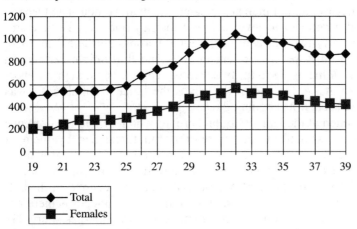

SOURCE: de Pencier, 'Enrolment of Women'

Women reached the fifty per cent plateau there in 1922, when they numbered 286 of the total membership of 546. Hovering consistently around half the total student population, they reached fifty-four per cent in 1932. Even in 1939, after almost a decade of continuous decline in

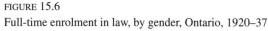

FIGURE 15.6

Full-time enrolment in law, by gender, Ontario, 1920–37

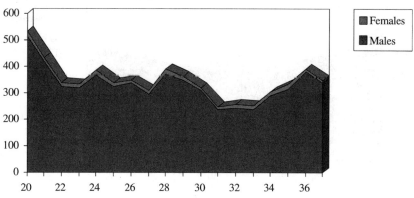

SOURCE: *Higher Education in Canada, 1936–38* (Ottawa 1939)

enrolment of female students at 'Vic,' women remained almost half of the student body (see Fig. 15.5).

Daily social life in Toronto's major colleges made it appear that university attendance almost reflected the equal balance of the sexes within the population as a whole. But the reality could differ depending on the classroom, for programs held varying proportions of men and women. In the traditional professions it was still a man's world, because so few women were in them. Among those studying medicine or law in Ontario between 1920 and 1937, for example, the presence of women was negligible, as it was in Canada as a whole (see Figs. 15.6–15.8).[77] Those women who possessed an aptitude for or an interest in traditional professional education were seldom encouraged. One woman recalled a conversation with her dean of arts, concerning her future: 'I explained to him that because I was doing well and had a strong penchant for medicine, I would like to transfer from the Arts College to the medical school. He was a likeable man, truly interested in all of his students, but he bristled at that and said he really would advise against such a move. "After all," he said, "you wouldn't get the use out of such a career, as you'll probably be a wife and a mother soon after graduation."'[78] The universities of Ontario were filled with such likeable men, just trying to help. As a result of such attitudes, the percentage of women in programs in law, medicine, and business continued to be small throughout the country.[79] So what did women study? The answer is as simple as it is hackneyed. They studied subjects that had come to be associated with their sex, its social attributes, and its instincts. The field of education provides the most striking example.

FIGURE 15.7

Full-time enrolment in law, by gender, Canada, 1920–37

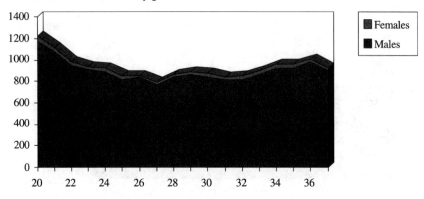

SOURCE: *Higher Education in Canada, 1936–38* (Ottawa 1939)

FIGURE 15.8

Full-time enrolment in commerce, by gender, Ontario, 1920–37

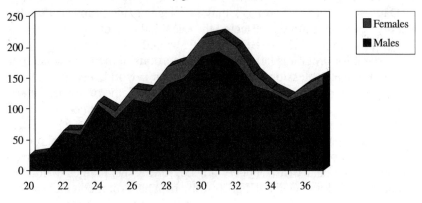

SOURCE: *Higher Education in Canada, 1936–38* (Ottawa 1939)

The feminization of teaching scarcely abated with the advent of the flapper and the bob. By the 1920s, in fact, the number of women seeking to enter the teaching profession had reached alarming proportions – alarming, at least, to some men. Educational experts were torn between recognizing financial common sense and giving voice to their opinions on the vocational place of women. School administrators complied with school boards concerned with fiscal responsibility by doing what their counterparts had done since the 1850s: they encouraged the hiring of even more female teachers. Meanwhile, at the Ontario College of Education and the University of Toronto, the teachers of the teachers lamented the lack of professional respect that resulted from its feminization. 'The greatest administrative need in modern education,' complained Dean Packenham of the recently created Ontario College of Education in 1922, 'is an adequate supply of trained teachers, trained *men* teachers. Let us be frank about it. Teaching lacks prestige. It does not attract men.'[80] A radical change had occurred since the days when the ablest of male students went into high school teaching, said one professor in 1930. 'The quality of the graduates, especially of the men, who now enter the profession has fallen almost to the level of those who enter the church.'[81]

In its lack of prestige, teaching threatened to become equal to the profession with which feminine attributes had most come to be associated: the clergy. The source of the problem was clear to male educators. More women in teaching meant less prestige for the profession, and women had swamped it. One professor estimated that in 1905 there had been 511 men and 178 women teaching in Ontario's secondary schools; in 1928 there were 880 men and 1,075 women. Many high schools in the smaller towns and villages of Ontario had a male principal but from three to eight women assistants. The women, moreover, were seen to be unreliable, and from a purely administrative point of view they were: the average length of service of women graduates in the pass course of the Ontario College of Education was under five years. Even those women who had graduated with honours degrees stayed in the profession only six and one-half years, compared with a little over twelve for the men. 'It would seem,' Professor J.F. Macdonald of the University of Toronto complained, 'that most of them have no intention of making the profession a life work but teach only long enough to earn the amount that will buy a satisfactory trousseau.'[82] The language of such complaints suggests that the problem rested less in the unreliability of women than in the social construction of gender. The maleness of men was threatened. The job had become sissified. Male students told Professor Macdonald why they turned to engineering or commerce instead of teaching. 'Oh, it's a kind of sissy job,' said one. 'The trouble is that most of the fellows think it's a sissy job,' said another. The sad fact was that 'the teacher has no longer the social standing he once had. In fact he belonged to a profession that is rapidly coming in this country, if indeed, it has not already come, to be regarded as a woman's occupation.'[83]

Of all those enrolled in full-time university undergraduate programs in education throughout Canada in 1920, 61.8 per cent were women. By 1930 this had increased to 64.4 per cent. Only the Depression, which

FIGURE 15.9

Enrolment in faculty of education, University of Toronto and Ontario College of Education, total and female, 1919–39

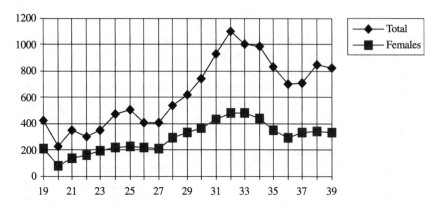

SOURCE: de Pencier, 'Enrolment of Women'

placed extraordinary pressure on women to return to the home so that men could have the few jobs available, halted the march of educated women into teaching. By the end of the 1930s, fifty-two percent of the nation's teachers were men.[84] Enrolment in education at the University of Toronto and (from 1920) the Ontario College of Education (OCE) reflects the trend. In 1920, total enrolment was 226, seventy-six of whom were women. By 1929 they comprised 335 of the total of 619. In a decade they had increased from thirty-four to fifty-four per cent of student teachers. Then came the Depression. Increasing numbers of men, possibly many who had lost jobs or who could see no prospects in other fields, began to enrol as secondary school teachers-in-training. Enrolment at OCE in 1932–3 was 624 men and 477 women. By the end of the decade, and of the Depression, the proportion of women had dropped to forty-one per cent of the OCE student population (see Fig. 15.9). This, however, was for training to teach in secondary schools. A much larger proportion of women taught in the primary grades after training in the province's normal schools. In 1926, Queen's University's dean of women, Hilda Laird, reported that of the 131 women students who had declared their professional intentions that year, 118 had said 'Teaching.'[85]

Next to faculties of education throughout Canada, women enrolled overwhelmingly in faculties of arts and science, usually concentrating on the humanities. Hilda Laird accounted for 257 women who had registered for honours work at Queen's in 1925–6 (concerning their choice of subjects, see Table 15.2).[86] This was the fundamental unit of academic

TABLE 15.2
Subjects chosen by women in honours arts program, Queen's University, 1925–6

Subjects	Number of Students
English and French	79
English and History	58
Mathematics and Physics	19
Latin and Greek	18
French and Spanish	15
French and German	12
Chemistry and Biology	12
Other 'less usual' combinations	44
TOTAL	257

SOURCE: Queen's University, *Report of the Principal, 1925–6*, 64

FIGURE 15.10
Enrolment in faculty of arts, University of Toronto, total and female, 1919–39

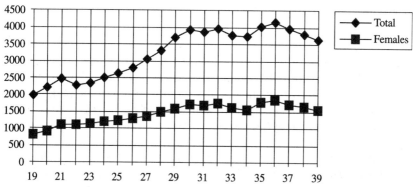

SOURCE: de Pencier, 'Enrolment of Women'

study for women in part because they found so few other avenues easily accessible or very hospitable to them (in 1930, women comprised fourteen per cent of Canadian undergraduates in commerce and business administration programs and under five percent in medicine and dentistry, for example).[87] Three hundred six of the 332 women at the University of Western Ontario in 1928 were enrolled in arts.[88] This was perhaps virtually inevitable at a university whose only other major program was the male-dominated medical school (in which six women registered that year). The University of Toronto, in contrast, had a rich and varied range of academic offerings. Yet here, too, women gravitated to arts. In 1929 1,603 of the 3,686 students enrolled in arts at the University of Toronto were women; a decade later the ratio was roughly the same, with 1,563 women and 3,648 men making up the faculty at the undergraduate level in 1939 (see Fig. 15.10).[89]

FIGURE 15.11
Enrolment in faculty of music, University of Toronto, total and female, 1919–39

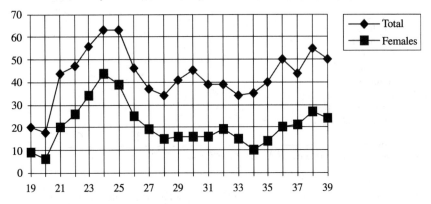

SOURCE: de Pencier, 'Enrolment of Women'

This streaming of students reflected a society that persisted in adjudicating professional or vocational potential by characteristics associated with gender as much as by actual possession of talent or skills. In this way, the replication of occupational structures also entrenched gender-based social attitudes. Music, for example, had been part of the Victorian and Edwardian lady's expected range of refined accomplishment, like watercolour painting or embroidery. When a faculty of music was founded at the University of Toronto in 1919, women immediately enrolled in sizeable numbers. Like English, languages, and (to a lesser extent) history, music provided invaluable preparation for a career in teaching. By 1924, with enrolment in the new faculty at its interwar peak, the forty-four female music students represented seventy per cent of its total student body. By 1928 their proportion had dropped to forty-four per cent. As usual the Depression took its toll, and in music the price was paid by women more than by men. By 1934 women constituted just twenty-eight per cent of the students enrolled in music, although after that their numbers slowly grew again until in 1938 they were sixty-one per cent of the faculty (see Fig. 15.11).[90]

If music was seen to reflect woman's refined nature, serving as a creative outlet for her emotional and aesthetic energies, social service (later social work) programs held abundant capacity to channel the empathetic sympathies and nurturing instincts that she was assigned by both the maternal feminist and 'man's domain' ideologies of the day. Social institutions such as the Young Women's Christian Association, founded in the 1870s and very early linked to university life, had long served as agencies that, in an evangelical Christian context, at once empowered women to seek active forms of professional and social service and reminded them that they could preserve their femininity even while assuming an active place in a troubled industrial society. 'The truest college woman,' said one YWCA pamphlet, 'does not crave a career in which she shall merely enjoy herself, or earn wealth, or gain a reputation. She hopes to be of the greatest real usefulness to the community, and so to the world.'[91] Even after college women began to criticize such overtly evangelical institutions in the second decade of the century for being too intrusive and conservative and overly zealous, they remained committed to active social service, and found an acceptable form in the kind of coeducational organization that culminated in the 1921 formation of the Student Christian Movement of Canada.

That reflected their extracurricular lives. They could equally channel energy into the University of Toronto's department of social service, founded in 1914 as the university's reaction to pervasive evidence within the student community of women's desire to serve the social good in a professional setting. Supported by the approach of its directors R.M. MacIver and E.J. Urwick, both of whom saw social service as a form of social philosophy more than a social science and whose loyalties remained firmly with the individual more than the group,[92] women who enrolled in the social service program found a professional haven and sympathetic professors. The department of social service – in fact a program within the larger department of political economy – became from the first almost exclusively a sphere for women of academic ambition and social commitment. In the years between the wars it was the University of Toronto's school of social work in all but name. At the time of its formal inauguration in September 1914, in quarters provided in the household science building, its enrolment was 293, and 274 of them were women. The balance scarcely changed for the next quarter-century. On the eve of the founding of the university's school of social work in 1941, seventy-eight of the ninety-three registrants were women (see Fig. 15.12).[93]

One advantage of social service as a profession was that it allowed women who wanted to work at a skilled occupation outside the home the capacity to do so but did not threaten either motherhood or the home itself. Indeed, it extended both institutions into society at large. At the turn of the century, Christian altruism, benevolence, and evangelical commitment had propelled young women into the slums, charity kitchens, settlement houses, and hospitals of the nation. In the 1920s and 1930s the daughters and granddaughters of that generation, no less idealistic, channelled similar energies in ways that professionalized mother-

FIGURE 15.12

Enrolment in department of social service / social science, University of Toronto, total and female, 1914–40

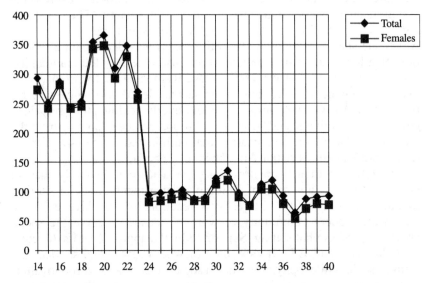

SOURCE: de Pencier, 'Enrolment of Women'

hood – or at least the sympathetic and nurturing instincts they were constantly told they had. In the quest for professions in which to channel their ambition, women continued to draw upon the vocabulary of maternal feminism. They should become librarians, said University of Toronto alumna Margaret Ray, because the new profession required 'peculiarly feminine attributes such as sympathy, intuition, patience in research, thoroughness in detail and a tendency to stress the human side of library work.' Little wonder that ninety-six per cent of those who studied librarianship in Toronto at the end of the 1930s were women.[94] Nor did other women's professions challenge the fundamental domesticity of woman. A basic objective of the professional social worker was, after all, to preserve the well-being of the family by making certain that women remained at home, just as graduates in household science attempted to convince house-bound women that they did not need to enter the work force in order to gain a sense of professional satisfaction in their work. The modern kitchen, women were told, required scientific management, and labour-saving electrical appliances would eliminate dirt and create leisure time.[95]

To be a mother, in the broad popular conception of the day, meant appearing to be in control of a woman's own sphere yet in fact subordinating herself to greater authority – that of the husband or father. Professional women in the interwar years scarcely escaped this nexus, for the professions they entered recapitulated in their own ways the nurturing and subordinate roles that prevailed at home. Yet the problem also involved relations of power and hence authority. Had academic credentials and the capacity to give comfort and aid been the sole prerequisites for recruitment into a profession, women could just as easily have entered medicine and dentistry as nursing or physiotherapy. But the former professions required an autonomy of action and independence of judgment inconsistent with women's perceived capacities or nature. As a result women comprised only 4.2 and 1.3 per cent of those enrolled in medicine and dentistry, respectively, in 1930. But they made up one hundred per cent of the national university enrolment in nursing and miscellaneous health programs (such as occupational therapy or physiotherapy). They graduated into professions where decisions of importance were deferred to the doctor in charge and where lines of authority were as patriarchal in practice as in any upright Victorian home. Few men would have argued that home and family were anything less than the most important institutions in society, yet not a single man in the country was sufficiently interested in the study of domestic management to enrol in a university course in household science during the interwar years.[96] None summoned sufficient courage to face the ridicule of his brothers. Men, as much as women, were prisoners of the social and occupational expectations placed upon their gender, and the university education of the day entrenched such attitudes much more than it questioned them.

Ideals and Realities

The Depression of the 1930s rocked the universities of Ontario, but it did not cause them to collapse. Throughout the country, university income fell by more than a quarter – from $22 million in 1930 to $15.4 million by 1935. Even by 1940, with the national economy on the verge of recovery, the income of institutions of higher education was significantly less than it had been in 1930. In order to compensate for this loss of revenue, the nation's universities increased tuition fees. Principal Hamilton Fyfe of Queen's spoke to the problems of all in charge of universities in the Depression when he commented on the consequences of financial exigency in his *Principal's Report* for 1934–5: classes were too large for effective teaching; assistants were too few in number; serious research was all but impossible.[97]

In the decade from 1929 to 1939 the average national increase in arts fees was fifty-three per cent. Because very little financial aid was available in the form of scholarships, loans, and bursaries – only 13.7 per cent of Ontario's undergraduates held scholarships in 1939 – students were forced to suspend their university educations.[98] Yet young adults in Ontario managed somehow to pursue academic study beyond the high school level. University enrolment in the province, as we have seen, did not grow but it did remain remarkably stable.[99] In some ways, so did the Ontario economy. Industrial productivity collapsed, yet so did the price level. If a man managed to keep his job, he might even be better off than he had been in the 1920s and so would his family. Many Ontarians did manage to remain employed. Production of commodities such as automobiles began to recover by 1933, and by the end of the decade as many cars were emerging from the factories as in 1929. In fact, one of the most distinctive features of the Depression, but one often overlooked, was that it did not impede the progress of the culture of consumption. People went to movies in unprecedented numbers, and they continued to spend on consumer durables such as autos, radios, washing machines, or refrigerators, especially after 1933. Many of these were manufactured in Ontario.[100]

Historian Paul Axelrod has observed that Canadian students who attended university during the Depression were 'relatively privileged' members of the broad middle class, but not necessarily 'uniformly affluent.' He concludes that 'most students came from modest middle-class as opposed to exceptionally privileged upper-class families.'[101] Many of them, male and female, worked in summers or at night so that they could remain students. They toiled in oil-tankers or fishing boats, in public libraries or department stores. Some, such as the group of enterprising students who formed a residential cooperative called the Group Planners Association, inadvertently discovered the virtues of primitive communism. That association aimed at a 'mutual benefit existence' by sharing 'profits from all work equally among its residents.' Such students, middle class or not, did not expect a free ride from their parents.[102]

The Great War had not disrupted student rites such as initiation or hazing, and neither did the Great Depression. Like war, they bred fellowship and loyalty, but at the cost of dignity rather than life. So they continued throughout the 1930s. As if to mark their entry into a higher level of existence as a university now that they were located in their new Hamilton campus, in 1930, for the first time, McMaster students began initiations, ranging from the consumption of cocktails made of epsom salts and castor oil (a sure sign that a Baptist presence tempered the Jazz Age in Hamilton) to the passing of torches from one generation of coed to another. Excess bred greater excess, culminating in the tarring and feathering of a student in 1932. (Actually, the concoction consisted of jam and feathers, but the truth proved insufficiently newsworthy for the Hamilton press).[103] In the same year, however, an Albertan university student suffered a nervous breakdown and was hospitalized after he was subjected to a particularly brutal and humiliating initiation. His father sued the University of Alberta, and the incident ultimately cost the university $15,000 plus court costs. After that university administrations throughout the country paid especially close attention to student rites of passage, and pressures increased upon student councils to control their constituency.[104]

Initiations and hazings nevertheless continued. For a year or so at Toronto they were subdued, confined to the privacy of residences and dormitories. Coloured berets and odd socks decorated student bodies; students of both sexes drank and then drove; windows got broken. Police confiscated the student cards of three undergraduates after a hundred of them 'crashed' a Toronto theatre. Traffic was held up for twenty minutes one day in 1934 when 'the entire manhood' of Trinity College descended on St Hilda's College. Yet the more excessive forms of rowdyism seemed to be abating.[105]

A change in student attitudes did seem to occur in the mid-1930s. Students were less rowdy and more serious. McMaster students abandoned their five-year experiment with autumnal initiations in 1935, and at the University of Toronto they were suddenly judged by *Varsity* to be rather juvenile. It declared that no one had ever really enjoyed initiations except sophomores, and then only while they remained sophomores. 'Present Day Students Are Little Gentlemen,' proclaimed a headline in the *University of Toronto Monthly* in 1936. 'I find the students very polite, responsive, and hard working,' said University of Toronto historian D.G. Creighton, not one to take an optimistic view of life.[106] Principal Fyfe of Queen's noted the change of attitude. If anything, Fyfe said, the new seriousness at Queen's threatened to produce a student generation of anxious note-takers and crammers overly concerned with examinations.[107] Yet this was but one face of student life during the Depression. Two years later he criticized them for the opposite reasons: 'it is not unreasonable to expect that intellectual interests should prevail. The modern comfortable notion that the greatest good comes from friendships and games and social functions and a variety of extra-curricular activities should have no place in a university; certainly not at Queen's.'[108]

One can scarcely escape noticing a distinct undercurrent of wistfulness in such declarations that students were guilty of either too much grinding or too much frivolity. Something, the professorial rhetoric hints, seemed to have soured at Queen's, and the blame lay with the students regardless of their actions or attitudes. But in fact the problem lay with the professors, for these were not the heroic 'Queen's Men' of the age just past. The University of Toronto had flourished under Falconer. McMaster and Western were renewed institutions on new sites. But the golden age of Queen's seemed to lie in its past. The days of the titans – of Principal Grant, John Watson, Adam Shortt, T.R. Glover, Nathan Dupuis, and James Cappon – were gone, and some of the best men of the new generation, such as O.D. Skelton and Clifford Clark, had found more rewarding work elsewhere. The grumblings of Queen's professors about their students were those of middle-aged men working in an institution middle-aged by Canadian standards, and both had lost their sense of academic direction.

The rift between professors and students at Queen's marked a larger divergence of cultural interests, even differences over the interpretation of culture. Fyfe spoke sarcastically in the early 1930s of the fact that 'the footballers ... [had] won their customary championship,' and congratulated those of them who used 'both their feet and their brains.' He complimented the Alma Mater Society for recognizing 'that an executive composed almost entirely of eminent footballers is not necessarily happy in the task of government.' He warned his students that 'the excessive demands of dancing' were even 'more inimical to work than football' and cautioned them that '"the pictures" ... fill a good many hours with little profitable result.' But when he said these things he was not so much addressing football, dancing, or movies as he was reacting to the flux of modern culture itself.[109] In the 1930s the confrontation of older and newer forms of culture had scarcely begun to be addressed seriously by members of the Ontario academic community, and they had yet to come to grips with the implications of the popular culture that now surrounded them.[110]

The sense of decline at Queen's intensified the confrontation of cultural definition and interests there, and Hamilton Fyfe became its prophet, a Kingston combination of Jeremiah and Job. Having arrived from his native Scotland in 1930, expecting to find a serious liberal arts college firmly set in the Calvinist tradition, he found himself instead surrounded by the world of Mencken's 'booboisie,' besotten by a huddle of footballers and a cuddle of dancers. He never quite adjusted to the fact that he had moved to North America. In his final report as principal he summarized his criticism: 'If a University is a centre of intellectual interests and enthusiasms, the students should themselves reflect this spirit. There are such interests among the students at Queen's; but they seem sometimes – particularly at the beginning of the year – to disappear beneath an all-consuming interest in sport.'[111] Students at Queen's would scarcely have disagreed. They certainly liked their dances and their football team, and they might even have added radio and movies to the list of things that consumed them and their generation. It was their principal who misread his students and his era, and he happily returned to Scotland in 1935 to become principal of the University of Aberdeen, where northern lights rather than city sights dominated the imaginative landscape.[112]

The students over whom he had presided, like those throughout the province, did not oscillate between being academic grinders and juvenile followers of supercilious fads. They were both: simply men and women coming of age in a decade of contradictions, not the least of which was the increasing availability of consumer goods and a flow of cheap popular entertainment at a time when so many other things were scarce or beyond one's means. The Depression made them aware of the educational privileges they enjoyed, and for that they were genuinely grateful; as a result, they took their examinations as seriously as they took their social lives. Many of them were acutely aware that a university degree might make the difference between poverty and prosperity, between breadlines and jobs. Yet at the same time, they could scarcely have escaped, even if they had wanted to, the pervasive influence of the great mass media of the day. They would only realize it later, but at the time they were direct witnesses to the golden era of radio and movies, an age for which many of them would become nostalgic after television ushered in a different world and their own children became instant experts on such media.

The gravitation of people, including university students, to entertainment provided by the institutions of mass culture had the effect of expanding the range of acceptable public behaviour. Hollywood *femmes fatales* such as Mae West scandalized the silver screen in the early 1930s by acting and speaking in ways that might have made even flappers blush. They smoked, they drank, they transformed sexual innuendo into an art form.[113] Advertisers in student newspapers, like the American-dominated mass media, began to reflect the changing moral images emanating from Hollywood and New York. The Hamilton firm of Northways, for example, placed an advertisement in the McMaster *Silhouette* in 1933. It was dominated by a line drawing of a woman clad only in undergarments. The text under the ad. read: 'TO THE MEN – of course you'll give "her" lingerie. No need to worry about buying it, you can sneak into Northway's Lingeries Shop. We know what to show you in Undies she'll love – at prices you can take!' This was characteristic of the age, although scarcely of McMaster, still firmly enough under Baptist control that coeds were refused a smoking room in 1934. 'University of Toronto women may smoke,' said a clearly disappointed McMaster woman, 'but here even dancing in the college buildings is frowned upon.' The university's men were equally downcast the next year when its board of governors rejected a student application for a wine and beer licence.[114]

The historical importance of such seemingly minor events lies not in the refusal but in the initiative. Students were eager to participate in the culture they perceived as their own, in newspapers, on the screen, and over the airwaves. Mixed groups allowed themselves to be seen on the edge of drunkenness in public. The automobile, not the parlour, was the new symbolic arena where boy snared girl in the mating ritual. Public dating had all but replaced private courting, a substitution also of process for place and the provisional for the permanent. Few young people in fact talked of courting any more, except with a conscious sense of the archaic intended to mollify anxious parents. In her 1934 report, one of her last as dean of women at Queen's, Hilda Laird remarked upon the change that had taken place since the mid-1920s. 'In 1926 ... dances were still called "Social Evenings" and held in Grant Hall at half-past seven,' she noted. 'They ended before midnight. Now it is fashionable to dance from nine to two, if not till three or four, and to go to a Chinese restaurant, the Kingston equivalent of a night-club, for supper or breakfast afterwards. Our "Main Street" has apparently an altogether new charm after midnight; grapefruit and bacon and eggs are tastier at the "Roy [sic] York" than in the residence dining-hall.' Missing were restraint, decorum, and dignity. Miss Laird did not exaggerate, for even Queen's students noted the 'mad dancing craze' that had gripped their generation. 'Let us have no more of the depression dance – couples close against each other shuffling their feet slowly in time to minor music,' said one student in 1937. 'All hail the Big Apple, the prosperity peck, the triumphant truck, the shining shag. Welcome the dance designed especially for swing music. For the Big Apple is the young person's dance.'[115]

By 1935, whether students smoked was not an issue on the University of Toronto campus, for smoking had become part of mainstream North American culture. Cigarette manufacturers successfully marketed the habit to youth by linking cigarettes, radio, popular music, and college. The programs of band leaders such as Tommy Dorsey, Benny Goodman, Kay Kyser, Artie Shaw, and Paul Whiteman were sponsored by cigarette companies. The announcer on Benny Goodman's 'Camel Caravan' program offered North America's college students 'a little post-graduate work in swing.' Tin Pan Alley linked the cigarette with youth and romance. Rudee Vallee sang about 'The Cigarette Lady,' Jerome Kern wrote 'Smoke Gets in Your Eyes,' and the lyrics of 'Two Sleepy People' linked the need for a smoke with a hint at post-coital relaxation: 'Here we are out of cigarettes.'[116] It is not surprising that by the mid 1930s smoking in itself had largely ceased to be a matter of major concern at larger universities. The issue was more likely to be, as it was in Toronto, whether the proposed new smoking room should be coeducational or for women only (Toronto's men had long been allowed to smoke in their common rooms). In 1937, University of Toronto officials unobtrusively but officially recognized the existence of female student smokers by allowing the University College alumni association to finance the restoration of the women's common room as a smoker.[117]

Signs could be seen that the unwritten rules of courtship were less certain than they had once been. Students debated in the pages of *Varsity* whether or not dutch dates (an equal sharing of expenses) were good, whether women should propose marriage, and whether Sadie Hawkins Week (when women initiated and paid for dates) was acceptable. 'It looks like a wow,' said one Toronto man concerning Sadie Hawkins Week.[118] He probably reflected the view of a majority of men. The majority of Toronto women declared their opposition. 'I certainly do not believe in Dutch Dates,' declared second-year student Miriam Inkster of University College. 'After all, it's a man's privilege to ask a girl out, whoever, whenever and wherever he likes – why shouldn't he pay for it?' In the mid-1930s Toronto women rejected the idea of a university uniform, in spite of its obvious financial advantages. The coeds of 1934 were socially competitive and style conscious – it was a year for tweed short-jacket suits and polo coats on campus.[119]

By the second half of the 1930s students were even willing to answer pollsters' questions concerning their private habits. One hundred fifty University of Toronto students selected at random by a Toronto *Star* reporter answered questions intended to establish their 'purity quotient.' Only fifteen refused to comply. The published results provide one of the only glimpses, however partial or flawed, of how Ontario students viewed that 'four-letter word' *sex*. Ninety-nine per cent of the girls interviewed admitted to having kissed a man at one time or another; eighty-five per cent admitted that they had kissed more than ten men. Ten per cent fewer of the men admitted to kissing, but only forty per cent admitted kissing more than ten girls. Both sexes tied on smoking: seventy-five per cent did. On the question of drinking, men again proved more cautious. Only fifty per cent admitted to imbibing, while sixty per cent of coeds claimed to have had the occasional drink. Eighty-five per cent of the women admitted that they told off-colour stories, a sin to which all the men pleaded guilty although only ten per cent said that they would tell them in mixed company. Fifty-three of the men admitted attending nude mixed bathing parties, ninety-per cent admitted to necking and fifty per cent to petting. The *Star* provided no information on women for these sensitive categories.[120] Perhaps its reporter was too embarrassed to ask the questions.

From the point of view of scientific social research, the *Star* survey was as flawed as University of Toronto professors in the social sciences said it was. The survey is nevertheless not without historical value. It shows that most students were willing to talk to strangers – and strangers from the press at that – about their private habits, even some of their bad ones. That made them different from their parents, and perhaps even from their older brothers and sisters. It also suggests, especially in some of its more obviously disingenuous responses, that in some ways men were more reticent, more 'Victorian,' than women – or perhaps in their own eyes simply more guilty. But that, too, was 'Victorian.'

The reciprocity that was slowly beginning to take place in the social conduct of the sexes did not alter male views about women's fundamental capacities or vocational place. As before, women were portrayed as distracting influences, hampering academic study. Women still found their presence resented in law courses; they were accused of not being intellectually capable of addressing political issues adequately, and they resented the hypocrisy of their male accusers, whose debating club they were not allowed to join. They were ridiculed when they showed a consequent lack of political interest, as when one man wondered why, if women could be emotionally aroused by a rugby game, they did not develop a similar passion for politics.[121] Commitment to their chosen profession was often publicly doubted.[122] A placard posted in the men's common room at McMaster University in the 1930s read, in part: 'Young ladies will not request the fraternity pins of their escorts. Don't paint your finger-nails red. Avoid absorption of liquids. When in doubt about wearing apparel, choose black and white ... Remember, a college boy's pocketbook will not allow caviar, box seats, or a slice of the moon. Do not play the lead. Remember, Eve had to leave the garden when she stole the show from Adam. Give the man the stage. Park your heart in your jewelry case, and throw away the key until you receive your diploma.'[123] Resentment fed such sarcasm, and the corrosive influence of the Depression on the myth of man the provider helps explain it. There was often good-natured humour in newspaper headlines about women students, as there was in the McMaster placard, yet they reflect the almost palpable anxiety and fear that increasingly swelled in the hearts of men.

Concern about national and international problems was a major reason for the increasing seriousness of students as the 1930s wore on. Their political activity in the 1920s had largely been confined to student literary and debating societies, although some students had attended lectures with overtly political messages, such as those given by American radical Paul Blanchard at the 1924 conference of the Student Volunteer Movement.[124] University of Toronto students were drawn into political controversy in 1931 when the infamous letter on police suppression of free speech and assembly in Toronto, signed by sixty-eight of their professors, was published. In spite of widespread public criticism of the professorial action, *Varsity* backed them. It went so far as to accuse the 219 professors who refused to express an opinion as lacking moral courage and proudly noted that students themselves voted to support their professors by a five-to-one margin. The Toronto student newspaper gave column space to those who supported the police, but scarcely concealed its own views to the contrary.[125]

Yet seventy-four per cent of the University of Toronto's students did not bother to vote in the 1931 *Varsity* survey,[126] an indication of how little politicized most students were even when events of serious political import came very close to home. In the middle of the controversy a Fellowship of Reconciliation speaker, whose subject was 'Youth Movements throughout the World,' chided his audience with the assertion that student activists were more likely to 'go galloping down the street with a great clatter' than to 'be scared into thought.'[127] The main Canadian student organization of the day, the National Federation of Canadian University Students, was more concerned with student exchanges and the promotion of national unity than it was with political action or issues. It remained studiously apolitical throughout the Depression years.[128]

By 1934, when Ontario university authorities began to notice the new student seriousness, much had changed. The year 1933 was marked by the depths of the Depression and the rise of Hitler. After the burning of the Reichstag it was difficult to avoid certain political realities. The Student Christian Movement, a decade old in 1931, building on its social-gospel legacy of Christian socialism, and inspired and propelled by the 'neo-orthodox' Christian realism of Reinhold Niebuhr and J. King Gordon, provided a vital forum for political discussion. The SCM was also a potential vehicle for the concerted political action that the national federation was unwilling or unable to provide.[129] By the mid-1930s student activists such as those involved in the SCM were prodded and provoked, on the one hand, by the rigid Marxism and call to action of members of the Young Communist League and, on the other, by the more palatable Fabianism of the League for Social Reconstruction. University authorities allowed a Communist club to be formed at the University of Toronto in December 1935, despite the fact that its parent organization, the Communist party of Canada, had earlier been declared an illegal organization and its leader, Tim Buck, jailed. Member groups of the League for Social Reconstruction existed and were very active at several Canadian universities, especially at Toronto and Queen's in Ontario.[130]

In contrast to the poor turnout of University of Toronto student voters in 1931, more than four thousand of them participated in a straw vote in 1935, meant to provide a hint at the possible result of the imminent Canadian federal election. The returns demonstrated that while Toronto students had begun to take their politics seriously the new political consciousness scarcely reflected a significant degree of radicalism in the student population at large. If the results of the federal election of 1935 had been left to the students of the University of Toronto, a minority Conservative government would have been returned to office: 1,415 students voted Tory, 1,194 Liberal, 518 Co-operative Commonwealth Federation, 392 Reconstruction Party, 128 Communist, and 62 Social Credit. In contrast, Canadian voters swept the Conservatives out of office and returned Mackenzie King's Liberals with a landslide. Varsity's students may not have been radical, but a good number of them were at least now politically aware, if not prescient.[131]

It was not so much the domestic scene that caught the political attention and concern of Ontario students as the international stage and the clash of ideologies that was then sweeping through Europe. As early as 1930 students at the University of Western Ontario debated whether or not to sign a peace pledge in conjunction with the formation of a League of Nations Society; a year later the society, now organized and active, petitioned Prime Minister R.B. Bennett to take a leading role in negotiations leading to the reduction of arms.[132] The prospect of another world war seemed imminent as the middle years of the decade approached, and students began to be more vocal in their views. Varsity declared in November 1934 that a majority of University of Toronto students were pacifists, after results of a poll on student attitudes to war and peace were published.[133] (Given that the poll was described as an anti-war one, the pacifism of Toronto students must be greeted with a degree of scepticism. It is more likely that, given a choice between war and peace, they simply chose to be reasonable people: they were against war in most circumstances more than they were for peace at any cost.) Nevertheless, the sentiment was real, and the anti-war movement, it was claimed, gathered widely based support on campus that autumn. A Hart House debate of the resolution 'that this house is of the opinion that pacificism [sic] is an economically impossible creed' was defeated 218 to 70. The result,

Varsity reported, 'would seem to have been the opinion of the house rather than a tribute to superlative debating methods ...'[134]

Concerned students and staff, not quite certain whether they were spearheading a movement against war or in favour of peace, found it easier to be critical than constructive. Meetings of anti-war supporters were plagued with sectarian squabbling over assumptions, definitions, and terminology. One disenchanted anti-war association member recalled interminable discussions about 'whether or not the word "imperialist" ... was a communist word.' Students agonized over the meaning of Armistice Day, and how to mark it. Should they demonstrate for peace at the Toronto memorial service, as Victoria College student Kenneth Woodsworth suggested? (Woodsworth was in the midst of his speech urging a demonstration against 'the militaristic character of Armistice Day and Empire Day' when a uniformed platoon of the local COTC arrived, intent on breaking up the meeting – an unwitting burlesque of the very storm-trooper mentality against which many of them would soon enough be fighting.) Professor N.A.M. Mackenzie, of Toronto's department of law, prevented mayhem at the meeting when he suggested that perhaps a simple wreath should be laid at the cenotaph. It would read: 'In memory of those who died in the last war – from those who are determined to prevent another war.'[135]

Only twenty pacifists ultimately joined the Armistice Day service to present the anti-war wreath on 11 November 1934, but ninety-nine out of the two hundred Toronto students polled by the Toronto *Telegram* later in the month declared themselves to be absolute pacifists. Early in the New Year, the November group, formerly known as the Anti-War Society, declared that henceforth they were to be called the Student Peace Movement. Angus Blair, its chairman, explained the change of name: 'The former name has consistently met with considerable disfavour because of the negative character which the uninformed ... were all too prone to ascribe to it and because, somehow, some sense in it a smacking of communism.' In fact, said Blair, most of the group belonged to the Student Christian Movement. One of the group's leaders, Kenneth Woodsworth, soon wrote to *Varsity* to plead for moral and financial support so that a University of Toronto representative could be sent to the 1935 International Students' Congress Against War in Geneva. Ten days later *Varsity* announced that, thanks to the twenty campus societies who had pooled their resources, Mr Woodsworth himself had won the free trip to Switzerland.[136]

Students at other universities were equally concerned about war. A poll taken at McMaster in the early winter of 1934 brought responses that may also have reflected the views of students elsewhere, although the pacifist element of McMaster's Baptist tradition must be taken into account. When asked the conditions under which war was justifiable, 256 men found adequate grounds; fifty answered that it was justifiable under no circumstances. Only twenty-nine of 145 McMaster women found no grounds for any war. Canadian patriotism was clearly strong, and it was not linked to residual strains of loyalty to the British Empire. Even the League of Nations, clearly failing in its task at the time, held more moral authority than the empire for these students, testimony perhaps to the strong development of internationalist sentiment in the decade. When asked what advice they would give to a brother or a fiancé if Canada declared war, ninety-seven men and fifty-three women stated that they should either refuse military service but render humanitarian aid or refuse all service altogether.[137] A year later, reflecting upon the 1934 student peace poll in light of subsequent events in Europe, the editor of the McMaster *Silhouette* had occasion to write: 'Then, war was a possibility; to-day it is an actual fact – disguised, perhaps, under the soubriquet of "necessary police measures" but nevertheless warfare with all its accompanying horrors.'[138] (On the question of the conditions under which war was justifiable, see Table 15.3. For their responses when asked what advice they would give to a brother or fiancé if Canada declared war, see Table 15.4.)

Peace activism gained further momentum in 1935. The newly-named Student Peace Movement of the University of Toronto announced in February the imminent release of its first official publication, *Student Front Against War*, with contributions by university staff members W. Woodside and Eric Havelock.[139] In March 1935 *Varsity* confidently declared that the Student Peace Movement had become 'the focus, the rallying point of an ever increasing anti-war sentiment,' at one moment helping send a delegate to a European peace conference, at another organizing for a similar conference to be held in Toronto itself.[140] Similarly, groups at Queen's, such as the Student Christian Movement, the League for Social Reconstruction, and the Student Peace Movement met collectively on various occasions to coordinate strategies over Armistice Day ceremonies and to discuss problems of peace and war 'such as Christianity and the war, the Fascist trend, the munitions racket and the part women can play in supporting or averting future conflicts.'[141]

Nurtured by their own moral convictions, given courage by the knowledge that students at other universities were engaged in similar activities, and perhaps inspired by some professors who were willing to express unpopular but necessary political views in public (men like Eric Havelock, Harry Cassidy, and Frank Underhill at Toronto, and Gregory Vlastos and Martyn Estall at Queen's), student peace activists continued

TABLE 15.3
McMaster University student survey, 1935: 'conditions under which war is
justifiable'

	Men	Women
When Canada is invaded	106	54
When Canadian life and property are endangered abroad	31	21
When Great Britain is invaded	43	23
When Great Britain declared any war	7	5
When the League of Nations requests assistance	51	34
When the U.S.A. is invaded	18	8
Under no circumstances	50	29
Totals	306	174

SOURCE: 'McMaster Students Will War Only if Canada Is Justified,' Toronto *Star*
(4 Dec. 1934)

TABLE 15.4
McMaster University student survey, 1935: 'advice given to brother or fiancé if
Canada declares war'

	Men	Women
Enlist voluntarily	28	17
Serve when conscripted	25	18
Serve when the alternative is imprisonment	6	6
Refuse military service but render humanitarian aid	64	4
Refuse all service	33	10
Totals	156	94

SOURCE: 'McMaster Students Will War Only If Canada Is Justified,' Toronto *Star*
(4 Dec. 1934)

to work hard to gain support. They attacked fascism in Europe and saw
signs of its incipient presence in Canada. They met Sir Edward Beatty's
attacks on radicalism in the universities with strong yet reasoned criticism. They attended speeches by communist Sam Carr and socialist
James Simpson. At meetings sponsored by the League for Reconstruction, Queen's students heard that poverty in Russia was overemphasized
and that nothing less than the socialization and control of private property by the state would bring about a just society. Frank Underhill urged
students to be suspicious of imperialist interests, and J.S. Woodsworth
urged them to enter the political field. By the end of the decade, the conservative National Federation of Canadian University Students had been
challenged not only by the existence of special ideological interest
groups such as the Student Christian Movement, campus branches of the
League for Social Reconstruction, the Young Communist League, and

Co-operative Commonwealth Federation clubs, but also by other national associations of students. The Canadian Youth Congress was founded in 1936 as an umbrella group and coordinating agency that organized annual conferences to express youth interests. The Canadian Student Assembly came into being two years later, after a well-attended national conference of university students held in Winnipeg. Both groups gave the political culture of youth a strong if minority voice.[142]

Students were by no means united in the second half of the 1930s about how to deal with momentous problems so remote from Sarnia or Gananoque or St Thomas. But half a century after the death of Karl Marx they had begun, in small circles at first, to discuss the Marxist critique of capitalist society. They debated the relation of militarism to Remembrance Day; they examined the legacy of the Versailles agreement of 1919. They worried about the Nazi treatment of Jews; they wondered about the compatibility of the new forms of fundamental social and ethical criticism, such as socialism, and the Christian inheritance in which they had been brought up. They fretted about their generation's ignorance of the Bible and expressed concern that so many of them had come to think of religion 'as a theory rather than a joyous experience,' just one academic discipline among others.[143]

Being radical usually means being party to a minority. The student radicals of the 1930s were few in number – only about ten per cent of Victoria College students in the mid-1930s were members of the Student Christian Movement, and 'Vic' was one of the centres of radical unrest. Yet these activists were organized and vocal. Those who lacked deep ideological commitment, or were suspicious of others who claimed it, probably tried to stay out of trouble by sticking to their books or going to the movies. Yet on occasion they too would organize to express their cynicism, their contempt, or perhaps just their boredom. One group of University of Toronto students managed to disrupt a communist rally led by Tim Buck by yelling 'Hurrah for Fascism' – the verbal display was meant as a joke, not a political statement – and barely managed to escape once the mood of the crowd began to grow ugly. Another group was led by a spirited coed who called herself 'Comrade Smith' and climbed the fountain in Queen's Park just as a nearby socialist rally was about to take place. Calling for the abolition of professors, classes, and examinations, the coed comrade atop the fountain managed successfully to draw the crowd's attention from the main rally.[144] She probably also drew some good-natured laughter.

Such humour masked the swelling tension. To general public chagrin, students at the University of Toronto and the University of Western Ontario formed branches of 'Veterans of Future Wars' in 1936, on the grounds that they were destined to fill the front trenches in the next war. Dedicated to the notion that by poking so much fun at war nobody would dare mention a battle in a serious tone of voice, they insisted that they did not require an expensive cenotaph. 'One of our members designed an appropriate one,' said group spokesman R.G. Anglin, 'along the simple lines of a park bench. It will not only be a thing of beauty, but will provide a place for the unemployed veteran of tomorrow to sit down.' Then he suggested that the student 'veterans' should receive a thousand-dollar federal government pension.[145]

Students of the 1930s were moderate idealists in the sense that some of them believed if they could muster the courage to express their convictions they could help prevent catastrophe, if not change the world. But compared with their parents' generation they were realists. A 1929 *Acta Victoriana* reviewer of Erich Maria Remarque's novel *All Quiet on the Western Front*, which quickly became an anti-war classic, declared bluntly: 'This book is not going to end war ... nor is it going to do much, if anything, in the way of anti-war propaganda ... We shall have universal peace when it comes to the mind of the vague plutocracy that war costs money. At present there are too many who nominally gain it in war-time. In addition to this, it will also be necessary for human nature to be revised.' Six years later, similar views could still be heard. 'The underlying cause of war,' said a Queen's student taking advantage of the *Queen's Journal*'s 'Soap Box' at the end of 1935, 'has always been that someone wants profits ... The masses pay for those gains in life and in decades to come in cash. To whom can the masses look for leadership in ridding themselves of this curse? To the newspapers? To politicians? To church leaders? No.'[146]

Student newspapers of the 1930s testify to the ambiguities of the decade. In issue after issue and on page after page, accounts of escapist trivia in the form of campus fun and frolics rival with items of the most serious import for student attention. The front-page article, 'Scavenger Search Staged as Greenies Are Greeted in Rollicking Reception,' doubtless found readers when McMaster students picked up their first issue of the *Silhouette* on 2 October 1935; but so, presumably, did the thoughtful piece on 'Italy and Ethiopia' on the editorial page of the same issue. The tragedy of the Spanish Civil War occupied the minds of some of the best students, such as Donald C. MacDonald and J.B. Conacher of Queen's, and they put their thoughtful assessments to paper for others to read.[147] Yet others found time to worry and complain about the cost and competition involved in the practice of the wearing of corsages on big dates, and they speculated openly whether any Western girl would be daring enough to risk the ire of university officials by wearing a strapless gown at the 1938 varsity ball. Western coeds wondered what all the fuss was about. Western men probably agreed with the London *Free Press*: 'Depends on Shoulders, Carriage and So on.' College life in the 1930s was captivated and worried about the unknown dangers of life, like strapless gowns and awkward dates and Hitler and Mussolini – and so on.[148]

An ironic fact dawned on one Toronto reporter. The peace activists of the mid-1930s were the war babies of the returned soldiers of 1917. Unlike their fathers, he noted, they were not 'filled with war propaganda and a certainty that Allies were right.' These young people bore little resemblance to the generation of 1914. No religious or fanatical fervor characterized them. These were the teenagers of the Depression, 'a determined, serious crowd who wouldn't bet a nickel on the theory of right and wrong, thought war was bunk, and whose knowledge of the Bible was variously and authoritatively stated to us as "appallingly slim" and "non-existent."' The *Silhouette*'s managing editor reflected this attitude. 'What our smug, bridge-and-golf society needs,' he wrote, 'is a reversion to the rock floor of ascetic idealism. But it must be a vigorous, liberal idealism, not a crabbed sentimentality over spiritual things.'[149] Even as Norman Ward, class of '41, wrote those words in October 1939, he must have wondered whether they had not been penned too late. The lesson of Ethiopia and Spain, and now Belgium and Poland, seemed to be that idealism did not work.

On the idealist road to pacifism in the 1930s, the war babies of the Great War became realists. In 1938, when the students of the nation were asked whether they would go to war, their overwhelming answer had been no. But within a year they had completedly reversed their opinion. Sixty per cent of the students at the University of Western Ontario, for example, now declared that they were 'in favour of military action to check the expansion of totalitarian states,' and fifty-seven per cent of them said they would heed the call of Great Britain if the Mother Country went to war. In the spring of 1939, nearly sixty per cent of the male graduating class at Western applied to join the Royal Canadian Air Force.[150] If they were meant to perish in war, they were going to make damned certain it would not be in trenches.

16

History and Humanities

In the autumn of 1932 a young graduate of Runnymede Collegiate Institute, a school located in what at the time was a suburb of Toronto, arrived at University College. He was armed with a fifty-dollar provincial cash scholarship. Gravitating to the disciplines of English and history, he soon came to distinguish himself – first as an honours student, later as a faculty member in the department of English. In 1958 he was to become the university's president. In spirit the young Claude Bissell never quite left what, by the time of his retirement in the 1970s, he had come to associate with the title of a Henry James short story: 'The Great Good Place.' For him, the University of Toronto in the 1930s had been 'a place of uncluttered intensity' and self-discovery, 'a place of which one could not say "if it were the last echo of the old or the sharpest note of the modern."'[1] His undergraduate world was filled largely with activities that took place in University College and with the academic personalities who dominated it – such as historian Frank Underhill and English professor A.S.P. Woodhouse. The University of Toronto was still, in Bissell's eyes, an institution akin to 'the feudalistic, ordered university that still "whispered from her tower, the last enchantments of the middle ages" ...'[2]

Claude Bissell knew very well, both as student and autobiographer, that by the 1930s the University of Toronto was a very complex institution. Had he been a graduate student in 1932–3 rather than a freshman, he would have been part of a community that included 730 other young men and women. By the end of the decade, in fact, he could have pursued a graduate education in any of forty-three academic fields, including anthropology, applied mathematics, Chinese, archaeology, food chemistry, law, metallurgical engineering, pharmacology, and psychiatry.[3] Bissell chose in fact to enroll in the faculty of arts and science, and that meant that he was part of the overwhelming majority of university students. However influential the culture of utility was in the outside world of mass circulation newspapers, consumerism, and public opinion, and however much of a purchase it was beginning to secure in the Ontario university community, the fact is that the faculties of arts and science continued to be central throughout the province, and their importance cannot be over-estimated. Here was the heart of Bissell's great good place, and it existed, in different measures, at universities throughout Ontario – a world where cultural inheritance and social change could be encountered in the college classroom as well as in the changing character of university architecture.

The Great War had seemed to have marked the permanent rupture of a civilization; the war in fact became a metaphor for it: 'the Great Divide.' In a ravaged post-war Europe, scholars who held elements of their history ultimately responsible for the carnage of 1914–18 began to chart an intellectual course that often rejected the historical and the progressive as a means of acceptable social or moral organization. The fruits of their labours ultimately resulted in forms of understanding that dominated an age ushered in by another world war: existentialism, structuralism, post-structuralism, even the *longue durée* of historians, usually French, who fled from the problem of human agency.

Yet for others the past was a means of recovery and at times of solace, embraced and treasured because it represented inherited traditions and values. The power of memory continued to run deep in Ontario academic life, and it served as a counterbalance to that aspect of the contemporary university dedicated to academic disciplines aimed at social utility and change. For many of those connected with the humanities, the past, with its attendant values, was a force that could mediate between the desire for empowerment and change and the need for stability and control. As in so many other matters, this precarious academic balance was most pronounced at the University of Toronto, for these were years when the increasing number of publications by its academic staff contributed to its rise to unchallenged pre-eminence in Ontario academic life. As it was the only major centre for post-graduate education in the humanities and social sciences in the province, the Canadian cutting edge of many disciplines resided there. In the practice of the humanities, the power of the past – of cultural memory – was a central element, for it held the potential both to liberate and to control the creative mind.

Arnold's Ghost

In 1919 Queen's University theologian Ernest F. Scott began a *Queen's Quarterly* article on 'The Effects of the War on Literature and Learning' by proclaiming that 'It can hardly be doubted that ... we have crossed one of the great dividing lines of the world's history, and men are all trying, from their different points of view, to make out the nature of the new prospect.' For Scott, the prospects were bleak: he foresaw no literary revival, no likelihood of a new synthesis of knowledge; only carping criticism and little else but 'conflicts and new experiments and endless debates over problems which at present appear insoluble.' The defeat of Germany had ushered in a general distrust of German scholarship; revolution in Russia meant that its literature and learning would largely 'lie outside the pale of European culture – to our grievous loss.' Scott concluded that the legacy of the war was 'a considerable narrowing of the intellectual field,' a diminution of concern for knowledge for its own sake. 'We shall find ourselves in a world pre-occupied with the present, and the studies we once associated with the higher culture will be more and more crowded out.'[4]

Almost two decades later, after the end of another great war with Germany, much of what Scott had foreseen with such sadness had come about. In 1947 the recently formed Humanities Research Council of Canada published *The Humanities in Canada*, a comprehensive survey of the liberal arts in Canada. During the Second World War, its editors noted, Canada as a nation had become the world's fourth largest trading power; but in the world of scholarship it was eclipsed even by tiny Denmark. On the whole Canada had not yet come of age in its academic life,[5] although the editors' bibliography of scholarly activity contained several examples of extraordinary scholarship. The Humanities Research Council's report also made a number of suggestions for the future of the humanities in Canada, ranging from curricular reform to higher professorial salaries. But the importance of *The Humanities in Canada* as a major document in the nation's intellectual history lies less in such practical suggestions than in its characterization of humanistic learning.

Watson Kirkconnell and A.S.P. Woodhouse, two of Canada's most pre-eminent humanists, began their review with a preface that outlined the compass and function of the humanities. Its domain was seen to include the study of language, literature, the fine arts, and aspects of history, religion, and philosophy. Mathematics and the social sciences were excluded, although the editors recognized that they – particularly mathematics – could be pursued in a humanistic fashion and be humanistic in influence. It was a measure of the realignment of scholarly authority over the past century that classics did not exist in the Kirkconnell and Woodhouse schemata as an independent element within the arts curriculum; instead, it was subsumed within the general study of languages, history, and culture. Similarly, they included religion only insofar as professional schools and seminaries dealt with these subjects.[6] The heart of contemporary humanistic understanding lay primarily in the study of languages, literatures, and history. 'In the past,' wrote Kirkconnell, 'it was with the great classics of antiquity that the student sought to merge his spirit. Association with the poets, orators and historians of the past detached him from the mere present, humanized his imagination and elevated his sentiments.'[7] The question was whether the contemporary humanities – particularly English, history, and philosophy – could fulfill this essential function.

What is most striking in *The Humanities in Canada*'s statement of the purpose of the humanities is how little that purpose was seen to have changed from the years when W.J. Alexander, James Cappon, and Maurice Hutton were in their prime. Kirkconnell and Woodhouse provided in their preface a concise and eloquent statement of the meaning of the humanities, with which none of these luminaries of a previous generation would have disagreed. The spirit of Matthew Arnold suffused their prose, and he was quoted with the kind of uncritical reverence usually accorded to Scripture. On the one hand, Kirkconnell said, the major focus of a liberal education was an intellectual one; the 'data' of 'ethics and politics, of arts and letters and of religion itself,' were made the subject of 'rational formulation and enquiry' by studies in the arts. Yet, on the other hand, he invoked the Arnoldian injunction that aesthetic and ethical concerns were of no less consequence. 'As Matthew Arnold pointed out to his own generation, the "power of beauty" and the "power of conduct" are integral parts of the cultured or liberal personality. The validity of literature and the arts is not merely rational. The taste, as well as the intellect, needs to become civilised; and the enrichment and refinement of the whole esthetic side of man will always be a major task of the humanities.' It was difficult to maintain such a view in the wake of Hitler's war, but it was necessary. 'That ethical sense of man that Arnold regarded as so vital an area of liberal education,' Kirkconnell insisted, 'can attain genuine maturity only as it apprehends moral values while confronting unflinchingly the terror and cruelty of our contemporary world.'[8]

The role of each major discipline within the humanities was cast in the mould of Arnoldian humanism. By making possible an imaginative projection of the self into 'the environment, the problems and the characters created for us by the great masters,' the study of literature allowed one to 'enter vicariously into the whole range of human experience – extending, refining and ennobling our feelings as we identify ourselves with this or that character, living with his life and growing with his growth.' The student of music engaged the spirit of Bach or Beethoven; the student of history gained an enlarged perspective by projecting himself into the 'artistic, moral and religious heritage of the past.' The philosopher's study of intellectual processes and his search for clarity of definition and meaning allowed him to 'co-ordinate his experiences of every sort into a well-rounded and coherent whole.' Such achievements in intellectual synthesis, Kirkconnell and Woodhouse believed, were the 'crowning achievement of a free personality.'[9]

To a significant extent this characterization of the function of the humanities encapsulated their place within the Ontario university curriculum between the two great wars of the twentieth century. Caught between a past increasingly distant to a public preoccupied with the present and a future that no one could predict, Ontario professors in the liberal arts sought to build upon the strengths of their cultural heritage. The biblical dictum to 'prove all things, hold fast that which is good' characterizes the orientation of their concerns.[10]

The pronouncements of Ontario university leaders between the wars on the meaning of a liberal education recapitulated, as often as not, the broad idealism of the pre-war years. In 1923, upon being installed as chancellor of McMaster University, H.P. Whidden proclaimed that 'liberal education should seek to relate the individual to his universe ... The mind of youth must be brought into sympathetic acquaintance with the best there is in the experience of man.' Seven years later, at his own inauguration as principal of Queen's University, W.H. Fyfe reminded his audience that 'the function of a University ... [was] to aid human beings in the growth of character, in the healthy development of all their faculties, physical, mental, moral, aesthetic and spiritual ...' Such declarations continued well into the decade of the Depression.[11] Yet the traditional academic disciplines nurturing such fulfilment, grounded in religion and the classics, did not have an easy time of it between the wars.

Religion and Classics

During the interwar years the traditional function of religious education to nurture denominational conviction continued, but it ceased to be the *raison d'être* of religious scholarship in Protestant denominational colleges. What became dominant, instead, was 'Biblical Studies,' a discipline requiring highly specialized linguistic and technical skills, in which scholarly interest and personal religious belief were increasingly separated. As one observer has noted: 'The increasingly formalized discussion, seemingly exclusively addressed to philosophers and social scientists, isolated clergymen-professors from their traditional constituency, the clergymen and congregations who demanded a message of doctrinal and moral certainty as the basis for human action.'[12]

Post-war clergymen or professors of religion were generally no less committed to religious principles than their Victorian predecessors had been, but they were not always certain what those principles should be or even what they were. The experience of the trenches had shaken and altered views of religion, and post-war journals of informed opinion to which members of the Ontario professoriate contributed convey a clear sense of uncertainty and doubt about the nature of religious authority. For some who survived the war to return to the pulpit or the lectern, the historical theology of the pre-war years had been thrown into disrepute. Such men at times sought solace in traditional ideas of personal redemption through divine transcendence. 'The tragic events of the times in which we live,' said the professor of New Testament at Knox College in 1918, 'are compelling us so to think and to-day the Hope of the Gospel is nearer and dearer to multitudes than ever before ... We feel the tragic incompleteness of all human life, feel that it cannot be a circle closing us in, it must be a path leading elsewhere.'[13]

The will to believe existed as it had before the war. Yet post-war popular judgments on theological matters often lacked the ring of conviction. As often as not they testified instead to a new mood of pessimism in the English-Canadian churches.[14] They also pointed to a rediscovery of the inscrutability and unpredictability of the Christian God – to the problem of Job rather than to the anger of Amos. Post-war Christians wanted a religion that would help them in the task of reconstruction. Many sought deeply for a personal and transcendent Christianity, but they did so as often as not with significant reservations or uncertainty about the divinity of Christ. Others continued on the pre-war path of conceiving of Him in down-to-earth terms, as a man's man, and used the lexicon of the new advertising man. 'Christ,' said E.A. Corbett in 1918, was the 'Great White Comrade of the Trenches ... the majestic man who faces a man's problems, meets a man's temptations and is compelled to make the decisions and choices of a man.' This call for a 'religion that would meet the tests of life' scarcely helped those in search of a renewed foundation for religious authority, for they were left with a theological foundation that resembled nothing so much as a chamber of commerce luncheon creed: 'Faith in God, as set forth by Jesus,' said church historian and chaplain A.E. Lavell. 'The practical unity of religion and "the square deal all round." Religion as right character, right thinking and willing, and human service. The complete reasonableness of real religion.'[15]

In the 1920s and 1930s, Canadian theologians searched earnestly – and at times, one senses, desperately – for some means of reconciling transcendence and immanence, for a god not dependent on the earthly whirlwind of changing values yet who could address material human needs and expectations. They did not find Him, at least in the theological colleges of Ontario. Ontario professors and clergymen between the wars found themselves confronted with the legacy of pre-war intellectual ferment, and it did not augur well for certainty in post-war religious thought. In a series of articles written for the *Canadian Forum*, for example, S.H. Hooke, professor of Oriental studies at Victoria College, expressed many of the concerns of the post-war generation. Hooke's 1919 book, *Christ and the Kingdom of God*, declared an unwillingness to accept either the historical Christ of the higher criticism or the redemptive Christ of traditional Christianity. Writing for a popular audience four years later, he proclaimed that the Kingdom of Heaven could be found nowhere within the institutional structures Christians called 'the Church.' It was found, if anywhere, instead 'in art, in philosophy, in all those activities which are fused in religion ... For true worship is life glorified; it is not merely the assertion that the Kingdom of Heaven exists, but the achieving of it by man; and when men see it so achieved they believe in it, they recognize the true purpose of their lives.'[16] Later, Hooke gave notice that modern doubters (like himself) were not so much making an organized attack on religion as reflecting instead their belief that 'the appeal to authority, whether of the Bible or of the Church, has lost its force.' As a result of his ardent social activism and his radical views of biblical exegesis, Hooke found himself *persona non grata* even at liberal Victoria. In 1924 he went on leave with the apparent understanding that he was not expected to return. When he threatened to do so in 1927, the Victoria board of regents arranged to send him $1,500. Officially, Hooke was not dismissed; but he did not return, and Victoria escaped public criticism for removing a popular professor.[17]

Caught between the traditional and the modern, challenged and buffeted by the religious vitalism of Henri Bergson, the experiential pragmatism of William James, the irrationalism of Freud, the relativism of German historicism, the dogmatism of American fundamentalism, and the escape from history proffered by the neo-orthodoxy of Karl Barth, all the while preoccupied by the vexations of 'Church Union,' Canadian Methodist and Presbyterian clergy and professors of religion found themselves proclaiming a middle way – as one preacher expressed it, a theology both traditional and modern, transcendent and immanent.[18] Ontario theological colleges did not become the repositories of any simple solution to the problem of religious certainty – whether fundamentalism or neo-orthodoxy – in the interwar years. Rather, as Michael Gauvreau states, they sought to reshape theology 'in relation to history and the "human sciences."' Even before the Great War, the provisional nature of religious truth had been conceded by professors such as A.B. Macallum. 'It follows,' Macallum said in an *Acta Victoriana* article, 'that the long discussions of the past on the nature of truth have been but vain dallyings with illusory ideas. There is no absolute truth knowable to the human mind.'[19] He was correct: the age of truth was dying; the age of the concept, provisional by definition, had arrived. Press and pulpit became highly indignant when the more extreme consequences of such views became public, as when the Toronto *Star* published questions that University College Oriental scholar William Andrew Irwin posed to his second-year students: 'Is the book of Jonah history, allegory or what is it? What do you think of the incident of the "big fish"?'[20]

The years between the wars were perplexing but challenging ones in the Protestant theological colleges attached to Ontario universities. Members of the Student Christian Movement – who celebrated the wonders of science and the human Jesus – kept alive the social gospel tradition of Christian social reform, inspired and encouraged by professors such as philosopher Gregory Vlastos at Queen's, and the Depression provided daily reminders of why reform continued to be necessary. Other students, more traditional in orientation and drawn from the evangelical unions at the universities of Manitoba, Toronto, and Western Ontario, formed the Inter-Varsity Christian Fellowship in 1928. It was consciously conceived to be an evangelical alternative to the SCM.[21] The appearance in 1924 of the *Canadian Journal of Religious Thought* testified to the willingness of Canadian religious thinkers to state publicly their difficulties with Christianity and to search earnestly for solutions. Principal Gandier of Knox College imported several Scottish professors of religion – John Baillie was one – in the hope that Scottish moderation would mediate between theological extremes. Baillie, whose specialty was systematic theology, did not disappoint. His book, *The Interpretation of Religion: An Introductory Study of Theological Principles* (1928), sought to disengage theology from the relativistic tangles of historicism and the Baconian distinction between facts and values upon which it rested. In turn, Baillie depended heavily, as did others such as William Morgan of Queen's Theological College, on the assumptions of late nineteenth-century neo-Kantian idealism. For them, facts and values were one, and history was essential as a record of the unfolding of spiritual progress. Baillie nevertheless believed, as Gauvreau has noted, that 'theology was in no way a mere client of historical study. It was a science "of the spirit," concerned with the empirical investigation of reality, not with metaphysics.' This was a view that John Watson, who introduced neo-Kantian idealism to Canada and who lived until 1939, would certainly have agreed with – if by metaphysics was meant the the traditional doctrines of the Christian church.[22]

A year after Watson's death, the principal of Queen's contributed an article to the *United Church Observer* on 'Christianity Today and Tomorrow.' 'Ours is not an irreligious age,' R.C. Wallace concluded, 'but it is a time when the influence of the Christian Church has weakened to an alarming degree. Young men and young women are waiting for an interpretation of the meaning of the message of Christ ... But it will not be found in assent to every phrase of the Apostles Creed.' Notions such as the Atonement, Wallace said, held validity only in times when men realized that they were 'desperately wicked' and powerless in the face of God. 'Must it not be frankly stated that there is no such conviction to-day, and that it would be impossible to bring it about by any artificial stimulation? A vital part of Christian dogma has therefore lost its appeal and, to a large extent, its meaning for the present generation.'[23]

In spite of the increasingly difficult problem of reconciling scholarship and faith, a number of major contributions to biblical studies were nevertheless made by Ontario scholars in these years. W.G. Jordan of Queen's published *History and Revelation* in 1921 and *Hebrew Origins*, by Theophile Meek of University College, appeared in 1936. *The Abingdon Bible Commentary* contained a number of articles by Canadian scholars. *The Canadian Journal of Religious Thought* published many thoughtful articles on religious and ethical subjects until its demise (because of a lack of funds) in 1932. The Canadian Society of Biblical Studies, founded in 1933 in Toronto, met annually for the reading and criticism of scholarly papers. Theophile Meek, along with W.R. Taylor and S.A.B. Mercer of Trinity College, made important contributions to biblical archaeology: Meek went on expeditions to Iraq and was affiliated with the American School of Oriental Research in Baghdad; Taylor held a similar position in Jerusalem; Mercer (the only Canadian present at the opening of King Tutankhamen's tomb) discovered a fourteenth-century manuscript of Ecclesiastes in 1930 while in Ethiopia. In these and other ways, biblical scholarship grew even as the importance of religion in the climate of opinion of Ontario universities slowly but inexorably became more marginal. Not until the 1960s would religious studies gain full departmental status within Ontario universities, and then usually as a branch of secular scholarship distinct from theology or divinity programs.[24]

In the universities of Ontario with Protestant origins, theological schools came to be seen as simply one academic unit among many. Faculty members within such institutions as Queen's Theological College and the University of Toronto's Emmanuel College (created in 1928 to house those professors from Knox and Victoria colleges who supported Church Union) were normally committed Christians of one stripe or another, but their truths, like all others in the academic environment between the wars, had to be subjected to critical scrutiny. The main exception to this tendency was the Institute of Medieval Studies, inspired and organized by the French philosopher and medieval historian Etienne Gilson at St Michael's College between 1927 and 1929. The Institute – a decade later renamed the Pontifical Institute of Medieval Studies after it received a papal charter – quickly became a world centre of Thomistic studies, and attracted such international Catholic scholars as Jacques Maritain.[25] In Roman Catholic institutions generally, scholarship and religious devotion were not yet divorced.

Like religion, classical studies were less under direct siege than they were gradually marginalized within the academic community between the wars. Since the days of Wilson and Loudon, the Ontario apostles of science had been claiming science as one of the most significant forces in the rise of Western civilization. In 1896, for example, Nathan F. Dupuis of Queen's began an article with the title 'Some of the Factors of Modern Civilization' with the sentence 'The past is our inheritance' – but then he proceeded to chronicle the history of Western science in a way that placed it on a plane equal to the Christian religion or the achievements of classical antiquity.[26] Possibly because of the presumed arrogance of scientists such as Dupuis, humanists such as historian William Lawson Grant at Queen's (son of Principal Grant) and classicist John Macnaughton at University College, Toronto, decried the cult of modern industrial science and the narrow specialization it fostered. 'Perhaps the most painful sight which a modern university can show,' wrote Grant bitterly soon after Dupuis's article appeared, 'is the clever young scientist, who, when the working of his own mind finally presents to him some of the great questions of thought and life, has no better means with which to solve them than the methods and results which he had used with success in the study of some petty branch of some petty science. The chemist or biologist turned metaphysician is surely a sight at which the Gods must weep – or laugh.'[27]

But even in 1897 Grant was fighting a rearguard action. Soon enough, chemists such as Grant's colleague W.L. Goodwin exacted their revenge, dismissing the Arnoldian notion of culture with disdain and adding the proposition that 'a man whose culture is limited to the thought and knowledge of the more or less remote past can hardly be a wise or competent critic of the life of to-day.' As to specialization, said Goodwin, the kind of specialization involving a 'wide and deep knowledge of some subject,' any subject, was a means to culture.[28] The obvious wartime triumph of scientific technology based on extreme forms of specialization was not lost on either camp, and it made each more amenable to the assumptions and goals of the other. Even before the end of the war scientists had begun to preach the humanistic nature of their ideal of pure science; by 1930 they were confidently addressing learned bodies such as the National Conference of Canadian Universities at discussion sessions on the humanism of science.[29]

Classics programs were propped up in the 1920s because in Ontario (and in the Maritimes) two years of Latin beyond junior matriculation continued to be required for university arts students. Moreover, the lengthy and close association of Maurice Hutton's classics program with the popular and prestigious four-year honours degree in arts at the University of Toronto guaranteed a steady stream of enrolments – as long as the school system of Ontario continued to offer instruction in Latin and Greek. Nevertheless, like theology, classics – however valuable its rhetorical stock – was in a state of relative decline in English-Canadian universities in the interwar years.[30] Some classicists at small institutions became champions of the teaching of classical texts in translation (William Lawson Grant was one), but in doing so they undercut the practical justification for classical study – that it provided training in the base languages of the Western tradition. Moreover, in 1934, with the election of the Liberal government of Mitchell Hepburn in Ontario, Duncan McArthur became deputy minister (and later minister) of education. McArthur, a 1912 graduate in 'honour classics' from the University of Toronto, championed French as opposed to Latin in the province's high schools, possibly for political reasons. Soon Latin was denied to students in the first year in the secondary school system (grade nine); Greek was limited to two schools. Students were allowed to choose between Latin and mathematics as the language of entry into university. Such reforms to the public school curriculum invariably undercut enrolment in classics programs throughout the province, even at the University of Toronto.[31]

The editors of *The Humanities in Canada* referred in 1947 to 'the flight from the classics which has been a mark of the twentieth century.'[32] Nevertheless, classics survived, if dethroned and generally diminished. Upon its move from Toronto to Hamilton, McMaster University appointed two classicists, Edward Togo Salmon and Marjorie Carpenter (who also served as its dean of women). Increasingly domi-

nated by its programs in business and medicine, the University of Western Ontario offered a classics program that was, and remained, very
modest. At Queen's the classics department suffered from the general
sense of inertia that characterized the humanities there in the interwar
years. By 1947 resignations had reduced the Queen's department to a
staff of three, students showed little interest in the subject, and 'it was
difficult to do more than maintain the current courses.'[33] Only at the
University of Toronto did study of the classics retain something of its
former lustre.

By the end of the 1920s the age of Hutton had, in a formal sense,
ended at Toronto. He retired from university service in 1928, after forty-
eight years of undiminished authority and great influence. His last years
– those from the end of the Great War to his death in 1940 – were bitter-
sweet ones. The optimistic nineteenth-century idealist had become a sar-
donic sage, almost revelling, one suspects, in the masque of twentieth-
century pessimism. Both democracy and science, in his view, had
reached a state of such excess that his only solace was to retreat into the
sanctuary of ancient Greece. Democracy had led to Lenin, science to
Passchendaele. His own enthusiastic pre-war militarism, born of idealism, had led to slaughter. But the war, he recognized, had not been the
cause of his alienation and ennui. 'We had learned from the Greek philosophers and from the New Testament, to find reason and purpose, and
mind and God in the world and then Darwin interposed and brought
back chance and luck and accident and the doctrine of casual survival of
the lucky ... until the world has again become all chaos and confusion
...'[34]

Yet in his prime, which lasted decades, Hutton had given distinct and
important shape and force and coherence to the classics program at Toronto. It was already strong in the federated colleges of Victoria and Trinity, and Hutton continued to structure the program around the strengths
of the honours degree – such as its acceptance of student specialization.
Without dismissing language training in Greek and Latin, he had conceived the acquisition of such skills to be the means to a specific end.
The twentieth-century University of Toronto classicists, like the language specialists there, did not teach or encourage much philological
research. The 'knowledge of words' in Hutton's department was instead
'... a key by which the student obtains access to the treasure-house of literature. The aim of the course is to bring him into contact with the main
forms of Greek and Latin literary art ...'[35]

In lock step with W.J. Alexander's English program, Hutton marched
his own offerings continuously and systematically away from language
towards literature, philosophy, and history, and he provided his students

with instructors who refused to divorce the sphere of one from those of the others. Hutton and his colleagues viewed their students as 'the spiritual heirs of Greece and Rome' and sent them to the sources to examine 'the foundations of [their] common culture.' Their approach was to ideas through literature, by means of what later would be called intellectual history. 'The fundamental unity of Greco-Roman culture,' they wrote, 'is accepted as a starting-point. The Greeks are important as the discoverers of the main forms of European thought and expression; the Romans, as the first of a long series of European peoples whose lives have been enriched by the reception of Greek culture, and also as the architects of that institutional framework within which Greek culture was preserved and perpetuated; both together as the *fons et origo* of much that is still current and vital in the life of Europe and the West.'[36]

This historical approach to the imaginative and philosophical literature of classical antiquity helped provide a supportive atmosphere in which the scholarship of professors such as Gilbert Norwood, for many years director of classical studies at University College, could flourish.[37] It also gained favour elsewhere in the province and the country, in public schools and in universities, as the academic diaspora of Toronto graduates in honours classics took place in the generations after 1880. By the time of Hutton's retirement, hundreds of advocates of the Toronto approach to classical studies were found throughout the professions in Ontario and abroad – as professors, school inspectors and principals, primary and secondary teachers, in the church, the legal and medical professions, business and finance, the civil service, journalism, libraries and museums.[38] One of these graduates, who stated that he remained 'a student of the history of ideas,' seems to have reflected the views of many when he recalled that he was happy that exposure to classical authors in the Toronto program had presented him 'with a total view of life when the world also was young ... The world was young enough and small enough in the classical age for a young student of the classics to get a view of it all as a whole, and to carry with him through life the feeling – so difficult to attain in these days – that all life is one and all truth is one.'[39]

The Errand of English

No subject enjoyed more prestige in the two decades after the Great War than English. In the imperial twilight of post-Edwardian England, study of the English language and its literature belatedly became not only a way of preaching about the greatness of British civilization and its literary heritage but also, beneath the imperial bravado, a potential means of cultural renewal in an era of mass democracy. In this way, it became a virtual substitute for alternative definitions of British national life.[40] The legitimation of 'English' – for language and literature were now subsumed within the noun – was complete when Henry Newbolt's 1921 report on *The Teaching of English in England* proclaimed that English had become a 'universally known language' and argued that the study of English should be an instrument of formal national policy.[41]

The appearance of the Newbolt Report in England coincided with the last few years of W.J. Alexander's tenure at the University of Toronto and of James Cappon's literary career at Queen's, and it seemed to have given official British sanction to their Arnoldian way of thinking. It spoke of English as the major means to 'the inner world of thought and feeling.' The study of English was 'not merely the medium of our thought, [but] the very stuff and process of it. It is itself the English mind, the element in which we live and work.' English, in its 'highest sense,' was 'the channel for formative culture for all English people, and the medium of the creative art by which all English writers of distinction, whether poets, historians, philosophers, or men of science, have secured for us the power of realising some part of their own experience of life.'[42] Such words were balm to romantic idealists of Alexander's generation, for they confirmed that the direction English studies had been given in Canada, away from 'sterile' and 'pedantic' Germanic philology and towards Arnoldian humanism, had been the proper one. In this way, at a time when American scholarship on the English language was bitterly divided between these two schools of specialists and generalists, English in Canada remained on a relatively tranquil plane.[43]

Although the Department of English at the University of Toronto rapidly became by far the largest in the province (and in the country), the first half of the twentieth century was marked there by a remarkable degree of continuity. This was mainly because Alexander first inspired students of like mind and then recommended the appointment of the best of them, most notably Pelham Edgar at Victoria College in 1897 and Malcolm Wallace at University College in 1905. Similar appointments followed during the tenures of his disciples as heads of English at their respective colleges. In this way, during the 1920s Victoria under Edgar gained E.J. Pratt and John Robins, and University College under Wallace secured R.S. Knox and H.J. Davis. The expansion continued into the Depression.

Within a year of the formal retirement of Alexander in 1928, Wallace appointed E.K. Brown and A.S.P. Woodhouse. Both were University of Toronto graduates. In 1931 Trinity College attracted the distinguished Shakespeare scholar G. Wilson Knight to its chancellor's chair in

English, and he remained there until he returned to England at the outset of the Second World War. The main appointment in English at St Michael's College was that of Laurence Shook in 1940. In the middle of the Depression (1936) the university managed to appoint Roy Daniels, a Victoria College graduate and a recent PHD recipient from Toronto. Kathleen Coburn and Northrop Frye were secured for Victoria; both were 'Vic' graduates. The general line of continuity in leadership had been struck, from Wilson and Alexander, to Edgar and Wallace, to Woodhouse, whose retirement did not take place until 1964.

It is no slight to other universities in the province, or to their scholars, to place emphasis on the University of Toronto when speaking of the study of English; for in no area in the humanities was the overwhelming dominance of the provincial university so transparently clear. The comic-opera proportions of the faculty struggle over the headship of the department of English at Queen's in the 1920s (when university authorities appointed journalist B.K. Sandwell against the wishes of the department) reflected its sad fall from the heights Cappon had reached. Only after the appointment of George Herbert Clarke in 1925 did departmental circumstances, including morale, change for the better. The University of Western Ontario did not appoint its first professor of English language and literature until 1928, when it hired William Ferguson Tamblyn. In the 1930s and early 1940s other significant scholars of English appeared at such institutions, notably Carl F. Klinck and William E. Collin at Western and Watson Kirkconnell at McMaster. But these were men struggling, often virtually on their own or with one or two colleagues, to teach English literature and grammar in departments that resembled nothing in size so much as Alexander's at the turn of the century. In contrast, by 1945 the combined full-time academic staff in English at Toronto numbered twenty-seven. Only three of the people appointed had not attended a Canadian school or university. In fact, two-thirds of them had graduated from the honours program at Toronto.[44]

The Toronto approach to English during and after the interwar years remained largely as it had been under Alexander: cultural and historical in orientation, an introduction to the great books and therefore to the great minds of English literature. Alexander, Edgar, and Woodhouse aspired to emulate the English man of letters, and they did their best to continue the broad approach of the man of letters to learning by speaking their minds not only in the academic classroom but also in public lectures and newspaper articles. It was not uncommon for Alexander to draw a thousand people or more to his popular Convocation Hall addresses. Edgar, like James Cappon, took his views to the daily press, writing popular pieces on a wide range of literary topics for the mass audience of the new century. Woodhouse also sought to disseminate the moral and social message of English literature, not least by his lengthy and careful stewardship of the 'Letters in Canada' section of the *University of Toronto Quarterly*, which began publication in 1931 and quickly became a major national forum for the publication of articles in the humanities.[45]

W.J. Alexander had believed in Arnoldian disinterestedness, yet throughout his life he remained a moral critic and he moved people. Perhaps it was the very plainness of his delivery, consciously avoiding the ornateness of the rhetorician; perhaps it was that his subjects had been early contemporaries such as Browning or Rossetti that gave literature, as he talked about it, a life and currency it did not previously possess. Perhaps the quiet force of his moral idealism met and mingled with the romantic nationalism of his Maple Leaf audiences. To his dying day, Alexander, said Woodhouse, was 'true to the best tradition of English Romanticism.'[46] So, in his own way, was his pupil and devotee Edgar, whose greatest literary debts were to Matthew Arnold, Thomas Carlyle, and the French critic Charles-Augustin Sainte-Beuve. Romantic moralist yet champion of the critical imagination, Edgar was consistent in his views: 'Perhaps only our poets will save us in the end,' he said, 'by this very quality of imagination, from the slough of materialism, that with hideous maw threatens to engulf us.' That was written in 1892; this in 1931: 'Romanticism is out of fashion, but is it too late to hope for the recovery of a sane idealism, a romanticism purged of its posturing egotism and sentimentality?'[47]

It was in Edgar's first-year class in 1930 that the eighteen-year-old Northrop Frye, fresh from his native Moncton, signed up to write on the topic of 'Eccentricity,' the only student in the class to do so. 'Next year,' Frye later recalled in a letter to Edgar, 'you made a remark about Blake in a lecture that kept him in my mind, and that summer, when I went home, I took some of the long prophecies with me, and used to take them out and stare at them and think how nice it would be if I could read them. The third year came your eighteenth century course, and I signed up for a paper on Blake. From then on I was hooked.'[48] Fourteen years later, in 1947, when Frye's illuminating study of William Blake, *Fearful Symmetry*, was published by Princeton University Press, the book was dedicated to Pelham Edgar. After Edgar's death it was Frye who edited his unfinished autobiography, *Across My Path* (1952).

E.K. Brown was touched by Alexander and Edgar for life. 'There was not a series of [Alexander's] lectures I did not hear at least twice,' he noted, 'and the course on nineteenth-century poets given to students in the final year of the Pass Course I heard four times.'[49] It is not, then, surprising that Brown trod the moralistic path of his masters, teaching that to understand literature was to understand society, or that he presented poetry as the highest form of literary expression. 'The function of a professor of English literature,' he wrote, 'is to know and to teach and to write about the best literature written in English. He seeks to spread among his students a delight in literature, a hunger for the best literature.'[50]

Since it was clear to even the most ardent of Canadian academic nationalists that Canada had not yet produced a literary record equal to that ideal, Canadian literature was slow to gain entrance into the academic canon in English departments. Privately, Pelham Edgar, W.J. Alexander, and James Cappon at Queen's quietly encouraged the development of Canadian letters. Edgar was the champion of E.J. Pratt, Morley Callaghan, Frederick Philip Grove, and Mazo de la Roche, among others. [51] But Canadian literature was not formally treated in the University of Toronto curriculum until 1934, and even then it was only in six lectures E.K. Brown gave near the end of his course on American literature. Whatever Canadian content had existed in the English curriculum at Queen's under Cappon, who had published *Roberts and the Influence of His Times* in 1905, was reduced by George Herbert Clarke in 1926. The first full course on the subject seems to have been given at the University of Western Ontario in 1928, when William Ferguson Tamblyn introduced a course called 'Canadian Literature: a study of Canadian prose and poetry before and since Confederation.' McMaster added a half-course on the subject in 1941, taught by Watson Kirkconnell. Only five per cent of the English theses written in Canada between 1921 and 1946 were on the country's literature, and the same period produced only three doctoral dissertations on the subject. The first graduate course, 'Studies in Canadian History and Letters,' appeared only after the Second World War. It was taught in its first year by A.J.M. Smith and Ernest Sirluck and later by Claude Bissell and Donald Creighton.[52] This was the academic environment Claude Bissell remembered as 'the great good place.'

The department in which Bissell studied was one he believed to be 'at the height of its powers,' and in the 1930s and 1940s the dominant force in it was A.S.P. Woodhouse. Having returned to his Alma Mater in 1929, after a few years teaching in colonial exile at the University of Manitoba, Woodhouse, an imposing and acerbic man whose idol was Samuel Johnson, embodied the best and the worst of the Toronto approach to the scholarly life. After Alexander's retirement it was Woodhouse, above all, who safeguarded the sanctity of the treasured Toronto honours program and sought to keep 'English language and literature' as its heart. 'The assumption,' Woodhouse wrote, 'is that English is one of the most valuable of humanistic disciplines but that to bring out its full value it requires to be grouped with others,' such as history or philosophy.[53]

This was no mere rhetoric. While Woodhouse was privately critical, like most scholars, of disciplines other than his own,[54] the honours program under his protective eye achieved a degree of intellectual integration that was clearly remarkable. 'From the standpoint of the student, it was not simply a matter of taking seventeenth-century British history in parallel with Milton and Dryden or a course in Locke, Berkeley, and Hume as a background to eighteenth-century poetry and prose. The cross references were often very detailed: lectures on Boileau's *L'Art Poétique* from the French Department in November, on Pope's *Essay on Criticism* in January.'[55] Students like Bissell, who were attracted by the broad cultural and historical orientation of the program, thrived. Under Woodhouse's direction, English language and literature was carefully amended in the 1930s and 1940s; but after his ascension to the headship of the department in 1944 it changed very little until the 1960s.

There was, however, a darker side to Bissell's 'great good place,' especially in English. Woodhouse was in all respects a despot, if a benign one to those he liked; he 'acted,' Bissell remembered, 'like an imperial emperor, dispatching his graduate students to serve in the outlying provinces.'[56] He was intensely protective of his own academic turf and distrustful of those whose approach differed from his own. He was suspicious of the idiosyncratic brilliance of G. Wilson Knight at Trinity and steered promising graduate students away from Northrop Frye and (after his appointment to St Michael's College in 1946) Marshall McLuhan. Woodhouse in fact actively attempted to prevent the hiring of McLuhan, whose Cambridge doctorate and eccentric ways had become known even before his arrival. (This was a double curse because Woodhouse detested the Cambridge 'new criticism' and he did not possess the degree.) He 'was not the sort of person we want at the University of Toronto,' Woodhouse told a St Michael's colleague.[57] For Woodhouse, University College was the very centre of the intellectual firmament at the university; the outlying colleges were local variations of the colonial outposts that were the other universities in the province and the country, particularly in the west.

Roman Catholics and women did not fare well in Woodhouse's imperium. McLuhan was particularly marginalized not only because (like Frye) he was seen as a 'new critic' but also because of his Roman Catholicism. McLuhan's conversion to the Church of Rome from the United Church of Canada was well known in academic circles, and this did not sit well with Woodhouse, historian and interpreter of the Puritan revolution.[58] Frye and McLuhan sensed the way they were marginalized and were well aware of the patronizing manner in which it took place. For his part, McLuhan came to dismiss the University College English professors as 'a ghastly crew,' and Frye, who disliked the dry historicism of many of his colleagues, wondered at Knight's willingness to be associated with 'all that Babbittry.'[59] Although women were present in great numbers as undergraduates, few were encouraged to undertake graduate work. Kathleen Coburn was an exception. Fortunately 'marked' by Pelham Edgar, as Frye was to be, she was encouraged to pursue work on Coleridge, and Edgar made certain that she was retained on the Victoria staff. Yet in her autobiography, *In Pursuit of Coleridge*, there is more than a hint of resentment at the imperious and condescending treatment she (and her students) received at the hands of colleagues in the University College imperium, particularly Woodhouse.[60] Women associated with other departments in the humanities were tolerated, but only just.[61]

Woodhouse, a life-long bachelor, was inclined to be disdainful and dismissive of women – except for his mother, with whom he lived until her death shortly before his own and to whom he dedicated his last book.[62] Given such an environment, few female scholars found a permanent place on the university academic staff. Thirteen women held teaching positions in English at the University of Toronto between 1920 and 1945; of these five were sisters affiliated with the women's division (Loretto's) of St Michael's College; five taught at St Michael's, Trinity, or Victoria. Only three women came to be associated with University College in these twenty-five years: two of them were married to professors of English (one of them at UC), the third was Mossie May Kirkwood, Dean of Women at University College between 1920 and 1936, and principal of St Hilda's College from 1936 until her retirement in 1959.[63]

History Lessons

Between the wars the discipline of history enjoyed considerable academic prestige within the spectrum of the humanities. Historians were, after all, the official chroniclers of the cultural and political traditions to which so many other disciplines in the arts were linked. The historical orientation of classics, religion, and English made historians the natural allies of these disciplines, and connections between Ontario's historians and other scholars were close. From George Wrong and O.D. Skelton at the beginning of the 1920s to Frank Underhill and Harold Innis at the end of the 1930s, the province's historians sought and found a high public profile and became the major academic interpreters of Canada's place in the contemporary world. They began to establish a significant publishing record, and as they did so they charted the country's changing place in relation to its European heritage and its North American environment. If, as historian Joseph Levitt has claimed, theirs was ultimately a vision beyond reach, it was still a vision. They spoke and wrote of their nation's uncertain destiny, and it was one for which they sought a wide public audience.[64]

From the beginnings of the practice of history in the country, initially by amateurs, history had always served some practical economic, moral, or political purpose – whether to promote commerce and settlement, to instill a sense of patriotism, or to legitimize a political point of view by recording the existence of a particular tradition and its struggle against adversity.[65] In the late nineteenth and early twentieth centuries, Canadian historians, especially those in Ontario, were usually unabashed apologists for the achievements of the British Empire and of Canada's place within it. The title of Carl Berger's book on the ideology of Canadian imperial nationalism – *The Sense of Power* (1970) – nicely conveys the well-spring of their motivations: they believed that by transmitting to Canadians the importance of the imperial ideal they could help Canada achieve its destiny as the North American inheritor of the British imperial destiny. As a result, history departments perhaps more than others tended to appoint people with social credentials and cultural backgrounds deemed appropriate for such a teaching mission. When a man named Bernstein applied in 1911 for a position in constitutional history at the University of Toronto, he was rejected (largely on the advice of board member Joseph Flavelle), in spite of his 'first' at Oxford, partly because his stutter made him socially unacceptable and partly because he was a Polish Jew.[66] Later, his name changed, he became one of Great Britain's best-known and most influential historians, Sir Lewis B. Namier. At the time of the Great War, Toronto's department was thus 'an entirely Anglo-Saxon institution, mainly Canadian-born, generally Oxford-trained, and mostly (but not entirely) Protestant.' Canadian history remained colonial – at times parochial – history well into the twentieth century.[67]

Yet even before the Great War, lines of fissure had emerged within the small community of Canadian historians. The hagiographic account of Canadian national heroes that found expression in publisher George Morang's 'Makers of Canada' series, beginning in 1903, testified to the hold of a Carlylean romantic nationalism; yet the multi-volume series 'Canada and Its Provinces,' directed by Adam Shortt and Arthur

Doughty, also published before the war, marked a distinct rejection of the idea of history as romantic art or as a form of moral judgment.[68] Instead, the volumes of 'Canada and Its Provinces' dealt with regional, economic, and thematic aspects of the Canadian historical experience. Theirs was a form of history largely shorn of the ornate Victorian adjective. Moreover, Edwardian interpreters of history such as the Ottawa lawyer J.S. Ewart and Queen's political scientist O.D. Skelton began to express a distrust of British imperial intention and of Canada's constitutional ties to it. They continued to do so in the decade after the war and found allies in the influential Manitoba journalist J.W. Dafoe and, later, in historian Frank H. Underhill.[69]

The doyen of Ontario's historians, George M. Wrong epitomized many of the profession's conflicting assumptions and priorities. Wrong, like Alexander and Woodhouse, helped extend the Anglo-Canadian tradition of public moralism into academic life well into the twentieth century.[70] He continued after the war to be a firm believer in the historian's obligation to render moral judgment, to draw lessons from the past. In 1932 the annual meetings of the American Historical Association were held in Toronto, and Wrong gave an address entitled 'The Historian's Duty to Society.' 'The historian is both the guardian and the interpreter of the past,' he began. Other animals possessed memory, but man alone built up a 'formal story' of his past and was therefore 'governed by its traditions.' And with this gift came his duty. Wrong went on to reject the notion that history held no lessons and that it was 'not the duty of the historian to indulge in moral judgments' but, rather, simply to tell 'what was done.' Wrong's creed, instead, was that of the great Roman Catholic historian Lord Acton, who had declared that 'the great achievement of history is to develop and perfect and arm conscience.' The historian, said Wrong, was the conscience of the race, his truth the expression of 'constructive standards of conduct.' His duty to society – 'a half-blind mass, living on its traditions, not knowing whither it is going, requiring leadership' – was to teach it that truth. To do so, Wrong warned his audience, the historian must avoid twin perils that had already begun to undermine his influence on society: 'the lure of the notebook,' in which documentation took precedence over style or audience,[71] and 'the fascination of the picturesque,' in which history became thinly disguised fiction in order to find an audience in the age of the mass-circulation newspaper and the radio.[72]

One of the American historians in Wrong's audience was Charles A. Beard, president-elect of the American Historical Association. A year earlier at the AHA meetings, Beard had listened to Carl Becker's presidential address, 'Every Man His Own Historian,' an eloquent and forceful statement of historical relativism. Now, maybe provoked by Wrong's address, he used the occasion of a banquet address sponsored by the University of Toronto to express his own views on the subject. He began with an apparent paradox: it was only 'by becoming unmoral that history serves the highest morality.' Judgments about right or wrong in history led neither to 'understanding nor reconciliation.' Only by 'putting aside the moral function of meting out damnation' could historians enter into 'the kingdom of comprehension.'[73]

This was no glib after-dinner speech, for Beard's essential message was that no modern historian could escape the ambiguities or complexities of contemporary historical practice. Narrow specialization was mere escapism, for the obligation of the historian was to broaden, not narrow, horizons – to move 'beyond the boundaries of nations, economic systems, and political jurisdictions.' This mandate, he said, was inescapable and it would bring little comfort, for the modern historian was caught in a conflict as old as Western civilization itself – a 'tragic conflict' between 'subjective idealism and objective reality' – from which there could be no resolution. 'Whatever may be the subjective ideal we accept,' Beard concluded, 'it is certain to be lacerated on the cruel world of deed and fact. Yet we cannot accept the cruel world of deed and fact as corresponding to any ideal satisfactory to the spirit. And all efforts at reconciliation lead us into scepticism and distress, scarcely less acute than the scepticism and distress of impassive neutrality.'[74]

Beard argued forcefully that historians must accept that the world of values was one of relative moral claims. History practiced by the serious-minded arbiters of moral finality would lead only to 'tragedy and tears'; and the light-minded would receive no greater reprieve from this morally-ambiguous world, for theirs would be the history of 'irony and cynicism.'[75] Donald Creighton and Frank Underhill were no doubt present when Beard spoke those words. They could scarcely have conceived that Beard, without knowing it, had just uttered their professional epitaphs.

Wrong remained an unrepentant public moralist, shaped when Queen Victoria still lived, in spite of Beard's own Toronto homily. So did most Canadian historians of the generation that Creighton and Underhill represented, coming to intellectual maturity in the 1930s and 1940s and dominating the profession into the 1960s. Whether liberal or conservative, their history took the form of secular sermons built on a nationalist historical testament. 'Historians – even the "specialists" among them using the tools of modern social science – could still offer moral and political guidance to students and the public. Indeed, the mere exercise of studying the past, whatever the lessons elicited, helped to preserve the high purpose of the liberal arts, and history's significant position within the humanities was thus secured.'[76]

The professionalization of Canadian history, which in practical terms meant the conscription of the past for academic purposes, took place within this milieu. Wrong himself embodied much of this impulse within the Ontario historical community. With University of Toronto Librarian H.H. Langton, an 1883 Toronto classmate, he was responsible for the creation in 1920 of the *Canadian Historical Review*, a revitalized version of the *Review of Historical Publications* he had launched in 1897 and had edited to 1919.[77] The Canadian Historical Association emerged in the wake of the new journal in 1922, at first associated with the activities of the Royal Society of Canada. The increasingly academic community of historians thus gained a professional association and a vehicle for publishing research well over a decade before their colleagues in economics or political science.

In the early 1930s Chester Martin, Wrong's successor as head of the history department at the University of Toronto, remarked on the fiftieth anniversary of the Royal Society of Canada that Canadian history was in a transitional stage. He meant that both the country and the historical profession had reached a new stage in their evolution. Martin's book, *Empire and Commonwealth: Studies in Governance and Self-Government in Canada* (1929), embodied both elements. A work of substantial scholarship, it also documented the fate of the imperial ideal and of Canada's newly voluntaristic association with it as an autonomous actor on the world stage. In Martin's view, the rise of Canadian liberty through the mechanism of responsible government was a gift made possible because it was an extension and modification of British institutions; and it was the most precious because it had been a gift freely given.[78] Other historians, such as Reginald Trotter of Queen's, in *Canadian Federation* (1924) and in *The British Empire-Commonwealth: A Study in Political Evolution* (1932), echoed such views.

Yet others, including Trotter himself,[79] had begun to comment on the need to examine Canadian history in a North American context. Harold Innis, Frank Underhill, and Donald Creighton at Toronto, and A.R.M. Lower, first at United College in Winnipeg and later at Queen's, began to examine Canadian history in the context of its North American economic, geographic, and political environments. Although they differed strongly on the nature and meaning of this cultural exchange, Canada was, for each, the site of an imperial conflict between British and American influences and values. Early in the 1920s Innis began his lengthy and solitary study of Canada's staple industries. He concluded that while geographic and economic circumstances were of overwhelming importance to the country's national development, those circumstances were transatlantic in nature: Canada, whether in French or British imperial orbits, was an economic, political, and cultural extension of European metropolitan influences. Underhill and Lower were more open to American scholarship, particularly the radical environmentalism of Frederick Jackson Turner's 'frontier thesis' (which argued that frontier conditions led to a process of acculturation that stripped away European assumptions and values but forged democratic – that is, American – ones). Yet neither historian denied the importance of Canada's British or French heritages. Underhill, in fact, lamented their stifling hold on the development of political thought and action. His life-long search for a Canadian liberalism as strong and vital as that of Jeffersonian and Jacksonian America began with an attempt to link George Brown and the 'Clear Grit' movement of the mid-nineteenth century to the Turnerian interpretation of sectional conflict. If Canada did not have a tradition of Jacksonian democracy, Underhill was determined to use the historical imagination to locate and popularize its Canadian equivalent.[80]

This reorientation of historical attention towards continental affairs reflected a subtle shift in the spiritual landscape of the Toronto department. As with his predecessors, George Wrong had studiously avoided appointing graduates of North American doctoral programs such as those offered at Harvard or Chicago. In his view, possession of an Oxford bachelor's degree or a Toronto MA was sufficient for Canadian academic life. While empowered to do so for much of Wrong's long tenure as head of history at Toronto, his department awarded no PHD until the eve of his retirement, in 1925, when W.B. Kerr and Walter Sage were granted them. Until the 1930s the only member of the history faculty holding an advanced research degree was W.P.M. Kennedy, who possessed a doctorate from Trinity College, Dublin. The first faculty member to hold an American PHD was George Brown, appointed in 1932. Only very gradually did the American commitment to intense archival research as the foundation for an advanced degree take hold, and in general Toronto continued to procure staff as it had in the past, from those of its graduates who had gone on to Oxford 'for training and finishing.'[81]

The sense of crisis brought on by the Depression and the escalation of political extremism in Europe drew the attention of Canadian historians away from the writing of history as a form of nationalist expression – whether imperialist or autonomist – and towards the need for a broader perspective. In 1929, with the appointment of Chester Martin as its new head, the University of Toronto history department embarked on a restructuring of its modern history offerings that resulted eventually in an expansion of American courses and the introduction of others such as 'medieval and renaissance Europe' in first year and 'English-Speaking World' in third.[82] This was consistent with concerns within the profession. In 1930, Maritime historian D.C. Harvey pleaded with his professional colleagues at the annual meetings of the Canadian Historical Association that they should get abreast of contemporary trends in international scholarship and listen to the demands of the public. 'The modern historian is being pressed from all sides to help in the solution of contemporary social, political, intellectual and international problems by the application of doses of history.' A 'two-fold revolt against the narrowness of history' was under way, said Harvey; a revolt brought on by its narrowly political and national nature. More attention was needed to the economic and social dimension of the historical record and more general (instead of national) history should be written.[83]

Harvey's plea reflected the views of others. Only a year earlier, Harold Innis had presented a paper on 'The Teaching of Economic History in Canada' to an audience of economics and commerce teachers at the National Conference of Canadian Universities. He, too, called for an expansion of the scope and conceptual framework of history. Serious study of economic history would, he said, anchor both history and economics. Like Harvey, Innis was tired of the well-worn path to nationhood that used the moral compass of responsible government.[84]

Innis had practiced what he preached since his appointment to the University of Toronto just after the Great War. His *History of the Canadian Pacific Railway*, a revision of his University of Chicago doctoral thesis, was published in 1924; but by then he had already turned his attention – and that of many of his students – to the history of the fur trade in Canada. By 1925 more than a dozen students, often from the university's department of extension, had written theses under his direction on various aspects of the fur trade, and something of a local fur trade 'industry' had developed.[85] Innis himself, working somewhat in isolation in a department presided over in the 1920s and 1930s by social philosophers suspicious of the very idea of social science yet populated also by colleagues whom he regarded as statistically oriented philistines, set the pace for fur trade research. His seminal work on the subject, *The Fur Trade in Canada*, was published in 1930.[86]

The scholarship of Innis was clearly a labour of love, and he was completely committed to the scholarly life. He had witnessed this commitment at first hand as a student of philosopher James Ten Broeke at McMaster University, and was inspired to follow the same lonely path. Innis did his best to instil scholarly commitment in others by example and by sharing his research and ideas with them. In the 1920s, for example, he helped A.R.M. Lower (then studying at Harvard) in various ways; and in the 1930s he did the same for Irene Biss (later Irene Spry).[87] Nor was it only graduate students for whom he was an academic model. In 1933, six years after Donald Creighton had joined the University of Toronto staff as an instructor in history, J.B. Brebner wrote to Innis: 'It is good that you are keeping an eye on Creighton. He is one of your true admirers and through you he has been infected with the most serious intentions, not only of knowing what Canadian history is about, but of writing lucidly about it.'[88]

Creighton's intentions were indeed serious, although the lucidity of his prose certainly stemmed much more from his reading of Victorian novelists and historians than it did from reading anything by Innis. Nevertheless, the intellectual mark of Innis's work was indelible in Creighton's own. Creighton's magisterial book *The Commercial Empire of the St Lawrence*, which appeared in 1937, took Innis's economic and geographic determinism beyond the level of his insights into the staple theory of Canadian development. In it, Creighton transformed the St Lawrence river system and its vast hinterland into a metaphor that at once captured the importance of Innis's ideas on metropolitan dominance and the impossibility of full control over the North American heartland. To the empiricism, the concrete detail, of *The Fur Trade in Canada*, Creighton engrafted techniques of romantic narrative and an essentially tragic vision. In doing so, he managed to balance Harold Innis's concern for environmental circumstance and George Wrong's insistence on the importance of individual moral character as a fundamental element in social change.[89] For the next quarter century, approaches to historical transformation were marked by this essentially liberal approach to historical studies; the assumptions and categories of Karl Marx made little mark on Ontario universities during these years.

Although Creighton and Innis came eventually to distrust American ideology and intentions, their concentration on the geographic environment within which Canada sought its place in the world helped shift the attention of historians to social, economic, and political connections within the transatlantic community, including continental ones. Two expatriate University of Toronto graduates in the United States also provided inspiration and leadership for a more cosmopolitan approach to history, one that transcended national borders and disciplinary boundaries. John Bartlet Brebner, son of the University of Toronto registrar allegedly thrown down a flight of stairs by Mackenzie King in the student strike of 1895, was one. Located at Columbia University, Brebner consistently undercut nationalist pretension and argued for the international –which for him in the 1930s primarily meant continental – nature of scholarly enterprise. In 1931, at the annual meetings of the Canadian Historical Association, Brebner called for historians to aspire to a 'continental interpretation' of their history.[90]

The second Canadian expatriate, James T. Shotwell, was well placed to bring Brebner's hopes to fruition. As director of the division of economics and history of the Carnegie Endowment for International Peace and of the program of research on international relations for the Social Science Research Council, the influential Shotwell secured a promise from the Carnegie Trust to underwrite the costs of a major series of studies, many historical in nature, on almost all aspects of relations between Canada and the United States. Thus was born the 'Carnegie Series,' which eventually ran to twenty-five volumes. For almost the first time in Canadian academic life, scholarship brought the extra income necessary for major research. It paid. As Shotwell wrote to a suspicious Harold Innis in 1932: 'That was a splendid letter I got from you yesterday, and one which I deeply appreciate. I heartily agree with you that research is not a thing to be bought and sold on the money market; nevertheless it is an encouraging sign of genuine appreciation when the funds are made available to viable projects.'[91] In the depths of the Depression, it was difficult to argue with such lucrative logic, and several Canadian scholars participated. One of them was Innis, his worries about the influence of the money market on scholarship sufficiently allayed that he produced *The Cod Fisheries: The History of an International Economy* for the series in 1940.[92] Remarkably enough, within the span of a decade of scarcity as much academic Canadian history had been researched and written as in the previous century. In the process, the axis of interpretation had begun to tilt, however slowly, and it pointed north and south.[93]

Accounts of Canadian historical scholarship between the wars, however much they reflect the growing interest of professors in using Canadian archives for the study of the Canadian past, somewhat misrepresent the undergraduate classroom reality. That reality was of students exposed to little Canadian history, at least initially, for few courses on the subject were offered. When Maurice Careless entered the University of Toronto as a freshman in 1936, Canadian history was given only in a combined Canadian-American survey course and in fourth-year seminars taught by Chester Martin and Frank Underhill. These were the last years when the Toronto department could be described as intimate in size, for the post-war demand for higher education would transform it, like others, out of all previous proportion.[94] Yet Toronto's department was large compared with that of McMaster or Western where, respectively, Chester New and Fred Landon found themselves teaching much of the history curriculum.[95] The department of history at Queen's University entered the 1950s with a full-time academic staff of five, including a senior tutor. As elsewhere, Canadian history was subsumed within a European perspective. Honours in history could be taken either in British and European history or in British and colonial history. The calendar description of A.R.M. Lower's third-year course in Canadian history read: 'Canadian History as a phase of the expansion of European civilization into the western hemisphere.'[96]

Along with English, the study of history was central to honours arts courses throughout the province. This was especially the case at the University of Toronto, whose program had long served as the model for others in the country, and whose graduates often provided other institutions with the Canadian-born complement on their teaching staffs.[97] Most students who enrolled in Toronto history courses in the 1930s did so in the English and history combination that was the core of the honours program. After the provincial ministry of education allowed a separation of the two by creating a specialist's certificate in modern history, the English and history stream was ended. By 1939 it consisted of English alone. The emphasis within the history department then shifted to the modern history area, where enrolments had grown significantly. Now in greater control over its own student clientele, the department gained greater autonomy in controlling the direction of its curricular destiny.[98] Course offerings began to expand in European, British, American, and Canadian fields, and they were supplemented by optional ones in ancient history or by historically oriented courses given in the departments of English, French, German, and political science and economics. Even historians who published primarily in Canadian history, like Innis, Underhill, and Creighton, had teaching responsibilities not primarily Canadian in orientation. The lengthy textbook by Toronto historian Ralph Flenley, *Modern Europe and the World*, first published in 1930, reflected the emphasis and orientation of the program his department offered.

Flenley's book was an exceptional achievement, for Ontario historians did not generally have the time, energy, or resources to engage in sustained research in British or European history leading to publication. For example, the first research interest of Donald Creighton was in eighteenth-century France, but lack of financial support allowing time to spend in European archives led him to work in Canada on Canadian subjects. In 1946, in his presidential address to the Canadian Historical Association, Frank Underhill lamented the absence of much historical writing other than of Canada's rather parochial past. He pointed to Charles Norris Cochrane's book *Christianity and Classical Culture: A Study of Thought and Action from Augustus to Augustine*

(1940) as one of the few important Canadian contributions to world history.[99]

Underhill was correct in judging Cochrane's book to be an instant classic of the profession, the culmination of a lifetime's work, and his assessment of the state of non-Canadian historical publications within the profession was not an unfair one. Nevertheless, other noteworthy works had appeared. McMaster historian Edward Togo Salmon had published *A History of the Roman World from 30 BC to AD 138* in 1944 and Underhill's Toronto colleague Bertie Wilkinson had made significant contributions to medieval history with *The Chancery under Edward III* (1929), *The Mediaeval Council of Exeter* (1931), and *Studies in the Constitutional History of the Thirteenth and Fourteenth Centuries* (1937). Ralph Flenley continued his work in modern European history, publishing *Makers of Nineteenth-Century Europe* (1937). For the most part, however, the major Ontario contributions to British, European, or American historical scholarship were not produced until after the Second World War.[100]

A division of professional labour in historical scholarship was beginning to take shape. The shift of emphasis by historians towards economic, social, and North American conditions, combined with the gradual emergence of political science from the twin shadows of the historians and the political economists, facilitated the gravitation of responsibility for the history of the Canadian political system (and with it Canadian constitutional history) to the political scientists. At the University of Toronto, W.P.M. Kennedy, first in the history department, then in political economy, took the historical approach dominant in so many other areas of the university into the new department (later faculty) of law in 1930. Major studies, beginning with Kennedy's *The Constitution of Canada: An Introduction to Its Development and Law* (1922) and R. MacGregor Dawson's *The Principle of Official Independence* (1922), and later Dawson's *The Civil Service of Canada* (1929) and J.A. Corry's *Democratic Government and Politics* (1946), reflected this new division of scholarly labour.[101] Another result, probably of more consequence, was that the breadth of approach to legal study provided by the choice of an historical rather than a case approach made the academic study of law, especially at Toronto, an integral part of the social sciences and humanities.[102]

The major spokesmen of the core disciplines in the humanities at Ontario universities between the wars held much in common. They lived in a fragmented and pluralistic world of industry, mass democracy, and mass media that many of them did not like. Few held any brief for an unknown future. Most grounded their work, instead, in a knowable past. Ontario humanists used various forms of historical practice as a means of preserving cultural memory. They lived in a country that by European standards was almost as new as that which John Graves Simcoe and other colonial governors had superintended a century and more earlier. In a sense, the professors of the humanities between the wars were the colonial administrators of a formally post-colonial era. Seneca had once said: 'They change their skies but not their minds who cross the sea in ships.' This, the hold of memory, was their means of preserving a new 'sense of power,' in the form of a continued connection to the meaning of Western civilization, as they understood it, after the end of formal imperial connection.

Such was the deep meaning of Claude Bissell's 'great good place,' where students could take courses in classics from Maurice Hutton or Charles Norris Cochrane or C.B. Sissons, in English from W.J. Alexander or Pelham Edgar or A.S.P. Woodhouse, in history from George Wrong or Harold Innis or Donald Creighton, and live and grow within essentially the same universe of values given force and meaning by the passionate intensity with which such men linked it to a rich and resonant past. This general pattern was replicated at the other universities in the province, although the names of the professors differed. Yet the scholarly work of most enduring value tended to be produced those by associated with the University of Toronto. Moreover, only the provincial university offered instruction in enough disciplines for a student in the humanities to be able to come to grips with the scope of the social sciences. Only the provincial university harboured scholars who between the wars directly addressed the nature and meaning of social science. Students there, moving from classes in the humanities to those in the social sciences, heard variations on familiar themes.

Social Philosophy and Social Science

Teaching and scholarship in the social sciences had existed in Ontario universities since the days of W.J. Ashley, James Mavor, Adam Shortt, and O.D. Skelton. Given the orientation, interests, and influence of such men, much of the work that appeared in the next several decades was in the fields of economics, political science, or political economy. It was usually intended to be of practical value, and often it carried strong implications for the creation of public policy. The nine volumes of the 'Canadian Frontiers of Settlement' series (1934–40), edited by W.A. Mackintosh and W.L.G. Joerg, combined economic theory with a geographic and historical approach; they also addressed economic problems brought to public consciousness by the Depression. At Queen's University, Mackintosh inspired and encouraged the field of applied economics, exemplified by his own books, *Economic Problems of the Prairie Provinces* (1935) and *The Economic Background of Dominion-Provincial Relations* (1939) – the latter undertaken as a research study for the Royal Commission on Dominion-Provincial Relations. Such books found counterparts elsewhere in the country, particularly in the work of Saskatchewan economic historians G.E. Britnell and V.C. Fowke. Studies in political economy by Ontario-based scholars tended to be surveys, at times with practical or political implications. These included H.A.Logan's and M.K. Inman's *A Social Approach to Economics* (1939), V.W. Bladen's *An Introduction to Political Economy* (1941), and Harold A. Innis's *Political Economy in the Modern State* (1946).

The story of other social sciences in Ontario universities between the wars once again testifies to the pre-eminence of the University of Toronto. Work in subjects such as psychology or sociology at other institutions, such as Queen's, McMaster, and the University of Western Ontario, was largely confined to teaching in areas such as economics, commerce, finance, and accountancy – those disciplines with the most demonstrably practical and professional results. Social science disciplines such as sociology, anthropology, and geography, when taught at all at these universities, existed only within the jurisdictions of traditional and well-established disciplines. At Queen's, for example, sociology and geography were established only in the 1950s within the department of economics and political science; in 1959, Principal W.A. Mackintosh declared to historian A.R.M. Lower that the development of anthropology was certainly not among his priorities.[1] At McMaster, sociology was paired with psychology until well after the Second World War, to the detriment of work in both disciplines. Social sciences in the Hamilton university had scarcely gained the respect of its president by the end of the 1940s. 'Your references to the social scientists,' wrote G.P. Gilmour, ' – if they can merit the term "science" at all – put the finger on the sorest spot in all educational work. Certainly I would not want to turn a lot of sociologists I know loose in an educational institution. A sensitive professor of English literature can often do more to disarm prejudice and correct psychoses than some of the polysyllabic experts in the field.'[2] In 1953 Gilmour did appoint a psychologist to his staff, but he expressed intense relief upon discovering that he was a practicing Anglican: 'we do not want work in ... Psychology to fall into the hands of men who are out of sympathy with the aims and convictions of Christian men.' The first permanent appointment in sociology at McMaster was not made until 1955. One former McMaster faculty member recalled that in the late 1950s 'only two half classes in sociology were offered. These were taught by Wreford Watson, a geographer and poet, and were known to students as Sex 303 and 304.' In short, scholarship in such disciplines throughout the province and the country was, on the whole, meagre in the first half of the twentieth century. An overview of them conducted in 1965 was less than two pages in length. It began: 'Political science is under-developed compared with economics; the other social sciences lag far in the rear. Many universities are even yet scarcely aware that there are such disciplines as sociology, anthropology, and criminology.'[3]

The reasons for the neglect of social science disciplines other than economics, political science, and political economy are complex. Given the penurious state of most Ontario universities, disciplines such as sociology and anthropology were considered luxuries that could not be afforded. Individual professors were at times encouraged to offer a course on such subjects if they had expressed an interest in them, but the creation of programs leading to departmental status was not. The continuing preference for the appointment of British- rather than American-educated professors perpetuated the commitment to traditional disciplines and traditional approaches.

Yet certain Ontario professors made exceptional contributions to the disciplines of philosophy, psychology, and sociology during this period. The most outstanding among them taught at the University of Toronto. They were remarkable precisely because they refused to separate the concerns of the social sciences from those of the humanities. Like their colleagues in classics, English, and history, theirs was usually an historical approach derived from earlier assumptions about the progressive nature of social evolution. Moreover, they refused to divorce their work not only from the past but also from the moral. They represented the persistence well into the twentieth century of the nineteenth-century search for synthesis. As such, they resisted the general direction of academic thought in North America, and eventually they found their views challenged even in the academic units they administered. In doing so, however, they made possible the continuance of a distinctive and comprehensive approach to the study of the social.

George Sidney Brett, R.M. MacIver, E.J. Urwick, and Harold Innis were collectively responsible for much of the temper and direction of social investigation at the provincial university in the first half of the twentieth century. They were not only prolific and influential scholars but also held positions of substantial power within the university. MacIver, Urwick, and Innis were the successive heads of Toronto's department of political economy from 1922 until Innis's death in 1952. Brett became the dean of its graduate school soon after its creation in 1923; Innis assumed the position in 1947. The institutional history of the University of Toronto in the twentieth century remains to be written, and when it is these four men will be dominant figures. Yet their importance lies in the connection that existed between their activities as administrators and their convictions as scholars. A very distinctive approach to social science was practiced in the provincial university between the wars, and it cannot be fully understood without taking these scholars and their ideas into account. Each was a major interpreter of the relationship between social philosophy and social science.

Historians usually trace the paths of those who prevail. This commonplace observation applies as much to the history of academic disciplines as it does to political dynasties. Yet occasionally it is instructive to investigate why a certain path was not taken, a deed not done, a choice not made. The question of how, when, and under what influences the social sciences developed in Ontario from the First to the Second World War represents at one level such a path not taken by these institutional leaders, although not always by those they led: a path not simply left unexplored but one that was consciously rejected in favour of another. The forsaken path was that of American social science, of which the behaviouralism of John B. Watson in psychology and of the 'Chicago School' in sociology were emblematic. The path these men chose was one that bore the marks of previous explorers of known reputation and of their own lineage. Put simply, social science in Ontario, as they envisioned it, looked to the British rather than the American way, to an evolved history and a European intellectual heritage. The question was: could the European direction they sought for their disciplines be maintained intact any more than could the British nature of English-speaking Canada itself in the dawn of the American century?

Matters on the Mind

Ideas about the nature of social change had been part of the magisterial edifice of late nineteenth-century mental and moral philosophy. Yet, eroded by the fragmentation of knowledge and the growth of specialized research, philosophy had slowly surrendered its intellectual territories to emergent academic disciplines. Most universities in the twentieth century boasted separate departments of political and economic science, history, and mathematics. Philosophy was largely shorn of its traditional association with Christian theology by the emergence of religion as a disciplinary unit of secular academic study, and in consequence had been narrowed to the study of logic, epistemology, metaphysics, and ethics. By the time of his retirement in the early 1920s, John Watson, the last lingering representative of the golden age of Queen's, was simply one member of a diverse and highly specialized academic staff.

Nineteenth-century British idealism, whether that of T.H. Green or Bernard Bosanquet or John Watson, had fought a rearguard action against several philosophical 'heresies,' such as Adam Smith's atomistic individualism, Jeremy Bentham's utilitarianism, August Comte's positivism, Herbert Spencer's evolutionary naturalism, and John Tyndall's scientific materialism. Philosophers such as John Watson and Bernard Bosanquet had insisted that man could not understand either himself or society unless the primacy of the social group – the community or the state – was recognized. For man was, above all, a social being, and his essence was realized in the consciousness that he was part of a larger social whole. Society was a single psychic entity driven by purposive human action; institutions within it were viewed as 'ethical ideas' that expressed the moral will. John Watson had expressed these ideas in the language of the civic humanism characteristic of the British idealist tradition: 'The citizen should not consider that he is any chartered libertine,' he said, following Plato and Aristotle, 'free to do whatever seems good in his eyes. There must indeed be freedom to live the higher life without interference from either neighbour or state; such freedom, however, does not mean licence, but subordination of all personal motives and conduct to the laws of the community. In such subordination there is no loss of real freedom, but on the contrary the realisation of the common will, which is on the whole a rational will.'[4]

President Robert Falconer was referring to this larger, social and ethical whole when, in an address called 'The Education of National Character,' he spoke of the need for the good teacher to make his pupils see 'the regular order in which things work,' to distinguish between 'mere knowledge and knowledge of what is worth knowing,' and to forge the disciplined intelligence necessary to establish such a perspective. What we are as a people, he said, 'is the result of a long process of education of the will rather than of the intellect ...'[5] By educating the will he meant not merely cultivating the habit of self-control but, more important, subordinating oneself to the social will. Only by doing so would one's individuality – and hence freedom – truly be established. Nor did Falconer's successor as president, H.J. Cody, change this moralistic emphasis. 'The university transmits the sacred fire of learning from the past,' he told members of the Canadian Educational Association in 1935; 'its present ideal is to discipline the intelligence ...'[6]

No Ontario scholar better embodied this general ideal than George Sidney Brett. Born in South Wales in 1879, Brett was appointed lecturer in classics and librarian at Trinity College, Toronto, in 1908. His book *The Philosophy of Gassendi* appeared that year, and he was quickly marked as a man of formidable intellectual and organizational capacity. Within a matter of months the new president of the University of Toronto, Robert Falconer, had secured his reappointment as professor of ethics and ancient philosophy.[7] A 1902 graduate of Oxford, with a first-class degree in *Litteræ Humaniores*, Brett became deeply acquainted (and remained fascinated) with the comprehensive philosophical testaments to the power of the rational mind written by the nineteenth-century Oxford idealists T.H. Green, F.H. Bradley, and Bernard Bosanquet; yet his Oxford tutor, John Alexander Stewart, had also impressed him with the presence and power of the irrational element in human nature.

Like the idealists, Brett believed in the essential unity of all knowledge, and the force of his erudition was such that he resolved to take much of the range of human thought as his compass. By the time he arrived in Toronto, he had already conceived his life's main project: to write a history of psychology from the days of the ancients to the present, as it was found in the history of religion, philosophy, the physical sciences, medicine, and much else. This was psychology in no limited sense: it was, rather, to be 'a study of the development of man's knowledge about himself and the influence of that knowledge on his conduct and his beliefs.' In short, it was an elaborate attempt, requiring three substantial volumes, to convey for his times the story of what the ancients had called the 'science of the soul.'[8] As preparation for this heroic task, Brett's education at Oxford stood him in good stead, for in their imperious manner British universities had resisted the encroachment of new disciplines into the traditional academic structures.

Brett did not object to specialization. In fact he saw it as inherent in the nature of social evolution. The very first words of his *History of Psychology* testified to this. 'The evolution of thought,' he began, 'has followed a course not unlike that which the ancient philosophers described when they traced the genesis of the world out of chaos.' But from chaos, even in 'primitive thought,' came classification and order, derived from 'the reflective attitude which desires to unify knowledge under the least possible number of headings or even find one category to include all ...' Knowledge preceded science; science grew out of knowledge as knowledge became progressively specialized. Psychology itself was the product of the 'slow process of specialisation,' and precisely because of this only the historical approach could illuminate it.[9] Brett's indebtedness to the ideas and assumptions of British social evolutionists such as Herbert Spencer is clear, especially in his use of an organic metaphor derived from biology – human thought, like life itself, proceeded in stages from the simple and homogeneous to the complex and heterogeneous. Yet he was equally indebted to his Oxford tutor Stewart; for from him he gained the idea that psychology was not so much a science as it was a critical stance upon the world. As Stewart had put it in an 1876 essay, it was a 'critique, a Method, a certain thoughtful attitude in science, morals, and literature. It is the critical examination of my own adult opinions, desires, and tastes in relation to present objects.'[10] From such a perspective, specialization posed less a threat than a challenge. The growth of modern knowledge had made it inevitable; but the duty of those with a philosophic temper and an historical approach was to synthesize the divergent approaches of the several disciplines.

Brett's *History* was his attempt at such a synthesis, and it took him well over a decade to complete. His first volume, covering ancient and patristic thought, was published in 1912; the second and third volumes, on the medieval and early modern period and on 'modern psychology' (from the Scottish common sense philosophers to the British social evolutionists), appeared in 1921. Addressing from the outset the relation of scientific views and religious beliefs, he resolutely refused to be circumscribed by either pluralistic or monistic views of the world – for human thought was more complex than this. 'From one point of view,' he wrote, 'all sciences are one science, the science of one universe. But from another point of view the sciences are manifold. Between the two hypothetical points, that of a world of objects regarded as containing implicitly a unity and intelligibility of its own and that of the same world transformed by the activity of thought into a system of knowledge, there lies all the process of reconstruction whose recorded steps make up the history of human thought.'[11] Brett assumed the task of enacting such a reconstruction, and his *History of Psychology* became a complicated and sustained act not only of synthesis but also of recovery and reconciliation.

Brett's view of psychology as a form of process made him a natural interpreter of extreme and at times conflicting views, whether of science and religion, of the particular and the general, of the empirical and the ideal, or of extreme relativism and extreme determinism. His approach was experiential and pluralistic rather than abstract and monocausal, and he believed that human experience could best be studied by historical examination of the record of human thought over the centuries. His style was more synoptic than analytical, his temper judicious. One of the most remarkable aspects of his *History* is that after its thousand pages it ends abruptly, without the slightest attempt to formulate a conclusion. This may, in fact, have been the point he was trying to make: that man's search for meaning, for his soul, has no closure but is continuous. It is as if Brett believed that his recovery of the psychological dimension of being through the ages would speak for itself, giving modern man an anchor for the courage necessary to face life in a complex and bewildering world. There are hints of this throughout the work.[12]

In his own way, Brett believed as much as Arnold had done in exposing public and student to the best that was known and thought in the world; his own history was drawn from a record of written philosophical expression that was every much as canonical as the literary tradition upheld by Arnold and, later, by F.R. Leavis and others. Brett anticipated Leavis, in fact, by referring to the record of humanistic thought on which he based his work as 'the great tradition.' The approach of the University of Toronto philosophy department under his leadership has been described, accurately, as a study of 'great men.'[13]

Like the nineteenth-century idealists who so fascinated him, Brett believed that science and religion operated on separate planes in the continuum of knowledge; but because he was less directly tied than they had been to the perceived necessity of reconciling them he had no use for reason as an instrument for demonstrating the superiority of philosophy to either. 'Religion and science,' he wrote, 'have no relations sufficiently exact to cause conflict or demand reconciliation. The conflict has been created by individuals who assume either that religion is a means by which scientific questions can be settled or that Science is the only method for the comprehension of life. The result has been that some individuals have been brought to think in terms of this opposition and this has produced in them a mental crisis.'[14] Brett was also intensely aware of the way personal and social factors determined the structure of philosophical systems.[15] History was his chosen means of demonstrating the flux of human thought in a manner as non-judgmental as possible. The course of that thought was one of insight and error, a process in which knowledge was continually made and remade.[16] This, for Brett, was the lesson of history.

To say that Brett consciously avoided giving readers of his *History of Psychology* his own moral judgments is not to say he was without moral concern. Midway through writing his *History*, he published a book that made this concern, if not his conclusions, clear. *The Government of Man* appeared in 1913, and it was sufficiently popular that it reached a second edition in 1920. In it he surveyed much of the same ground he was covering in his larger work, from the ancients to John Stuart Mill; but his focus was different. His attention now was given to theories of conduct. Concerned with the relation between the political and the ethical realms, he linked his historical overview to those aspects of life most closely related to them – social, psychological, economic, and religious: '... life exhibits a process towards unity of system, and we may accept the formula that life begins in action and ends in conduct. Conduct, in this terminology, signifies action brought under a rule, and corresponds therefore to what we mean by moral as opposed to non-moral action. In this context "moral" means simply "regulated by principle."'[17]

The Government of Man, like the *History*, was synoptic and judicious, with Brett rendering judgment on the strengths and weaknesses of particular theories of conduct; but he studiously refused to be prescriptive. 'The story has its moral,' he concluded, 'but it is no part of the volume to dictate that moral.'[18] His was the responsibility to provide the historical evidence; the reader's was to think for himself. He rendered judgment on many philosophers, yet seldom did he relate those personal views to contemporary problems. He hoped, simply, that the combination of his book and his reader's intelligence would be sufficient to make the connections between two millennia of ethical theorizing and 'our present problems' clear. 'Innumerable questions suggest themselves at once,' he warned, 'the future of democracy, the relation of public to private morality, the meaning of religion for the State and for the individual, the power and weakness of reason or of feeling ...'[19]

Such concerns were scarcely Brett's alone in the Edwardian twilight.

On both sides of the Atlantic thoughtful social observers such as England's Graham Wallas and America's Walter Lippmann expressed their disquiet over the relation between the individual and the social good and the implications of the new mass society for democratic leadership and government. In spite of his steadfast refusal to impose himself as moral arbiter of competing psychological or ethical theories in his books, Brett clearly regarded himself as having a purpose akin to theirs: to articulate a vision of the good society and to formulate a new liberalism out of the best elements of the old. When he reviewed Wallas's book *The Great Society* in 1915, he found much in it he admired. It was an original and 'outstanding' book, written from the viewpoint of an author with practical experience and concerned with group psychology in the era of mass democracy. Such works were essential. 'Mankind is ever changing, and that change is not merely a change of spirit which the sociologist, the philosopher and the psychologist estimate reflectively, each under his own rubric. Here we have to deal with the psychology of the subject, that subtle evasive aspect of life which everyone thinks important but few have the courage to face honestly.'[20] If this was the age of man in the mass, he concluded, it was the task of the social psychologist to sort out which commonly held beliefs were sound and which unsound; only then would generalizations about 'collective feeling and willing ... be true and serviceable.' Brett found Wallas's work to be a major accomplishment, yet by the 1920s Brett himself had contributed as much of enduring value as Wallas to such an understanding.

By the time Brett became head of the University of Toronto's philosophy department and dean of its graduate school in the 1920s he was a figure of international stature in the scholarly community. He also became a close and trusted adviser of presidents Falconer and Cody, providing suggestions on academic appointments, administration and structures, and much else. Several of his students remained at Toronto as colleagues, possibly as a result of Brett's personal encouragement or even his intervention with university authorities. Fulton H. Anderson and Thomas A. Goudge continued their mentor's great man approach to philosophy, writing books such as Anderson's *The Argument of Plato* (1934) and Goudge's *The Thought of C.S. Peirce* (1950). They also produced works on subjects close to Brett's own special interests, such as Marcus Long's *Introduction to Systematic Philosophy* (1948) and *The Spirit of Philosophy* (1953), John A. Irving's *Science and Values* (1952), Goudge's study of contemporary evolutionary theory, *The Ascent of Life* (1961), and Derwyn R.G. Owen's *Scientism, Man, and Religion* (1952). A.H. Johnson of the University of Western Ontario was a self-proclaimed 'Brett man,' and the author of *Whitehead's Theory of Reality*

(1952) and *Whitehead's Philosophy of Civilization* (1952).[21] Brett's concern for the historical and the biographical, for overview and synthesis, for the nature of social evolution, and for the relationship between science and values, is the dominant note in these books.

'The history of psychology,' wrote a contributor to *Queen's Quarterly* in 1939, 'falls into two great divisions, the study of the soul and the study of behaviour without a soul.'[22] George Brett's *History of Psychology*, which devoted much of its attention to ideas of the soul in the ancient through the early modern eras, and his *The Government of Man*, dedicated to ideas of the ethical, made it evident that he believed the existence of the soul and the search for the good were inherent and enduring elements of the psychological history of humankind. Yet his work also demonstrated that many of the practitioners of modern psychology did not share such a view. Much of the third volume of his *History* gave attention to developments in nineteenth-century German physiological psychology and its influence on others. Brett was judicious yet sceptical in his treatment of this kind of psychology, for it clearly led in the direction of 'behaviour without a soul.' The rise of experimental psychology, which sought to measure behaviour under controlled conditions, had introduced 'a spectre' that haunted 'the halls of psychology.' The spectre, said Brett, was 'the question whether experimental work is not fundamentally a matter of quantity, whether quantity is really ever given in the sphere of psychology, and whether, if it is not, there is anything except illusion and physiology in the "new psychology."'[23]

The formal separation of psychology from the Toronto department of philosophy after the Great War was to a considerable extent an unavoidable necessity; yet it is testimony to Brett's openness of mind that in spite of his belief in the essential unity of philosophy and psychology he encouraged this development and helped arrange for an advocate of the experimental psychology of which he was so sceptical to be its first head. E.A. Bott, one of Brett's former students and the author of *Studies in Industrial Psychology* (1920), took charge of the new department and its laboratory when it came into existence in 1926.[24] Brett may have had serious misgivings about the value of behavioural measurement by psychologists, but he did not doubt the practical utility and popularity of applied psychology in such areas as education, mental health, and criminology.

Bott had made the importance of modern psychology clear during the Great War, when he had opened a rehabilitation clinic for casualties in the west wing of University College. Work on such a scale required skilled psychologists, and Bott recruited them in large numbers. By the end of the war, a de facto psychology department existed in the University of Toronto. By the early 1920s, psychologists taught more students than the rest of the philosophy department combined and Bott continued to recruit staff, including William Blatz, imported from the University of Chicago in 1925 to take charge of the new nursery school project at Toronto (it later became the Institute of Child Study). When the department of psychology was formally recognized in 1926 it was already very much dedicated to the 'applied' aspects of the discipline such as that represented by Peter Sandiford's *Educational Psychology* (1928), and it remained so.[25]

Bott's appointment marked the triumph of measurement and a general dismissal of metaphysics from the domain of the psychological. His American-style behaviourism was a science of the psyche without use for the soul. By 1930, when Bott was privately inveigling Rockefeller Foundation funding for the study of behaviour and personality,[26] the difference of perspectives between Bott and Brett had become an unbridgeable rupture. When Brett discovered the nature of Bott's entrepreneurial initiatives from Carleton Stanley, he replied: 'Bott seems to be afflicted with the American (or late Chicago) idea of efficiency. He is a go-getter by nature. The result is that we have a nursery school, an educational programme and a social science programme all being engineered from one angle.' When Brett complained in the same letter that 'the main part of the racket is Mental Hygiene – the Hincks organization wants to establish *independent* agents, with *independent* money, under the rooftree of a University which gives the show prestige'[27] – he was not criticizing the health care movement; rather, he was lamenting the debasing of his discipline. 'The practical difficulty at the present time,' he wrote in 1919, 'lies in the simple fact that, with the present point of view, too much emphasis falls on mere exchange value; in other words, people only value what they pay for.'[28]

E.A. Bott remained head of the department of psychology at the University of Toronto until 1956, presiding over thirty years of substantial departmental growth when psychology elsewhere in the province was still generally taught within the jurisdiction of philosophy departments (Queen's University, for example, did not formally create a department of psychology until the 1949–50 academic year).[29] As the continuing head of the philosophy department and later as dean of the University of Toronto graduate school, George Brett did his best to encourage a breadth of scholarly vision and a desire for historical and cultural synthesis in the students for whom he was directly and indirectly responsible. However much he may have regretted certain directions his university had taken, sometimes at the hands of former students such as

Bott, he doubtless took great satisfaction in the knowledge that others of them even beyond the disciplinary boundaries of philosophy, such as Northrop Frye and C.B. Macpherson, had come to understand what he had been trying to teach.

The Sociological Ideal

Because its fundamental message was so profoundly a social one, the creed of the British idealists contained the elements of a sociological perspective. The idealists rejected entirely the notion that standards of morality, individual or social, could be explained as natural products of cultural evolution. This, they said, confused moral origins with moral standards and denied the idea of man's moral nature. Yet their own understanding of the nature and formation of culture and society also assumed a course of progressive social evolution in human history. Their argument with nineteenth-century 'sociologists' was not that their work was historical, but that it was sloppy. As the British idealist philosopher D.G. Ritchie put it: 'The sociologist (especially when he is simply the biologist sociologizing) is apt to regard the historian as merely occupied with the higher gossip; on the other hand, the contempt for distinctions of time and place, and the unscholarly use of authorities, which too often characterize the sociologist, are apt to make the very word "evolution" stink in the nostrils of the genuine historian. "Evolution" and "development" seem only grand names for history treated inaccurately.'[30]

These were serious charges, made worse by the fact that the new sociologists had assumed one of the most fundamental tasks traditionally undertaken by philosophers: they sought to understand the mind and actions of man in systematic terms and on a scientific basis. To idealists, the sociologists' fundamental heresy was that they tended to marginalize or to dismiss altogether the place of conscious ends – human intention – in the sociological scheme of things. Yet the idealists' own optimistic account of social evolution as spiritual progression held little capacity to account for the disjunction of social ideals and social reality. The supreme irony is that they were as dependent as any evolutionary naturalist on a basically biological metaphor for social growth; thus, like the Spencerians, the British idealists failed to provide an adequate theoretical explanation of the origins and growth of social conflict. The stillborn nature of a discipline-based British academic sociology was a direct result. Not until the 1950s would sociology come to be recognized as an academic social science in Britain.[31]

In contrast, academic sociology in the United States flourished in the same period. The University of Chicago was the organizational and conceptual fulcrum of the emergent discipline. Chicago sociologists used their city as a social laboratory for direct empirical investigation, but Chicago sociology, at first scarcely separable from the moral and social reform movement of the 'progressive era,' gradually became instead the examination and explanation of social problems, a preoccupation not necessarily reformist in character. Like most American social scientists before and after him, Albion Small, founder of the *American Journal of Sociology* in 1895, worked within the categories of American exceptionalism – the deeply rooted set of assumptions that America had a special place in history because of its republican government and economic opportunity.[32] Yet the age of industrial conflict and urban unrest between 1890 and 1920 belied this exceptionalist vision, for America experienced many problems common to all industrial societies. Small and others searched for, and found, theories and methods that appeared to resolve the contradiction. He managed to avoid confronting the possibility that class conflict existed in America by insisting that the essence of the practice of sociology lay instead in its study of 'the process of association in groups, a pluralistic process of conflict and accommodation that issued in wider harmony.' Similarly, at Columbia University (the other major centre of sociological research in America) Franklin Giddings established a sociological tradition that sidestepped the problematic nature of American exceptionalism. The Giddings approach was highly statistical. In fact, 'the more fearful Giddings was of the American future, the more he propagandized for the scientific method of exact measurement ... In one sense this was the familiar American ocean of atomistic individuals. In another, it was the last resort for someone who could no longer trust where America stood in time.'[33]

The settlement houses had been the centre of social action for late nineteenth-century American or English reformers such as Jane Addams or Canon S.A. Barnett, but Chicago academic sociologists of the twentieth century viewed them in increasingly astringent terms: as 'social observing stations where invaluable supplementary experience should be sought by students, and where material is to be gathered by mature investigators.'[34] Theirs was a concern for human ecology and social indicators, their emphasis by the 1920s distinctly on method rather than ameliorization. The professional language of Small drew little, if at all, from the moralistic vocabulary of the nineteenth century; it pointed, instead, towards the profession's future in North America: 'A sociologist, properly speaking, is a man whose professional procedure consists in discovery or analysis of categories of human group composition or reaction and behavior, or in use of such categories as means of interpreting or controlling group situations.'[35] The language of the sentence marks the gradual disengagement of American sociology from historical change and social reform, away from 'development' towards the study of 'inter-relationships,' from Christian or progressivist teleology to the elucidation of social *being*, away from design, towards pattern. The fundamental metaphor of the new American sociologist was not the evolving organism. It was not the spider; it was the spider's web.

The Chicago approach to sociology was successfully marketed and exported. Albion Small, its founder-leader, presided over the department of sociology (the first in the world) from its creation in 1892 until he retired in 1924 at the age of seventy. Having launched the *American Journal of Sociology*, he then became instrumental in the founding of the American Sociological Society in 1905. Small's department and his journal facilitated disciplinary cohesion and provided forums for the dissemination of ideas and research. Most professional sociologists in the formative years of the discipline graduated from Chicago.[36]

The publication of *Introduction to the Science of Sociology* in 1921, by Robert E. Park and Ernest W. Burgess, was a landmark in the history of the profession. Their popular textbook told post-war students of sociology to 'observe and record their own observations' and to 'organize and use ... their own experience.' The Park and Burgess 'green bible,' as it came affectionately to be known, sought to lay out the framework for a systematic sociological understanding of human nature, and viewed that nature in instrumentalist rather than hereditarian terms as socially constructed in the complexity of competitive relations. This book also facilitated the organizational division of labour within academic sociology, for it laid out the disciplinary territory. Its chapters provided the emergent discipline, in short, with a kind of geography. Henceforth, American sociologists searching for fields of specialty would choose, as often as not, from conceptual maps first found in the Park and Burgess atlas – such as culture and personality, group formation, interaction processes, organization, social forces, or social change.[37]

In Canada, the Chicago approach to sociology was strongest at McGill University. In 1922 the Maritime-born but Chicago-trained sociologist Carl Dawson was appointed as an assistant professor of social science and director of its social-work program. Within three years he presided over a newly created department of sociology. For the next thirty years, Dawson remained at McGill and practiced a social science consciously disengaged from social action and from the earlier moral reform tradition of liberal Protestantism. On his way to a 'calling' to the Baptist ministry, Dawson had witnessed a divine truth; but it was of the science of sociology and of the research ideal. His Maritime Baptist heritage makes it possible to claim that there were certain indigenous Canadian elements in the pathway to his chosen profession. Certainly he sought to apply his knowledge and methods to Canadian society – in the words of one scholar 'to develop it as a Canadian venture'[38] – and his example and approach significantly influenced other Canadian disciplines, such as history.[39] Yet Dawson's achievements at McGill came about in the face of much opposition and suspicion on the part of university authorities and professors in other disciplines. That the research creed in which he believed began gradually to find serious support within the academic community between the wars should not blind us to the fact that sociology – especially 'Chicago Sociology' – was anathema to most Canadian scholars of the day.

It is difficult not to agree with the retrospective view of sociologist S.D. Clark: 'One legacy of the British influence remained: a deeply rooted attitude of hostility to sociology as it was now developing in the years after the First World War in the United States. There lingered on in a few Canadian universities teaching that went by the name of sociology, but, with its heavy reformist bent and tie to social work, it was not a sociology that secured standing in the Canadian university community in the way that modern history, economics, political science and even anthropology did. On the other hand, the Chicago School of Sociology which was now gaining strength in the United States and which, under Dawson's leadership, became established at McGill, aroused in Canadian academic circles the same sort of scorn that it roused in British academic circles.'[40] For such reasons, sociology remained a marginal enterprise in English-Canadian universities for the first half of the twentieth century, much as it had done in Great Britain.

The University of Toronto had nevertheless given it a distinct sense of direction. Toronto's earliest social analysts, W.J. Ashley and James Mavor, working within the environment of political economy, had been firmly located within the British tradition, empirical in bent yet essentially moralistic in outlook. Its University Settlement, established in 1910 and patterned after Toynbee Hall in London's slum-ridden East End, came into existence soon after the arrival of Robert Falconer, a philosophical idealist, as the university's president. As in mother England, the ideas of Christian moral and social reform and of the civic idealism of philosophers such as T.H. Green and Bernard Bosanquet found fertile soil in Ontario, for they were crystallized in the social thought of Falconer and in his university's scheme for creating an institution that would alleviate the material and moral plight of the poor and the dispossessed of Ontario's capital city in order to transform them into enlightened and useful citizens.[41]

In 1914, with the notion of social analysis in Toronto still firmly committed to the idea of moral and social reform and with the social gospel in Canada near the peak of its influence, the provincial university created its department of social service. As the intellectual arm of the university's settlement work, almost immediately the new department attracted the academic attention of many women associated with reform activities in such groups as the Women's Undergraduate Association of University College and the YWCA. As an academic enterprise it was an immediate success. This, in turn, helped maintain in Ontario the traditional British link between the practice of social work and an academic sociology that steadfastly refused to divorce moral reform and social investigation from ethical questions, embodied by the Toynbee Hall ideal that had been rooted in a communitarian desire for human fellowship.[42] This ideal of settlement and sociological work was replicated in Toronto, and for many years it remained an expression of social philosophy.

The intellectual baggage R.M. MacIver brought with him to Toronto in 1915 was well suited to this general approach to the study of society. His first published essays, a two-part series on 'The Ethical Significance of the Idea Theory,' appeared in the major British philosophical journal *Mind* in 1909 and 1912. In them, MacIver sought a middle ground between two kinds of limitation: the tendency of science to dismiss purpose in favour of process, and the inadequacy of Plato's 'absolute' philosophy in dealing with the nature of change or movement. MacIver's intention was to accommodate social philosophy to the study of interrelated forms of change while maintaining the importance of Plato as 'primarily an ethical thinker.'[43]

It was, however, the problems he had with the British idealist view of the state that were ultimately responsible for his decision to uproot himself from his position in the University of Aberdeen and move to Toronto. After publishing a highly critical review of Bernard Bosanquet's neo-Hegelian book *The Philosophical Theory of the State*,[44] he found that his mentor at Aberdeen, J.B. Baillie (holder of the university's chair in moral philosophy and translator of Hegel's *Phenomenology*), had taken the review to be a thinly veiled personal attack upon himself. The withdrawal of Baillie's academic patronage was disastrous. MacIver's position at Aberdeen was precarious in spite of the young scholar's growing publishing record in a number of internationally renowned philosophy journals,[45] since he seemed to fit into no existing departmental or disciplinary boundaries. He had read deeply in philosophy and the classics, and in so doing had become interested in the 'central study of society,' sociology. 'It was regarded by the pundits,' he later wrote of this period in his life, 'as outside the pale, a bastard, quasi subject with a bastard name – the purists scorned its title derived half from a Greek and half from a Latin word. It was the kind of subject that caught on in the woolly American Midwest.'[46]

By the autumn of 1914 MacIver had completed a large manuscript on the idea of community, the latest of many British studies of social evolution, and was preparing it for publication. He had become suspicious of contemporary nationalism and was now deeply critical of European leadership, including that of Britain. He felt unwelcome and uncomfortable in British academic life. His wife was pregnant for the second time. Europe was at war. He worried about being drafted, although he was willing to serve if called upon to do so. After canvassing some British colleagues, he learned from Edinburgh philosopher James Seth (who had been contacted by James Mavor) that a suitable opening might exist in North America. He was psychologically prepared for major personal change.[47]

Testimonials on his behalf crossed the Atlantic, and he was offered the job.[48] When he arrived in late summer 1915, his new academic position was not in America's woolly Chicago, but in Ontario's stolid Toronto. From the point of view of a later economic historian it was a strange appointment, since MacIver arrived to teach in Toronto's department of political economy with an Oxford degree in classics and without having studied or taught economics. Moreover, his interest was in sociology, a subject not taught at Toronto.[49] Yet from the perspective of the historian of social thought the choice of MacIver was not odd at all, for his academic convictions were perfectly in tune with Robert Falconer's view of the world and Toronto's president took a direct interest in virtually all academic appointments.

MacIver's manuscript on community won a Carnegie award open to all Scottish universities and was soon published. Well received in Great Britain but less so in the United States (Robert Park condemned it as 'jejune'), by 1924 *Community: a Sociological Study* (1917) was into its third edition. In it, MacIver advocated the kind of syncretic social philosophy so admired by those of the idealist tradition, such as Falconer. To MacIver, sociology was nothing less than 'the science of community.'[50] It transcended the boundaries of existing disciplines – indeed, it assimilated many of their concerns. 'The social sciences,' he wrote, 'have their sphere within sociology, just as associations have their sphere within community. The specific social sciences are *sciences of associational forms of life*, and, therefore, can never ascend the throne reserved for sociology, a throne tenantless until she enter into her kingdom ... The special social sciences – politics, economics, jurisprudence,

the study of the associational aspects of religion, education, art, literature, and every other activity of men – exist as such owing to the relative
isolability of certain kinds of social fact, the relative interdependence of
social phenomena belonging to the same series and their relative independence of social phenomena belonging to other series.'[51] The notion
of interdependence is a key to MacIver's thought. He used it throughout
his long academic life, sometimes refracted in terms such as 'interrela-
tion' or 'interactive,' especially when he spoke of associational activity
or of government.[52]

MacIver's brand of sociology, which sought to study all social relations yet posited that they remained part of a 'great communal unity,'
embraced all the special social sciences. It was not merely one of them.
'The common determinants of all specific activities, their greater interre-
lations and their communal resultants, constitute a subject-matter the
study of which is the heroic and endless task of sociology. It is concerned with the nature and development of community.'[53] It sided with
Plato, declaring *The Republic* to be 'the first and greatest of sociological
treatises,' while lamenting Aristotle's treatment of ethics and politics as
separate realms leading to the modern study of economics, politics, religion, and so forth, as discrete, seemingly unrelated entities. The task of
contemporary sociology, MacIver wrote, was to recover the integrative
vision of Plato and to build upon Comte's nineteenth-century attempt to
restore it. 'The growth of sociology since the time of Comte is a witness
that men are beginning to realise again that there is a unity of social life,
and are seeking to restore the lost synthesis of community.'

MacIver's sociology was a disciplinary newcomer that appeared to
conscript much of the traditional terrain of ethics and psychology. Sociology combined the ethical and the social, and the sociologist was 'an
ethical philosopher' who could 'never divest himself of his philosophy.'
Nevertheless, MacIver insisted that the ethical could never be reducible
to the social, or be identified with it. The sociologist could be interested
in moral and social reform – 'the relation of social means to ethical
ends' – yet also be engaged in the practice of one or several 'specific
social sciences.' The fate of sociology as a science was not tied to the
rise and fall of specific ethical systems. 'At a certain point our sociologies will take different directions according to our ethical ideals. Not
that where our ideals conflict our sociologies will also conflict, but
rather that we are answering different sociological questions. It is our
social interests that conflict. The conflict of ethical ideas is, therefore, no
ultimate problem for sociology.' MacIver's sociology was a science, but
a science of life itself including both its social relations and its moral
dynamics. He wished to see no narrowing of this mission: 'Those who

would make sociology a "natural" science, unconcerned with values, would leave out of account the special characteristics of the world of which it treats, in a vain attempt to ape those sciences where such characteristics are unknown.' Life was purposeful. That which was most knowable was least measurable, 'purposes, passions, desires, and the complex social world built out of their conflicts and co-ordinations. In truth, you can measure only what you cannot understand. You can measure only the external, that which lies outside the grasp of the imagination ... The very existence of society means ethical purpose in its members. The sociologist who has no ethical interest, no interest in social conditions as relative to values, is a dilettante. He is like a grammarian who studies the letters and syllables of words but never thinks of the words themselves as meanings ... Putting it in the most summary form, we may say that sociology is concerned with facts as values, ethics with values as facts.'

The realm of MacIver's sociology therefore included not only social action but also social conduct – action regulated by ethics – the operation of mind in relation to the exterior world. MacIver shared much with the general ethos of British idealism, but there were also significant points at which he parted company with the tradition of Green, Watson, and Bosanquet. As with his objection to the absolutist character of Bosanquet's Hegelian state, he rejected the idealists' monistic epistemology. He was a psychological dualist. Mind is known in relation to the world; the division between the two is real; the key lay in the relationship. 'In so far as we can know mind at all, it must be through some kind of analysis of its realisations in subject-object relations.' Here, in MacIver's view, the assumptions and functions of psychologists and sociologists differed. The psychologist sought to view the object as an entity that manifests the character of a perceiving, thinking, knowing, feeling, and willing being; the sociologist's object was law and custom and other social institutions. 'Forms of association or community,' he concluded, 'are in their nature objective things ... They are what mind thinks, not what mind is. They reveal mind, but they are not mind, and their laws are not the laws of mind.' Hence, sociology was essentially the study of interrelationships, including those of individual and society. 'There are no individuals who are not social individuals, and there is no social mind that is not individual mind.' As a social animal, man became more individualized in the very process of becoming socialized.[54] Here was a sociology that sought to build upon the best of the British idealist tradition but differed in important aspects from it. It was liberal-democratic and reformist in orientation and recognized – as the idealists also did – the complex network of social structures and social relations. But it did not subsume the destiny of the individual within the larger organic whole.

MacIver spent twelve productive years in Toronto as a professor of political science. From the outset he was also active in the department of social service, becoming acting director upon the departure of Franklin Johnson, Jr, in 1918. His previous interest in settlement and extension work continued in Canada. During the war he channelled his abundant energy and infectious enthusiasm in this direction. He provided a rounded, philosophically oriented education for students in social service. He gave courses of evening lectures to members of the Workers' Educational Association (his 1919 book *Labor in the Changing World* was written for WEA students in Canada and England). He attempted in 1917 to establish a National Problems Club, with the help of academic colleagues and Toronto businessmen and journalists, and served during the war as co-chairman of the Dominion of Canada War Labour Board. He spoke in 1918 to the Royal Canadian Institute (and probably to other such groups) on 'Capital and Labour – the New Situation.' He gave lectures on economic theory and philosophy to returned soldiers in 1919.[55]

Invariably the intentions of MacIver's writing, lectures, and speeches were to facilitate social harmony by means of cooperation, reconciliation, and mutual understanding. The practical suggestions for reform provided in *Labor in the Changing World* appear less than revolutionary to the observer of the late twentieth century, consisting as they do of measures such as maximum work hours and a minimum wage, child labour regulations, health and safety legislation, security against unemployment and arbitrary dismissal, and joint worker-management boards. It is a measure of the industrial and social tension of 1918 and 1919 that MacIver saw his reforms as part of 'a drastic revision of the whole industrial order' whose alternative was 'drift and chaos.'[56] It is easy to see how critics such as Colonel Reuben Wells Leonard lost sight of MacIver's peaceful intentions and ameliorist reform proposals, confusing them with his harsh assessment of social and industrial problems that seemed to point to revolution. The preface to *Labor in the Changing World* spoke overtly of revolution made necessary by the evil of the industrial wage system, but it was to be a revolution of ends not means. The revolution would result from peaceful reform. Robert MacIver's kind of revolution was that of Arthur Henderson and the gradualism of the British Labour Party, not that of Leon Trotsky and his revolutionary vanguard. Such subtleties were understandably lost on men such as Colonel Leonard, for whom revolution was revolution pure and simple.[57]

As a champion of labour in the new industrial order and as a source of inspiration for students in the University of Toronto's department of social service, Robert MacIver was an unqualified success. His academic sociology and his reformist political convictions complemented each other. But with war's end the university community was changing. The great influx of students in 1919, particularly war veterans, taxed the diminished resources of the university. In 1919 he was asked to return full-time to the department of political science. Petitions to President Falconer from extension course students of the department of social service and from social service alumni in Toronto, urging the university to spare no effort in keeping MacIver as social service director, failed.[58] President Falconer created a chair of social science in 1920, to be held by the new director of social service, but the appointee was James Alfred Dale, professor of education at McGill University.

Falconer had other things in mind for MacIver. James Mavor's retirement was imminent and MacIver, by 1920 one of the political science department's senior scholars, was an obvious choice as his successor. In spite of the attacks upon MacIver (and the university) by Colonel Leonard and others for his radical views, Falconer may have favoured him for another reason. The post-war demand for training in economics, commerce, and political science pointed in the direction of increased specialization. Departmental appointments in the immediate post-war years made this clear: Harold Innis in economic history, Gilbert Jackson in commerce and finance, William Jackman in transportation and rural economics, Herbert Marshall in statistics. Nowhere else in the provincial university was an arts department as divided into areas of specialization – some virtually approximating different disciplines – than political science. As one who believed that educational expertise should be grounded on a broad and humanistic basis in the arts and sciences, Falconer may well have seen MacIver's philosophical and inclusive definition of the social sciences as a means of combatting the worst excesses of academic specialization. 'I thought of myself as a social scientist,' MacIver later reminisced of this period in his life, '–not as a sociologist or a political scientist or an economist. I had come to the conclusion that the demarcation of the social sciences into separate departmental boxes was artificial, mainly a device for the convenience of administration.'[59] If Falconer did see MacIver's broad perspective on the social sciences as an essential requisite for academic leadership at Toronto, the publication of MacIver's book *The Elements of Social Science* in 1921 provided Falconer with much evidence that the Scottish social philosopher was the man for the job.

The Elements of Social Science covered much of the ground explored earlier in *Community*, and its author confessed as much.[60] Yet in *Ele-*

ments MacIver had shifted focus from the idea of community to that of society. *Elements* was cast as a study in social evolution. From examining the nature of society in its first chapter, the book moves to stages of community through which societies pass – village, city, feudal, and national. It outlines the relationships between society and its physical, economic, and social environments. Subsequent chapters deal with the 'interests and associations' that characterize societal relations, the institutional basis of the structure of society, and the search for a principle of social evolution. *The Elements of Social Science*, like *Community* before it, shared the propensity to large-scale system-building that characterized the work of British sociologist L.T. Hobhouse.[61]

MacIver also shared with Hobhouse similar views of the nature and scope of social science, at once denying that it could be limited to the methods of the physical sciences and insisting on its fundamentally ethical character and inclusive – what MacIver called its 'architectonic' – compass. 'The feature that makes Sociology a distinct science,' Hobhouse wrote in 1908, 'is the web of purpose wherein men act on one another and react on the conditions that make them. But purpose and the relations of purpose also constitute the subject of the ethical judgment. Ethics and social science have, generically, the same subject matter ...' MacIver defined society in *The Elements of Social Science* along identical lines. 'Society,' he wrote, 'means likeness, interdependence, co-operation, economy, but in so saying we have not penetrated to the meaning of society. For society is an infinitely interwoven series of relationships, issuing from the wills and purposes of beings who realize their likeness and their interdependence, in a word, their community. It is, therefore, in the first place *a state or quality of mind*, not a mere means or agency for the comfort or convenience of the beings so minded.'[62]

Robert Falconer appointed R.M. MacIver as head of the political science department of the University of Toronto in 1922 upon the retirement of James Mavor. For the next five years the Scottish sociologist presided over an increasingly fractious group of colleagues that showed little inclination to profess his holistic view of social science or his idealistic notion of community. The new department head never found the occasion to introduce or to teach a course on sociology, and he spent much of his time overseeing a revision to the undergraduate student curriculum that pointed in the direction of increased specialization in the senior years for those who wanted intensive study of economics or political science, but not both. Attempts were made to ensure that such students, as well as those in marketing and production, were provided with a broad liberal education in the first and second years rather than with mere training in business techniques. But one senses that this was a kind of rearguard action: the many appointments made to the department's ranks, with the exception of Harold Innis in 1919 and Vincent Bladen in 1921, were in the direction of narrower circles of expertise. Even Innis, who later championed a broad and integrative conception of the social sciences, practiced a narrowly focused and severely empirical economic history in the 1920s.[63]

Robert MacIver found few kindred spirits in his own department, British in orientation but empirical rather than speculative in its research practice. Still, its very Britishness meant that Toronto social analysis would not move in the direction of the ecologically oriented and ahistorical Chicago School. What can perhaps be claimed is that MacIver's holistic social philosophy and his commitment to the study of social evolution as a central element in it claimed general academic respect, if few practitioners. As such, it probably helped keep alive as an academic ideal the interconnected nature of the social sciences, a link with its idealist past in an era when disciplinary boundaries were becoming rigid and exclusive and when academic knowledge was more fragmented than ever before. The sheer size of the University of Toronto guaranteed a certain degree of narrow specialization across the range of disciplines. What is most striking about the major contributions of Toronto academic thinkers in the interwar years is that the most significant among them managed to give voice to a broad and essentially humanistic vision. MacIver's early role in maintaining the general acceptability of such views should not be underestimated.

Possibly frustrated at his relative intellectual isolation, MacIver resigned from the University of Toronto in 1927 to take a position as head of the department of economics and sociology at Barnard College in the United States. His book *The Modern State* (1926) had just been published, and MacIver had emerged as a leading North American exponent of a variety of sociology that stood in significant contrast to that of the Chicago School. By decade's end he was Franklin H. Gidding's successor as chairman of the department of sociology at Columbia University, the University of Chicago's nearest rival in the subject. At Toronto, MacIver's replacement as head of the department (officially renamed the Department of Political Economy in 1924) was another émigré British social philosopher.

As William Jackman and Gilbert Jackson, two competitors for the headship vacated by MacIver, preferred to see it, the department of political economy was about to be run either by an expert in transportation and rural economics (Jackman) or in commerce and finance (Jackson). President Falconer chose neither.[64] The appointment went instead to E.J. Urwick, a sixty-year-old Englishman who had retired from an

English academic career in 1924 and chosen to spend his remaining years in Toronto. But Urwick was no ordinary ex-don.

The son of a Congregational minister, Edward Johns Urwick had been born in Cheshire and educated at Uppingham under its great headmaster, Edward Thring. He had received a first in *Litteræ Humaniores* at Oxford in 1890 and an MA in 1892. Caught up in the Settlement movement while at Oxford, from 1897 to 1903 he served as sub-warden of Toynbee Hall and was also extremely active in the organization and administration of a number of social agencies, including the Charitable Organization Society. Here was a social philosopher with much practical experience, a pioneer in the development of the theory and practice of twentieth-century English social work who had helped establish the subject at the Universities of Liverpool, Edinburgh, Birmingham, and Glasgow.[65]

Urwick had been more than merely well acquainted with the apostles of the New Liberalism. He had been part of the inner circle. William H. Beveridge, whose famous study of unemployment would later provide the rationale and legislative framework for the welfare state (for example the National Insurance Act), had been Urwick's successor as Sub-Warden of Toynbee Hall. L.T. Hobhouse, three years older than Urwick, had studied social philosophy at Oxford during Urwick's years there. Later, after both had moved to London, Hobhouse to work as a journalist with the *Guardian* and the *Nation* and Urwick to become the first director of the London School of Sociology, forerunner of the London School of Economics (a position he held from 1902 to 1910), they worked together as founding members of the Sociological Society. After 1907, when Hobhouse was appointed professor of sociology at the University of London, their interests and careers converged still further. Urwick was in great demand as a professor at the time and held several posts. These years, the apogee of Liberal England, were those in which Urwick worked closely on various reform committees and study groups with other 'graduates' of Toynbee Hall and its ethic of civic idealism, such as J.A. Spender, Clement Attlee, Max Beer, and R.H. Tawney.[66]

For men such as Falconer and MacIver, Urwick's unexpected move to Toronto – it was thought for family reasons – must have brought the mixture of surprise, delight, and anticipation that urban reformers in the city experienced a half-century later when American social critic Jane Jacobs arrived there. Falconer and MacIver had strong connections to the Oxford and London academic circles Urwick had just left, so he scarcely needed to introduce himself either to the university's president or the head of its political science department. Within a year of taking up residence in Toronto, MacIver had conscripted Urwick as a special lecturer, and there can be little doubt that Urwick was present at the farewell dinner given for MacIver in 1927. Given the overt divisions in the department at the time – it would get worse – it is not surprising that President Falconer took advantage of Urwick's presence by asking him to become the new head of his political science department. Probably reluctantly, Urwick accepted. For the next ten years he was in charge of the largest academic department in the University of Toronto.

Urwick's involvement in Toynbee Hall, his role in the development of British social work, and his association with the New Liberals of Edwardian England would have been well known to Falconer. Perhaps less obvious, however, was the fact that his had often been a dissenting and at times even eccentric voice. He had left Toynbee Hall in 1902, for example, because he had become disenchanted at the decline of the settlement ideal. 'The texts are worn too threadbare to cover any more sermons,' Urwick had written in a frank and discouraging 1902 assessment of the settlement ideal; 'the phrases which inspired the Settlement movement twenty years ago will not serve our purpose today.'[67]

Deeply involved in social work as an honourable and important vocation, Urwick came to be at odds with certain directions the new profession had taken. With economist Alfred Marshall, he found himself defending the idea that social workers should be provided with a broad humanistic education against a number of university officials who believed that practical, technical training was sufficient and that this should not be a university's responsibility. Urwick's 1902 proposal for a comprehensive social-work curriculum aimed to provide 'an adequate basis of social theory' for students, with lectures on such subjects as 'social science and obligation,' the development of society, economics, social psychology, and ethics. But it had been harshly criticized by those committed to empirical social analysis. His later efforts at providing social-work students with a broad base in social philosophy also ran into strong opposition, and this resistance continued after the School of Sociology amalgamated with the London School of Economics, under Urwick's direction, in 1912.[68] A strong advocate of a philosophical 'academic' approach to social work, Urwick found himself steering an administrative middle course between the two. This tension between advocates of social ethics and social statistics – between academic and professional approaches – went unresolved. As with the settlement ideal, so by 1912 Urwick had come to be critical of directions taken by British social science in general.

Urwick's book *A Philosophy of Social Progress* (1912) must be understood as a study in disenchantment. 'All through this book,' his preface stated bluntly, 'there will be found a very marked antagonism to the current conception of a general sociology, or science of social phenomena.' He promised to give an unequivocal statement of his 'heresies,' and he did. 'Sociology is commonly described as the science of social life,' founded upon rationality and intellect. 'I do not believe that there is or can be any science of social life; nor do I believe that sociology is or can be a science.' This was because, in his view, social understanding was not driven by reason. What passed for sociology was little more than a 'collection of generalizations' of very limited value, a range of 'dignified guesses' derived from the 'more or less disguised expressions of the hopes and fears, the prejudices and beliefs, of their originators.' Sociology as science was impossible; but 'a philosophy of social life – or rather, of social change – ' was not, because it transcended rationality and was 'very closely analogous to a religious faith.'[69]

Urwick believed that the individual was essentially 'supra-social,' and that because of this the spiritual element in social progress was of supreme importance. Like the objective idealists before him, he strenuously rejected the Comtean positivist tradition in sociology in favour of a philosophical approach to social change. Yet he did not attack the positivist's search for a comprehensive explanation of social causation. His point of disagreement was, rather, with the Comtean notion that the 'positive' (or scientific) stage of social evolution necessarily displaced the earlier ones – the theological and the metaphysical. Positivist science could at best provide only a partial explanation of society or social development; inevitably, in Urwick's view, it must 'turn back to both religion and philosophy for an interpretation of the real significance of all the processes which it reveals.'

This was why, for Urwick, social philosophy inherently held more authority than did sociology. The scientific sociologist's investigative province was and should be a wide one. But even the most accurate and comprehensive studies of social conditions could not explain social purpose; nor could the best examinations of the actions of people tell of their feelings or address their conduct – action with purpose. 'No social science of any department of social phenomena is decisive in the sense of being in a position to dictate to us the necessary or the best lines of conduct. We go to each for a little help; but the question, "How shall we live well?" is never answered by any science. And it is clear that no list of separate sciences can cover the ground.'

In contrast, the social philosopher could take advantage of all the limited yet significant findings of the social scientists and go beyond them. Social scientists dealt with causal processes; social philosophers dealt with 'the *significance* of those processes and their results in relation to an ideal scheme of life.' Urwick assumed that human activity was part of a purposive struggle towards some ideal that was not part of the sociologist's capacity to understand, because it was allied not with science but with religion. The role of the social philosopher was to attempt to interpret the quest for this ideal: 'it involves a strong conception of a master aim and master plan of our life; a fervid idealism is the core of it; its essence is to lay hold of a dream of a City of God; and to make all its reasonings, all its linkings of effect to cause, all its groupings of change under the laws of sequence or causation, dependent from beginning to end upon the spirit and purpose of the dominating ideal.'

This claim to explain the ethical significance of human conduct by linking it to the religious order made Urwick certain that the authority of the social philosopher would always be greater than that of the social scientist. Social philosophy was nothing less than 'an attempt to present social phenomena as an ordered system or process dominated by a purpose which gives to the whole and all the parts their true significance.' The social philosopher was therefore more important than the social scientist, for he sought to elaborate for the public 'a coherent scheme which gives meaning to the social process – the meaning which he no doubt finds truest and best. But into the making of it there has entered the bias of his own mental and moral nature and experience; of his own spiritual attitude.'

Urwick and MacIver each published major books in social philosophy on the eve of the latter's departure from Toronto. Urwick's *The Social Good* appeared in 1927, MacIver's *The Modern State* in 1926.[70] Urwick read MacIver's *Community* and *The Modern State* as preparation for his own book, and in turn MacIver read and made extensive comments on *The Social Good* in manuscript. The two men shared many assumptions. What Urwick called 'the social good' and MacIver 'the social sense' lay for both (as MacIver put it) in 'the sense of solidarity, the sense of common interest' of which the state was only one form. The essence of this social unity lay 'in the sphere of values, which must be felt before they are established.'[71] MacIver wrote that 'the initial difficulty of all social theory' was that 'of reconciling an objective or scientific understanding of its character with the necessary appreciation of its ethical value,' for he believed that without that ethical value the social structure had 'no foundation, no validity in its values.' For both, the individual was the fundamental unit of society. 'In our search for unity we come at last to the individual,' wrote MacIver in 1926. 'We find that unity where many have discovered only its opposite, disharmony and strife, in the will of each to be himself and achieve the objects that are dear to him ... The deeper bond of community is the character not of class or nation, but of free human personality which from within its own small circle is capable of reconciling in one community the whole world.' 'It is the individual –

you or I – who is the unit of society,' said Urwick in 1927. 'Our souls are the arena in which the social struggle is for ever going on; from our souls issue the forces of co-operation and of competition, of harmony or of disharmony, which make or mar our social life ... *Nothing* wills or acts except the minds of living individuals: social action is never more than this; the full explanation of social action needs the introduction of no other factor.'[72]

In this way, when the headship of the University of Toronto's department of political economy shifted from MacIver to Urwick, certain fundamental views of the nature and purpose of social science continued in the office. Not the least of these was a belief in the limitations of 'scientific sociology.' Urwick had been present at the birth of Fabian socialism in England, and was in general sympathy with its intentions if not its means. He had come to believe, however, that any attempt at systematic reform of society by instrumental means (means divorced from ethical concern), in economic life, education, or health care, would meet only with failure.[73] Both MacIver and Urwick were fundamentally concerned with the place of the individual in a complex and pluralistic industrial society, and they sought to establish the means by which the meaningful moral agency of the individual could continue to be expressed. MacIver searched for ways the state could be shaped and directed so that its potential as an 'instrument of repression' would be minimized.[74] Urwick sought some way of minimizing the sense of dissatisfaction that resulted from 'the natural expansion of desire' encouraged by a culture of consumption.[75] Both believed that the good society would be realized only when the individual good and the social good were harmonized.

MacIver's *The Modern State* was academic in form, substance, and tone, but it was written to find a way of empowering the man on the street. Urwick's *The Social Good* spoke from the perspective of that man, and for the same purpose. The author and the man on the street ('Smith and me,' as Urwick put it) were in a sense the joint authors of his book; and 'you and me – and God' were the essential elements of society. Yet for the most part Urwick ignored God, because he believed that no religion (or philosophy) had 'grasped the full significance of the Great Society of To-day.' The old shibboleths were tired and failed to move people. Science, to which people often turned, had proven to be 'that most excellent of helpers, but least excellent of guides, for the simple reason that it has no sure knowledge of the values upon which life depends.' Such a vacuum of ethical guidance made the need of social philosophy more essential than ever, and its basic advice was very practical. 'Go on doing what you are doing now,' Urwick advised his friend Smith, ' – only do it better and more completely.'

Such were the values and priorities of those at the helm of the University of Toronto's department of political economy from 1922 to 1937, and they are important for the stamp they left upon it. Urwick presided over a department that at his initiative, and through his personal recruitment, expanded from ten to eighteen members in his decade as head, necessitating its move to larger quarters first in Baldwin House and later (1933) to the old McMaster University building on Bloor Street West. 'He was a social philosopher rather than an economist,' political economist Vincent Bladen reflected, 'he was a prophet rather than a scientist, but he was a wise, kindly gentleman, the Department flourished under him.' His broad philosophical interests made him, like George Brett, a champion of the 'Soc. and Phil.' course of studies for first-year students. In fact, according to Bladen, it was 'largely through Urwick's influence' that it was established. He introduced the subject of sociology into the honours program, but his suspicion of academic practitioners who masqueraded as scientists made him teach the subject himself – for he appointed no sociologist to the department.[76]

When social-work expert Harry M. Cassidy proposed in the depths of the Depression to establish a Canadian Institute of Social-Economic Research, in affiliation with the University of Toronto (and with Rockefeller Foundation money),[77] Urwick was polite in reply but less than enthusiastic. To Urwick, Cassidy would have appeared to be exactly the kind of well-intentioned but naive pseudo-scientist of which he had been so critical in *A Philosophy of Social Progress*. When Cassidy wrote in a preliminary outline of the institute that it 'would aim at the best academic standards of scientific accuracy' he should have known that to Urwick this was not the solution to society's ills. It was part of the problem. Hence Urwick's cool reply to one of Cassidy's inquiries: 'Our feeling at present is that we ought ... to do something, even though we still think that the scheme outlined by you has certain rather grave objections, not only in connection with finance but also in connection with the particular aims of the researches and the possible difficulties which may arise through political complications.'[78] No institute for social and economic research was created at the University of Toronto in the 1930s. When in 1944 the university announced that it planned to appoint Cassidy, Harold Innis, an ally of Urwick, presented President Cody with his resignation as chairman of the university's school of social work.[79]

Academic sociology along American lines developed at the University of Toronto between the wars no more than did academic psychology. The department of political economy, that omnibus unit which at various points housed even such subjects as anthropology, held no more brief for Chicago's ecological approach to sociology than philosophy under Brett did for John B. Watson's behaviouralism. Yet E.J. Urwick found himself hiring experts in statistical measurement, as did Brett. Both experienced a gap between their personal beliefs and their administrative responsibilities, but they recognized that the institution they worked for served a plurality of individual and social interests that transcended their own. Brett put up with Bott and Blatz, and Urwick with Jackman and Jackson – measurers of a society whose moral basis, in their view, could not be measured.

Were men such as Brett and Urwick merely reactionaries, out of touch with their times? In a sense they were, if we take the empirical and behavioural orientation of American social science as the model and its values as normative. Yet measured in its own terms, this apparently anachronistic environment whose leaders prized values before 'facts' was not without merit. It showed in the recruitment. Northrop Frye and Kathleen Coburn had been appointed on Pelham Edgar's gut instinct alone: neither was a safe or even a likely appointment in most English departments, and for a long time they did not 'produce.' This was also the case with Charles Norris Cochrane in classics, the author of less than a handful of articles in journals of local interest until *Christianity and Classical Culture* appeared shortly before his death. The corridors of the provincial university contained many such people in these years, including Douglas Bush in English and Eric Havelock in classics (both ultimately lost to major universities in the United States).

The department of political economy was no exception. In the mid-1930s the university appointed one of its own graduates, Crawford Brough Macpherson. Like so many others at Toronto who ultimately became scholars of international reputation and authority, Macpherson was nurtured in an academic environment that rewarded sustained if unpublished reflection. When almost thirty years later he did produce the result of his intellectual labour, *The Political Theory of Possessive Individualism: Hobbes to Locke* (1962), the book proved well worth the wait. Hailed as a study that changed the intellectual landscape of its discipline, it testified in part to its author's many years of careful research and deliberation. Yet the seeds of its concern for the intellectual history of seventeenth-century England may well have been sown in the daily fare offered to the young Macpherson by the honours program at Toronto. Whether he studied philosophy or psychology with Brett, English with Woodhouse, history with Underhill (who had purchased and read MacIver's *The Modern State* while still teaching in Saskatchewan and had paid careful attention to MacIver's detailed discussion of Hobbes and Locke),[80] or social philosophy with MacIver or Urwick, he would have learned some common lessons about the past and its ideas, the ethical and the social, the individual and society.

Intelligence and the Social Process

The idea of inviting the heads of the two largest departments of political science to contribute to the first number of the new *Canadian Journal of Economics and Political Science* must have seemed a very good one at the time. In 1934 Stephen Leacock and E.J. Urwick, of McGill University and the University of Toronto respectively, were at the pinnacle of their profession and were well known not only to members of the social-science community but also to the public. Thanks to his many volumes of humorous fiction, Leacock was even famous. Yet beyond the common sense of asking men of such distinction to provide contributions lay a more practical motive. After the founding of the Canadian Political Science Association in 1929,[81] the need for a regular Canadian outlet for professional publications in the field had been actively considered. Toronto's President Cody encouraged this and wanted his institution to take the lead. It was immediately recognized, however, that any initiative by the University of Toronto to launch a new journal should be seen as a cooperative venture, involving other universities but particularly McGill. Late in 1934 the CPSA arranged with the University of Toronto Press to publish a new journal. Vincent Bladen from the University of Toronto, secretary-treasurer of the CPSA, was appointed its managing editor. The first issue of *Canadian Journal of Economics and Political Science* appeared in February 1935.[82] It contained the articles solicited from Leacock and Urwick.

No one could quite have anticipated the results. Leacock's piece was masked coyly as a review of Adam Smith's *Inquiry into the Nature and Causes of the Wealth of Nations* (1776) and Immanuel Kant's *Critique of Pure Reason* (1781). But that was merely Leacock's deadly humour at work, for nowhere in his essay did he cite either philosopher. His first sentence was: 'Here are two sciences –Philosophy and Political Economy – both bankrupt.' The article, 'What is Left of Adam Smith,' written in Leacock's inimitably attractive informal prose, went on to dismiss philosophy as meaningless and irrelevant to modern life and to attack political economy as an intellectually bankrupt discipline that 'cites a wilderness, not of opinion, but of statistics and facts, all apparently bearing on nothing, gets confused, breaks down and cries – a very picture of senile collapse.'[83] Whether philosophy was capable of rehabilitation from its 'huge catalogue of the opinions of the past, and of the opinions held about other opinions,' Leacock cared not a whit. But the collapse of the social order in the 1930s, he said, made it essential that the discipline of political economy search for answers. Classical economics had outlined the nature of production of national wealth but had produced no solution to what Leacock had earlier called 'the unsolved riddle of social justice.' It failed to account for capitalist overproduction, its theory of cost (rooted in the myth of the 'natural price') explained nothing, and the gravitation of the discipline towards mathematical model-making overlooked the one valuable insight of Adam Smith: economic man, who sought to maximize personal wealth at least personal cost. *Laissez-faire* was irrelevant if not dangerous in the 1930s; *'faire-faire'* was necessary. 'Make things happen.' Leacock's essay was, as he put it, 'an SOS' to his profession.[84]

Urwick's lengthy article attacked the very historical and intellectual foundations on which the 'science' of political economy was based. Entitled 'The Role of Intelligence in the Social Process,' it decried the persistence of the Age of Reason into the twentieth century and lamented its intellectualization of social thought and the triumph of scientific instrumental reason that followed from it. The result had been a narrowing of the 'rational' to a point that any form of human thought beyond that of scientific reason – such as Faith – was now equated with credulity. 'The intelligentzia [*sic*] of the British world,' Urwick wrote, 'who had already proved their intelligence by swallowing as final truth a political economy which was much less than half true, embraced the new vision with enthusiasm.[85]

Urwick's view was that as the problem-solving element of the human mind, intellect dealt only with 'static existences' – the realm of the dead. It was akin to a chessmaster, putting pieces on a board, moving them about, and solving problems delimited by the rules of the game. Governed by myths converted into scientific rules, such as the uniformity of nature, causality, and objectivity, intellect was incapable of seeing life as it is actually lived – in the world of the subjective. It was incapable of understanding or dealing with the life of sentient beings. 'So we may define scientific truths,' Urwick wrote, 'as statements concerning observed or inferred relations among objects which are themselves nonsignificant, unconnected with feeling or purpose, neutral – and dead.'

The very term 'political science' was a contradiction in terms to Urwick, 'beyond the pale.' Political philosophy, at least, sought to discuss the life that intellectuals skilled in political 'science' moved callously around their conceptual chessboards. Economic science was no better than its political twin, for it too was concerned not with real people but with bloodless social forces. 'Your chessmen in fact are just copies of the economic man, whom nobody ever supposed to be human ... It is all very triumphant – though, of course, it *means* nothing – so far. It is the work of pure intelligence in its own sphere.' The science of statistics, similarly, dealt only with 'data that are dead and meaningless,' for it bore no relation to 'the real inner life which moves ...'

Urwick was no less scathing in his denunciation of sociology and psychology. The former, he said, was 'not yet a fit subject for intelligence' and if it bore any relation to the social process it was only because it was 'a glorious and fascinating mass of speculation about what is unlikely to happen.' Whenever it tried to be scientific, adopting the guise of objectivity, it merely became ludicrous. Unlike sociology, psychology was not even on trial – it was only 'waiting for its death-sentence,' denying the very idea of mind. The psychologist 'empties out, not only the baby with the bath water, but the whole bath as well; and then proceeds to fill what isn't there with water which never was anywhere.'

Intellectualized intelligence, in short, could tell us nothing about the social process because it excluded the realm of feeling, the world as it is actually lived, the values of life and the 'sediment of experience' by which those values are formed. Scientific understanding was incapable of understanding or explaining the way the mind builds judgments and constructs purposes with which the will identifies itself. 'You may call the process, if you like, the progressive determination of my particular life-impulse, and that of my society so far as I am a significant part of it. *Feeling* is quite definitely the dominant element in the process: what I *like*, what I desire, determines not only my choices, but my judgment of ends to be chosen and of values to be accepted.' Hobbes understood this when he said that reason was the servant of the emotions, but the Age of Reason had lost this essential insight.

Leacock and Urwick had assailed the dominant assumptions and methods of the social sciences to the point of outright ridicule. Some of the members of the Canadian Political Science Association no doubt dismissed the two articles as the work of cranks from a generation still rooted in the morality and beliefs of the nineteenth century. Yet Harold Innis was not one of them. He took their diatribes seriously, and his response appeared in the next issue of the journal. This took no little courage, especially since Leacock was capable of a devastating rebuttal and Urwick was the head of his own department. For Innis, the thoughtful if irreverent articles of Leacock and Urwick raised general problems and tendencies within the social sciences. Moreover, these senior members of the profession had raised other questions that had begun to trouble him. Was the liberal tradition really incapable of defining, much less addressing, liberty and democracy? Was the scientific study of society possible, or desirable? To what extent did social forces determine or circumscribe human thought and action? Could the social scientist be objective? What was the function of the modern university, and what should be the place of the social sciences in it? What was, or should be, the function of the intellectual in society? What in fact *was* the role of intelligence in the social process?

Innis's article, 'The Role of Intelligence: Some Further Notes,' was as elliptical and as cumbersome as those of Leacock and Urwick had been straightforward and clear. Of most immediate concern to him was the way Leacock's call for social scientists to make things happen seemed also to be a call for their direct engagement in the political process as activists offering political solutions to economic problems. If that happened, he said, the capacity of the political scientist or economist to engage in a dispassionate, scholarly assessment of the problem at hand was undermined. The problem, said Innis, was that the social scientist was part of the very social process he presumed to study and was therefore capable of being co-opted by its vested interests – whether those of the politician or of the university administrator. 'The importance of vested interests and of rigidities in thought in the social sciences weakens the position of the social scientist in relation to impacts of cultural importance. For example, the current belief in progress reinforces the importance of *change* in the thinking of the social sciences ... Vested interests are implied in the resistance to *change* and the demand for *change*.'[86] Given such pressures and imperatives, Innis admitted, objectivity in its pure form was probably impossible for the social scientist.

Yet Innis did not wish to abandon hope. Self-awareness, critical reflection on its own role in the social process, could become one of the strengths of social science rather than its fatal flaw. Institutions acted as agents of control by the state and, therefore, had a 'corrosive' effect on the social scientist. Social scientists' knowledge of the role they themselves played in such forms of constraint would make them recognize that when they took definite views of the direction society should take, or when they offered specific (that is, political) objectives to effect social change, they became part of the social process they studied and were therefore closely associated with the very problems they sought to solve.[87] Only by learning to recognize their own biases could political scientists and economists recognize their own limitations and try to correct them. That their explanatory capacity had thus far been limited, and their use of statistics of minor value, was sad but beside the point. They sought only to understand the very 'sediment of experience' that Urwick had so prized. That sediment was in fact the ground on which the social scientist did his work.[88]

By and large, the part of Innis's article that replied to Urwick did so obliquely. In many respects he agreed with his department head about the problems inherent in social science. It was the continuing duty of the social scientist, however, even in the knowledge of his discipline's limitations, to continue in the spirit of inquiry and to keep abreast of the various approaches of social analysts – such as those of Marx and Veblen – into the foundations of social life, however elusive. Not to do so, Innis concluded, would be to abdicate one's intellectual duty and to contribute to a decline of the role of intelligence in the social process.[89]

The differences of assumption about the nature, role, and potential of the social sciences expressed in this 1935 exchange of views reveal much about the ambivalent place of those sciences in the academic scheme of things in Ontario, but especially in Toronto. Academic social scientists had become increasingly involved in the formation of public policy between the wars. This was particularly the case at Queen's University, whose professors found permanent positions or contract work so regularly that the institution appeared to have a virtual 'pipeline' to places of power in Ottawa. In large measure this was the result of the power and influence of O.D. Skelton. Yet even at the University of Toronto, whose department of political economy was presided over by a man overtly hostile to the very idea of social science and was increasingly dominated by Harold Innis, whose academic ideal was that of the scholar consciously separated from the political process, a similar pattern held. In the 1930s and 1940s members of their department also actively sought and obtained contracted work in the public sector.[90]

No figure in Canadian social science reflected the discrepancy between the social scientist's intellectual and social functions more than Harold Innis himself. The apostle of academic detachment, who in 1935 contributed an article bitterly critical of those professors involved with the League for Social Reconstruction (calling them 'Political Adventurers in Universities, using language which suggested they resembled travelling salesmen peddling nostrums'), Innis nevertheless took appointments on public bodies and commissions when it suited him. A man whose public pronouncements warned of the malignant nature of centralized power and control, Innis was at the same time a scholar of consummate ambition who sought, obtained, and centralized whatever forms of power came his way and would adopt whatever means it took to obtain and consolidate that power. (When he was passed over for promotion in 1929 he threatened to resign; he was promoted. When the university announced its intention to hire Harry Cassidy in the 1940s he again threatened to resign; the appointment of Cassidy was postponed. When the Royal Society of Canada gave the Lorne Pierce Medal in 1939 to Wilfrid Bovey for his contributions to French-English understanding he

resigned his position as secretary of section II of the society.) By the
1940s he was head of the department of political economy, chairman of
the school of social work, dean of the University of Toronto's graduate
school, chairman of the grants-in-aid committee of the Canadian Social
Science Research Council, and held important positions as a chief coun-
cillor of the division of social sciences of the Rockefeller Foundation and
as a frequent evaluator of grants awarded by the John Simon Guggen-
heim Memorial Foundation. Scholarship was free, it seems, as long as
Innis was a major instrument of control.[91]

The pursuit of power and dedication to scholarship are by no means
mutually exclusive. Innis was a man driven in both directions by an
abundant reserve of inner resources. He was also a scholar of extraordinary dedication and enormous physical energy. Not only did he keep up
his research on the role of staple products in the development of Canada
(*The Cod Fisheries* appeared in 1940), he also facilitated the work of
others, organized conferences, and contributed to edited volumes or
edited them himself. One of the latter was *Essays in Political Economy
in Honour of E.J. Urwick* (1938), published by the University of Toronto
Press shortly after Urwick's retirement. Some of the contributions to the
volume were on subjects that held little interest to the man being
honoured – on the tariff and Canadian butter, for example. But others,
such as Vincent Bladen's 'Adam Smith on Value,' C.W.M. Hart's
attempt to find a means of rehabilitating social evolution for modern
anthropology, and political philosopher C.B. Macpherson's argument
that the study of politics in Canada must concentrate on the interaction
of men's ideas and men's actions had been central to Urwick's life-long
concerns.[92]

Innis's initiative in organizing this festschrift for Urwick as the first
volume of his university's 'Political Economy Series' was not simply
done out of duty, but out of deep respect and possibly out of a sense of
personal indebtedness. Urwick had postponed his retirement until he
could be certain that Innis rather than a narrow specialist like Gilbert
Jackson would succeed him. No one could have doubted after Innis's
1935 intervention on the role of intelligence in the social process that
there was more than a hint of the social philosopher about him. Here was
a scholar of genuine breadth of vision and of uncompromising views, as
critical in his own way of the directions taken by scholarship in the
social sciences as Urwick had been himself.[93]

In 1940 the seventh volume of the University of Toronto's 'Political
Economy Series' appeared. Edited by C.W.M. Hart, whose interests
spanned sociology and anthropology, it was entitled *Essays in Sociology*. It marked formal recognition by members of the Canadian Political

Science Association of the need to develop sociology in the Canadian context, for the editorial board of the *Canadian Journal of Economics and Political Science* had published the papers in its May 1940 number. Second, its contributors were, or were shortly to become, the premier members of their profession.[94] The Canadian contributors were Carl A. Dawson of McGill, and Hart and S.D. Clark of Toronto. Some of the essays recapitulated and at times modified well-known approaches;[95] others provided interesting glimpses of views that would only later become influential. These latter essays are a particularly fascinating study in contrasting assumptions. In 'The Motivation of Economic Activities,' the American sociologist Talcott Parsons argued that this motivation came not from any aspect of human nature such as 'the moral sentiments' but instead from 'the structure of social systems of action.' S.D. Clark's argument, in 'Economic Expansion and the Moral Order,' was virtually the reverse. 'Moral codes,' for Clark, changed as a result of socio-economic transformation, but morality remained rooted in sources extrinsic to social structure.[96]

The third reason the publication of *Essays in Sociology* was significant is that its foreword was written by Harold Innis. The purpose of the volume was to create Canadian interest in the discipline of sociology; yet his argument was a warning against the entrenchment of disciplinary attitudes and boundaries, even against the idea of attempting formal definitions of disciplines. New disciplines, he noted, come about because of the vested interests of older ones. Older disciplines, with their entrenched attitudes, narrowing circles of specialization, and self-serving sense of preservation, resist new approaches and ideas. To counter this, the brave academic leader is one who appoints scholars in a new discipline, even if the initial result must be interdepartmental friction and the draining of energy away from scholarly activity. Lacking such biases, and perhaps *because* of its lack of adequate disciplinary definition, Innis said, sociology held an advantage over older disciplines. Its great obstacle was the sociologist, 'and his persistence as a political scientist, economist, anthropologist, or whatever he may have been ...' Disciplines arise when a systematized body of knowledge comes into existence, but this reflects the propensity to co-ordinate, to synthesize knowledge; and the result, said Innis, was the death of philosophy, 'the basis of the social sciences.'[97]

In an addendum to his 1935 rejoinder to Leacock and Urwick, a 'Note on Universities and the Social Sciences,' Innis had made it clear that his quarrel was not with individuals but with institutional imperatives. The structure and departmental routines of universities hampered the social scientist more than the scientist. 'Equipment and buildings are tangible indications of "scientific work" and of the importance of more equipment and buildings, whereas a social scientist [in the eyes of administrators] is just another social scientist.' In search of tangible but scarce rewards, and encouraged by university authorities, social scientists no less than scientists became inclined to offer categorical judgments that held out to politicians and public the aura of authority and certainty. In this way, 'the social sciences tend to become the opiate of the people' even as they compromise their own ability to pursue truth. 'The problem of the social scientist,' Innis had concluded, 'is the problem of the University.'[98]

And so, five years later, Innis found inspiration in Urwick and MacIver. 'Exponents of the individual disciplines of the social sciences, including philosophy,' he concluded, 'one by one, wash their hands of the problem of philosophy[99] or offer spurious remedies and alternatives. It is a pleasure to refer to the efforts of Professor MacIver, Professor Urwick, and others to maintain an interest in the fundamental problems of civilization. It is this which offers hope of life in each of the social sciences.'[100] By the time Innis penned those words no one needed to be convinced that civilization was imperilled, that science – natural or social – had failed to usher in a world in which hope would prevail, or that anyone really understood the role of intelligence in the social process. The world of humane values seemed to be held hostage to that of industrial and military might, that of democracy to dictatorship. For by the summer of 1940 Europe was in flames and Canada was once again at war.

18

War and Recovery

'This time it is different.' Those were the words of the editor of the *Queen's Journal* in November 1939, in an editorial called 'Courage of a Different Nature.' It was clear to him and to everyone else that Canadian participation in the Second World War would not repeat the naive romantic enthusiasm of 1914. 'When people go to war this time they have some idea what they are going to; they expect not romance and high adventure but discomfort, drab weariness, suffering, death. Nor are they very sure that the world will become Utopia even when the war is won.' Earlier, the editor of the McMaster *Silhouette* had greeted the news of war in a similar fashion. 'Now, no one in Canada can reasonably believe that war can solve the ills of the economic and social world. Nor can democracy really be saved by war ...' Even so, the student journalist added, 'We are fighting this war for honourable as well as for selfish reasons, and it is, therefore, our struggle.'[1]

Ontarians, like most Canadians, adjusted to the fact of a Second World War with gritty realism such as this. Memories of the degree of human suffering exacted by the Great War of 1914–18 remained starkly present in the Canadian consciousness, for 'the war to end all wars' had ended less than a generation earlier. Moreover, when war again broke out in September 1939, with Hitler's invasion of Poland and Great Britain's declaration of war against Germany some fifty hours later, Canada remained in a state of serious economic depression. The decade of the 1930s had provided all Canadians with lessons in the harsh realities of the international economic and political orders. The combined memories of war and depression provided little room for romantic idealism.

The outbreak of war in 1939, unlike the experience of 1914, came as no surprise. Activists of the left had been fearing it since Hitler's rise to power in 1933, and predicting it since the massive use of the Luftwaffe in the Spanish Civil War and the German invasion of the Sudetenland.

In England, Winston Churchill had been warning that the policy of appeasement advocated by Neville Chamberlain would lead only to war. President Cody of the University of Toronto caught the sense of imminent catastrophe that prevailed in the late 1930s in his address to returning students at the end of September 1939. 'Last year we began the year under the shadow of a threatening war. For the time the cloud was lifted, a respite was given. Today the storm has broken upon us ...'[2]

The Canadian government declared war on Germany within days of Great Britain's own commitment. Prime Minister Mackenzie King announced in September that Canada would raise an infantry division for service in Europe, and by mid-December it was overseas. By then the prime minister had formed a cabinet war committee consisting of key government ministers. It quickly drew upon the resources of major government departments and recruited the most competent civil servants from them to mobilize the resources of the nation. Virtually from the outset of the war politicians and civil servants alike recognized that its outcome would depend on the extent of that mobilization, particularly of scientific and technical personnel. Moreover, unlike the situation in 1914, the institutional infrastructure now existed to provide it. The National Research Council had almost a quarter-century of experience behind it, and the nation's universities were equipped with a variety of engineering programs, science faculties, and medical schools. 'It became clear,' said the principal of Queen's late in the war, 'that Canada was to be a great arsenal for the allied arms, and that trained technical men were needed for all the fighting forces as well as for the war industry plants that were springing up all over the country. It became clear as well that the country possessing the newest and best devices would have a very great advantage in this kind of technical warfare.'[3]

National Service

At the outbreak·of war, no state-coordinated system of higher education existed in any province of Canada. Yet the organizational basis for immediate cooperation between Canadian universities and the federal government for the purpose of wartime mobilization was in place. The National Conference of Canadian Universities (NCCU) had met eighteen times since its founding in 1911 as an association of university presidents. By the end of the 1930s some thirty-one institutions were members, and the conference (by then an annual event) was attended not only by their presidents but also, at times, by a variety of deans and invited guests. During the Depression the conference had continued along its original lines, as a kind of men's club for senior educational executives.

Discussion took place on academic standards, the meaning of a liberal education, the need for more university scholarships, and other matters of concern, but for the most part the group remained unresponsive to the degree of social despair that surrounded it.[4]

A series of wartime initiatives by the federal government, however, galvanized the NCCU to action. Even early in the war, Ottawa was concerned with establishing post-war policies related to demobilized soldiers. It is clear that members of the federal cabinet and the civil service were intent that the veterans of the second war would not be treated as poorly as those of the first had been.[5] Accordingly, it initiated a number of studies aimed at their reintegration into post-war society, including institutions of post-secondary education, and consulted several chief executive officers, particularly H.J. Cody of Toronto, Cyril James of McGill, and R.C. Wallace of Queen's.[6] This process of consultation was expanded after the end of the 'phoney war' and the disaster at Dunkirk in 1940, when the heads of universities were summoned to Ottawa to discuss a wide range of ways they could effectively contribute to the war effort. For the remainder of the war, relationships between universities and the federal government grew closer; those with provincial administrations became secondary. For the first time it could truly be said that politicians believed the nation's universities to be of national importance.

At meetings between university presidents and federal officers in July and September 1940 it was decided that students' courses of studies were to be disrupted as little as possible, but that on-campus military training of all physically fit male students should strongly be encouraged. Universities and their students acted quickly. The Canadian Officers' Training Corps, formed during the Great War, was revived and infantry battalions created or expanded on each campus.[7] By fall 1939 two full companies of 150 McMaster men had volunteered for the campus COTC. The entire student population of the university numbered approximately 600. Membership in the University of Western Ontario unit rose to 391 from less than 200 in the first year of the war. At the University of Toronto, enlistment in the four companies of the campus COTC jumped from 327 members in 1938–9 to 1,800 (including 500 graduates) within two weeks of the beginning of the war. Principal Wallace urged all Queen's men to join. By November 1939, 842 students were in training.[8]

The federal government passed the National Resources Mobilization Act in June 1940, requiring registration of all able-bodied single men and childless widowers between the ages of twenty-one and forty-five. Eight hundred thousand Canadian men proved eligible to serve in home defence, and it appeared likely that the universities might largely be emptied of male undergraduates. After inquiries from the universities, however, the Department of War Services (established to administer the National Resources Mobilization Act) replied that the highly technical nature of the war made it imperative for students, particularly in the sciences, to continue their education. The government concluded that compulsory military training in the universities would, for the time being, be sufficient, and at its 9 September 1940 meeting, the NCCU overwhelmingly agreed to the plan. 'It was the nearest thing to a unanimous voice of the universities which we have yet had in Canada,' said President Cody to his students. 'We felt we should give a lead right across Canada. And so the young men, trained for what some term the "soft white-collar jobs," will be the first group in the Dominion to be trained as a body for military service.'[9]

Those students anxious to serve actively in the war against Hitler were understandably pleased at this coordination of academic study and military training by governments and universities. So were the ones who had no desire to fight in a European war, for the terms of the National Resources Mobilization Act stipulated not only that students who did their six weeks of training were not required to work for the home service but also that if they were successful academically they would not be called up for active war service until their education was finished. The best way for a university student to avoid becoming a casualty of war was, in short, to enlist in the COTC – and then study hard. By 1943 it was also possible for students to enlist in university Air Training Corps or Naval Training Divisions at McMaster, Queen's, and Toronto. In this way, the province's campuses came quickly to resemble army barracks as much as universities. Queen's had forty platoons of thirty men attending classes and taking drill by the opening of its fall 1940 term, and by Christmas 1,271 of its 1,692 intramural students were in uniform. Three thousand University of Toronto students underwent compulsory military training that year. Commenting on the many Toronto students in uniform at the university's annual Remembrance Day service that November, the Toronto *Globe and Mail* noted that the sight was probably 'sufficient answer to charges heard in some quarters that the University has become the breeding ground for ideologies, subversive in nature.'[10]

Lecture halls did not empty as the war went on. Overall university enrolment declined but remained relatively stable. Registration at the University of Western Ontario, for example, dropped from 2,141 to 1,979 in the years 1941 and 1942. Queen's awarded 392 degrees at its 1939 convocations, and 354 at those of 1944. Total registration at the University of Toronto (including affiliated colleges) was 7,960 in

1938–9; it dropped to 7,811 the next year, declining to a low of 6,779 in 1943–4 before it rose again with the arrival of the first war veterans.[11]

While men drilled, receiving minor academic credit for doing so, female students participated in the war effort in many other ways. At McMaster University a Women's Service Training Detachment was created late in 1940, the inspiration of the university's athletic director Arthur Burridge. Some women drilled (forty-eight McMaster women ultimately served in auxiliary units of the regular armed forces), but most took training with the St John Ambulance brigade or the Red Cross. By the end of the war McMaster's Red Cross Corps, formed in 1941, was the second largest in the country. Such activities were common on each campus of the province. The Levana Society at Queen's marshalled its members, setting up a Red Cross room on the top floor of the old arts building in which it required all Queen's women each week to make bandages, quilts, and socks. Charlotte Whitton, executive director of the Canadian Welfare Council and a graduate of Queen's, urged Queen's women to 'hold the home front against sickness, need and unemployment.' At Toronto, Mrs H.J. Cody, wife of the university's president, was instrumental in forming the Women's War Service Committee (WWSC), which she then chaired. Addressing the group, Adelaide M. Plumptre, vice-president of the Red Cross Women's Voluntary Service Corps, suggested that Toronto women could best serve by knitting socks, speaking to women's groups, and transporting nurses. One of the first acts of the WWSC was to organize a registration of the voluntary war service intentions of the university's women. One indication of their priorities rests in the fact that 170 women registered in the course offered in motor mechanics, compared with seventy for that given by the St John Ambulance and only forty-five for home nursing. It is clear that, unlike the older women who led them, a good number of university women did not necessarily view their war work as an extension of traditional roles.[12]

As the war got worse, women became increasingly discontented with traditional forms of social duty. The Levana Society at Queen's was instrumental in attempting to convince those in authority that there were ways women could contribute to the war effort other than those derived from their presumed nurturing instinct. By the beginning of 1941 a Women's Voluntary Service Corps (WVSC) of about thirty women had been founded, similar to the University of Toronto's Women's War Service Committee, where more than a thousand campus women worked on the Toronto war effort. Sanctioned by the Canadian Red Cross, women began to be trained in skills such as switchboard operations, motor mechanics and transportation, and orderly operation. The Toronto Red

Cross WVCS, which issued women with uniforms patterned along the lines of the Red Cross, also provided a certificate course in air raid precaution that included the protection of food supplies, preparation for gas warfare, and provision of first aid. Queen's followed in 1942–3 with a compulsory course of a similar nature, administered by the Kingston fire department. (At the University of Western Ontario, the situation was reversed: there, the department of university extension co-sponsored an air-raid course to train firemen.) By 1942 some form of compulsory war training for women existed on most Canadian campuses, and the range of activities in which they were involved was very visible to the public. 'To-day's girl student,' wrote a Toronto *Globe and Mail* reporter in 1942, 'is more interested in gas masks and stirrup pumps than new hairdos; she would rather ... cook a meal for refugees during a blitz than acquire the smoothest party tricks.'[13]

The sight of women in uniform constituted a challenge to the traditional stereotype of the campus coed. The response of the press to women in paramilitary gear reflected its ambivalent attitude towards them. Newspaper treatments of women's contributions to the war often spoke positively of women's new roles. Yet such articles usually did so by contrasting the frivolity of coeds, previously depicted as normal, with their new-found and, it was alluded, obviously temporary seriousness. The net effect was that at best such writings were backhanded compliments; at worst, they were patronizing and hypocritical pieces that merely subjected women to public ridicule. 'No longer inhabitants of a delightful dream world in which nothing has to be done unless you want to do it,' wrote a female reporter for the *Globe and Mail*, '... co-eds are real people.' Gone, she continued, were the girls who played bridge all day and skipped lectures to go to the drugstore for Cokes. 'Listen to a representative group of co-eds talking at lunchtime. You will find that the conversation not once touches on dates. They discuss anything from psychology tests to the new social betterment plan. They argue as heatedly about the second front as they do about the ballet, and they know their stuff.' Evidence that military involvement by women was viewed as a necessary but temporary deviation from woman's normal duty emerges from the debate in *Varsity* that arose out of the possibility that compulsory training of women might lead to full conscription. Such a notion, the student newspaper declared, 'is utterly foreign to our precious ideals of civilization and culture. The strength of our system of government is rooted in the individual family and home, thus in the central figure of that home, the mother ... [women's] best service in the interest of the war effort is to preserve the home.'[14]

Normal student activities were significantly curtailed throughout the war. Fearing the possibility of some incident that might be exaggerated by the daily press, a University of Toronto committee reluctantly suspended the Hart House debates. The university's medical society cancelled its bawdy and irreverent yearly review, the 'Daffydill.' At the request of McGill, the University of Toronto, and Queen's, the Senior Intercollegiate Rugby Football Union cancelled its 1940–1 season and resolved to continue to do so for the duration of the war. This resulted in the suspension of all intercollegiate sports. Compulsory military training took more than enough time and energy from university athletes. (Even so, intramural sports greatly increased everywhere: there were seventeen women's basketball teams at the University of Toronto by the fall of 1942.) In order to maintain morale, dances were not banned, but they were fewer in number. The Student Administrative Council at the University of Toronto, for example, recommended that 'formals' be limited to one per year. Often, ballrooms were decorated in a military motif. At the Queen's arts formal of January 1940, for example, food was distributed in gas-mask containers by uniformed attendants. As the war dragged on, the tendency was for such events to be more modest. Few students supported banning such events, but many recognized that this was not a time for extravagant corsages and evening clothes or expensive dance bands and decorations. The money could be better spent on war bonds.[15]

University officials attempted to act *in loco parentis*, as they always had. Dances were allowed on campus at McMaster after 1942 only because the university was concerned about deteriorating standards of student conduct, mainly relating to alcohol consumption, at events held in downtown Hamilton hotels. Yet there were problems for the university as moral guardian. McMaster's dean of arts and science complained of random car-parking, and incidents of booze parties in the men's residence occasionally got out of hand. At Trinity College the provost and dean condoned the opening of suites and rooms to mixed groups of men and women. 'Here,' one former student later recalled, 'cocktail parties were held throughout the evening. The atmosphere was compelling. Indeed couples were known never to have seen the dance floor, so utterly absorbing were the residences under these circumstances.'[16]

The war exacted a psychological toll on university students. Engineers and medical students felt overworked by the combination of many hours in the classroom, in the laboratory or hospital ward, and on the parade square. Women felt underutilized, at least initially, because their extracurricular hours lacked coordinated forms of war service. Arts students, made constantly aware of how much the federal military and civil authorities valued the skills of engineers, scientists, and physicians, publicly and privately questioned their own usefulness in prosecuting the war. The result was a number of incidents, particularly at Queen's, where the mixture of military personnel, professional faculties, and arts students in the setting of a small town increased the potential for conflict. Verbal altercations led to outright brawls in movie houses and restaurants between students and soldiers stationed in the Kingston area. This was alleviated only when university authorities granted soldiers limited access to university facilities, such as its swimming pool and library, and issued members of its COTC with battledress to make the university's military contribution more visible. Tension between engineers and artsmen at Queen's reached a breaking-point in fall of 1940, when, after several days of egg and tomato fights between the two groups, the engineers stormed the new arts building, broke through the front doors, and proceeded to wreak havoc. When Principal Wallace emerged from his office in the library he was greeted with a flour bomb to the shoulder.[17]

The view of the Canadian military and the federal government from the outset of the war had been that the nation's universities could best contribute by producing a trained reservoir of officers and a highly skilled pool of scientists, engineers, and medical men. No general mobilization of troops for immediate transportation overseas was to take place. Federal civil servants continued to encourage universities to keep students at their studies and reminded them that the Second World War would be won by the combatant power that best marshalled its scientific and technical personnel. In contrast to earlier university leaders, who during the Great War had done their best to encourage massive enlistment in the Canadian Expeditionary Force, those of the Second World War sought mainly to assemble a trained domestic army of engineers, scientists, dentists, and doctors. They became recruiting officers for their own professional faculties.

The resulting maintenance of student enrolment placed great demands on an academic staff that was increasingly depleted by secondment to government service or outright enlistment in the armed services. 'I am getting quite used ... to my economics department being shot to pieces,' McMaster economics professor Humfrey Michell wrote to Harold Innis in 1941. Three years later he was still complaining to Innis. 'Hurd and I ... do our best to teach our classes ... everybody else runs off to Ottawa ... Principal Wallace of Queen's was here the other day and was telling us, what we know already, how the Queen's economists were winning the war in Ottawa. To which I innocently asked whether anybody was doing any teaching at Queen's.'[18]

The drainage of professors from their university offices to those in the increasingly bureaucratic environment of wartime Ottawa hampered instruction at every Ontario university. Political scientist C.B. Macpherson left Toronto to serve in the Wartime Information Bureau. Economists J.F. Parkinson, H.R. Kemp, and K.W. Taylor left Toronto and McMaster to work for the Wartime Prices and Trade Board (McMaster's Taylor became its director). The federal Department of Finance absorbed many university social scientists, including A.F.W. Plumptre and Vincent Bladen of Toronto and C.A. Curtis and F.A. Knox of Queen's. This kind of commitment was part of what Principal Wallace had in mind when in the summer of 1942 he noted that 'the University has become, in a real sense, a service department of the Government as far as the technical requirements of war are concerned.' In addition to those seconded to domestic war service, faculty resources were further depleted by enlistment. By autumn 1942 the University of Toronto, for example, had lost 190 members of its academic staff to the armed services. 'No more is the university a haven of peace and leisurely study,' the *Globe and Mail* observed. 'Rather, it is a place of bustling activity, of wartime problems, of crowded classrooms ...'[19]

Disciplines with practical value had risen in size and stature within university communities throughout the interwar period. The Second World War was the ultimate proof of their crucial importance to an industrial society. Students recognized this. Enrolment in practical science at the University of Toronto rose from 924 in 1938–9 to 1,388 in 1942–3. In spite of extraordinary demand for trained physicians to serve overseas, enrolment in medicine at Toronto managed to remain fairly stable, increasing from 835 in 1938–9 to 844 in 1941–2. Registration in both faculties fell off only in the last, desperate years of the war: to 1,184 and 701 students respectively in 1944–5. In contrast, registration in the faculty of arts and science declined steadily from 1938–9, when total enrolment stood at 3,806, until it reached a wartime low of 3,126 in 1943–4 (see Fig. 18.1).[20]

Government and military demand for trained scientific personnel became especially strong after 1941 when the federal minister of labour wrote to university presidents: 'Now that our manpower resources must be considered in their entirety and in detail ... [my] Department ... feels that cognizance of the key position held by universities and their alumni is of national importance ... I think that university authorities should advise all graduates and undergraduates that they can serve the national interests best by practising their professions, whether in war industries or the armed forces.' Whole graduating classes in science, such as that of McMaster University in 1941, were absorbed by the Wartime Bureau of Technical Personnel for domestic war service in production plants and laboratories.[21]

FIGURE 18.1

Enrolment in arts and science, practical science, and medicine, University of Toronto, 1938–51

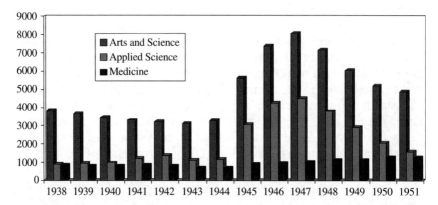

SOURCE: Marni de Pencier, 'A Study of the Enrolment of Women in the University of Toronto,' research paper, University of Toronto (1973), PUH A83-0036/001, University of Toronto Archives

Every Ontario university made curricular adjustments to reflect this heightened emphasis on the importance of professional and scientific skills, but none more dramatically than McMaster University. Even before the German invasion of Poland, Chancellor Whidden had warned his university community that 'we may be compelled to drop some of our cultural, but not essential educational courses ... If war does come we must have the courage to curtail or delete something that is not of absolutely primary ... importance.' By spring 1942 its popular department of fine arts was closed down. In the same year, with George P. Gilmour appointed chancellor upon Whidden's retirement, the faculty of arts was renamed the faculty of arts and science, and a chemist named as dean. After 1941 the university's Baptist supporters came reluctantly to accept the eventual necessity of what they had long opposed: government funding for university departments. It was clear to the university's officials that its scientific work could not continue unless a new means of financing its operations was found. As Chancellor Gilmour later reflected: 'McMaster had gone as far as she could with her original and available resources and must change or decline.'[22]

Professors of science in the province were engaged throughout the war on a variety of war-related projects. The whole physics program at the University of Toronto in the summer of 1941 was geared to radio training for Royal Canadian Air Force personnel. Five hundred radar mechanics from across the country, living and dining in Hart House, took the three-month course. It required forty university instructors as lecturers.[23] Undergraduate courses were often taught by student assistants while professors did top-secret research on radar and long- and short-wave radio techniques, electronics, chemical warfare, submarine detection, radioactive isotopes, the analysis of heavy water and nuclear fission, and synthetic rubber. 'This is a war which may well be won or lost in the laboratories,' declared Principal Wallace of Queen's. The inventory he took of his university's scientific resources included research in the departments of bacteriology, chemistry, chemical engineering, pharmacology, physics, physiology, and psychology. Major research projects conducted in Queen's laboratories, or elsewhere (such as the atomic research laboratories in Montreal or in Chalk River), were similar to those conducted elsewhere: on nuclear fission, radar detection, the design and construction of microwave devices, chemical warfare, the spectrographic analysis of explosives, the study of metals and alloys (done for the Aluminum Company of Canada), and the design of psychological tests for military personnel.[24]

The clamour for trained scientists, engineers, and health-care professionals by government and the military was clearly of great help in mobilizing the province and the nation for global war. It gave universities an unprecedented level of public regard and institutional self-esteem. Yet for some, both academic staff and students, the massive reorientation of public and academic priorities was profoundly troublesome. When Principal Wallace of Queen's announced in 1942 that 'The trend today is to science, applied science and medicine, and our best students follow that path,' he belaboured the obvious. When he added that 'The humanities are in eclipse in university life' he struck at the heart of what, by then, had become a problem of national values.[25]

Values under Siege

The universities of Ontario did their best to let politician and public alike know how much they were contributing to the technology of warfare and to the relief of the suffering that resulted from it, but many of their students took degrees in the liberal arts. On the eve of the war, in 1937–8, the University of Toronto's total enrolment stood at 7,960; of this number, 3,803 were taking an arts degree of one sort or another (see Fig. 18.1). At the other universities the proportion of arts students to others was much higher. Of the total registration of 4,714 at Queen's in the same year, 3,616 were arts students.[26] These students had no clearly defined role in the war effort, and the many exhortations by the leaders of their universities for more doctors, engineers, and scientists scarcely helped them. Moreover, the Department of Labour and the Wartime Bureau of Technical Personnel said little, if anything, in the first years of the war about the kind of contribution they might make. As the dean of arts at Queen's observed in 1941: 'Not a few young men were unsettled as to what they should do, as to their share, in the war.'[27]

Canadian university presidents had no answers for such students. At the 1942 meetings of the NCCU a special session was held on 'The Future of the Arts Course,' and several institutional leaders spoke on the subject. Principal Wallace of Queen's professed the centrality of arts in an ideal university, but pronounced the reality to be that 'an increasing number of our students, particularly men students,' found arts unnecessary. 'The studies in the humanities are thought by the great majority of students to lead nowhere in particular ...' Wallace was not exactly consistent in his analysis of the situation. At one moment he lamented the 'cult of the utilitarian which [was] so much a part of modern thinking'; in the next he advocated a closer association between arts faculties and professional ones, for 'an arts college of the old type, devoted to the humanities and to culture, splendid in its own isolation, is frankly going out because it is no longer adjusted to our modern ways.' So little did Wallace, a geologist by training, value the actual contribution of a general arts education to the contemporary world that he ended his address by advocating the creation of an Associate in Arts certificate to be granted to those students not in honours programs after the second or third year of university enrolment. The clear implication was that these students would be released into the world of work and of war without a university degree.[28]

Other implications arose out of Wallace's suggestion, and they soon were of enormous consequence for those engaged in the academic arts. Wallace and Cyril James of McGill had been members of a federal cabinet-appointed committee examining post-war construction since 1941 (James was its chairman), and continued to meet virtually weekly in Ottawa. One issue, not directly linked to their mandate, was apparently the role of the arts faculty in wartime. The conclusion they reached by the end of 1942 was that arts programs throughout the country should be severely curtailed. British and American universities had by then virtually suspended instruction in arts, but the leaders of Queen's and McGill concluded that Canadian war needs could best be met if enrolment in arts courses was restricted to the first two years of undergraduate study. (Was this the intention of Wallace's proposal for an arts diploma to be awarded after second year?) Thereafter, students would presumably have been released for full-time military service, thereby demonstrating that the artsman, too, was of some value to society. This idea found public support.[29]

The NCCU held an extraordinary meeting in Ottawa early in January 1943. Specially invited guests from a number of government departments attended, as did a large delegation from the universities. Its ostensible purpose, as recorded in Department of Labour records, was to review the government's plans concerning 'the manpower situation in Canada and ... the Government's policy towards the problem with particular reference to those phases that affect universities.'[30] The major spokesman of the government was the deputy minister of labour and director of the national selective service, Arthur MacNamara.

Rumours that the future of instruction in the arts was in peril at Canadian universities had circulated in academic circles for the last several months of 1942. A.R.M. Lower at United College in Winnipeg, Watson Kirkconnell at McMaster, and Harold Innis at Toronto, among others, became convinced that Wallace and James intended to obtain NCCU sanction for the closing of the nation's faculties of arts, as well as programs in commerce, law, and education, for the remainder of the war, and that this was the reason for the special meeting. Innis had been in conflict with James in particular for over a year, when James, acting as chairman of the Committee on Reconstruction, had invited the Social Science Research Council to participate fully in forming government peacetime policy. Innis strongly objected to this 'collaboration' of the new council with the state and the compromise of scholarly pursuit of truth it would entail. As it had in the past, the submission of a letter of resignation by Innis worked: the SSRC declined James's offer and Innis stayed on the council.[31]

Innis greeted news of the apparent connivance of James and Wallace concerning the future of the liberal arts with disdain. The rumour also circulating that prime minister King was willing to put the scheme into immediate effect resulted in a SSRC petition to the prime minister in November 1942, on behalf of history, political science, political economy, sociology, psychology, geography, and related subjects, to convince him not to do so. In addition, as president of Section II of the Royal Society of Canada, Innis convened an informal gathering of humanists – who had no national equivalent to the SSRC. Robert Falconer, George Brett, A.S.P. Woodhouse, and others met in the Hamilton home of Watson Kirkconnell (who chaired the meeting) to draft a petition similar to that of the SSRC. Ultimately signed by forty-one 'anxious humanists,' it, too, was forwarded to Mr King. It stressed 'the vital importance' of humanistic studies, and urged the government to maintain an adequate level of instruction in the arts. Theirs, they said, was a long-range view, 'the perspective of civilization itself.' 'If the civilized values of the race are to survive, we shall need to have at least a fair number of men in our communities who have a strong grasp of principles, and whose minds, while appreciating practical details, can rise above these details to a sense of their broad, human significance.'[32]

If Deputy Minister MacNamara thought that the scheme of James and Wallace represented the views of the majority in the Canadian academic community, he had been badly misled. Speaking to an audience that ranged from the sceptical to the hostile, he was defensive from the first. He claimed that he was not certain why the meeting had been called, and he assured his audience that 'persistent rumours that the Government is planning to recommend or require the discontinuance, at least for physically fit male students, of courses in liberal arts which do not give specific training that can be of no immediate use in the war effort,' were false. Yet almost in the same breath he told his audience that the rumours probably reflected 'a growing feeling on the part, not only of the general public, but perhaps even of educators, that at this time when all our institutions stand in peril, liberal education like some other necessities may have to be rationed.' MacNamara's words clearly, if perhaps inadvertently, indicated that he was well aware of why the meeting had been called. He urged the conference to 'weigh the problem *as I know you intend to during this conference*, and ... give to the Government your considered judgment about the manner in which this necessary balance [between the ideal and the practical] may best be struck and the immediate and long-run interests of our nation best furthered.' To provide the high-minded academicians some food for thought, he added: 'For the present ... speaking quite unofficially, I venture the personal conviction that if the universities will ruthlessly weed out the incompetent and mediocre students, if we continue to require that all students take their military training while at the universities, and if it can be understood that, when the requirements of the Armed Forces or the industrial war effort so necessitate, National Selective Service would be authorized to call up students even though that interrupts their course, no immediate further restriction would be necessary.' If the universities wished to avoid draconian action taken by government, MacNamara seemed to say, perhaps they should themselves take the severe measures necessary to serve the national interest.[33]

The government officials no doubt went away from that meeting dismayed at the uncooperative nature of the academic community. Cyril James and R.C. Wallace left chastened: they had badly misread the mood of their constituency and in so doing misled the government officials they now served. Representatives of the arts left the meeting satisfied that for the time being, at least, an education in the humanities and social sciences remained possible in Canada. Social scientists in attendance concluded that weakness in the humanities entailed a possible threat to activity in their own fields and that this problem had to be addressed immediately. Humanists now recognized that had it not been for the existence of the SSRC, and the lobby it was able to generate at short notice, a much different conclusion to the meeting might have been reached. The result, by the end of 1943, was the creation of the Humanities Research Council of Canada, initially funded by its social-science equivalent and organized – again at the initiative of R.H. Coats and Harold Innis – by a few members of section II of the Royal Society of Canada led by Watson Kirkconnell and A.S.P. Woodhouse. One of its first tasks was to survey the state of the humanities in Canada, published as *The Humanities in Canada* two years after the war. One of its early decisions was to bar deans and presidents from membership. This, too, was a legacy left by Innis.

Even before the federal government made clear how much it valued the war services of those with practical skills over others, universities in Ontario had made similar discriminations. In 1941, fourth-year chemical engineering students at the University of Toronto were released from their studies without having to take final examinations so that they could work in munitions factories. From early 1942 students at Queen's and Toronto who passed the COTC examinations were awarded a three-mark bonus in each of their academic courses. (The University of Western Ontario refused to do so; one of its deans called the scheme a 'sympathy racket'.)[34] At the University of Toronto, students in the applied sciences whose marks were not in the honours or scholarship class were given a credit of up to ten per cent of the total marks for each academic subject if they worked with the Officers' Training Battalion of the COTC. If they enrolled instead in the Training Centre Battalion their maximum credit was five per cent. The five year course of medical students was compressed into four. No general rules applied to arts students. Then, shortly after the emergency meeting of government and university officials in January 1943, the federal government finally announced those categories of students it considered vital to the 'national interest.'[35] Students in the designated programs were to be exempt from conscription; any others would be afforded this status only if they placed in the top half of the classes at final examination.

The ruthless weeding out of the weak and the incompetent called for by deputy minister MacNamara had begun, and universities complied in kind. Amendments in 1942 to the National War Students Regulations had provided that any student who failed a term or year course was to be reported to the federal government. These students would then be subject to immediate call-up. A good deal of internal discretion lay with the universities in determining what constituted a failing grade, yet the sympathies of their presidential offices clearly favoured government needs over student interests. Queen's under Wallace was particularly harsh. Toronto reported male students who failed, but let them continue in their programs until whenever they might be called for military service. Queen's sent the names of male and female failures – ninety in number, fifty-six of them in arts – to the government. Its prompt report left the undergraduates with no time to appeal, and university authorities refused to allow them to continue their studies.[36]

One of the grating ironies of the situation for students was that a number of those who failed had been arts students who the previous autumn had heeded a national call by the federal Department of Labour for volunteers to help in the harvest of the western Canadian wheat crop. Armed with the promise of four dollars a day in pay, free board and rail transportation, and all the presidential rhetoric of national service they could have wished for, more than twelve hundred students from Queen's, McMaster, Toronto, McGill, Western, and Laval, mainly from arts and commerce programs, had assembled at Union Station in Toronto. Self-proclaimed 'saviours of the harvest,' they were determined to bring in the sheaves. Finally, they had a concrete way of contributing to national life, and their journey westward in the eighteen railway cars provided for them was a rollicking affair that looked like an ongoing football pep rally.[37] Life on prairie farms, however, was no game. The harvest was late, and harvesting continued into mid-November in freezing temperatures. The daily four dollars pay required steady work from five in the morning until nightfall. By mid-October many student labourers were ill or had quit. They also found themselves described by drought-toughened western farmers as something less than saviours of their crops.[38]

For some, worse consequences lay in store. Those who had left from Queen's were told on their return that they had to make up time missed in military drill and academic classes, and that because of the new regulations they had to catch-up or risk being permanently suspended from university because of the conscription regulations. Before their departure Principal Wallace had assured them that their professors 'would lean over backwards to give them consideration in the Christmas and final exams'; after the fact, he spoke of their 'costly experience.' The *Queen's Journal*, which earlier had supported the Order-in-Council that made the reporting of student failures mandatory, now condemned it. Queen's had failed a higher proportion of its students than any other

Canadian university; the ninety students comprised five per cent of its student population.[39]

The Second World War would be won by physicists, it was said, as the Great War had been won by chemists. This view did not help the arts student. War remained what wars had always been: fundamentally a man's game, if a deadly one. The dominant images of man at war in North American popular culture during these years were those of Gary Cooper and Humphrey Bogart – tough, resolute, silent, and strong – in movies such as *Sergeant York* or *Casablanca*. In stark contrast, the image of the man on the domestic front during the war resembled nothing so much as Mickey Rooney in the several 'Andy Hardy' movies he made with Judy Garland – the naïve (usually Midwestern) 'virginal boy' untutored in the ways of a real man's world, whose primary interest in females was the girl next door, a non-sexual idealization of Mom. If Andy Hardy had gone to college he would have enrolled in arts, for he was the artsman personified in a non-academic setting. One McMaster graduate fondly recalled going 'to one event at a converted barn in the country in the rumble-seat of a friend's car.' It was, he said, 'the closest I ever came to the Andy Hardy / Joe College model either before or since.'[40]

The academic Andy Hardys of the 'true north' were surrounded by women. The assault on their sense of scholarly self-worth embodied in the constant emphasis on the military importance of the professions was strong enough; that they had enrolled in a faculty where most women chose to take their courses gave contours to their identity that served to distance their own sense of self still further from the occupations of 'real' men. At the University of Toronto, with by far the most diverse offerings in the province, the number of women in arts courses steadily increased throughout the war years. By war's end fully 61.5 per cent of arts registration was female, 2,025 out of 3,289 students in 1944–5 (see Fig. 18.2). Relatively few of these women concentrated on unconventional academic subjects. The proportion of women to men in arts was similar in Ontario's smaller universities. Intramural registration in the faculty of arts at Queen's in the same year consisted of 345 women and 249 men – fifty-eight per cent female.[41]

The presence of so many women in Ontario universities did little to alter conceptions of their social role. Even after 1942, when compulsory campus military service for draft-age men resulted in equivalent forms of mandatory service for women, the kinds of courses and duties they were given reflected traditional views of woman's essentially domestic and nurturing disposition: they became dieticians' aids, experts in the preservation of textiles and in domestic budgeting, repairers and remod-

FIGURE 18.2

Total and female enrolment in arts and science, University of Toronto, 1938–51

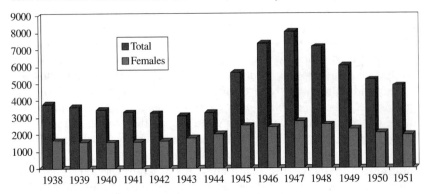

SOURCE: de Pencier, 'Enrolment of Women'

ellers of clothes, service-camp leaders, and so forth. Moreover, when women enrolled in programs other than arts they did so in courses of study that complemented the prevailing view that their post-war careers would essentially be nurturing ones, as wives, mothers, or volunteer workers. Few took courses in medicine, dentistry, law, engineering, or the sciences. Instead they continued to gravitate in large numbers to ones in nursing (including public health and dental nursing), education, household science, social work, occupational therapy, and physiotherapy. Both forms of educational activity – compulsory war work and academic programs – had the ultimate effect of entrenching rather than challenging conventional stereotypes. 'The programs that the women helped to establish worked against them in the end, for those programs reinforced their inferior status and popular conceptions of femininity.'[42]

The general confusion about the value of arts programs reflected a crisis of confidence within the academic community in the Western liberal tradition. Ontario scholars wrote many anxious articles during the Second World War, but whether they spoke about the problems of the university, the future of the arts faculty, the plight of the humanities, the stifling of dissent, the course or corruption of democracy, or the transmutation of the liberal tradition, they invariably addressed elements of the same fundamental problem. How had liberal values come to be so precarious, so little treasured? Would they survive in the post-war world?

In 1943, a year before his death, Sir Robert Falconer drew attention to the most fundamental problem of the scholar as citizen. 'How to preserve in totalitarian war the cultural ideals even of one's own people, which have been patiently won, has been giving concern to the most thoughtful.' Falconer's subject was 'The Humanities in the War-time University,' and he seems clearly to have written it, in spite of failing health, to address the besieged mentality of academic humanists in the wake of the threatened suspension of arts programs the previous year. In the wake of the Great War, a generation earlier, he had spoken eloquently of the need for 'a disciplined intelligence,' one that channelled the intellect by the force of moral authority and individual will. Now, a generation later, he drew attention to the consequences of failing to regulate the intellect. The Hitler war, he said, was not simply a conflict between brute forces. It was a conflict, instead, of intellectual powers requiring economic and organizational measures unprecedented in scale. The flame of intellect had burned 'with an ever brightening flame in the indefatigable work of scientists, workers, engineers, agronomists and doctors.' This was a war of 'brain-workers' as much as of 'manual workers.'[43] A few years earlier, scholars at Falconer's own university had debated the role of intelligence in the social process. Now the harvest of unencumbered intellect had been reaped.

Falconer nowhere alluded to the exchange that had taken place in 1935 between Urwick and Innis in the pages of the *Canadian Journal of Economics and Political Science*, but echoes of the substance of their argument resonated in his article. The intellect had proven not to be a neutral arbiter, a pure seeker after truth. It had been harnessed instead to the most ruthless kinds of service to the state system, with practicality as its end and instrumental reason its guide. Lost in the reorientation of the priorities of governments towards these ends was the ultimate purpose the humanities were meant to serve: to provide that 'most sacred freedom ... the spiritual autonomy' of the human personality. 'The humanities,' Falconer said, 'are so called because they concern man as a person, his real self. They provide a liberal education because they liberate his spiritual freedom.' The humanities, like the world, were in crisis because new ideas of the origin, nature, and destiny of humankind had undermined belief. Scepticism had replaced the older sense of the inherent value of human character and the forces that traditionally had shaped it. Democracy was impossible unless the universality of such values could somehow be recovered. An education in arts had come to be seen as a mere accessory to university life. Lacking any form of visible proof acceptable to those enamoured with science, it had lost its cultural legitimacy. [44]

Even as he uttered these dearly held truths Falconer must have recognized that the words probably sounded like tired platitudes. Yet it was necessary to state them. The fact was that when his successor, H.J.

Cody, now used the phrase 'a disciplined intelligence' he did so when trying to convince 'university girls' that they had the necessary mental equipment to 'master the intricacies of military work, in both drill and lectures.'[45]

Other humanists addressing similar subjects scarcely fared better than Falconer in trying to find something to say that had not already been said. Were the faculties of arts themselves to blame? English professor C.R. Tracy argued that they were largely the mistresses of their own misfortunes, because in order to service the professional faculties each had transformed itself into 'an emporium of miscellaneous branches of knowledge,' divided by competition between departments. As a result, the average student was no longer offered 'a way of life, but a meaningless collection of musty respectabilities ... He cannot understand how this curriculum will foster in him that philosophic understanding of life about which he has been told on solemn occasions by college dignitaries ... The fact is that a modern faculty of Arts resembles nothing so much as Vanity Fair, full of clamorous voices and confusion ... It has become a prey to overspecialization, and has lost its own sense of the oneness of its mission.'[46] Nevertheless, Tracy concluded, if the nation's faculties of arts did not survive the war, neither would the university.

The confusion over the place of the liberal arts in the contemporary world reflected a similar lack of confidence in the durability of liberal-democratic values. Professors in the humanities and social sciences throughout North America witnessed from afar the collapse of democratic governments throughout the European continent in the face of German and Italian fascism, and were profoundly uneasy when Stalin's communist empire changed to the side of the Allies after Hitler's invasion of Russia in 1941. At home, the Depression had given rise to political movements of the right and the left in the form of the Social Credit Party in Alberta and the Cooperative Commonwealth Federation; in 1935 the former was elected to govern Alberta and late in the war, in 1944, the latter became the government of Saskatchewan. Even the older provinces of Ontario and Quebec had succumbed to the demagogic, in the persons of premier Mitchell Hepburn and Duplessis. What had gone wrong?

In their search for the meaning and possible consequences of such events, scholars in English-speaking Canada found themselves operating in what had become a dark hiatus in the relations with Great Britain and the United States, the two imperial powers that had always provided them with political and cultural models. When they looked at Canada and its place in the world, they saw their nation caught up in a massive shift in imperial authority and power. The British Empire, struggling virtually alone early in the war against the combined might of the Axis powers, seemed to be in irreversible decline. In contrast, the United States seemed on the threshold of global dominance. The virtual collapse of liberal democracy in continental Europe, the sea change in the structure of Anglo-American power relations, and the lack of confidence in their own institutions caused the most thoughtful of Ontario's scholars, particularly its historians, to agonize throughout the war and long after it about the fate of their nation. No one was tormented more about the Canadian condition than Frank Underhill.

In August 1940 the Canadian Institute of Public Affairs held its annual conference at Geneva Park on Lake Couchiching. The sense of urgency at the 1940 conference was acute, for since the spring Denmark and Norway had been invaded by the Germans, France had fallen, the British disaster at Dunkirk had taken place, and the Battle of Britain was reaching its height. During the conference, as a member of a panel comprised of Americans and Canadians, Underhill made a twenty minute informal presentation of his views. Canada, he said, was now committed to two loyalties: those of its British inheritance and of its American geographic circumstance. The nation, he added, should not put all its 'eggs in the British basket' because British importance in the world was sinking. No doubt he thought he was simply making a common-sense observation.[47] A garbled account of his words was soon published by Underhill's old enemies, the Orillia *Packet and Times* and the Toronto *Telegram*, which accused him of treasonous abandonment of Mother England at a time of her greatest peril. Press, public, and politicians called for his dismissal from the University of Toronto, as they had in the past. Former Prime Minister Arthur Meighen called for his internment. At the request of Ontario minister of education, Duncan McArthur, provincial Attorney-General Gordon Conant got the Ontario Provincial Police to investigate his background and to place his home under surveillance. Chancellor William Mulock and others on the provincial university's board of governors unanimously demanded his dismissal. The Toronto *Telegram* kept the issue in the public eye, at one point running editorials on the subject for a full week. He was asked to resign and refused. The crisis took a year and many meetings of Underhill's friends and enemies to resolve.[48]

In the end, two groups of lobbyists on Underhill's behalf made it possible for him to keep his position. The first was the university community, which overwhelmingly supported him. Underhill's undergraduate and graduate students petitioned President Cody urging his retention. Former students and alumni of the university sent letters and telegrams. Underhill's personal friends, Charles Cochrane, J.B. Brebner, and Carlton McNaught, rallied to his cause, as did other colleagues less close to him, like Gilbert Norwood, Griffith Taylor, Ralph Flenley, George Brown, George Brett, and Malcolm Wallace. Even those who bitterly opposed Underhill's political activism and pronouncements, such as Harold Innis and Donald Creighton, came to his defence. Innis was an especially strong defender of his colleague, partly because the questions of freedom of speech and academic freedom were at issue. More personally, however, Innis rose to Underhill's defence because of the intangible but deep bond that continued to exist among those who had served in the Great War.[49] Underhill and he also held something else in common beyond their war wounds: an uncompromising intellectual fearlessness. For this reason, too, Underhill had gained Innis's respect.

The second group that helped save Underhill's position was a coterie of his friends in positions of power and influence in Ottawa. Hugh L. Keenleyside, in a senior position in the Department of External Affairs, and O.D. Skelton, still undersecretary of state for external affairs, wrote to Prime Minister King reminding him of the damage that could be done to Canadian-American relations if Americans discovered that a Canadian professor was seen to be fired because of his pro-American views. The dismissal of Underhill would then become a political weapon for the isolationist cause. One of Mr King's secretaries, Jack Pickersgill, also became involved. Aware that the associate minister of defence, C.G. 'Chubby' Power, was friendly with Premier Mitchell Hepburn yet also strongly supported the cause of civil liberties, Pickersgill asked Power to speak with Hepburn. 'Later that day,' Pickersgill recalled, 'Power called me, and, in a thick husky voice said: "Jack, I called Mitch about your friend Longbottom. That isn't the right name but he knew who I meant and said he would try to do something."'[50] A majority of members of the board still favoured dismissing Underhill, but Cody recognized the political impossibility of such action and at length obtained the board's very reluctant consent to do nothing.

The situation was ironic in several ways. First, although Underhill disliked Cody and detested Hepburn (who he believed had been the source of the movement to have him dismissed), it had in fact been Cody's refusal to act on the demands of the board of governors and Hepburn's instruction that no action to dismiss should be taken that had saved his academic hide. Second, the case had become an instance of external political pressure from both Ottawa and Queen's Park that was the reverse of previous instances of such interference in academic autonomy. In this case, it was the provincial university's own board that insisted on the dismissal of the professor and it was the interfering external parties that ultimately preserved his academic position. Academic freedom could be a two-way street, and the path of angels did not point only in one direction.

The situation was also ironic because by the time Underhill's dismissal from the university was sought he had come to question his anti-imperial and socialist views himself. 'The course of the war since May 10th,' he had written in the *Canadian Forum* in August 1940, 'has destroyed all our familiar ideas about the kind of world in which we are likely to live for the rest of our lives.'[51] The collapse of Europe demonstrated the dangers of unwavering isolationism. The battle he had been fighting, between capitalism and socialism, had proven to be the wrong one, for the world's struggle was instead between totalitarianism and democracy. The intellectuals involved in the socialist movement, epitomized by the League for Social Reconstruction he had helped to found, now seemed too dogmatic and more concerned with centralization and efficiency than with true social democracy. Thus, when he gave a keynote speech to the national convention of the League for Social Reconstruction in 1941, a year before it was dissolved, the league's secretary recorded that his performance had shown the intellectual confusion of a man tormented by a bewildering world. The speech, wrote the secretary, 'contained so many opposing ideas that one would not have known ... just whether he was an enemy alien, a tired radical or an agent provocateur.'[52]

The world of the Enlightenment that Underhill had so admired, a world of rationality and progress and liberalism, had collapsed around him. He remained committed to these virtues, but by the end of the war they reflected his understanding not of the way the world worked but what it must continually work towards. By 1945 it was not Marx or Bentham or even Mill who inspired him, as they had earlier, but the late-Victorian liberal critic John Morley, author, among other writings, of a well-known essay on 'Compromise.' The liberal ideal had proven to be just that – an ideal – and Underhill resolved to devote the rest of his life to the recovery of its flame.[53]

Other Ontario scholars, no less concerned than Underhill about the fate of liberal democracy but usually more circumspect in public gatherings, also agonized over the fate of the nation. The crisis of values epitomized in the struggle between totalitarianism and democracy, combined with the recognition that Canadians were caught politically and culturally between rising and falling imperial powers, had the effect of focusing their attention on North Atlantic civilization and Canada's inheritance from it. At Queen's University, political scientist J.A. Corry undertook during the war to study Canadian political institutions. Published in 1946 as *Democratic Government and Politics*, it began and

ended with Corry's concern with preserving democracy from dictatorship.[54] Recalling the origins of his book, he later noted how the 1930s
had witnessed the 'spectacular show' made by the rise of European dic-
tatorships at the very time that the remaining democracies in Europe and
America were 'hesitating and floundering ... In these circumstances, it
seemed essential to undertake a more searching study of liberal democracy, to examine more carefully its inner strengths, account for its
defects and limitations, consider how far the defects could be remedied,
and how far they were an inevitable price to be paid, if we were not to
fall into the embrace of authoritarian regimes.'[55] Throughout the war,
and after it, Watson Kirkconnell at McMaster University also acted as an
interpreter of Canadian freedoms. He was a diligent and indefatigable
watchdog over them, scouring the ethnic press for evidence of communist (or for that matter fascist) subversion.[56]

Previously dominant approaches of Ontario's historians, ones that had
emphasized imperial-colonial conflict, frontier influences, or economic
determinants, gave way to a reorientation towards the traditions, ideas,
and beliefs that had given rise to Canada's political and social institutions. In a 1942 article on 'The Course of Canadian Democracy,' for
example, Donald Creighton lamented 'the complete absence of native
speculation on the nature of political democracy,' and argued that it was
necessary for historians to undertake such a task. 'The inheritance, of
course, comes chiefly from England. It happens to be a remarkably
good, and justly celebrated, inheritance.'[57] Creighton's own contributions to this cause were substantial. His survey of Canadian history
Dominion of the North, which stressed the nation's transatlantic and
British rather than its American ties, appeared in 1944. Next, he began
almost single-handedly to rehabilitate the conservative tradition in Canada by embarking on a magisterial two-volume biography of Sir John A.
Macdonald. After the war students of Creighton and of the somewhat
chastened Underhill began to re-examine the nineteenth-century political tradition in the context of the transatlantic world. J.M.S. Careless
was one such student. His studies of George Brown, culminating in a
two-volume biography equal to Creighton's own achievement with
Macdonald, began to appear shortly after the war. Careless's scholarship
and his growing stature and influence helped direct the reorientation of
Canadian historiography after the war away from the North American
frontier experience towards the urban and metropolitan, and combined a
deep awareness of the geographic circumstances of Canadian history
with a recognition of, and sensitivity to, the European origins of many of
the nation's ideas and institutions.[58]

The Second World War helped Ontario scholars in the humanities and social sciences rediscover or appreciate anew their own institutions and heritage. It did not, however, resolve the question of the scholar's role in public life. If anything, the combination of crisis in the liberal arts yet substantial involvement of academic men in service to the state refracted the sense of scholarly purpose still further. Moreover, this vexing question seemed to be linked to fundamental changes in Western life and thought of which the rise of totalitarianism was but a symptom. When Harold Innis said in 1935 that 'the problem of the social scientist is the problem of the University' he had been talking about the way institutional imperatives and entrenched forms of thought compromised the disinterested pursuit of truth, thereby controlling it.

By 1941 his friend A.R.M. Lower was also thinking about the problem of control in society and its relation to the future of the social sciences. The era of liberal individualism ushered in by the Renaissance and the Reformation seemed to be over, he wrote in the *Canadian Historical Review*; but the interwar decades had found nothing to put in its place. 'What Hitler did in Germany, essentially, apart from his cruelties, was to end the confusion of purpose, the irresolution, the fumbling, that necessarily attend the senility of a social philosophy.' A 'new order,' he said, was 'struggling to be born.' But who would shape it, control it? The fundamental problem of the day was 'in what kind of hands is the new society to be and how can it be built without losing the enduring values that our civilization has created?' The war had ushered in a 'vast increase in the edifice of control' over all aspects of life: over opinion, personal freedom, assembly, movement and residence, and due process. The only way society could be protected against abuse of its freedoms was for the social scientist to take an active part in public life.[59] Lower could be inspirational, and after the war he set some of his best students to work on these problems. One of them was Ramsay Cook, whose MA thesis completed at Queen's under Lower's direction was on civil liberties in wartime. Like Lower, in a distinguished career Cook sought to bring the judgment of the historian to a wide public audience.

Lower denied that the social scientist was, or should aspire to be, a 'detached observer' unaffected by circumstances. All social science could ever provide was an interim report on the ongoing problems of society; it had no firm blueprint for the future. Yet it was the social scientist's public duty to help shape that future. Did this compromise scholarship? Lower denied that true scholarship in the social sciences was ever a matter of detached observation and recording. The social scientist did not simply write for other scholars, but helped create and affect society even as he described it. He was an artist as well as a scientist. His responsibility was to resist unwanted forms of control, to educate rather than to train, and to understand and shape the national culture. 'The social scientist in these pregnant days and in this malleable society of ours, cannot, if he is to exist, be a mere spectator, a mere dissector of society: he must also be a formative agent in society.'[60]

Lower's article prompted a debate within and beyond the community of Canadian historians. Responses to it were published in the next number of the *Canadian Historical Review*, and discussion of the subject took place at the June 1941 meetings of the Canadian Historical Association. Their reactions mirrored the larger uncertainty about the role of the scholar in public life.[61] The most vigorous reactions to Lower's vision of the role of Canadian social scientists in the post-war world came, not unexpectedly, from Frank Underhill and Harold Innis. At a CHA panel disussion, Underhill expressed his wholehearted agreement with Lower's view that the social scientist must be fully engaged in current affairs and should examine and help shape the values of society.[62] The rebuttal by Innis was in writing and was brief, but it was blunt. The social scientist, he said, could 'make his most effective contribution to the maintenance of morale on the home front, to the advancement of his interests, and to the solution of problems of democracy by showing confidence in the traditions of his subject and minding his own business.' It was the duty of the scholar, Innis added, to be an example of 'active, mental alertness' as he faced the difficult problems associated with intellectual work and he must be prepared to devote his life to it. Participation of scholars in government resulted in benefits for the state but lowered the standards of academic achievement of a 'fundamental character.'[63]

No Canadian scholar was more profoundly disturbed by the events of the Second World War, or had subjected his own beliefs to closer scrutiny during it, than Harold Innis. Shortly after the collapse of France he had suddenly redirected his research away from staples and towards the history and economics of various forms of communication, with particular emphasis on the press, censorship, advertising, and propaganda. By the end of the war he had produced a thousand-page manuscript on the subject. This quest for understanding the ways the biases of communication – particularly the press and radio – shaped and distorted contemporary life preoccupied him to the point of obsession for the remainder of his life.[64] He also became intensely aware of the influence of American culture on Canadian life, and he was critical of it. It kindled his sense of nationalism. But there was a direct link between this redirection in his thinking and his concern over the fate of scholarship in such a society. Both involved the problem of external control over individual initiative, and therefore freedom. He was scathing in his denunciation of the willingness of professors, particularly those born in the British isles, to accept government posts. 'This has reached such a point, that in [a] lighter vein it has been said Canadian birth, participation in the last war, and non-attendance at Queen's University present a combination practically precluding an appointment with the federal government.' As the war got longer, Innis's criticisms of the nation's universities intensified, particularly of the British-born men who governed them and helped perpetuate a snobbish yet essentially colonial frame of mind within them. The memory of the Great War and of the Canadian men who had fought and died in it was on his mind as he penned these thoughts. 'Scholarship,' he concluded, 'provides the essentials for that steadiness and self-respect by which Canada can become a nation worthy of those who have fought and given up their lives in the last war or in this.'[65]

Recovery

Of the million men and fifty thousand women who served in the Canadian armed services during the Second World War, about 175,000 chose to further their education after they returned to civilian life at war's end. Some 33,000 of them entered the nation's universities. University enrolment in the country, which had been 38,000 in 1944–5, expanded to over 80,000 by 1947-8. By the end of the 1940s enrolment in Ontario universities was more than double that of a decade earlier.[66] An era in the history of Ontario – and Canadian – higher education was drawing to a close.

After the successful Allied offensive of 1944 the attention of universities and governments began to turn from mobilizing the nation for war to preparing it for peace. Government officials anticipated an economic recession, as there had been after the Great War a generation earlier. They also recognized, as before, that the demand for trained scientific and technical personnel would be greater than ever. A central problem was that, as one government memorandum put it, 'throughout North America, and indeed, the world, there is uncertainty as to the fundamental purpose of university education' – whether along liberal or practical lines – and the confusion must be addressed if a coherent philosophy of higher education was to be articulated for post-war national life.[67] But the first priority was to increase economic productivity in the face of the anticipated recession, and to give the returned veterans a central role in it.

Federal initiatives concerning veterans and higher education were in place by the time the first of them made their presence felt in universities in the autumn session of 1944. Through the Department of Veterans

Affairs, arrangements were made for tuition fees and a living allowance for every qualified veteran seeking educational betterment.[68] No university, however, had the capacity to project just how many returned men would take advantage of this unparalleled opportunity, and different institutions responded with different degrees of interest and efficiency. The associate dean of arts and science at McMaster anticipated an enrolment of 850 in the fall 1945 session, more than 300 more than attended in 1940–1 and 150 more than the university (which consisted of three buildings) could accommodate. His guess proved accurate: 853 students registered for the 1945–6 year. The university's senate, which had already been discussing the problem, was 'feverishly active' during the year, not least because the anticipated creation of a separate (and publicly funded) science facility had become its central object of attention and returned veterans were seen to be its prime clients.[69]

At Queen's, by contrast, post-war planning was weak. Hampered by an ineffectual Senate, two decades of straitened circumstances in its faculty of arts, and with a generally demoralized professoriate, particularly in the humanities, it was slow in addressing post-war problems. Its faculty of applied science sought more space and staff from the board of trustees but was met with silence; its faculty of arts focused on the problem of electives in the pass course as its central post-war problem and managed to produce only an interim report by the end of 1945. 'Invited by the principal to look ahead and define its goals,' wrote the university's official historian, the Queen's faculty of arts 'responded with a timid conservatism.' Nearly half of the 2,242 intramural students at Queen's in the fall of 1945 (1,030) were returned veterans, but when the university's registrar reported these figures in September 1945 its senate appeared 'startled.' Within a year, the enrolment of veterans (including those in special summer sessions) exceeded intramural registration at any point in the years before the war. Little wonder that the post-war era at Queen's began 'in an atmosphere of frenzy': its administrators and staff were engaged in a sustained exercise in what a later generation would call damage control. Some of the damage was of the university's own making.[70]

The University of Toronto little doubted that because of its size and the variety of its programs it would bear the brunt of any increase in post-war enrolment. On the eve of the war, the total undergraduate population of the province was approximately 12,000 students, and 7,000 of them were enrolled at the provincial university.[71] The matter was one of grave concern not only to the university but also to the provincial government of George Drew, whose Conservative party had defeated that of one of Mitch Hepburn's successors, Harry Nixon, in August 1943.

Drew's first government was an activist one: he promised an unprecedented degree of provincial planning, in part because the interventionist
nature of the war-time federal government had reduced the economic
role of its provincial counterparts to a secondary level even in the
administration of its own affairs. Drew wanted to regain lost ground.[72]

When it came to official planning in higher education, policy under
Drew nevertheless remained as it always had been, ad hoc and unsys-
tematic, with universities left to provide their own direction and to articulate their individual financial needs.[73] Behind the scenes, however, the
premier was more directly involved than at first appeared. In the centennial year of the first King's College convocation, the University of Toronto was led by its seventy-five-year-old president, H.J. Cody, and its
101-year-old chancellor, Sir William Mulock, the latter central to the
affairs of the university since the days in the previous century when Sir
Daniel Wilson referred to him in exasperated diary entries as 'Mule.'
Members of the university's board of governors clearly recognized that
new – and presumably younger – leadership was needed if the University of Toronto was successfully to meet the challenges of the post-war
years. Accordingly, when the imminent retirement of seventy-year-old
Malcolm Wallace (principal of University College since Hutton's retirement in 1929) was considered by the board it instructed Cody to search
for a successor 'keeping in mind some one who might later succeed to
the office of President in the University.'[74]

Whether or not this announcement of the forthcoming end of Cody's
term as president came as a surprise to him is not known. In the event, he
approached forty-seven-year-old Sidney Earle Smith, president of the
University of Manitoba since 1934 and Cody's successor as president of
the NCCU in 1942. His overture was for Smith to assume the principalship of University College for an acclimatizing period, to act also as
executive assistant to the president, and to succeed to the presidency at
an appropriate point (understood within the university community to be
after two years). Smith responded favourably to the initiative, and the
board of governors approved it. Cody and the chairman of the board
were summoned by George Drew to his office, and the premier personally endorsed the university's actions. Smith moved into University College in time for the beginning of the fall term of 1944.[75]

Some members of the academic community took exception to the fact
that no other people had been considered for the appointment, which
appeared to them as a *fait accompli* of the board at the behest of the premier. But they were effectively silenced by the endorsement the premier
had given. Other critics were concerned about the suitability of Smith's
background, which was in legal education rather the arts or sciences. As

Maclean's magazine noted: 'What place his genial qualities have in academic circles is not clear to Torontonians, who are inclined to contrast him with his predecessors, Presidents Cody and Falconer, two gentlemen cut from clerical cloth. That Sidney Smith is different cannot be questioned. His background is legal, not clerical, his talents administrative rather than academic. Aside from his firm stand in favor of a liberal education as against professional courses he might be described as a president – American plan.'[76] A Cape Bretoner by birth, with a decade of life in the prairies recently behind him, he was a big man with a glad-handing, avuncular style, a social and political animal not an academic one. In short, his 'Rotarian' manner was completely alien to the idealized image of the Oxbridge don.

The premier and his friends on the university's board of governors got a second opportunity to shape the University of Toronto's leadership when Chancellor Mulock died in October 1944. Cody was quickly appointed to the position in his place. A matter of days later, a provincial Order-in-Council appointed W. Eric Phillips to the university's board of governors. A wealthy businessman with a reputation for being brilliant but ruthless, Phillips was a supporter and confidant of George Drew, Leslie Frost, and others in the Conservative party. Within four months the chairman of the university's board, D.B. Macdonald, had submitted his resignation (it was thought at the suggestion of the premier himself) and Phillips took his place. Finally, in May 1945 it was announced that as of 1 July 1945 – a year early – Sidney Smith would assume the university's presidency. It was unexpected news to President Cody, who expressed his regret at the change of events in a letter to Harold Innis.[77]

The return of the veterans to the University of Toronto coincided with a thorough reconstitution of the university's governors, led by Phillips but with the complete approval of Premier Drew and his cabinet. In Phillips's first twelve months as chairman of the board of governors no fewer than nine of its members were replaced, including the vice-chairman and Howard Ferguson, former premier and Harry Cody's former room-mate at University College in the distant days of the late nineteenth century. The new board included Henry Borden (nephew of the former Conservative prime minister), Toronto accountant Walter L. Gordon, Arthur Kelly, Edward Johnson, Beverly Matthews, Norman Urquhart, Mr Justice J.A. Hope, and O.D. Vaughan.

They took two immediate initiatives that significantly affected the university's governance. First, the university's administrative structure was reorganized with the appointment of a comptroller responsible not to the president but to the board through its chairman. The result was what Claude Bissell later described as a 'dual system of administration' which, in his view, stripped the president of 'a good deal of authority' and placed him 'under the threat of a veto from an administrative colleague [the comptroller, later a vice-presidential position] who was junior to him.'[78] A few years later, in 1947, Phillips's board enacted the final stage of this administrative near-revolution. It obtained cabinet approval to change the method of selecting the chancellor and to shorten the term of office from four years to three. Formerly elected by the university's graduates, the chancellor was now to be chosen by a committee of nomination, comprised of representatives of the board of governors, the senate and the alumni federation. In this way, yet more power was invested in the board by means of its influence on the committee of nomination, and when a choice for chancellor had to be made in 1947 between either Cody or Vincent Massey (whose term as Canadian high commissioner in London had just ended) it was the committee's choice, made over the objections of the university's senate, that held sway. On 21 November 1947 Vincent Massey was installed as the twentieth chancellor of the university.[79]

Such changes, however ambiguous their long-term consequences, made possible quick executive action on important post-war matters. The university was inundated with students after the war, many of them veterans. At no time had full-time enrolment at Toronto ever reached 8,500. In 1944–5 it stood at 7,265, excluding 228 ex-service men enrolled in a course especially designed for them. But as the university entered the era of its new administrative dispensation, enrolment virtually doubled, to 13,157 in 1945–6. Of these, 4,727 were veterans, excluding the 701 enrolled in the special session of the faculty of arts from April to September 1946. That was only the beginning. Of the 17,007 students who enrolled in 1946–7, 8,723 were were ex-service personnel. Post-war enrolment at the University of Toronto peaked in 1947–8 at 17,723, a level not to be surpassed until the 1962–3 academic year. This was also the session when the highest number of veterans – 8,392 – attended. Enrolment declined in 1948–9 to 16,635 and continued to do so until it reached its post-war low of 10,919 in 1953–4. By then the last of the 480 veterans still in attendance in 1951–2 were gone.[80]

The great influx of university students taxed each institution in the province well beyond its capacity. Professors with salaries virtually frozen for a decade and a half now taught year-round and often. Classes were unprecedented in size. Those in undergraduate English and philosophy courses at Queen's, where enrolment rose from 2,242 to 3,197 between the 1945–6 and 1947–8 terms, exceeded six hundred; those at Toronto sometimes surpassed a thousand, with course lectures delivered in Convocation Hall. J.A. Corry returned to Queen's from wartime work in the federal civil service only to find himself teaching for thirty consecutive months and with virtually no break between terms. His experience was a common one. In 1949 Principal Wallace wrote: 'The heavy strains of the war years and the postwar influx of students have taken their toll in the health of our staff ... Too many breakdowns have taken place, and several others are at the breaking point.'[81] If ever there was a time when professors were indisputably overworked and underpaid, it was in the half-dozen years that followed the Second World War.

University administrators frantically sought to accommodate the thousands of post-war students. Campuses were transformed throughout the province. At Queen's, attics were converted into lecture rooms and an old machine shop became a drafting room. For the first time, universities found it necessary to find accommodation for married students, and university housing offices became permanent parts of the administrative apparatus. Portable buildings appeared on the edge of the University of Toronto, on the site where Massey College was later built. Eleven barrack-like H-huts appeared on McMaster's grounds. Meant for temporary accommodation, they served their purpose, and since a number of them remained 'temporary' for many years after the war (the last H-hut at McMaster disappeared only in 1972) they became fixtures of campus life, part of the folklore of student culture. The residential H-hut that McMaster's chancellor designated the 'Edwards Hall Annex' became known in student memory as 'The Shambles,' where a late-night beer could be purchased by the right knock on a certain door. Another such temporary building at McMaster – the 'Rec Hut' – served as a student centre, complete with snack bar, reading rooms, a bowling alley, and other amenities.[82]

For several years, post-war exigencies made the engineering student's fondest dreams come true. University of Toronto administrators knew that the heaviest student demands would be in the sciences, in commerce, and particularly in engineering. Accordingly, by the summer of 1945 the university had acquired the site and facilities of a large munitions plant at Ajax, a war-created town twenty-five miles east of Toronto. With its 446 acres and 111 buildings, 23 lecture rooms, 14 drafting rooms, 7 chemical laboratories, and much else, it became the main location of the university's faculty of applied science and engineering. It was a world of its own, where green, flatbed trucks constantly shuttled students to and from the widely separated facilities and where the sub-culture of the engineer existed in unadulterated form. Its architecture was military drab, its ethos was 1940s masculine, and its atmosphere was that of the mining town or logging camp. DVA credits became tokens in common-room bridge games; girls from insurance companies and Bell

Telephone were imported from Oshawa or Toronto by the busload for Thursday-night bashes; cafeteria waitresses were dismissed as 'kitchen wenches.' Cafeteria fights with grapes, known as 'Tits and Rivets,' became outright donnybrooks culminating in thunderous table-thumping when, as one graduate recalled, 'the first-named walked in.'[83]

Ajax was a Greek hero of the Trojan War, but the Ajax division of Toronto's faculty of applied science and engineering was named after a less remote symbol, *HMS Ajax*, the British cruiser that had defeated the German battleship, *Graf Spee*. In 1948 the British Admiralty presented the ship's crest, taken from its forward turret, to the University of Toronto as a token of its contribution to the war effort. Ajax dormitory talk at times involved personal recollections of bailing out of a crippled Lancaster or Halifax while a crewmate sacrificed his life to dislodge a flight-boot entangled in the hatch, of misadventures in the brothels of Brussels, and of 'telephone girls' from Oshawa. Ajax graduate Alan Heisey later recalled that the mood of Ajax was fundamentally that of 'the inevitable winding down of the wastes and passions of a cruel war.'[84]

The substantial presence of veterans on university campuses throughout the province – at the University of Western Ontario they comprised 47.6 per cent of the student body in arts and science in 1946–7[85] – brought a degree of seriousness and maturity that served as a counterweight to the more jejune aspects of student culture. Post-war initiations at Queen's paled in comparison with those that had preceded them, although at the first 'away games' of the reinstated football season in 1945, at Toronto and McGill, Queen's students did substantial damage to the opponents' stadia and to their own reputation. In Hamilton the Military Ball became what it had been before the war, the Mac Formal, and in London a capacity audience listened to a New Orleans jazz band performing in the University of Western Ontario's convocation hall. Jazz, once a four-letter word that embodied immoral conduct, was now pronounced to be 'one of the arts.' Students, wrote a reporter, got 'the shivers' as they listened to the seductive tones of Harvey Lamberts's tenor sax in 'I Surrender, Dear.' The fear at McMaster and the University of Western Ontario that returned veterans would be an 'unwholesome' influence on other students did not materialize. Few 'civilian' students seriously resented their older veteran colleagues or their no-nonsense approach to campus life. Instead, social divisions within the student body continued in pre-war grooves, between students in arts and those in the professional faculties and also between men and women – both made worse after the war because of the marginalization of an arts education as a form of national service during it. But other sources of division and segregation were new: between 'vets' who had served overseas and those who had not, and between married and unmarried students.[86]

For all that they were often overworked to the point of exhaustion, professors in the immediate post-war years came to prize the veterans' presence and, perhaps somewhat unfairly, to contrast their attitudes, deportment, and behaviour with those of the teenage products of the local high schools. More than one professor – especially, it seems, historians – stopped in mid-lecture to express their gratitude and pleasure. McMaster historian Chester New was one of them, interrupting a lecture on the period from the Great Reform Bill to the advent of Lord Durham (his favourite topic) to compliment the veterans on their "'healthy scepticism,' their maturity, and their improvement of the tone of the university.' One former Queen's student remembered that while 'Teaching a class in military history crowded with ex-majors and ex-captains,' Professor A.E. Prince of the department of history stopped one February in the middle of a lecture. "'I would like you to know," he said, "that I have never had such a class as this one." His voice broke but he continued: "It has been the high point of my teaching career."'[87]

Veterans rapidly assumed positions of leadership within student institutions and associations. They knew how to organize and to operate within a chain of command, and rapidly they came to dominate student unions and newspapers, whether Toronto's *Varsity*, McMaster's *Silhouette*, or the Queen's *Journal*. By February 1945 a number of them at Queen's had managed to get the university's public affairs club, the international relations club, and the Queen's debating union to co-operate in the publication of a new journal, the *Queen's Commentator*. They supported the movement to reinvigorate the National Federation of Canadian University Students, founded in 1926, but became impatient of its loosely knit and ineffectual nature and of its incapacity to represent the practical interests of students, such as increasing the level of student aid. Before the first term after the war was over they had held the First National Conference of Student Veterans in Montreal. At it, they began to formalize a student lobby of the Department of Veterans Affairs aimed at increasing their DVA allowances because sixty per cent of them, they estimated, would not be able to complete their studies with the existing level of funding. (One estimate was that the grants met half the living costs of single students and less than this in the case of married students.) They also displayed a keen interest in campus clubs with a political orientation. Many of them had seen the world, or enough of it for their liking, and they now wanted to understand and help shape it. Student veterans tended to support clubs with international relations or political economy as their focus, preferring them to the more traditional party political groups – Conservative, Liberal, Co-operative Common-wealth Federation – favoured by 'civilian' students.[88]

A cynical edge, a certain world-weariness, marks their writings, whether in columns of opinion or in fiction. A short story written by a lieutenant and dedicated to a dead colleague last seen 'somewhere in Italy' begins: 'Fiendishly hidden. Diabolically hidden. Maiming. Killing. Bastardly mines. Mines. We hit them. The three of us.' Another short story begins: 'My story is not very moral. Virtue isn't rewarded, in fact there isn't much virtue in this story and sin, which there is plenty of, is not served with hellfire as is only just and right.' It is a story about another battle, that of the sexes.[89]

The cult of domesticity reached new heights in North American society after the war. Released briefly from traditional gender roles during it, women were barraged in the post-war years with a massive campaign to make men happy by serving on the kitchen front. Governments seeking increased productivity and full employment, businesses with a host of new consumer products to sell, and men yearning for nothing more than a stable life at home participated equally in this new offensive.[90] The winner of the *National Home Monthly*'s 1945 contest for the best letter on whether women wanted a job in industry after the war wrote: 'One thing I would like to make clear, I do not feel I am sacrificing myself for housekeeping. The thing I wanted most was a husband and home of my own.' An article in the *Canadian Home Journal* on what happened to Canada's 48,000 'Ex-Girl-Soldiers' was entitled 'When Fluffy Clothes Replace the Uniform.' A former officer in the CWAC, Lieutenant-Colonel Joan Kennedy, was quoted in it saying that 'Many who two years ago were giving orders now are taking orders from their husbands and loving it.' The proportion of advertisements in *Maclean's* magazine aimed at women as homemaker rose from about forty per cent in 1939 to over seventy per cent in 1950.[91]

This gender-driven ideology understandably found social and institutional expression on Canadian campuses. 'Does a BA Fit Women for Marriage?' was the title of a student article written in 1946. 'Is her degree,' asked its male author, 'going to make the home – be it in a room or a house – or cook or wash floors? ... The good wife of to-day is not one who only mends or cooks well and tells her husband how wonderful he is: she must be able to tell him why.' Another student, writing about 'The Feminine Folly,' lamented the rise of the career girl. 'Not only has femininity gone masculine with slacks, whiskey sours and cigarettes but over-ambitious women with radical ideas have attempted to snatch the sceptre from Man's firm grasp and make this a woman's world.'[92] Advertisements placed by INCO in *Queen's Journal* showed several variations on pictures of young mothers taking freshly-baked muffins from gleaming ovens and displaying them before adoring children. The freedom of women, said the implicit message, lay in the ease of working in a stainless-steel kitchen. In 1947 eighteen year-old Barbara Ann Scott of Ottawa won the women's world figure-skating championship. Shortly thereafter the Alpha Kappa Psi fraternity of the University of Western Ontario declared her to be its official 'sweetheart' and she arrived in London to accept the fraternity's pin.[93]

Given such attitudes, it is not surprising that the 'liberation' of the war years was followed by another false dawn for feminism and a decline in the percentage of women who sought higher education. In 1940 approximately 8,000 women represented twenty-three per cent of full-time undergraduate enrolment in the nation's universities; by 1945 they had almost doubled in number, to 14,000, but the influx of veterans had reduced their proportion to twenty-one per cent. At the University of Toronto the proportion of women had risen to 44.4 per cent in 1944–5, but by the 1950–1 academic year it had fallen to 27.2 per cent, a figure identical to that of 1913–14. At no point for more than twenty years after 1950 would the number of women at the University of Toronto reach the forty per cent level. Moreover, the programs chosen by women followed the general pattern of the interwar years. Their percentage in the university's faculty of arts increased.[94]

The post-war campaign to convince women that they could most nobly serve their country in the environment of home and family worked. Marriage rates rose greatly. Women married younger, had children sooner, and had more of them than before the war. By 1954 twice as many women than in 1937 married in the fifteen-to-nineteen age group, that of normal university entrance.[95] In a literal sense, the seeds of the revolution that would take place in university life a generation later were being planted.

Along with the campaign for female domesticity was another, addressed to young men. Both the Ontario and federal governments had assumed that the main post-war problem would be to find employment for demobilized soldiers in conditions of economic recession. But that recession did not materialize. Instead the Ontario economy, which even before the war was the wealthiest and most diversified in the country, boomed. The task of government planners therefore became one of providing the services and skilled personnel needed to build roads and electric power stations, run mines, mills, factories, and businesses – in short, to meet the social needs of a highly urban and industrial society. Their problem had unexpectedly become not one of finding jobs for men but of finding enough men for the jobs that post-war prosperity had produced.[96]

Accordingly, educators in the sciences, in industrial and business management, and in engineering extolled the virtues and the importance of their professions, and journalists discovered that their appeal was of great public interest. The Second World War had given the nation's universities an unprecedented degree of publicity and the universities, for their part, had demonstrated the indispensable contributions they made to national life. The war had seen the advent of federal financial support for higher education and in the post-war years this continued as university education remained a national issue. By 1944 *Saturday Night* was asking: 'Will Canada's Universities Meet [the] Needs of Post-war?' It concluded the next year that 'Learning as an end in itself [was] no longer valid in a nation which needs the minds of its youth for leadership in the rough new world to come ...'[97] Newspapers and journals called for the universities to provide increased training of future financiers and business leaders, and tracked the entry of university graduates into the job market, as did the federal Department of Labour.[98]

Engineering educators such as C.R. Young, dean of the University of Toronto's faculty of applied science and engineering, spoke of the coming of age of the engineering profession. 'Between 1931 and 1945,' Young noted, 'the graduates in applied science and engineering from Canadian universities increased by 81 per cent. In the same period the graduates in arts, including those in the science course, increased by only 23 per cent.'[99] Young's many dinner addresses and public lectures were emblematic of the enhanced prestige of the engineer. He chronicled with pride the profession's arduous increase in status from that of the untutored mechanic to that of the highly trained practical scientist and noted with evident satisfaction the fact that many engineering graduates now assumed prominent managerial positions in commerce, industry, and finance. He spoke of the relative decline in the purely empirical aspects of the profession because of the growing need for a sound knowledge of basic science and the conduct of complex laboratory research. He spoke sincerely, too, of the need for the engineer to keep in touch with the humanistic side of higher education. In this respect he differed from those of his American colleagues who at best paid lip service to the liberal arts and at worst were outright disdainful of their social value.[100] Young sought genuine balance in engineering education, but even to him, one senses, this appeared to be an increasingly distant ideal, ever difficult to attain when the public cry was for deeper levels of specialization and a better return on its educational investment.

The government of Ontario acknowledged the importance of the province's universities in its 1944 budget. Premier George Drew and his treasurer Leslie Frost were known friends of education. Drew's '22 point' political manifesto of 1943 had promised a reorganization of the province's educational system so that 'every child in this province will have an opportunity to be educated to the full extent of their mental capacity, no matter where they live or what the financial circumstances of their parents may be.' Frost's budget speech seemed to extend this into the realm of higher education. In order for academic science to best serve industrial needs, he announced, the universities had to be relieved from their 'burden of debt.' Accordingly, grants were to be made to the University of Toronto ($816,000), Queen's, and Western ($250,000 each). The clear import of the message was that such relief from debt would continue permanently. Privately, Drew and Frost worried about the costs of unnecessary expansion of universities and duplication of programs, but given the problems created by the influx of veterans they were powerless to prevent whatever measures the universities might individually undertake. The absence of leadership and direction from the province meant that decisions about physical or program expansion remained with the universities, but at the expense of continuous financial uncertainty. The kind of planning that went on in the province's Department of Education even in the Drew and Frost years (from 1949 to 1961) consisted mainly of exercises in the coordination of bureaucratic effort. Meanwhile, the universities went individually cap in hand, as they always had, to Queen's Park. Much to the annoyance of the premier and his treasurer, an exasperated president of the University of Western Ontario, G.E. Hall, finally vented his frustration publicly in 1949. 'The presidents, deans and other officials in our universities,' he told the *Globe and Mail* in 1949, 'have had to forsake education to become executive supersalesmen, leaders of delegations and beggars, so that universities may even remain in existence.' He was not the only dissatisfied university governor. Even Eric Phillips felt prompted to write to the premier that such a haphazard, piecemeal, and arbitrary process surely had to end.[101]

One reason why university officials were dissatisfied with the Drew government was that its grants covered operating costs only.[102] Any capital improvement of the universities had to be borne by them. And since educational administrators recognized that the veterans' 'bulge' would end they were reluctant to build facilities that would be under-utilized, they believed, when enrolment fell. Universities thus embarked on fund-raising ventures aimed at private patrons, industrial and financial corporations, and local communities, with varying degrees of success. Queen's University managed to save money by spending only $38.60 per student veteran out of the $150 granted for each by the federal government. This, along with a niggardly salary policy, subsequent increases in provincial operating grants, and the gifts of Colonel R.S. McLaughlin ($1.2 million dollars in the late 1940s alone), allowed the university to erect a new administration building, expand its medical facilities, replace the Students' Memorial Union building (destroyed by fire in 1947), and extend its women's residence. The University of Western Ontario found the resources to add to its physics laboratories in 1947, build the Collip research laboratory in 1949, construct Thames Hall in 1950, and begin planning for an addition to the Lawson Memorial Library (completed in 1954). The University of Toronto launched a building program in 1945, but it had not begun to change the shape of the St George campus by the time the last of the veterans had graduated. Spearheaded by chemist Harry Thode, Hamilton College – in effect McMaster's science program – was chartered under the Companies Act in 1947. Since it was independent of the Baptist Convention it allowed the university for the first time to qualify for provincial aid in the programs where it was most needed. Aided also by the philanthropy of the Davella Mills Foundation of New Jersey and grants from the National Research Council, the three-building McMaster campus doubled in size by 1951, with the construction and opening of the David B. Mills Library, a student union and recreational centre, the Alumni Memorial Building, and a facility for nuclear research.[103]

Hamilton College was not the first institution of higher education to be chartered under the Companies Act. That distinction was held by the Ottawa Association for the Advancement of Learning, which secured incorporation in 1943. In the late 1930s a number of people associated with the Ottawa Young Men's Christian Association recognized that a strong demand for college-level education existed within the federal civil service; this became even more pronounced during the war, when many people interrupted or postponed university educations to serve in Ottawa, particularly at the Department of Defence. Moreover, no local post-secondary institution existed to serve the needs of the English-speaking, non-Roman Catholic population of the city. The University of Ottawa, where the language of instruction was French (except at its affiliated college, St Patrick's), remained under the tutelage of the Oblate order. By the fall of 1942, led by civil servant H.L. Keenleyside and by Henry Marshall Tory, former chairman of the National Research Council and founding president of the University of Alberta and the University of British Columbia, the group had applied for letters patent under the provincial Companies Act, and had privately raised a quarter of a million dollars in $5,000 donations from individuals. It found a pool of highly qualified part-time instructors, mainly employed in the civil service, and registered 779 people for evening classes at levels ranging

from grade 13 to first-year university. Meanwhile, Tory solicited acceptance of the new institution's courses by Canadian universities as credit
towards their degrees. From the first those involved in the venture called
the new organization Carleton College.[104]

The institution became Carleton College formally in 1952, when it
was empowered by the provincial government to grant degrees. It gained
university status in a change to its charter in 1957. In one respect, Carleton was unique, for it was the last of the old and the first of the new. It
was the last of the institutions of higher education to be founded in
Ontario prior to those created because of the imminent arrival of the war
babies in the late 1950s and 1960s; but it was the first in the province
that at its founding did not initially have the traditional arts subjects as
its focus or view recent high school graduates as its primary constituency. Its first full-degree programs were in public administration and
journalism, and its approach from the outset emphasized what later
would be called 'continuing education' as a fundamental element of its
mission.[105]

While Carleton College struggled to find its first permanent facilities,
leaders of the established universities struggled to come to grips with the
problems of size. None of them unambiguously welcomed substantial
growth. Sidney Smith of Toronto was disturbed at the size of his university in the peak veterans' year of 1947. He echoed the sentiments of
other leaders when in his annual report he wrote: 'While we willingly
accept the obligation of serving the large number of students ... we
should not contemplate without dismay the development of a large institution that could be properly compared to a factory with methods of
rapid and mass production. Should the very size of a student body make
it necessary to deal with students in the mass and to regard them as inan-
imate counters, we would then forfeit the classification as an institution
of higher learning – a university.'[106] Chancellor Gilmour of McMaster
also wanted his institution to remain manageable in size, under a thousand students. The plans he laid before the Baptist Convention in 1945
stated that there was no need to contemplate new schools of engineering,
medicine, or law. Yet a year later he was speaking of the way the incorporation of a secular Hamilton College under the Companies Act would
harness business to the 'chariot wheels' of his institution. When a representative of the Westinghouse Company was asked about a corporate
contribution to it, his impatient response was to suggest that the new science program simply 'take over the entire [University] operation ...' and
provide appropriate compensation to the Baptist Convention.[107]

To critics of the new corporate rather than denominational path taken
by Gilmour's chariot, it must have seemed that the exotic vehicle was

driven by Icarus. Some, such as Toronto lawyer Evan Gray, said as much, and did so bluntly: 'The prospect is that the *new McMaster* would be just another of the chain of "across-Canada Universities," all accommodated to a single pattern, which we already see taking form. It is the chain-store principle in national education at the university level, without the uniformity of quality which chain-stores provide.' As McMaster University's official historian put it, these words were prophetic.[108]

Epilogue

Towards the Educative Society

By 1951 the latest of several chapters in the history of higher education in Ontario had come to an end. From the 1790s to the 1840s, university life in the province existed largely as a form of denominational aspiration operating in the political domain. It lacked the tangible reality of students and professors. The half-century between 1840 and 1890 marked the founding of the universities – the University of Toronto, Queen's University, the University of Ottawa, McMaster University, and (to use its later name) the University of Western Ontario – that collectively offered higher education in Ontario until the middle of the twentieth century. Associated with them were the colleges whose origins also lay in these years: University, Victoria, Trinity, Huron, Wycliffe, Knox, and St Michael's. These Victorian decades witnessed the emergence and development of the liberal arts curriculum – derived from the heritage of classical antiquity but shaped by the power of evangelical Christianity – as the core of instruction at each institution. From the 1880s to the end of the Great War of 1914–18, Ontario universities were transformed, in varying degrees, by imperatives generated by the industrialization of central Canada. A modern economy required scientists, engineers, and other experts with theoretical and practical skills. Each Ontario university, but especially the University of Toronto, responded to this demand by providing programs – secular in orientation and intention – that would meet such needs. The Great War demonstrated the public utility and the crucial function of scientific research and professional training in industrial society. By 1920 government and university alike recognized that adequate higher education, particularly in the sciences, could not be provided without aid from the state. Accordingly, provincial support for Ontario universities (since 1868 guaranteed only to the University of Toronto and provided to other institutions only on a yearly, ad hoc basis) came to be established as an annual commitment to any university of a non-denominational character. Between 1939 and 1945 war once again demonstrated the importance of university-based expertise; but the truly global nature of the Second World War, and later the challenge of Sputnik, pointed also to the fact that without the development of that expertise national security itself was at grave risk. By 1951 only McMaster and Ottawa remained universities outside the orbit of provincial financial commitment to the funding of higher education. The former had already begun to move irrevocably in the direction of secularity, and in the 1960s the latter would also do so.

The report of the Royal Commission on National Development in the Arts, Letters and Sciences in 1951 not only marked the end of a chapter in the history of higher education in Canada, but also heralded the beginning of one so different in its demographic, social, economic, and intellectual imperatives as to constitute a revolution in matters of mind. The insecurities brought about by the advent of the atomic age and the Cold War, made worse by the increasing economic and cultural integration of Canada into the American imperial orbit, lay beneath many of the commission's concerns. In the face of such threats what would become the fate of Canada in the second half of the twentieth century? Led by the University of Toronto's chancellor, Vincent Massey, the commissioners concluded that the universities were essential to the nation's future as never before. They were the 'nurseries of a truly Canadian civilization and culture.'[1] Supported by strong submissions from the National Conference of Canadian Universities and by many cultural and university organizations both voluntary and institutional (such as the Humanities Research Council, the Royal Society of Canada, and individual universities), they brought a liberal humanist creed to bear on the problems they faced. The conclusions they reached and the recommendations they put forward reflected the assumptions of that creed.[2] In doing so, the commissioners found common cause with a rising tide of cultural nationalism in English-speaking Canada. Both were central to their argument for national support for education. 'All civilized societies,' the commission's report asserted, 'strive for a common good, including not only material but intellectual and moral elements. If the Federal Government is to renounce its right to associate itself with other social groups, public and private, in the general education of Canadian citizens, it denies its intellectual and moral purpose, the complete conception of the common good is lost, and Canada, as such, becomes a materialistic society.'[3]

Such deeply held sentiments marked the mid-twentieth century expression of an Anglo-Canadian moral imperative that had first been given force and direction generations earlier in evangelical Christianity and in the desire to cultivate the life of the mind in the face of inhospitable colonial circumstance. It had been given academic shape by the rise of the Victorian liberal arts curriculum, and had been propelled into the twentieth century by idealist intellectual sympathies linked to a cultural disposition that was kindred in spirit to the thought and sentiments of Matthew Arnold. Philosophical in its underpinnings, it was secular but moralistic in its twentieth-century ambience.

An initial concern of the Massey Commission for the provision of scholarships and research grants for university students quickly became an examination of the relationship between institutions of higher education and the federal government. Its conclusion was that since federal involvement in education already existed in areas such as aid to veterans by means of the Direct Veterans Assistance Plan (due to end in 1951), a strong argument could be made for substantial aid for university finances in general. The universities lobbied intensively for such support, fearful that with the end of the DVAP they would no longer be able to finance expanded facilities and staffs, and they found strong support in the English-Canadian press.

In October 1949 Prime Minister Louis St Laurent, standing beside Chancellor Vincent Massey at a University of Toronto convocation, announced his acceptance of the principle of federal support for higher education. 'Many of us,' he told his audience, 'recognize increasingly that some means must be found to ensure to our universities the financial capacity to perform the many services which are required in the interest of the nation.' The Massey Commission, he added, would hopefully 'be able to help us find a proper solution to that difficult problem.'[4] The solution reached by the commission was to recommend per capita provincial grants in amounts to be determined by provincial populations and distributed to universities according to their full-time enrolment. It was a measure, applauded by universities and accepted by government and public alike, that suited the expansive and generally optimistic atmosphere of post-war Canada. In an age of economic growth as remarkable as it was unexpected, it provided financial incentives to expansion; in an era of rising expectations in other aspects of national life, such as the provision of health care and pensions, it seemed to declare that higher education was a form of public entitlement, not a matter of private privilege.

Other recommendations of the Massey Commission also held the potential to affect higher education in profound ways, but were implemented only later or not at all. The commissioners urged the creation of a Canada Council to support the arts, humanities, and social sciences, for example, but this was acted upon only in 1957. In contrast, the federal per capita support for Canadian universities began almost immediately.

By 1954–5, federal funding totalled $5,390,000; of this amount, $2,523,000 went to universities in Ontario. It continued and was increased until by 1967 the state proportion of total post-secondary educational expenditures in Canada was seventy-one per cent.[5]

By 1951 most of the veterans had graduated. University enrolment in Ontario declined as a result, dropping from 23,000 in 1950 to just over 20,000 in 1953.[6] Yet university and government officials worried less about this decline than about the desirability of an unprecedented expansion of enrolment in the not-so-distant future, when the children born after the war came of age. In 1954 G.E. Hall, president of the University of Western Ontario, told his community: 'There is no mystery. Those who will be seeking higher education in 1960 and 1965 are already born; we can count them now; they are already in our schools ... It can be said then, with considerable accuracy, that we do know the time of the coming of students from the secondary schools to the universities. And the numbers are large.'[7] The numbers were large because the provincial birth rate had risen from seventeen or eighteen per thousand population in the late 1930s to over twenty-six by 1954. The campaign to get Canadian women back into the home after the war had accomplished its task, and not far from the kitchen was the bedroom. The provincial population increased from four to five million in the decade after the Second World War, and the number of Ontario children eligible by age for school entrance rose from 59,000 in 1941 to 122,000 in 1956. How could one estimate the number of these 'war babies' who might choose to pursue a higher education? That was the major problem faced by university administrators as a demographically driven revolution in university life loomed on the horizon.[8]

In its own response to the problem, the Canadian Conference of Canadian Universities organized a symposium on 'the expansion of university enrolment' in 1955. Edward Sheffield, of the Dominion Bureau of Statistics, was called upon to make some demographic projections. He warned his audience that full-time enrolment in Canadian universities would very likely double in the following decade. The 64,200 Canadian university students of 1953–4, might well increase to 128,900 or more by 1964–5.[9] His conclusions were so alarming that the NCCU hosted a conference the next year on 'the crisis in higher education' to examine the implications of the projections. What Sheffield and others could not have predicted was the degree to which the nation's youth would come to have great expectations for themselves. Experiencing neither economic depression nor war, they would hold the view that a university education was a right to which they were entitled by birth and citizenship, and they quickly recognized that rising incomes and a buoyant economy now provided the means of obtaining it. Sheffield was forced to revise his predictions upward in 1957, 1959, 1961, and 1963. Actual enrolment in Canadian universities in 1964–5 was 178,200 students, 50,800 of them studying in Ontario. In 1950 roughly one in twelve Canadian primary school pupils entered the first year of university; by 1965 about one in six did so. Twenty-five years later, such numbers appeared meagre. In 1990, when the children of the 'baby boomers' were of university age, full-time university enrolment in Ontario reached 216,000. Most high school students in the province expected to attend a university.[10]

By 1991, the bicentennial of Ontario's existence as a province, the era in the history of higher education in Ontario that began in the early 1950s had by no means ended. The number of Ontario universities trebled in the 1960s. Regional needs and aspirations, the expanding population of metropolitan Toronto, and an ever-increasing demand for a university education by the baby boomers resulted in the founding of the University of Waterloo (1957), Waterloo Lutheran University (1959, later re-named Wilfrid Laurier University), York University in Toronto (1959), Laurentian University in Sudbury (1960), the University of Windsor (1963), Trent University in Peterborough (1963), Brock University in St Catharines (1964), the University of Guelph (1964, an outgrowth of the Ontario Agricultural College), and Lakehead University in Thunder Bay (1965). Carleton College had become Carleton University, and the Royal Military College, in existence since 1876, was awarded degree-granting powers by the Ontario legislature (1959). The University of Toronto added two new campuses, Scarborough (1965) and Erindale (1967). In some cases the new universities emerged from a previous existence as a college, religious or vocational; in others, their appearance seemed to be the instant products of an age of affluence. In each instance they served a particular constituency, and at times they met different academic needs with distinctive programs. All of them received massive state aid. Together, they constituted the crowning achievement in what educator and historian W.G. Fleming labelled 'Ontario's educative society' in his 1971 multi-volume testimonial to the wisdom of provincial Conservative leaders Premier John P. Robarts and Minister of Education William G. Davis. The comprehensive story of higher education in this 'educative society' has yet to be written, and awaits its own historian.[11] It is difficult to think of a more daunting, or more important, task for the intellectual and cultural historian of the province.

In these years, Ontario higher education, like that of the nation, was transformed as profoundly as it had been in the three decades that preceded the Great War of 1914–18. Yet the historian of Ontario's universities in the second half of the twentieth century will discover that, however unique the story appears to be, it contains certain inescapable elements of continuity with the previous 150 years of past experience in higher learning in the province. University administrators continued to search for stability in times of unpredictable growth or contraction, whether of funds or of students. They worked, as usual, in an uneasy relationship between universities and the state, seeking to maintain aca demic autonomy while also hoping to obtain a sufficient level of operational funding. Clear to all of them was the fact that the state alone held the capacity to provide such support. The tension between liberal and practical forms of education continued, eventually exacerbated by an increasing reliance by universities on industrial corporations and research foundations for patronage. At various points in the 1970s through the early 1990s, governments themselves declared that they were no longer capable of providing the level of financial support necessary to sustain the system whose growth they had earlier encouraged. Tensions continued to exist between institutions in 'imperial' Toronto and those in the Ontario 'hinterlands,' especially in the 1970s, when resources became scarce, and funding diminished, yet students continued to enrol in high numbers. Just as the state could give, the state could also take away, and it was discovered that as much political capital could be made in the legislature by preaching restraint as by being generous in university affairs. This, too, had been witnessed before.

Professors taught and wrote articles and books in flush times and lean, as they had always done, and they found themselves challenged by reorientations in their many disciplines as exciting yet as disturbing as any inaugurated in the heyday of Darwin or Marx. Some 'traditional' disciplines – not so long ago themselves new – lost a measure of intellectual authority and prestige. The empire of English, for example, slowly began to dissolve in the face of interdisciplinary initiatives in the direction of 'cultural studies' and 'mass communications' as a post-industrial, multi-cultural, information-driven society took shape. Arnoldian notions of culture, and even the very idea of an academic 'canon' of knowledge, belief, and values, yielded to a concatenation of pluralistic interests committed to equality, first in relations between professors and students, and later in matters of ethnicity, gender, and sexual preference. Except at divinity schools, religion was present in the Ontario university only as a branch of secular study or as one extracurricular activity among many, in competition with the squash court and the campus pub. Student generations, three or four years in duration, were variously activist and conformist, radical and conservative, romantic and cynical. Women continued to struggle for an equal place on both sides of the lectern. The

search of women for their rightful place within the academic community, as students, as professors, and as administrators, and across the full
range of the disciplinary and faculty spectrum, became the main symbol
of a larger hope for democracy and justice in academic life. By the
1990s, two centuries after the first words urging the creation of an educated citizenry in what is now Ontario were uttered, that hope had been
only partially realized.

The modern university has inescapably become the social, intellectual, and moral site on which the competing imperatives of past and
future, of tradition and innovation, are played out, whether in the arts,
the sciences, or the professions. The university in Ontario has been, and
is, no exception. At times ignored, at others pampered or neglected, it
has nevertheless continued to reflect the regional community from
which – in various institutional forms – it arose. Like the culture of the
province itself, its main characteristics continue to embody 'the tension
between a rapid adaptation to the processes of modernization and industrialization in western society and a reluctance to modify or discard traditional values and attitudes.'[12] It encompasses all of this, and yet it
remains linked also to a more ancient lineage, to conversations that took
place before the nation-state was conceived, to a time centuries earlier
and under distant skies, when teachers with something to profess and
students eager to learn began to gather together to examine human
affairs and to seek to turn darkness and shadow into light.

Abbreviations

AV	*Acta Victoriana*
AO	Public Archives of Ontario
CEM	*Canada Educational Monthly and School Chronicle*
CF	*Canadian Forum*
CHA	Canadian Historical Association
CHR	*Canadian Historical Review*
CJ	*Canadian Journal*
CJEPS	*Canadian Journal of Economics and Political Science*
CJRT	*Canadian Journal of Religious Thought*
CM	*Canadian Monthly and National Review*
CRSA	*Canadian Review of Sociology and Anthropology*
DEC	Department of Education Correspondence, Ontario
DPE	Department of Political Economy, University of Toronto
GM	*Globe and Mail*
IC	*Industrial Canada*
IJE	*International Journal of Ethics*
JCS	*Journal of Canadian Studies*
JEIC	*Journal of the Engineering Institute of Canada*
LFP	*London Free Press*
MUM	*McMaster University Monthly*
NAC	National Archives of Canada, Ottawa
NCCU	National Conference of Canadian Universities
OH	*Ontario History*
PQ	*Political Quarterly*
PR	*Philosophical Review*
PUH	Papers of the University Historian, University of Toronto
QJ	*Queen's Journal*
QC	*Queen's Commentator*
QQ	*Queen's Quarterly*

QUA	Queen's University Archives, Kingston
RBCM	*Rose-Belford's Canadian Monthly and National Review*
ROP	*Report of the Principal*, Queen's University
SN	*Saturday Night*
SR	*Sociological Review*
TG	*Toronto Globe*
TM	*Toronto Mail*
TN	*Toronto News*
TS	*Toronto Star*
TSW	*Toronto Star Weekly*
TT	*Toronto Telegram*
TW	*Toronto World*
UCCA	United Church of Canada Archives, Toronto
UTA	University of Toronto Archives
UTM	*University of Toronto Monthly*
UTQ	*University of Toronto Quarterly*
UWO	University of Western Ontario
VLS	*Varsity Literary Supplement*

Notes

CHAPTER I *Education and Authority*

1 Quotations and descriptions on the subject of this convocation are from the *Patriot* (27 Dec. 1844); see also *Patriot* (24 Dec. 1844).
2 *Fasti Academici: Annals of King's College, Toronto* (Toronto 1850), 1–14; *Patriot* (27 Dec. 1844). See also *Patriot* (24 Dec. 1844).
3 *Patriot* (27 Dec. 1844)
4 Quoted in Gerald M. Craig, *Upper Canada: The Formative Years, 1784–1841* (Toronto 1963), 21. See also Ged Martin, 'The Simcoes and Their Friends,' *OH* 69 (June 1977), 110–12.
5 Simcoe to Banks (8 Jan. 1792), quoted in Marni de Pencier, 'The Evolution of the Idea of the University in English-Speaking Canada,' PHD thesis, U of T (1974), 134
6 Simcoe to Mountain (30 Apr. 1795), quoted in E.E. Stewart, 'The Role of the Provincial Government in the Development of the Universities of Ontario,' EDD thesis, U of T (1970), 20
7 Quoted in Craig, *Upper Canada*, 39
8 Simcoe to Mountain (27 Feb. 1796), quoted in E.A. Cruikshank, ed., *The Correspondence of Lieut. Governor John Graves Simcoe, with Allied Documents Relating to His Administration of the Government of Upper Canada* 5 (Toronto 1923–31), Supplement, 264
9 By 1832 George Markland, secretary to the General Board of Education, could report that 225,944 acres had been 'reinvested in the Crown in lieu of scattered Reserves granted as an endowment to the University of King's College ...' (Markland to the secretary of Lieutenant-Governor Sir John Colborne [14 Dec. 1832], in J. George Hodgins, ed., *Historical and Other Papers and Documents, Illustrative of Education in Ontario* 1 [Toronto 1911], 32). It should also be noted that during the first two decades of the 19th century Strachan had largely been preoccupied with matters of public education, both as schoolmaster and as educator/politician. See J.D. Purdy, 'John Strachan's Educational Policies,' *OH* 64 (Mar. 1972), 45–54.

10 Bathurst, against Strachan's strenuous objections, insisted that the presidency of King's College be united with the Archdeaconry of York. See Purdy, 'Strachan's Policies,' 55–7; Stewart, 'Provincial Government,' 31–2.

11 See Hodgins, *Documents* 1, 223–24, for a list of these bills.

12 See S.F. Wise, 'Sermon Literature and Canadian Intellectual History' and 'Upper Canada and the Conservative Tradition,' in S.F. Wise, *God's Peculiar Peoples: Essays on Political Culture in Nineteenth-Century Canada*, ed. A.B. McKillop and Paul Romney (Ottawa 1993), 3–18, 169–84.

13 See Terry Cook, 'John Beverley Robinson and the Conservative Blueprint for the Upper Canadian Community,' *OH* 64 (June 1972), 79–94; S.F. Wise, 'The Rise of Christopher Hagerman' and 'John Macaulay: Tory for All Seasons,' in Wise, *God's Peculiar Peoples*, 61–90.

14 Stewart, 'Provincial Government,' 57–8

15 Upper Canada Academy charter quoted in de Pencier, 'Idea of the University,' 171

16 William Westfall, *Two Worlds: The Protestant Culture of Nineteenth-Century Ontario* (Montreal/Kingston 1989), passim. On the nature and influence of 'optimistic materialism,' see Phillip Graham Reynolds, 'Race, Nationality and Empire: Aspects of Mid-Victorian Thought, 1852–1872,' PHD thesis, Queen's (1978), 17–74.

17 Lord Durham, *The Report of the Earl of Durham, Her Majesty's High Commissioner and Governor-General of British North America*. 3rd ed. (London 1922), 5. The quotations in the next few paragraphs are drawn from this *Report* at 136, 193–4, 202, 109–10, 231.

18 Regarding the availability and nature of pre-Confederation statistics relating to denominational affiliation in Upper Canada, information was recorded only in the years 1842, 1849, 1851–2, and 1861–2. As found in *Censuses of Canada, 1665 to 1871. Statistics of Canada* (Ottawa 1976), 135, these data provided the basis for Fig. 1.1. The standard modern source of Canadian historical statistics, M.C. Urquhart and K.A.H. Buckley, eds., *Historical Statistics of Canada* (Toronto 1965), partly because of the paucity of the statistical record, is inadequate in this respect. It includes only two brief tables relating to any aspect of religion in Canada (and for any period), and neither makes any attempt to discriminate by region. The category 'Sheep and Lambs' is bleatingly fulsome by comparison and regional breakdowns of the woolly population are happily provided.

19 The conclusion should not be drawn, however, that members of the Compact were not engaged in business ventures. They were, but they tended to speculate in land (as befits aspiring aristocrats). See David Gagan, 'Property and "Interest": Some Preliminary Evidence of Land Speculation by the "Family Compact" in Upper Canada,' *OH* 70 (Mar. 1978), 63–70: H. Pearson Gundy, 'The Family Compact at Work: The Second Heir and Devisee Commission of Upper Canada, 1805–1841,' *OH* 66 (Sept. 1974), 129–46; Leo A. Johnson, 'Land Policy, Population Growth and Social Structure in the Home District, 1793–1851,' *OH* 63 (Mar. 1971), 41–60; J.K. Johnson. 'The U.C. Club and the Upper Canadian Elite, 1837–1840,' *OH* 69 (Sept. 1977),

151–68. Johnson's article shows the existence by the late 1830s of 'overlapping elites' making their fortunes both from land and from trade. It argues that by then members of the Compact were coming to share a 'developmental' economic vision. This suggests that the old Upper Canadian oligarchy was not vanquished by Mackenzie's attacks but was instead absorbed and transmogrified by Cobden's commercial vision.

20 See George Metcalf, 'William Henry Draper,' in J.M.S. Careless, ed., *The Pre-Confederation Premiers: Ontario Government Leaders, 1841–1867* (Toronto 1980), 32–7.

21 D.C. Masters, *Protestant Church Colleges in Canada: A History* (Toronto 1966), 30–1; C.B.Sissons, *A History of Victoria University* (Toronto 1952), 22–37

22 C.B. Sissons, *Egerton Ryerson: His Life and Letters* I (Toronto 1937), 122

23 Ibid., 274–311

24 Sissons, *Victoria*, 33–5

25 Quoted in Sissons, *Ryerson* 2 (Toronto 1947), 11, 17

26 This was curious logic, since the charter granted by the Legislature of Upper Canada had necessarily received royal assent. According to Hilda Neatby, the rationale of the legal authorities of the Crown was: 'First, the colonial legislature could not ... incorporate a university, that being a prerogative of the Crown. Second, this irregular act having received royal assent through the governor general, the Crown could not gainsay itself by issuing a charter to amend its own act' (Hilda Neatby, *Queen's University*, vol. I, *1841–1917: And Not to Yield*, ed. Frederick W. Gibson and Roger Graham [Montreal/Kingston 1978], 27).

27 Masters, *Protestant Colleges*, 44–5; Neatby, *Queen's*, 43–8

28 On the university reform issue see John S. Moir, *Church and State in Canada West: Three Studies in the Relation of Denominationalism and Nationalism, 1841–1867* (Toronto 1959), 85–98.

29 Macdonald to Ogle Gowan (30 Apr. 1847), in Frederick H. Armstrong, 'The Macdonald-Gowan Letters, 1847,' *OH* 63 (Mar. 1971), 6, emphasis in original

30 Armstrong, 'Letters,' 92

31 Metcalf, 'Draper,' 57–9; Moir, *Church and State*, 93–5

32 Quoted in Moir, *Church and State,* 96; see also Macdonald to Gowan (3 Nov. 1847), in Armstrong, 'Letters,' 12

33 Moir, *Church and State*, 97

34 Brown and Baldwin quoted in ibid., 97–8

35 Oliver Mowat to John Mowat (8 Dec. 1843), in Peter Neary, ed., ' "Neither Radical Nor Tory Nor Whig": Letters by Oliver Mowat to John Mowat, 1843–1846,' *OH* 71 (June 1979), 100

36 See Richard Sennett, *Authority* (New York 1980), 43–4; Reg Whitaker, 'Images of the State,' in Leo Panitch, ed., *The Canadian State: Political Economy and Political Power* (Toronto 1977), 34–43.

37 Hodgins, *Documents* I, 254

38 Ibid., 253–61
39 Quoted in R.M. and Janet Baldwin, *The Baldwins and the Great Experiment* (Don Mills 1969), 188
40 Quoted in Goldwin S. French, *Parsons and Politics: The Role of the Wesleyan Methodists in Upper Canada and the Maritimes from 1850 to 1855* (Toronto 1962), 260
41 Ibid., 267
42 Quoted in Nathanael Burwash, *The History of Victoria College* (Toronto 1927), 516
43 Sissons, *Victoria*, 93
44 Quoted in William Ormsby, 'Sir Francis Hincks,' in Careless, ed., *Pre-Confederation Premiers*, 175
45 Quoted in Stewart, 'Provincial Government,' 123
46 See the text of the 1853 act in Hodgins, *Documents* I, 300–14.
47 John Langton, *Early Days in Upper Canada: Letters of John Langton from the Backwoods of Upper Canada and the Audit Office of the Province of Canada*, ed. W.A. Langton (Toronto 1926), 281–2

CHAPTER 2   *The One and the Many*

1 J. George Hodgins, ed., *Historical and Other Papers and Documents, Illustrative of Education in Ontario* I (Toronto 1911), 314, emphasis in original
2 William Westfall, *Creating a Protestant Ontario: The Anglican Church and the Secular State* (London 1982), passim. For the 'denominationalism' of Anglicanism in the British context during this period, see A.D. Gilbert, *Religion and Society in Industrial England: Church, Chapel, and Social Change, 1740–1914* (London 1976), 138–43.
3 Janet C. Scarfe, 'Letters and Affection: The Recruitment and Responsibilities of Academics in English-Speaking Universities in British North America in the Mid-Nineteenth Century,' PHD thesis, U of T (1982), 210–16
4 F.A. Moure, 'Outline of the Financial History of the University,' in W.J. Alexander, ed., *The University of Toronto and Its Colleges, 1827–1906* (Toronto 1906), 74–5
5 Following C.B. Sissons, in *A History of Victoria University* (Toronto 1952), 90, conversions from pounds sterling to dollars for this period are made at a ratio of 1:4.
6 Scarfe, 'Letters and Affection,' 159; Hilda Neatby, *Queen's University*, vol. I, *1841–1917: And Not to Yield*, ed. Frederick W. Gibson and Roger Graham (Montreal/Kingston 1978), 65–6; Sissons, *Victoria*, 90–1, 104
7 At the end of the 1840s the government had allocated $2,000 annually to Queen's, Victoria, and Regiopolis. With the grant of a charter to Bytown College in 1849, $600 was awarded to it, commencing in 1852. St Michael's College was added in 1855, with an amount of $1,400. At this point the grants to Queen's, Victoria, and Regiopolis were increased to $3,000. See E.E. Stewart, 'The Role of the Provincial Government in the Development of the Universities of Ontario,' EDD thesis, U of T (1970), 133–4.

8 Quoted in Alexander, *Toronto*, 105

9 James Loudon, 'The Memoirs of James Loudon,' 9, UTA. Loudon was recalling President McCaul's account of the affair.

10 Scarfe, 'Letters and Affection,' 439, 444, 446, 448

11 C.B. Sissons, *Egerton Ryerson: His Life and Letters* 2 (Toronto 1947), 398–9. For the history of University College, see Douglas Richardson with J.M.S. Careless, G.M. Craig, and Peter Heyworth, *A Not Unsightly Building: University College and Its History* (Oakville 1990).

12 John Langton, 'A Letter about University Affairs, 12 November, 1856,' in W.A. Langton, ed., *Early Days in Upper Canada: Letters of John Langton from the Backwoods of Upper Canada and the Audit Office of the Province of Canada* (Toronto 1926), 279–80

13 Stewart, 'Provincial Government,' 130–1; Moure, 'Outline of the Financial History,' in Alexander, *Toronto*, 73

14 *Journal of the Assembly of the United Canadas, Second Session of the Fifth Parliament* (Toronto 1856), 359

15 *TG* (1 June and 11, 25 July 1859); Stewart, 'Provincial Government,' 140; *Wesleyan Conference Memorial on the Question of Liberal Education in Upper Canada, Explained and Defended by Numerous Proofs and Illustrations, by a Committee* (Toronto 1860), 10. For further criticism, see 24–5, 37, 38.

16 See *University Question: The Statements of John Langton, Esq., MA, Vice-Chancellor of the University of Toronto; and Professor Daniel Wilson, LLD, of University College, Toronto; with Notes and Extracts from the Evidence taken before the Committee of the Legislative Assembly on the University* (Toronto 1860); *Dr Ryerson's Reply to the Recent Pamphlet of Mr Langton & Dr Wilson, on The University Question, in Five Letters to the Hon M. Cameron, MLC, Chairman of the Late University Committee of the Legislative Assembly* (Toronto 1861). For a detailed listing of pamphlets arising from the Select Committee proceedings, see Sissons, *Ryerson* 2, 402–3n.

17 *University Question*, 52–3; *Dr Ryerson's Reply*, 27–8. Only these short titles are used in later chapters.

18 To obtain such aid, however, the colleges would have had to demonstrate an annual income of $8,000 from voluntary contributions and 'hold in abeyance their University powers.' See 'Draft Reports Prepared on Behalf of the University of Toronto and of the Memorialists for the Select Committee of the House of Assembly on the University Question, 1860,' in Hodgins, *Documents* 15, 306–7.

19 Hodgins, *Documents* 15, 307–14. Ryerson, of course, responded to the reply (214–15).

20 For more detail, see Stewart, 'Provincial Government,' 146–50.

21 The recommendations of the commission are ably summarized in ibid., 'Provincial Government,' 151–4

22 *TG* (20 Jan. 1863), quoted in Stewart, 'Provincial Government,' 156

23 Robin S. Harris, *A History of Higher Education in Canada, 1663–1960* (Toronto 1976), 108

24 *Journal of the Ontario Legislative Assembly, First Session of the First Legislature* (Toronto 1868), 68

25 *Provincial Statutes of Ontario*, 31 Vict., 1868, c. 4

26 Ibid.

27 These events are examined in detail by David John Ayre in 'Universities and the Legislature: Political Aspects of the Ontario University Question, 1868–1906,' PHD thesis, U of T (1981), 16–39. *TG* (26 Nov. 1868)

28 *TG* (26 Nov. 1868)

29 *'The College Question': Being the Debate in The Legislative Assembly of Ontario, on December 2nd, 1868, on 'The Outlying Colleges,' and 'Sectarian Grants.'* Reported by J.K. Edwards (Toronto 1869). The text of the proposed resolution is reproduced on p. 3 of the pamphlet.

30 William Snodgrass to S.S. Nelles (19 Dec. 1868), quoted in Stewart, 'Provincial Government,' 165

31 Sissons, *Victoria*, 138–40

32 Neatby, *Queen's*, 117–18

33 W.S. Wallace, *A History of the University of Toronto* (Toronto 1927), 244–5; Alexander, *Toronto*, 195–7

34 See Laurence K. Shook, *Catholic Post-Secondary Education in English-speaking Canada* (Toronto 1971), 129–46, 242–52; *University of Ottawa: A Tradition for Tomorrow* (Ottawa 1990), 3–5.

35 Quoted in Alexander, *Toronto*, 140, 146

36 John R.W. Gwynne-Timothy, *Western's First Century* (n.p. 1978), 65–6

37 Ibid., 76–7

38 Ibid., 79–80

39 See Ayre, 'Universities and the Legislature,' 66–75.

40 Generalizations made in the previous three paragraphs are based on Gwynne-Timothy, *Western*, 82–127.

41 See Jakob Jocz, 'The Principalship of James Paterson Sheraton 1877–1906,' in Arnold Edinburgh, ed., *The Enduring Word: A Centennial History of Wycliffe College* (Toronto 1978), 7–8. Whitaker's six articles for *Dominion Churchman* appeared from 11 July to 15 Dec. 1878.

42 Jocz, 'Sheraton,' 13–17; Wallace, *Toronto*, 246–7; Alexander, *University of Toronto*, 192–4

43 See Michael C. Stokes, *One and Many in Presocratic Philosophy* (Washington 1971), passim.

44 Egerton Ryerson, *Inaugural Address on the Nature and Advantages of an English and Liberal Education ... June 21, 1842 ...* (Toronto 1842), 46–7

45 *University Question*, 31

46 Goldwin Smith, 'Current Questions in Education,' *Minutes of the 22nd Annual Con-*

vention of the Ontario Teachers' Association (Toronto 1882), 48. See also J. Millar, 'National Education and Its Relation to Religion and Morality,' *CEM* 1 (Dec. 1879), 599.

47 'A Provincial University,' *QJ* (10 Apr. 1875), 4

48 Harris, *Higher Education,* 609

49 Ayre, 'Universities and the Legislature,' 59–60

50 R., 'Revenues of Toronto University,' *Varsity* (24 Feb. 1883), 202, quoted in Ayre, 'Universities and the Legislature,' 90

51 Ibid.

52 See 'Reasons for Appeals' (2 Dec. 1882), 75; 'Urgency' (16 Dec. 1882), 99. Ross provides an account of anti-university public sentiment very similar to that given by 'R.' From the vantage point of 1913, however, he found public opposition to state funding of universities 'humiliating' because it represented 'such a narrow view.' See George W. Ross, *Getting into Parliament and After* (Toronto 1913), 201. It is highly likely, however, given his subsequent actions as a popular minister of education, that he shared precisely such a 'narrow view' in the 1880s.

53 See H. Snelgrove to G.W. Ross (23 Nov. 1883), DEC, box 14, AO. For the Toronto perspective see 'Memoirs of James Loudon,' 54–6, UTA.

54 For these quotations from Loudon, Wilson, and Nelles, see, respectively: Loudon, 'Memoirs,' 53; Wilson, 'The Diary of Daniel Wilson' (both in UTA); S.S. Nelles to John George Hodgins (9 Jan. 1884), Nelles Papers, box 1 file 14, UCCA. Daniel Wilson regarded Vice-Chancellor Mulock as lacking in tact and diplomacy, so he asked Loudon also to represent the university. This suited Mulock, who wanted Loudon to act as a 'firebrand' on a possible commission while he served as 'peace-maker.' See Loudon, 'Memoirs,' 54–6.

55 Nelles to Hodgins ('Monday' [probably 1 Jan. 1884]), Nelles Papers, box 1, file 14, UCCA, underscoring in original

56 The following four paragraphs include material from S.S. Nelles, *Address of President Nelles at Victoria University Convocation, Cobourg, Wednesday, May 13th, 1885* (n.p. 1885), 1–3, 6–8.

57 Daniel Wilson, 'University College: President Wilson's Address,' *CEM* 7 (Nov. 1885), 338, 340–1, 341–3, 343–4; here and in following paragraphs.

58 'A Provincial University,' *QJ* (1 May 1875), 4–5. See also 21 Dec. 1878, 50–1; 25 Jan. 1879, 74–5; 6 Mar. 1880, 101–2.

59 Neatby, *Queen's,* 160–2

60 This and the following excerpts, from *Principal Grant's Inaugural Address, Delivered at Queen's University, Kingston, on University Day* (Toronto 1885), 3–5, 9, 11–12.

61 Quotations that follow on McMaster are from Charles M. Johnston, *McMaster University,* vol. 1, *The Toronto Years* (Toronto 1976), 10–17, 18–19, 24, 28–9, 32, 40, 44, 11. Unless otherwise noted, material on the founding of McMaster has been drawn from this source.

62 For a lengthy account of the arguments on behalf of McMaster, as well as of the government's response, see 'McMaster University: The Claims of the Baptists to an Arts College ...,' *TM* (19 Mar. 1887). See also the file 'McMaster University no. 1,' A73–051/box 001(15), UTA.

CHAPTER 3   *Professions and Politics*

1   For theoretical discussions of professionalism, see Magali Sarfatti Larson, *The Rise of Professionalism: A Sociological Analysis* (Berkeley 1977); Randall Collins, *The Credential Society: An Historical Sociology of Education and Stratification* (New York 1979).
2   35 Geo. III (1795), c.1 (UC)
3   37 Geo. III (1797), c.13 (UC)
4   A.A. Travill, *Medicine at Queen's, 1854–1920: A Peculiarly Happy Relationship* (Kingston, n.d.), 8
5   See G. Blaine Baker, 'Legal Education in Upper Canada 1785–1889: The Law Society as Educator,' in David H. Flaherty, ed., *Essays in the History of Canadian Law* 2 (Toronto 1983), 58ff; Brian D. Bucknall, T.C.H. Baldwin, and J.D. Lakin, 'Pedants, Practitioners and Prophets: Legal Education at Osgoode Hall to 1957,' *Osgoode Hall Law Journal* 6 (Dec. 1968), 142–4; Joseph F. Kett, 'American and Canadian Medical Institutions, 1800–1870,' in S.E.D. Shortt, ed., *Medicine in Canadian Society: Historical Perspectives* (Montreal/Kingston 1981), 194–6.
6   Quoted in C. Ian Kyer and Jerome E. Bickenbach, *The Fiercest Debate: Cecil A. Wright, the Benchers, and Legal Education in Ontario, 1923–1957* (Toronto 1987), 26
7   The account of this case is drawn from *Authentic Report of the Proceedings of a Coroner's Inquest, Held on the Body of Job Broom, with the Committal of Dixon, One of the Students of the Toronto School of Medicine, for Manslaughter* (Toronto 1855). Several surnames of the principal figures in the case were mis-spelled in the newspaper reports that formed the main text of *Authentic Report*. I have corrected them accordingly. See also Jacalyn Duffin, 'In View of the Body of Job Broom: A Glimpse of the Medical Knowledge and Practice of John Rolph,' *Canadian Bulletin of Medical History* 7 (1990), 9–30. Duffin's article appeared after this chapter was written.
8   For superb brief biographical treatment of Rolph, see G.M. Craig, 'Rolph, John,' in *Dictionary of Canadian Biography,* vol. 6, *1861–1870* (Toronto 1976), 683–90.
9   Quoted in Marian A. Patterson, 'The Life and Times of the Hon John Rolph, MD (1793–1870),' *Medical History* 5 (1961), 25. See also S.E.D. Shortt, 'The Canadian Hospital in the Nineteenth Century: An Historiographical Lament,' *JCS* 18 (Winter 1983–4), 3–14.
10 Travill, *Medicine at Queen's,* 9; Elizabeth MacNab, *A Legal History of Health Professions in Ontario* (Toronto 1970), 4–9
11 See W.G. Cosbie, *The Toronto General Hospital, 1819–1965: A Chronicle* (Toronto

1975), esp. ch. 3, 'The Tory and the Radical,' and ch. 4, 'The Rival Medical Schools,' 36–61; Patterson, 'John Rolph,' 28–9.

12 Quoted in Patterson, 'John Rolph,' 28

13 *Hamilton Gazette* (2 Aug. 1855); *Daily Colonist* (6 Aug. 1855); *Quebec Mercury* (7 Aug. 1855); and *Montreal Gazette* (4 Aug. 1855)

14 *Authentic Report*, 33

15 'An Inquest – Medical Professors,' *Daily Colonist* (18 Aug. 1855); Cosbie, *Toronto General Hospital*, 60

16 C.B. Sissons, *A History of Victoria University* (Toronto 1952), 141–2; Patterson, 'John Rolph,' 31–2; Kett, 'Medical Institutions,' 196–7

17 George W. Spragge, 'The Trinity Medical College,' *OH* 58 (June 1966), 73–5

18 Travill, *Medicine at Queen's*, 15–16, 40–1, 43, 46–50, 63–6

19 D.D. Calvin, *Queen's University at Kingston* (Kingston 1941), 190–210. See also 'The Medical School,' *QJ* (25 Oct. 1873).

20 For problems in Lower Canada at mid-century, e.g., see A. Hall, MD, *An Apology for British and Colonial Medical Degrees ...* (Montreal 1853).

21 Registered doctors were elected from 12 territorial districts within the province; there were only five degree-granting institutions at the time. See MacNab, *Health Professions*, 10.

22 These medical acts, culminating in the Ontario Medical Act of 1869, marked the rise to dominance of allopathic (or 'regular') practitioners, advocates of 'heroic' medicine based on surgical intervention, and the gradual marginalization of alternate forms, such as those that stressed 'botanical' or 'natural' remedies. Called 'irregulars' by the 'regulars' they were variously called 'eclectics, 'botanics,' 'Thomsonians,' or 'homeopaths.' See Jane Alexandra Gordon, 'The Debate Over Medical Systems and Incorporation in Ontario, 1839–1869,' MA research essay, Carleton (1986); see also R.D. Gidney and W.P.J. Millar, 'The Origins of Organized Medicine in Ontario 1850–1869,' in C. Roland, ed., *Health, Disease, and Medicine* (Toronto 1983), 65–7 passim.

23 MacNab, *Health Professions*, 12–14

24 Baker, 'Legal Education,' 73–5; Bucknall et al., 'Pedants,' 145

25 See, e.g., entrance 'examination' given to Patrick McGregor by William Warren Baldwin and John Beverley Robinson in 1834, noted in Bucknall et al., 'Pedants,' 146.

26 Kyer and Bickenbach, *Debate*, 25; Bucknall et al., 'Pedants,' 150

27 Curtis Cole, '"A Hand to Shake the Tree of Knowledge": Legal Education in Ontario, 1871–1889,' *Interchange* 17 (Autumn 1986), 17; Bucknall et al., 'Pedants,' 150–1, 158

28 Harris, *Higher Education,* 156

29 Quoted in J.W. Gwynne-Timothy, *Western's First Century* (n.p. 1978), 428

30 Baker, 'Legal Education,' 49

31 R.C.B. Risk, 'The Law and the Economy in Mid-Nineteenth Century Ontario: A Per-

spective,' in Flaherty, *Essays* 1, 91. See also William N.T. Wylie, 'Instruments of Commerce and Authority: The Civil Courts in Upper Canada 1789–1812,' in Flaherty, *Essays* 2, 7; Paul Romney, *Mr. Attorney: The Attorney General for Ontario in Court, Cabinet, and Legislature, 1791–1899* (Toronto 1986): 'We must remember that Upper Canada was a frontier colony, in which ways of making a secure living were scarce. Together with public office, the legal profession was the provincial elite's preferred way of setting its sons up for life' (75–6).

32 Patrick Brode, *Sir John Beverley Robinson: Bone and Sinew of the Compact* (Toronto 1984); Patterson, 'John Rolph,' 18–24; Colin Read, *The Rising in Western Upper Canada, 1837–8: The Duncombe Revolt and After* (Toronto 1982)

33 Quoted in Bucknall et al., 'Pedants,' 147

34 See David Howes, 'Property, God, and Nature in the Thought of Sir John Beverley Robinson,' *McGill Law Journal* 30 (1985), 365–414.

35 See Daniel J. Boorstin, *The Mysterious Science of the Law: An Essay on Blackstone's COMMENTARIES Showing How Blackstone, Employing Eighteenth-Century Ideas of Science, Religion, History, Aesthetics, and Philosophy, Made of the Law at Once a Conservative and a Mysterious Science* (Gloucester, Mass. 1973 [1941]).

36 See Janice Potter, *The Liberty We Seek: Loyalist Ideology in Colonial New York and Massachusetts* (Cambridge, Mass. 1983), 101–6; Terry Cook, 'John Beverley Robinson and the Conservative Blueprint for the Upper Canadian Community,' *OH* 64 (1972), passim; S.F. Wise, 'Upper Canada and the Conservative Tradition,' in *Profiles of a Province: Studies in the History of Ontario* (Toronto 1967), 20–33.

37 Risk, 'Law and the Economy,' 108

38 Lawrence M. Friedman, *A History of American Law* (New York 1973), 529–30; Kyer and Bickenbach, *The Fiercest Debate*, 8–9

39 Robert Stevens, 'Two Cheers for 1870: The American Law School,' in Donald Fleming and Bernard Bailyn, eds., *Law in American Society* (Toronto 1971), 416–24. See also Robert H. Wiebe, *The Opening of American Society* (New York 1984), 222–9, 307–9.

40 See Cole, 'Tree of Knowledge,' 18; Baker, 'Legal Education,' in Flaherty, *Essays* 2, 100–1.

41 See Kyer and Bickenbach, *The Fiercest Debate*, 26–8; Bucknall et al., 'Pedants,' 154–5; Cole, 'Tree of Knowledge,' 18-19ff.

42 George S. Holmested, 'The Law of Succession to Land in Ontario,' *CM* 12 (Nov. 1877), 475

43 *CM* 12 (Dec. 1877), 642

44 *Ibid* 643–4

45 *CM* 13 (Jan. 1878), 92–3. The author of the offending thoughts subsequently declared himself to be 'Lester Lelan' in a lengthy and thoughtful elaboration of his initial accusations, entitled 'Law and the Study of Law,' *CM* 13 (Jan. 1878), 190–201.

46 Thomas A. Gorham, 'No Law School,' *RBCM* 4 (Feb. 1880), 119–23

47 Nicholas Flood Davin, 'Legal Education,' *RBCM* 4 (Mar. 1880), 287–8

48 Thomas A. Gorham, 'The Law Students' Grievance,' *RBCM* 4 (May 1880), 531–3

49 Gorham, 'Law Students' Grievance,' 536–7. Curtis Cole discusses the controversy in the context of 'geographical conflict of interest.' See Cole, 'Tree of Knowledge,' 19–22

50 Quoted in Bucknall et al., 'Pedants,' 158. See also Cole, 'Tree of Knowledge,' 20–1.

51 Bucknall et al., 'Pedants,' 159; Cole, 'Tree of Knowledge,' 23–5

52 J. George Hodgins, ed., *Historical and Other Papers and Documents, Illustrative of Education in Ontario* 2 (Toronto 1911), 169; Spragge, 'Trinity Medical,' 88

53 See, e.g., Geikie to the Vice Chancellor and Members of Senate of the University of Toronto (6 Apr. 1887), DEC, box 12, AO, RG2D7.

54 See Geikie, 'A Letter to the Minister of Education' (22 Mar. 1890); Geikie to Ross (27 Mar. 1897), DEC, box 9, AO, RG2D7; Spragge, 'Trinity Medical,' 88–9.

55 Spragge, 'Trinity Medical,' 93–5

56 Hilda Neatby, *Queen's University*, vol. 1, *1841–1917: And Not to Yield*, ed. Frederick W. Gibson and Roger Graham (Montreal/Kingston 1978), 126, 128–9, 201, 211–13; Travill, *Medicine at Queen's*, 82–100

57 Gwynne-Timothy, *Western*, 92–114

58 Harris, *Higher Education*, 16

59 See David Gagan, 'For "Patients of Moderate Means": The Transformation of Ontario's Public General Hospitals, 1880–1950,' *CHR* 70 (1989), 152–9ff.

60 This paragraph and the next two are based upon the work of R.D. Gidney and W.P.J. Millar, in 'The Reorientation of Medical Education in Late Nineteenth-Century Ontario: The Proprietary Schools and the Foundation of the Faculty of Medicine at the University of Toronto,' *Journal of the History of Medicine* (forthcoming). I wish to thank Gidney and Millar for allowing me to examine and to use material from their unpublished article.

61 Paul Starr, *The Social Transformation of American Medicine* (New York 1982), 198. Nevertheless, late 19th-century medical students, like law students, at times found their facilities and the instruction less than adequate. See 'The Sanitary Condition of the Royal Medical College,' *QJ* (3 Feb. 1886), 93; Beemer, 'Medical Education,' 634.

62 Wylie, 'Instruments of Commerce and Authority,' 39

63 Quoted in James Forbes Newman, 'Reaction and Change: A Study of the Ontario Bar, 1880 to 1920,' *University of Toronto Faculty of Law Review* 32 (1974), 157

64 Baker, 'Legal Education,' 111

CHAPTER 4   *Character and Conduct*

1 L.P. Hartley, *The Go-Between* (Harmondsworth 1973), 7

2 See Gregory S. Kealey, 'Toronto's Industrial Revolution, 1850–1892,' in Michael S. Cross and Gregory S. Kealey, eds., *Canada's Age of Industry* (Toronto 1982), 20–30 passim; W.L. Morton, 'Victorian Canada,' in W.L. Morton, ed., *The Shield of*

Achilles (Toronto 1968), 311–33. For statistics on rural and urban populations see John McCallum, *Unequal Beginnings: Agriculture and Economic Development in Quebec and Ontario until 1870* (Toronto 1980), 55.

3 T.C. Keefer, *Philosophy of Railroads*, ed. H.V. Nelles (Toronto 1972), 9

4 See Susanna Moodie, *Roughing It In the Bush*, ed. Carl F. Klinck (Toronto 1962 [1852]), and 'Education the True Wealth of the World,' in *Victoria Magazine, 1847–1848*, ed. W.H. New (Vancouver 1968), 89–92; following extracts from 89–90, 91, 89, 91.

5 W.S. Wallace, *A History of the University of Toronto* (Toronto 1927), 70–4. See also Douglas Richardson with J.M.S. Careless, G.M. Craig and Peter Heyworth, *A Not Unsightly Building: University College and Its History* (Oakville 1990).

6 See Peter G. Goheen, *Victorian Toronto, 1850 to 1900* (Chicago 1970), Fig. 2, 82–3; Wallace, *Toronto*, illustration facing 102: 'View to the South from the Tower of University College *circa* 1870.'

7 Loudon, *Studies of Student Life* 5 (Toronto 1923), 222

8 T.A. Reed, ed., *A History of the University of Trinity College, Toronto, 1852–1952* (Toronto 1952), illustrations following 52. Published without designated authors as a 'Special Centennial Issue' of the *Trinity Review*, Trinity College, Toronto.

9 John Watson, 'Thirty Years in the History of Queen's University,' *QQ* 10 (Oct. 1902), 188

10 Ibid., 188–9

11 Robin S. Harris, *A History of Higher Education in Canada, 1663–1960* (Toronto 1976), 609

12 Ibid., 609

13 McCallum, *Unequal Beginnings*, 55. Studies of the historical demography of Ontario students are virtually non-existent. The one major exception is David R. Keane, 'Rediscovering Ontario University Students of the Mid-Nineteenth Century: Sources for and Approaches to the Study of the Experience of Going to College and Personal, Family and Social Backgrounds of Students,' PHD thesis, U of T (1981).

14 Loudon, *Studies* 5, 223

15 See Harvey J. Graff, *The Literacy Myth: Literacy and Social Structure in the Nineteenth-Century City* (New York 1979), 51–116, 132–46.

16 Bruce W. Hodgins, 'Democracy and the Ontario Fathers of Confederation,' in *Profiles of a Province* (Toronto 1967), 88

17 The latent anti-Americanism of Ontario political culture helped prevent the kind of democratization of higher education witnessed in the United States during and after the Jacksonian era. See Daniel Walker Howe, *The Political Culture of the American Whigs* (Chicago 1979), passim; Robert H. Wiebe, *The Opening of American Society* (New York 1984), 127ff.

18 Alison Prentice, *The School Promoters* (Toronto 1977), 144

19 See Robert L. Fraser, 'Like Eden in her Summer Dress: Gentry, Economy, and Society: Upper Canada, 1812–1840,' PHD thesis, U of T (1979), esp. 207–27.

20 See Janet C. Scarfe, 'Letters and Affection: The Recruitment and Responsibilities of Academics in English-Speaking Universities in British North America in the Mid-Nineteenth Century,' PHD thesis, U of T (1982), passim.

21 For full details surrounding the backgrounds of Ontario professors in this period, see Scarfe, 'Letters and Affection.'

22 Nathanael Burwash, *The History of Victoria College* (Toronto 1927), 460–2. See William Westfall, 'Order and Experience: Patterns of Religious Metaphor in Early Nineteenth Century Upper Canada,' *JCS* 20 (Spring 1985), 5–24, for an examination of the religious culture of Upper Canada / Canada West. See also Westfall's *Two Worlds: The Protestant Culture of Nineteenth Century Ontario* (Montreal/Kingston 1989).

23 Hilda Neatby, *Queen's University*, vol. 1, *1841–1917: And Not to Yield*, ed. Frederick W. Gibson and Roger Graham (Montreal/Kingston 1978), 47

24 *University Question* (Toronto 1860), 76

25 Reed, *Trinity*, 50. I am grateful to William Westfall for information and insight concerning the Diocesan Theological Institute.

26 Loudon, *Studies* 5, 234–5: reminiscence of James H. Coyne '70

27 Reed, *Trinity*, 58; Loudon, *Studies* 5, 235

28 Burwash, *Victoria*, 181

29 Ibid., 180

30 J. Campbell, 'The Rev Prof James Beaven,' *UTM* 3 (Dec. 1902), 69–72; C.R.W. Biggar, 'The Rev William Hincks,' *UTM* 2 (June 1902), 232–3

31 A.B. McKillop, *A Disciplined Intelligence: Critical Inquiry and Canadian Thought in the Victorian Era* (Montreal/Kingston 1979), 86. Student copies of these lectures became a major source of evidence for the 1860 accusation by Bishop Benjamin Cronyn of Huron that dangerous Romish doctrines were being taught at Strachan's Trinity. In spite of Whitaker's vehement denials, the resulting rift within college and church was serious enough to help precipitate the founding in 1863 of Cronyn's broad church alternative to Trinity, Huron College, at London. See R.T. Appleyard, 'The Origin of Huron College in Relation to the Religious Questions of the Period,' MA thesis, Western (1937), 50–123; Reed, *Trinity*, 62–9.

32 Neatby, *Queen's*, 92–7

33 For an examination of the susceptibility of adolescents to religious conversion, see Joseph F. Kett, *Rites of Passage: Adolescence in America 1790 to the Present* (New York 1977), 62–85.

34 Burwash, *Victoria*, 180–1

35 James George, *What Is Civilization?* (Kingston 1859), 4–6, 13

36 For the transatlantic dimensions of evangelicalism, see Bernard Semmel, *The Methodist Revolution* (New York 1973); W.R. Ward, *Religion and Society in England, 1790–1850* (London 1972); Alan Heimert, *Religion and the American Mind: From the Great Awakening to the Revolution* (Cambridge, Mass. 1966); William G. McLoughlin, ed., *The American Evangelicals, 1800–1900* (New York 1968); Rich-

ard L. Bushman, *From Puritan to Yankee* (Cambridge, Mass. 1965). For treatment of the Canadian context, see Michael Gauvreau, *The Evangelical Century: College and Creed in English Canada from the Great Revival to the Great Depression* (Montreal/Kingston 1991).

37 Quoted in Ian C. Bradley, *The Call to Seriousness* (New York 1976), 20
38 Quoted in ibid., 202
39 Nathanael Burwash, 'Sunset Thoughts,' Diary entry (2 Sept. 1861), Burwash Papers, UCCA
40 See McKillop, *Disciplined Intelligence*, 1-22ff; Gauvreau, *Evangelical Century*, passim; D.C. Masters, *Protestant Denominational Colleges in Canada* (Toronto 1966); D.H. Meyer, *The Instructed Conscience* (Philadelphia 1972).
41 Rev Thomas Gisborne, quoted in Bradley, *Call to Seriousness*, 149
42 See George M. Marsden, *The Evangelical Mind and the New School Presbyterian Experience* (New Haven 1970), xii, 230–49; William R. Hutchison, *The Modernist Impulse in American Protestantism* (New York 1966), 41–75.
43 Trygve Tholfsen, *Working Class Radicalism in Mid-Victorian England* (London 1976), 168. See also Richard D. Altick, *Victorian People and Ideas* (Toronto 1973), 165–202; Walter E. Houghton, *The Victorian Frame of Mind* (New Haven 1957), esp. 'Earnestness' and 'Enthusiasm,' 218–305.
44 See Meyer, *Instructed Conscience*, 135–8.
45 Bradley, *Call to Seriousness*, 154–5. See also A.B. McKillop, 'Canadian Methodism in 1884,' Canadian Methodist Historical Society *Papers* 4 (1984), 19–23; Neil Austin Semple, 'The Impact of Urbanization on the Methodist Church in Central Canada, 1854–1884,' PHD thesis, U of T (1979).
46 For the English background, see Sheldon Rothblatt, *Tradition and Change in English Liberal Education: An Essay in History and Culture* (London 1976); for American evidence, see Burton J. Bledstein, *The Culture of Professionalism: The Middle Class and the Development of Higher Education in America* (New York 1976), 129–58.
47 Trinity College, *Aims and Objects of Trinity* (Toronto 1902), 4
48 John McCaul, 'Inaugural Address,' in University of King's College, *Proceedings* (Toronto 1843), 55–6
49 H. Melville, *The Rise and Progress of Trinity College, Toronto, with a Sketch of the life of Bishop Strachan* (Toronto 1852), 155
50 'University Day,' *QJ* (25 Oct. 1873), 7
51 'The Principal's Address to the Graduates of 1873–1874,' *QJ* (2 May 1874)
52 E.L. Burn, *The Age of Equipoise: A Study of the Mid-Victorian Generation* (New York 1965), 128. For the internalization and social application of the mid-Victorian moral code, see Burn's chapter, 'Social Disciplines,' 232–94. But see E.P. Thompson, *The Making of the English Working Class* (London 1963), 350–400, for a more critical assessment of the evangelical inheritance for British class relations.
53 James George, *An Address Delivered at the Opening of Queen's College, 1853* (Kingston 1853), 11

54 'Thoughts on Civilization,' *QJ* (31 Jan. 1874), 2

55 George, *Address* (1853), 16–17, emphasis in original

56 'Custom and the Moral Sentiments,' *QJ* (20 Dec. 1873), 4–5

57 'Choosing a College,' *QJ* (3 May 1886), 149

58 *QJ* (10 Dec. 1890), 33

59 'The Objects of the University Curriculum,' *QJ* (20 Oct. 1874), 1

60 James George, *The Value of Earnestness* (Kingston 1854), 4–5. See also his *Moral Courage* (Kingston 1856). Both were addresses given to students at the opening of the school year.

61 George, *Address* (1853), 8

62 *QJ* (28 Nov. 1874), 1–3

63 *QJ* (10 Dec. 1890), 33. Quotations have here been drawn from Queen's University sources, but similar examples could as easily have been given from the newspapers of other colleges. From the Methodist Victoria College, e.g., see: 'Religion and Social Life,' *AV* (Oct. 1885), 8–10; 'Denominational Colleges,' *AV* (Nov. 1888), 4–5; 'Life's Mission,' *AV* (Feb. 1889), 9–12; 'Relation of Faith to Character,' *AV* (Mar. 1889), 8–10. See also C. MacMillan, 'The University and the Freshman,' *University Magazine* 10 (Apr. 1911), 207–21.

CHAPTER 5   *Mid-Victorian Arts and Sciences*

1 See Trygve R. Tholfsen, *Working Class Radicalism in Mid-Victorian England* (London 1976), 46–7. For detailed treatment of the ways evangelical religion, particularly Methodism, helped instil the values associated with industrial capitalism, including work-discipline, see E.P. Thompson, *The Making of the English Working Class* (London 1963), 350–400.

2 Egerton Ryerson, *Inaugural Address on the Nature and Advantages of an English and Liberal Education ... June 21, 1842 ...* (Toronto 1842), 12. For sustained examination of the mimetic tradition, see Eric Auerbach, *Mimesis: The Representation of Reality in Western Literature*, trans. Willard R. Trask (Princeton 1953).

3 See A.B. McKillop, *A Disciplined Intelligence: Critical Inquiry and Canadian Thought in the Victorian Era* (Montreal/Kingston 1979), 5–16.

4 Perry Miller, *The New England Mind*, vol. 1, *The Seventeenth Century* (Boston 1961), 21. See also Clifford Geertz, 'Religion as a Cultural System,' in his *The Interpretation of Cultures* (New York 1973), 95–7; George Santayana, *The Life of Reason*, 1-vol. ed. (New York 1955), 258; Robert S. Nisbet, *The Sociological Tradition* (New York 1968), 261–3.

5 James George, *The Relation Between Piety and Intellectual Labor: An Address Delivered at the Opening of the Fourteenth Session of Queen's College* (Kingston 1855), 9. See also Ebenezer E. Ross, *The Manliness of Piety* (Halifax 1860).

6 See McKillop, *Disciplined Intelligence,* passim.

7 For extensive treatment of the 19th-century liberal arts curriculum in English Can-

ada, see Patricia Jasen, 'The English Canadian Liberal Arts Curriculum: An Intellectual History, 1800–1950,' PHD thesis, Manitoba (1987), 37–50 passim.

8 Ryerson, *Liberal Education*, 14–20, 27

9 Robin S. Harris, *A History of Higher Education in Canada, 1663–1960* (Toronto 1976), 41–2

10 Sheldon Rothblatt, *Tradition and Change in English Liberal Education: An Essay in History and Culture* (London 1976), 100

11 Douglas Sloan, *The Scottish Enlightenment and the American College Ideal* (New York 1971), viii; Henry F. May, *The Enlightenment in America* (New York 1976), 358; Wilson Smith, *Professors and Public Ethics: Studies of Northern Moral Philosophers before the Civil War* (Philadelphia 1972); D.H. Meyer, *The Instructed Conscience: The Shaping of the American National Ethic* (Philadelphia 1972). Michael Gauvreau argues that the Anglo-Canadian professoriate did not import the Scottish Enlightenment into British North America in a programmatic sense, but in doing so he undervalues its general influence. See Gauvreau, *The Evangelical Century: College and Creed in English Canada from the Great Revival to the Great Depression* (Montreal/Kingston 1991), 14–17 passim.

12 Meyer, *Instructed Conscience*, 4–11

13 McKillop, *Disciplined Intelligence*, 91; Harris, *Higher Education*, 52. For a general estimation of the importance of the Scottish contribution to Canadian education, see R.S. Harris's ironically titled essay, 'English Influences on Canadian Education,' *CF* (Apr. 1966), 289–91. One of the foremost American exponents of a moral philosophy derived from Scotland was Francis Wayland, whose works were frequently used in Ontario universities in the 19th century. See Francis Wayland, *The Elements of Moral Science*, ed. Joseph L. Blau (Cambridge, Mass. 1963 [1835]). Gauvreau, in *Evangelical Century*, properly notes that in Canada the common sense tradition was 'at once reverent and practical,' because it was 'filtered through spectacles coloured by the evangelical Awakening' (19).

14 See Ryerson, *Liberal Education*, 60.

15 Ibid., 22. Both common sense and natural theology are discussed extensively, within the Canadian context, in McKillop, *Disciplined Intelligence*.

16 *University Question* (Toronto 1860), 60

17 Hilda Neatby, *Queen's University*, vol. 1, *1841–1917: And Not to Yield*, ed. Frederick W. Gibson and Roger Graham (Montreal/Kingston 1978), 124

18 C.B. Sissons, *A History of Victoria University* (Toronto 1952), 124. For a survey of public education in classics in Upper Canada / Canada West in the first half of the 19th century, see Percy J. Robinson, 'Classical Teaching in Ontario,' *University Magazine* 13 (1914), 126–47.

19 Rothblatt, *Tradition and Change*, 40–1. See also Frank M. Turner, *The Greek Heritage in Victorian Britain* (New Haven 1981), 4.

20 Rothblatt, *Tradition and Change*, 46

21 'Academical Notes,' *QJ* (20 Dec. 1873)

22 *Quebec Mercury* (8 Jan. 1856). See also Burton J. Bledstein, *The Culture of Profes-sionalism: The Middle Class and the Development of Higher Education in America* (New York 1976), 146–52, for similar American pronouncements.

23 See Nan Johnson, 'English Composition, Rhetoric, and English Studies at Nine-teenth-Century Canadian Colleges and Universities, '*English Quarterly* 20 (Winter 1987), 296–304, and 'Rhetoric and Belles Lettres in the Canadian Academy: An His-torical Analysis,' *College English* 50 (Dec. 1988), 861–73. For a comprehensive and insightful historiographical survey, see Heather Murray, 'English Studies in Canada to 1945: A Bibliographic Essay,' *English Studies in Canada* 17 (Dec. 1991), 438–67.

24 Harris, *Higher Education*, 45. See the reply to Ryerson's charges by Daniel Wilson and John Langton, in *University Question*, 30–43, passim. See also Jasen, 'Liberal Arts Curriculum,' 61–71.

25 For Wilson, see Robert Bothwell, *Laying the Foundation: A Century of History at University of Toronto* (Toronto 1991), 10–22. I am indebted to Henry Hubert's book, *Harmonious Perfection: The Development of English Studies in Nineteenth-Century Anglo-Canadian Colleges* (East Lansing 1993), for insights into the nature of the rise of English and the transformation of the traditional role of rhetoric in this period. (Because Hubert's book was examined in manuscript, I am unable to present page references.) See also Jasen, 'Liberal Arts Curriculum,' 78–82.

26 'Academical Notes.' See also David Tucker, BA, 'Intellectual Tendencies and Train-ing,' *RBCM* 6 (Feb. 1881), 161–70. See also 'The Study of the Classics,' *Dalhousie Gazette* 4 (27 Jan. 1872), for an example drawn from another province.

27 Rev Professor (John) Mackerras, *The Progress of Classical Learning During the Present Century. A Lecture Delivered as an Installation Address ... Oct. 16, 1867* (Kingston 1867), 12–16 passim. See also John King, *McCaul, Croft, Forneri: Per-sonalities of Early University Days* (Toronto 1914), 74–6, for an overview of John McCaul's approach to classical study and examination.

28 John Fletcher, 'Benefits of Classical Study,' *CEM* 3 (1881), 417–20

29 Edward Hartley Dewart, *Selections from Canadian Poets; with occasional Critical and Biographical Notes, and an Introductory Essay on Canadian Poetry* (Montreal 1864), x–xi. See also F. Louise Morse, 'The Poetry of Shelley,' *CM* 12 (Sept. 1877), 247–57; Angus M'Kinnon, MD, 'Reading,' *New Dominion Monthly* 1 (Feb. 1868), 282–5; Carol Gerson, *A Purer Taste: The Writing and Reading of Fiction in English in Nineteenth-Century Canada* (Toronto 1989).

30 W.J. Alexander, *The Study of Literature: Inaugural Lecture ... Oct. 12th, 1889* (Tor-onto 1889), 7, 9, 12–15

31 J. Henderson, MA, St Catharines, 'The Study of History in the Schools,' *CEM* 1 (1879), 214–16, emphasis in original

32 G.W. Field, BA (head master, Elora High School), 'History and Its Study in Our Schools,' *CEM* 2 (1880), 382–6

33 *Final Report of the Commissions of Inquiry into the Affairs of King's College Uni-versity and Upper Canada College* (Quebec 1852), 82

34 Harris, *Higher Education*, 53–4; Neatby, *Queen's*, 69

35 Quoted in Harris, *Higher Education*, 54

36 See, e.g., C.R.W. Biggar, 'The Reverend William Hincks, MA,' *UTM* 2 (June 1902), 232.

37 See Charles Coulston Gillispie, *Genesis and Geology: A Study in the Relations of Scientific Thought, Natural Theology, and Social Opinion in Great Britain, 1790–1850* (New York 1959); Herbert Hovenkamp, *Science and Religion in America, 1800–1860* (Philadelphia 1978); McKillop, *Disciplined Intelligence*; Carl Berger, *Science, God, and Nature in Victorian Canada* (Toronto 1983).

38 Ramsay Wright, 'The Arts Faculty,' in W.J. Alexander, ed., *The University of Toronto and Its Colleges, 1827–1906* (Toronto 1906), 86, 234

39 Alexander, *Toronto*, 236. See also W.H. Ellis, 'Henry Holmes Croft, DCL,' *UTM* 2 (Nov. 1901), 29–32

40 Alexander, *Toronto*, 238. See also Henry Scadding, 'The Late Professor Hincks,' *CJ*, new series, 13 (1872), 253–4.

41 Alexander, *Toronto*, 238

42 (Some historical themes do appear to be timeless.)

43 William Hincks, 'Thoughts on Belief and Evidence,' *CJ*, series 2, 10 (1865), 239. Hincks's chosen subject, a century after David Hume had tackled the problem of causation, brings to mind a commentary by Leslie Stephen on Hume's influence: 'The soul of the nation was stirred by impulses of which Hume was but one, though by far the ablest, interpreter; or, to speak in less mystical phrase, we must admit that thousands of inferior thinkers were dealing with the same problems which occupied Hume ...' Leslie Stephen, 'English Thought in the Eighteenth Century,' in Noel Annan, ed., *Leslie Stephen: Selected Writings in British Intellectual History* (Chicago 1979), 2

44 William Hincks, 'On the True Aims, Foundations and Claims to Attention of the Science of Political Economy,' *CJ*, series 2, 6 (1861), 26

45 Ibid., 23. See also his 'An Attempt at a New Theory of Human Emotions,' *CJ*, series 2, 7 (1862), 103–8, for evidence of his commitment to associationist psychology. The Victorian fascination with collecting and classifying all manner of plants, rocks, and animals is discussed in Berger, *Science, God, and Nature,* passim.

46 Hincks, 'Belief and Evidence,' 240–1

47 James Loudon, 'Memoirs of James Loudon,' 9, UTA. See also W.H. Ellis, 'Edward John Chapman, PHD, LLD,' *UTM* 2 (June 1902), 229–31

48 For extended treatment of natural theology in English Canada, see McKillop, *Disciplined Intelligence*, 58–91, and Berger, *Science, God, and Nature*, 31–50, Gauvreau, *Evangelical Century*, passim. See also William Leitch, *God's Glory in the Heavens* (London 1862). Leitch was principal of Queen's from 1859 to 1864. For the British background, see Gillispie, *Genesis and Geology*, 3–40.

49 Harvey Cushing, *The Life of Sir William Osler* 1 (London 1925), 57–8. Much of Cushing's ch. 3, 'Trinity College and the Toronto Medical School,' 47–69, concerns Bovell's extraordinary influence on Osler.

50 The passage from *Religio Medici* serves as the title-page epigraph to the first volume of Cushing's biography of Osler.

51 William Hincks, review of *On the Origin of Species, or the Causes of the Phenomena of Organic Nature: A Course of Lectures to Working Men* (1863), by T.H. Huxley, *CJ*, series 2, 8 (1863), 391

52 See Hovenkamp, *Science and Religion in America*, 10, 17-18 passim; George H. Daniels, *American Science in the Age of Jackson* (New York 1968) and *Science in American Society: A Social History* (New York 1971); McKillop, *Disciplined Intelligence*, 93–5 passim. See also Rev E.K. Kendall, *Theory and Experiment: A Lecture Delivered before the Board of Arts and Manufacturers for Lower Canada, on the Connection between Experiment and Theory ..., Dec. 20, 1858* (Montreal 1859), 1–63. Kendall was then professor of mathematics at Trinity College, Toronto.

53 Hincks, review of *On the Origin*, 393. See also his review of *Contributions to the Natural History of the United States* (1857), by Louis Agassiz, in *CJ*, series 2, 3 (1858), 243–7; William Hincks, 'Attempted Improvement in Arrangement of Ferns, and in Nomenclature of their Divisions,' *CJ*, series 2, 12 (1868–70), 358–69. See also Henry Scadding, 'On Museums and Other Classified Collections, Temporary or Permanent, as Instruments of Education in Natural Science,' *CJ*, new series, 13 (1871), 1–25. The 'hypothetico-deductive method' so criticized by Canadian (and other) opponents of Darwin was an essential element in the Darwinian revolution. See Michael Ghiselin, *The Triumph of the Darwinian Method* (Berkeley 1969). For comprehensive treatment of the Darwinian legacy, see David Kohn, ed., *The Darwinian Heritage* (Princeton 1985).

54 Daniel Wilson, 'The President's Address,' *CJ*, series 2, 5 (1860); series 2, 6 (1861)

55 Daniel Wilson, *Convocation Address* (Toronto 1889), 21–2. For detailed treatment of Wilson, see McKillop, *Disciplined Intelligence*, 99–101, 104–110. Darwin was in fact very interested in expression of the emotions and wrote a book on the subject, *Expression of the Emotions in Man and Animals* (1872). See Janet Browne, 'Darwin and the Expression of the Emotions,' in Kohn, *Darwinian Heritage*, 307–26.

56 Wilson, *Convocation Address*, 21–2

57 Daniel Wilson, *Spring Wild Flowers* (London 1875), 69. See also Goldwin Smith, 'The Consolations of Science,' *CM* 1 (Jan. 1872), 53–4, for another poetic treatment of the same theme.

58 E.J. Chapman, review of *The Geological Evidences of the Antiquity of Man*, by Sir Charles Lyell, *CJ*, series 2, 8 (1863), 378–90

59 Daniel Wilson, 'Vestiges of the Natural History of Creation,' *Week* 1 (12 June 1884), 440

60 'Finality and Opinion,' *QJ* (6 Dec. 1873); 'Belief and Knowledge' (Mar. 1874) and (Apr. 1874), 'Faith and Opinion' (27 Mar. 1875)

61 'Finality and Opinion'

62 'Belief and Knowledge'

63 'Faith and Opinion'

64 'Academical Notes,' *QJ* (17 Jan. 1874)

65 See, e.g., A.B. McKillop, ed., *A Critical Spirit: The Thought of William Dawson LeSueur* (Toronto 1977); Ruth Compton Brouwer, 'The "Between-Age" Christianity of Agnes Machar,' *CHR* 65 (Sept. 1984), 347–70.

66 See H.D., review of *What Is Technology?* by George Wilson, *CJ*, series 2, 1 (1856), 53–8. I have been unable to determine the identity of this reviewer.

67 Wilson, 'President's Address' (1860), 124, 114–16

68 Ibid., 106–8

69 'Current Literature,' *CM* 4 (Sept. 1873), 268

70 'The Progress of Science,' *Belford's Monthly* 1 (Dec. 1876), 116–17. See Berger, *Science, God, and Nature*, for the popularization of science in the late Victorian period.

71 'Thoughts on Civilisation,' *QJ* (31 Jan. 1874)

72 See Richard Hofstadter, *Social Darwinism in American Thought* (Boston 1970 [1944]); Cynthia Eagle Russett, *Darwin in America: The Intellectual Response, 1865–1912* (San Francisco 1976), 83–124; J.D.Y. Peel, *Herbert Spencer: The Evolution of a Sociologist* (New York 1971); McKillop, *Critical Spirit*, 69–152.

73 'A Bystander,' *Week* 1 (24 July 1884), 532

74 'Self-Culture,' *QJ* (20 Dec. 1873)

75 'Should There Be Optional Subjects in a College Course?' *QJ* (14 Mar. 1884)

76 Hannah Arendt, *Between Past and Future* (New York 1968), 32–3

CHAPTER 6 *The Arrival of Women*

1 Quoted in Ramsay Cook and Wendy Mitchinson, eds., *The Proper Sphere: Woman's Place in Canadian Society* (Toronto 1976), 9, 19. See also Martha Vicinus, ed., *A Widening Sphere: Changing Roles of Victorian Women* (Bloomington 1980), ix–x; Nancy F. Cott, *The Bonds of Womanhood; 'Woman's Sphere' in New England, 1780–1835* (New Haven 1977), 63–100; Deborah Gorham, *The Victorian Girl and the Feminine Ideal* (London 1982).

2 See Wendy Mitchinson, *The Nature of Their Bodies: Women and Their Doctors in Victorian Canada* (Toronto 1991), 16.

3 See Mari Jo Buhle, *Women and American Socialism, 1870–1920* (Urbana 1983), xiii–xv.

4 A Bystander [Goldwin Smith], 'The Woman's Rights Movement,' *CM* 1 (Mar. 1872), 249–64; Alison Prentice, Paula Bourne, Gail Cuthbert Brandt, Beth Light, Wendy Mitchinson, and Naomi Black, *Canadian Women: A History* (Toronto 1988), 194

5 A Bystander, 'Woman's Rights Movement,' 252

6 'The Woman Question,' *CM* 2 (May 1879), 568–79; in Cook and Mitchinson, *The Proper Sphere,* 51–64

7 Cook and Mitchinson, *Proper Sphere,* 52–60

8 Constance Backhouse, *Petticoats and Prejudice: Women and Law in Nineteenth-Century Canada* (Toronto 1991), 298; Mitchinson, *The Nature of Their Bodies*, 40, 82–7. See also N. Allen, MD, LLD, Lowell, Mass., 'The Education of Girls, as Connected with their Growth and Physical Development,' *CEM* 1 (Sept. 1879), 413–20. Allen's article was originally delivered as a paper to the American Institute in July 1879.

9 Principal [G.M.] Grant, 'Education and Co-Education,' *RBCM* 3 (Nov. 1879), 509

10 Grant, 'Education and Co-Education,' 516

11 See Leslie Armour and Elizabeth Trott, *The Faces of Reason: An Essay on Philosophy and Culture in English Canada, 1850–1950* (Waterloo 1981), 133–8; also Margaret Gillett, *We Walked Very Warily: A History of Women at McGill* (Montreal 1981), 113–48.

12 Catherine M. Kendall, 'Higher Education and the Emergence of the Professional Woman in Glasgow *c.* 1890–1914,' *History of Universities* 10 (1991), 201

13 Susan E. Houston and Alison Prentice, *Schooling and Scholars in Nineteenth-Century Ontario* (Toronto 1988), 14–16, 34, 41–3, 55 passim; Alison Prentice, 'Scholarly Passion: Two Persons Who Caught It,' *Historical Studies in Education* 1 (Spring 1989), 8–14

14 See Ian E. Davey, 'Trends in Female School Attendance in Mid-Nineteenth Century Ontario,' *Histoire sociale / Social History* 8 (Nov. 1975), 238–54; Alison Prentice, 'The Feminization of Teaching in British North America and Canada 1845–1875,' *Histoire sociale / Social History* 8 (May 1975), 5–20, reprinted in S. Trofimenkoff and A. Prentice, eds., *The Neglected Majority: Essays in Canadian Women's History* (Toronto 1977); Marta Danylewycz, Beth Light, and Alison Prentice, 'The Evolution of the Sexual Division of Labour in Teaching: A Nineteenth-Century Ontario and Quebec Case Study,' *Histoire sociale / Social History* 16 (May 1983), 81–109.

15 John Squair, *Admission of Women to the University of Toronto and University College* (Toronto 1924), 1–4

16 See Anna Sonser, '"A Respectable English Education": Innovation and Tradition in Literary Studies at Wesley Ladies' College (1861–1897),' *English Studies in Canada* 19 (Mar. 1993), 87–103. The college was led by a series of energetic and progressive principals during its existence: Mary Electra Adams, Rev S.D. Rice, and Dr Alexander Burns. It was closed in 1897 for financial reasons, having educated more than two thousand women. Whether or not the Mistress of Liberal Arts and Mistress of English Literature 'degrees' can be equated with Bachelor of Arts degrees given elsewhere must remain the subject of further study. The quality of education provided at the Wesley Ladies' College was nevertheless high.

17 Hilda Neatby, *Queen's University*, vol. 1, *1841–1917: And Not to Yield*, ed. Frederick Gibson and Roger Graham (Montreal/Kingston 1978), 133

18 Daniel Wilson, 'Higher Education for Women,' *CJ* 12 (Nov. 1869), 316–18

19 See, e.g., 'Principal Dawson on University Culture,' *QJ* (23 Oct. 1875), 5–6. The occasion was a lecture to the Ladies' Educational Association of Toronto on 'The

Ideal of Education of Women.' For extended discussion of Dawson's views, see Gillett, *We Walked Very Warily*, 26–38 passim.

20 Jo LaPierre, 'The Academic Life of Canadian Coeds, 1880–1900,' *Historical Studies in Education* 2 (1990), 227

21 Henrietta Charles to the president and members of the university council, University of Toronto (31 Dec. 1881), quoted in Squair, *Admission of Women*, 6–7

22 For sustained treatment of the academic and social experience of these and other students, see Lapierre, 'Academic Life,' 228–31 passim.

23 Chaviva M. Hosek, 'Women at Victoria,' in Goldwin S. French and Gordon L. McLennan, eds., *From Cobourg to Toronto: Victoria University in Retrospect* (Toronto 1989), 57–8

24 Quoted in Squair, *Admission of Women*, 7–9

25 Ibid., 10–11

26 The correspondence is published in ibid., 12–23.

27 Ibid., 13

28 Daniel Wilson to G.W. Ross (20 June 1884), DEC, box 14, AO

29 Squair, *Admission of Women*, 20

30 Ibid., 25

31 Daniel Wilson to G.W. Ross (29 Dec. 1885), DEC, box 14, AO

32 Squair, *Admission of Women*, 25–6

33 William Mulock to G.W. Ross (13 Dec. 1895), DEC, box 9, AO

34 William Mulock to William Harcourt (21 Dec. 1899), DEC, box 9, AO

35 Mitchinson, *Nature of Their Bodies*, 27–8

36 The limitations of a summer program were stressed by Dr Stowe in the advice she gave to Elizabeth Smith. See Stowe to Smith (2 July 1879), quoted in Veronica Strong-Boag, ed., *A Woman with a Purpose: The Diaries of Elizabeth Smith, 1872–1884* (Toronto 1980), xxiii

37 Neatby, *Queen's*, 214

38 Diary entry (22 Nov. 1882), quoted by Smith in Elizabeth (Smith) Shortt, 'Historical Sketch of Medical Education of Women in Kingston,' read before the Osler Club, Queen's (14 Sept. 1916), reprinted in Cook and Mitchinson, *Proper Sphere*, 160–1

39 Cook and Mitchinson, *Proper Sphere*, 162–3. See also Neatby, *Queen's*, 214–16

40 Wayne Roberts, '"Rocking the Cradle for the World": The New Woman and Maternal Feminism, Toronto, 1877–1914,' in Linda Kealey, ed., *A Not Unreasonable Claim: Women and Reform in Canada, 1880s–1920s* (Toronto 1979), 34

41 Neatby, *Queen's*, 214–15

42 Shortt, 'Historical Sketch,' 163. For stylistic purposes, I have enjoined two paragraphs of Elizabeth Shortt's text in this citation.

43 In her history of Queen's, Hilda Neatby placed the best possible interpretation on the events of the previous years. 'Short as its history was,' wrote Neatby, 'the Women's Medical College was a distinguished example of the cooperation of doctors, citizens of Kingston, and the faculty of Queen's, especially Grant, Watson, Dupuis, and

Knight, in rebuking narrow prejudice and supporting the best liberal principles of the age' (*Queen's*, 217). The medical faculty at Queen's would not admit women again until 1943. See Veronica Strong-Boag, 'Canada's Women Doctors: Feminism Constrained,' in Kealey, *A Not Unreasonable Claim*, 118

44 Lykke de la Cour and Rose Sheinin, 'The Ontario Medical College for Women, 1883 to 1906: Lessons from Gender-Separatism in Medical Education,' *Canadian Woman Studies* 7 (Fall 1988), 73–7. At the Medical College for Women 18 women had taught in a 16-year period prior to its closure; thereafter, they were 'essentially excluded from teaching positions' (Alison Prentice, 'Bluestockings, Feminists, or Women Workers? A Preliminary Look at Women's Early Employment at the University of Toronto,' *Journal of the Canadian Historical Association: Kingston 1991*, new series, no. 2 [Ottawa 1992], 237).

45 Veronica Strong-Boag, 'Introduction' to *A Woman with a Purpose*, xxix

46 Kealey, 'Introduction' to *A Not Unreasonable Claim*, 7–8

47 Shortt, 'Historical Sketch,' 163

48 'Educated Women's True Duties,' *QJ* (9 Dec. 1885), 51

49 Strong-Boag, 'Canada's Women Doctors,' 118–19

50 Backhouse, *Petticoats and Prejudice*, 294–314

51 Ibid., 314–21

52 *Annual Report of the Chief Superintendent of Schools for Upper Canada* (1865), part 1, 7.

53 John Abbott, 'Accomplishing "a Man's Task": Rural Women Teachers, Male Culture, and the School Inspectorate in Turn-of-the-Century Ontario,' *OH* 78 (Dec. 1986), 313. See also Prentice, 'Feminization of Teaching'; Marta Danylewycz, et al., 'Sexual Divison of Labour in Teaching'; Wendy E. Bryans, 'Virtuous Women at Half the Price: The Feminization of the Teaching Force and Early Teacher Organizations in Ontario,' MA thesis, U of T (1974). For the important role played by women's academies, see Johanna Selles-Roney, '"Manners or Morals"? Or "Men in Petticoats"? Education at Alma College, 1871–1898,' in Ruby Heap and Alison Prentice, eds., *Gender and Education in Ontario: An Historical Reader* (Toronto 1991), 247–68.

54 'If men cannot be got to teach our boys,' complained one rural Ontario school trustee in 1912, 'and hence leave their training to girls I fear it will tend towards effeminacy and eventually breed a generation more fit to be apparelled in petticoats than pants' (William Corbett to L.A. Green [29 Aug. 1912], quoted in Abbott, 'A Man's Task,' 314).

55 Robert M. Stamp, *The Schools of Ontario, 1876–1976* (Toronto 1982), 15

56 See Robin S. Harris, *A History of Higher Education in Canada, 1663–1960* Toronto 1976), 179–80. See also Harris, *Quiet Evolution: A Study of the Educational System of Ontario* (Toronto 1967), 79–81.

57 See Susan Gelman, 'The "Feminization" of the High School: Women Secondary Schoolteachers in Toronto: 1871–1930,' in Heap and Prentice, *Gender and Educa-*

tion, 76; R.D. Gidney and W.P.J. Millar, *Inventing Secondary Education: The Rise of the High School in Nineteenth-Century Ontario* (Montreal/Kingston 1990), 299–300. The Toronto Conservatory of Music was founded in 1887 and affiliated with the U of T in 1896; the Toronto College of Music was founded in 1888 and obtained affiliation in 1890. In the 26-year-period ending 1920–1, 371 women appear to have taught at these music schools. . See Prentice, 'Bluestockings,' 236.

58 See Robert M. Stamp, 'Teaching Girls their "God Given Place in Life",' *Atlantis* 2 (1977), 18–34; Diana Pedersen, '"The Scientific Training of Mothers": The Campaign for Domestic Science in Ontario Schools, 1890–1913,' in Richard A. Jarrell and Arnold E. Roos, eds., *Critical Issues in the History of Canadian Science, Technology, and Medicine* (Thornhill/Ottawa 1983), 178–94.

59 This view is set forward by Stamp and Pedersen, above, and by T.R. Morrison, '"Their Proper Sphere": Feminism, the Family, and Child-Centred Social Reform in Ontario, 1875–1900,' *OH* 68 (Mar. and June 1976), 45–64, 65–74. See also Marta Danylewycz, 'Domestic Science Education in Ontario, 1900–1940,' in Heap and Prentice, *Gender and Education,* 127–45

60 Stamp, 'Teaching Girls,' 20

61 Pedersen, 'Scientific Training,' 184

62 See Carol Christ, 'Victorian Masculinity and the Angel in the House,' in Vicinus, *Widening Sphere,* 146–62.

63 Quoted in Stamp, 'Teaching Girls,' 33

64 Quoted in Pedersen, 'Scientific Training,' 186. See also Terry Crowley, 'The Origins of Continuing Education for Women: The Ontario Women's Institutes,' *Canadian Woman Studies* 7 (Fall 1986), 78–81.

65 Harris, *Higher Education,* 284–5; C.B. Sissons, *A History of Victoria University* (Toronto 1952), 269–70

66 The ambiguous nature of the household science movement is reflected in the primary sources concerning it. A representative example is a 'Report on Home Science' (n.d., but approximately 1903), prepared for the Ontario minister of education. The anonymous author argues strongly that schools and institutes of Home Science should not be mere technical 'Cooking Schools,' but should be based on sound academic requirements. The report then adds: 'Home Science aims to establish at an early age a respect for and an intelligent idea of the Home as the most important factor in civilization. To try and secure greater cooperation between the home and the school. To secure better food and sanitary conditions in the home; to teach respect for the duties to be performed in the home; to apply the theories acquired in the other departments of school work to everyday life; to understand the principles of economics as applied to household management, and the relation of the home and the state' ('Report on Home Science,' DEC, box 3, AO). See also the 13-page prospectus for the Normal School of Domestic Science and Art, in Hamilton (Sept. 1899), for an identical wedding of science and domesticity: 'In introducing the subject into the schools of Ontario, the educational value of the subject is the first thing to be considered. To

increase the intelligence and form character; to lead girls to be observant, thoughtful and exact; to carry out the household functions with greater ease and consequently more pleasure; to prevent waste and promote health and comfort; in short, to bring a scientifically trained intellect to bear on the management of a home are the objects to be kept in view' (4).

67 Harris, *Higher Education*, 626, 628

68 Lynn Marks and Chad Gaffield, 'Women at Queen's University, 1895–1905: A "Little Sphere" All Their Own?' *OH* 78 (Dec. 1986), 333–4,336–40. See also Chad Gaffield, Lynne Marks, and Susan Laskin, 'Student Populations and Graduate Careers: Queen's University, 1895–1900,' in Paul Axelrod and John G. Reid, eds., *Youth, University, and Canadian Society: Essays in the Social History of Higher Education* (Montreal/Kingston 1989), 12.

69 Gaffield et al., 'Student Populations,' 13–14

70 Marks and Gaffield, 'Women at Queen's,' 340

71 Ibid., 341–4

72 Gaffield, et al., 'Student Populations,' 16

73 Marks and Gaffield, 'Women at Queen's,' 331–2

74 'Levana History,' *QJ* (12 Jan. 1917); *QJ* (10 Mar. 1890)

75 *QJ* (3 Dec. 1889), quoted in D.D. Calvin, *Queen's University at Kingston: The First Century of a Scottish-Canadian Foundation, 1841–1941* (Kingston 1941), 238. Calvin gives the date of Levana's founding as Jan. 1888.

76 Helen L. Horowitz, *Alma Mater: Design and Experience in the Women's Colleges from Their Nineteenth-Century Beginnings to the 1930s* (New York 1984)

77 'Levana History,' *QJ* (12 Jan. 1917)

78 Ibid.

79 Quoted in Marks and Gaffield, 'Women at Queen's,' 331

CHAPTER 7:   *The Gospel of Research*

1 W.S. Wallace, *A History of the University of Toronto* (Toronto 1927), 133

2 Ian Drummond, *Progress without Planning: The Economic History of Ontario from Confederation to the Second World War* (Toronto 1987), ch. 7, 'Ontario's Industrial Revolution, 1867–1914,' 103–33. See also ch. 2, 'What People Did,' 19–26.

3 Bryan D. Palmer, *Working-Class Experience: The Rise and Reconstitution of Canadian Labour, 1800–1980* (Toronto 1983), 97. See also Peter D. Goheen, *Victorian Toronto, 1850 to 1900* (Chicago 1970), 64–70.

4 *Census of Canada, 1931* 1 (Ottawa 1931), Table 9, 'Numerical distribution of the population, by quinquennial age groups and sex, Canada and provinces, 1881–1931'

5 Population statistics from *Census of Canada, 1931;* production percentage increase from Drummond, *Progress without Planning*, Table 7.4, 'decennial percentage growth, industry groups, current prices, 1870–1910,' 398

6 See A.B. McKillop, *A Disciplined Intelligence: Critical Inquiry and Canadian*

Thought in the Victorian Era (Montreal/Kingston 1979), 110–16 passim. Daniel Wilson, 'The President's Address,' *CJ*, series 1, 6 (Mar. 1861), 119.

7 Wilson, 'President's Address,' 120

8 'Extract from Exhibition Lectures,' *CJ*, series 1, 1 (1853), 158–9

9 See T.C. Keefer, *Philosophy of Railroads*, ed. H.V. Nelles (Toronto 1972); Pierre Berton, *The National Dream* (Toronto 1970).

10 See McKillop, *Disciplined Intelligence*, 95–8, 105–10.

11 Daniel Wilson, 'Address at the Convocation of University College, 1884,' *CEM*, 6 (Nov. 1884), 418–19

12 Senate Reform Act, Apr. 1873, 36 Vict., c. 29. See also 'Minutes of the University Senate,' U of T, 15 Sept. 1873, 3, UTA.

13 Frank Underhill, *The Image of Confederation* (Toronto 1963); Carl Berger, *The Sense of Power: Studies in the Ideas of Canadian Imperialism, 1867–1914* (Toronto 1970)

14 See A.B. Macallum, 'Huxley and Tyndall and the University of Toronto,' *UTM* (Dec. 1901).

15 Daniel Wilson, 'Journal,' part 1, 56 (6 Oct. 1881), UTA

16 W.J. Loudon, *Sir William Mulock: A Short Biography* (Toronto 1932), 64

17 See, e.g., Hon J.M. Gibson to G.W. Ross (2 June 1887), DEC, box 4, AO.

18 See, e.g., another letter by J.M. Gibson to George Ross, concerning an appointment in Latin: 'It is true his political leanings have been very decidedly the other way – the wrong way – but you will acknowledge that an appointment of that kind would go a long way to silence any suggestion of a political favouritism in these matters' (J.M. Gibson to G.W. Ross [10 May 1887], ibid.).

19 James Reaney, *The Dismissal: Or Twisted Beards and Tangled Whiskers* (Erin, Ont. 1978)

20 William Dale to G.W. Ross (9 Dec. 1890), DEC, box 2, AO

21 'Memoirs of James Loudon,' 5–6, UTA

22 James Loudon, 'The President's Address,' *CJ*, new series, (Apr. 1877), 376–7

23 William Hincks, 'The Sensationalist Philosophy,' *CJ* (Sept. 1859), 399

24 The years 1914–18 were not easy ones for professors of the German language and culture. See Barbara Wilson, ed., *Ontario and the First World War, 1914–1918* (Toronto 1977), 162–4; see also ch. 11, below.

25 E.E. Stewart, 'The Role of the Provincial Government in the Development of Universities in Ontario,' EDD thesis, U of T (1970), 255–6

26 Legislative Assembly of Ontario, *Sessional Papers*, no. 74, vol. 7, part IX, First Session of the Eighth Legislature (Toronto 1895)

27 *TG* (2 Apr. 1897)

28 See Peter N. Ross, 'The Establishment of the PHD at Toronto: A Case of American Influence,' *History of Education Quarterly* 12 (Fall 1972), 364–6.

29 See Yves Gingras, 'Financial Support for Post-Graduate Students and the Development of Scientific Research in Canada,' in Paul Axelrod and John G. Reid, eds.,

Youth, University, and Canadian Society: Essays in the Social History of Higher Education (Montreal/Kingston 1989), 303.

30 See R.D. Gidney and W.P.J. Millar, 'The Reorientation of Medical Education in Late Nineteenth-Century Ontario: The Proprietary Medical Schools and the Foundation of the Faculty of Medicine at the University of Toronto,' *Journal of the History of Medicine*, forthcoming.

31 For more details on this controversy, see Tory Hoff, 'The Controversial Appointment of James Mark Baldwin to the University of Toronto in 1889,' MA thesis, Carleton (1980).

32 See *TW* (26, 27 Sept. 1889).

33 Wilson, 'Journal' (21 Oct. 1889). See also Robert Bothwell, *Laying the Foundation: A Century of History at University of Toronto* (Toronto 1991), 20–2.

34 James Mark Baldwin, *Philosophy: Its Relation to Life and Education* (Toronto 1890)

35 For Baldwin, see R. Jackson Wilson, *In Quest of Community* (New York 1968); for Ashley, see Anne Ashley, *William James Ashley* (London 1932).

36 Peter N. Ross, 'The Origins and Development of the PHD Degree at the University of Toronto, 1871–1932,' EDD thesis, U of T (1972), 372

37 See Stewart, 'Provincial Government,' Table 2, 'Provincial assistance to higher education in Ontario, 1891–1916,' 556.

38 James Loudon, *Convocation Address, October 1, 1900* (Toronto 1900)

39 James Loudon, 'Convocation Address, October 2, 1899,' typescript in Loudon Papers, file c22, 7, UTA

40 James Loudon, 'The Universities in Relation to Research,' *Proceedings of the Royal Society of Canada* (1902), Appendix A, XLIX

41 Robin Harris, 'Pages for a History Book,' *Varsity Graduate* (Summer 1965), 108; Stewart, 'Provincial Government,' 255–8

42 *Provincial Statutes of Ontario*, 5 Edward VII (1905), c. 37. See also *Speech Delivered by the Hon J.P. Whitney, Premier and Attorney General, in the Legislative Assembly of Ontario, on Introducing the Act Respecting the University of Toronto, on Wednesday, May 17, 1905* (Toronto 1905), 21.

43 See S.H. Blake to J.P. Whitney (18 May 1905), quoted in Charles W. Humphries, *'Honest Enough to Be Bold': The Life and Times of Sir James Pliny Whitney* (Toronto 1985), 109.

44 *Report of the Royal Commission on the University of Toronto* (Toronto 1906), xx

45 The only significant change was that the government increased appointed membership to the new board from the recommended number of 15 to 18.

46 *Report of the Royal Commission*, lx

47 W.L. Goodwin, 'The Signs of the Times,' *QJ* (30 Nov. 1895), 42. See also 'The March of Science,' *Dominion* (Sept.–Oct. 1911), 188.

48 See David F. Noble, *America By Design: Science, Technology, and the Rise of Corporate Capitalism* (New York 1977). See also Burton J. Bledstein, *The Culture of Professionalism* (New York 1976), 193–5; Magali Sarfatti Larson, *The Rise of*

Professionalism: A Sociological Analysis (Berkeley / Los Angeles 1977), 25–31, 122–36 passim.

49 'Report of the Technical Education Committee,' *IC* (Oct. 1906), 216–17
50 Robert M. Stamp, 'Technical Education, the National Policy, and Federal-Provincial Relations in Canadian Education, 1899–1919,' *CHR* 52 (Dec. 1971), 404–23
51 'Do our Schools Produce Artisans?' *IC* (July 1907), 916. For other examples, all published in *IC*, see: 'Technical Education' [Speeches by D.F. Monk, MP, President Loudon, and Principal Peterson] (Nov. 1901), 154–6; 'Technical Education' (Jan. 1902), 292; 'Technical Education in Montreal' (July 1902), 427; 'Technical Education' (Aug. 1902), 5–6; 'Technical Education' (Sept. 1902), 113–14; 'Technical Education' (Nov. 1902), 202; 'Technical Education in London; Report of a Committee of the London County Council' (Nov. 1902), 207–8; 'Technical Education' (Jan. 1903), 282–3; 'Report of the Nominations and Resolutions Committee' (Oct. 1904), 163–4; 'Technical Education in Canada' (Jan. 1905), 375–7; 'National Technical Schools' (Jan. 1906), 368–9; 'Technical Education' (June 1906), 717; 'Ask Commission on Technical Education – Deputation Presents Petition to Government' (June 1906), 725–8; J.P. Murray, 'Apprenticeship and Technical Education' (Sept. 1906), 106–8; James A. Emery, 'Technical Education – An Industrial Necessity' (Oct.1907), 180–3; 'Report of Technical Education Committee' (Oct. 1908), 262–9; 'Germany and Technical Education' and 'Canada and Technical Education' (Feb. 1909), 576; 'Progress of Technical Education Abroad' (Jan. 1910), 586–7; 'Technical Education in Toronto' (Jan. 1910), 607–8; 'Some Requirements for Technical Education in Toronto' (Dec. 1911), 603–6; James W. Robertson, 'The Value of Technical Education' (Oct. 1912), 454–64; 'Industrial Education; Its Methods, Problems and Dangers' (Jan. 1913), 860–1; 'Industrial Education in Ontario' (Apr. 1913), 121–3.
52 *Report of the Royal Commission on Industrial Training and Technical Education* 1 (Ottawa 1913), 30–8
53 Stamp, 'Technical Education,' 417–23
54 C.R. Young, *Early Engineering Education at Toronto, 1851–1919* (Toronto 1959), 25–7
55 Larson, *Rise of Professionalism*, 26
56 Quoted in ibid., 28
57 Quoted in Robin S. Harris, *A History of Higher Education in Canada, 1663–1960* (Toronto 1976), 165
58 Young, *Early Engineering Education*, 42–3
59 Quoted in ibid., 48. See also Yves Gingras, *Physics and the Rise of Scientific Research in Canada*, trans. Peter Keating (Montreal/Kingston 1991), 15.
60 Young, *Early Engineering Education*, 76–80
61 Ibid., 88
62 'New Ontario,' *QJ* (22 Oct. 1906), 5–7. See also Charles A. Grant, '02, 'A Surveying Tour in New Ontario,' *MUM* (Mar. 1901), 248–55.

63 H.V. Nelles, *The Politics of Development: Forests, Mines, and Hydro-electric Power in Ontario, 1849–1941* (Toronto 1974), 138–9

64 Ibid., 140

65 See Dianne Newell, 'Technological Change in a New and Developing Country: A Study of Mining Technology in Canada West-Ontario, 1841–1891,' PHD thesis, UWO (1981)

66 Hilda Neatby, *Queen's University, vol. 1, 1841–1917: And Not to Yield*, ed. Frederick W. Gibson and Roger Graham (Montreal/Kingston 1978), 217–18. See also W. George Richardson, *Queen's Engineers: A Century of Applied Science, 1893–1993* (Kingston 1992), 1–23.

67 James Loudon to Richard Harcourt (6 June 1903). DEC, box 7, AO; G.M. Grant to Richard Harcourt (7 Mar. 1901), ibid., box 12; Grant to Harcourt (6 Mar. 1901), ibid.

68 'School of Mines Grant is Large,' *TM* (4 Apr. 1901). See also 'Joy Reigns at Varsity,' *TS* (22 Mar. 1901).

69 'An Insidious Conspiracy,' *TW* (8 Nov. 1901)

70 See 'Memorial to the Government of Ontario, Presented by the Legislation Committee of the Senate of the University of Toronto, Respecting the Rumoured Application of the Kingston School of Mining,' DEC, AO.

71 Quoted in Stewart, 'Role of the Provincial Government,' 288

72 *Report of the Royal Commission*, xxx–xxxix. See also Stewart, 'Provincial Government,' 289. The strong emphasis on 'practical science,' particularly mining and forestry, in the report was in part due to the presence of B.E. Walker on the commission. Walker had been a member of the 1891 Royal Commission on the Mineral Resources of Ontario and was a strong advocate of scientific forestry. See H.V. Nelles, *Politics of Development*, 143.

73 'Prof Goodwin,' *IC* (Sept. 1902), 113

74 'Technical Education: An Address Delivered by Principal N.E. Miller, of the Philadelphia Textile School ...,' *IC* (Jan. 1903), 202–3

75 'Industrial Fellowships and Laboratory Work,' *IC* (Oct. 1909), 309; 'Industrial Fellowships,' *IC* (Dec. 1909), 502–3; Clifford S. Griffin, *The University of Kansas: A History* (Lawrence/Manhattan/Wichita 1974), 337–8

76 'President Loudon, University of Toronto,' *IC* (Nov. 1901), 155; 'Ask Commission on Technical Education: Deputation Presents Petition to Government,' *IC* (June 1906), 725

77 'Campus and Corridor,' *UTM* 2 (Nov. 1901), 50; 'The University and the Manufacturer,' *IC* (Mar. 1905), 478–9

78 T. Linsey Crossley, 'A Canadian Bureau of Chemistry,' *IC* (May 1913), 133

79 T.H. Wardleworth, 'The Society of Chemical Industry in Canada,' *IC* (Dec. 1914), 493–5

80 'Technical Education in Canada,' *IC* (Jan. 1905), 377

81 Gingras, *Physics and Scientific Research*, 50–1

82 Quoted in Humphries, *'Honest Enough to Be Bold,'* 129

83 R.A. Falconer, 'The Relation of the University to the Industrial Life of the Nation,' *IC* (May 1911), 1059–61

84 David S. Landes, *The Unbound Prometheus: Technological Change and Industrial Development in Western Europe from 1750 to the Present* (Cambridge 1969), 33 passim

CHAPTER 8   *Understanding Social Change*

1 See Ramsay Cook and Robert Craig Brown, *Canada, 1896–1921: A Nation Transformed* (Toronto 1974).

2 Henry Steele Commager, *The American Mind: An Interpretation of American Thought and Character Since the 1880's* (New Haven 1950), 53

3 Commager, *American Mind*, 41

4 See John Higham, 'The Reorientation of American Culture in the 1890's,' in Higham, *Writing American History: Essays on Modern Scholarship* (Bloomington/ London 1970), 73–102; Robert H. Wiebe, *The Search for Order, 1877–1920* (New York 1967); Thomas L. Haskell, *The Emergence of Professional Social Science: The American Social Science Association and the Nineteenth-Century Crisis of Authority* (Urbana 1977); T.J. Jackson Lears, 'From Salvation to Self-Realization: Advertising and the Therapeutic Roots of the Consumer Culture, 1880–1930,' in Richard Wightman Fox and T.J. Jackson Lears, eds., *The Culture of Consumption: Critical Essays in American History, 1880–1980* (New York 1983), 3–38.

5 S.E.D. Shortt, *The Search for an Ideal: Six Canadian Intellectuals and Their Convictions in an Age of Transition* (Toronto 1976)

6 'Christmas,' *Dominion Illustrated* (22 Dec.1888), 386–7

7 Shortt, *Search*, 3

8 Memorandum (1903), DEC, box 9, AO

9 See Talcott Parsons, *The Structure of Social Action* (New York 1937); Morton G. White, *Social Thought in America: The Revolt against Formalism* (Boston 1957); H. Stuart Hughes, *Consciousness and Society: The Reorientation of European Social Thought, 1890–1930* (New York 1958); Haskell, *Professional Social Science*.

10 See Parsons, Hughes, and Haskell, above; see also Mary O. Furner, *Advocacy and Objectivity: A Crisis in the Professionalization of American Social Science, 1865–1905* (Lexington 1975).

11 Frank Miller Turner, *Between Science and Religion: The Reaction to Scientific Naturalism in Late Victorian England* (New Haven 1974)

12 A.M. Machar, 'Prayer for Daily Bread,' *CM* 7 (May 1875), 415–25

13 W.D. LeSueur, 'Prayer and Modern Thought,' *CM* 8 (Aug. 1875), 145–55

14 For a complete listing of these and other articles on the prayer question and on morality in general, see A.B. McKillop, ed., *A Critical Spirit: The Thought of William Dawson LeSueur* (Toronto 1977), 91–2.

15 W.D. LeSueur, 'Morality and Religion,' in McKillop, *Critical Spirit*, 115

16 Lorraine Daston, *Classical Probability in the Enlightenment* (Princeton 1988),

xi–xii. One of the great strengths of Daston's book is that she relates her subject to changing legal ideas and forms (such as the notion of risk), and, in a general way, to emergent forms of social knowledge such as moral science and political economy. For the thematic purposes of this chapter, see esp. ch. 2, 'Expectation and the Reasonable Man,' 49–111, but note her caveat not to 'identify the Enlightenment moral sciences narrowly with their twentieth-century descendants' (110). See also Ian Hacking, *The Emergence of Probability: A Philosophical Study of Early Ideas about Probability, Induction, and Statistical Inference* (Cambridge 1975), for the philosophical context of the 17th and 18th centuries.

17 See Lorraine J. Daston, 'The Domestication of Risk: Mathematical Probability and Insurance, 1650–1830' (237–60) and her 'Rational Individuals versus Laws of Society: From Probability to Statistics' (295–304), in Lorenz Kruger, Lorraine J. Daston, and Michael Heidelberger, eds., *The Probabilistic Revolution*, vol. 1, *Ideas in History* (Cambridge, Mass. 1987). Several other articles in this volume deal directly with the relationship between the probabilistic revolution and the social sciences, but see esp. Stephen M. Stigler, 'The Measurement of Uncertainty in Nineteenth-Century Social Science' (287–92) and M. Norton Wise, 'How Do Sums Count? On the Cultural Origins of Statistical Causality' (395–425). In Lorenz Kruger, Gerd Gigerenzer, and Mary S. Morgan, eds., *The Probabilistic Revolution*, vol. 2, *Ideas in the Sciences* (Cambridge, Mass. 1987), see Anthony Oberschall, 'The Two Empirical Roots of Social Theory and the Probability Revolution' (103–37).

18 Daston, 'Domestication of Risk,' 237–8

19 See Haskell, *Professional Social Science.*

20 Ibid., 13–14

21 Neil Austin Semple, 'The Impact of Urbanization on the Methodist Church in Central Canada, 1854–1884,' PHD thesis, U of T (1979), 169–206 passim. See also A.B. McKillop, 'Canadian Methodism in 1884,' Canadian Methodist Historical Society *Papers* 4 (1984), 23 passim.

22 Nathanael Burwash, *The History of Victoria College* (Toronto 1927), 469–70

23 Ibid.

24 Allan Smith, 'The Myth of the Self-made Man in English Canada, 1850–1914,' CHR 59 (June 1978), 203 passim. See also Michael Bliss, *A Living Profit: Studies in the Social History of Canadian Business, 1883–1911* (Toronto 1974).

25 See *QJ* (20 Nov. 1890); Charles M. Johnston, *McMaster University*, vol. 1, *The Toronto Years* (Toronto 1976), 73; 'Exchanges,' *QJ* (9 Nov. 1910). See also J.B. Hicks, 'Christian Success,' *AV* (4 Jan.1886); (anon.), 'A Plea for the Small College,' *In Cap and Gown* (UWO) (Feb. 1908); C. Macmillan, 'The University and the Freshman,' *University Magazine* 10 (Apr. 1911).

26 W.J. Alexander, ed., *The University of Toronto and Its Colleges, 1827–1906* (Toronto 1906), 90

27 'About the Origin and Development of Some Subjects of University Study Here and Elsewhere,' *QJ* (16 Dec. 1893)

28 Hilda Neatby, *Queen's University*, vol. 1, *1841–1917: And Not to Yield*, ed. Frederick W. Gibson and Roger Graham (Montreal/Kingston 1978), 217–22, 275–8

29 John Watson, 'Thirty Years in the History of Queen's University,' *QQ*, 10 (Oct. 1902), 193–5

30 Watson, 'Thirty Years'

31 Alan Franklin Bowker, 'Truly Useful Men: Maurice Hutton, George Wrong, James Mavor and the University of Toronto, 1880–1917,' PHD thesis, U of T (1975), 16

32 Alexander, ed., *Toronto*, 86–8

33 A.B. McKillop, *A Disciplined Intelligence: Critical Inquiry and Canadian Thought in the Victorian Era* (Montreal/Kingston 1979), 23–58, 161–2, 263

34 *QJ* (26 Nov. 1898)

35 McKillop, *Disciplined Intelligence*, 171–84

36 John Watson, 'Edward Caird as Teacher and Thinker,' *QQ* 16 (Apr., May, June 1909), 304–5

37 See Clifford J. Williams, 'The Political Philosophy of Two Canadians: John Watson and Wilfred Currier Kierstead,' MA thesis, UWO (1952), 1.

38 McKillop, *Disciplined Intelligence*, 206–12

39 See *QJ* (18 Feb. 1886).

40 Maurice Mandelbaum, *History, Man, and Reason: A Study in Nineteenth-Century Thought* (Baltimore 1971), 263

41 John Watson, *An Outline of Philosophy* (Glasgow 1901), 229

42 Ibid., 228–31

43 Ibid., 232

44 George Paxton Young, *The Ethics of Freedom: Notes, Selected, Translated and Arranged by His Pupil James Gibson Hume* (Toronto 1911). See Leslie Armour and Elizabeth Trott, 'George Paxton Young and the Foundations of Ethics,' in *The Faces of Reason: An Essay on Philosophy and Culture in English Canada, 1850–1950* (Waterloo 1981), 85–104; McKillop, *Disciplined Intelligence*, 200.

45 I.M. Greengarten, *Thomas Hill Green and the Development of Liberal-Democratic Thought* (Toronto 1981), 5

46 Reba N. Soffer, *Ethics and Society in England: The Revolution in the Social Sciences, 1870–1914* (Los Angeles 1978), 25. See also Melvin Richter, *The Politics of Conscience* (London 1964), 176.

47 For the example of Watson, see McKillop, *Disciplined Intelligence*, 206–8, 212–16. By the 1890s the assumptions of liberal Protestantism had penetrated substantially beyond the rarified atmosphere of the universities. See for example the summary of its tenets by the Protestant Chaplain of the Reformatory for Boys at Penetanguishene, Rev Stephen Card, in *The Atonement and Modern Liberalism* (Toronto 1892), 1–7.

48 Mandelbaum, *History, Man, and Reason*, 263

49 J.G. Hume, 'Professor George Paxton Young,' *UTM* 28 (Oct. 1927), 21–2

50 Lilian Vaux MacKinnon, *Miriam of Queen's* (Toronto 1921), 122, 263, 220, 66. Bio-

graphical details on MacKinnon are from the finding aid for her papers in QUA. See also Lillian (*sic*) Vaux MacKinnon, "'We Only Followed Geordie,'" *Queen's Alumni Review* (July/Aug. 1968), 98–9, 115.

51 Paul Rutherford, *A Victorian Authority: The Daily Press in Late Nineteenth-Century Canada* (Toronto 1982), 176–81 passim

52 Ibid., 19, Table 6, 'Comparative salary and wage levels in manufacturing 1901'

53 Ibid., 16–24; Gregory S. Kealey, *Toronto Workers Respond to Industrial Capitalism, 1867–1892* (Toronto 1980)

54 Robin S. Harris, *A History of Higher Education in Canada, 1663–1960* (Toronto 1976), 141–2; J.G. Bourinot, 'The Study of Political Science in Canadian Universities,' *Transactions of the Royal Society of Canada* (1880), 3–16. See also J.W. Burrow, *A Liberal Descent: Victorian Historians and the English Past* (Cambridge 1983); T.W. Heyck, *The Transformation of Intellectual Life in Victorian England* (London 1982).

55 William Houston to G.W. Ross (17 Sept. 1884), DEC, box 6, AO. Houston, a person of 'advanced' political views, was an active worker for the Liberal party and a vocal advocate of coeducation in his Alma Mater. He also desperately coveted a university appointment and during the 1880s applied for appointments in political science, English, and history at the U of T. That he was a constant bother to President Wilson is evidenced in numerous derogatory references in Wilson's diary throughout the decade. See also Ian M. Drummond, *Political Economy at the University of Toronto: A History of the Department, 1888–1982* (Toronto 1983), 17–18.

56 William Houston to G.W. Ross (n.d. Nov. 1887), DEC, box 6, AO

57 See Furner, *Advocacy and Objectivity*, ch. 1, 'Reform versus Knowledge,' 10–34.

58 William Mulock to G.W. Ross (7 Apr. 1888), DEC, box 9, AO

59 Daniel Wilson to G.W. Ross (21 Apr. 1887), DEC, box 14, AO

60 Tory Hoff, 'The Controversial Appointment of James Mark Baldwin to the University of Toronto in 1889,' MA thesis, Carleton (1980). ch. 2, n58 (unpaginated)

61 Drummond, *Political Economy*, 18–19, 25

62 See Oliver Mowat to Edward Blake (6 and 12 June 1888), DEC, box 9, AO

63 W.J. Ashley to G.W. Ross (21 Mar. 1889), DEC, box 1, AO

64 W.J. Ashley to G.W. Ross (n.d. Sept. 1888), DEC, box 1, AO

65 W.J. Ashley to G.W. Ross, (n.d. Sept. 1888), DEC, box 1, AO

66 W.J. Ashley to G.W. Ross (23 Mar.1891), DEC, box 1, AO

67 Shortt, *Search*, 95–6

68 This is the premise of S.E.D. Shortt (in *Search*), whose equation of late 19th-century idealism with a commitment to intuition causes confusion in his book. For criticism along these lines, see A.B. McKillop, 'Moralists and Moderns,' JCS 14 (Winter 1979–80), 144–50. For a discussion of Watson's 'objective idealism,' see McKillop, 'John Watson and the Idealist Legacy,' *Canadian Literature* 83 (Winter 1979), 72–89.

69 Quoted in Shortt, *Search*, 103

70 Quoted in ibid., 104

71 For bibliographical listing of published pieces by Shortt on these and other topics, see Shortt, *Search,* 198–200. For an indication of the curricular reorientation of the teaching of political economy, compare the *Calendar of Queen's College and University, 1886–7,* part 1 (Kingston 1886), 51, when Watson taught the subject, with that of 1904–5 (83–5), when Adam Shortt taught it. 'The lectures,' said the calendar in the latter year, 'will include a critical examination of the leading theories of the State, and a discussion of the nature of Social and Political Relations.'

72 Ashley's close links with late 19th-century British idealism are examined in Sara Z. Burke's doctoral thesis, '"Seeking the Highest Good": Social Service at the University of Toronto, 1888–1940,' Carleton (1993).

73 Quoted in Drummond, *Political Economy,* 21

74 Ibid.

75 Quoted in Paul Craven, *'An Impartial Umpire': Industrial Relations and the Canadian State, 1900–1911* (Toronto 1980), 44

76 Copy of a petition to G.W. Ross, signed in Toronto (4 Aug. 1892), DEC, box 13, AO

77 Drummond, *Political Economy,* 29

78 The telephones book was 'edited' and published by the American Telephone and Telegraph Company; the hydro book was financed by the National (USA) Electric Light Association. By the time of the publication of these books, Mavor had cultivated influential friends in the business community, including Sir Edmund Walker, Zebulon Lash, and Sir William Mackenzie (Shortt, *Search,* 123).

79 Quoted in Craven, *'Impartial Umpire,'* 47. As for Shortt: 'In economics he considered the "whole commercial network of the country ... one vast co-operative society" requiring only minimum intervention to function smoothly. Industrialization, far from being a step towards social disintegration, was both an inevitable and progressive step for man' (*Search,* 108).

80 Drummond, *Political Economy,* 110. Adam Shortt was also committed to the role of the expert: 'We should have in this country a body of experts to pass upon the plans and premises that are brought forward by the corporation ... to see that the public are being told the facts ...' (quoted in Shortt, *Search,* 110).

81 Drummond, *Political Economy,* 30

82 Quoted in Craven, *'Impartial Umpire,'* 61. The diary entry is that of 27 Aug. 1895. Craven makes a convincing case that the 'intellectual formation' of King was rooted in his studies at Toronto as much as it was in his later graduate work at the University of Chicago and Harvard University. See ch. 2, 'The Intellectual Formation of Mackenzie King,' 31–73; see also Drummond, *Political Economy,* 33–4.

83 William Lyon Mackenzie King Papers, 'Speeches,' MG26, J5 vol. 5, D3021, NAC

84 Craven, 'Excursus: *Industry and Humanity,'* in *'Impartial Umpire,'* 74–89. See also Ramsay Cook, 'The Modern Pilgrim's Progress,' ch. 11 in *The Regenerators: Social Criticism in Late Victorian English Canada* (Toronto 1985), 196–227.

85 Antonio Gramsci, *Selections from the Prison Notebooks* (New York 1971), 5. Gram-

sci distinguishes between 'traditional' and 'organic' intellectuals. An example of the former is the clergy; of the latter, 'professionals' such as engineers.

86 See Ralph Miliband, *Marxism and Politics* (Oxford 1977), 57–9.

87 See Furner, *Advocacy and Objectivity*, 14–18.

88 Biographical details have been drawn from Barry Glen Ferguson, 'The New Political Economy and Canadian Liberal-Democratic Thought: Queen's University, 1890– 1925,' PHD thesis, U of T (1982), 30–3.

89 Neatby, *Queen's*, 273

90 Skelton to Shortt (27 July 1907); quoted in Ferguson, 'Political Economy,' 36

91 See Ferguson, 'Political Economy,' 57.

92 'The Philosophy of History,' *QJ* (2 Feb. 1912)

93 'Philosophy of History.' See also Doug Owram, 'Economic Thought in the 1930s: The Prelude to Keynesianism,' *CHR* 66 (Sept. 1985), 352–3.

94 'Political Science Teaching,' *TG* (28 Aug. 1905)

95 'University Plans a Broad Course in Social Service ...,' *TS* (23 Feb. 1912)

CHAPTER 9   *Christianity and Culture*

1 Michael Gauvreau, *The Evangelical Century: College and Creed in English Canada from the Great Revival to the Great Depression* (Montreal/Kingston1991), 91–124. The question of the degree to which English-Canadian culture and society was 'secularized' between 1850 and 1940 is contentious and unresolved. See Marguerite Van Die, *An Evangelical Mind: Nathanael Burwash and the Methodist Tradition in Canada, 1839–1918* (Montreal/Kingston 1989); David B. Marshall, *Secularizing the Faith: Canadian Protestant Clergy and the Crisis of Belief, 1850–1940* (Toronto 1992); Phyllis D. Airhart, *Serving the Present Age: Revivalism, Progressivism, and the Methodist Tradition in Canada* (Montreal/Kingston 1992). For brief treatment of major interpretive differences, see also Chad Reimer, 'Religion and Culture in Nineteenth-Century English Canada,' *JCS* 25 (Spring 1990), 192–203; Michael Gauvreau, 'Beyond the Half-Way House: Evangelicalism and the Shaping of English Canadian Culture,' *Acadiensis* 20 (Spring 1991), 158–77; A.B. McKillop, 'Culture, Intellect, and Context,' *JCS* 24 (Autumn 1989), 7–31.

2 *QJ* (18 Jan. 1901), 132

3 Ibid., 133

4 See Richard Allen, *The Social Passion: Religion and Social Reform in Canada, 1914–28* (Toronto 1973); William R. Hutchison, *The Modernist Impulse in American Protestantism* (London 1976).

5 For the accommodating influence of idealism, see A.B. McKillop, *A Disciplined Intelligence: Critical Inquiry and Canadian Thought in the Victorian Era* (Montreal/ Kingston 1979), 205–32; on higher criticism see, e.g., Lawrence Burkholder, 'Canadian Methodism and Higher Criticism, 1860–1910,' essay (n.p., n.d.), UCCA; Gauvreau, *Evangelical Century*, passim; Charles M. Johnston, *McMaster University*,

vol. 1, *The Toronto Years* (Toronto 1976), 95–6 passim.

6 For Dewart's views on biblical criticism, see E.H. Dewart, *The Bible Under Higher Criticism: A Review of Current Evolution Theories about the Old Testament* (Toronto 1900). See also Van Die, *Evangelical Mind*, 102–5.

7 See G.C. Workman, 'Messianic Prophecy,' *AV* (May 1890), 10–12.

8 See C.B. Sissons, *A History of Victoria University* (Toronto 1952), 192–3. For discussion of Burwash, see Van Die, *Evangelical Mind*, 89–113 passim.

9 Van Die, *Evangelical Mind*, 106

10 Burkholder, 'Canadian Methodism,' 24. Late in his life Workman indicated some of the theological implications of his liberal Protestantism: 'Historical exegesis makes it possible to prove that the accounts of the virgin birth of Jesus are traditional, that his oneness with the Father was ethical, that his resurrection from the dead was spiritual, that his state of pre-existence was impersonal, and that his place in the Trinity is experimental' (*Jesus the Man and Christ the Spirit* [New York 1928], 10–11).

11 Burkholder, 'Canadian Methodism,' 28–30, 35

12 S.D. Chown, 'The Light and the Lantern,' *Canadian Methodist Magazine* (Mar.-Apr. 1895), 115. See also Airhart, *Serving the Present Age*, 57–8.

13 Gauvreau argues that evangelical leaders in religious colleges attempted to 'tame' both higher criticism and evolutionary theory by forging a 'reverent' criticism that attempted to reconcile scriptural authority and historical accuracy (*Evangelical Century*, 150).

14 Van Die, *Evangelical Mind*, 111–13. For a brief but judicious account of the Jackson controversy, see also Sissons, *Victoria*, 233–9.

15 'Principal Grant's Address,' *QJ* (5 Mar. 1892), 125. See also 'Dr Briggs' Monday Address,' in the same issue. William Briggs, the steward of the Methodist Book Room in Toronto, had been invited to Queen's to address a mixed class of divinity and arts students on the subject 'Problems, Methods and Results of Higher Criticism' (126–7). Briggs also held liberal views regarding the Bible, choosing to regard the first two chapters of Genesis as 'two different poems' and 'Esther, Job and Jonah to be fiction.' The philosophical and theological foundations of G.M. Grant's thought are discussed in Hubert R. Krygsman, '"Practical Preaching," The Liberal Theology of George M. Grant,' MA thesis, Calgary (1986): 'To reconcile reason, religion, and practice [Grant] adopted an objective idealism that was based on divine immanence. For Grant, secular reality was the progressive manifestation of God's spirit, and all of life was religion' (iii). Michael Gauvreau stresses Grant's evangelical credentials while diminishing the influence of idealism upon him (*Evangelical Century*, 155–60).

16 John Watson, 'Some Remarks on Biblical Criticism,' *QJ* (17 Nov. 1894), 23–7

17 Watson, 'Biblical Criticism,' 26. The higher criticism receives virtually no mention in the official history of Queen's Theological College. See George Rawlyk and Kevin Quinn, *The Redeemed of the Lord Say So: A History of Queen's Theological College, 1912–1972* (Kingston 1980).

18 'Strife' is the title of Charles M. Johnston's excellent chapter on these years (*McMaster* 1, 90–113).

19 Johnston, *McMaster* 1, 90–2

20 For background on Harper and the University of Chicago, see Laurence R. Veysey, *The Emergence of the American University* (Chicago 1965), 366–80.

21 Johnston, *McMaster* 1, 96

22 Ibid., 99

23 Ibid., 103. For an alternate view of modernism at McMaster, as well as a defence of Harris, see Clark H. Pinnock, 'The Modernist Impulse at McMaster University, 1887–1927,' in Jarold K. Zeman, ed., *Baptists in Canada* (Burlington 1980), 193–207.

24 Johnston, *McMaster* 1, 104

25 Quoted in ibid., 105, italics in original

26 Ibid., 106–7

27 'Influence of College Life Upon Personal Religion,' *AV* (Oct. 1890), 10–12

28 'Valedictory for Divinity, Read by Neil M'Pherson, MA,' *QJ* (6 May 1893), 176, italics in original

29 Quoted in Rawlyk and Quinn, *Redeemed*, 7. See also Hilda Neatby, *Queen's University*, vol. 1, *1841–1917: And Not to Yield*, ed. Frederick W. Gibson and Roger Graham (Montreal/Kingston), 231–5.

30 *QJ* (17 Mar. 1894), 147

31 *QJ* (15 Dec. 1894), 54

32 *QJ* (27 Nov. 1897), 38–9

33 See 'Reason, Religion, and the Idea of Nature: George Blewett and James Ten Broeke,' in Leslie Armour and Elizabeth Trott, *The Faces of Reason: An Essay on Philosophy and Culture in English Canada, 1850–1950* (Waterloo 1981), 231–60.

34 A.L.B., '10, 'Editorial, "The Old Order Changeth, Yielding Place to New,"' *AV* (Mar. 1909), 486–7

35 'A Student Problem – Losing One's Religion,' *QJ* (11 May 1907), 447–9

36 F.L. Farewell, BA, 'The Relation of the Church to Human Needs and Forces,' *AV* (Apr. 1910), 454

37 'Religion in the College,' *AV* (Oct. 1904), 52

38 Albert H. Abbott, 'Essential Christianity,' *AV* (Jan. 1911), 212–18, emphasis in original

39 Ibid., 214, 216

40 Ibid., 218. See also Albert H. Abbott, BA, 'Thoughts on Philosophy,' *UTQ* 2 (Jan. 1896), 133–47, for an indication of his commitment to absolute idealism.

41 See, e.g., A Graduate, 'The Class in Theology, 1900,' *MUM* (Nov. 1900), 69–73; W.E. Matthews, '05 (Arts), 'What M'Master Means to the Student for the Ministry,' *MUM* (Apr. 1906), 289–93.

42 Barton quoted by T.J. Jackson Lears, 'From Salvation to Self-Realization: Advertising and the Therapeutic Roots of the Consumer Culture, 1880–1930,' in Richard

Wightman Fox and T.J. Jackson Lears, eds., *The Culture of Consumption* (New York 1983), 31. See esp. the section of Lears's essay entitled 'Therapy, Advertising, and Doubt: Bruce Barton,' 30–8.

43 W.T. Herridge, '"Baccalaureate Sermon,"' *QJ* (5 May 1896), 193–4

44 Armour and Trott, *Faces of Reason*, 354–60

45 Lears, 'Salvation to Self–Realization,' 3–38

46 Ibid., 15. See also Jackson Lears, *No Place of Grace: Antimodernism and the Transformation of American Culture, 1880–1920* (New York 1981); Christopher Lasch, *The Culture of Narcissism* (New York 1979) and his *The Minimal Self: Psychic Survival in Troubled Times* (New York 1984).

47 Quoted in McKillop, *Disciplined Intelligence*, 222

48 *QJ* (9 Nov. 1910), 82

49 See Henry Wilkes Wright, *Self-Realization: An Outline of Ethics* (New York 1913), 209; *Faith Justified by Progress* (New York 1916). Wright was professor of philosophy at the University of Manitoba and was largely responsible for founding its department of psychology.

50 Rev Joseph F. McFadyen, MA, *Jesus and Life* (New York 1917), 13–14

51 Ibid., 15–20

52 Rev James Binnie, MA, 'The Basis of a Working Theology,' *QJ* (8 Feb. 1911), 326

53 Ibid., 327

54 Matthew Arnold, *Culture and Anarchy* (Cambridge 1948), 45

55 See Henry Hubert, *Harmonious Perfection: The Development of English Studies in Nineteenth-Century Anglo-Canadian Colleges* (East Lansing 1993); Patricia Jasen, 'Arnoldian Humanism, English Studies, and the Canadian University,' *QQ* 95 (Autumn 1988), 550–3; Malcolm Bradbury, *The Social Context of Modern English Literature* (Oxford 1971), 36–66.

56 See ch. 5, above.

57 Hubert, *Harmonious Perfection*, ch. 5: 'Specialization, Idealism, and British Literature in Canada: 1884–1900.' For the complementarity of philosophical idealism and the study of literature, see John Watson, 'The Study of Literature,' *CEM* 8 (1886), 48–53. At times, the linkage was direct. The host of the first of several 'English Conferences,' held at Saskatoon in 1926, was R.A. Wilson, head of the English department of the University of Saskatchewan. He was described by Watson Kirkconnell, who attended, as 'an old disciple of John Watson, [who] had just completed an erudite volume on the metaphysical implications of language ...' (quoted in Heather Murray, 'English Studies in Canada to 1945: A Bibliographic Essay,' *English Studies in Canada* 17 [Dec. 1991], 449).

58 When Arnold visited Toronto in 1884 he met with a decidedly mixed reception. The elitist nature of his view of culture rankled some in his audience. See Barbara Opala, 'Matthew Arnold in Canada,' MA thesis, McGill (1968). On the occasion of Arnold's arrival in 1884, The Toronto *Evening News*, for example, published the following doggerel, entitled, 'To Mr. Arnold ... Greetings!' to welcome the famous poet:

Dear friend, if thou would'st so be called
Talk on the topics of the place
Tell us what votes, and how, were polled
In that corrupt Algoma case.

Alas! not sweetness and not light,
Can ever in our ears supplant
Your views upon the boundary fight,
Or that Pacific railway grant.   (quoted in Opala, 33)

59 Daniel Wilson quoted in Robin S. Harris, *English Studies at Toronto: A History* (Toronto 1988), 29
60 Archibald Lampman quoted in Margerie Fee, 'English-Canadian Literary Criticism, 1890–1950: Defining and Establishing a National Literature,' PHD thesis, U of T (1981), 206–7
61 See Anna Sonser, '"A Respectable English Education": Innovation and Tradition in Literary Studies at Wesleyan Ladies' College (1861–1897),' *English Studies in Canada* 19 (Mar. 1993), 96–101
62 *Varsity* (5 Dec. 1885)
63 Editorial, 'The Study of English' *Varsity* (21 Feb. 1885)
64 'The Claims of Nationality,' *Varsity* (17 Nov. 1888)
65 Pelham Edgar, 'Modern Authors in the English Course,' *Varsity* (23 Mar. 1889), letter to editor
66 Alexander quoted in Hubert, *Harmonious Perfection*
67 Alexander quoted in Harris, *English Studies*, 34–5
68 See W.J. Alexander and M.F. Bibby, *Composition from Models for Use in Schools and Colleges* (Toronto 1894).
69 Chris Baldick, *The Social Mission of English Criticism, 1848–1932* (Oxford 1983), 53
70 Matthew Arnold, 'The Study of Poetry' (1880), quoted in Patricia Jasen, 'The English Canadian Liberal Arts Curriculum: An Intellectual History, 1800–1950,' PHD thesis, Manitoba (1987), 176–7
71 W.E. McNeill, 'James Cappon,' in *Some Great Men of Queen's* (Kingston 1941), 74
72 S.E.D. Shortt, *The Search for an Ideal: Six Canadian Intellectuals and Their Convictions in an Age of Transition, 1890–1930* (Toronto 1976), 64–7
73 Quoted in Shortt, *Search*, 66
74 Chris Baldick's definition of ideology bears noting: '... those usually unspoken assumptions upon which the most untheoretical, undogmatic, and "common-sense" arguments rest; in particular the assumption that the existing institutions and values of society are natural and eternal rather than artificial and temporary' (*Social Mission*, 2).

75 Quoted in Shortt, *Search*, 74

76 Hutton quoted in ibid., 82–3

77 See Carl Berger, *The Writing of Canadian History: Aspects of English-Canadian Historical Writing since 1900*, 2nd ed. (Toronto 1986), 11–13.

78 Cappon quoted in Shortt, *Search*, 63. See also Harris, *English Studies*, 33, for enrolment statistics in the U of T English department, 1890–1905.

79 Robin S. Harris, *A History of Higher Education in Canada, 1663–1960* (Toronto 1976), 247

80 See Baldick, *Social Mission*, 62–3. The connection between criticism and appreciation is examined in Bruce Robbins, *Secular Vocations: Intellectuals, Professionalism, Culture* (London 1993), 62. For an indication of the impact of the Arnoldian approach to culture and literature on the teaching profession – which speaks to its diffusion into the secondary school system in Ontario – see D.R. Keys, 'Our Debt as Teachers to Matthew Arnold,' *Proceedings of the 35th Annual Convention of the Ontario Educational Association: Held in Toronto on the 7th, 8th, and 9th of April 1896* (Toronto 1896), 126–36. David R. Keys, an unsuccessful applicant for the English chair at Toronto in 1889, became W.J. Alexander's assistant. Until his promotion to associate professor in 1903 he had spent 20 years at the rank of lecturer. See Harris, *English Studies*, 29–32.

81 J.F. Macdonald, 'The Philosophy of Matthew Arnold,' *QQ* 20 (Jan., Feb., Mar. 1913), 333–4

82 Alfred Reynar quoted in Hubert, *Harmonious Perfection*. See also Alfred H. Reynar, 'Literature and Culture,' *CEM* 11 (1889), 125–31.

83 For general treatment of this theme see Ramsay Cook, *The Regenerators: Social Criticism in Late Victorian English Canada* (Toronto 1985).

84 'The Alumni Conference,' *QJ* (3 Nov. 1910), 48–9

85 'Christian Culture,' *AV* (Nov. 1895), 49–50, and (Dec. 1895), 90–93. See also 'Culture and Victoria,' *AV* ((Jan. 1913), 214.

86 Daniel Miner Gordon, 'Culture and Religion,' *Theologue* (Jan. 1901), 195

87 Gordon, 'Culture and Religion,' 196–205

CHAPTER 10   *Marching as to War*

1 'Conversazione Was Brilliant – Successful Function at Western University – Concerts and Promenade,' unidentified clipping in 'University of Western Ontario Scrapbook' 1 (1903–6), 'presented by Mr Fred Landon,' UWO Archives. See also 'Brilliant Event at the University – Annual Conversazione a Delightful Function – Five Hundred Guests Present,' ibid., identified as 1903.

2 'Conversazione Was Brilliant'

3 See 'Jap Supremacy – Interesting Debate Between Students of OAC and Western University' (1905) and 'Have Non-Church University or None at All – Students of Western Do Not Want It Run by Diocese of Huron – Strong Reasons Given' (1906), ibid.

4 William Ferguson Tamblyn, *These Sixty Years: An Unconventional Chronicle of the Lives, the Faith, the Labour and the Comradeship that Have Gone into the Building of 'Western's' Household of Learning* (London 1938), esp. ch. 2, 'General Student Life, 1895–1908,' 19–34, and ch. 4, 'General Student Life, 1908–1924,' 68–88. See also James J. Talman and Ruth Davis Talman, *'Western' – 1878–1953: Being the History of the Origins and Development of the University of Western Ontario during Its First Seventy-Five Years* (London 1953), 53

5 J.R.W. Gwynne-Timothy, *Western's First Century* (n.p. 1978), 209. Gwynne-Timothy provides no account of student activities or concerns for these years.

6 *University of Ottawa: A Tradition for Tomorrow* (Ottawa 1990), 18–19. For examination of one Ontario convent academy, see Elizabeth Smyth, '"A Noble Proof of Excellence": The Culture and Curriculum of a Nineteenth-Century Ontario Convent Academy,' in Ruby Heap and Alison Prentice, eds., *Gender and Education in Ontario: An Historical Reader* (Toronto 1991), 269–85.

7 *Tradition for Tomorrow*, 12; Laurence K. Shook, *Catholic Post-Secondary Education in English-Speaking Canada* (Toronto 1971), 253–4

8 See Franklin A. Walker, *Catholic Education and Politics in Ontario: A Documentary Study* (Toronto 1964), 126–296 passim; Roger Guindon, *Coexistence Difficile: La dualité linguistique à l'Université d'Ottawa*, vol. 1, *1848–1898* (Ottawa 1989). See also Margaret Prang, 'Clerics, Politicians, and the Bilingual Schools Issue in Ontario, 1910–1917,' *CHR* 41 (1960), 281–307; Marilyn Barber, 'The Ontario Bilingual School Issue: Sources of Conflict,' *CHR* 47 (1966), 227–48; John H. Taylor, *Ottawa: An Illustrated History* (Toronto 1986), 150–4.

9 C.C. Sinclair, '02, 'College News: Around the Hall,' *MUM* (Nov. 1900), 86–95

10 J.F. Ingram to A.C. McKay (6 Jan. 1908), quoted in Charles M. Johnston, *McMaster University*, vol. 1, *The Toronto Years* (Toronto 1976), 115

11 Ibid., 117

12 Quoted in ibid.

13 R.E. Freeman, '14, 'College News: Around the Hall,' *MUM* (Nov. 1913), 68

14 T.A. Reed, ed., *A History of the University of Trinity College, Toronto, 1852–1952* (Toronto 1952), 92. Published without designated authors as a 'Special Centennial Issue' of the *Trinity Review*, Trinity College, Toronto. Material in this and following paragraph from 62–3, 77, 93–4, 94, 97.

15 Maurice Hutton, 'The Arts Colleges: University College,' in W.J. Alexander, ed., *The University of Toronto and Its Colleges, 1827–1906* (Toronto 1906), 120–1

16 B.K. Sandwell, 'Student '97,' in Claude T. Bissell, ed., *University College: A Portrait, 1853–1953* (Toronto 1953), 114–16

17 Sandwell, 'Student '97,' 116

18 Ibid.; Alan Franklin Bowker, '"Truly Useful Men": Maurice Hutton, George Wrong, James Mavor, and the University of Toronto, 1880–1927,' PHD thesis, U of T (1975), 18–19

19 Sandwell, 'Student '97,' 117

20 As president, Wilson took an active interest in preventing students from being tainted by heterodox political and religious views. From an entry for 4 Nov. 1886 in the university's Natural Science Association Minute Book, 1: 'The Secretary read a communication from the College Registrar to the effect that none but Undergraduates in actual attendance at the College should take part in any of the College Associations without first having obtained the sanction of the President. Dr Wilson explained that this rule would not be enforced in our case, and was primarily intended for societies such as invited wild communists like Henry George' (200, UTA).

21 *Report of the Commissioners on the Discipline and Other Matters in the University of Toronto* (Toronto 1895), 7–10, 23–6 passim; Peter Razgaitis, 'A Synopsis of Events Surrounding the Student Strike of 1895,' in James Reaney, *The Dismissal: Or Twisted Beards and Tangled Whiskers* (Toronto 1977), 56–7; Robert Bothwell, *Laying the Foundation: A Century of History at University of Toronto* (Toronto 1991), 29–32; Paul T. Phillips, *Britain's Past in Canada: The Teaching and Writing of British History* (Vancouver 1989), 36–8; Paul Craven, *'An Impartial Umpire': Industrial Relations and the Canadian State, 1900–1911* (Toronto 1980), 50–1

22 *Report of the Commissioners*, 26

23 William Lyon Mackenzie King Diary (17 June 1895), NAC. For accounts of the extent to which King would go to prevent critical historical interpretations of his maternal grandfather's place in the Canadian liberal tradition, see A.B. McKillop, ed., *A Critical Spirit: The Thought of William Dawson LeSueur* (Toronto 1977), 247–64; W.D. LeSueur, *William Lyon Mackenzie: A Reinterpretation* (Toronto 1979), vii–xxvii.

24 Keith Walden, 'Respectable Hooligans: Male Toronto College Students Celebrate Hallowe'en, 1884–1910,' *CHR* 68 (Mar. 1987), 6

25 See Maurice Hutton, 'The Arts Colleges: University College,' in Alexander, *Toronto*, 121–2; R.E. Kingsford, 'Restoration of the Residence,' *Report of the Royal Commission on the University of Toronto* (Toronto 1906), 195.

26 Kingsford, 'Restoration of the Residence'

27 Sandwell, 'Student '97,' 117–18

28 *Report of the Royal Commission*, 182

29 Ibid., xix, 165

30 *QJ* (8 Nov. 1890), 2; (10 Dec. 1890), 34; (1 Dec.1894), 48

31 *QJ* (16 Nov. 1910), 93. In the official report from the Queen's department of history for the academic year 1911–12, Professor Morison wrote: 'I could wish that apart from definite examination and essay work, there was more real interest in reading for its own sake; apart from that want on the part of the students, which concerns not History alone, but all the Departments, I have no reason to complain. If anything could be done to cut down social functions, work would greatly gain' (*ROP, 1911–12* [Kingston 1912], 10).

32 'Enthusiasm in the University – An Interview Criticized by President Loudon,' *TM*

(18 Nov. 1899); 'Varsity's Big Program Ready for Next Week – Lectures and Tennis Tournament Begin Monday – Receptions to Freshies and Freshettes Follow – The Difficulties of Enrollment – Students Awed by Display of Faculty Robes,' *TS* (1 Oct. 1910)

33 'The Week at Varsity,' *TT* (6 Feb. 1911)

34 On partyism, see *QJ* (20 Mar. 1891), 145; (20 Jan. 1892); 'Political Partyism at Queen's,' *QJ* (27 Nov. 1913). On socialism, see *QJ* (4 Apr. 1896), 17?; review of Agnes Maule Machar's *Roland Graeme, Knight, QJ* (21 Jan. 1893), 74–5. On American Expansionism, see 'American Expansion,' *QJ* (24 Dec. 1898), 56–7. On prohibition, see 'The Present Phase of the Prohibition Question,' *QJ* (1 Apr. 1899), 152–3. On combines, see 'Editorial,' *QJ* (12 Feb. 1914), 4–5. Although illustrations have here been drawn from Queen's, other universities also exhibited degrees of social concern. See, e.g., W.A. Lamport, 'Is the Baptist Position in Reference to the Manitoba School Question Consistent?' *MUM* (Apr. 1896), 296–304; George J. Menge, 'The Social Problem,' ibid. (Mar. 1901), 255–60. For Victoria University, using *AV* as a source, see 'Looking Backward' [review of Edward Bellamy's *Looking Backward* (1888)] (Jan. 1890), 14–15; 'Editorial' [re labour–capital relations] (Dec. 1892), 3–4; W.G. Watson, 'Christian Socialism' (Feb. 1894), 154–9; W.J. Conoly, 'Compulsory Arbitration' (Dec. 1894), 84–6; A.H. Sinclair, 'Labour and Capital' (May 1896), 380–4; J.B. Gibson, 'Prohibition as a Problem of Individual and Social Reform' (Dec. 1890), 105–11, and (Feb. 1901), 248–56; F.L. Farewell, 'The Church and Social Problems' (Oct. 1903), 31–8; W.E. Gilroy, 'Christian Socialism' (Dec. 1903), 224–9. The list could be expanded greatly.

35 See, e.g.: 'The Student's Attitude Toward the Everyday World,' *AV* (Nov. 1900), 71–2; 'What a College Course Should Be,' *AV* (Feb. 1899), 367–70; R.H. Bell, 'Some Manifestations of Our College Life,' *AV* (Apr. 1899), 455–62; 'The Student's Attitude to College Activities,' *AV* (Oct. 1902), 37; 'Student Life at Victoria,' *AV* (June 1905), 556–9.

36 'Missionary Association,' *QJ* (22 Nov. 1873), 6; 'Queen's College Missionary Association,' ibid. (16 Mar. 1886), 122–3; 'Intercollegiate Missionary Alliance,' *AV* (Dec. 1887), 6–7; 'The Sixth Annual Convention of the Canadian Inter-Collegiate Missionary Alliance,' *AV* (Dec. 1890), 19–21; 'Ninth Annual Report of the Fyfe Missionary Society,' *MUM* (Nov. 1891), 69–73; 'Thirteenth Annual Report of the Fyfe Missionary Society,' *MUM* (Jan. 1896), 170–7; 'Canadian Inter-Collegiate Missionary Alliance, Thirteenth Biennial Convention,' *MUM* (Dec. 1900), 121–5

37 See Rosemary R. Gagan, *A Sensitive Independence: Canadian Methodist Women Missionaries in Canada and the Orient, 1881–1925* (Montreal/Kingston 1992), 7–8. See also Ruth Compton Brouwer, *New Women for God: Canadian Presbyterian Women and India Missions, 1876–1914* (Toronto 1990); Jane Hunter, *The Gospel of Gentility: American Women Missionaries in Turn-of-the-Century China* (New Haven 1984).

38 C.B. Sissons, *A History of Victoria University* (Toronto 1952), 197. Nevertheless, it

should be noted that most Canadian women who became missionaries were not university graduates, particularly before the 20th century. The exception in the Methodist case was missions to Japan (Gagan, *A Sensitive Independence*, 36).

39 'Re-organization of the Missionary Society,' *AV* (Jan. 1892), 19
40 See Diana L. Pedersen, '"Keeping Our Good Girls Good": The Young Women's
Christian Association of Canada, 1870–1920,' MA thesis, Carleton (1981); Donald
Layton Kirkey, Jr, '"Building the City of God": The Founding of the Student Christian Movement of Canada,' MA thesis, McMaster (1983). Each issue of every student
newspaper contained missionary notices, but see, e.g.: 'The Origin of the Young
People's Forward Movement for Missions,' *AV* (May 1902), 446–8; 'Great Conven-
tion of Students Will Meet in Toronto,' *AV* (Jan. 1902), 239–40; A.B. Williams (Stu-
dents' YMCA Secretary for Canada and the East), 'A Significant Student
Movement,' *AV* (Mar. 1903), 401–3; J.G. Hume, 'The Canadian Colleges' Mission,'
AV (Dec. 1907), 198–200; 'A Summer in New Ontario,' *In Cap and Gown* [UWO]
(19 Feb. 1908), 102–4; 'Intercollegiate YMCA,' *QJ* (19 Nov. 1906), 88; 'Peregrine
Preachers or Practical Experiences in New Ontario,' *QJ* (15 Jan. 1907), 209–11;
'Protestant Missions,' *QJ* (1 Feb. 1907), 317–18; 'The Student Volunteer Band,' *QJ*,
16 Nov. 1910), 95; 'University Service – Rev J.D. Byrnes, Supt. of Missions, Gives
Us a Vivid Account of Conditions in Great North Country, and Future Prospects –
An Appeal for Help,' *QJ* (26 Jan. 1914), 1.
41 Alfred Fitzpatrick, *The University in Overalls* (Toronto 1920)
42 For examination of the connection between the English public school ethos and
'muscular Christianity,' see David Newsome, *Godliness and Good Learning* (London 1961), 80–2.
43 Reed, *Trinity*, 28; Hilda Neatby, *Queen's University*, vol. 1, *1841–1917: And Not to
Yield*, ed. Frederick W. Gibson and Roger Graham (Montreal/Kingston 1978), 143
44 A parallel occurrence should be mentioned. Keith Walden notes that the Toronto
male celebration of Hallowe'en began in 1884. This was only weeks after the first
female students attended lectures at the University of Toronto. Walden provides evidence in his article that the annual Hallowe'en ritual was not only very much a men's
affair, but also that student scorn was often directed at women, especially in the theatre: 'Instead of treating women with dignified respect, they blew kisses at actresses,
made loud smacks during love scenes, and embarrassed their fellows who dared to
bring female guests to the show.' After the annual episode at the theatre, noise-mak-
ing on the streets apparently reached its peak when the student mob reached the girls'
schools (Walden, 'Respectable Hooligans,' 15, 17, 25–6). See also K.G. Sheard and
E.G. Dunning, 'The Rugby Football Club as a Type of "Male Preserve": Some
Sociological Notes,' *International Review of Sport Sociology* 8 (1973), 5–21.
45 See 'The Foot-Ball Club,' *QJ* (31 Oct. 1874), 7; also (5 Apr. 1879), 1; (25 Oct.
1879), 1; (20 Dec. 1879), 50.
46 *QJ* (25 Nov. 1885), 30
47 Reed, 27–34; Sissons, *Victoria*, 202–3, 212–13; Neatby, *Queen's*, 200, 212–13; D.D.

Calvin, *Queen's University at Kingston* (Kingston 1941), 277–87

48 See J.A. Mangan, *Athleticism in the Victorian and Edwardian Public School: The Emergence and Consolidation of an Educated Ideology* (Cambridge 1981); J.A. Mangan, *The Games Ethic and Imperialism: Aspects of the Diffusion of an Ideal* (New York 1986).

49 See Ann Douglas, *The Feminization of American Culture* (New York 1977).

50 Quoted in Stow Persons, *The Decline of American Gentility* (New York 1973), 275

51 Joseph F. Kett, *Rites of Passage: Adolescence and Youth in America, 1790 to the Present* (New York 1977), 173; David I. Macleod, *Building Character in the American Boy: The Boy Scouts, YMCA, and Their Forerunners, 1870–1920* (Madison 1983), 44–5, passim; Carol Christ, 'Victorian Masculinity and the Angel in the House,' in Martha Vicinus, ed., *A Widening Sphere: Changing Roles of Victorian Women* (Bloomington 1980), 146–62

52 Charles Gordon, *Postscript to Adventure: The Autobiography of Ralph Connor* (Toronto 1975), 39–40

53 Senior, 'First Things in College Life,' *AV* (Oct. 1904), 27

54 Douglas, *Feminization*, 12, 23, 48–9

55 'Western Girls – Beware of Cosy Corners,' *In Cap and Gown* (Mar. 1908), 150–1. This item was signed: 'The One Who Peeped.'

56 A.P. Addison, 'The Ministry and Athletics,' *AV* (Apr. 1897), 361–2

57 R. Pearson, '04, 'Athletics and Religion,' *AV* (Mar. 1907), 366–70

58 N. Davies, '14, 'Athletics,' *MUM* (Feb. 1914), 222

59 *QJ* (2 Dec. 1893), 35. Symptomatic of the crassness of the American approach to organized athletics was the appearance of the 'professional coach' on its campuses, thereby undermining the assumption that organized 'manly games' should best be left to gentleman-amateurs. The innovation was roundly condemned in Canadian college circles, but by 1913 schools originally critical, such as Queen's, were coming to change their views, especially after suffering defeats by scores of 49–2. See 'Professional Coaching in Football,' *QJ* (19 Nov. 1906), 84; 'The Failure of Our Rugby Team – The Sporting Editor Gives His Views – Advocates Recognition of Athletes by Faculty, More Liberal Financial Support, and the Hiring of a Professional Coach,' *QJ* (16 Oct. 1913), 1; 'The Rugby Situation,' *QJ* (21 Oct. 1913), 2, 5.

60 'The College Man and Business,' *AV* (Feb. 1904), 333

61 'Editorials – Physical Education,' *QJ* (1 Mar. 1907), 342

62 R. Tait McKenzie, MD (professor of physical education and director of the department of physical education, University of Pennsylvania), *QJ* (1 Feb. 1907), 247. See also W.H.M., 'A History of the Gymnasium Movement in Queen's,' *QJ* (1 Feb. 1907), 243–6. On the connection between moral values, athletics, and militarism in the context of American higher education for this period, see Michael Pearlman, 'To Make the University Safe for Morality: Higher Education, Football and Military Training from the 1890s through the 1920s,' *Canadian Review of American Studies* 12 (Spring 1981), 37–56.

63 See Paul Fussell, *The Great War and Modern Memory* (New York 1975), 18–23 passim.

64 *QJ* (9 Nov. 1900), 50; *QJ* (7 Dec. 1900), 85

65 'Intercollege Football,' *In Cap and Gown* (Dec. 1907), 41

66 Rev S.W. Dyde, 'University Sermon – "The Game of Life,"' *QJ* (9 Dec. 1899), 66–7

67 Ibid., 67

68 *QJ* (16 Nov. 1910), 89–90

69 N. Davies, '14, 'Athletics,' *MUM* (Dec. 1913), 129. See Robert M. Stamp's treatment of imperialist ideology in the contents of the 1910 edition of the Ontario Fourth Reader, in Stamp, *The Schools of Ontario, 1876–1976* (Toronto 1982), 93–4.

70 O.D. Skelton to D.M. Gordon (17 Dec. 1913). D.M. Gordon Papers, box 3, section A, QUA. Gordon's 18-page unpublished speech, 'Universal military Training' (undated but clearly written around this time, and found in the same source), provides an elaborate rationale for extensive military training on campus. See also: Neatby, *Queen's*, 292; Hartley Munro Thomas, *The History of the UWO Contingent, COTC* (London 1956), 3–6.

71 William Peterson, *Canadian Essays and Addresses* (London 1915), 87–154; Cappon and Hutton quoted in S.E.D. Shortt, *The Search for an Ideal: Six Canadian Intellectuals and their Convictions in an Age of Transition* (Toronto 1976), 74–5, 91. See also Bowker, '"Truly Useful Men": Maurice Hutton, George Wrong, James Mavor and the University of Toronto, 1880–1917,' PHD thesis, U of T (1975), 50–71; Carl Berger, *The Sense of Power: Studies in the Ideas of Canadian Imperialism, 1867–1914* (Toronto 1970) passim.

72 *Varsity* did so in 1908; *QJ* in 1911.

73 The 'Gibson Girl,' the creation of lithographer Charles Dana Gibson, first appeared in *Life* magazine in the mid-1890s, marking a departure in the portrayal of American feminine beauty in mass magazines. For some feminists, she embodied the image of the new woman, for she was often portrayed in situations where either her independence and athletic capacity or her social graces were evident. See Lois W. Banner, *American Beauty* (New York 1983), ch. 8, 'The Gibson Girl,' 155–74.

74 'A Splendid Address – Principal Gordon Thinks Women's Sphere Has Now Extended to the State,' *QJ* (19 Jan. 1912), 3; *ROP, 1912–13* (Kingston 1913), 14–15; *ROP, 1911–12* (Kingston 1912), 23

75 *QJ* (3 Dec. 1906), 144

76 'Editorial Notes,' *MUM* (Mar. 1914), 255; 'Women's Department,' *MUM* (Apr. 1914), 315–16

77 Miss Mary Fowler, '14, 'Women's Department,' *MUM* (Feb. 1914), 7

78 Peter Ward, 'Courtship and Social Space in Nineteenth-Century English Canada,' *CHR* 68 (Mar. 1987), 56, 60–1. For revealing and sustained illustration of the academic life and undergraduate social arena of one Edwardian woman student (at Victoria College), see Kathleen Cowan, *It's Late, and All the Girls Have Gone: An Annesley Diary, 1907–1910*, ed. Aida Farrag Graff and David Knight (Toronto 1984).

79 See William R. Leach, 'Transformations in a Culture of Consumption: Women and Department Stores, 1899–1925,' *Journal of American History* 71 (Sept. 1984), 319–42. See also Paul Greenhalgh, *Ephemeral Vistas: The Expositions Universalles, Great Exhibitions and World's Fairs, 1851–1939* (Manchester 1988), 191. I am grateful to Keith Walden for drawing the works of Leach and Greenhalgh to my attention.

80 'Students Plead for Dancing at the Agricultural College – Largely Signed Petition Urging Its Permission Sent to the Minister of Agriculture,' Toronto *Mail and Empire* (9 Jan. 1911); 'About Our Social Affairs,' *QJ* (4 Dec. 1911), 1; 'Students May Dance at the University School,' *TG* (9 Oct. 1912)

81 'Tango Party Reprimanded – President Falconer Is Preparing a Statement,' *TN* (6 Dec. 1913)

82 See Ellen K. Rothman, *Hands and Hearts: A History of Courtship in America* (New York 1984), 211–12; Paula S. Fass, *The Damned and the Beautiful: American Youth in the 1920s* (New York 1977), 23–5.

83 'No Objectionable Tangoing at Varsity – Report of "Toronto Star" – Fancy Dances at Varsity Are Not of Indelicate Kind – President Falconer's Opinion,' *Varsity* (17 Dec. 1913)

84 'Flowers and Tango Under Student Ban – "Sentimental Corsages" Will Not Be Allowed at the Undergraduates' Dance,' *TN* (5 Feb. 1914); 'Cold Shoulder for Tango,' *TT* (14 Feb. 1914). Even at this – pre–lyric – stage of the social history of the tango, associations indeed abounded between the dance and sexuality, for the bordellos of Rio de Janiero were its home; prostitution became an important theme in tango lyrics. 'The tango,' wrote historian Donald S. Castro, 'both as a dance and as a song is filled with latent sexuality.' See Castro, 'Popular Culture as a Source for the Historians: The Tango in Its *Epoca de oro*, 1917–1943,' *Journal of Popular Culture* 20 (Winter 1986), 58. See also Castro, 'Popular Culture as a Source for the Historian: The Tango in Its Era of *La Guardia Vieja* [1870–1917],' *Studies in Latin American Popular Culture* 3 (1984), 70–85.

85 'When Students' Fancies Clash With Religion – What Will Methodists Do about Dancing? – Victoria College Craze,' *Montreal Star* (clipping, Dec. 1913), in 'Student Activities – General' file, vol. 20, file 1, UTA

CHAPTER 11   *The Great Divide*

1 Quoted in C.P. Stacey, *Canada and the Age of Conflict* 1 (Toronto 1977), 175. See also Ramsay Cook and Robert Craig Brown, *Canada, 1896–1921: A Nation Transformed* (Toronto 1974), 275. See also A.J.P. Taylor, *The First World War: An Illustrated History* (Harmondsworth 1966), 24, 20. For other recent studies of the war, see John Terraine, *The First World War, 1914–18* (London 1984); James L. Stokesbury, *A Short History of World War I* (New York 1981). For Canada's involvement in it, see Stacey, *Canada*, 172–239; Desmond Morton, *A Military History of Canada* (Edmonton 1985), 130–72.

2   Morton, *Military History*, 136

3   Ibid., 156, 158. Morton properly points out, however, that claims for the failure of conscription are based on hindsight, for 'no one in 1917 knew that the war would be over in a year.'

4   The national census of 1911 showed Ontario to be a province of 2,527,292 people; a decade later its population stood at 2,933,622.

5   Joseph Schull, *Ontario since 1867* (Toronto 1978), 214

6   *Census of Canada, 1931*, 1 (Ottawa 1931), Table 9

7   Falconer quoted in *University of Toronto Roll of Service, 1914–1918* (Toronto 1921), xi; also *TS* (29 Sept. 1914). For similar addresses by Falconer to students, given in the academic year 1914–15, see his *The German Tragedy and the Meaning for Canada* (Toronto 1915).

8   'Principal's Foreword,' *QJ* (15 Oct. 1914), 1; see also 'The University and the War' and 'The Moral Effects of the War' (undated typescripts), D.M. Gordon Papers, boxes 126 and 5, respectively, QUA. Both speeches were given by Gordon during the war and view the call to service and self-sacrifice as the hightest form of duty: e.g., 'the best thing about war, with all its horrors, the thing that even redeems and glorifies it in the eyes of many, is that it spells service to the uttermost, service to the extent of self-sacrifice' ('Moral Effects,' 2). See also Robert Bothwell, *Laying the Foundation: A Century of History at University of Toronto* (Toronto 1991), 58; Paul T. Phillips, *Britain's Past in Canada: The Teaching and Writing of British History* (Vancouver 1989), 57–8.

9   Charles M. Johnston, *McMaster University*, vol. 1, *The Toronto Years* (Toronto 1976), 130–1

10   Quoted in Thomas P. Socknat, *Witness against War: Pacifism in Canada, 1900–1945* (Toronto 1987), 38–9, 42, 46–7. See also *AV* (Oct. 1915) for Horning's pacifist article called 'The Two Ideals.'

11   O.D. Skelton, 'The European War and the Peace Movement,' *QQ* 22 (Oct., Nov., Dec. 1914), 205–14. See also Doug Owram, *The Government Generation: Canadian Intellectuals and the State, 1900–1945* (Toronto 1986), 87–8; 'Philosophical Society: "Laws of War" by Prof. Skelton,' *QJ* (8 Feb. 1915); Arthur R.M. Lower, *My First Seventy-five Years* (Toronto 1967), 48; 'Mr Glazebrook's Address to Political Science Club – Pacifism,' *QJ* (8 Feb. 1915).

12   Quoted in Socknat, *Witness to War*, 44

13   W.G. Jordan, 'The British Empire,' *QJ* (15 Oct. 1914). See also 'Stories of War a Hundred Years Ago,' *QJ* (16, 26 Nov. 1914).

14   'The University Sermon,' *QJ* (26 Oct. 1914)

15   'Stand Up and Meet the War' and 'By Tennyson,' *QJ* (2 Nov. 1914)

16   For example, 'The Reapers,' *QJ* (17 Oct. 1916)

17   See, e.g., John Watson, 'German Philosophy and Politics,' *QJ* 22 (Apr., May, June 1915), 329–44.

18   Rev Dr Strachan, 'Convocation Address – the Blessings of Purity,' *QJ* (17 Oct.

1916); Dr Bruce Taylor, 'The Sunday Sermon,' *QJ* (19 Oct. 1914); Rev Dr Herridge, 'The University Sermon,' *QJ* (25 Jan. 1915); Rev Principal Griffith-Jones (Airedale [Congregational] College, Bradford, England), 'Convocation Service,' *QJ* (9 Jan. 1917); Dr Welsch, 'University Service,' *QJ* (9 Nov. 1914). Although these examples have been chosen from Queen's sources, they are typical of exhortations elsewhere at Ontario universities. See, e.g., Johnston, *McMaster* 1, 129–32.

19 Editorial, *QJ* (15 Oct. 1914)

20 'Our Affinity for War,' *AV* (Oct. 1915)

21 *TG* (4 Aug. 1914), quoted in Barbara Wilson, ed., *Ontario and the First World War, 1914–1918* (Toronto 1977), xix

22 The seven were John Squair, J.H. Cameron, Richard Davidson, J.L. Wile, J.B. Allan, H.J. Boultbee, and A.B. McCallum.

23 'Harbord Collegiate Has Its Own Wee War.' See also 'Prof Mueller's Position,' *TG* (25 Sept. 1914).

24 See, e.g., letters to the editor such as 'No Need to Mince Matters,' James Applegate to editor, *TT* (22 Sept. 1914), and 'Should Talk of the War,' Canadian to editor, *TT* (23 Sept. 1914).

25 'Student Organ Rises in Indignant Protest,' *TG* (20 Dec. 1913). The wording of the headline reflects the extent to which English usage has changed – some would say, has been impoverished – in the 20th century.

26 'Germans in Canada deserve courtesy, but not coddling,' *TT* (19 Sept. 1914)

27 'Shall the Toronto School Teachers Bow ... to a German Professor?' *TT* (23 Sept. 1914)

28 'University Teaching and the Nation,' *TG* (6 Oct. 1914). See also 'Trustees Condemn Varsity Professors,' *TS* (2 Oct. 1914).

29 See B.E. Walker to E.B. Osler (19 Nov. 1914), Walker Papers, box 33, UTA.

30 Falconer to *TG* (17 Nov. 1914); 'German Teachers Hard to Replace – President Falconer Explains Attitudes of University Towards Three Professors – Have Done No Wrong,' *TW* (16 Nov. 1914)

31 *TG* (12 Nov. 1914). Stories with headlines reading 'Toronto Man's Story of German Atrocities – Saw Two Belgian Boys with Hands Cut Off' now appeared routinely in the Toronto press. Toronto's City Council had voted to remove enemy aliens from its payroll. Politicians at the provincial level were also under public pressure to bring the provincial university under control.

32 '"Varsity vs King George,"' *TW* (26 Nov. 1914); 'University of Toronto Must Face the Question,' *TT* (25 Nov. 1914). See also 'Anti-British Germans in the University,' *TW* (14 Nov. 1914); 'German Professors at the University,' *TW* (18 Nov. 1914).

33 'Call Back the President – To Decide German Question,' *TT* (27 Nov. 1914). See Osler to Walker (18 Nov. 1914), Walker Papers, box 21, UTA; Walker to Osler (19 Nov. 1914), ibid., box 33.

34 This document is reprinted in Wilson, *Ontario and the First World War*, 162–4.

35 Emotions may have been heightened by the publication in Toronto newspapers on 2

December of a letter to Falconer by a prominent Toronto banker, Col D.R. Wilkie, expressing his outrage over Falconer's October letter in defense of Mueller, 'in which you encourage the employment of German subjects as leaders and teachers of our youth.' The letter had been penned on the day Falconer's letter had appeared; within hours Wilkie died. (Of apoplexy?) See 'Col Wilkie and German Professors,' *TG* (2 Dec. 1914).

36 'If we can't get university professors of British blood,' provincial politician Thomas Hook told a North Toronto audience, '... then let us close the universities' (Osler and Hook quoted in Wilson, *Ontario and the First World War*, cii).

37 'The Canadian Reign of Terror,' *Varsity* (4 Dec. 1914). *Varsity*'s editor was in part defending the loyalty of his own newspaper. See 'Varsity Defends Germans – Call Attacks an Insult – Student Organ Says Newspapers are Unfairly Influencing People – Surprised at Persecution of Germans,' *TT* (2 Dec. 1914).

38 'The University and the Public,' *TW* (2 Dec. 1914)

39 'President Inspires Entire University,' *TS* (3 Dec. 1914). The story of Falconer's handling of problems with 'the German professors' is fully told in James G. Greenlee, *Sir Robert Falconer: A Biography* (Toronto 1988).

40 Quoted in Johnston, *McMaster* I 137. The fact was, however, that official appointment of Mueller to the chair of German was deferred until after the war, 'out of respect for the condition of public opinion.' During it, he survived on a series of sessional appointments 'subject to possible adjustment,' said the McMaster senate, 'which may be necessary if war continues' (137–8).

41 See Marilyn Barber, 'The Ontario Bilingual Schools Issue: Sources of Conflict,' in Ramsay Cook, ed., *Minorities, Schools, and Politics* (Toronto 1969), 63–84.

42 See Margaret Prang, 'Clerics, Politicians, and the Bilingual Schools Issue in Ontario, 1910–1917,' in Cook, *Minorities*, 85–111; Franklin A. Walker, *Catholic Education and Politics in Ontario* (Toronto 1964), 263–96.

43 Laurence K. Shook, *Catholic Post-Secondary Education in English-Speaking Canada* (Toronto 1971), 249, 252–4

44 J. Castell Hopkins, *The Province of Ontario in the War* (Toronto 1919), 30

45 'The University and the War,' *TG* (14 Sept. 1914)

46 Hilda Neatby, *Queen's University*, vol. I, *1841–1917: And Not to Yield*, ed. Frederick W. Gibson and Roger Graham (Montreal/Kingston 1978), 296; Kathryn M. Bindon, *Queen's Men, Canada's Men: The Military History of Queen's University, Kingston* (Kingston 1978), 20–4; 'QQ,' *Queen's Quarterly* 22 (Apr. May, June 1915), 384–5; *ROP, 1914–15*, 20

47 Hartley Munro Thomas, *UWO Contingent COTC: The History of the Canadian Officers' Training Corps at the University of Western Ontario* (London 1956), 8–12 and (next two paragraphs) 15, 17, 17–19

48 In short, they were given a traditional and – from the military perspective – entirely appropriate basic training. See Richard Holmes, *Firing Line* (Harmondsworth 1987), 36–56; Denis Winter, *Death's Men: Soldiers of the Great War* (Harmondsworth 1978), 37–69. Quotation from Winter, *Death's Men*, 65

49 J.L. Morison, 'Military Training at Queen's,' *QJ* (19 Oct. 1914); addresses by Dr
   Thornton and George Foster were reprinted in the same issue.
50 'Military Training,' *QJ* (26 Oct. 1914)
51 'Military Drill,' *QJ* (29 Oct. 1914); but see the student editorial reply in *QJ* (9 Nov.
   1914)
52 Bindon, *Queen's Men*, 28–32
53 Quoted in PUH, UTA, A83-0036/001. 'University at War.' This archival collection
   comprises the research notes, memoranda, and typescripts related to the authorized
   history of the University of Toronto which engaged University Historian Robin S.
   Harris between the early 1970s and 1983. At times I have utilized information from
   various draft chapters. Since these chapters exist in variant forms, have different
   numerical designations, and at times are not paginated (e.g., the chapter noted
   above), precise citation is not always possible. All materials I have used, however,
   may be found in A83-0036/001.
54 Robert Falconer to 'Officer Commanding,' 2nd Div, Toronto (30 Sept. 1914). Falconer Papers, UTA, A67-0007/037
55 Adjutant-General, Canadian Militia, to Falconer (17 Oct. 1914). Falconer Papers,
   UTA, A67-0007/037. This letter granted the university formal permission to form
   a COTC contingent, 'provided arms[,] equipment and ammunition not demanded
   until after embarkation second contingent Canadian Expeditionary Force ...' See also
   Roll of Service, xxxvi; G. Oswald Smith, 'Canadian Educational Institutions in the
   Great War. VIII – University of Toronto,' *Canadian Defence Quarterly* 5 (1927–8),
   227.
56 C.B. Sissons, *A History of Victoria University* (Toronto 1952), 271; Johnston,
   McMaster University 1, 132
57 Falconer to Officer Commanding 2nd Div, Toronto (30 Mar. 1915). Falconer Papers,
   UTA, A67-0007/037
58 The 253rd (Queen's University) Highland Battalion, in the words of the Official
   Historian of Canada's military participation in the Great War, 'had little connection
   with Queen's except for its name, drawing its personnel from the general public'
   (Colonel G.W.L. Nicholson, *Canadian Expeditionary Force, 1914–1919* [Ottawa
   1962], 229).
59 Ralph Hodder-Williams, *Princess Patricia's Canadian Light Infantry, 1914–1919*,
   2nd ed. (Edmonton 1968), 83. See also Nicholson, *Canadian Expeditionary Force*,
   228–9; Smith, 'Canadian Educational Institutions,' 227.
60 Johnston, *McMaster* 1, 133, 148; Bindon, *Queen's Men*, 46, 160–1; John R.W.
   Gwynne-Timothy, *Western's First Century* (London 1978), 238–9. Some of Bindon's statistics: in 1917, of 235 arts undergraduates 187 did not hold commissions;
   but of 133 arts graduates 93 were commissioned officers. In science, 88 undergraduates were privates and non-commissioned and 61 were officers; 38 graduates held no
   commission and 96 did. Only in medicine did the number of officers exceed that of
   other ranks both for undergraduates and graduates. Of the former, 82 of 157 were
   officers; of the latter, only 4 of 132 were not officers (160–1).

61 'The University at War' (unpaginated), PUH A83-0036/001

62 Neatby, *Queen's*, 297–9; D.D. Calvin, *Queen's University at Kingston* (Kingston 1941), 175–7; 'Queen's and the War,' *QQ* 22 (Apr., May, June 1915), 384–7

63 Quoted in 'The University at War'

64 Queen's extension work with bankers was initiated in 1913, with the approval of the Canadian Bankers' Association, by O.D. Skelton. Patterned after similar programs at the universities of Chicago and Wisconsin, Skelton's course took advantage of a provision in the CBA's by-laws allowing for lectures and examinations to be administered when deemed 'proper.' As a result, under Skelton's direction and with professors such as Clifford Clark as instructors, the university prepared a syllabus in association with the CBA, and assumed responsibility for conducting examinations and awarding diplomas. Successful candidates were entitled to use the initials 'ACBA' (Associate of the Canadian Bankers' Association) after their names. See 'The Banking Courses of Queen's,' *QJ* (14 Nov. 1916), 5; *ROP, 1914–15*, 6, 11–12.

65 *ROP, 1915–16*, 3

66 'University Registration Statistics,' *QJ* (21 Nov. 1916), 1; *ROP, 1916–17*, 4–5

67 See also Neatby, *Queen's*, 303.

68 Overall, female Canadian participation in the academic work force in 1901 had been 13.5%; by 1931 it rose to 19.19%, an increase of almost 6%. University figures indicate a 10% increase in general female participation in the academic work force in the same period. See Marni de Pencier, 'Women Faculty at the University of Toronto,' research study (1972), U of T, 18 (copy in PUH A83-0036/001).

69 de Pencier, 'Women Faculty,' 23

70 Ibid., Chart D, 'Distribution in Ranks'

71 Ibid., 8

72 Ibid., 22, 26

73 See Ian Drummond, *Political Economy at the University of Toronto: A History of the Department, 1888–1902* (Toronto 1983), Fig. I, 'Enrolments in the department ...,' and Fig. III, 'Full-time academic staff and graduate enrolment,' 4, 9.

74 'Liberal Education' (unpaginated), PUH A83-0036/001

75 During the 1915–16 academic year the U of T's faculty of medicine decided to extend basic medical training from five to six years, to begin in Sept. 1918. The lengthened program was not, however, implemented until Sept. 1919.

76 'Professional Education' (unpaginated), PUH A83–0036/001

77 'The University at War'; Johnston, *McMaster* I, 134–5; Frederick W. Gibson, *Queen's University*, vol. 2, *1917–1961: To Serve and Yet Be Free* (Montreal/Kingston 1983), 12. Douglas agreed to contribute $500,000 if the university raised an equal amount. The Chancellor did, however, write a cheque to the university for $63,000 to eliminate its current deficit.

78 E.E. Stewart, 'The Role of the Provincial Government in the Development of the Universities of Ontario,' EDD thesis, U of T (1970), 301–2

79 *Provincial Statutes of Ontario*, 8 Edward VII, 1908, c. 145; *Statutes of Canada*, 2

Geo. V, 1912, c. 138. See Canada. *Statutes*, 2 Geo. V, 1912, c. 139, for the Theological College legislation; see also George Rawlyk and Kevin Quinn, *The Redeemed of the Lord Say So: A History of Queen's Theological College, 1912–1972* (Kingston 1980), 7–15, for details of the controversy.

80 *TG* (13 Feb. 1913); quoted in Stewart, 'Provincial Government,' 308

81 *TG* (18 Apr. 1914); quoted in Stewart, 'Provincial Government,' 310

82 Stewart, 'Provincial Government,' 311–14

83 Ibid., 345. See also untitled typescript memorandum focusing on physical expansion and finances at the U of T, 1906 to 1951 (unpaginated), PUH A83-0036/001.

84 Johnston, *McMaster*, 1, 87, 138–40; *ROP, 1916–17*, 16–17

85 'Research' (unpaginated), PUH A83-0036/001

86 Ibid.; memorandum from J.E. Fitzgerald to Falconer (27 May 1915), Falconer Papers, UTA. For the next 20 years the province also provided an annual statutory grant of $3,750 to the university for the services of the Connaught Laboratories.

87 *TG* passage quoted in 'Editorial – Universities and the Public,' *QJ* (23 Jan. 1917)

88 *Royal Canadian Institute Centennial Volume*, ed. W. Stewart Wallace (Toronto 1949), 160–2

89 'Made-in-Canada Education' (editorial), *IC* (Aug. 1915), 473. For accounts of the proceedings of the 1915 NCCU, see: 'Great Prosperity Awaits Canadians: Country Will Have More Development Than Ever After the War,' *TW* (2 June 1915); 'Canada Must Provide Young Men with Education At Home: President Falconer Deprecates Necessity of Western Youth Going to US Colleges,' *TN* (2 June 1915). See also Gwendoline Pilkington, 'A History of the National Conference of Canadian Universities, 1911–1961,' PHD thesis, U of T (1974).

90 Mel Thistle, *The Inner Ring: The Early History of the National Research Council of Canada* (Toronto 1966), 4–5. Information on the founding of the Advisory Research Council is taken from this source.

91 University representatives were as follows. From McGill: F.D. Adams, Dean of the Faculty of Applied Science; H.T. Barnes, Director of Physics; H.M. MacKay, Professor of Civil Engineering; W. Peterson, Principal; R.F. Ruttan, Director of Chemistry. From Toronto: W.E. Ellis, Dean of the Faculty of Applied Science; R.A. Falconer, President; J.C. McLennan, Professor of Physics. From Queen's: W.L. Goodwin, Dean of the Faculty of Applied Science. G.T. Chown, Registrar of Queen's, also attended, but as a representative of the Canadian Manufacturers' Association.

92 See, e.g., 'Projects of Industrial Research' and 'Research Bureaus to Be Recommended' (editorials), *IC* (Mar. 1917), 1273–4; R.F. Ruttan, 'Organizing for Industrial Research,' *IC* (July 1917), 401–3.

93 J.D. McLennan, 'The Problem of Industrial Research in Canada,' *IC* (July 1916), 354–5; Thistle, *Inner Ring*, 33–4

94 Quoted in Thistle, *Inner Ring*, 42. The letter from Murray was written on 9 Nov. 1918.

95 A.S.P. Woodhouse, 'The Humanities – Sixty Years,' *QQ* 60 (Winter 1954), 542–3

96 'War Kills Dancing Season – University Ladies Refuse to Be Gay This Winter,' (unidentified *Varsity* clipping, Nov. 1914); in 'Student Activities – General' files, A73-052, box 20, file 1, UTA. For Richards's (d. 13 Nov. 1914) obituary, see *Roll of Service*, 118. Richards was the first U of T combat casualty, not the first death. That unfortunate distinction belonged to Andrew Russell Campbell (Applied Science '02), who left Winnipeg with the Princess Patricia's Canadian Light Infantry on the outbreak of war. In Ottawa arranging for an appointment in the Engineers, he drowned in the Rideau Canal (20 Aug. 1914). See *Roll of Service*, 22. See also 'Dancing Is Banned at Class Meetings,' *Varsity* (7 Dec. 1918).

97 'Athletics-sport situation,' *QJ* (3 Nov. 1916). 'Soldiers and Athletics,' *QJ* (9 Jan. 1917): 'The first requisite of a good army is "esprit de corps." The best trained army in the world is beaten if they don't play the game together.' See also the inspirational memoir by Coningsby Dawson, *The Glory of the Trenches* (Toronto 1918), 102: 'The worst thing you can say of a man at the Front is, "He doesn't play the game."'

98 'Science Men Stole Barrel Used in the Medical Rush – Sophomores Won from Freshmen on Campus: About Two Hundred in the Event,' *TN* (5 Oct. 1914); 'OAC Students Fight Police and Soldiers; Trouble Arose during Show in Opera House – Many Hurt on Both Sides,' *TG* (22 Mar. 1915); *ROP, 1916–17*, 48. 'Med Stude [*sic*] Favours "Scrap,"' *Varsity* (17 Oct. 1917).

99 Editorial, *QJ* (11 Dec. 1917)

100 See 'COTC at McGill,' *QJ* (17 Nov. 1916); editorial [regarding the national military inventory], *QJ* (19 Dec. 1916); 'The Case for National Service,' *QJ* (5 Jan. 1917).

101 'Merry Battle at Varsity – Medical Students Line Up Against SPS and Arts Men,' *TG* (14 Mar. 1918). War forged some untraditional academic alliances. With approximately 500 medical students on the Toronto campus, compared with only about 150 students of the School of Practical Science, arts students found themselves supporting their traditional rivals – the engineers – against 'the meds' in the 1918 interfaculty student battles. This marriage of necessity did not survive much beyond the Armistice.

102 Falconer quoted in *Canadian Annual Review, 1916* (Toronto 1917), 549

103 'The Suggestion to Close the University of Toronto during the Next Academic Year' broadside, undated and unpaginated, Falconer Papers, UTA

104 'Dr Watson Lectures to the Philosophical Society – German Idealism and Nationality,' *QJ* (28 Jan. 1915); 'Germany's Contribution to Culture,' *QJ* (14 Jan. 1915); 'Professor Scott Addresses YMCA,' *QJ* (11 Feb. 1915); Falconer, *The German Tragedy*, passim

105 'Editorial,' *QJ* (7 Nov. 1916); Johnston, *McMaster* 1, 137; *Roll of Service*, 87

106 E.F. Scott, 'The Effects of the War on Literature and Learning,' *QQ* 27 (Oct., Nov., Dec. 1919), 152

107 Robert Falconer, 'What about Progress?' in Falconer, *Idealism in National Charac-*

ter (Toronto 1920), 94–116; Maurice Hutton, *The University in War and Peace* (Winnipeg 1916), 3, 5; Robert Law, *Optimism* (Winnipeg 1918), 11. For further evidence of the demoralizing effect of the Great War on professors, see S.E.D. Shortt, *The Search for an Ideal: Six Canadian Intellectuals and Their Convictions in an Age of Transition, 1890–1930* (Toronto 1976); David B. Marshall, *Secularizing the Faith: Canadian Protestant Clergy and the Crisis of Belief, 1850–1940* (Toronto 1992), 156–80. For the European context see, e.g., Robert Wohl, *The Generation of 1914* (Cambridge, Mass. 1979).

108   'Convocation Address,' *QJ* (27 Apr. 1917)

109   Merlin, 'Values,' *Rebel* 2 (Feb. 1918); *QJ* (8 Feb. 1918). See also 'Science, Authority, and the American Empire,' in A.B. McKillop, *Contours of Canadian Thought* (Toronto 1987), 113.

CHAPTER 12   *Reconstruction, Consolidation, Expansion*

1   George Pearson quoted in Desmond Morton and Glenn Wright, *Winning the Second Battle: Canadian Veterans and the Return to Civilian Life, 1915–1930* (Toronto 1987), 117

2   *ROP, 1918–19*, 48; 'University Buildings Closed by Order of Caput on Account of Influenza Epidemic – No Lectures Will Be Delivered from 1 PM Today until Nov. 5 at 9 AM,' *Varsity* (18 Oct. 1918); 'Flu Epidemic Continues to Spread Here,' *TG* (3 Feb. 1920)

3   C.B. Sissons, *A History of Victoria University* (Toronto 1952), 273–4. Sissons notes that of the 67 Victoria men who died in the war, 15 fell in its last months as the Allies pushed back the German lines (272).

4   UTA, A-73-051, box /001(07), 'Canadian Universities Conference'; UTA, A-73-052, box /001(07)

5   W.S. Wallace, *A History of the University of Toronto* (Toronto 1927), 187

6   E.E. Stewart, 'The Role of the Provincial Government in the Development of the Universities of Ontario,' EDD thesis, U of T (1970), 405–6

7   At the U of T, registration had dropped by 1917–18 to 2,799, from a 1913–14 total of 4,141. But by the 1919–20 academic year, numbers had soared to an all-time high of 5,237. Similarly, in spite of the declines of the war years, enrolment at Queen's had increased from 2,009 to 2,578, at UWO from 192 to 255, and at McMaster from 268 to 281 between the autumn of 1914 and that of 1919. Wallace, *Toronto*, 188; *Canadian Annual Review 1913*, 423

8   See *Canada Year Book* (Ottawa 1914–1920).

9   E.E. Stewart, 'Provincial Government,' 383

10   *ROP, 1919–20*, 6

11   G.M. Wrong to A.L. Smith, Oxford (30 Sept. 1919); quoted in James G. Greenlee, *Sir Robert Falconer: A Biography* (Toronto 1988), 259

12   Albert Hellyer to W.E. Raney (26 Feb. 1921). Quoted in Charles M. Johnston, *E.C.*

Drury: Agrarian Idealist (Toronto 1986), 90. Hellyer was brother-in-law to J.J. Morrison.

13 Hearst to Falconer (18 June 1919), quoted in Greenlee, *Falconer*, 258

14 R.H. Grant to Falconer (14 Sept. 1920), quoted in Greenlee, *Falconer*, 261

15 *Report of the Royal Commission on University Finances* (Toronto 1921), 3

16 Frederick W. Gibson, Q*ueen's University*, vol. 2, *1917–1961: To Serve and Yet Be Free* (Montreal/Kingston 1983), 31, 42

17 Opposition had arisen in some London and university quarters to Western's lack of progress, especially in the faculty of arts and science. 'Some ... have contended that we have been far too slow in securing the recognition of our honor degrees for specialist standing...,' wrote Braithwaite, responding to criticism in the press. 'In reality it was absurd to suppose that this recognition could be had by a university which had no laboratories for its science departments, with the single exception of chemistry, and was at the same time so undermanned in its staff.' He added: 'I am not blind to the fact that there have been forces working against me behind the scenes, especially for the last couple [of] years. But as the fighting has not been in the open there has been no way to combat this which I have cared to adopt.' 'Dr Braithwaite States Position; Makes Explanation in Regard to University,' *LFP* (17 Feb. 1919). See also 'Dr Fox Appointed Head of Western Arts Faculty; Selected to Hold Position Temporarily by Board of Governors; Committee of Three to Govern University,' *LFP* (12 Aug. 1919).

18 James J. Talman and Ruth Davis Talman, *'Western' – 1878–1953: Being the History of the Origins and Development of the University of Western Ontario during Its First Seventy-Five Years* (London 1953), 69–71

19 William Sherwood Fox, *Sherwood Fox of Western* (Toronto 1964), 116. Recruited as professor of classics by President E.E. Braithwaite, Fox was appointed dean of arts and science in 1919; he became the university's president in 1927.

20 John R.W. Gwynne-Timothy, *Western's First Century* (London 1978), 226–7. Talman and Talman, *'Western,'* 92

21 Gwynne-Timothy, *Western,* 230–1; Greenlee, *Falconer,* 262

22 *Report of the Royal Commission on University Finances,* 8–9

23 Gwynne-Timothy, *Western,* 233. The local and regional nature of the pool of students also applied to the university. Although, like Queen's, it consistently claimed to be a 'national university,' in the mid-1920s half of its students were from Toronto; 30% more came from a 30-mile radius of the city. Peter Oliver, *G. Howard Ferguson: Provincial Tory* (Toronto 1977), 242

24 *Report of the Royal Commission on University Finances,* 15

25 *TG* (15 Apr. 1921), quoted in Stewart, 'Provincial Government,' 351

26 Quoted in Gwynne-Timothy, *Western,* 232

27 Fox, *Sherwood Fox,* 137

28 Even before the appointment of the Cody Commission the London City Council was prepared to make a substantial contribution to the university. Its finance committee

approved a grant of $55,000 in 1920 (up from $20,000 in 1919). See '$55,000 Grant to Western Varsity; Finance Committee of the London Council Makes Recommendation,' *LFP* (12 Feb. 1920).

29 See Fred Landon, 'First UWO Buildings Were Started 40 Years Ago,' *LFP* (23 Mar. 1963).

30 Fox, *Sherwood Fox*, 135

31 Gwynne-Timothy, *Western*, 246

32 'Varsity Cornerstones "Well and Truly Laid" by Ontario Premier,' *LFP* (19 June 1923)

33 13–14 Geo. V c. 105

34 *ROP, 1921–2*, 22–6; *ROP, 1925–6*, 4. Gibson, *Queen's* 2, 29–82

35 Wallace, *Toronto*, 177, 188–9; unpaginated typescript on physical expansion and finances, 1906–1932, PUH, UTA, A83-0036/001

36 T.A. Reed, ed., *A History of the University of Trinity College, Toronto, 1852–1952* (Toronto 1952), 121–2, 134

37 Ian Montagnes, *An Uncommon Fellowship: The Story of Hart House* (Toronto 1969), 6–8. The following material on Hart House is from this source.

38 Claude Bissell, *The Young Vincent Massey* (Toronto 1981), 53

39 Montagnes, *Uncommon Fellowship*, 2. Of women at Hart House, Montagnes writes: 'Yet their presence in the building as planned would have been as inappropriate as cast iron or reinforced concrete. Women were still accorded a respect and separateness which would have inhibited the sense of community on which the House was based. This decision too was functional' (18–19).

40 See 'Discuss Moving of McMaster – Niagara-Hamilton Baptist Association Meeting at Welland,' *TG* (2 June 1921); 'Mountain Site for McMaster – What Hamilton Has to Offer the Baptist University – Use Ontario Hospital,' *TG* (28 July 1921); 'McMaster, Hamilton? Latter Would Be Glad – Ambitious City Alumni Brochure Urges College Be Taken from Toronto,' *TS* (12 Oct. 1921); 'Location of McMaster,' *TS* (20 Oct. 1921); 'Big Problems Face Baptists – McMaster University Discussing Removal from Present Site – Seeks New Chancellor,' *TG* (19 Sept. 1922).

41 Charles M. Johnston, *McMaster University*, vol. 1, *The Toronto Years* (Toronto 1976), 216–17

42 From its inception the executive head of McMaster was its Chancellor: it had no office of vice-chancellor, president, or principal as elsewhere. This remained the case until 1950, when, in keeping with practice at most other universities, the office of chancellor was made honorific and the position combining the offices of president and vice-chancellor was introduced. See Charles M. Johnston, *McMaster University*, vol. 2, *The Early Years in Hamilton* (Toronto 1981),170, 171.

43 G.A. Rawlyk, 'A.L. McCrimmon, H.P. Whidden, T.T. Shields, Christian Education, and McMaster University,' in G.A. Rawlyk, ed., *Canadian Baptists and Christian Higher Education* (Montreal/Kingston 1988), 31–127

44 Rawlyk, 'McCrimmon, Whidden, Shields,' 42, 47, 52–3

45 Quoted in ibid., 58
46 See 'McMaster May Forfeit Near Million in Gifts if It Leaves Toronto,' *TS* (27 Dec. 1926); 'Governors of McMaster Weigh University's Future,' *TG* (29 Dec. 1926)
47 'McMaster Secures Site – 70 Acres at Hamilton,' *TT* (9 Nov. 1927); Johnston, *McMaster* 1, 228–9
48 'New McMaster University Cornerstone Has Been Laid,' *TS* (9 Oct. 1929); 'Whidden – the Moving Spirit,' *Silhouette* (19 Nov. 1965); 'McMaster Opens Its Doors in Hamilton for First time – Expects Record Enrolment of Five Hundred Students at Starting To–day – Is Well Equipped,' *TS* (1 Oct. 1930); 'McMaster's Doors Open at Hamilton,' *TM* (15 Nov. 1930); 'Doors of New Home Open to McMaster as Golden Key Turns,' *TG* (15 Nov. 1930); Johnston, *McMaster* 2, 8–19
49 'McMaster Undergrads Reach Promised Land After Forty Years,' *Silhouette* (2 Oct. 1930)
50 Oliver, *Ferguson*, 235–6
51 Quoted in ibid., 241
52 *Census of Canada, 1931* 1: 'Numerical distribution of the population by quinquennial age groups and sex, Canada and the provinces, 1881–1931'
53 Robert Bothwell, Ian Drummond, and John English, *Canada 1900–1945* (Toronto 1987), 219; e.g., the real GNP increased by 20% between 1926 and 1929, while prices tended to fall throughout the decade.
54 Ian Drummond, *Progress without Planning: The Economic History of Ontario from Confederation to the Second World War* (Toronto 1987), 245

CHAPTER 13   *The Culture of Utility*

1 See John Herd Thompson with Allan Seager, *Decades of Discord: Canada 1922–1939* (Toronto 1984); 'Science, Authority, and the American Empire,' in A.B. McKillop, *Contours of Canadian Thought* (1987), 111–28; Mary Vipond, 'The Nationalist Network: English-Canada's Intellectuals and Artists in the 1920s,' *Canadian Review of Studies in Nationalism* 7 (1980); Robert Bothwell, Ian Drummond, and John English, 'The Making of Modern Times: Culture and Communications, 1919–39,' in Bothwell et al., *Canada 1900–1945* (Toronto 1987), 279–94. Hopkins quotations in this and the next paragraph from *Canadian Annual Review 1919* (Toronto 1920), 558–9
2 See David O. Levine, *The American College and the Culture of Aspiration, 1915–1940* (Ithaca and London 1986), 13–22 passim.
3 'Educational Link: English and American University Life,' *TM* (25 Aug. 1923)
4 'Students in Vacation: Canada's Novel Example – Earning the Fees,' *Daily Telegraph* (15 Aug. 1929); 'English Boys for Canada,' London *Times* (16 Mar. 1929); 'A Case for Intellectual Co-operation,' *Spectator* (29 June 1929). See also 'Britain Has Good Opinion of Canadian Universities,' *TM* (5 Jan. 1926); 'Canadian Universities Praised By Englishman,' *TM* (23 Mar. 1929)

5 *Irish Independent* quoted in *TS* (17 Sept. 1927); 'Universities in Canada: Openings for Boys From Britain: A Scholarship Plan,' London *Times* (7 July 1930)

6 See Marni de Pencier, 'The Evolution of the Idea of the University in English-Speaking Canada,' PHD thesis, U of T (1974), 654–63.

7 See Burton R. Clark, *The Higher Education System: Academic Organization in Cross-National Perspective* (Berkeley 1983), 11–26.

8 Reba Sofer, 'Why Do Disciplines Fail? The Strange Case of British Sociology,' *English Historical Review* 97 (1982), 774

9 See Harold Perkin, *The Rise of Professional Society: England Since 1880* (London/New York 1989), esp. 1–16.

10 The institutional histories of Ontario's major universities fully document the ways in which, after the Great War, university administrators at times felt powerless to control the directions in which their institutions were headed. See, e.g., Frederick W. Gibson, *Queen's University*, vol. 2, *1917–1961: To Serve and Yet Be Free* (Montreal/Kingston 1983), esp. ch. 5, 'Principals Don't Carry Weight,' 109–32.

11 Ian M. Drummond, *Progress without Planning: The Economic History of Ontario from Confederation to the Second World War* (Toronto 1987), 22, 24, and Tables 2.3, 'Occupational distribution, Ontario, main groups (percentage)' and 2.5, 'Gainfully employed, Ontario, 1941, classified by years of schooling completed,' 364–5

12 G.Y. Chown to R.B. Taylor (27 Oct. 1917), quoted in Gibson, *Queen's*, 30. See also Allan Smith, 'The Myth of the Self-Made Man in English-Canada 1850–1914,' *CHR* 59 (June 1978), 189–219.

13 Quoted in Levine, *American College*, 45–8

14 'Editorial,' *QJ* (7 Dec. 1917)

15 This *TG* editorial, 'Universities and the Public,' was reproduced (presumably at the initiative of editor-in-chief Charlotte Whitton) as the lead editorial in *QJ* (23 Jan. 1917).

16 'Memorandum on Economic Research and Social Business Training,' dated 15 Oct. 1918, copy in Daniel Miner Gordon Papers, box 2, file 9, QUA. This typescript copy of the four-page foolscap memorandum is unsigned.

17 James Loudon, 'Commercial Education,' *UTM* 1 (1901), 243–4

18 S.J. McLean, 'The School of Commerce Idea,' *UTM* 7 (1907), 214–15. McLean, author of a study of the regulation of railway rates, was later appointed a railway commissioner. See Vincent Bladen, *Bladen on Bladen: Memoirs of a Political Economist* (Toronto 1978), 25.

19 Quoted in Doug Owram, *The Government Generation: Canadian Intellectuals and the State, 1900–1945* (Toronto 1986), 50

20 Ian M. Drummond, *Political Economy at the University of Toronto: A History of the Department, 1888–1982* (Toronto 1982), 5. Drummond notes that the BCOMM program scarcely differed from the BA degree in commerce and finance.

21 Robin S. Harris, *A History of Higher Education in Canada, 1663–1960* (Toronto 1976), 383. Harris points to the difficulty of establishing with accuracy the number

of undergraduates enrolled in commerce courses. The problem is that often (as with the U of T, Queen's, and UWO) statistics for these students were included under their host faculty, arts and science.

22 See Fig. I, 'Enrolments in the department of political science, economics, commerce, sociology B.A., B. Com., Graduate and Service Teaching,' in Drummond, *Political Economy*, 4, for general trends within the Toronto department.

23 See Drummond, *Political Economy*, 63–6.

24 *ROP, 1913–14*: 'Extension Courses in Banking,' 9–12

25 *ROP, 1919–20*, 46. More precisely, enrolment in banking courses was 1,943.

26 See 'Memorandum on Economic Research and Social Business Training,' 1.

27 *ROP, 1918–19*, 15

28 James Cappon to W.L. Grant (19 Sept. 1919), quoted in S.E.D. Shortt, *The Search for an Ideal: Six Canadian Intellectuals and Their Convictions in an Age of Transition, 1890–1930* (Toronto 1976), 64

29 *ROP, 1921–2*, 35, 17

30 Gibson, *Queen's,* 39. Clifford Clark had left Queen's to join a Chicago investment banking firm in 1923, leaving another Skelton protégé appointed in 1920 – the 30-year-old economic historian W.A. Mackintosh – as heir apparent. Going against the advice of Skelton and others, the Queen's board of trustees appointed Herbert Heaton of the University of Adelaide, Australia, as head. Reflecting upon even greater and continuing discontent in the English department over the board of trustees' appointment in 1923 of another outsider (B.K. Sandwell) as head, against the recommendation of the principal and faculty members, Skelton wrote to Mackintosh: 'The only explanation I can give is that after the wrecking of the English Department it has been felt that it would be invidious not to wreck the Economics Department also' (Skelton to Mackintosh [9 June 1925], quoted in Gibson *Queen's*, 57).

31 J.A. Corry, *My Life and Work: A Happy Partnership – Memoirs of J.A. Corry* (Kingston 1981), 72–4, 85

32 *ROP, 1937–8*, 20

33 'Business course for Western U; Dean Fox Outlines Plans At the Chamber of Commerce,' *LFP* (2 Apr. 1920)

34 James J. Talman and Ruth Davis Talman, *'Western' – 1878–1953: Being the History of the Origins and Development of the University of Western Ontario during Its First Seventy-Five Years* (London 1953), 176

35 Philip H. Hensel, 'Business Administration Training at the University of Western Ontario, London, Canada,' *Bostonia: The Boston University Alumni Magazine* (Feb. 1935)

36 John R.W. Gwynne-Timothy, *Western's First Century* (London 1978), 464; 'University Men in Business,' *LFP* (17 May 1930)

37 Hensel, 'Business Administration Training,' 8

38 Harris, *Higher Education,* 388

39 *ROP, 1931–2*, 52

40 Quoted in Gibson, *Queen's*, 129

41 Harold Perkin, 'The Historical Perspective,' in Burton R. Clark, ed., *Perspectives on Higher Education: Eight Disciplinary and Comparative Views* (Berkeley / Los Angeles / London 1984), 41

42 Harold Perkin, 'The Pattern of Social Transformation in England,' in Konrad H. Jarausch, ed., *The Transformation of Higher Learning, 1860–1930: Expansion, Diversification, Social Opening, and Professionalization in England, Germany, Russia, and the United States* (Chicago 1983), 218

43 Gilbert E. Jackson, 'The Course in Commerce and Finance: Just What It Is and What It Does,' *UTM* (Apr. 1929), 261

44 See J. Rodney Millard, *The Master Spirit of the Age: Canadian Engineers and the Politics of Professionalism* (Toronto 1988).

45 *QJ* (28 Feb. 1916). Only slightly less effusive were the words of Brigadier-General C.H. Mitchell in his 1919 inaugural address as dean of the faculty of applied science and engineering at the U of T, esp. when discussing the contribution of technical knowledge to the war effort. See C.H. Mitchell, 'The Future of Applied Science,' *JEIC* 3 (Jan. 1920), 2. Such metaphors, however, were part of the mythic, as much as of the rhetorical, structure of the world of the Canadian engineer. See T. C. Keefer, *The Philosophy of Railroads*, ed. H.V. Nelles (Toronto 1972).

46 'Engineers Hear Instructive Talk – C.V. Corliss, Prominent Mining Man, Addresses Science Men,' *QJ* (20 Jan. 1917); 'The Engineers,' *QJ* (1 Mar. 1918); 'Engineers,' *QJ* (15 Mar. 1918); 'Professional Ethics,' *QJ* (26 Feb. 1918)

47 Millard, *Master Spirit*, Table A7: 'Apprentices and university students 1887–1922,' 152

48 Ibid., 8

49 Mitchell, 'The Future of Applied Science,' 3, 4. For a substantial discussion of the role of the chemist in post-war society, see W.L. Goodwin [of Queen's, chairman, Canadian section, Society of Chemical Industry], 'Place of the Chemist in Canadian Industry,' *IC* 19 (July 1918), 175–9.

50 P.B. Hughes, 'The Faculty,' in Robin S. Harris and Ian Montagnes, eds., *Cold Iron and Lady Godiva: Engineering Education at Toronto, 1920–1972*, Fig. 1, 'Faculty of applied science and engineering 1920–21 to 1970–71,' following 6

51 *ROP, 1925–6*, 22

52 For extensive discussion of the problems of engineers in establishing a professional identity, see Millard, *Master Spirit*. For discussion of the American experience, see David F. Noble, *America by Design: Science, Technology, and the Rise of Corporate Capitalism* (New York 1979).

53 R.W. Brock, dean of the faculty of applied science at the University of British Columbia, told the Vancouver branch of the Engineering Institute of Canada in 1926 that 'not one-half of the present students [presumably in his faculty] will ever enter the engineering profession' ('The Relation of the University to the Engineering Profession,' *JEIC* 9 [July 1926)], 345). For this reason, he concluded, a faculty of

applied science should not be regarded as a professional school in the sense that those in medicine and law were – nor even an 'engineering school.'

54 Mitchell, 'Applied Science,' 7

55 Frank D. Adams, 'The Problems of Engineering Education,' *JEIC* 3 (Apr. 1920), 192

56 Mitchell, 'Applied Science,' 5

57 R.W. Brock, 'Engineering Profession,' 345

58 Dean Clark, 'Report of Committee on Engineering Education,' NCCU *Proceedings* (1923), 86–8

59 E. Geoffrey Cullwick, Jr, 'Engineering Education in Canada,' *JEIC* 15 (July 1932), 341

60 Cullwick, Jr, 'Engineering Education,' 337, 346–8. See Appendix, Tables 3–14.

61 Quoted in Philip C. Enros, 'The Technical Service Council's Origins: A "Patriotic Experiment" in Selling Engineers,' *JCS* 24 (Winter 1989–90), 88

62 See, e.g.: J.C. Maclennan, 'The Problem of Industrial Research in Canada,' *IC* 17 (July 1916), 354; Arthur D. Little, 'The Relation of Research to Industrial Development,' *IC* 17 (Dec. 1916), 929; editorial, 'Projects of Industrial Research,' *IC* 17 (Mar. 1917), 1273–4; R.F. Ruttan, 'Organizing for Industrial Research,' *IC* 18 (July 1917), 401–3; John C. Kirkwood, 'Solving Our Reconstruction Problems,' *IC* 19 (June 1918), 43; Thomas Roden, 'Our Duty with Respect to Research Work,' *IC* 19 (June 1918), 48–9; A.B. Macallum, 'A Year's Work in Industrial Research,' *IC* 19 (July 1918), 168–72; Sir John Willison (president, Canadian Industrial Reconstruction Association), 'Organization for After-the-War Problems,' *IC* 19 (July 1918), 187–9; Sir John Willison, 'The Progress of Industrial Reconstruction,' *IC* 19 (Aug. 1918), 50–1; Thomas Roden, 'Science and Research in Reconstruction,' *IC* 20 (May 1919), 65–6.

63 See Enros, 'Technical Service Council,' Table 3: 'Number of Bachelors of Applied Science or equivalent degrees granted in Canada, 1921–1938,' 98. In no year between 1921 and 1938 did the nation's universities graduate fewer than 329 Bachelors of Applied Science: that low figure occurred in 1926, with the effects still lingering in Ontario of the rise of entrance standards; the high enrolment figure was at the very depths of the Depression – 1935 – when 682 engineers graduated. This exceeded even the 1923 war-veteran year, when 643 engineers faced public life after the university.

64 F. McArthur, 'Employment for Engineers,' *Canadian Engineer* 40 (1923), 596, quoted in Enros, 'Technical Service Council,' 89

65 Enros, 'Technical Service Council,' 90; A.R. Randall-Jones, 'Let's Keep Our Best Brains at Home!' *SN* (4 Jan. 1930), 21, 28

66 See, e.g., the attitude of Arthur Meighen, leader of the federal opposition, in 1924 (M. Christine King, *E.W.R. Steacie and Science in Canada* [Toronto 1989], 51).

67 Peter Oliver, 'Government, Industry and Science in Ontario: The Case of the Ontario Research Foundation,' in Peter Oliver, *Public and Private Persons: The Ontario Political Culture, 1914–1934* (Toronto 1975), 161–2

68 'Boss Ferguson' is the title of ch. 16 of Peter Oliver's book, *G. Howard Ferguson: Ontario Tory* (Toronto 1977), 339–70.

69 Mel Thistle, *The Inner Ring: The Early History of the National Research Council of Canada* (Toronto 1966), 213

70 Henry Marshall Tory to the Hon James Malcolm (20 Apr. 1927), quoted in ibid., 224

71 Oliver, 'Ontario Research Foundation,' 170

72 These were the words of Sir Joseph Flavelle quoted in Oliver, 'Ontario Research Foundation,' 172. On the question of Ferguson's dedication to the Foundation, Oliver writes: 'One may even question the extent of Howard Ferguson's commitment ... to the cooperative ideal [between government and industry as a means of furthering scientific research]' (176). These were the very years in which American research universities were established by substantial investments by donors, private and institutional. See Roger L. Geiger, *To Advance Knowledge: The Growth of American Research Universities, 1900–1940* (New York 1986).

73 Taylor became the subject of the privately and publicly expressed venom of the NRC's protectors. 'He [Taylor] is a dangerous man, evidently trying to get the Council to play his game by publicity thus giving him an opportunity of airing the imaginary grievances of Queen's' (R.F. Ruttan to A.B. Macallum [2 Mar. 1919]; 'He [Taylor] ... indulges in insinuations regarding his opponents' motives and he resorts to the rhetoric which occasionally characterizes a certain type of politics which he ostentatiously affects to despise' ('Statement to the Press by A.B. Macallum' [Mar. 1919]). Both quoted in Thistle, *Inner Ring*, 64–5

74 Henry Marshall Tory to H.S. Congdon (5 May 1926), quoted in Thistle, *Inner Ring*, 201

75 See Yves Gingras, 'Financial Support for Post-Graduate Students and the Development of Scientific Research in Canada,' in Paul Axelrod and John G. Reid, eds., *Youth, University, and Canadian Society: Essays in the Social History of Higher Education* (Montreal/Kingston 1989), 311. Because financial aid for graduate studies was so little available, the NRC fellowships became an essential element in the development of scientific research between the wars, particularly in physics and chemistry (Gingras, 315).

76 Macallum quoted in R. Bruce Taylor to R.F. Ruttan (27 Feb. 1919), in Thistle, *Inner Ring*, 62. In 1925 W.J. Brown of Western suggested that 'instead of putting up a large plant immediately and engaging a staff for this particular line of work [agricultural and industrial research] ... the universities and colleges of the country might be called upon to cooperate with the National Research Council and place, as far as practicable, their laboratory equipment and their trained personnel at the disposal of the Council in order to carry out an aggressive program of research work.' In his successful recommendation that the proposal be rejected, Tory fell back upon a favourite line of defence: 'in the 35 years that I have been associated with university life and in which I have been actively engaged in promoting research, I have not found it possible to have the university laboratories do work very far removed from the work

associated with their teaching activities ... Only a few of the universities are giving teaching courses suited to the training of men for higher research.' This, no doubt, was true; but Tory's rejection of such suggestions as Brown's helped perpetuate such a state of academic affairs. See W.J. Brown to the Hon James A. Robb (9 Dec. 1925) and Henry Marshall Tory to the Hon James A. Robb (18 Dec. 1925), in Thistle, *Inner Ring,* 176–8. The description of Tory and Macallum as 'arch-enemies' is by no means too strong, as their increasingly vitriolic, petty, and self-serving correspondence in Thistle, *Inner Ring,* makes clear.

77 Quoted in Mario Creet, 'H.M. Tory and the Secularization of Canadian Universities,' *QQ* 88 (Winter 1981), 728

78 Harris, *Higher Education,* 390; King, *Steacie and Science,* 58

79 Principal Fyfe ultimately obtained the required amount from a private benefactor (Senator A.C. Hardy, a member of the university's board of trustees), but the order for the accelerator was rejected by the firm of Metropolitan Vickers because too much time had elapsed between the company's tender for the contract and the date of the university's order (see Gibson, *Queen's,* 120–7). Gibson is properly critical of the university's board of trustees for its 'casual indifference' to Hardy's project. But beyond its parsimonious attitude, extreme even during an economic depression, lay the broader lack of outside funding for scientific research.

80 Yves Gingras, *Physics and the Rise of Scientific Research in Canada,* trans. Peter Keating (Montreal/Kingston 1991), 71–3

81 Unpaginated typescript on graduate studies 1905–1932, PUH, UTA, A83-0036/001

82 See Dean J. P. McMurrich, 'The Distribution of Canadian Men of Science,' NCCU *Proceedings* (1928), 63. Of the other Ontario universities, Queen's had trained 47, McMaster 22, UWO 2, and Ottawa 1. McGill had produced 100; the total from the rest of the country was 88.

83 McMurrich, 'Distribution of Canadian Men of Science,' 64–5. Gingras notes that between 1900 and 1916, Canadian universities awarded only six doctorates in physics (*Physics,* 71).

84 King, *Steacie and Science,* 46

85 Gingras, *Physics,* Figs. A1 and A2, 156–7

86 Harris, *Higher Education,* 428–31; Gingras, *Physics,* 71

87 Harris, *Higher Education,* 429

88 Charles M. Johnston, *McMaster University,* vol. 1, *The Toronto Years* (Toronto 1976), 22, 42–3, 61–2

89 Michael Bliss, *Banting: A Biography* (Toronto 1984); Michael Bliss, *The Discovery of Insulin* (Toronto 1982). The highly condensed and necessarily simplified account provided here is drawn from these judicious books.

90 William Sherwood Fox, *Sherwood Fox of Western* (Toronto 1964), 129–31; Bliss, *Banting,* 65

91 Bliss, *Banting,* 65

92 That insulin was first produced not in a single moment by a heroic genius alone in his

laboratory but by a group of competitive researchers with different skills is not the exception in scientific discovery but the norm: 'the idea that skills lie at the heart of science is reinforced by recent work by historians and sociologists of science. Many in science studies now see knowledge as *constructed* in laboratories rather than "discovered" in any simple way. And the sharing of know-how, of ways of getting things done which are never fully spelt out, often seems crucial to the formation of groups which agree that they have defined something new and important about the world' (Jon Turney, 'Sorcerer's Apprentice,' *Times Higher Education Supplement* [2 Nov. 1990], 15).

93 See S.E.D. Shortt, '"Before the Age of Miracles": The Rise, Fall, and Rebirth of General Practice in Canada, 1890–1940,' in Charles Roland, ed., *Health, Disease, and Medicine: Essays in Canadian History* (Hamilton 1984), 128–9. See also R.D. Gidney and W.P.J. Millar, 'The Reorientation of Medical Education in Late Nineteenth-Century Ontario: The Proprietary Medical Schools and the Founding of the Faculty of Medicine at the University of Toronto,' *Journal of the History of Medicine*, forthcoming.

94 See Mary Vipond, 'A Canadian Hero of the 1920s: Dr Frederick G. Banting,' *CHR* 63 (Dec. 1982), 482.

95 Bliss, *Banting*, 71, 97, 117, 120

96 Unpaginated typescript on 'Professional Education, 1906–32,' PUH, UTA, A83-0036/001

97 Ibid. By way of contrast, the medical school of Western was described by Flexner as being 'as bad as anything on this side of the line.' See Harris, *Higher Education*, 267.

98 James G. Greenlee, *Sir Robert Falconer: A Biography* (Toronto 1988), 266

99 'Professional Education'

100 Greenlee, *Falconer*, 264–6

101 D. Graham, 'The Department of Medicine, University of Toronto,' *UTM* 21 (Apr. 1921), 296; quoted in 'Professional Education,' above.

102 Quoted in Greenlee, *Falconer*, 267

103 J.R. Nicholson to E.C. Drury (13 Feb. 1922), Drury Papers, AO RG3, series 7, file 'U of T 1922.' In the same source see also J.F. March (dominion secretary, Grand Army of United Veterans) to Drury (2 Feb. 1922).

104 See Greenlee, *Falconer*, 267–9.

105 'Professional Education'

106 Greenlee, *Falconer*, 269–73; Bliss, *Banting*, 92

107 'Professional Education'

108 Flexner wrote: 'The future of Queen's depends on its ability to develop halfway between Toronto and Montreal, despite comparative inaccessibility, the Ann Arbor type of school' (quoted in Gwynne-Timothy, *Western*, 191–2).

109 A.A. Travill, *Medicine at Queen's, 1854–1920: A Peculiarly Happy Relationship* (Kingston 1988), 227–8

110 Ibid., 229
111 *ROP, 1918–19*, 33
112 Travill, *Medicine at Queen's*, 232
113 *ROP, 1919–20*, 8–9. See also Travill, *Medicine at Queen's*, 233–4
114 Gibson, Queen's, 32–4 (Taylor quotation from 32)
115 Gwynne-Timothy, *Western*, 188–92; Flexner quotations from 192
116 See C. David Naylor, 'Rural Protest and Medical Professionalism in Turn-of-the Century Ontario,' *JCS* 21 (Spring 1986), 5–20. Unpublished research by R.D. Gidney and W.P.J. Millar suggests that Naylor has over-estimated the degree of cohesion and control of the medical community by the early twentieth century.
117 Principal W.H. Fyfe, 'The Art and Science of Medicine,' *Queen's Review* (7 (Aug. 1933), 161
118 Gwynne-Timothy, *Western*, 206. After the Second World War the curricular pendulum swung briefly back towards emphasis on the liberal arts in medical education.
119 Dean Hattie, 'The Preliminary Education of the Medical Student,' NCCU *Proceedings* (1925), 42–3
120 Gwynne-Timothy, *Western*, 207
121 'Professional Education,' Harris, *Higher Education*, 403
122 Figures drawn from *Canadian Annual Review*, 1921–2 to 1931–2
123 Bliss, *Banting*, 100–1
124 Jews comprised 1.5% of the Canadian population in the 1930s (at least as reflected in the census of 1941). The percentage of Jews at major universities was Dalhousie 11.3, Toronto 7.2, UWO 1.9, Manitoba 11.4, Alberta 4.2. See Paul Axelrod, *Making a Middle Class: Student Life in English Canada during the Thirties* (Montreal/ Kingston 1990), Table 6, 'Religious denominations of Canadian university students, 1930s (%),' 31.
125 J.J.R. Macleod to Robert Falconer (10 Dec. 1928), quoted in Bliss, *Banting*, 179
126 Axelrod, *Making a Middle Class*, 32–4
127 H.J. Cody to General C.F. Winter (8 Feb. 1934). Typescript memorandum on Cody administration, 9–10, in PUH, UTA, A83-0036/001

CHAPTER 14   *The Piper and the Tune*

1 E.E. Stewart, 'The Role of the Provincial Government in the Development of the Universities of Ontario,' EDD thesis, U of T (1970), 341
2 See Jeffery M. Taylor, 'Dominant and Popular Ideologies in the Making of Rural Manitobans, 1890–1925,' PHD thesis, Manitoba (1988).
3 R. Bruce Taylor, 'Academic Freedom,' *QQ* 27 (July, Aug., Sept. 1919), 1–3
4 In the 1880s and 1890s several well-known professors whose radical public criticisms of political, social, and economic injustice were deemed unacceptable had been tried or dismissed by the universities that employed them. Economists Henry Carter Adams at Cornell and Michigan in 1886, Richard T. Ely at Wisconsin in

1894, John R. Commons at Indiana in 1896, and E.A. Ross at Stanford in 1900, were only the most prominent and controversial of those whose trials became matters of public scandal in progressive journals such as the *Nation*. See Richard Hofstadter and Walter P. Metzger, *The Development of Academic Freedom in the United States* (New York 1955), 413–67; Laurence R. Veysey, *The Emergence of the American University* (Chicago 1965), 384–418; Frederick Rudolph, *The American College and University: A History* (New York 1962), 410–16; Ellen W. Schrecker, *No Ivory Tower: McCarthyism and the Universities* (New York 1986), 15–16.

5 Quoted in Hofstadter and Metzger, *Academic Freedom*, 452

6 Ibid., 8

7 Taylor, 'Academic Freedom,' 7, 11

8 See Taylor, 'Dominant and Popular Ideologies,' passim.

9 E.E. Braithwaite, 'Academic Freedom,' *TG* (4 June 1919)

10 Taylor, 'Academic Freedom,' 4. It had been Leonard (see ch. 10) who, before the war, had summarily withdrawn his offer to finance a men's residence at Queen's when Principal Gordon refused to allow the building to be superintended by an officer from the military rather than the university. It may well have been Leonard, too, who was on the mind of Gordon's successor, Bruce Taylor, when he stated in his 1919 Winnipeg address on academic freedom: 'Personally, I prefer the pious donors dead!'

11 James G. Greenlee, *Sir Robert Falconer: A Biography* (Toronto 1988), 275. Greenlee provides a sustained account of Falconer and issues of academic freedom in ch. 10, 'Skylarking on the Ragged Edge of Folly,' 274–304.

12 R.M. MacIver, *Labor in the Changing World* (New York 1919)

13 R.W. Leonard to R.A. Falconer (9 Dec. 1921). The Rev H.J. Cody Papers, AO, MU 4964–4966, A–3. A collection of materials related to Cody also exists in the UTA (Department of Graduate Records, A73-0026/063), dealing with Cody's years as university president and chancellor.

14 R.A. Falconer to R.W. Leonard (12 Dec. 1921), Cody Papers, AO

15 R.W. Leonard to H.J. Cody (15 Dec. 1921), Cody Papers, AO

16 See R.M. MacIver, *As a Tale That Is Told: The Autobiography of R.M. MacIver* (Chicago 1968); R.M. MacIver, *On Community, Society, and Power: Selected Writings*, ed. with intro. by Leon Bramson (Chicago 1970), 2–3.

17 'The Ethical Significance of the Idea Theory,' *Mind* 18 (Oct. 1909), 552–69; 21 (Apr. 1912), 182–200; 'Ethics and Politics,' *IJE* 20 (Oct. 1909), 72–86; 'Society and State,' *PR* 20 (Jan. 1911), 30–45; 'War and Civilization,' *IJE* 22 (Jan. 1912), 127–45; 'Do Nations Grow Old?' *IJE* 23 (Jan. 1913), 127–43; 'What Is Social Psychology?' *SR* 6 (Apr. 1913), 147–60; 'Society and "the Individual,"' *SR* 7 (Jan. 1914), 58–64; 'Institutions as Instruments of Social Control,' *PQ* no. 2 (May 1914), 105–16; 'The Foundations of Nationality,' *SR* 8 (July 1915), 157–66; 'Personality and the Suprapersonal,' *PR* 24 (Sept. 1915), 501–25; 'Supremacy of the State,' *New Republic* 12 (13 Oct. 1917), 304

18 *Community – A Sociological Study: Being an Attempt to Set Out the Nature and Fundamental Laws of Social Life*, 5th ed. (London 1965 [1917]); *The Elements of Social Science,* 9th ed. (London 1949 [1921])

19 MacIver, *Community,* 272

20 Michiel Horn, *The League for Social Reconstruction: Intellectual Origins of the Democratic Left in Canada, 1930–1942* (Toronto 1980), 11

21 Evidence exists to suggest that Leonard was aware of MacIver's apparent radicalism prior to his reading of *Labor in the Changing World,* for as early as Jan. 1921 he had written to B.E. Walker, a member of the university's board of governors, warning of MacIver's disruptive presence (Greenlee, *Falconer,* 276).

22 Sir Robert Falconer, *Academic Freedom* (Toronto 1922), here 3–16, and in the following pages.

23 Ibid., 9. Graham Wallas, *Human Nature in Politics,* Introduction by A.L. Rowse, 3rd ed. (London 1948 [1908]). The first sentence of the first chapter reads: 'Whoever sets himself to base his political thinking on a re-examination of the working of human nature, must begin by trying to overcome his own tendency to exaggerate the intellectuality of mankind' (45). See also Terence H. Qualter, *Graham Wallas and the Great Society* (London 1980).

24 Charles Forcey, *The Crossroads of Liberalism: Croly, Weyl, Lippmann, and the Progressive Era, 1900–1920* (New York 1961), 297

25 Falconer, *Academic Freedom,* 10–11, and next paragraph from 11–12

26 See Rudolph, *American College,* 412–13; Veysey, *Emergence of the American University,* 384.

27 Falconer, *Academic Freedom,* 14, and following excerpts from 15, 16

28 MacIver was director of the American Academic Freedom Project at Columbia University in the 1950s and was therefore responsible for the publication of the landmark study, *The Development of Academic Freedom in the United States* (New York 1955), by Richard Hofstadter and Walter P. Metzger. See also Morroe Berger, Theodore Abel, and Charles H. Page, eds., *Freedom and Control in Modern Society* (New York 1978). The volume was written by former students and colleagues of R.M. MacIver, and was in honour of him. See esp. Harry Alpert, 'Robert M. MacIver's Contributions to Sociological Theory' (286–92), and David Spitz, 'Robert M. MacIver's Contributions to Political Theory' (293–312).

29 The voluntaristic nature of such self-censorship is central to Antonio Gramsci's notion of hegemony, in which 'that what is thereby consented to is a negotiated version of ruling class culture and ideology.' See Tony Bennett, 'Introduction: popular culture and "the turn to Gramsci,"' in Tony Bennett, Colin Mercer, and Janet Woollacott, eds., *Popular Culture and Social Relations* (Milton Keynes 1986), xv.

30 Rudolph, *American College,* 413

31 *AV* (Feb. 1924)

32 See *Financial Post* (21 Dec. 1923).

33 'Let Mounties Search Varsity Is Attitude of Colonal MacLean [*sic*] – "Varsity"

Replies to Charges of Sedition, But Colonel Would Like Officers to Search Hart House Cellars for Bomb Classes,' *TSW* (26 Jan. 1924)

34 'League of Industrial Democracy Has No Official Connection at U of T,' *Varsity* (18 Jan. 1924)

35 'Complain University Students Subjected to False Teaching – "Financial Post" Replies to "Varsity" Editorial on Free Speech – Attacks Dr Eddy – Calls Natural Radicalism of Students a Very Good Symptom,' *Varsity* (30 Jan. 1925)

36 J.T. Hull to Harold A. Innis (12 Nov. 1924), in reply to Innis to Hull (9 Oct. 1924), DPE Papers, UTA, box 6, file 1924

37 See ch. 12 for details of the royal commission of 1921. The idea of a 'University Day,' a proposal of the U of T Alumni Association to the commission, was ultimately rejected as impracticable. See E.C. Drury Papers, AO, RG3, series 7, box 37, file: 'University of Toronto 1923,' half-page internal memorandum entitled 'Tentative Suggestions – University Day in the House,' n.d.

38 See E.C. Drury Papers, AO, RG3, series 7, box 37, file: 'University of Toronto 1923'

39 Quoted in Peter Oliver, *G. Howard Ferguson: Ontario Tory* (Toronto 1977), 238

40 G. Howard Ferguson to H.J. Cody (27 Nov. 1925), G. Howard Ferguson Papers, AO, RG3 series 7, box 77, file: 'University of Toronto 1925'

41 G. Howard Ferguson to R.A. Falconer (2 June 1924), quoted in Greenlee, *Falconer*, 284

42 Ibid., 285–6

43 James Brebner to D.O. Ferris (31 Aug. 1925); W.G. Willson, MPP, to G. Howard Ferguson (n.d.); Ferguson to Willson (9 Oct. 1925). G. Howard Ferguson Papers, AO, RG3, series 7, box 77, file: 'University of Toronto 1925'

44 Harry W. Anderson to Ferguson (26 Aug. 1930); Ferguson to Anderson (28 Aug. 1930); J.G. Althouse to Mrs Stocks (8 Sept. 1930). For further instances of favours wanted, see box 77: Ferguson to J.G. Althouse (8 June 1925); box 90, file 'McMaster University 1926': R.J. Flynn to Ferguson (30 June 1926); Ferguson to W.S.W. McLay (6 July 1930); McLay to Ferguson (12 July 1926); Ferguson to Flynn (17 July 1926); box 77: Dr H.A. Clarke, MPP (Brockville) to Mr C.C. Heale (9 Sept. 1925); box 97, file 'University of Toronto 1926': Charles Hoare to Mr C.C. Heale (5 June 1926); Ferguson to Althouse (10 June 1926); box 109, file 'University of Toronto 1930.' All in G. Howard Ferguson Papers, AO, RG3 series 7

45 Underhill was Wrong's replacement in the sense that his appointment was solicited by Wrong for the term following Wrong's retirement. As head of the department, Wrong was replaced by Chester Martin in 1929.

46 Many years later, historian C.B. Sissons – a member of the university's faculty in 1911 – wrote of Underhill: 'He was a member of our finest year in Honour Classics, 1911, in which there were seven firsts. Here I am tempted to quote scripture – "And now abideth these three" – Stanley, Cochrane, and Underhill, "but the greatest of these is" Underhill' (quoted in R. Douglas Francis, *Frank H. Underhill: Intellectual Provocateur* [Toronto 1986], 20). Sissons refers to Carleton Stanley and Charles Norris Cochrane.

47 G.M. Wrong to Walter Murray (7 Jan. 1927); quoted in Francis, *Underhill*, 72

48 R.D. Francis, 'Frank H. Underhill at the University of Saskatchewan: Formative Years in His Intellectual Development,' *Saskatchewan History* 34 (Spring 1981), 41–56; Carl Berger, *The Writing of Canadian History: Aspects of English-Canadian Historical Writing since 1900*, 2nd ed. (Toronto 1986), 56–72

49 Berger, *Writing History*, 34–44

50 W.P.M. Kennedy to H.J. Cody (28 Mar. 1927), 'Private and Confidential,' Cody Papers, AO MU 4964-4966, A-3; underscoring (here italicized) in original

51 Quoted in Greenlee, *Falconer*, 286

52 G. Howard Ferguson to H.J. Cody (6 Apr. 1929), quoted in Oliver, *Ferguson*, 327. See also Michiel Horn, 'Professors in the Public Eye: Canadian Universities, Academic Freedom, and the League for Social Reconstruction,' *History of Education Quarterly* 20 (Winter 1980), 427.

53 Horn, 'Professors in the Public Eye,' 428

54 Mary Vipond, *The Mass Media in Canada* (Toronto 1989), 10–22. See also D.L. LeMahieu, *A Culture for Democracy: Mass Communication and the Cultivated Mind in Britain Between the Wars* (Oxford 1988), 7–99. Well before the Great War, 65.5% of the space in the Hamilton *Spectator* (1902) and 76.1% of *TN* (1906) was given over to advertisers. See Vipond, *Mass Media,* above.

55 Michiel Horn, '"Free Speech within the Law": The Letter of the Sixty-Eight Toronto Professors, 1931,' *OH* 72 (Mar. 1980), 31–2. Horn provides a detailed account of this controversy.

56 For a sense of the atmosphere of 1920s and 1930s at the level of municipal politics, see A.B. McKillop, 'The Communist as Conscience: Jacob Penner and Winnipeg Civic Politics, 1934–5,' *Cities in the West* (Ottawa 1975), 181–203; McKillop, 'The Socialist as Citizen: John Queen and the Mayoralty of Winnipeg, 1935,' *Historical and Scientific Society of Manitoba Transactions,* ser. III no. 30 (1973–4), 61–77.

57 Frank H. Underhill to J.W. Dafoe (30 Nov. 1930); quoted in Francis, *Underhill*, 79

58 Quoted in Horn, 'Free Speech,' 27

59 See 'Appendix' to Horn, 'Free Speech within the Law,' 45–7, for a full list of the signatories with departmental and faculty affiliations. The letter did not indicate institutional affiliation, but many were well-known U of T staff; 23 of the 68 people who signed the letter were from the departments of history or political economy.

60 Horn, 'Free Speech,' 28–9, 33–7; Greenlee, *Falconer*, 291–2. For discussion of anti-communist views, see McKillop, 'The Communist as Conscience.'

61 Quotations from Horn, 'Free Speech,' 37–8; Greenlee, *Falconer*, 293

62 George Henry Papers, AO, RG3 series 7, box 149, file: 'University of Toronto 1931'

63 Horn, 'Free Speech,' 39

64 George Henry to Rev F.J. Moore (3 Mar. 1931), George Henry Papers, AO, RG3 series 7, box 149, file: 'University of Toronto 1931.' Henry's reference to 'parents of under-graduates' was drawn from personal experience. On 23 Mar. 1931 (see same source) he noted in a letter to Alfred T. DeLury: 'I have a daughter taking an Arts

Course and she sometimes brings home ideas to her Mother who gets very much concerned about it at times. I sometimes feel there are discussions in the classes with the youths that are being trained that would be better confined to more mature minds.' In this letter, Henry notes that he looks 'forward to getting more closely in touch with the affairs of the University' and trusts that 'things will right themselves and that the confidence of the public will not be disturbed by similar incidents in the future.' It is clear from the context, as Greenlee has also suggested (*Falconer*, 296), that such words reflected Henry's genuine concern for the University of Toronto's fortunes, and were not intended as a veiled threat.

65 Quoted in Greenlee, *Falconer*, 297

66 Francis, *Underhill*, 79; Greenlee, *Falconer*, 298

67 Frank H. Underhill to R.A. Falconer (24 Sept. 1931) and Falconer to Underhill (28 Sept. 1931), Carleton Stanley to R.A. Falconer (22 Dec. 1931); quoted in Greenlee, *Falconer,* 299

68 Frank H. Underhill to Brooke Claxton (15 Apr. 1931); quoted in Francis, *Underhill,* 195. Cody had in fact been offered the archbishopric of Melbourne, Australia, in 1921. He had also been a serious candidate for the presidency of the U of T, with significant support from alumni, when James Loudon's successor was sought in 1906.

69 W.P.M. Kennedy to H.J. Cody (10 Oct. 1931); W.L. Grant to H.J. Cody (10 Oct. 1931), Cody Papers, AO

70 'Appointment of Cody As Head of University Criticized by Sinclair – Opposition Leader Terms Rector Political Partisan – Fears for Varsity: Premier to Defence,' *TM* (18 Mar. 1932); 'Dr Cody and University of Toronto,' *SN* (26 Mar. 1932)

71 Francis, *Underhill*, 83–4

72 See Horn, 'Professors in the Public Eye,' 432.

73 George Henry to H.J. Cody (30 July 1932), in reply to Cody's letter to Henry of 29 July 1932, Cody Papers, AO; Horn, 'Professors in the Public Eye,' 433; Sir Arthur Currie to H.J. Cody (29 Mar. 1933), Cody Papers, AO. For details on problems of academic freedom at McGill, see Marlene Shore, *The Science of Social Redemption: McGill, the Chicago School, and the Origins of Social Research in Canada* (Toronto 1987).

74 Harry Cassidy to H.J. Cody (22 June 1934), quoted in Horn, 'Professors in the Public Eye,' 433. To conclude from the evidence of Cassidy's letter, as Horn has done, that 'for unknown reasons, under Cody's presidency a measure of freedom was permitted which went beyond the cloistered version sanctioned by Falconer,' one must ignore the possibility that the letter was disingenuous as well as fawning. As Horn notes, Cassidy was angling for a permanent position at Toronto. Horn's generous conclusion is supported by the absence of any firings of academic staff as a direct result of political activity or utterance, but it discounts the matter of academic self-censorship. As will be seen when discussing Cody's utterances of late 1933 and early 1934, the university president lived in a glass house constructed of his own rhetoric and was therefore in a weak position to gain much support for criticism of professors for their political views.

75 'University Will Aid in Economy Program – Cody Pledges Support of Ontario Gov't Efforts,' *TM* (11 Nov. 1932); 'Alumni Are Asked to Support U of T – Dr Cody Sees Greater Extension of Research Work,' *TG* (18 Jan. 1933); 'The President of the University,' *Varsity* (17 Mar. 1933)

76 G. Howard Ferguson to H.J. Cody (22 Mar. 1933), Cody Papers, AO

77 Quoted in Francis, *Underhill*, 95

78 Quoted in ibid., 96

79 'Europe So Hot and Noisy Cody Speeds to Barrie,' *Varsity* (5 Aug. 1933); 'Mussolini Praised by Hon Dr Cody, *TG* (27 Oct. 1933)

80 Henry Pratt Fairchild, ed., *The Obligation of Universities to the Social Order: Addresses and Discussion at a Conference of Universities under the Auspices of New York University at the Waldorf-Astoria in New York November 15–17, 1932* (New York 1933), 411–14. Since he was one of a diminishing number of ordained clergymen holding presidential appointments at prominent North American universities, Cody was asked by the convenors to provide the invocation at the closing dinner of the conference.

81 'Respect for Education Growing Declares President in Address,' *Varsity* (28 Sept. 1933)

82 'Dr H.J. Cody Under Critical Barrage – Evangelical Board of United Church Resents Recent Remarks Here – Feud about Politics,' *Montreal Gazette* (30 Dec. 1933); 'Church, University Urged by Dr Cody to Avoid Politics – Can Serve Best by Giving Trained Minds to World,' *TG* (19 Dec. 1933)

83 *Enterprise* (Chesley, Ont.; 28 Dec. 1933); 'Dr Cody – Now and Then' (letter to editor from George Simmer), *TG* (28 Dec. 1933)

84 'Dr H.J. Cody Under Critical Barrage'

85 'Dr Cody Answered by Queen's Scholar – Toronto President's Policy of Political Non-Interference Criticized,' *TG* (17 Jan. 1934)

86 'The Means or the End?' *TG* (20 Dec. 1933)

87 'Cody Lays Stress on Rights of State – Individual Duty Often Forgotten in Scoring Governments: Co-operation Need [*sic*] – Italy Teaching Lesson to World, He Declares,' *TM* (9 Jan. 1934)

88 'Italy Week Opens with British Amity Being Emphasized – Commendatore Villari and President Cody Are Speakers – Near-Capacity Audience,' *TG* (9 Jan. 1934)

89 'Christianity Needs Youth – Hope of Church Lies in Organization of Young People,' unidentified clipping from Toronto daily press, published between 24 and 29 Jan. 1934, in UTA, A-73-052, clippings, box 20, file 1: 'Student Activities – General.' See also Lita-Rose Betcherman, *The Swastika and the Maple Leaf: Fascist Movements in Canada in the Thirties* (Toronto 1975).

90 'Progressive Ideas Control Toronto University,' *TM* (29 Jan. 1934)

91 Quoted in Francis, *Underhill*, 96–7

92 J.H. MacBrien to H.J. Cody (4 Apr. 1935). 'Secret,' Cody Papers, AO. MacBrien went on to note that there were 'a number of eminently respectable people on the

Executive' of the League Against War and Fascism, but warned that 'there are sufficient Communists on the Directorate to effectively control the league.'

93 See Robert Bothwell, Ian Drummond, and John English, *Canada 1900–1945* (Toronto 1987), 266.

94 Donald Kerr and Deryck W. Holdsworth, eds., *Historical Atlas of Canada*, vol. 3, *Addressing the Twentieth Century* (Toronto 1990), plate 40; Bothwell, Drummond, and English, *Canada*, 251

95 Stewart, 'Provincial Government,' Table 3, 'Provincial assistance to higher education in Ontario 1917–1947,' 559

96 Ibid., 368

97 Copy in Mitchell Hepburn Papers, AO, RG3, box 301, file: 'University Decrease 1939.' This thick file contains many letters of protest against Hepburn's budget and several supporting it. It also contains a number of unidentified newspaper clippings on the subject. Uncited quotations below are from this file.

98 'Western Makes a Noise,' *SN* 54 (22 Apr. 1939), 3. The $90,000 reference is to the fact that whereas the provincial grant to Western had been $356,000 in 1931, it had dropped to $267,000 by the end of the decade. See Stewart, 'Provincial Government,' Table 3, 559. See also 'University Hit by Cut in Grant' and 'Western Hit' (editorial), *LFP* (29 Mar. 1939); 'Protest Cut in Western's Grant – Student Bodies Send Telegram to Premier Hepburn,' *LFP* (30 Mar. 1939).

99 Mrs Herbert S. White to Hepburn (7 Apr. 1939); Byron F. Wood to Hepburn (11 Apr. 1939); D.F. Glass to Hepburn (6 Apr. 1939)

100 'Convocation Address by Sir Edward Beatty,' London *Advertiser* (26 Oct. 1935); Horn, 'Professors in the Public Eye,' 437; Frank H. Underhill, 'Beatty and the University Reds,' *CF* 15 (Dec. 1935), 385. Beatty was at the time chancellor of McGill University. For his relationship with academic staff at McGill University on the matter of academic freedom, see Shore, *Science of Social Redemption*, passim. For the controversy see 'The Universities and Economics,' *LFP* (26 Oct. 1935): '[Beatty's address was]... thought provoking and one which the universities of this country should take to heart.' 'Radicalism in Colleges and at a Funeral,' Toronto *Mail and Empire* (29 Oct. 1935): 'Such men [radical professors] have apparently absorbed more knowledge than they have been able to digest and assimilate. Hence their economic dyspepsia.' Economic historian Harold A. Logan, head of the University of Western Ontario's department of economics, was strongly critical of Beatty's address and issued a written rebuttal of its assumptions. See 'Socialism Explained, but no Propaganda in Colleges,' *LFP* (30 Oct. 1935); 'Lauds Reply of Prof H.A. Logan; T.& L. Council Pleased with Reply to Sir Edward Beatty,' *LFP* (7 Nov. 1935); 'Back Criticism of Sir Edward: Railway Brotherhood Supports Dr H.A. Logan,' *LFP* (18 Nov. 1935). The dean of arts and science at Queen's also rejected Beatty's criticisms: 'He stated that Sir Edward knew not of what he spoke and emphasized that it was impossible for any man who was concerned almost solely with one phase of life to make correct judgments regarding an entirely

diverse field of activity.' 'Exception Is Taken to Beatty's Remark: Dean Matheson Refers to Criticism of Radical Professors,' *QJ* (12 Nov. 1935)

101 Douglas Francis, 'The Threatened Dismissal of Frank Underhill from the University of Toronto – 1939–1941,' Canadian Association of University Teachers *Bulletin* 24 (Dec. 1975), 5; Berger, *Writing History*, 81; Francis, *Underhill*, 101

102 Editorial, Montreal *Gazette* (20 Aug. 1938); 'Kick the Professor Out,' *SN* 53 (20 Aug. 1938), 3; 'Professional Hired Men,' *SN* 54 (10 Dec. 1938)

103 McCullagh and Cody quoted in Francis, 'Threatened dismissal,' 5

104 Berger, *Writing History*, 81; Oliver, *Ferguson*, 434, 438

105 Dr L.J. Simpson quoted in Francis, *Underhill*, 109, and the following from 109, 110, 197

106 B.K. Sandwell, 'New "Prexy" for Varsity,' *SN* 54 (22 Apr. 1939), 7. See also Politicus, 'At Queen's Park: Professors Beware,' *SN* 54 (22 Apr. 1939), 6; M.L. Ross, 'University Zone: Silence,' *SN* 54 (29 Apr. 1939), 24; Politicus, 'At Queen's Park: Keeping an Even Keel,' *SN* 54 (6 May 1939).

107 H. Carver, 'Premier Hepburn and the Professors,' *CF* 19 (May 1939), 41

108 Francis, *Underhill*, 112–13

109 Francis, 'Threatened Dismissal,' 6; Francis, *Underhill*, 114

110 Underhill quoted in Francis, *Underhill*, 113; Oliver, *Ferguson*, 438

111 Hunter quoted in Francis, *Underhill*, 109

112 See Balmer Neilly (a member of the university's Board of Governors) to C.E. Higginbottom (8 May 1939), quoted in Francis, 'Threatened Dismissal,' 6. Cody had by then already told Underhill in person that he was 'a trouble-maker who was costing the University untold sums of money ...' (quoted in Francis, *Underhill*, 111).

113 Horn, 'Professors in the Public Eye,' 435–6. Gregory Vlastos spoke of the Queen's administration's 'proper attitude' during the 1930s and 1940s (see Horn, above, 435). In 1934 Principal Hamilton Fyfe of Queen's spoke on academic freedom in a vein similar to that prevailing at the University of Toronto in the Falconer and Cody years. He dismissed the notion that Canadian universities were 'nurseries of anarchy and revolution,' and defended the importance of free speech in universities, but added: 'If we are to stimulate in our pupils objective thinking, we must be equally free in speech and thought ourselves – but not equally rash. Propaganda is no part of a teacher's function. He is not concerned to produce opinion, a temporary state of conviction which can be quickly changed by counter-propaganda. His aim is to stimulate the growth of intelligence, the power of detached judgement. To that end he may exercise in the classroom every art of sophistry, but if he blinks his way into the outer world, where opinions clash unanchored both from fact and reason, it behoves him to remember what astonishing weight that world attaches to a professorial pronouncement. The dignity of the University stalks beside him on the platform, sternly demanding judicial sobriety. A University teacher should certainly be clever; he needs also to be wise; and of the factors of wisdom not the least are self-restraint and kindliness and patience' (*ROP, 1933–4*, 7). There can be little doubt

that Fyfe addressed the academic controversy that took place in Toronto the previous autumn and winter, or that its practical object was to nip any Kingston Underhills in the bud.

114 Laura Hunter (secretary, Toronto branch, Canadian Civil Liberties Union) to Mitchell Hepburn (24 Apr. 1939); Harold Buckingham (secretary, Labour Party of Ontario) to Hepburn (15 Apr. 1939); J.R. Mutchmor (secretary, Board of Evangelism and Social Service, United Church of Canada) to Hepburn (17 Apr. 1939); all in Mitchell Hepburn Papers, AO, RG3, box 299, file 'Legislation 1939'

115 T.M. Medland (secretary, Canadian Corps Association) to Mitchell Hepburn (15 Apr. 1939); George E. Fisher (secretary-treasurer and manager, Canadian Brass Co.) to Hepburn (15 Apr. 1939); H.E. Mason (secretary, Stratford Board of Trade) to Hepburn (15 Apr. 1939); Elton M. Plant (district secretary-treasurer, Lions International of Canada, Ltd., Ontario and Quebec) to Hepburn (18 Apr. 1939); all in Mitchell Hepburn Papers, AO RG3, box 299, file 'Legislation 1939'

116 Charles Hallowell (Paris, Ontario) to Mitchell Hepburn (14 Apr. 1939); J.W. Hagen, DDS (Kitchener) to Hepburn (14 Apr. 1939); John Ferguson (Toronto) to Hepburn (14 Apr. 1939); A. Ives (president, New Market Lions Club) to Hepburn (13 Apr. 1939); all in Mitchell Hepburn Papers, AO, RG3, box 299, file: 'Legislation 1939'

117 J. Tassie (Hamilton) to Mitchell Hepburn (14 Apr. 1939), Mitchell Hepburn Papers, AO, RG3, box 299, file 'Legislation 1939'

118 Clifford Sifton to Mitchell Hepburn (10 Jan. 1941), Mitchell Hepburn Papers, AO, RG3, box 319, file 'University of Toronto 1941'

CHAPTER 15   *Students between Wars*

1 See F. Scott Fitzgerald, *This Side of Paradise* (London 1963 [1920]) and *The Beautiful and Damned* (London 1966 [1922]).

2 Paula S. Fass, *The Damned and the Beautiful: American Youth in the 1920s* (New York 1977), 17, 26–7

3 Roderick Nash, *The Nervous Generation: American Thought, 1917–1930* (Chicago 1990 [1970]), 6–7. Nash provides a comprehensive survey of the portrayal of the 1920s by historians, journalists, and novelists in his second chapter, 'Reputation,' 5–32.

4 Fitzgerald, *Paradise*, 253

5 Nash, *Nervous Generation*, vi; Fass, *Damned and Beautiful*, 368

6 Vipond, *The Mass Media in Canada* (Toronto 1989), 24

7 *SN* (17 Dec. 1927); copy in UTA, A-73-052, clippings, box 20, file 1 'Student Activities – General'

8 This was the finding of a 1918 board of education survey. It should be noted, however, that enrolment losses in American agricultural and engineering schools were substantially higher. See David O. Levine, *The American College and the Culture of Aspiration, 1915–1940* (Ithaca 1986), 25–6.

9 Levine, *American College*, 31

10 Keith Walden, 'Hazes, Hustles, Scraps, and Stunts: Initiations at the University of Toronto, 1880–1925,' in Paul Axelrod and John G. Reid, eds., *Youth, University, and Canadian Society: Essays in the Social History of Higher Education* (Kingston/Montreal 1989), 96

11 'Students Doused by Firemen in Rear of Trinity College – Small Fire Spread beyond Control and When Young Men Thought It a Joke, the Firemen Turned the Hose on Them and Party Broke Up,' *TW* (15 Dec. 1913). See also 'Science Men Stole Barrel Used in the Medical Rush – Sophomores Won From Freshmen on Campus: About Two Hundred in the Event,' *TN* (5 Oct. 1914).

12 'OAC Students Fight Police and Soldiers: Trouble Arose during Show in Opera House – Many Hurt on Both Sides,' *TG* (22 Mar. 1915)

13 Walden, 'Hazes, Hustles,' 108

14 'Med. Stude [*sic*] Favours "Scrap,"' *Varsity* (17 Oct. 1917), letter to editor

15 'Merry Battle at Varsity – Medical Students Line Up against SPS and Arts Men,' *TG* (14 Mar. 1918)

16 'More Initiations Coming: Scraps in a New Guise – Authorized Inter-Year Contests in Arts and Science to be Athletic or Burlesque,' *TT* (27 Oct. 1919)

17 'Guilty and Innocent Pay for Med. Scrap: Discipline Committee Condemns Rash Action of Med. Sophs,' *Varsity* (29 Oct. 1919); 'Medicals Make Midnight Merry – Sophomores and Freshmen Run Amok in Theatre and Restaurant,' *TW* (6 Nov. 1919); 'Medical Students Must Pay for Their Fun at Gaiety Theatre,' *Varsity* (15 Dec. 1919)

18 'Old-Timers Deplore the Red Tape Method of Initiating the Freshmen Nowadays – Too Much Organization – Not Enough Enthusiasm,' *Varsity* (19 Nov. 1920). Perhaps to remind the reader of the degree to which such conclusions were built on nostalgia, Leacock added: 'But I suppose the reason why I dislike it is because I am over half a century old. Of this much I am convinced, that when I was an undergraduate the professors were wiser, the college girls more beautiful, and the grass on the campus greener than ever it is to-day.'

19 *ROP, 1921–2*, 10, 16; *ROP, 1918–19*, 51; *ROP, 1921–2*, 60. The concern of Queen's authorities over initiations did not diminish. As a result of the 1922 initiations, a woman student with a history of heart disease died. In 1926, the AMS, after 'prolonged negotiations' with the university's senate, voted to abolish physical initiations, but found it difficult to enforce the prohibition. Moreover, the controversy bred distrust between students and administrators that lasted throughout the decade. See Frederick Gibson, *Queen's University*, vol. 2, *1917–1961: To Serve and Yet Be Free* (Montreal/Kingston 1983), 74.

20 C.M. Johnston and J.C. Weaver, *Student Days: An Illustrated History of Student Life at McMaster University from the 1890s to the 1980s* (Hamilton 1986), 27. Initiation quotation at 33–5. See also 'A Code of Ethics for University Students,' McMaster *Silhouette* (27 Nov. 1930).

21 'Students Celebrate Elections with 2-Hour Scrap,' *TT* (19 Mar. 1924); 'Jubilant Students Parade Streets – Mounted Constable Said to Have Slashed One of Crowd with Whip,' *TG* (18 Oct. 1924); 'Tradition Upheld in Annual College "Scrap,"' *TS* (26 Mar. 1928); '500 Rioting Students Storm Downtown Show – Eight Arrested after Wild March up Yonge Street,' *TM* (15 Nov. 1929); 'Students Engage in Fierce Combat – Trail of Wreckage Left When SPS Cohorts Raid Burwash – Tree Rams in Door – One Man Badly Beaten, One Missing, Others Nursing Bruises,' *TM* (24 Oct. 1930)

22 W.L. Morton, 'The 1920s,' in *The Canadians, 1867–1967*, ed. J.M.S. Careless (Toronto 1968), 229–30

23 'Tradition!' *VLS* (18 Jan.1924)

24 J. Pijoan, 'Sursum Corda!' *CF* 1 (May 1921). See also Edward Sapir, 'I Seek Returning Steps,' *CF* 6 (Oct. 1925); A.B. McKillop, 'Science, Authority, and the American Empire,' in A.B. McKillop, *Contours of Canadian Thought* (Toronto 1987), 111–28.

25 'Are College Students "Snobs?"' *Varsity* (14 Oct. 1921)

26 Editorial, 'The Student and College Activities,' *Varsity* (29 Sept. 1922)

27 Editorial, *AV* (Oct. 1929)

28 *QJ* (22 Oct. 1929)

29 'The Old Order Changes,' *Varsity* (5 Feb. 1923). See also 'Robots and Robotism,' *AV* (Feb. 1924), 8–10, in which the problem of regimentation in contemporary university education (aimed at 'making you a better money-making Robot') is linked to the incursion of American values.

30 *ROP, 1929–30*, 4–5. See also *AV* (Apr. 1924); 'Our Misguided Universities,' *Varsity* (5 Mar. 1929).

31 *AV* (Feb. 1927)

32 *QJ* (18 Oct. 1929); *ROP, 1929–30*, 76–8. See discussion of the 1928 student strike at Queen's, below, for context.

33 Editorial, 'Student Government,' *Silhouette* (9 Oct. 1930)

34 Ibid.

35 T.A. Reed, ed., *A History of the University of Trinitiy College, Toronto, 1852–1952* (Toronto 1952), 128–30

36 Alison Prentice, Paula Bourne, Gail Cuthbert Brandt, Beth Light, Wendy Mitchinson, and Naomi Black, *Canadian Women: A History* (Toronto 1988). See Table A.19, 'Female enrolment as a percentage of full-time university undergraduate enrolment, 1891–1975,' 427. Elsewhere in *Canadian Women* (162) a percentage of 13.9 is given for the 1919–20 academic year.

37 See Peter Ward, *Courtship, Love, and Marriage in Nineteenth-Century English Canada* (Montreal/Kingston 1990), 86

38 Reed, 130

39 See also 'Cost of Living for Co-eds $650,' *TS*(14 Oct. 1925); 'Rich Men's Sons Don't Make a Mark at College,' *TSW* (17 Oct. 1925). The average estimated annual cost for male students at Toronto in 1925 was $700, roughly $150 more than at Queen's. As a *Varsity* editorial stated in 1926, on the subject of students' difficulty in

obtaining loans: 'it is a cold and unrelenting fact that, generally speaking, it is as easy for a rich man to get into Heaven as it is for a self-supporting student to proceed to a degree in four consecutive years' ('Economically and Socially Indefensible,' *Varsity* [11 Feb. 1926]). See also 'Students from the Country Specially Considered,' *TM* (Jan. 1926).

40 See, e.g., *AV* 51 (1926–7), or *QJ* 61 (1929–30). For a good general overview of the cultivation of a North American consumer society in the 1920s, see Loren Baritz, *The Good Life: The Meaning of Success for the American Middle Class* (New York 1990), 76–83.

41 'Varsity Girls Lead the War,' *TS* (31 Jan. 1923); 'Queen's Hall Coeds in Favour of Taxis: Nearly All Seem to be Opposed to Riding From Dances in TTC Cars – NOT THE PROPER THING,' *Varsity* (9 Feb. 1923). Security as well as comfort was probably on women's minds, for the possibility of assault on unescorted women existed. In 1925 Mossie May Kirkwood, dean of women at University College, issued a proclamation forbidding women students to go unaccompanied after dark because a 'Peeping Tom' had been sighted by at least eight people. He was later arrested. See 'Women Students Advised Not to Walk Unaccompanied after Dark,' *Varsity* (7 Dec. 1925); 'Annoyances Stopped by Timely Arrest,' *Varsity* (10 Dec. 1925).

42 'Dilemma of the Co-eds' Academic Garb Problem,' *TT* (29 Dec. 1924); 'Gowns Become More Popular,' *Varsity* (28 Nov. 1924); 'Co-eds Asked to Wear Gowns,' *Varsity* (8 Jan. 1925); 'Gowns Coming Back to Varsity Campus,' *TS* (9 Jan. 1925); 'Wearing of Flowing Gowns Grows Popular with Co-eds,' *TG* (13 Jan. 1925). The fate of academic gowns was probably summed up by a person writing to *Varsity* in 1921. After briefly outlining the history and meaning of academic gowns, he concluded: 'Perhaps the discontinuance of this venerable custom is another evidence of the practical age in which we live. After all, if a thing has outlived its usefulness, why prolong its life?' See letter to editor from 'Tradition,' *Varsity* (7 Dec.1921).

43 'What Does It Cost Student for a Year?... ,' *Varsity* (25 Oct. 1922)

44 'Wise Girls and Foolish Fellow,' *TS* (16 Feb. 1923)

45 Quotation from *Printers' Ink*, in Baritz, *The Good Life*, 78. For examples of advertising aimed at Canadian women between the wars, see Veronica Strong-Boag, *The New Day Recalled: Lives of Girls and Women in English Canada, 1919–1939* (Toronto 1988), 13–15.

46 Helen Lefkowitz Horowitz, *Campus Life: Undergraduate Cultures from the End of the Eighteenth Century to the Present* (Chicago 1987), 127. Evidence on the sexual activity of Ontario students in the 1920s is scant, but see John English, *Shadow of Heaven: The Life of Lester Pearson*, vol. 1, *1897–1948* (Toronto 1989), 102–11 passim, for brief characterization of the ambiguity and tension in sexual attitudes and social expectations at Victoria College in the 1920s. Horowitz's characterization is probably applicable to the Ontario case, although (as will be seen) the continued strictness of the supervision of female students would likely have made sexual contact more difficult.

U of T students may or may not have been chaste in the 1920s, but they were usually 'clean.' In 1924, e.g., Dr George D. Porter, director of the University Health Service, reported to Premier Ferguson: 'It is gratifying to state that according to our examinations there is a clean bill of health in regard to Venereal Diseases in our University' (G. Howard Ferguson Papers, AO, RG3 series 7, box 112, file 'University of Toronto Reports #2'). Similarly, when Dr Edith Gordon, medical adviser of women at the U of T, reported for the year 1923–4, she noted many ailments and diseases suffered by the 516 students who had been examined, but none was of a sexual nature ('Report of the Medical Advisor of Women for the Year 1923–24 [12 June 1924], in ibid., AO, RG3 series 7, box 112, file 'University of Toronto Reports #2').

47 'Coeducation Changes from the Early Days: Fair "Coeds" Now Are a Multitude and Individual Is Inconspicuous; STILL, THEY MARRY!' *TS* (2 Feb. 1923); 'They Have Travelled a Long Road from the Bluestocking Era,' *TT* (24 Apr. 1923)

48 'Co-Ed at Last Differentiated with [*sic*] Woman Undergraduate,' *Varsity* (18 Nov. 1924)

49 'Hectic Years Gone Hence: Paint, Booze, Petting, Myths – Various Heads of University Find No Traces of 'Drink and Fast Set' which Alarms US Prof.,' *TT* (15 Jan. 1924); 'Dissolute College Boy Unknown in Real Life – Representative Authorities Disprove Prevalent Hip Flask Theory – Considered as Fad,' *Varsity* (5 Nov. 1926); 'Not Much Gambling about University,' *TG* (15 Oct. 1927); 'Charges Students Have Manners of Night Clubs,' *Varsity* (18 Jan. 1928). See also Ellen K. Rothman, *Hands and Hearts: A History of Courtship in America* (New York 1984), 287–90; Baritz, *The Good Life*, 89–90.

50 Quoted in Gibson, *Queen's*, 72

51 Ibid., 75–6

52 Ibid., 79

53 'College Girl of 1925 Has Common Sense – More Definite Aim in Life than Co-Ed of 25 Years Ago: Full, Happy Life,' *TSW* (7 Feb. 1925)

54 'Coeducation Changes from the Early Days,' *TS* (2 Feb. 1923)

55 Prentice et al., *Canadian Women*, 218–19, 240–1 passim. See also Strong-Boag, *New Day Recalled*, 7–13; Lynn D. Gordon, 'The Gibson Girl Goes to College: Popular Culture and Women's Higher Education in the Progressive Era, 1890–1920,' *American Quarterly* 39 (Summer 1987), 225–6.

56 See Strong-Boag, *New Day Recalled*, Table 1, 'Percentage of each sex aged 15 to 19 at school,' 21.

57 See Prentice et al., *Canadian Women*, Table A.19, 'Female enrolment as a percentage of full-time university undergraduate enrolment, 1891–1975,' 427.

58 'Woman Students and Their Responsibilities,' *Varsity* (24 Nov. 1921); 'Fatigue Brings Co-Eds Incapacity,' *Varsity* (3 Mar. 1925)

59 'Practical Politics,' *Varsity* (17 Oct. 1921); 'College Lawns are Quiet Now; Carefree Co-eds Off to Try Conclusions in World's Mills of Toil,' *TG* (23 May 1922)

60 'Colleges Draw Girls by Many and Varied Means: Different Motives Impell the

High School Grad to Universities,' *Varsity* (3 Mar. 1925); 'Do Varsity Co-Eds Agree with This Attitude to Marriage?' *Varsity* (5 Feb. 1925)

61 'Character Strongest Matrimonial Factor,' *TS* (6 May 1925). The personal costs to women as a result of such pressure are clear in the case of Maryon Pearson. See English, *Shadow of Heaven*, 108–11.

62 'Marriage Prime Object of Many College Women,' *Varsity* (3 Mar. 1925)

63 Marni de Pencier, 'Women Faculty at the University of Toronto,' research study, U of T (1973), Chart C, 'Distribution of women faculty within the university' (PUH, UTA, A83-0036/001)

64 Editorial, *AV* (Oct. 1929)

65 'Co-eds Are Becoming Decidedly Athletic,' *TS* (18 Feb. 1924); 'Varsity Co-eds Vote in Favour of Athletics,' *TSW* (20 Nov. 1926)

66 'Co-eds Gym Seems Inadequate,' *Varsity* (28 Oct. 1935); 'Women Lack Credit in Outdoor Sports; Inadequate Grounds Make Training Compulsory for Co-eds; Needs Central Locale,' *Varsity* (22 Oct. 1935); 'Physical Training Should Be Source of Enjoyment to Co-eds,' *Varsity* (24 Jan. 1939)

67 Johnston and Weaver, *Student Days*, 39

68 'Dedicate "Wallingford,"' *TT* (2 Nov. 1920)

69 'Co-Education Losing Favour at Varsity: Even Class Parties May Be Abolished,' *TS* (31 Jan. 1923); 'To Be or Not to Be? Co-Education? The Women Gossip Over It, the Men Discuss It, It Is on Every Tongue,' *Varsity* (28 Feb. 1923); 'Reorganization of UC Executive Councils to Satisfy Co-Eds: According to Friday's Referendum Women Favour Separate Activities,' *Varsity* (5 Mar. 1923); Marni de Pencier, 'A Study of the Enrolment of Women in the University of Toronto,' research study, U of T (July 1973), Appendix A: 'Master chart: enrolment from 1904–1970' (PUH, A83-0036/001)

70 *ROP, 1931–2*, 8

71 *Student Handbook, 1926–7* (Kingston 1926); *QJ* (20 Nov. 1928); *QJ* (29 Jan. 1929). Quotations from original sources in this paragraph have been drawn from Nicole Neatby, 'Women at Queen's in the Twenties: A Separate Sphere,' MA thesis, Queen's (1988), 46, 48ff

72 Articles in *QJ* (18 Feb. 1930), (23 Nov. 1928), (20 Mar. 1923); cited in Neatby, 'Women at Queen's,' 50–2

73 Taylor quoted in *QJ* (5 Oct. 1927); cited in Neatby, 'Women at Queen's,' 55

74 *QJ* (23 Nov. 1928)

75 See Ian M. Drummond, *Progress without Planning: The Economic History of Ontario from Confederation to the Second World War* (Toronto 1987), 40, 182–3 and passim.

76 See also 'More and More Co-eds Are Attending U of T,' *TG* (24 Jan. 1935). *TG*'s estimation of a 30% enrolment of women in the university as a whole appears to be an underestimate, and its estimation of 50% female enrolment an overestimate (my figures suggest that women constituted 41.7% of the Toronto arts enrolment in 1934–5, for which see Fig. 15.10).

77 In medicine, only 75 of the 986 U of T students were women, and the number declined to 69 (of 844) a decade later. In the 1939–40 academic year, women numbered only 64 in a class of 817. Full-time enrolment by women in Ontario commerce courses was negligible between the wars. The peak in female enrolment was 1931, when 30 women were enrolled: the total number of commerce students at the time was 216. See also de Pencier, 'Enrolment of Women.'

78 Quoted in Paul Axelrod, *Making a Middle Class: Student Life in English Canada during the Thirties* (Montreal/Kingston 1990), 91

79 In 1930 women comprised, respectively, only 3.4, 4.2, and 14.3% of the national undergraduate enrolment in those fields. Prentice et al., *Canadian Women*, Table A.19, 427

80 Dean Packenham, 'The University and the Training of Teachers,' NCCU *Proceedings* (1922), 37–8, italics in original. In 1919, the provincial ministry of education suspended funding for the faculty of education at Queen's, and transformed the U of T's faculty of education into the Ontario College of Education, located in Toronto, to be staffed by former members of the U of T's faculty of education, and becoming the U of T's education faculty in all but name. Queen's objected strongly, for it was forced for financial reasons to close its own faculty at the end of the 1920–21 academic year. See D.D. Calvin, *Queen's University at Kingston: The First Century of a Scottish-Canadian Foundation* (Kingston 1941), 214–16.

The origins of the decision to create the OCE lay in the years of the Great War, when the superintendent of education for Ontario, John Seath, had condemned existing structures for teacher training in the province. Long a believer that a faculty of education at Queen's was an unnecessary luxury, and concerned with declining enrolment in secondary teacher training, Seath saw the solution in centralization. The OCE was intended to concentrate on the training of secondary school teachers; training of primary school teachers was assigned to the normal schools. The result, as Robin S. Harris has noted, was that for the half-century after 1920 a clear separation existed between the training of primary and secondary school teachers. See 'Professional Education' (unpaginated), PUH, UTA, A83-0036/001.

81 Professor J.F. Macdonald, 'Can First Class Honour Graduates Be Induced to take Up Secondary School Teaching as a Life Work?' NCCU *Proceedings* (1930), 103

82 Macdonald, 'Honour Graduates,' 104–5

83 Ibid., 107

84 Prentice et al., *Canadian Women*, Table A.19, 427

85 *ROP, 1925–6*, 64–5. Of the remainder, five considered secretarial work, three library work, two journalism, one law, one social work, and one household economics. During the 1931–2 summer school at Queen's, in education classes sanctioned by the provincial Department of Education, there were 23 men and 72 women. At the time, women comprised 40% of the university's net total registration of 2,062, and they began to outnumber men as extramural students when the financial pressures of the Great Depression made full-time university for women a luxury that few families

could afford (*ROP, 1931–2*, 44, 15). Extramural summer registration at Queen's in 1936 was 590 men and 623 women. During the winter term of 1936–7, 737 men and 893 women were registered (*ROP, 1936–7*, 45).

86 *ROP, 1925–6*, 64

87 See Prentice et al., *Canadian Women*, Table A.19, 427.

88 Ruby C.E. Mason (dean of women at UWO), *The Education of Women* (London 1928), 2

89 The number of women acting in an instructional capacity at U of T between the wars more than doubled, but most of them held junior positions, often temporary in nature, as laboratory instructors in the natural and medical sciences or in modern languages. See Alison Prentice, 'Bluestockings, Feminists, or Women Workers? A Preliminary Look at Women's Early Employment at the University of Toronto,' *Journal of the Canadian Historical Association: Kingston 1991*, new series, no. 2 (Ottawa 1992), 243–8.

90 See also Susan Gelman, 'The "Feminization" of the High School: Women Secondary Schoolteachers in Toronto: 1871–1930,' Table 4, 'Subjects taught by women secondary schoolteachers in Toronto: 1900–1930,' in Ruby Heap and Alison Prentice, eds., *Gender and Education in Ontario: An Historical Reader* (Toronto 1991), 92.

91 Diana Pederson, '"The Call to Service": The YWCA and the Canadian College Woman, 1886–1920,' in Axelrod and Reid, *Youth, University, and Canadian Society*, 187–9, 196–7 passim

92 This subject is treated at length in ch. 16, but see E.J. Urwick, *A Philosophy of Social Progress* (London 1912); R.M. MacIver, *The Elements of Social Science* (London 1921); E.J. Urwick, *The Social Good* (London 1927) and *The Values of Life* (Toronto 1948).

93 See also 'Professional Education' (unpaginated), PUH UTA, A83-0036/001.

94 Ray quoted in Axelrod, *Making a Middle Class*, 93; de Pencier, 'Enrolment of Women'

95 This was the kind of message peddled by appliance manufacturers and professional home economists hired by North American electrical generating companies in the 1920s. See Baritz, *The Good Life*, 78. By the 1950s, Baritz notes, the dream had proven to be illusory: 'The American house in the fifties contained seven times as much equipment as it had had in the twenties. The result was a slight increase in the amount of time the housewife spent doing her work: the fifty-two hour week of the twenties housewife became fifty-six hours thirty years later. New standards of cleanliness and the dispersion of stores created more work' (192–3). See also Dianne E. Dodd, 'Delivering Electrical Technology to the Ontario Housewife, 1920-1939: An Alliance of Professional Women, Advertisers and the Electrical Industry,' PHD thesis, Carleton (1988).

96 See Prentice et al., *Canadian Women*, Table A.19, 427; de Pencier, 'Enrolment of Women'

97 *ROP, 1934–5*, 4; see also *ROP, 1931–2*, 10; *ROP, 1933–4*, 4–5; 'University Gets Through Year with a Deficit,' *LFP* (15 Jan. 1936)

98 Axelrod, *Making a Middle Class*, 20, 26–7

99 Gibson notes that 'The decline in enrolment at Queen's between 1930 and 1935 was far from precipitous' (*Queen's*, 102–3). The *TT* reported in Oct. 1934 that in the past four years enrolment in arts at McMaster had doubled ('Fear Theology on a Side Track at McMaster,' *TT* [26 Oct. 1934]).

100 Drummond, *Progress without Planning*, Table 2.1, 'Gainful Workers, Ontario,' following 359. Robert Bothwell, Ian Drummond, and John English, *Canada 1900–1945* (Toronto 1987), 251–2, 258. See also Donald Kerr and Deryck W. Holdsworth, eds., *Historical Atlas of Canada*, vol. 3, *Addressing the Twentieth Century* (Toronto 1990), plates 40 (concerning the Ontario Employment Index) and 41 (concerning price and wage indices). Both demonstrate that the economy was severely depressed between 1929 and 1933, but recovered thereafter.

101 Axelrod, *Making a Middle Class*, 21–6. See also Gibson, *Queen's*, 103, 448. Gibson concludes that in the 1930s Queen's became 'a more homogeneous, a more heavily urban middle-class, institution' (103).

102 'Students in Mutual Benefit Camp Build Road in Exchange for Aid: Pay themselves from Common Fund,' *TM* (17 Sept. 1932). In the mid-1930s some Queen's students also started a cooperative scheme. Described as a group of 'amateur communists,' they pooled their money and redistributed a larger allowance to each in return. *QJ* (11 Oct. 1935) noted wryly: 'The latest reports have it that both Stalin and Premier Aberhart are in town to look over the feasibility of this scheme.' See also 'Versatile Students Earn University Fees: Oil Tankers, Fisheries, Music Sales Posts Studded with Ambitious Youths,' *TS* (12 Oct. 1935); 'Many Co-eds Take Jobs to Meet College Fees,' *Varsity* (20 Oct. 1937).

103 Johnston and Weaver, *Student Days*, 45. The first two volumes of *Silhouette* (1930–2) show very little evidence of the impact of the Depression on students.

104 'Up to Varsities to Halt Hazing Dangers, Says Court: Initiations Unpopular Following Decision of Alberta Appeal Judges,' *TS* (22 May 1934); 'Hazing of Freshmen Excluded at Varsity,' *TM* (24 Dec. 1933); Axelrod, *Making a Middle Class,* 104–5

105 'Initiations "On Quiet" Continue at "Varsity,"' *TS* (15 Sept. 1934); '"Ordeal by Fire" Faces Freshmen: Many Original Methods of Reception to be Tried Out,' *Varsity* (27 Sept. 1934); 'In Mock Ministerial Garb Freshman Visits Beer Room: College Initiation Party Park and Drink, Then Motor Off; Many Imbibe, Drive,' *TS* (27 Sept. 1934); 'Students Must Foot Bill of 49 Broken Windows,' *TT* (3 Oct. 1934); 'Students Crash Gate at Show: 100 Are Ejected by Police,' *TM* (10 Oct. 1934); 'Campus the Place for Student Pranks,' *TT* (11 Oct. 1934); 'Trinity Frosh "Take the Cake": Songs Keep Sleepy Saints Awake,' *Varsity* (30 Nov.1934); 'Co-eds Locked in Whitney Hall: University Students Celebrate Hallowe'en,' *TT* (1 Nov. 1934); 'Rowdyism at U of T Is Seen on Decline: President Cody Speaks Highly of New Spirit of Students,' *TM* (24 Dec. 1934)

106 'Improvement Seen in Student Body Say Professors: Less Rowdyism, More Honesty but Gum Chewing Is Still Prevalent: Civil and Well Mannered,' *Varsity* (6

654 Notes to pages 439–43

Dec. 1935); 'Bold Initiation Now Abolished – McMaster Sophomores Must Observe Milder Tactics – Students Approve,' *Varsity* (10 Oct. 1934); 'Varsity Initiations Undergo Reform,' *TT* (30 Sept. 1935); 'Present Day Students Are Little Gentlemen,' *UTM* (Jan. 1936)

The new student seriousness did not preclude student pranks or the continuation of initiations. The cycle continued, with student governments attempting to curb excess. See, e.g., 'Iron Gates Torn Off as Students of SPS Hold Annual Elections,' *TG* (29 Feb. 1936); *ROP, 1936–7*, 79–82; 'Varsity Bans "Rough Stuff," Say Student Leaders,' *TS* (19 Oct. 1938); 'Gun Booms in U of T Ballot Battle, Strikes Terror in Nervous Hearts,' *TGM* (4 Mar. 1939).

107 *ROP, 1933–4*, 6; Gibson, *Queen's*, 104

108 *ROP, 1935–6*, 19. The dean of applied science expressed similar views that year: he complained of 'too many students of the careless indifferent sort' who 'should be weeded out. The present generation is rather indisciplined ... I wish we might bring back some of the old-time respect for the trained mind.'

109 *ROP, 1930–1*, 12–13

110 Canadian journalistic commentators had lamented the influences of American mass culture for many years. See McKillop, 'Science, Authority, and the American Empire.' For the impact of 'international' influences on Anglo-Canadian elite culture, see Maria Tippett, *Making Culture: English-Canadian Institutions and the Arts before the Massey Commission* (Toronto 1990), 127–55.

111 *ROP, 1936–7*, 7

112 Gibson, *Queen's*, 128–31. Fyfe left behind him a report to the Queen's board of trustees extremely critical of education at Queen's and in Canada. The report was never circulated beyond the university's board of trustees, and a more innocuous one was written for the official university record. The chairman of the board, J.M. Macdonnell, wrote: 'I am afraid we were never able to innoculate [*sic*] him with the Queen's spirit' (131).

113 Baritz, *The Good Life*, 153–65

114 Advertisement from Northway's in *Silhouette* (5 Dec. 1933); 'Coeds at McMaster Won't Have Smoker,' *Varsity* (11 Oct. 1934); 'Refuses Sale of Beer at University Campus,' *TT* (25 Feb. 1935)

115 Laird quoted in Gibson, *Queen's*, 104; *QJ* of 1937 quoted in Axelrod, *Making a Middle Class*, 114. See also 'Learn to Do the Big Apple: Professor Hamill Here on Friday Night – This is a new American Dance Craze,' *QJ* (30 Nov. 1937); also editorial on 'The Big Apple' in same issue.

116 For treatment of the growth of linkages between the cigarette and radio industries in North America, making it almost impossible in the 1930s to listen to a Big Band or popular crooner without also being besieged by the message to smoke, see 'Smoke Rings,' ch. 8 in Philip K. Eberly, *Music in the Air: America's Changing Tastes in Popular Music, 1920–1980* (New York 1982), 114–24. The romance of cigarettes was not invented in the 1930s: in 1908, Victor Herbert had written the tune 'Love Is

Like a Cigarette.' For an evocative and beautifully written personal account of the rise and decline of the Big Band era, see 'Pavilion in the Rain,' in Gene Lees, *Singers and the Song* (New York 1987), 70–100. Lees was born in Canada, and when young lived in St Catharines, Ontario.

117 'Students Favour Co-Educational Smoking Room: A Few Dissent from General Point of View in Some of the Colleges ...,' *Varsity* (4 Dec. 1935); 'Ash Trays Oust Lunch Boxes in Girl's Room at Varsity,' *TT* (14 Jan. 1937). Previously, U of T women who wanted to smoke had to do so on the front steps of University College. Since they were still 'strictly prohibited' from eating in their common room even after it was open to smokers, those who wanted to do both still found themselves on the front doorstep of the college or in its cloakroom.

118 'To-Day Marks Beginning of Sadie Hawkins Week: Campus Said Enthusiastic about Plan for Co-Ed Dating and Paying,' *Varsity* (31 Oct. 1938). This instant 'tradition' of the 1930s was inspired by the voluptuous and forward character in Al Capp's popular syndicated comic strip, 'L'il Abner.' See also 'Sadie Hawkins Real Live Girl: Arrives in Flesh and Blood This Evening – Plans to Stay for Week – Undergrads to Welcome Her at Capitol Theatre,' *LFP* (21 Nov. 1938); 'Sadie Hawkins Week for "U": Social Conventions Go into Reverse for Western Students – And Woman Must Pay ...,' *LFP* (18 Nov. 1940).

119 'Modern Girl Prefers Dutch Date Rather Than Lonely Fate,' *Varsity* (13 Nov. 1934); 'Co-Eds Averse to Dutch Dates: Difference of Feminine Opinion between British Columbia and Toronto,' *Varsity* (2 Nov. 1934); 'Co-Eds Fear a Spinster's Fate: Determine How to Snare a Mate,' *Varsity* (28 Nov. 1934); 'University Students Don't Favour Uniform,' *TS* (14 Nov. 1934); 'Co-Eds Are Lauded for Taste in Dress,' *TM* (15 Nov. 1934)

120 'Varsity Co-eds 66 PC "Pure," Men 59 PC Inquiry Shows: Latter Make Bad Showing Compared with 71 PC in New York – Ask 18 Questions,' *TS* (11 Dec. 1936). Public discussion of sex in more formal settings occurred obliquely, as when the Trinity College Literary Institute debated the following: 'Resolved that women are as yet incapable of friendship.' The man taking the affirmative side argued that 'Woman uses her men acquaintances as a means to an end – usually a week-end.' The woman for the negative side asserted that 'man's passion prevented him from thinking of platonic friendship' *QJ* (26 Oct. 1935). See also Joe Scoop, 'Growing Generation in Need of Sex Education,' *QJ* (11 Jan. 1938.), which, in spite of its flippant tone, spoke to a real need.

121 'Girls Disturbing to Academic Work Say Varsity Men: Political Leaders Are Cited as Examples of Value of Celibacy – Women Said Irrational – Some Less Biased Males Are Willing to Tolerate Fairer Sex,' *Varsity* (14 Feb. 1935); 'Women Make Good Lawyers University Professor Says ... Male Members of Profession Said Trifle Resentful,' *TS* (21 Nov. 1938); 'University Men Agree Co-Eds Can't Debate Well on Politics,' *Varsity* (6 Dec. 1935); 'Further Weakness of the Weaker Sex,' *Varsity* (9 Oct. 1936)

122 'Women Study Mining Just "For Pastime": They Are Interested in Rocks but Will Not Go "Prospecting,"' *TS* (8 Jan. 1935); 'Seeking Science Honors, but Pack Dimples, Too: Dozen of 'Em Going through Engineering and Architectural Courses but They're Still Eager for Dances – One Would Go to Great Bear Lake,' *TS* (10 Feb. 1940)

123 UTA, A-73-052, box 1, file 16 'McMaster University no. 2'

124 See *AV* (Feb. 1924, Oct. 1926); *ROP, 1929–30*, 9

125 'University Staff Backs "68" by 3 to 1 Vote: 70% of Staff Reached by "Varsity" but 219 Refuse to Express Opinion,' *Varsity* (21 Jan. 1931); 'The Most Inglorious,' *Varsity* (21 Jan. 1931); 'The Student Speaks,' *Varsity* (23 Jan. 1931); 'Fotheringham Vents Disgust with University in Scathing Diatribe,' *Varsity* (26 Jan. 1926)

126 See 'Student Speaks.' The demands of academic work should not be discounted as a significant factor in students' lack of participation in the political process. See 'Lectures Overburden Students: No Time for World Affairs – More Time for Lectures than World Affairs, Opine Professors,' *Varsity* (18 Feb. 1935).

127 'Students Always Hub of Ferment; FOR Speaker Deplores Lack of Original, Unafraid Thinking,' *Varsity* (26 Jan. 1931). The speaker was J. Woodrington of Pickering College. See also 'Why Not a Political Career?' *Silhouette* (16 Feb. 1932).

128 See Axelrod, 'The Student Movement of the 1930s,' in Axelrod and Reid, *Youth, University, and Canadian Society*, 216–17. The NFCUS was founded in 1926.

129 See Margaret Beattie, *SCM: A Short History of the Student Christian Movement in Canada* (Toronto 1975); Axelrod, 'Student Movement,' 217–18.

130 'New Communist Club Formed Here First in Any Canadian University: Will Have Same Position on Campus as Other Political Groups,' *Varsity* (5 Dec. 1935); Axelrod, 'Student Movement,' 219–20; Michiel Horn, *The League for Social Reconstruction: Intellectual Origins of the Democratic Left in Canada, 1930–1942* (Toronto 1980)

131 'Majority of Students Air Political Opinions: Result of Straw Vote Shatters All Former Charges of Apathy and Radicalism on the Part of Students at the University of Toronto – Approximately 4,000 Voters Appear at Polls,' *Varsity* (11 Oct. 1935). The federal election was held on 14 Oct.

132 'University Students May Sign Pledge Not to Participate in a War,' *LFP* (25 Nov. 1930); 'University Students Ask Statesmen, Not Experts in Armed Service, at Geneva,' *LFP* (19 Oct. 1931)

133 'Anti-War Questionnaire Arouses Varied Comments: Members of Faculty Do Not Consider Opinion of Students Now Would Determine Their Action in Time of War: Co-Eds Are on the Whole Pacifists – Function of Questionnaire in Stimulating Thought Lauded,' *Varsity* (16 Nov. 1934)

134 'Anti-War Sentiment among Students,' *Varsity* (4 Dec. 1934)

135 'Anti-War Wreath to Honor Soldiers,' *TT* (8 Nov. 1934); letter to editor from Claude de Mestral, *Varsity* (4 Dec. 1934); letter to editor from M. Wayman (Chem-

istry III), *Varsity* (14 Dec. 1934); 'Anti-War Meeting Raided by Cohorts of COTC,'
TM (8 Nov. 1934). See also editorial, 'The Purpose of Armistice Day,' *QJ* (8 Nov.
1935), 'Remembrance Day,' *QJ* (9 Nov. 1937).

136 'Twenty Varsity Pacifists Join Memorial Service,' *TT* (12 Nov. 1934); '99 of 200
Students Absolute Pacifists,' *TT* (27 Nov. 1934); 'Anti-War Society to Call Con-
gress to Further Peace,' *Varsity* (16 Jan. 1935); letter to editor from K.C. Woods-
worth, *Varsity* (4 Dec. 1934), 'Anti-War Society Decides to Send Delegate to
Europe – Ken Woodsworth is elected to Represent U of T at Congress – Is "Typical
Student"...,' *Varsity* (14 Dec. 1934)

137 For student recognition of waning support for British imperial interests and support
of the League of Nations, see 'Anomalies Vanquished,' *QJ* (7 Feb. 1930); 'The
League at Work,' *QJ* (1 Oct. 1935); 'First Prevent World War,' *QJ* (4 Oct. 1935);
'Force Needed in Securing of Peace – Strength in League,' *QJ* (26 Oct. 1935).

138 'McMaster Students Will War Only if Canada Is Justified,' *TS* (4 Dec. 1934); 'Justify War – Then Only Will We Fight,' *Silhouette* (4 Dec. 1934); 'Echoes,' *Silhouette* (9 Oct. 1935)

139 'Anti-War Experts Give Views Today – Professor W. Woodside Contributes Article, Also Havelack [*sic*] Ellis,' *Varsity* (23 Feb. 1935). This student's mistake in
remembering Eric Havelock's name, together with the 'Freudian slip' he made,
suggests that he had other things on his mind.

140 'Student Peace Movement,' *Varsity* (1 Mar. 1935); 'Students Arranging for Peace
Conference,' *TM* (26 Feb. 1935)

141 'Campus Societies to Hold Armistice Meeting,' *QJ* (1 Nov. 1935); editorial, 'The
Purpose of Armistice Day,' *QJ* (8 Nov. 1935); 'SCM and LSR Will Meet Together,'
QJ (8 Nov. 1935); 'Campus Clubs Have Discussion on Peace: Meeting Held in
YWCA Sunday Many Speeches,' *QJ* (12 Nov. 1935)

142 'Wide Developments for Peace League are Anticipated,' *Varsity* (30 Sept. 1935);
'Sees Trend Toward Fascism in Canada,' *QJ* (19 Nov. 1935); 'Radicalism in Col-
leges,' *QJ* (1 Nov. 1935); Donald C. MacDonald, 'Conservatism vs. Radicalism,'
QJ (29 Oct. 1937); 'Proletarian Rule Deemed Necessity,' *Varsity* (12 Feb. 1935);
'Mayor Asks That Students Be Radicals: Considers It a Compliment When Term Is
Applied to Himself, Says Simpson,' *TT* (9 Jan. 1935); 'Poverty in Russia Is Over-
emphasized G.B. Reed States ...,' *QJ* (18 Oct. 1935); 'Vlastos Criticises Capitalistic
Rule: Sees Need for Property Socialization and Control – At LSR Meeting,' *QJ* (15
Oct. 1935); 'Underhill Favours Careful Policy,' *Varsity* (5 Dec. 1935); J.S. Wood-
sworth, 'Youth Needed in Political Field,' *QJ* (16 Nov. 1937). See also Axelrod,
'Student Movement,' 218–19.

143 'Professor Knox Outlines Significance of Marxism,' *QJ* (25 Jan. 1938); 'Graduates
and Undergraduates Hold Separate Armistice Services,' *Varsity* (12 Nov. 1936);
'Pertinent to Peace,' *QJ* (26 Nov. 1935); 'Radical Schools of Thought Challenging
Religious Beliefs ...,' *QJ* (16 Nov. 1937); 'Religion Should Be an Experience Dr
Jones States,' *QJ* (29 Oct. 1935) ; 'SCM Panel,' *QJ* (26 Oct. 1935)

144 'Buck Listeners Rush University "Fascists": College Men Yell "Hurrah for Fascism" – Crowd Turns on Group,' *TS* (2 May 1935); 'Mischievous Co-Ed on Fountain Diversion at Queen's Park Rally,' *TS* (4 Apr. 1935); Axelrod, 'Student
Movement,' 217–19

145 'Veterans Divided over University Students' Group to Satirize War,' *LFP* (30 Mar.
1936); 'War Veterans of Future Meet,' *LFP* (30 Mar. 1936); 'Students Plan to
Make War Laughing Stock of North American People,' *LFP* (30 Mar. 1936)

146 Review, *AV* (Oct. 1929); 'The Soap Box,' *QJ* (15 Nov. 1935); 'Peace and the
Present,' *QJ* (3 Dec. 1935); 'Students Divided, Too,' *TG* (22 Mar. 1935)

147 Articles by Donald C. MacDonald: 'War Torn Spain,' *QJ* (21 Oct. 1937); 'Propaganda in Italy,' *QJ* (2 Nov. 1937); 'International Origins of the Spanish Civil War,'
QJ (9 Nov. 1937). J.B. Conacher, letter to editor, *QJ* (13 Nov. 1937); 'Controversy,' *QJ* (19 Nov. 1937)

148 'No More Orchids for Co-Eds Say College Men Figuring Costs ...,' *LFP* (29 Jan.
1937); 'Well-Dressed Man Will Wear Vegetable Corsage According to "Co-Ed
Prom,"' *LFP* (17 Feb. 1938); 'Strapless Gown Gets Approval: University Co-eds
Say They're All Right; If a Girl Can Wear Them – Depends on Shoulders, Carriage
and So On,' *LFP* (1 Dec. 1938). See also 'Student Social Life Defended,' *LFP* (5
Feb. 1937).

149 'Lad Starts College Broke But Determined; 1935 Freshmen Made of Stern Stuff ...,'
TS (26 Sept. 1935); 'Storm in the Streets,' *Silhouette* (20 Oct. 1939). Norman Ward
subsequently became a distinguished political scientist at the University of
Saskatchewan.

150 'University Students Will Be Asked Opinions on War, Conscription: Poll To Be
Taken in All Canadian Universities ... – Year Ago Large Majority Opposed to Supporting Any War,' *LFP* (21 Mar. 1939); 'Opinion Changes on War Action: Poll
Shows 57 p.c. of "U" Students Would Support Britain in Hostilities: Think Civilization Doomed if War Comes,' *LFP* (23 Mar. 1939)

CHAPTER 16   *History and Humanities*

1 Claude Bissell, *Halfway Up Parnassus: A Personal Account of the University of
Toronto, 1932–1971* (Toronto 1974), 16. Bissell borrowed these phrases from
Henry James.

2 Bissell, *Parnassus*, ix

3 Unpaginated typescript on graduate studies, section 'Developments: 1932–39,'
PUH, UTA, A83-0036/001

4 Ernest F. Scott, 'The Effects of the War on Literature and Learning,' *QQ* 27 (Oct.,
Nov., Dec. 1919), 147–53

5 Watson Kirkconnell and A.S.P. Woodhouse, eds., *The Humanities in Canada*
(Ottawa 1947), 203

6 Ibid., 5

7 Ibid., 7

8 Ibid., 10–11

9 Ibid., 8–9

10 It is invoked, e.g., in W.G. Jordan, 'The Higher Criticism in Canada II: The Canadian Situation,' *QQ* 36 (Winter 1920), 47.

11 H.P. Whidden, 'What Is a Liberal Education?' *CJRT* 1 (Feb. 1924), 36–7; W.H. Fyfe, 'Inaugural Address' (24 Oct. 1930), typescript in W.H. Fyfe Papers, box 2 file 9, QUA; Paul Axelrod, *Making a Middle Class: Student Life in English Canada during the Thirties* (Montreal/Kingston 1990), 39–41

12 Michael Gauvreau, *The Evangelical Century: College and Creed in English Canada from the Great Revival to the Great Depression* (Montreal/Kingston 1991), 282

13 Gauvreau, *Evangelical Century,* 262–3

14 David B. Marshall, *Secularizing the Faith: Canadian Protestant Clergy and the Crisis of Belief, 1850–1940* (Toronto 1992), ch. 6, 'Battling with the Great War,' 174–80. See also Robert A. Wright, 'The Canadian Protestant Tradition, 1914–1945,' in George A. Rawlyk, ed., *The Canadian Protestant Experience, 1760–1990* (Burlington 1990), 145–6. Wright's argument is elaborated in his book *A World Mission: Canadian Protestantism and the Quest for a New International Order, 1918–1939* (Montreal/Kingston 1991).

15 E.A. Corbett and E.A. Lavell, as quoted in Gauvreau, *Evangelical Century,* 264

16 S.H. Hooke, 'The Saving of the Church,' *CF* 3 (Mar. 1923), 169–70. Hooke was quoting from another source.

17 S.H. Hooke, 'A Modern Lay Apologia,' *CF* 3 (Aug. 1923), 335. See also Hooke, 'The Religion of a Scientist, I,' *CF* 5 (Dec. 1925), 81–2; John S. Moir, *A History of Biblical Studies in Canada: A Sense of Proportion* (Chico, Calif. 1982), 62–3.

18 This very Canadian resolution to a thorny problem was that of the Rev Richard Roberts, minister of Sherbourne Street United Church, Toronto. See Gauvreau, *Evangelical Century,* 265.

19 Macallum quoted in ibid., 275

20 See Moir, *Biblical Studies,* 63

21 Wright, 'Canadian Protestant Tradition,' 165

22 Baillie quoted in Gauvreau, *Evangelical Century,* 281. This is ironic, since Gauvreau discounts the impact of neo-Kantian idealism (filtered as it was through Hegelian lenses) on English-Canadian Protestant thought.

23 R.C. Wallace, 'Christianity Today and Tomorrow' (1940), 5, 2, manuscript in R.C. Wallace Papers, box 3, file 16, QUA. See also W.H. Fyfe, 'Religious Pragmatism,' *CJRT* (Jan.-Feb. 1932), for further evidence from Queen's of the theological confusion of the day.

24 Moir, *Biblical Studies,* 66–77, 90–1

25 See Laurence K. Shook, *Catholic Post-Secondary Education in English-Speaking Canada* (Toronto 1971), 210–28. Maritain lectured at the institute from 1932 to 1938. See also Laurence K. Shook, *Etienne Gilson* (Toronto 1984), 175, 180, 192–5.

26 N.F.D. (Nathan F. Dupuis), 'Some of the Factors of Modern Civilization,' *QQ* 4 (July 1896), 45–55. For a similar conflict in 1901, when in an address Dupuis appeared to dismiss the significance of Greek, see 'The Prospects of Greek,' *QJ* (29 Mar. 1901), 251–3, a defence of the intrinsic value of the subject, and Dupuis's 'A Reply,' *QJ* (17 May 1901), 284–5.

27 W.L.G. (William Lawson Grant), 'Specialization,' *QJ* (13 Mar. 1897), 134–5. See also Grant's later article, 'A Plea for the Wider Study of Classical Life and History,' *QQ* 24 (1917), 478–83. In it Grant pleaded for greater use of English translations of the classical texts. See also John Macnaughton, 'A Modest Plea for the Retention in Our Educational System of Some Tincture of Letters' (*Essays and Addresses*, selected by D.D. Calvin (Kingston 1946), 105–27). A cantankerous old soul, Macnaughton was a peripatetic man of letters: at Queen's 1889–1903, McGill 1903–4, Queen's 1904–8, McGill 1908–19, U of T 1919–25.

28 W.L. Goodwin, 'Culture and Specialization,' *QQ* 19 (Apr. 1912), 348–58

29 J.K. Robertson, 'Pure Science and the Humanities,' *QQ* 26 (1917), 54–65; R.C. Wallace (at the time President of the University of Alberta), 'The Humanism of Science,' Appendix A, in NCCU *Proceedings* (1930), 32–40; H. Wasteneys (Professor of Biochemistry, U of T), 'Humanism of Science,' Appendix B, ibid., 41–6

30 Robin S. Harris, *A History of Higher Education in Canada, 1663–1960* (Toronto 1976), 399, 386; Patricia Jasen, 'The English Canadian Liberal Arts Curriculum: An Intellectual History, 1800–1950,' PHD thesis, Manitoba (1987), 157–66; Axelrod, *Making a Middle Class*, 51

31 See *The Memoirs of C.B. Sissons: Nil Alienum* (Toronto 1964), 129–35

32 Kirkconnell and Woodhouse, *Humanities*, 46

33 S.E. Smethurst, 'Classics at Queen's: The First 150 Years,' *Queen's Alumni Review* (Nov.-Dec. 1992), 24. See also S.E. Smethurst, *Classics at Queen's: A Brief History* (Kingston 1992).

34 Maurice Hutton quoted in S.E.D. Shortt, *The Search for an Ideal: Six Canadian Intellectuals and Their Convictions in an Age of Transition, 1890–1930* (Toronto 1976), 92. See also, Maurice Hutton, *The Sisters Jest and Earnest* (Toronto n.d.)

35 *Honour Classics in the University of Toronto* (Toronto 1929), 32, 36, 28. The book was written by 'a Group of Classical Graduates.'

36 Ibid., 29, The orientation of the Toronto program towards intellectual history was noted by the American philosopher Charles W. Hendel in 'The Character of Philosophy in Canada,' *UTQ* 20 (Jan. 1951), 129–30. William Dale, Hutton's assistant until he was dismissed by President Loudon in 1895, was also instrumental in the late 19th-century reorientation of the Toronto classical program towards literature and history. For an indication of his views, see William Dale, 'The Gods of Greece,' *QQ* 3 (Jan. 1896), 217–31. For a similar approach, see also A. B. Nicholson, 'The Pre-Homeric Age of Greek Civilization,' *QQ* 4 (July 1896), 30–44.

37 A complete listing of Norwood's many books, articles, and reviews is contained in Mary E. White, ed., *Studies in Honour of Gilbert Norwood* (Toronto 1952), xi–xvii.

For a brief overview and estimation of classics scholarship in Canada, see Millar MacLure, 'Literary Scholarship to 1960,' in Carl F. Klinck, ed., *Literary History of Canada: Canadian Literature in English,* 2nd ed., vol. 2 (Toronto 1976), 59–68.

38 See 'Graduates in Honour Classics 1881–1928,' in *Honour Classics,* 69–83. I am grateful to Blair Neatby for lending me his copy of *Honour Classics,* not least because it once belonged to Frank Underhill (one of its authors) and contains Underhill's marginalia.

39 Ibid., 39–40. The book contains extracts from many former students of Hutton.

40 Brian Doyle, *English and Englishness* (London / New York 1989), 31–40. See also Chris Baldick, *The Social Mission of English Criticism, 1848–1932* (Oxford 1983), 86–9 passim.

41 Newbolt quoted in Baldick, *Social Mission,* 89–90. The mission of the Newbolt Report to make English an instrument of national policy ultimately failed, but few people after 1921 voiced reservations about its 'intrinsic value.' See Doyle, *English,* 40–67.

42 Newbolt quoted Doyle, *English,* 45, 47

43 See Gerald Graff, *Professing Literature: An Institutional History* (Chicago/London 1987), 65–97 passim; Robin S. Harris, *English Studies at Toronto: A History* (Toronto 1988), 199–201; Laura Groening, 'Modernizing Academica: An American and a Canadian Vision,' *Dalhousie Review* 67 (Winter 1987–8), 511–22.

44 Near the end of the 1940s McMaster and Western appear to have had only three faculty members in English, Queen's five. See Appendix D in Kirkconnell and Woodhouse, *Humanities,* 256–8, 282–3. See also G.B. Harrison, 'Department of English,' *QQ* 51 (1944–5), for a plea for understanding and support by an over-worked English professor from Queen's. For Toronto's growth, see Harris, *English Studies,* 115.

45 See John Gross, *The Rise and Fall of the Man of Letters: Aspects of English Literary Life since 1800* (London 1969); Margerie Fee, 'English-Canadian Literary Criticism, 1890–1950: Defining and Establishing a National Literature,' PHD thesis, U of T (1981), 215; Pelham Edgar, 'Some Canadian Poets: Archibald Lampman,' *TG* (14 Jan. 1905); 'Some Canadian Poets: Bliss Carman,' *TG* (4 Feb. 1905); 'Some Canadian Poets: Duncan Campbell Scott,' *TG* (4 Mar. 1905); 'New Stars in Our Literary Firmament,' *TSW* (2 Nov. 1929). For Cappon's popular publications see Shortt, *Search,* 188–9.

46 A.S.P. Woodhouse, 'Staff,' in *University College: A Portrait,* ed. Claude T. Bissell, (Toronto 1951), 81; A.S.P. Woodhouse (with Malcolm Wallace), 'In Memoriam: William John Alexander,' *UTQ* 14 (Oct. 1944), 11

47 Pelham Edgar, 'Walt Whitman,' *TM* (9 Apr. 1892); 'The Drift of Modern Fiction,' *UTQ* 1 (Oct. 1931), 128, quoted in Fee, 'Literary Criticism,' 240

48 Pelham Edgar, *Across My Path,* ed. Northrop Frye (Toronto 1952), 85. See also John Ayre, *Northrop Frye: A Biography* (Toronto 1989), 68–70.

49 Pelham Edgar, *Rhythm in the Novel* (Toronto 1950), ix–x

50 E.K. Brown, 'Recent Canadian Literature,' quoted in Fee, 'Literary Criticism,' 333;
   E.K. Brown, *Matthew Arnold: A Study in Conflict* (Toronto 1948), and 'Matthew
   Arnold and the Elizabethans,' *UTQ* I (1931–2), 333. Brown wrote a sympathetic
   biography of Arnold and became, with Columbia University's Lionel Trilling,
   Arnold's major interpreter in North America.

51 See Edgar, 'New Stars'; Fee, 'Literary Criticism,' 217. Frederick Philip Grove was
   so grateful to Alexander for his inspiration and help that he dedicated *The Master of
   the Mill* (Toronto 1961 [1944]) to him. Alexander's recent death, the dedication said,
   had 'deprived Canada of its acutest mind and left a void in the hearts of all who loved
   him' (v).

52 Fee, 'Literary Criticism,' 216–18, 225–35; Robert H. Blackburn, *Evolution of the
   Heart: A History of the University of Toronto Library* (Toronto 1989), 139–50, 176.
   It appears that the first course on Canadian literature taught at a Canadian post-secondary institution was a summer course taught at the Macdonald Institute, affiliated
   with the Ontario Agricultural College, in 1907. See Margery Fee, 'Canadian Literature and English Studies in the Canadian University,' *Essays on Canadian Writing*,
   number 48 (Winter 1992–3), 22–3.

53 Harris, *English Studies*, 84, but esp. Appendix 3, Woodhouse's 'The University
   Preparation of Teachers of English,' a previously unpublished lecture delivered in
   1951 (292–6). See also Patricia Jasen, 'Educating an Elite: A History of the Honour
   Course System at the University of Toronto,' *OH* 81 (Dec. 1989), 269–88.

54 Bissell, *Parnassus*, 8

55 Harris, *English Studies*, 84. This integration was facilitated by the 1936 introduction
   of a common first-year program, 'Social and Philosophical Studies' – usually abbre-
   viated to 'Soc and Phil,' and affectionately pronounced by its students as 'Sock and
   Fill' (ibid., 85).

56 Bissell, *Parnassus*, 8–9. For reiteration of this imperial theme, see also the introduction in Millar MacLure and F.W. Watt, eds., *Essays in English Literature from the
   Renaissance to the Victorian Age: Presented to A.S.P. Woodhouse* (Toronto 1964),
   vi: 'His office in University College was an imperial secretariat, from which procon-
   suls departed to Canadian universities from coast to coast, and to universities outside
   Canada.'

57 Ayre, *Frye*, 185; Philip Marchand, *Marshall McLuhan: The Medium and the Mes-
   senger* (Toronto 1989), 85. For Woodhouse's hostility to the 'new criticism,' see
   Woodhouse, *The Poet and His Faith: Religion and Poetry in England from Spenser
   to Eliot and Auden* (Chicago 1965), 2–4, 258–61.

58 F.E.L. Priestley quoted in Marchand, *McLuhan*, 84

59 Marchand, *McLuhan*, 85; Ayre, *Frye*, 112

60 Kathleen Coburn, *In Pursuit of Coleridge* (Toronto 1977), 58–9. When Coburn suggested to George Whalley that he should take a PHD at the University of London, she
   discovered that Woodhouse 'was making difficulties if Whalley did not decide on
   Toronto ... I also had some reason to fear that the anti-feminism of the head of the

department [Woodhouse] would not make life any easier for my students than for me' (88).

61 Laurence K. Shook notes that women were not 'really welcome in strictly philosophy courses' at St Michael's College in the 1930s and 1940s (*Catholic Education*, 190).

62 See A.S.P. Woodhouse, *The Heavenly Muse: A Preface to Milton*, ed. Hugh MacCallum (Toronto 1972), xii–xiii. The dedication – '*Ad matrem*' – acknowledged that he owed his mother 'the greatest of all' his debts. In *Parnassus*, Claude Bissell writes that Woodhouse was a man 'whose affection for his mother, with whom he lived, was beautiful and moving' (10). Marshall McLuhan's biographer, Philip Marchand, writes of a curious disdain in Woodhouse for 'the biology of procreation' and claims that he 'barely recovered from the trauma of having to serve, on one occasion, as an examiner at the PHD orals of a pregnant woman' (*McLuhan*, 83). Marchand provides no evidence to substantiate the veracity of this anecdote.

63 See Harris, *English Studies*, Appendix 1, 'Full-Time Staff Members with Appointments for at Least Two Years, 1853–1984,' 213–40. For a discussion of the ideology of English as a 'masculine profession,' in spite of its female undergraduate clientele, see Doyle, *English*, 68–93.

64 See Joseph Levitt, *A Vision Beyond Reach: A Century of Images of Canadian Destiny* (Ottawa n.d.), 77–124. See also Carl Berger, *The Writing of Canadian History*, 1st ed. (Toronto 1976).

65 See Peter Novick, *That Noble Dream: The 'Objectivity Question' and the American Historical Profession* (Cambridge 1988); M. Brook Taylor, *Promoters, Patriots, and Partisans: Historiography in Nineteenth-Century English Canada* (Toronto 1989).

66 Robert Bothwell, *Laying the Foundation: A Century of History at University of Toronto* (Toronto 1991), 48

67 Carl Berger, *The Sense of Power: Studies in the Ideas of Canadian Imperialism* (Toronto 1970); Paul T. Phillips, *Britain's Past in Canada: The Teaching and Writing of British History* (Vancouver 1989), 47; Levitt, *Beyond Reach*, 19–62; W.L. Grant, 'The Teaching of Colonial History,' *QQ* 18 (1911), 181–8

68 For discussion of the 'Makers of Canada' series, see the editorial introduction to William Dawson LeSueur, *William Lyon Mackenzie: A Reinterpretation*, ed. A.B. McKillop, (Toronto 1989); see also 'The Critic as Historian,' in A.B. McKillop, ed., *A Critical Spirit: The Thought of William Dawson LeSueur* (Toronto 1977). On the 'Canada and Its Provinces' series, see Berger, *Writing*, 28.

69 Levitt, *Beyond Reach*, 77–101 passim; J.W. Dafoe, 'The Views and Influence of John S. Ewart,' *CHR* 14 (June 1933), 136–42; Berger, *Writing*, 49 passim

70 For 19th-century background of this 'moral imperative' in Canadian thought, see A.B. McKillop, *A Disciplined Intelligence: Critical Inquiry and Canadian Thought in the Victorian Era* (Montreal/Kingston 1979).

71 Wrong was severely critical of the heavy documentation produced by research in American graduate schools. 'The Americans pursue a very rigorous and, to me, one-sided method,' he wrote in 1923. 'If you wish to see an illustration of it, look at the

History of the CPR just issued by Innis of our Dept. of Pol. Econ. It is a sound piece of research but it is almost formless in respect to literary quality and the text is overburdened by footnotes to an absurd extent. And this excess of method is what the American School of History glories in' (quoted in Bothwell, *Foundation*, 65).

72 George M. Wrong, 'The Historian and Society,' *CHR* 14 (Mar. 1933), 4–8. See also E.F. Scott, 'History as a Guide to the Present,' *QQ* 24 (Dec. 1916), 153–62. The pessimistic Scott believed that history was a very fallible guide at best, yet he concluded by saying that it nevertheless 'enables us to see the present in its true character, as part of a great movement which must be understood as a whole' (162).

73 Charles A. Beard, 'The Historian and Society,' *CHR* 14 (Mar. 1933), 1

74 Beard, 'Historian and Society,' 2–3

75 Ibid., 2

76 Axelrod, *Making a Middle Class*, 53

77 Robert H. Blackburn, 'Origins of the *Canadian Historical Review*,' *CHR* 65 (1984), 542–6; editor, 'The Beginnings of Historical Criticism in Canada: A Retrospect, 1896–1936,' *CHR* 17 (1936), 1–8, to which is appended an account by George M. Wrong of the founding of the *CHR*. Initiative for the new journal appears to have come from Langton, but it was Wrong's academic prestige and authority that gave legitimacy to the project.

78 Chester Martin, 'Fifty Years of Canadian History,' in Royal Society of Canada, *Fifty Years Retrospect: Anniversary Volume, 1882–1932* (n.p. 1932), 63–9; Berger, *Writing*, 36–8

79 Reginald G. Trotter, 'Canadian Interest in the History of the United States,' *QQ* 36 (1929), 92–107

80 See F.H. Underhill, 'Some Aspects of Upper Canadian Radical Opinion in the Decade before Confederation,' CHA *Annual Report* (1927), 47. See also J.M.S. Careless, 'Frontierism, Metropolitanism and Canadian History,' in J.M.S. Careless, *Careless at Work: Selected Canadian Historical Studies* (Toronto 1990), 112–13.

81 Bothwell, *Foundation*, 47–8, 66–8, 73–5

82 Ibid., 90–1

83 D.C. Harvey, 'Canadian Historians and Present Tendencies in Historical Writing,' CHA *Annual Report* (1930), 17–24

84 Harold A. Innis, 'The Teaching of Economic History in Canada' (1929), reprinted in Innis, *Essays in Canadian Economic History* (Toronto 1956)

85 W.J. Dunlop (department of university extension) to H.A. Innis (16 July 1925), DPE Papers, box 6, file 1925, UTA

86 For an overview of Innis's activities during these years, see Donald Creighton, *Harold Adams Innis: Portrait of a Scholar* (Toronto 1978 [1957]), 61–73. Innis's reputation was made with its publication, but his fortune was not. In its first year *The Fur Trade in Canada* sold 136 copies. Innis's royalties came to $48.75 in 1931; in 1932 he received $65.00 on 160 sales. See royalty statements in DPE Papers, box 7, files 1932 and 1933, UTA.

87 James Ten Broeke to H.A. Innis (25 Sept. 1932), DPE Papers, box 7, file 1932; A.R.M. Lower to H.A. Innis (19 Nov. 1928), ibid., box 7, file 1928; Irene Biss to H.A. Innis (10 June, 6 Sept. 1935), ibid., box 7, file 1935, UTA

88 J.B. Brebner to H.A. Innis (20 Dec. 1933), DPE Papers, box 7, file 1933, UTA

89 See Donald Creighton, *Towards the Discovery of Canada: Selected Essays* (Toronto 1972), passim.

90 J.B. Brebner, 'Canadian and North American History,' CIIA *Annual Report* (1931), 32

91 James T. Shotwell to Harold A. Innis (6 Oct. 1932), DPE Papers, UTA, box 7, file 1932

92 For treatment of the Carnegie Series, see Berger, *Writing*, 140–59.

93 As Berger points out, J.B. Brebner's summation volume in the series, *North Atlantic Triangle: The Interplay of Canada, the United States, and Great Britain* (1945), was consciously written to counter the emphasis on Canadian-American historical relations at the expense of two centuries of the British connection. In this way, a series on bilateral relations was triangulated. See Berger, *Writing*, 157–8.

94 See Frederick H. Armstrong, 'Maurice Careless,' in David Keane and Colin Read, eds., *Old Ontario: Essays in Honour of J.M.S. Careless* (Toronto 1990), 14–15.

95 New could therefore turn, without any sense that he had shifted fields, from writing a much-needed biography of Lord Durham to studying the life of the English Whig reformer Henry Brougham. See Charles M. Johnston, *McMaster University*, vol. 2, *The Early Years in Hamilton, 1930–1957* (Toronto 1981), 68–9.

96 *Queen's University Undergraduate Calendar, 1950–1*, 183–5

97 Harris, *Higher Education*, 381; Kirkconnell and Woodhouse, *Humanities*, 58–62

98 Bothwell, *Foundation*, 91–3.

99 E.R. Adair made much the same point in 1943, when he wrote that 'there has not been during the past fifty years, so far as I know, one single work of real historical distinction produced by historians in Canada which does not deal with Canadian history' (Adair, 'The Canadian Contribution to Historical Science,' *Culture* 4 [1943], 65). A graduate of the U of T in 1911, Cochrane taught Classics in University College from 1913 (with the exception of his war service) until his death in 1945. See the tribute by Harold Innis, 'Charles Norris Cochrane, 1889–1945,' *CJEPS* 12 (1946), 95–7. See also Charles N. Cochrane, 'The Latin Spirit in Literature,' *UTQ* 2 (1932–3), 315–38; 'The Mind of Edward Gibbon,' part 1, *UTQ* 12 (1942–3), 1–17, and part 2, 146–66.

100 See William Kilbourn, 'The Writing of Canadian History,' in Klinck, *Literary History,* 2nd ed., vol. 2, 41–2.

101 See H. McD. Clokie, 'Canadian Contributions to Political Science,' *Culture* 3 (1942), 467–74; Jasen, 'Liberal Arts,' 237. For a useful survey, see C.B. Macpherson, 'On the Study of Politics in Canada,' in H.A. Innis, ed. *Essays in Political Economy: In honour of E.J. Urwick* (Toronto 1938), 147–65.

102 Axelrod, *Making a Middle Class*, 84–7 (Wright quoted, 84). This stood in great

contrast with conventional teaching practice at Osgoode Hall, the teaching arm of the Upper Canada Law Society. After some liberalization of its curriculum under Dean John Falconbridge in the 1920s, it reverted during the Depression to what had been its basic approach since the 19th century: a heavy reliance on articling in law firms. Students at the U of T interested in law, such as Bora Laskin (later Chief Justice of the Supreme Court of Canada), contrasted this emphasis on narrow training for professional employment with Toronto's much more broadly humanistic approach to law within its faculty of arts. Even the occasional member of the Osgoode Hall staff came to lament the sterility of the Law Society's conception of legal education. Law, said Osgoode professor Cecil Wright, should be more than 'a collection of skills and rules that had to be learned by rote and applied precisely in practice.' It was, instead, 'a living rather than the stagnant well of technicalities which it has always seemed to the man in the street.' Such discontent led in the 1950s first to the establishment of a faculty of law at the U of T and, shortly thereafter, recognition by the Upper Canada Law Society of the legitimacy of the new faculty's offerings. This victory for those who wanted a more academic approach to legal education came three-quarters of a century after Ontario law students and others had first voiced their concerns. See also C. Ian Kyer and Jerome E. Bickenbach, *The Fiercest Debate: Cecil A. Wright, the Benchers, and Legal Education in Ontario, 1923–1957* (Toronto 1987).

CHAPTER 17   *Social Philosophy and Social Science*

1 Frederick W. Gibson, Queen's University, vol. 2, *1917–1961: To Serve and Yet Be Free* (Montreal/Kingston 1983), 24, 26, 35, 484n113. The first sociology course at Queen's was taught by John Meisel in the department of political and economic studies in 1951–2; in 1957–8 the sociology offerings remained Meisel's single course. The university's department of sociology was not founded until 1969. See *Queen's University Undergraduate Calendar, 1951–2*, 230; *Queen's University Undergraduate Calendar, 1957–8*, 192; 'Sociology, Department of,' in Ian Malcolm and Allison Dawe, eds., *Queen's Encyclopedia* (Kingston 1993), 181. The 1957–8 Queen's undergraduate calendar lists only three geography courses, given within the department of political and economic studies (192–3).

2 G.P. Gilmour to S.G. Cole (31 Mar. 1948); quoted in Charles M. Johnston, *McMaster University*, vol. 2, *The Early Years in Hamilton* (Toronto 1981), 221–2

3 Gilmour quoted in Johnston, *McMaster* 2, 224; Goldwin S. French to author (24 Nov. 1992); Henry B. Mayo, 'Sociology, and Anthropology, etc.,' in Carl F. Klinck, ed., *Literary History of Canada: Canadian Literature in English*. 2nd ed., vol. 2 (Toronto 1976 [1965]), 51–2

4 John Watson, *The State in Peace and War* (Glasgow 1919), 48. In *Philosophy, Politics, and Citizenship: The Life and Thought of the British Idealists* (Oxford 1984), authors Andrew Vincent and Raymond Plant note: 'The Idealists ... saw the role of

the state not merely as a set of instrumentalities for securing material welfare but as the focus of a sense of community and citizenship, an institution in which a good common to all classes and recognizable by all interest groups could be articulated. The purpose of the state was to promote the good life of its citizens and to develop the moral nature of man' (2).

5 Sir Robert Falconer, *Idealism in National Character: Essays and Addresses* (Toronto 1920), 30, 38, 13. See also A.B. McKillop, *A Disciplined Intelligence: Critical Inquiry and Canadian Thought in the Victorian Era* (Montreal/Kingston 1979), 231–2.

6 H.J. Cody, 'The Place of the University in National Life,' *UTQ* 4 (1934–5), 433

7 Biographical material on Brett is drawn from John A. Irving, adapted by A.H. Johnson, 'Philosophical Literature 1910–1964: Part 1, The Achievement of G.S. Brett,' in Klinck, *Literary History of Canada*, 1st ed. (Toronto 1965), 556–86; Michael Gauvreau, 'Philosophy, Psychology, and History: George Sidney Brett and the Quest for a Social Science at the University of Toronto, 1910–1940,' CHA *Historical Papers* (1988), 209–36. For another view of Brett's contribution, see Leslie Armour and Elizabeth Trott, *The Faces of Reason: An Essay on Philosophy and Culture in English Canada, 1850–1950* (Waterloo 1981), 430–48.

8 George Sidney Brett, *A History of Psychology*, vol. 1, *Ancient and Patristic* (London 1912), x. This was the first in Brett's three-volume history. For comments on the evolution of ideas about the soul as the object of his book and the meaning of psychology to the ancients, see ix, 5.

9 Brett, *History* 1, 3–7

10 John Alexander Stewart, 'Psychology – A Science or a Method?' *Mind* 1 (Oct. 1876), 445–51, quoted in Gauvreau, 'Brett,' 216. For Brett's appreciation of Spencer, for example, see his *History*, vol. 3, *Modern Psychology* (London 1921), 213–15.

11 Brett, *History* 1, 16

12 As when, after quoting Augustine's *Confessions*, he says: 'Here we have clearly a state of feeling, the awakening of thoughts that lie too deep for words, vivid realisation of limitless possibilities, and a condition charged with greater power than is found in the detached thinking of daily life' (Brett, *History* 1, 347). This passage is mistakenly ascribed to vol. 2 by Irving and Johnson, in Klinck, *Literary History*, 1st ed., 580. Subsequent references to this source are from this edition unless otherwise noted.

13 Gauvreau, 'Brett,' 212; A.H. Johnson, 'Philosophical Literature 1910–1964. II. Other Philosophers,' in Klinck, ed., *Literary History*, 587

14 G.S. Brett, 'The Evolution of Orthodoxy,' *CJRT* 3 (Mar./Apr. 1926), 99. See also G.S. Brett, 'The Limits of Science,' *UTM* 14 (Nov. 1913), 34–8. For Brett's estimation of the legacy of 19th-century idealism, see his 'Arms and the Nation,' *UTM* 16 (Jan. 1916), 232–7.

15 Irving and Johnson, 'Philosophical Literature 1,' 584

16 George Sidney Brett, *History*, vol. 2, *Mediaeval and Early Modern Period* (London 1921), 6

17 G.S. Brett, *The Government of Man: An Introduction to Ethics and Politics*, 2nd ed. (London 1920), 1

18 Brett, *Government of Man*, 314

19 Ibid.

20 G.S. Brett, 'Concerning the Common Mind,' *UTM* 15 (Mar. 1915), 243. See also Terence H. Qualter, *Graham Wallas and the Great Society* (London 1980).

21 Irving and Johnson, 'Philosophical Literature 2,' 586–8

22 Peter Hampton, 'Schools of Psychology,' *QQ* 46 (1939), 289, quoted in Paul Axelrod, *Making a Middle Class: Student Life in English Canada during the Thirties* (Montreal/Kingston 1990), 56. While the separation of the humanistic and experimental approaches to psychology was not formalized until the 1920s, it was certainly present in the late 19th-century U of T. See, e.g., James Gibson Hume, 'Value of Psychology,' *CEM* 19 (1897), 260–4, and Albert H. Abbott, 'Experimental Psychology and the Laboratory in Toronto,' *UTM* 1 (1900), 85–9.

23 Brett, *History* 3, 275–7. In contrast, Brett applauded psychoanalysis as practiced by Sigmund Freud for its clear sense of causality: 'Freud's position involves the principle that no effect lacks its cause, and this can only be regarded as a truly scientific standpoint' (307).
　　The first psychiatric clinic in Canada was established in 1909, under the direction of Dr C.K. Clarke, superintendent of the Toronto Asylum and dean of the U of T's faculty of medicine. Between 1908 and 1913, he was aided by Dr Ernest Jones, a British expatriate whose increasingly close association with Sigmund Freud ultimately made him Freud's biographer and alter ego. Before returning to Europe in 1913, Jones spent much of his time 'selling' Freudian theories to North American psychologists. See Vincent Brome, *Ernest Jones: Freud's Alter Ego* (New York and London 1983); Ernest Jones, *Free Associations: Memories of a Psycho-Analyst* (New York 1959); Nathan G. Hale, Jr ed., *James Jackson Putnam and Psychoanalysis: Letters between Putnam and Sigmund Freud, Ernest Jones, William James, Sandor Ferenczi, and Morton Prince, 1877–1917* (Cambridge, Mass. 1971); Cyril Greenland, *Charles Kirk Clarke: A Pioneer of Canadian Psychiatry* (Toronto 1966).

24 Gauvreau, 'Brett,' 230–2. See also C. Roger Myers, 'Psychology at Toronto,' in Mary J. Wright and C. Roger Myers, eds., *History of Academic Psychology in Canada* (Toronto 1982), 79–81.

25 Myers, 'Psychology at Toronto,' 81–5ff

26 The instrumentalist study of 'personality,' which came to resemble a kind of cult within American psychological circles by the 1920s, was resisted by some in Ontario – not least because its replacement of 'conduct' with 'behaviour' seemed to denigrate the importance of moral 'character.' See 'G.R.B.' (G. Richard Brisay), 'Personality,' *AV* 48 (Oct. 1923), 20–24. For the emergence of the cult of personality in American life, see Warren I. Susman, '"Personality" and the Making of Twentieth-

Century Culture,' in John Higham and Paul K. Conkin, eds., *New Directions in American Intellectual History* (Baltimore 1979), 212–26.

27 G.S. Brett to Carleton Stanley (24 Jan. 1931); quoted in Marlene Shore, *The Science of Social Redemption: McGill, the Chicago School, and the Origins of Social Research in Canada* (Montreal/Kingston 1987), 217, emphasis in original. Bott was of the late 19th- and early 20th-century generation of Ontario university graduates discussed by Nancy J. Christie in 'Psychology, Sociology and the Secular Moment: The Ontario Educational Association's Quest for Authority, 1880–1900,' *JCS* 25 (Summer 1990), 119–43. Christie argues that in their search for academic respectability (and university positions), such men became reformist champions of specialized secular 'science,' esp. psychology and sociology, and adopted its language in order to fulfill their ambitions. Prior to the Great War, they failed to reorient Ontario social science along the empirical and inductive American model championed by Richard T. Ely, G. Stanley Hall, and John Dewey, because they 'underestimated the strength of the classical humanities within the Canadian university setting' (135) and the continuing authority of its guardians.

28 G.S. Brett, 'The New Materialism,' *AV* 43 (Mar. 1919), 262

29 For a general overview of academic psychology in Canada at the beginning of the Second World War, see H.W. Wright, 'Psychology in Canada,' *Culture* 1 (1940), 327–32. Wright makes no mention of the extent of resistance to psychology – at times an attitude of dismissive scorn – within traditional disciplines such as history and English. For psychology at Queen's, see James Inglis, 'Psychology at Queen's,' in Wright and Myers, *Academic Psychology*, 100. In 1951–2 the *Queen's University Undergraduate Calendar* listed a staff in psychology of 1 professor of psychiatry, 2 assistant professors, 4 instructors, and 1 clinical assistant in psychiatry (234). Bott of U of T was the founding president of the Canadian Psychological Association in 1938, and his role in the Second World War was even more substantial and of greater influence than it had been in the First World War, for he became one of the main exponents and practitioners of the use of psychological tests for the evaluation of service personnel. See Terry Copp and Bill McAndrew, *Battle Exhaustion: Soldiers and Psychiatrists in the Canadian Army, 1939–1945* (Montreal/Kingston 1990), 27–33.

30 D.G. Ritchie, 'Social Evolution,' quoted in Stefan Collini, 'Sociology and Idealism in Britain, 1880–1920,' *Archives Européennes de sociologie* 19 (1978), 22

31 Collini, 'Sociology and Idealism,' 22–4; Reba Soffer, 'Why Do Disciplines Fail? The Strange Case of British Sociology,' *English Historical Review* 97 (1982), 781–4

32 Dorothy Ross, *The Origins of American Social Science* (Cambridge, Mass. 1991), xiv–xv

33 Ross, *American Social Science*, 224–9

34 Lester R. Kurtz, *Evaluating Chicago Sociology: A Guide to the Literature, with an Annotated Bibliography* (Chicago 1984), 13

35 Albion Small, *Origins of Sociology* (1924), quoted in Peter T. Manicas, *A History and Philosophy of the Social Sciences* (Oxford 1987), 226

36 The Chicago department produced no fewer than 36 PHDs between 1895 and 1915, and these informal agents of the 'Chicago School' taught sociology in newly established departments throughout the United States. Of the 27 people who served as presidents of the American Sociological Society between 1924 and 1950, only 11 had not either received their doctorates from the University of Chicago or been a member of its staff. Martin Bulmer, *The Chicago School of Sociology: Institutionalization, Diversity, and the Rise of Sociological Research* (Chicago 1984), 34–43

37 Robert E. Faris, *Chicago Sociology, 1920–1932* (San Francisco 1967), 37–50; Bulmer, *Chicago School*, 1–10, 36–44

38 Oswald Hall, 'Carl A. Dawson, 1887–1964,' *CRSA* 1 (1964–5), 116

39 See Marlene Shore, 'Carl Dawson and the Research Ideal: The Evolution of a Canadian Sociologist,' CHA *Historical Papers* (1985), 45–73; Shore, *Science of Social Redemption*, passim.

40 S.D. Clark, 'Sociology in Canada: An Historical Over-view,' *Canadian Journal of Sociology / Cahiers canadiens de sociologie* 1 (1975), 226–7; Hall, 'Dawson,' 117

41 See Sara Z. Burke, 'Seeking the "Highest Good": The Creation of the University of Toronto Settlement, 1907–1910,' graduate research essay, Carleton University (1990). I am grateful to Ms Burke for allowing me to cite her paper.

42 See Andrew Vincent and Raymond Plant, *Philosophy, Politics, and Citizenship: The Life and Thought of the British Idealists* (London 1984), 135; Burke, 'Seeking the "Highest Good,"' 4–6.

43 See R.M. MacIver, 'The Ethical Significance of the Idea Theory,' I (*Mind* 18 [1909], 552–69) and II (*Mind* 21 [1912], 182–200). Quotation from I, 552

44 'In no modern work,' MacIver wrote of *The Philosophical Theory of the State*, 'are the inconsistencies and contradictions of applied Hellenism more apparent.' MacIver's critique was first published in *PR* (Jan. 1911), and republished in part as Appendix B, 'A Criticism of the Neo-Hegelian Identification of "Society" and "State,"' in *Community*, 424–33. Quotation above at 429

45 'Ethics and Politics,' *IJE* 20 (Oct. 1909), 72–86; 'Society and State,' *PR* 20 (Jan. 1911), 30–45; 'War and Civilization,' *IJE* 22 (Jan. 1912), 127–45; 'Do Nations Grow Old?' *IJE* 23 (Jan. 1913), 127–43; 'What Is Social Psychology?' *SR* 6 (Apr. 1913), 147–60; 'Society and "the Individual,"' *SR* 7 (Jan. 1914), 58–64; 'Institutions as Instruments of Social Control,' *PQ* no. 2 (May 1914), 105–16; 'The Foundations of Nationality,' *SR* 8 (July 1915), 157–66; 'Personality and the Suprapersonal,' *PR* 24 (Sept. 1915), 501–25

46 R.M. MacIver, *As a Tale That Is Told: The Autobiography of R.M. MacIver* (Chicago 1968), 65. See also Leon Bramson, 'Introduction' to Bramson, ed., *Robert MacIver on Community, Society, and Power: Selected Writings* (Chicago 1970), 8–9.

47 MacIver, *Autobiography*, 75–6; R.M. MacIver, 'Foundations of Nationality,' in Bramson, *MacIver on Community*, 94–105 (originally published in *SR* 8 [July 1915], 157–66); Ian M. Drummond, *Political Economy at the University of Toronto: A History of the Department, 1888–1982* (Toronto 1983), 43–4

48 See R.M. MacIver to Robert A. Falconer (20 July 1915), Falconer Papers, box 39,
    UTA. MacIver's testimonials were from Lancelot R. Phelps, provost of Oriel College,
    Oxford ('His views were always his own. They were fresh and unconventional,
    arrived at by reasoning process, and were not rigidly final.') and from George Adam
    Smith, principal of Aberdeen University ('has always been ready to take part in the
    organisation and conduct of schemes of University Extension').
49 This is Drummond's view (*Political Economy*, 46).
50 R.M. MacIver, *Community: A Sociological Study, Being an Attempt to Set Out the
    Nature and Fundamental Laws of Social Life* (London 1917), 48. Quotations are
    from the 3rd ed., 1924. A book of enduring value, it went into a 5th ed. as late as
    1965. On Park's view of *Community*, see MacIver, *Autobiography*, 87.
51 MacIver, *Community*, 49, emphasis in original
52 See, e.g., R.M. MacIver, *The Web of Government*, rev. ed. (New York 1965 [1947]).
53 MacIver, *Community*, 53, and on the following pages from 55, 56–60, 64, 65
54 Ibid., 64, 65. See also MacIver, *Autobiography*, 73.
55 R.M. MacIver, *Labor in the Changing World* (New York and Toronto 1919); R.M.
    MacIver to Robert A. Falconer (8 Mar. 1917) regarding National Problems Club,
    Falconer Papers, box 43, UTA; R.M. MacIver, 'Capital and Labour – the New Situa-
    tion,' *UTM* 18 (Mar. 1918), 209–11; R.M. MacIver to Registrar, U of T (24 May
    1919), regarding lectures to returned soldiers, Falconer Papers, box 53, UTA
56 MacIver, *Labor in the Changing World*, 212
57 Ibid., ix–x; ch. 4, 'The Widening of the Idea of Labor,' specifically contrasts Marx-
    ism and British Labour (64–76). When called upon in 1921 by Falconer to defend his
    'economic position in its relation to the problem of economic unrest' (Leonard was
    on the warpath and wanted MacIver's academic scalp), MacIver replied: 'All that
    should be required from the outside of a teacher of economics is that he should not
    advocate or support any proposals which strike at constitutional ways and means. I
    have always condemned any such proposals, in my book (c. IV), in articles, and in
    addresses where the subject was relevant' (MacIver to R.A. Falconer [27 Jan. 1921],
    Falconer Papers, box 65, UTA). MacIver's mention of 'articles' referred principally to
    a seven-article sequence published by the *Montreal Star* as part of its 'Canada in the
    Building' series in 1919. His contributions centred on the theme of building the new
    industrial order.
58 The petition to R.A. Falconer and university senate (2 June 1919) from extension
    course students in social service contained 61 signatures; the second, from social ser-
    vice alumni ((2 June 1919), was signed by 44 employees of such agencies as the
    Neighbourhood Workers' Association, Infants' Home and Infirmary, Military Head-
    quarters, Dominion Council of the YWCA, the Trades and Labour Branch, the Univer-
    sity Settlement; the Department of Public Health, and the Juvenile Court (Falconer
    Papers, box 53, UTA).
59 MacIver, *Autobiography*, 73
60 R.M. MacIver, *The Elements of Social Science* (London 1921), 180: 'The reader will

find that this book [*Community*] deals from the same standpoint with many of the topics treated in the present text.'

61 MacIver's sociological concerns at this stage in his career are strikingly similar to those of Hobhouse in, e.g., the latter's seminal essay 'Sociology, General, Special, and Scientific,' published in *SR* in 1908, or his book *The Metaphysical Theory of the State: A Criticism*, which appeared in 1918. Hobhouse's essay is reprinted in Philip Abrams, *The Origins of British Sociology, 1834–1914* (Chicago 1968), 247–59. MacIver characterized the work of Wallas and Hobhouse sympathetically in 'Sociology,' an overview of the discipline written at the end of the 1920s and published in Dixon Ryan Fox, ed., *A Quarter Century of Learning, 1904–1929* (New York 1931), 62–91. It may more easily be found in Bramson, *MacIver on Community*, 219–44.

The place of Hobhouse is a major one in the history of British sociology, for with sociologist Morris Ginsberg and economist J.A. Hobson he was one of the leaders of the 'New Liberalism' in England. Together they were largely responsible for giving articulate voice to a moral and philosophical justification for a positive and interventionist state, thereby helping bring about a fundamental reorientation of liberal thought and action. MacIver is seldom situated within this context, because, as historian Stefan Collini has observed, much of his published writing was done only after he had left Great Britain. Yet in fact he was central to the development of the 'New Liberalism.' The 1911 critique of Bosanquet's Hegelian identification of state and society that found its way into an appendix to *Community* in 1917 anticipated Hobhouse's similar agenda in *The Metaphysical Theory of the State*, and probably influenced it. In this way, MacIver played his part in the New Liberal disengagement from the British idealist tradition. See Collini, 'Sociology and Idealism in Britain,' 24n48, 28–9. See also Stefan Collini, 'Hobhouse, Bosanquet and the State: Philosophical Idealism and Political Argument in England 1880–1918,' *Past and Present* 72 (1976), 86–111. For extended examinations of Hobhouse's social thought, see Peter Weiler, *The New Liberalism: Liberal Social Theory in Great Britain, 1889–1914* (New York 1982) and Stefan Collini, *Liberalism and Sociology: L.T. Hobhouse and Political Argument in England, 1880–1914* (Cambridge 1979).

62 Hobhouse, 'Sociology, General, Special, and Scientific,' in Abrams, *British Sociology*, 253; MacIver, *Elements*, 3, 14–19, emphasis in original. MacIver's reference to the 'architectonic' character of social science occurs in *Elements*, 13.

63 See Vincent Bladen, *Bladen on Bladen: Memoirs of a Political Economist* (Toronto 1978), 34–6.

64 Shortly before his departure, MacIver was given a farewell dinner at the High Table of Victoria College. The occasion was later remembered mainly for the way in which some speakers, particularly Jackman and Jackson, used their speeches less as testimonials to their departing colleague than as a thinly veiled means of lobbying for the chairmanship of the department. As Innis wrote to his wife: 'It developed into a most interesting duel – interesting to those who knew' (Innis quoted in Donald Creighton,

Harold Adams Innis: Portrait of a Scholar [Toronto 1978 (1957)], 69). See also Bladen, *On Bladen*, 31.

65 For biographical details concerning Urwick, see John A. Irving, 'The Social Philosophy of E.J. Urwick,' the introductory essay in Irving's edition of Urwick's essays, *The Values of Life* (Toronto 1948), xi–lxv; H.J. Cody, 'Introduction' to *Essays in Political Economy in Honour of E.J. Urwick*, ed., H.A. Innis (Toronto 1938), v–vii; H.A. Innis, 'Edward Johns Urwick, 1867–1945,' *CJ* 11 (May 1945), 265–8. For personal appreciation of Urwick's role as counsellor and organizer at Toynbee Hall, see the memoir by Canon Barnett's widow: Mrs S.A. Barnett, *Canon Barnett: His Life, Work, and Friends – By His Wife* (London 1921), 317.

66 These positions included: Tooke professor of economic science at King's College, London (1907–14); professor of social philosophy at the University of London (1914–24); president of Morley Memorial College (1903–23); director of the department of social science and administration in the London School of Economics (1910–23). For Urwick's close association with other advocates of the new liberalism set, see Vincent and Plant, *Philosophy, Politics, and Citizenship*, 147; for biographical details concerning Hobhouse, see Weiler, *New Liberalism*, 20–1.

67 Urwick quoted in Standish Meacham, *Toynbee Hall and Social Reform, 1880–1914: The Search for Community* (New Haven 1987), 122. See also, Barnett, *Canon Barnett*, 338.

68 Marjorie J. Smith, *Professional Education for Social Work in Britain: An Historical Account* (London 1965), 37–65

69 E.J. Urwick, *A Philosophy of Social Progress* (London 1912), vi–vii. The following pages on Urwick are from this source, viii–ix, 4–8, emphasis in original

70 *The Social Good* was published in London by Methuen; *The Modern State* in Oxford at the Clarendon Press.

71 MacIver, *Modern State*, 481; Urwick, *Social Good*, 6

72 MacIver, *Modern State*, 426, 492; Urwick, *Social Good*, 46, 48, emphasis in original

73 Both MacIver and Urwick were marginally associated with contemporary movements in health-care reform. MacIver supported the birth control movement, attending the organizational meeting of the Ontario Birth Control League in 1925. Urwick supported the general aims of the eugenics movement, particularly because of the eugenicists' individualist approach to social reform. He was, however, severely critical of their assumptions and methods. See R.M. MacIver, 'Civilization versus Culture,' *UTQ* 1 (1931–2), 325–6; Urwick, *The Social Good*, ch. 11: 'The Problem of the Unfit,' 218–31. See also Angus McLaren, *Our Own Master Race: Eugenics in Canada, 1885–1945* (Toronto 1990), 83, 113.

74 MacIver, *Modern State*, 493. See also Doug Owram's discussion of *The Modern State* in *The Government Generation: Canadian Intellectuals and the State, 1900–1945* (Toronto 1986), 117–21.

75 Urwick, *Social Good*, 40–2, and next paragraph from 2, 240, 241, 238

76 Bladen, *On Bladen*, 39, 62–7; Drummond, *Political Economy*, 45, 56–9

77 H. M. Cassidy to E.J. Urwick (4 Aug. 1936), DPE Papers, UTA

78 E.J. Urwick to Dr H.M. Cassidy (25 Sept. 1936), DPE Papers, UTA

79 H.M. Cassidy to E.J. Urwick (27 Aug. 1936), DPE Papers, UTA. See also Carl Berger, *The Writing of Canadian History: Aspects of English-Canadian Historical Writing, 1900–1970,* 1st ed. (Toronto 1976), 68, 109–10; Owram, *Government Generation,* 166.

80 The copy of MacIver's *The Modern State* I consulted was Underhill's own, now in the collection of the Underhill Reading Room in the department of history at Carleton. Its inscription indicates that Underhill obtained it in September 1926; its marginal notes demonstrate that it was carefully read.

81 An earlier Canadian Political Science Association was founded in 1913, but after James Mavor launched a personal attack on Stephen Leacock at its first meeting the association quickly floundered. See Drummond, *Political Economy,* 74.

82 Bladen, *On Bladen,* 74–5. The new journal succeeded the U of T's *Contributions to Canadian Economics,* launched at the initiative of Harold Innis in 1928.

83 Stephen Leacock, 'What is Left of Adam Smith?' *CJEPS* 1 (Feb. 1935), 41

84 Leacock, 'Adam Smith,' 41–51

85 E.J. Urwick, 'The Role of Intelligence in the Social Process,' *CJEPS* 1(Feb. 1935), 64–5, and in the following passages from 65–8, 69–70, 72 (emphasis in original), 73, 74–6

86 H.A. Innis, 'The Role of Intelligence: Some Further Notes,' *CJEPS* 1 (May 1935), 281–2, emphasis in original

87 Innis had in mind here not only the articles by Leacock and Urwick, but also 'Social Science and the Political Trend,' by Frank H. Knight, (*UTQ* 3 [1934], 407–27). Like Leacock, Knight attacked the tradition of classical political economy and its incapacity to deal with contemporary problems. Knight also provided a substantial two-part critique (less directly polemical) in the first issues of the *CJEPS*: 'The Ricardian Theory of Production and Distribution,' 1 (Feb. 1935), 3–25, and (May 1935), 171–96.

88 Innis, 'Further Notes,' 281–4

89 Ibid., 284–5

90 For example, Gilbert Jackson's advice on the gold standard was obtained by the federal minister of finance; A.F.W. Plumptre tendered advice on central banking and exchange policy and served as secretary to the royal commission that recommended the creation of the Bank of Canada; D.C. MacGregor was active in the examination of federal income and expenditure accounts; Vincent Bladen wrote a study for the Stevens Royal Commission on price spreads and was an adviser to the Royal Commission on the Textile Industry. See Owram, *Government Generation,* 135–220 passim; Drummond, *Political Economy,* 77.

91 Little wonder that when he declined an offer from the University of Chicago, the reason he gave to his wife was that in Canada 'I have all the threads in my hands' (Berger, *Writing History,* 108–10). Little wonder, also, that when Eric A. Havelock (a close friend of Frank Underhill and one of those Toronto members of the LSR so

excoriated in Innis's 1935 *UTQ* article) gave a lecture on Innis to the members of the Harold Innis Foundation in 1978, he found it difficult to accept Donald Creighton's anodyne account in *Harold Innis: Portrait of a Scholar* (1957). 'The exercise of power and influence,' Havelock said, 'was something he valued, and sought, and achieved' (*Harold A. Innis: A Memoir* [Toronto 1982], 24).

92 See H.A. Innis, ed., *Essays in Political Economy in Honour of E.J. Urwick* (Toronto 1938): V.W. Bladen, 'Adam Smith on Value' (27–44); Agatha Chapman, 'The Tariff and Canadian Butter' (59–74); C.W.M. Hart, 'Social Evolution and Modern Anthropology' (99–116); C.B. Macpherson, 'On the Study of Politics in Canada' (147–165).

93 Drummond, *Political Economy*, 78; Bladen, *On Bladen*, 40

94 The American contributors were Robert E. Park, doyen of the 'Chicago School' of sociology and a dominant force in the subject between the wars, and Harvard sociologist Talcott Parsons, whose magnum opus *The Structure of Social Action* had appeared three years earlier and whose 'structural-functionalist' approach to sociology was to dominate American sociology in the quarter-century after the Second World War.

95 See Robert E. Park, 'Physics and Society' and C.A. Dawson, 'Sociology as a Specialized Science,' in C.W.M. Hart, ed., *Essays in Sociology* (Toronto 1940), 1–35.

96 Talcott Parsons, 'The Motivation of Economic Activities' and S.D. Clark, 'Economic Expansion and the Moral Order,' in Hart, *Essays*, 53–91. C.W.M. Hart's contribution was entitled 'Some Obstacles to a Scientific Sociology' (36–52).

97 H.A. Innis, 'Foreword' to Hart, *Essays*, v–viii

98 Innis, 'Further Notes,' 286–7

99 Here Innis referred to an article by F.H. Knight, 'Ethics and Economic Reform,' in *Economica* (Feb., Aug., Nov. 1939).

100 Innis, 'Foreword,' viii. By 1940 Urwick and MacIver had nevertheless had a serious disagreement in print. In 1938 Urwick published a lengthy review of MacIver's *Society: A Textbook of Sociology* (1937) admonishing him for subordinating his skills as philosopher (and by clear implication also abandoning his principles) in order to pose as the apostle of 'scientific' sociology for his American audience ('Review Article: Is There a Scientific Sociology?' *CJEPS* 4 [May 1938], 231–40). MacIver's brief reply reasserted the claim of sociology to be scientific. He did not disagree with Urwick about the continuing importance of social philosophy, but concluded: 'I would maintain, however, that unless philosophy seeks to build on the data and the conclusions of science it becomes a kind of dilettante theology, supporting our interests or our prejudices, but offering neither the enlightenment of science nor the sustenance of religion' ('Science and Sociology: A Reply to Professor Urwick,' *CJEPS* 4 [Nov. 1938], 549–51).

CHAPTER 18 *War and Recovery*

1 *QJ* quoted in Frederick W. Gibson, *Queen's University*, vol. 2, *1917–1961: To*

Serve and Yet Be Free (Montreal/Kingston 1983), 180; editorial, 'About the War,' McMaster *Silhouette* (6 Oct. 1939)

2 Quoted in 'Chapter Six,' PUH, UTA, A83–0036/001

3 R.C. Wallace, 'The Canadian Universities in the War' (n.d.), R.C. Wallace Papers, box 3, file 13, QUA. While the typescript of this address is not dated, it refers to 'the fourth year of the war.'

4 Gwendoline Pilkington, 'A History of the National Conference of Canadian Universities, 1911–1951,' PHD thesis, U of T (1974), 218

5 See Desmond Morton and Glenn Wright, *Winning the Second Battle: Canadian Veterans and the Return to Civilian Life, 1915–1930* (Toronto 1987).

6 NCCU *Proceedings* (1942), 82

7 See J.S. Thomson, *Yesteryears at the University of Saskatchewan, 1937–1949* (Saskatoon 1969), 37. Thomson was president of the NCCU during the war.

8 Charles M. Johnston, *McMaster University*, vol. 2, *The Early Years in Hamilton, 1930–1957* (Toronto 1981), 88; C.M. Johnston and J.C. Weaver, *Student Days: An Illustrated History of Student Life at McMaster University from the 1890s to the 1980s* (Hamilton 1986), 61; 'Organized in Last War – Contingent Has History of Invaluable Activity,' *LFP* (29 June 1942); 'Chapter Six,' PUH, UTA, A83-0036/001; Gibson, *Queen's*, 181

9 'Universities Will Give Military Training Lead,' *GM* (11 Sept. 1940)

10 Gibson, *Queen's*, 184–5; 'On Active Service – 3,000 U of T Students to Take Military Training during Academic Year and Camp Afterward,' *TT* (31 Aug. 1940); 'Require Direct Quota of Varsity Students – Soldiers to Go on Active Service,' *Varsity* (13 Jan. 1942); 'U of T Students, Grads Pay Impressive Tribute,' *GM* (12 Nov. 1940)

11 'University Registration of 1,979 Shows Decrease of 162 From Last Year, *LFP* (24 Oct. 1942); *ROP, 1939–40*, 130, and *ROP, 1944–5*, 9; Marni de Pencier, 'A Study of the Enrolment of Women in the University of Toronto,' research study, U of T (1973), Appendix A, 'Master chart: Enrolment from 1904–1970,' PUH A83-0036/001

12 Johnston, *McMaster* 2, 91–2; Gibson, *Queen's*, 185; Kathryn M. Bindon, *Queen's Men, Canada's Men: The Military History of Queen's University, Kingston* (Kingston 1978), 77; Nancy Kiefer and Ruth Roach Pierson, 'The War Effort and Women Students at the University of Toronto, 1939–45,' in Paul Axelrod and John G. Reid, eds., *Youth, University, and Canadian Society: Essays in the Social History of Higher Education* (Montreal/Kingston 1989), 164–5

13 'Chapter Six,' PUH, UTA, A83-0036/001; 'Drilling, Sewing, Typing War Courses for Co-Eds,' *Varsity* (27 Jan. 1943); '1,000 University Women Work on War Effort,' *GM* (19 Mar. 1941); 'Possibility of Air Raids Makes First Aid Knowledge Essential, Firemen Told,' *LFP* (9 May 1942); Bindon, *Queen's Men*, 84–5; 'University Girls Abandon Gaiety, More Take War-Important Courses,' *GM* (30 Oct. 1942)

14 Janet Tupper, 'Wartime College Girls More Mature in Outlook,' *GM* (1 Apr. 1943); *Varsity* (26 Oct. 1943), quoted in Kiefer and Pierson, 'The War Effort and Women Students,' 174–5

15 Gibson, *Queen's*, 188; 'Arts Dance Is Enjoyable Event,' *LFP* (28 Mar. 1941); 'Think Co-eds Sweet Enough: Frown on Corsages for Arts Ball Tonight,' *LFP* (27 Mar. 1941); 'Dances at "U" Cut in Half: Several Traditional Functions Dropped as Total Reduced From 15 to 7,' *LFP* (2 Oct. 1942); Johnston, *McMaster* 2, 113

16 Johnston, *McMaster* 2, 113; T.A. Reed, ed., *A History of the University of Trinity College, Toronto, 1852–1952* (Toronto 1952), 167

17 Bindon, *Queen's Men*, 88 9; Gibson, *Queen's*, 187–8

18 Humfrey Michell to Harold Innis (22 Nov. 1941, 4 Apr. 1944), quoted in Johnston, *McMaster* 2, 98–9

19 Gibson, *Queen's*, 194; Owram, *The Government Generation: Canadian Intellectuals and the State, 1900–1945* (Toronto 1986), 456–7; 'New Problems Endless as University of Toronto Widens Its Important Part in Nation's War Effort,' *GM* (28 Oct. 1942)

20 See *ROP, 1939–40*, 132, and *ROP, 1944–5*, 94.

21 Minister of labour quoted in Johnston, *McMaster* 2, 93

22 Ibid., 84, 98, 119–20

23 'Varsity Plans Training 500 for RCAF Radio Activity,' *TS* (15 Apr. 1941); 'U of T Halls Echo as RCAF Arrives – 500 Begin Special Wireless Course – "Work Hard," Urges Cody,' *TS* (26 May 1941)

24 Johnston, *McMaster* 2, 100–5; Gibson, *Queen's,* 194–6. For the important role of academic psychologists, see Terry Copp and Bill McAndrew, *Battle Exhaustion: Soldiers and Psychiatrists in the Canadian Army, 1939–1945* (Montreal/Kingston 1990); Mary J. Wright and C. Roger Myers, eds., *History of Academic Psychology in Canada* (Toronto 1982), 88–9, 108–9, 119–20.

25 Quoted in Gibson, *Queen's*, 191

26 See *ROP, 1939–40*, 131.

27 John Matheson quoted in Gibson, *Queen's*, 191. Matheson was dean of arts at Queen's from 1924 to 1943.

28 R.C. Wallace, 'The Arts Faculty,' NCCU *Proceedings* (1942), 118–21. For a more positive view of Wallace's concerns, see Robin S. Harris, *A History of Higher Education in Canada, 1663–1960* (Toronto 1976), 497–8. See also N.A.M. MacKenzie, 'The Future of the Arts Course,' NCCU *Proceedings* (1942), 128.

29 On 15 Aug. the *Financial Post* announced the results of a poll that had asked: 'Should we close all university courses except those training war specialists?' The consensus seems to be reflected by the Toronto chartered accountant who said: 'It seems absurd that fit young men and women should have facilities to pursue their studies as in peace-time while their contemporaries are fighting for them or engaged in war work.' On Christmas Eve, 1942, the *GM* published an editorial, 'Arts Courses in Wartime.' Noting American university practice, it admitted that 'curtailment of arts courses involves some danger for the future,' but concluded that 'there will be no future unless the war is won.' The *GM* viewpoint was rejected by some other newspapers. See, e.g., 'Should We Liquidate Universities?' *LFP* (26 Dec. 1942).

30　Quoted in Pilkington, 'National Conference,' 323
31　The Social Science Research Council was formed in 1940 at the initiative of Dominion Statistician R.H. Coates, but was organized largely by Innis. See Donald Fisher, *The Social Sciences in Canada: 50 Years of National Activity by the Social Science Federation of Canada* (Waterloo 1991), 12–13. Innis had once written to a friend that he looked upon government officials 'with contempt.' See Donald Creighton, *Harold Adams Innis: Portrait of a Scholar* (Toronto 1978 [1957]), 107.
32　Watson Kirkconnell, *A Slice of Canada: Memoirs* (Toronto 1967), 236–8
33　MacNamara quoted in Pilkington, 'National Conference,' 324–5, 327, emphasis added
34　'Plan to Release Students Early, No Formal Exams,' *Varsity* (13 Jan. 1941); Bindon, *Queen's Men*, 102–3
35　The categories were a) medicine; b) dentistry; c) engineering and applied science; d) architecture; e) agriculture; f) pharmacy; g) forestry; h) education; i) commerce; j) veterinary science; k) specialized courses in mathematics, physics, chemistry, biology, or geology.
36　Bindon, *Queen's Men*, 112–13. For the view of a McMaster student journalist that the regulations discriminated against arts students, see the editorial 'Reflection On Selection,' *Silhouette* (25 Feb. 1944).
37　Bindon, *Queen's Men*, 110–11; Johnston, *McMaster* 2, 110–11; Gibson, *Queen's*, 203–4
38　'Our employers saw us, I am sure,' recalled McMaster's Bernard F. Trotter, '... as soft, eastern city-bred boys who didn't know one end of a pitchfork from the other – incapable of an honest day's work ...' The *QJ* noted that 'Many farmers blamed the eastern authorities who sent inexperienced college boys out to do an experienced man's work.' Trotter quoted in Johnston, *McMaster* 2, 110; *QJ* quoted in Gibson, *Queen's*, 204
39　Gibson, *Queen's*, 203–6
40　See Loren Baritz, *The Good Life: The Meaning of Success for the American Middle Class* ((New York 1990), 168–73. Baritz points out that the American male took 'the cultural power of Mother' into military service, as often as not fighting for Mom. See also Johnston and Weaver, *Student Days*, 69.
41　*ROP, 1944–5*, 95
42　de Pencier, 'The Enrolment of Women,' 70; Kiefer and Pierson, 'The War Effort and Women Students,' 176–8. See also Ruth Roach Pierson, *'They're Still Women after All': The Second World War and Canadian Womanhood* (Toronto 1986); Alison Prentice, Paula Bourne, Gail Cuthbert Brandt, Beth Light, Wendy Mitchinson, and Naomi Black, *Canadian Women: A History* (Toronto 1988), 295–303.
43　Sir Robert Falconer, 'The Humanities in the War-Time University,' *UTQ* 13 (1943), 1–2
44　Falconer, 'Humanities,' 3–8
45　H.J. Cody quoted in Kiefer and Pierson, 'The War Effort and Women Students,' 170

46 C.R. Tracy, 'The Future of the Faculty of Arts,' *QQ* 50 (1943–4), 175–83. For other examples, see B.K. Sandwell, 'Religion and Education,' *SN* (16 Aug. 1941); R.D. Maclennan, 'The Continuing Aims of Higher Education,' *Culture* 4 (Dec. 1943), 495–503; H.L. Stewart, 'University Life in Canada,' *Culture* 6 (Sept. 1945), 333–48. J. Macmurray, 'Functions of a University,' *Public Affairs* (Winter 1945), 79–84.

47 Only days earlier, Prime Minister Mackenzie King had signed a bilateral agreement establishing a Permanent Joint Advisory Board, aimed at coordinating the defence of North America, with American President Franklin Delano Roosevelt at Ogdensberg, New York. Underhill welcomed the development, although he also said that the new pact did 'not necessitate a breach with our old connection' (quoted in R. Douglas Francis, *Frank H. Underhill: Intellectual Provocateur* [Toronto 1986], 115).

48 Francis, *Underhill*, 116–27. See also Carl Berger, *The Writing of Canadian History*, 1st ed. (Toronto 1976), 79–84, for a concise account of this episode.

49 'It is possibly necessary to remember,' Innis pointedly told President Cody at one tense meeting, 'that any returned man who has faced the continued dangers of modern warfare has a point of view fundamentally different from anyone who has not. Again and again have we told each other or repeated to ourselves, nothing can hurt us after this' (quoted in Francis, *Underhill*, 123). Eric Havelock and Donald Creighton both noted this bond, particularly as it marked Innis. See Eric A. Havelock, *Harold A. Innis: A Memoir* (Toronto 1982); Donald Creighton, 'The Ogdensburg Agreement and F.H. Underhill,' in his *The Passionate Observer: Selected Writings* (Toronto 1980), 133–4. Creighton's memoir reflects the views of a direct witness to the Underhill affair.

50 Pickersgill quoted in Francis, *Underhill*, 124

51 Underhill quoted in Joseph Levitt, *A Vision Beyond Reach: A Century of Images of Canadian Destiny* (Ottawa n.d.), 134. See also Francis, *Underhill*, 127; Berger, *Writing History*, 197–9.

52 Quoted in Francis, *Underhill*, 133

53 See Underhill's book, *In Search of Canadian Liberalism* (Toronto 1960), esp. 'Some Reflections on the Liberal Tradition in Canada,' his 1946 presidential address to the CHA.

54 J.A. Corry, *Democratic Government and Politics* (Toronto 1946), 1–8, 426–40

55 J.A. Corry, *My Life and Work A Happy Partnership: Memoirs of J.A. Corry* (Kingston 1981), 90–1

56 See, e.g., Watson Kirkconnell, *Seven Pillars of Freedom* (Toronto 1944); Kirkconnell, 'Confronting Communism,' in *Slice of Canada*, 314–30.

57 D.G. Creighton, 'The Course of Canadian Democracy,' *UTQ* 11 (1941–2), 256. Profoundly disturbed by the continental integration he thought to be implicit in the Ogdensburg Agreement, Creighton warned against succumbing to the American-style plebiscitary democracy. Clearly he had the spring 1942 national referendum on conscription in mind.

58 See J.M.S. Careless, *Careless at Work: Selected Canadian Historical Studies* (Tor-

onto 1990); Frederick H. Armstrong, 'Maurice Careless' and Kenneth McNaught, '"Us Old-Type Relativist Historians": The Historical Scholarship of J.M.S. Careless,' in David Keane and Colin Read, eds., *Old Ontario: Essays in Honour of J.M.S. Careless* (Toronto 1990), 12–70

59 A.R.M. Lower, 'The Social Sciences in the Post-War World,' *CHR* 22 (Mar. 1941), 1–6

60 Lower, 'Social Sciences,' 7–13. For elaboration of Lower's views, see his 'The Social Sciences in Canada,' *Culture* 3 (Dec. 1942), 433–40.

61 These various responses are presented serially in 'The Social Sciences in the Post-War World,' *CHR* 22 (June 1941), 117–32; Wallace is quoted on 129.

62 Francis, *Underhill*, 133

63 'The Social Sciences in the Post-War World,' 118–20

64 Berger, *Writing of History*, 187–9

65 Harold A. Innis, 'Some English-Canadian University Problems,' *QQ* 50 (Spring 1943), 34

66 Donald Creighton, *The Forked Road: Canada 1939–1957* (Toronto 1976), 116; Paul Axelrod, *Scholars and Dollars: Politics, Economics, and the Universities of Ontario, 1945–1980* (Toronto 1982), 19; W.G. Fleming, *Ontario's Educative Society*, vol. 1, *The Expansion of the Educational System* (Toronto 1971), 174

67 'The Problem of Education in Post-War Canada,' section IV (a) of an undated memorandum of the Committee of Reconstruction. R.C. Wallace Papers, QUA, box 10, file 24

68 Order-in-Council PC 7633, of Oct. 1941, had provided for $60 per month if single or $80 if married as an allowance for each month of military service.

69 Johnston, *McMaster* 2, 141

70 Gibson, *Queen's*, 233–4 passim

71 Fleming, *Ontario's Educative Society* 1, 174

72 See Robert Bothwell, *A Short History of Ontario* (Edmonton 1986), 164.

73 Roger Graham, *Old Man Ontario: Leslie M. Frost* (Toronto 1990), 247

74 'Appointment of Sidney Smith as President' (unpaginated typescript memorandum), PUH, UTA, A83-0036/001

75 'Appointment of Sidney Smith'

76 Thelma Lecocq, 'Varsity's Mr Smith,' *Maclean's Magazine* (1 Jan. 1945), 13

77 See 'Appointment of Sidney Smith.' See also Claude Bissell, *Halfway Up Parnassus: A Personal Account of the University of Toronto, 1932–1971* (Toronto 1974), 28–9. An indication of Phillips's administrative manner is provided by Bissell when discussing the circumstances of his appointment as Sidney Smith's successor. In a telephone conversation with Bissell, Phillips told him that several candidates were being considered for the position. 'But at the proper time, I shall take your name to the committee. I will get unanimous support and discussion will end' (*Parnassus*, 36). See also Axelrod, *Scholars and Dollars*, 90.

78 Bissell, *Parnassus*, 30

79 Cody, it appears, did not retire gracefully. He had many loyalists, and he seems to have called upon them in his bid to retain the chancellorship. 'I am inclined to think we have written "finis" to the active issue,' Eric Phillips wrote to Sidney Smith in 1948, 'but believe that there will be plenty of need to watch his activities. However, I do sincerely hope that they will not give us any more concern on the same level that they did last year.' Phillips was talking about Harry Cody. Unnamed memorandum on research in Sidney Smith Papers, in PUH, UTA, A83-0036/001. The press speculated that the new legislation was drafted specifically to shorten Cody's term as chancellor. Phillips to Smith (19 Aug. 1948); quoted in ibid. See also Bissell, *Parnassus*, 20.

80 Statistics on full-time veteran enrolment are from an unpaginated and untitled type-script memorandum, in PUH, UTA, A83-0036/001. Figures on page headed '1945–1951: How Did the University Fare?' Full-time total enrolment figures are from de Pencier, 'Enrolment of Women,' 71

81 Gibson, *Queen's*, 259

82 *ROP, 1945–6*, 11; Gibson, *Queen's*, 248–9; Johnston, *McMaster* 2, 151–3

83 Alan Heisey, 'The Ajax Years,' in Robin S. Harris and Ian Montagnes, eds., *Cold Iron and Lady Godiva: Engineering Education at Toronto, 1920–1972* (Toronto 1973), 73–6

84 Heisey, 'Ajax Years,' 78, 82

85 The proportions of the 1,021 returned veterans in different programs were as follows: arts and science 47.6%; medicine 50.9%; theology 58.6%; nursing 27.7%. Of these students, 28% were married. See '1,021 Veterans at UWO: Affiliates Have 208 More,' *LFP* (10 Feb. 1947).

86 Gibson, *Queen's*, 253; Johnston, *McMaster* 2, 141–2; Johnston and Weaver, *Student Days*, 73–5; 'U Jazz Debut Highly Pleasing,' *LFP* (10 Dec. 1946); John R. Gwynne-Timothy, *Western's First Century* (n.p. 1978), 343

87 Johnston, *McMaster* 2, 142; Gibson, *Queen's*, 252. For an excellent contemporary assessment of the student veteran, including academic strengths and weaknesses, see C.L. Bennet, 'What the Veteran Student Is Teaching the Universities,' *Dalhousie Review* 27 (1948), 311–22.

88 'On the NFCU,' *QC* (Feb. 1945); G.T. de Hueck, 'The Student Veterans,' *QC* (Jan. 1946); Ken Binks, 'Young Men in Politics,' *QC* (Mar. 1948); Gwynne-Timothy, *Western*, 344; Johnston and Weaver, *Student Days*, 75

89 Each is from the *QC*: Lieutenant Leo Mergler, 'The Three of Us' (Jan. 1946); Ken Lendon, 'Portrait of Jackie' (Spring 1948).

90 The federal Committee on Reconstruction, which had refused to appoint women to any of its main subcommittees, marginalized women's concerns during the war by creating a special 'advisory' sub-committee on women's issues, headed by Margaret McWilliams of Manitoba, and then ignoring most of its recommendations. See Advisory Committee on Reconstruction, 'Report of Subcommittee on Post-War Problems of Women' (30 Nov. 1943), copy in R.C. Wallace Papers, QUA. See also Prentice et al., *Canadian Women*, 304–5.

682 Notes to pages 555–60

91 *National Home Monthly, Canadian Home Journal*, and Kennedy quoted in Pierson, *'They're Still Women'*, 217–18; Prentice et al., *Canadian Women*, 307–8

92 Leslie McNaughton, 'Does a BA Fit Women for Marriage?' *QC* (Feb. 1946); J.F., 'The Feminine Folly,' *QC* (Spring 1948)

93 'Barbara Greeted in City: Meets "Frat" Brethren' and 'Who Is College Fraternity Sweetheart Anyway?' *LFP* (7 May 1947)

94 Prentice et al., *Canadian Women*, 327; de Pencier, 'Enrolment of Women,' 65, 67, 71–2

95 Prentice et al., *Canadian Women*, 311–12

96 K.J. Rea, *The Prosperous Years: The Economic History of Ontario, 1939–75* (Toronto 1985), 14–22

97 Janet R. Keith, 'Will Canada's Universities Meet Needs of Post-war?' and U. Hill, 'Canadian Universities Train Youth for War ... and Leadership in Critical Postwar Period,' *SN* (15 Jan. 1944), 4–5, and (20 Jan. 1945), 12–13

98 See, e.g., *Financial Post*: 'Here's Job Outlook for U, School Grads' (3 June 1950); V. Kolby, 'Will We Have Enough College Grads? University Enrolment Dip May Spell Economic Trouble Ahead' (27 Oct. 1951); *Canadian Business*: E. Murray, 'Business Eyes Joe College' (21 Feb. 1948); F.R. Clarke, 'From Campus to Business' (23 Mar. 1950); also 'Employment Prospects for Students in Engineering and Commerce,' *Labour Gazette* (Jan. 1949)

99 C.R. Young, 'The Engineer in the Days Ahead,' *JEIC* 32 (Nov. 1949), 752

100 For example, see these articles published by Young in *JEIC*: 'The Education of Engineers,' 29 (Apr. 1946), 240–2; 'Developing Professional Attitudes amongst Undergraduates,' 29 (Dec. 1946), 722–3; 'Professional Advancement in Canada,' 30 (Dec. 1947), 357–9. For American views, see William E. Wickenden (former dean of the Case School of Applied Science), 'Shall Higher Education Be Expanded on the Technological Pattern?' 30 (Sept. 1947), 427–31; Dr Harry S. Rogers (President of Brooklyn Polytechnic Institute), 'What the War Has Done to Engineering Education,' 31 (Oct. 1948), 545–7.

101 Rea, *Prosperous Years*, 17–20; Graham, *Old Man Ontario*, 246–8; Axelrod, *Scholars and Dollars*, 79–81

102 See Table 2, 'Operating and capital expenditures of universities by source of funds, Ontario, 1945–79,' in Axelrod, *Scholars and Dollars*, 258–9.

103 Gibson, *Queen's*, 264–71 passim; Gwynne-Timothy, *Western*, 284–5; 'How Did the University Fare?' in PUH, UTA, A83-0036/001; Johnston, *McMaster* 2, 154–6, 184–6

104 See 'Carleton College Vastly Enhances Ottawa's Cultural Future: Splendid New Opportunity Provided for Youth of Capital and Employes [*sic*] in Wartime Work to Advance Status,' Ottawa *Evening Citizen* (12 Sept. 1942), 92–4; *University of Ottawa: A Tradition for Tomorrow* (Ottawa 1990), 12.

105 See W.G. Fleming, *Ontario's Educative Society*, vol. 4, *Post-Secondary and Adult Education* (Toronto 1971), 91–3.

106 'University Expansion,' *LFP* (25 Feb. 1947)
107 Quotations in Johnston, *McMaster* 2, 154, 172–3
108 Ibid., 128, emphasis in original

EPILOGUE   *Towards the Educative Society*

1 Quoted in Imelda Mulvihill, 'From Patron to Manager: The Canadian State and Higher Education in the Post-War World,' MA thesis, Carleton (1987), 110
2 See Paul Litt, *The Muses, the Masses, and the Massey Commission* (Toronto 1992).
3 *Report of the Royal Commission on National Development in the Arts, Letters, and Sciences* (Ottawa 1951), 8
4 Louis St Laurent quoted in Litt, *Muses, Masses, and Massey*, 163
5 *Financing Higher Education in Canada: Being the Report of a Commission to the Association of Universities and Colleges of Canada* (Toronto 1965), Table 9, 'Federal per capita grants, value of university grants and tax abatements, and value per full-time student, 1954–55 to 1964–65,' 99. (The commission was chaired by U of T political economist Vincent W. Bladen.) See also Mulvihill, 'Patron to Manager,' 113.
6 *Financing Higher Education*, Table 1, 'Full-time university grade fall enrolment at Canadian universities and colleges ...,' 93
7 G.E. Hall quoted in John R.W. Gwynne-Timothy, *Western's First Century* (London 1978), 345
8 W.G. Fleming, *Ontario's Educative Society*, vol. 2, *The Expansion of the Education System* (Toronto 1971), 44–7
9 E.R. Sheffield, 'Canadian University and College Enrolment Projected to 1965,' NCCU *Proceedings* (1955), 39–46
10 *Financing Higher Education in Canada: Being the Report of a Commission to the Association of Universities and Colleges of Canada* (Toronto 1965), 12–18. See also Fleming, *Ontario's Educative Society* vol. 1, 42–8 passim; Statistics Canada, *Universities: Enrolment and Degrees, 1990* (Ottawa 1990), 16.
11 See Fleming, *Ontario's Educative Society*, vols. 1 to 7 (Toronto 1971). Brief surveys of institutional development are provided in Fleming, *Ontario's Educative Society*, vol. 4, *Post-Secondary and Adult Education* (Toronto 1971), 86–211. The general background has been well established by Paul Axelrod, in *Scholars and Dollars: Politics, Economics, and the Universities of Ontario, 1945–1980* (Toronto 1982).
12 *Ontario Historical Studies Series* (Toronto 1990), statement of purpose, unpaginated

Index